THE FRENCH DESCENT INTO

RENAISSANCE ITALY

The French Descent into Renaissance Italy 1494-95

Antecedents and Effects

edited by

David Abulafia

*Reader in Mediterranean History in the University of Cambridge
and Fellow of Gonville and Caius College*

VARIORUM
1995

Published by   VARIORUM
                   Ashgate Publishing Limited
                   Gower House, Croft Road
                   Aldershot, Hampshire GU11 3HR
                   Great Britain

                   Ashgate Publishing Company
                   Old Post Road
                   Brookfield, Vermont 05036-9704
                   USA

0-86078-550-5

British Library Cataloguing in Publication Data
                   French Descent into Renaissance Italy, 1494-95:
                   Antecedents and Effects
                   I. Abulafia, David
                   945.05

US Library of Congress Cataloging in Publication Data
                   French Descent into Renaissance Italy, 1494-95:
                   Antecedents and Effects / edited by David Abulafia
                        p.   cm.   Includes index.
                   ISBN 0-86078-550-5
                   1. Italy-History-Expedition of Charles VIII, 1494-96.
                   2. France-History-Charles VIII, 1483-98. I. Abulafia, David.
                   DG541.F74 1995
                   945'.06-dc20   95-34786
                                                                       CIP

This book is printed on acid free paper.

Printed and bound by Athenaeum Press, Ltd.,
Gateshead, Tyne & Wear.

Contents

Preface

Recent years have seen a proliferation of commemorative conferences marking the anniversary of the fall of Granada, the expulsion of the Jews from Spain, the European discovery of America, all in 1492; or, more recently, the birth of Frederick II of Hohenstaufen at the end of 1194 has been celebrated by so many conferences and events throughout Sicily and the rest of Italy that the published collective programme is nearly an inch thick. It may thus seem surprising that an event in the history of southern Italy, indeed in the whole history of the peninsula and of Europe, as much debated as the French invasion of Italy in 1494-5 has bestirred little comment in 1994-5 and has given rise to no conferences on the scale of several of those concerned with the events of 1492. Perhaps, indeed, it is only wise not to allow the interests of historians to be guided by ephemeral commemorations. Such events (notably the anniversary of the end of the Second World War) have their significance in the public domain, but those concerned with more remote times may not reflect the predominant interest of historians in our own day.

Still, it is hard to forget the words of Francesco Guicciardini, who insisted on the contrast between the peace and prosperity, the 'desirable condition', 'happy state', 'tranquillity' of Italy around 1490 and the disastrous events of 1494, 'a most unhappy year for Italy, and truly the beginning of the years of wretchedness', marking the start of a lengthy series of invasions. The focus of this book is the first of the invasions, that of King Charles VIII of France, which culminated in the fall of Naples in February 1495 and the retreat out of Italy, itself marked by the much debated battle of Fornovo. Yet it will be seen from this book that Charles' invasion cannot simply be seen as the start of a cycle; it was also in many ways the end of another cycle, since the French king came into Italy as the heir to the claims of the house of Anjou-Provence, which had been persistently asserting its right to the throne of Naples, seized by the Aragonese in the 1440's. No excuse is thus needed for the presence in this volume of studies of the Angevin claim to Naples, nor of the reign of King Ferrante of Naples, even though he died a few months before Charles' invasion force began its long trek.

This book is the outcome of a feeling, in which I have been energetically supported by the contributors, that this would be a good moment to bring together a series of articles on aspects of the French invasion and its antecedents. The aim has quite deliberately been to combine survey articles, such as that on the links between the French crown and Italy before 1494, and more detailed studies of particular moments and issues. It is thus hoped that this book will be of value to those who are in need of an introduction to the intricate complexities of Italian diplomacy in the late fifteenth century, while it is also intended to satisfy those wishing to see some of the results of modern research in this arena. It has recently been observed by George Holmes that a particular strength of modern British historiography of Renaissance Italy has been the study of the political history of Quattrocento Italy, and this area is well represented; but at the same time efforts have been made to include contributions on the cultural and institutional history of the period, and a special welcome is also extended to several distinguished French, Italian and American contributors. Another aim has been to represent Milan, Naples and a few lesser centres rather more fully than has been the case in several collections of essays about Italy in this period, where an understandably heavy emphasis has been laid on Florence, Venice and the papacy, though these too are represented by important contributions. Fortunately, too, the appearance in 1994 of Riccardo Fubini's magisterial collection of essays on *Italia Quattrocentesca* (Milan: FrancoAngeli) has meant that a secure guide to the diplomatic position of Florence within late fifteenth-century Italy is now readily at hand.

With the intention of making this book into a research tool of permanent value, a lengthy appendix has been included containing an index to the remarkable collection of microfilms at the Sterling Library, Yale University. This collection was built up by Vincent Ilardi, whose name it rightly carries, and covers the materials for the history of Italian diplomacy in the archives of Italy and many other countries. It can be used not simply as an index to the Ilardi collection, but as a guide to the relevant archival material in Milan, Modena, Florence, the Vatican and many other places; it is a great pleasure to thank Professor Ilardi not merely for his kind permission (together with that of the Sterling Library) to use this material, but also for his enthusiasm from the earliest stages of the planning of this book, and for his many helpful suggestions. Sincere thanks are also due to Dr A.V. Antonovics and to the Society for Renaissance Studies for their role in the organisation of a colloquium in Cambridge devoted to the French invasion in March 1995; several of the contributors to this volume were present and spoke about either the work presented here or other themes. The colloquium and several expenses arising from the preparation of this book were supported financially by the Master and Fellows of Gonville and Caius College, Cambridge; and it was there that Mrs Edna Pilmer expertly prepared a complex manuscript for the press.

Sandra Smith translated Georges Peyronnet's article from the French; I am responsible for the translations from Italian of the articles by Giorgio Chittolini and Paolo Margaroli. The sketch maps of Italy in 1492 and of the Papal State were drawn by K.C. Jordan for *At the Court of the Borgia*, a selection from the diary of Johann Burchard edited and translated by Geoffrey Parker, and published by the Folio Society Ltd., London, to which I am very grateful for kind permission to reproduce copies here. John Smedley's level-headed support and advice as publisher has been invaluable throughout; without his help, this project could not have met the deadline of publication in the year that Naples fell to the French.

David Abulafia

Gonville and Caius College, Cambridge

List of abbreviations

Note: archival references, particularly those to material in Milan, reflect a variety of practices; some authors prefer to offer more detailed references than others. The aim here has been to ensure clarity rather than absolute consistency.

State archives

ASF	Archivio di Stato, Florence
ASFe	Archivio di Stato, Ferrara
ASMa	Archivio di Stato, Mantua
	AG Archivio Gonzaga
ASMi	Archivio di Stato, Milan
	SCI Sforzesco Carteggio Interno
	SPE Sforzesco Potenze Estere
ASMo	Archivio di Stato, Modena
	ASE Amb. Archivio Segreto Estense, Carteggio Ambasciatori
ASS	Archivio di Stato, Siena
ASV	Archivio di Stato, Venice

Other archives

AOrsini	Archivio Capitolino, Rome, Archivio Orsini

Maps and illustrations

List of contributors

David Abulafia, *Cambridge University*
A. V. Antonovics, *University of Bristol*
Joël Blanchard, *Université du Maine*
Humfrey Butters, *University of Warwick*
David Chambers, *Warburg Institute, University of London*
Giorgio Chittolini, *Università degli Studi di Milano*
Cecil H. Clough, *University of Liverpool*
Trevor Dean, *Roehampton Institute*
Vincent Ilardi, *University of Massachusetts*
Carol Kidwell, *American University in Paris*
David Laven, *Keele University*
Michael Mallett, *University of Warwick*
Paolo Margaroli, *Università degli Studi di Milano*
Simon Pepper, *University of Liverpool*
Georges Peyronnet, *Université de la Bretagne occidentale*
Alan Ryder, *University of Bristol*
Eleni Sakellariou, *Cambridge University*
Christine Shaw, *University of Warwick*
Evelyn Welch, *University of Sussex*

ITALY IN 1492

Bormio

Como
OF Monza
Milan REP
MONT Vigevana O F
Casale
MILIAN
Tortona
FERRAT
Fornova
Genoa

Sarzana
Pietrasanta
Pisa Lucca
Leghorn REP.
OF FLORENCE
Florence

Corsica
(Genoese)

Piombino
Elba

Siena
REP.
OF
SIENA

DUCHY
OF
FERRARA
Ferrara
Bologna Ravenna
Imola

PUBLIC
VENICE
Venice

Mantua

Pesaro
Urbino Ancona
Perugia
Camerino
PAPAL
Spoleto
Viterbo
STATE
Civitavecchia
Rome
Ostia Velletri
Sora

(Venetian)

Aquila Pescara

Venafre

Sardinia

Cajazzo
Capua
Aversa Benevento
Pozzuoli Nola (Papal)
Ischia Naples
Atella

KINGDOM
Basilicita
OF
NAPLES

Bisceglia
Gravina
Altamura

Taranto

Cosenza

Squillace

Palermo

Reggio

Sicily

Boundaries ....
Papal State
Spanish
  Possessions
Milanese
  Territory

THE PAPAL STATE

AND CENTRAL ITALY

UNDER ALEXANDER VI

Introduction:
From Ferrante I to Charles VIII

David Abulafia

I

The French invasion of Italy under Charles VIII has acquired a special reputation as the start of a new era in Italian politics after the forty-year settlement that supposedly followed the Peace of Lodi in 1454.[1] The idea that this period was one of harmony and co-operation in the Italian peninsula has long been discounted; and yet the sense that Charles VIII's invasion was different in character and scale to previous French intervention in Italy has persisted, under the influence of Guicciardini's insistence that 1494 marked the beginning of an unending Italian tragedy, continuing through the reigns of Louis XII and Francis I of France and of Ferdinand II and Charles I of Spain. This collection of studies seeks to question such an assumption. It will be apparent that a clearer understanding of Charles' policies can only be gained by looking more closely at the intricate politics of the Italian states in the half century before the arrival of the French king. Particular emphasis has to be placed on the role of the kingdom of Naples and southern Italy (technically known as the *Regnum Sicilie citra Farum*, that is, the 'Kingdom of Sicily this side of the straits of Messina' or simply the *Regno*, the Kingdom par excellence); this kingdom, after all, was the first target of Charles VIII's armies, even though he aimed also to validate the traditional claim of the kings of Naples to Jerusalem by leading a crusade eastwards. Milan too, the source of an invitation to Charles VIII to enter Italy (as if any were needed), figures prominently in this volume; its relations with Naples are not merely particularly well documented, but they also were of signal importance in maintaining a rough balance within the peninsula in the late fifteenth century. These attempts to secure peace within Italy, though always to the best advantage of one's own state, were

---

[1] For the political condition of Italy in this period, see G. Pillinini, *Il sistema degli stati italiani 1454-1494* (Venice, 1970); P. Margaroli, *Diplomazia e stati rinascimentali. Le ambascerie sforzesche fino alla conclusione della Lega italica (1450-1455)* (Florence/Milan, 1992).

placed at risk by the intervention of outsiders. In particular, the career of the ruler of Anjou, Provence and Lorraine, *le bon roi* René, was punctuated by serious attempts to lay claim to the *Regno* and then to wrest it from its Aragonese rulers; René failed to understand that his own ambitions threatened to unsettle delicate power relations within Italy.[2] By stressing the antecedents, it becomes easier to answer the question why this invasion succeeded when earlier attempts by René's family to gain control of southern Italy failed.

The history of the French invasion is not merely one of French success. It is also one of the failure of the Aragonese dynasty in Naples.[3] Even when the French under Louis XII were finally expelled from southern Italy, this was achieved not by the Neapolitan branch of the house of Aragon, but by the Spanish branch under Ferdinand II, king of Aragon. The shifting loyalty of the south Italian barons and cities can be demonstrated throughout the fifteenth century. External interests, not least those of Venice, also sought to capitalise on troubles in the south to achieve advantage, a point made plain in Carol Kidwell's account of the continual attempts by the Venetians to gain lordship over the Apulian coastal towns. It is, indeed, essential to turn back to the long reign of Ferrante in order to explain Charles' ephemeral success in conquering Naples in 1495; even the moment of his accession contained the germ of his dynasty's defeat, as Milan, the papacy and other major powers deliberated on whether to sink or save the new king of Naples. Throughout the late fifteenth century, as studies in this volume by Vincent Ilardi, Giorgio Chittolini, David Chambers, Trevor Dean, Paolo Margaroli, Christine Shaw all make plain, the Milanese, the Mantuans, the Ferrarese, the Roman barons possessed their own specific agenda which determined whether, and for how long, they might be prepared to tolerate a French presence in Italy. The career of Ludovico il Moro as duke of Milan is clear testimony to the shifting interests and close calculation that underlay Italian support for Charles, when it was on offer.

This introductory chapter offers a short description of the invasion by Charles VIII, as a setting for more closely focussed studies of its antecedents and effects. However, to narrate the events of 1494-95 without paying attention to the career of the king of Naples who played so large a part in Italian politics and diplomacy before his death early in 1494 would mean making the familiar mistake of treating Charles VIII's invasion out of context: the fact that Ferrante I of Naples died early in 1494, and did not witness the tearing apart of his

---

[2] The classic biography of René is that by A. Lecoy de la Marche, *Le roi René*, 2 vols. (Paris, 1875); it is not especially illuminating on his Italian expeditions, however. More recent lives include J. Levron, *Le bon roi René* (Paris, 1972); M. Miquel, *Quand le bon roi René chevauchait en Provence* (Paris, 1979), and many more popular studies which do not add anything of significance to Lecoy's work. There is clearly more to be done here.

[3] For an overview of this dynasty, see G. Galasso, *Il Regno di Napoli*, vol. 1, *Il Mezzogiorno angioino e aragonese*, in the UTET Storia d'Italia (Turin, 1992).

kingdom, does not mean that he was an insignificant actor in the French-Aragonese confrontation that was looming at the end of his life.

II

King Ferrante or Ferdinand of Naples, whose long reign stretched from 1458 to 1494, early acquired a reputation for subtle diplomacy, duplicity and cruelty that has been vividly perpetuated in Jacob Burckhardt's characterisation of him in *The Civilization of the Renaissance in Italy*: 'it is certain that he was equalled in ferocity by none among the princes of his time', and yet he was 'recognised as one of the most powerful political minds of the day', who avoided all other vices in order to concentrate on the destruction of his political opponents. He enjoyed above all having his enemies near him, 'either in well-guarded prisons, or dead and embalmed, dressed in the costume which they wore in their lifetime. He would chuckle in talking of the captives with his friends, and made no secret whatever of his museum of mummies'.[4] It is essential therefore to stress that Burckhardt's presentation of Ferrante formed part of an argument concerning the legacy of Emperor Frederick II, whose imitation of oriental despotism was seen as a fundamental element in the creation of the state as a work of art; Ferrante thus emerges as his worthy successor in managing the economy, in restraining the feudal nobility and in setting a standard of royal cultural patronage.

This appalling reputation has its origins in the violent controversies that raged over the legitimacy of Ferrante's claim to the throne, and in the constant attempts of French princes to assert their own right to the kingdom of Naples. Yet the claim to rule of Ferrante could easily enough be faulted; as Alan Ryder shows in this book, the French king had a genuine claim to the throne of Naples which originated in the conquest of southern Italy, at papal behest, by Charles count of Anjou and Provence in 1266, and it was to Charles of Anjou that commentators such as Francesco Guicciardini, the great sixteenth-century Florentine historian, pointed when trying to explain what the French were doing in Italy. The discussion by Georges Peyronnet of French relations with Italy in this volume makes clear the exceptionally long history of French intervention in the peninsula, even if it was only with Charles VIII that a king of France actually led his own armies into Italy. The mid-fifteenth-century claimant René of Anjou-Provence was on more than one occasion widely accepted as ruler of the south Italian kingdom, and his chivalric order, the *Croissant*, became a haven for fugitive, dispossessed south Italian barons in search of a patron. Distinguished by its strict emphasis on the highest birth, the Order of the

---

[4] Jacob Burckhardt, *The Civilization of the Renaissance in Italy*, trans. S.G.C. Middlemore, ed. P. Burke and P. Murray (Harmondsworth, 1990), 40-41.

Croissant stands in interesting comparison alongside Ferrante's Order of the Ermine, similarly an attempt to bond south Italian barons to their leader: an order in which there was understandably no such emphasis on unalloyed nobility of birth, since the king of Naples himself was a love-child.[5]

Ferrante was born in Valencia in about 1425, but raised in southern Italy and recognised as duke of Calabria, that is, royal heir, by the south Italian barons.[6] Ferrante's illegitimacy gave rise to hostile rumours that his real father was a Spanish Moor or a converted Jew; apart from anything else, the strong physical resemblance between Alfonso and Ferrante visible in their portraits gives the lie to this accusation, and his mother can almost certainly be identified as a Catalan gentlewoman, Gueraldona Carlina Reverdit.[7] Illegitimate birth was not an irremovable obstacle to political success in fifteenth-century Italy, as the career of any number of Italian *signori* will make plain. More problematic, however, was the suitability of a bastard as heir to a real throne. If there was one kingdom where precedents for kings of bastard origin existed, it was the *Regnum Sicilie*; in the late twelfth century the illegitimate Norman prince Tancred briefly ruled Sicily and southern Italy with papal approval, and the thirteenth-century bastard prince Manfred of Hohenstaufen was elected king in the face of stiff papal opposition.

Here salvation could be found in Rome. Not merely could the pope be invited to legitimise Ferrante, but the kingdom of Naples itself was a dependency of the Holy See: the crown of Naples was technically in the gift of the pope, despite a long history of refusal by the rulers of the south to countenance serious papal intervention in their succession plans; indeed, it was only because the pope chose him (and rejected Manfred) that Charles of Anjou had been invested with the kingdom that his fifteenth-century successors now also claimed.[8] This time such papal intervention would be crucial; yet the pope, Calixtus III Borgia, from Valencia, a close associate of Alfonso V, ignored his predecessors' acceptance of Ferrante as heir to the throne and obstinately refused to accept him as king of Naples, planning, so rumour insisted, to

---

[5] M. Reynolds, 'René of Anjou, King of Sicily, and the Order of the *Croissant*', *Journal of Medieval History*, 19 (1993), 125-61 and, for the Ermine, D'A.J.D. Boulton, *The Knights of the Crown. The monarchical Orders of Knighthood in later medieval Europe, 1325-1520* (Woodbridge, Suffolk, 1987), 402-26, and also British Library Additional MS 28,628 for the statutes in Latin.

[6] There is no proper biography in any language of Ferrante, despite his agreed importance in Italian fifteenth-century politics, and despite the existence of biographies of his father, daughter, cousin, grandson, etc. A good introduction to the period is Jerry H. Bentley, *Politics and Culture in Renaissance Naples* (Princeton, NJ, 1987). For the antecedents, see A. Ryder, *Alfonso the Magnanimous* (Oxford, 1990).

[7] E. Pontieri, 'La giovinezza di Ferrante I d'Aragona', *Studi in onore di Riccardo Filangieri* (Naples, 1959), 531-601.

[8] Steven Runciman, *The Sicilian Vespers. A history of the Mediterranean world in the thirteenth century* (Cambridge, 1958).

proclaim one of his own nephews as ruler instead.[9] He seems to have gloried in the chance to act independently now that Alfonso was no longer alive, and he may, as a Valencian like Ferrante, have looked down on the king's mother and her family. It was only with the unexpected death of Calixtus late in 1458 and the election as pope of the great scholar Aeneas Sylvius Piccolomini as Pope Pius II that Ferrante received the recognition he craved, largely because Pius was anxious to maintain the peace of Italy while planning a great crusade against the Turks, who had only recently seized Constantinople.[10] At the Council of Mantua in 1459 Pius was thus careful to keep open his channels of communication with the house of Anjou, since the pope's major interest at the Mantua meeting was the new crusade, which earned many promises but very little concrete help; however, he refused to bow to eloquent French demands at the congress for the recognition of René of Anjou's claim to Naples.[11] His dilemma was clear. If he promised support to the house of Anjou, he might expect greater assurances of aid from the French; but the price would surely be that disruption of Italy which would delay still further the crusade against the Turk.

In any case, Ferrante had effective replies to the French claim. In the first place, Ferrante had been nominated as king of Naples by his father Alfonso the Magnanimous, whose own rights to the south of Italy originated not simply in conquest but in the will of the profligate last Angevin ruler of Naples, Joanna II, who died in 1434. Duke René of Anjou saw the death of Alfonso as an opportunity simply to reassert the rights that had been denied him by the king of Aragon, and so the accession of Ferrante saw renewed assaults on Italy by Angevin armies.[12] Their first place of concentration was Genoa, which was fortunate for Ferrante since both the king of France and the duke of Milan possessed clashing claims to overlordship over Genoa, and there were justifiable fears that it could be used as a base from which a naval assault on the *Regno* would be launched. Thus Angevin interference in Genoa pushed Francesco

---

[9] On Calixtus, see M. Mallett, *The Borgias. The rise and fall of a Renaissance dynasty* (2nd ed., London, 1971), 60-78, (3rd ed., Chicago, 1987), 67-89.

[10] The biographies of Ferrante by C.M. Ady, *Pius II* (London, 1913), and by R.J. Mitchell, *The laurels and the tiara* (London, 1962) both have rather little to say on Pius' relations with Ferrante, another example of the tendency to marginalise the history of southern Italy even when it is highly relevant to that of central and northern Italy as well. However, Pope Pius himself was more forthcoming: see his *Commentaries*, transl. F.A. Gragg, L.C. Gabel, *Smith College Studies in History*, vols. 22, 25, 30, 35, 43; abridged ed., *Memoirs of a Renaissance Pope. The Commentaries of Pius II* (New York, 1959; London, 1960; new ed., with new pagination, as *Secret Memoirs of a Renaissance Pope, the Commentaries of Aeneas Sylvius Piccolomini, Pius II*, Folio Society, London, 1988).

[11] Joycelyne G. Russell, *Diplomats at Work. Three Renaissance Studies* (Stroud, Gloucestershire, 1992), 60-67.

[12] For a detailed study, see E. Nunziante, 'I primi anni di Ferrante I d'Aragona e l'invasione di Giovanni d'Angiò', *Archivio storico per le province napoletane*, 17-23 (1892-98).

Sforza, duke of Milan, even more decisively into co-operation with Ferrante, who sent his own fleets (with all too little success) against Genoa and who tried to ensure that his cousin John (or Joan) II of Aragon would give him full naval support; it should be stressed that Francesco Sforza had earlier been well disposed to René of Anjou at the time of his own struggle with Alfonso V for Milan.[13] The danger that the French enemies of the house of Aragon would acquire an important naval base in northern Italy was one which remained a source of concern right up to the early sixteenth century.

As well as facing an external enemy, Ferrante faced internal foes who were only too glad to seize the opportunity offered by the renewed Angevin challenge to the house of Aragon. Several key barons, such as the Orsini Prince of Taranto, were reluctant from the start to recognise Ferrante as king; René's son Jean arrived in Italy and fostered revolt among the south Italian barons. Ferrante worked hard to contain this first baronial revolt, building close ties to the most important Italian princes, such as Francesco Sforza, duke of Milan, to whose daughter Ippolita his own son Alfonso was betrothed (for her subsequent role, see the study in this volume by Evelyn Welch); Ferrante's persistent message was that he had no ambitions within Italy beyond the maintenance of the peace of the peninsula. Ferrante keenly realised that his major task was simply that of imposing order in southern Italy; unlike his father, Alfonso, he possessed no great empire in Spain and the Mediterranean which could offer him the means to dominate all of Italy. Several times Ferrante was on the verge of being destroyed; the battle of Sarno in July 1460 resulted in devastating defeat not far from Naples, from which Ferrante only recovered because the Angevins failed to follow up their advantage. The Angevin forces tended to withdraw into the Abruzzi, where they possessed some loyal allies; but the northernmost region of the *Regno* was not an ideal base from which to organise the conquest of Naples and the entire south. Moreover, the great Albanian military commander Skanderbeg, who spent much of his career fighting the Turks in his homeland, at the start of Ferrante's reign, saved the king from almost certain defeat at the hands of Jean d'Anjou, using his Albanian *stradiot* soldiers to wear away the opposition by constant attrition.[14] Two years later the tables were turned at the battle of Troia in August 1462, but all the same Jean d'Anjou was not seen off until 1465, after a joint Neapolitan and Aragonese fleet destroyed the Angevin navy.

---

[13] See the comments in the article in this volume on the inception of Ferrante's reign. For the duke of Milan, see F. Catalano, *Francesco Sforza* (Milan, 1983), C. Santoro, *Gli Sforza* (2nd ed., Milan, 1992), while it is still worth referring to C.M. Ady, *A History of Milan under the Sforza* (London, 1907).

[14] The lack of an up-to-date study of Skanderbeg is surprising, not least in view of the reputation that he still possesses in Albania. See meanwhile Fan Noli, *George Castrioti Skanderbeg* (New York, 1947).

Revolt spelled treachery, and Ferrante was merciless to those who had stabbed him in the back. His treatment of the great mercenary captain Jacopo Piccinino is a famous example of how, when Ferrante believed he was performing a service for the peace of all of Italy, he earned instead obloquy. Piccinino had been seeking to carve out a principality for himself around Assisi, in the papal state, a position perilously close not merely to the borders of the kingdom of Naples but to other influential lordships, such as that of Sigismondo Malatesta, lord of Rimini and that of Federigo da Montefeltro, count of Urbino, a very close ally of King Ferrante.[15] Frustrated in his ambition (partly because Ferrante himself failed to lend support for fear of damaging relations with the papacy), Piccinino served with his mercenaries in the Angevin armies that were attempting to unseat Ferrante; a recommendation of papal support for Piccinino was an ill-considered clause in the presentation of the French case against Ferrante at the Congress of Mantua. At the end of the war, in 1465, the victorious Ferrante invited Piccinino to his court in what was assumed to be an act of magnanimity. Nearly a month of feasting in honour of Piccinino, who had just married an illegitimate daughter of Ferrante's ally the duke of Milan, ended abruptly with the arrest of Piccinino, who then fell in suspicious circumstances out of a high window and died of his injuries. It was also a message to those south Italian barons who contemplated further resistance; if a mercenary captain from outside the kingdom was dispensable, how much more so were they.

The ambition of maintaining the peace of Italy was more easily proclaimed than achieved. Ferrante's persistent professions of friendship towards the other major powers within Italy, Sforza Milan, Venice, Medicean Florence and the papacy, were thrown off balance in 1478 when the enemies of Lorenzo de' Medici sought by assassination to put to an end the ascendancy of the Medici within Florence. The Pazzi conspiracy against the Medici, from which Lorenzo himself escaped, culminated in a joint campaign by Ferrante's son Alfonso duke of Calabria and the forces of Ferrante's grudging ally Pope Sixtus IV against Florence; under pressure from the Neapolitan armies, the Florentine government allowed Lorenzo de' Medici to travel to see Ferrante in Naples and to negotiate a peace. This was portrayed at the time, in a letter from Lorenzo to the government of Florence, as a heroic gesture by a private citizen of Florence who was well aware how capricious the king of Naples could be, and who could easily find himself sharing the fate of Jacopo Piccinino: 'if our adversaries aim only at me, they will have me in their power'.[16] Indeed, Machiavelli recounts that some of Lorenzo's enemies within Florence were

---

[15] C.H. Clough, 'Federico da Montefeltro and the kings of Naples: a study in fifteenth-century survival', *Renaissance Studies*, 6 (1992), 113-72.

[16] Cited by C.M. Ady, *Lorenzo dei Medici and Renaissance Florence* (London, 1955), 76.

hoping Ferrante would treat him like Piccinino. Yet it is also plain that Lorenzo and Ferrante knew the time had come for peace; Ferrante drew honour from his generous treatment of so famous a foe as Lorenzo, while Florence was granted an equitable peace which also confirmed the Medicean ascendancy in the city. Ferrante began to regard Lorenzo as one of the chief guarantors of stability within Italy, constantly protesting his friendship and admiration for Lorenzo, even elevating him to the high office of Grand Chamberlain of the kingdom in 1483; in 1492, the king prophetically recognised the dangers to all Italy that followed from the death of Lorenzo.[17]

Yet the price of friendship for Florence was open papal enmity after years of tension beneath the surface; this break culminated in an ugly war between Naples, Florence and Milan on the one hand and Venice and the papacy on the other over control of Ferrara (1482-84), a territory that had long been a focus of disagreement between the north Italian states.[18] The conflict further generated discord within the Neapolitan kingdom, resulting in the outbreak of a second baronial revolt in 1485-86, directed in large measure against royal attempts to rein in the power of the nobility.[19] Duke Alfonso of Calabria was credited with plans to break the nobility by establishing direct royal control over a great swathe of territory around Naples. Faced with dispossession of lands and with increasing limitations on their political freedom, the nobles conspired to replace Ferrante and more particularly his heir Alfonso; an offer of the crown to Ferrante's wise and experienced brother Federigo or Frederick was flatly rejected; there was no obvious source of support among the Angevin claimants to Naples, for Good King René was dead and had been predeceased by his son Jean, with the result that his lands had soon passed into the hands of the French king, Louis XI. Content to have acquired Provence at long last, the 'Universal Spider' was reluctant to draw the French into potentially limitless conflicts within Italy, showing a degree of statesmanship that, arguably, his son Charles VIII was not to share. Yet there were still Angevin shadows over the *Regno*:

---

[17] There are several invaluable intersecting studies of these events: H. Butters, 'Lorenzo and Naples', in G.C. Garfagnani, ed., *Lorenzo il Magnifico e il suo mondo. Convegno internazionale di studi (Firenze, 9-13 giugno 1992)* (Florence, 1994), 143-51; H. Butters, 'Florence, Milan and the Barons' War (1485-1486)', in G.C. Garfagnani, ed., *Lorenzo de' Medici. Studi* (Florence, 1992), 281-308; H. Butters, 'Politics and diplomacy in late Quattrocento Italy: the case of the Barons' War (1485-1486)', in P. Denley and C. Elam, eds., *Florence and Italy. Renaissance Studies in honour of Nicolai Rubinstein* (London, 1988), 13-31. Useful material on Ferrante and Florence can also be found in Paula C. Clarke, *The Soderini and the Medici. Power and patronage in fifteenth-century Florence* (Oxford, 1991).

[18] Recent studies of this war and its aftermath include M. Mallett, 'Venice and the War of Ferrara, 1482-1484' and T. Dean, 'After the War of Ferrara: relations between Venice and Ercole d'Este, 1484-1505' both in D.S. Chambers, C.H. Clough, M.E. Mallett, eds., *War, culture and society in Renaissance Venice. Essays in honour of John Hale* (London, 1994), 57-72, 73-98.

[19] For this, see C. Porzio, *La congiura dei Baroni*, in various editions: Naples, 1964, Milan, 1965, Venosa, 1989, etc.

the father of the new pope, Innocent VIII, had actually fought for René of Anjou against the Aragonese; Innocent now eagerly supported the rebels.[20] Ferrante had been right that the stability of his own lands depended on the wider stability of the Italian peninsula. It was the papacy that had sanctioned his succession to the throne; and disputes with the Holy See, over border territories and over the payment of annual tribute by the king of Naples, had particularly serious consequences in a kingdom whose barons were suspicious of attempts at royal centralisation and of the king's fiscal policy. Yet what is particularly striking about the revolt is that the ringleaders included new men who had risen to prominence from relatively modest backgrounds only as a result of royal favour: the millionnaire Francesco Coppola, count of Sarno, and Antonello Petrucci, who served as royal secretary.

Apart from the pope, then, the rebels lacked really decisive external support, and 'how many legions has the pope?', as Stalin's famous question goes. Unable to crack royal power, the rebels decided to come to terms. They hoped that they had taught the king a lesson, and that government policy would be tailored to their needs. Ferrante appeared compliant. But in time honoured fashion, he destroyed the opposition by inviting his leading foes, supposedly forgiven, to a conciliatory marriage feast in honour of the son of the leading rebel, the count of Sarno, and Ferrante's own grand-daughter. In the midst of the feasting he arrested the count and his allies, later also arresting many other powerful noblemen who had resisted him, and reputedly murdering them and their families.

Ferrante's wish for stabilisation within Italy reflected wider Mediterranean concerns; there was simply no time for the luxury of internal squabbles when a powerful external threat to all Italy existed in the east. A few years before the second baronial rebellion, the arrival of a Turkish fleet at Otranto in 1480-81 served as a bitter reminder that the kingdom of Naples now lay on the edge of the Ottoman world. The capture of Otranto was followed by the massacre of many of its inhabitants; twelve thousand out of its population of twenty thousand (including all the males in the town) were reportedly put to death, and on one occasion eight hundred Otrantines were marched up a hill and executed for refusing to become Muslims.[21] But the fall of Otranto also proved that the Turks were very nearly able to shut the vital sea lanes down the Adriatic. The death of the sultan meant that the Turks suddenly lost interest in their Italian campaign; they were chased away by Alfonso of Calabria with the naval help of Ferrante's cousin Ferdinand king of Aragon, and Italy (including

---

[20] E. Pontieri, *Venezia e il conflitto tra Ferrante I d'Aragona e Innocenzo VIII* (Naples, 1969), reprinting material published in the *Archivio storico per le province napoletane* in 1966-67.

[21] F. Babinger, *Mehmed the Conqueror and his time*, ed. W.C. Hickman, trans. R. Manheim (Princeton, NJ, 1978), 390-92.

even the irate Pope Sixtus IV) united for once in support of Ferrante; but the strategic issue of control of the Adriatic ports of the kingdom of Naples remained an important one throughout the late fifteenth and sixteenth centuries, a worry in particular to the Venetians (a point well illustrated in Carol Kidwell's contribution to this book). Concern with the Turkish threat is also visible in Charles VIII's insistence that it was his aim to use Naples as a base for a grand crusade for the recovery of Constantinople and Jerusalem. Ferrante's close political and cultural links to Matthias Corvinus, king of Hungary, who married his daughter Beatrice, must also be seen as part of a far-sighted wider strategy of building a vast barrier against the Ottomans in the Balkans and the Adriatic.[22] His longstanding attempts to secure the crown of Cyprus for his family, and even to win the favour of the Mamluk sultans of Egypt, is all surely part of the same grand scheme.[23] In this sense Ferrante was not entirely forgetful of his claim to be king of Jerusalem, a claim reiterated every time the royal armns were raised, carrying the distinctive cross of the kingdom of Jerusalem.

It was natural that, as an Aragonese prince, Ferrante should seek good relations with his Spanish cousins, who in any case controlled the neighbouring island of Sicily, which might also suffer badly if the Turks gained a stranglehold on the southern Adriatic and the Ionian Sea. Relations with Aragon were generally smooth, and there was little sense that Ferrante was in any way subordinate to his father's successors in Spain. Ferrante counted on Aragonese assistance against Jean d'Anjou in Genoa and off Ischia. Yet Ferrante was immune to one major feature of Spanish policy in these years. In 1492 Ferdinand and Isabella expelled the Jews from all their lands in Spain and Italy; there was a massive influx of Sicilian and Spanish Jews into the kingdom of Naples which Ferrante openly welcomed.[24] He saw the Jews as a valuable source of artisan skills, for many Spanish and Sicilian Jews were active in such crafts as cloth production; he also reveals, in his public documents, a genuine desire to protect the Jews in southern Italy from increasing persecution at the hands of their Christian neighbours.

Certainly Ferrante was keen to establish manufacturing industries in southern Italy, notably the silk industry; and he aimed to fit out a royal fleet whose galleys could reach as far afield as England, entering into a treaty with Edward IV in 1468. He attempted to limit the sale of the Catalan and Majorcan

---

[22] On Beatrice, see the rather old-fashioned biography by Berzeviczy, of which an abridged Italian translation, Beatrice d'Aragona, is available in two editions (Milan, 1931 and 1974) which leave out most of the section on the Neapolitan background.

[23] M. Jacoviello, *Venezia e Napoli nel Quattrocento* (Naples, 1992); D. and I. Hunt, eds., *Caterina Cornaro, Queen of Cyprus* (London, 1989), 80-81, 92-3, 99, 106-7, 112, 119, 128-9.

[24] The literature on the expulsion of Spain is vast; as a brief starting point, see David Abulafia, *Spain and 1492. Unity and uniformity under Ferdinand and Isabella* (Headstart History Papers, Bangor, 1992).

cloths which were flooding into southern Italy, to give breathing space to local producers. Peace with Florence in 1479 brought with it handsome privileges for Florentine merchants, who offered invaluable financial help in the struggle against the Turks encamped at Otranto. There may be some validity in the suggestion that Ferrante was conducting an 'anti-feudal policy', that he saw the cities and their potential wealth as a powerful counterweight against the barons; he was, in a sense, a *roi bourgeois* anxious to create an alternative power base that did not depend on noble approval, a policy that would mark a break from his father's ready acceptance of the nobles as partners in government. Ferrante's close adviser Diomede Carafa (himself a great Neapolitan nobleman) wrote a tract on economic policy advising Ferrante to moderate taxes so that business could flourish unhampered, 'for a king cannot be poor to whose power wealthy men are subject'; Carafa insisted that 'where one just rule flourishes, there the cities flower and the riches of the citizens grow'. Moreover, 'money is struck not for the profit of the prince, but for ease of buying and selling, and for the advantage of the people'. Carafa thus moves beyond the straightforward fiscalism of earlier south Italian governments towards the enunciation of a liberal economic policy based on the principle that the crown will reap more benefits the less it intervenes through heavy taxation in the economic life of the kingdom. There are indeed signs that Carafa's ideals were put into practice under Ferrante, who also had the chance to benefit from growing population, expansion of the massive sheep flocks (a major source of revenue to the crown), and commercial recovery in the western Mediterranean. The fair of Salerno in 1478 is particularly well documented; there, north Italian businessmen congregated in sizeable numbers, and, although few southerners could compete with them in scale of business (except for Francesco Coppola, future count of Sarno), the fair provided a base for over two hundred south Italian merchants, and was a centre of exchange for cloths from Majorca, Languedoc, Florence and elsewhere; the impression is of a lively market, even though Ferrante's hopes of reviving manufactures within the *Regno* proved more difficult to achieve. In economic terms, the reign of Ferrante does not deserve the bad press it has traditionally received.[25]

Diomede Carafa was one of a group of distinguished men of letters who gathered at Ferrante's court. Alfonso the Magnanimous had already established a lively court in Naples, and under Ferrante the emphasis shifted slightly; Ferrante himself had been trained to a high pitch in law, and there was a shift towards what might be called more practical learning and away from the patronage of lyric poetry and the fine arts. But this was a movement of degree

---

[25] David Abulafia, 'The Crown and the economy under Ferrante I of Naples (1458-1494)', in T. Dean, C. Wickham, eds., *City and Countryside in late medieval and Renaissance Italy. Essays presented to Philip Jones* (London, 1990), 125-46.

only; Naples continued to attract artists of the stature of the painter Antonello da Messina and the sculptor Guido Mazzoni, whose life-size terracotta depiction of the entombment of Christ in the church of Monteoliveto in Naples incorporates portraits of the royal family. As Simon Pepper points out in his contribution to this volume, the participation of the Catalan Sagrera family of architects in Neapolitan building projects was particularly notable; it was Guillem Sagrera who built the extraordinary Exchange (*llonja* or *llotja*) in Palma de Mallorca, and the evidence this provides for Neapolitan cultural links to the Catalan world is of some interest. The sculptured triumphal gateway to the Castelnuovo in Naples was completed under Ferrante, who commisioned portrayals in this complex of his own escape from the rebellious barons and of his coronation; Duke Alfonso of Calabria initiated plans for the rebuilding of Naples which promised to make the town into a model city, furnished with fountains, streams and straight streets, which 'would, besides giving the city beautiful proportions, have turned it into the cleanest and most elegant in Europe', to cite the Neapolitan humanist Summonte, a figure who gave the Aragonese kings of Naples an unusually good press.[26] Important innovations in court music resulted from the arrival in Naples of Flemish composers such as the royal cantor Johannes Tinctoris, who spent twenty years at Ferrante's court, and whose influence lay not merely in his compositions and his performances, but also in his treatises on the art of music. Tinctoris, according to the major authority on Neapolitan Renaissance music, 'put Naples in the centre of the musical mainstream'; he was 'one of the seminal figures in Renaissance music theory'. Ferrante's policy was to offer salaries to the best musicians he could find in Europe. The humanist Raffaelle Brandolini wrote in about 1513 that

> Ferdinand pursued musical science with such affection that not only did he cultivate it himself most frequently in his private leisure but also attracted from all over Europe by means of most excellent rewards men most learned in this discipline.

Brandolini singles out for special praise the international team of singers, drawn from France, England, Germany and Spain, in the royal chapel, which contained two organs. Dance was much cultivated, under the eye of Giovanni Ambrosio da Pesaro, a converted Jew (also called Guglielmo Ebreo), who trained the royal princesses. Secular music also flourished, stimulated by the vigorous Italian poetry of Sannazaro and others.[27]

Distinguished literary figures at court included the eminent poet and administrator Giovanni Gioviano Pontano, who was active in the literary circle that still persists as the Accademia Pontaniana of Naples; Antonio Beccadelli, or Panormita, a reformed pornographer, wrote an elegant history of Ferrante's life

---

[26] On art, see G.L. Hersey, *The Aragonese arch at Naples* (New Haven, 1973), G.L. Hersey, *Alfonso II and the artistic renewal of Naples* (New Haven, 1969).

[27] A. Atlas, *Music at the Aragonese court of Naples* (Cambridge, 1985).

up to his assumption of the crown; the royal librarian Giovanni Brancati built up a splendid collection of books, and was himself the author of several political tracts and translations of key classical works. Ferrante took an interest in the new craft of printing, extending his protection to such figures as the immigrant German printer Sixtus Riessinger, and Naples became one of the major centres not merely for the printing of Latin and Italian works, but also for Hebrew printing. Given his legal interests, it is not surprsing that Ferrante stimulated the dormant university of Naples into new life, a policy which had a knock-on effect on demand for printed books. One of the early printed books to survive from Naples is Riessinger's edition, dated 1475, of the famous law-book of 1231 composed for Ferrante's predecessor as ruler and as patron of Naples University, Emperor Frederick II. In intellectual circles considerable thought was given to the problem how to adapt the predominantly civic republican ideals expressed in the political tracts of early fifteenth-century Florentine humanists to the political structure of a large Italian kingdom. Indeed, Naples became a magnet for Florentine intellectuals, with Ferrante himself earning elegant praise from Francesco Bandini in the 1470's on the grounds that he had brought justice, stability and prosperity to his kingdom at a time when Florence was lacking all three.[28]

Ferrante I died early in 1494 as the sound of French war drums began to be heard from across the Alps. The history of the French invasion and of the fall of the Neapolitan house of Aragon will be examined in a moment. What needs to be asserted here is that the destruction of the Aragonese dynasty resulted in a propaganda victory for Ferrante's enemies. He was illegitimate by birth; but so were many contemporary Italian rulers, and he had the benefit of papal sanction as they generally did not. He was duplicitous and cruel; but his enemies gave in equal kind; he was, after all, a contemporary of Louis XI and Richard III. Yet he also had ideals which were not simply self-centred: the preservation of peace within Italy, which only occasionally proved achievable; the stabilisation of his kingdom in the face of baronial power; the prosperity of his subjects. He was conscious enough of the precarious nature of south Italian politics not to allow himself, in imitation of his father, to be bewitched by vainglory and grandiose ambition; as has been seen, at the start of his reign he insisted in his letters to Francesco Sforza that he had one aim only: to exercise power within his south Italian inheritance, for unlike his father he was not, and had no real claim to be, a Mediterranean emperor controlling half a dozen kingdoms. His barons gave him little pause in which to dream of acquiring further lands, whether in Cyprus or within Italy itself. It was enough to manage to stay on the throne, which, after all, he did for nearly thirty-six years.

---

[28] Bentley, *Politics and culture in Renaissance Naples*; Carol Kidwell, *Pontano. Poet and Prime Minister* (London, 1991), and other studies by the same author.

III

It has been seen that Ferrante's son Alfonso, duke of Calabria, was already exceedingly unpopular with some of the barons in the 1480's, so that he rather than his father appears to have been the primary focus of complaint during the Second Barons' War. His accession in 1494 was therefore less smooth than appearances suggested: the papal chronicler Burchard offers a glittering description of Alfonso's coronation in May (though Ferrante had died in January), at the hands of Cardinal Giovanni Borgia, whose uncle was Pope Alexander VI.[29] The alliance between the papacy and Naples seemed still to have some meaning; marriage alliances linked the Borgia family with the house of Aragon, and attached to them were assignments of grand titles and lands in the deep south of Italy. In reality, however, Pope Alexander VI was constantly wavering between the desirability of showing some friendship to France and the advantages of maintaining close influence over his vassal and neighbour the king of Naples.

So too in recent years other props of the Italian League had been seriously weakened. It has been seen that the death of Lorenzo de' Medici in 1492 had already been recognised by Ferrante as a blow to the peace of Italy, for, despite Lorenzo's lack of a permanent official position at the head of Florence's government, his counsel had been crucial since 1479 in maintaining peace with Naples, and (as far as it was possible to do so) within Italy. More serious still was the erosion of Neapolitan influence at the court of Milan, first under Duke Galeazzo Maria (d. 1476), and eventually under Ludovico Sforza. The young duke Giangaleazzo Sforza was the husband to Ferrante's grand-daughter Isabella, and the ratification of their betrothal had at first restored the warmth of relations between Milan and Naples.[30] The reality was, however, that power in Milan was exercised by Giangaleazzo's uncle, Lodovico 'il Moro', 'the Moor', supposedly so called because of his swarthy complexion.[31] The Neapolitans were aware of his standing at the Milanese court, and recognised his succession to the Sforza duchy of Bari; and he took as wife Beatrice d'Este, a much loved grand-daughter of Ferrante, who had been brought up at the Neapolitan court (though she was not actually Ludovico's first choice).[32] It hardly seemed likely, though, that Ludovico would turn into an enemy of the house of Aragon, and

---

[29] G. Parker, trans., *At the Court of the Borgia being an account of the reign of Pope Alexander VI written by his Master of Ceremonies Johann Burchard* (Folio Society, London, 1963), 70-81; original ed. Johanni Burchardi, *Liber Notarum ab anno 1483 usque ad anno 1506*, ed. E. Celani, *Rerum italicarum scriptores*, ser. 2 (Città di Castello, 1906), 2 vols.

[30] Ady. *History of Milan*, 126.

[31] F. Catalano, *Ludovico il Moro* (Milan, 1985).

[32] With characteristic aplomb, Maria Bellonci describes her life in 'Beatrice and Isabella d'Este', in J.H. Plumb, ed., *Renaissance profiles* (New York, 1965), 139-56.

yet all this was insufficient inducement for the retention of his loyalty in the 1490's.[33] It was Ludovico who saw in the arrival of French armies a chance to bolster his position in Milan, to counter Neapolitan influence in the peninsula, and, no less urgently, to fend off Venice's attempts to secure its influence in the cities of the Lombard plain. In sum, Italy was the object of competition between two ruthless princes, the king of Naples and Ludovico, and the solution adopted by the latter was to call in as arbiter of Italian affairs an outside agency, France.

The moment was a propitious one. The death of King Louis XI (1461-83) marked the end of a reign in which a firm emphasis had been placed on the consolidation of royal authority within France and along its immediate borders: the ending of the hundred year long conflict with England, the resolution of difficulties with the Valois dukes of Burgundy, past arbiters of Anglo-French relations, the assertion of French interests in Provence and Roussillon, all were sizeable objectives in themselves, whether or not Louis 'always loathed everything Italian', as the great sixteenth-century Florentine historian Francesco Guicciardini tendentiously asserted.[34] Louis did, however, mediate when appropriate in the affairs of Italy, helping to broker peace between Naples, Florence and Milan in 1479.[35] Despite shocking Italians with his earthy allusions to the doubtful parentage of King Ferrante, and supporting Florence when it was threatened by Ferrante, Louis had the political acuteness to realise that he would gain nothing from further instability in the peninsula. He was even prepared to lease the city of Genoa to Milan, putting an end by an imaginative compromise to the bitter dispute, itself largely fuelled by factionalism within Genoa, that had soured relations between Milan and France at the start of his reign, and that had offered the Angevins a jumping-off point for an invasion of the south of Italy. Louis was certainly not prepared to let René of Anjou mould his Italian policies, though he seized the opportunity on René's death to incorporate Provence into the French realm for the first time in the county's history.[36]

By contrast, Louis' son Charles VIII has generally been portrayed as an enthusiastic devourer of historical romances, who shared with his father a direct and passionate piety, but who looked beyond France to redeem Christendom as

---

[33] The Sforza duchy of Bari has long attracted attention. See L. Pepe, *Storia della successione degli Sforzeschi negli stati di Puglia e Calabria* (Bari, 1900); N. Ferorelli, 'Il ducato di Bari sotto Sforza Maria Sforza e Ludovico il Moro', *Archivio storico lombardo*, 41 (1914), 389-468; cf. the review of Pepe's book by L. Rollone in the same journal, 29 (1902), 412-22. Vito A. Melchiorre, *Il ducato sforzesco di Bari* (Bari, 1990), is stronger on the sixteenth century.

[34] *History of Italy*, Book 1, cap. 4. (Citations in this chapter are from the translation by C. Grayson, ed. J.R. Hale, *History of Italy and History of Florence* (Chalfont St Giles, 1964).)

[35] P.M. Kendall, *Louis XI* (London, 1971), 417-18.

[36] R. Duchêne, *La Provence devient française* (Marseilles, 1986).

the new Charlemagne; dreaming of the recovery of Constantinople and Jerusalem, Charles VIII well knew that Naples was traditionally seen as the base from which a massive eastern crusade could best be launched.[37]   Though mocked by his foes in his own lifetime for his dwarfish stature and his large head with its massive nose atop a skinny body, Charles was not in fact the idiot king who is often portrayed; his concerns were well established ones that had occupied generations of Capetian kings of France and of Angevin kings of Naples, and which seemed to have gained rather than lessened in urgency now that the Turk was knocking on the gates of western Europe, having, indeed, overwhelmed Otranto in 1480-81.   The absorption of most of René of Anjou's claims brought Charles the title to Jerusalem and Sicily (i.e. Naples), and so his plans for the conquest of southern Italy were not an end in themselves, but part of a fantastic strategy aiming to wrest the Mediterranean from the Turks and the Mamluks.   Lord already of Brittany, through his marriage to the heiress to this previously autonomous territory, Charles seemed to have all France in his grasp. His father had created a French realm that stretched across the whole landmass between the Atlantic, the Pyrenees, the Alps and the western Rhineland; it was to be his task to create a French empire that stretched across all Christendom. As Guicciardini says:

> Charles was not at all unwilling to attempt to acquire by force the Kingdom of Naples as his own rightful property. The idea had been with him almost instinctively since childhood, and had been nourished by the encouragement of certain people who were very close to him. They filled him up with vain ideas and made him believe this was an opportunity to surpass the glory of his predecessors, as, once he had conquered the kingdom of Naples, he could easily defeat the empire of the Turks.[38]

It was on these sentiments that Ludovico Sforza could play, in trying to defend himself against the imagined threat to his authority posed by the Aragonese in Naples.   Yet it is a moot point whether Ludovico had in mind the massive expedition that actually reached Italy in 1494.   Attuned to subtle diplomatic bargaining, Ludovico was in the first place seeking to use Charles as a mighty counterweight against his enemies in Italy, to secure his dubious claims to authority over Milan, and to enable Milan to withstand regional threats.   There is no reason to suppose that he sought to make France the true master of Italy. Perhaps it was the threat of French aid, rather than its reality, which he proposed to use against his enemies.

---

[37] The authoritative study of Charles VIII is Y. Labande-Mailfert, *Charles VIII. La jeunesse au pouvoir (1470-1495)* (Paris, 1975); a further, shorter biography by the same author is Y. Labande-Mailfert, *Charles VIII. Le vouloir et la destiné* (Paris, 1986); see also I. Cloulas, *Charles VIII et le mirage italien* (Paris, 1986); A. Denis, *Charles VIII et les italiens: histoire et mythe* (Geneva, 1979).

[38] *History of Italy*, Book 1, cap. 4.

There is some reflection of these priorities in a grandiloquent speech that Guicciardini put into the mouth of Ludovico's ambassador to Charles; all the emphasis is placed on the glory that will accrue to Charles from a war against Naples, which will surely be far easier to accomplish than the wars of René of Anjou and Jean de Calabre, who had lacked resources and yet always came perilously near to destroying the Aragonese dynasty in Naples. But now 'it is God who leads you with such wonderful opportunities', while it is a matter of law that the house of France, as successor to that of Anjou, has a just claim to Naples, and a duty to remove from it the Catalan tyrants who oppress Charles' south Italian subjects.[39] This is thus a just war of liberation, whether of the victims of despotism in southern Italy or of the Church itself which has lost control of the holy places in the East. Yet the sub-text is plain: 'Ludovico would gain nothing but a just revenge against the intrigues and offences of the Catalans'. By insisting how little direct benefit this campaign would supposedly bring the master of Milan, Ludovico's ambassador was attempting to by-pass Ludovico's real concern to establish himself more securely in Milan. And not surprisingly opinion at the French court was sharply divided. The longstanding presence of south Italian exiles at court helped stimulate belief in the justice of the enterprise. Was Ludovico any more to be trusted than the other Italian princes? The reality was that the rulers of Milan had shifted back and forth in and out of friendship with Naples, while the expedition would undoubtedly cost a vast fortune. How would the conquered area be secured in the long term? To opponents of the scheme, the risks were over-riding.

Nor were Ludovico's protestations of friendship towards France fully supported by his actions. In his dealings with Ferrante or Alfonso and with Piero de' Medici, Ludovico tried to present himself as yet another potential victim of French aggression, arguing that he had little choice but to appear to co-operate with Charles VIII, in the light of the ancient alliance binding France and Milan, and in view of his wish to hold on to Genoa:

> Sforza, in his usual way, ingeniously fed Alfonso with various hopes, but gave him to understand that he was forced to proceed with the greatest skill and care so that the war planned against others should not begin against himself.[40]

At this time Ludovico's primary aim seems to have been to secure his investiture as duke of Milan, setting Giangaleazzo to one side, and this meant careful negotiation not with the French king but with the Holy Roman Emperor Maximilian. In other words, Ludovico's aims were not the resolution of an Italian issue, the claim to Naples, but of his own status as lord of Milan.

---

[39] *History of Italy*, Book 1, cap. 4.
[40] *History of Italy*, Book 1, cap. 6.

The pope too sought to play off the different sides, negotiating with France and Naples, offering tentative promises, though agreeing in secret that he would defend Naples if Ferrante would defend the papal states. It has been seen that after Ferrante's death the coronation of Alfonso did not take place at once; yet it did occur, and with considerable splendour, while Alexander insisted that he would not grant the kingdom of Naples to Charles until the legal rights of the French king and his rivals had been properly investigated, which was a neat way of evading the whole issue: since Charles claimed the kingdom by right of inheritance, and Alexander claimed the right to dispose of the kingdom as its overlord, the pope had clearly resolved to wait and see what the outcome of a French invasion would be. What made the complex diplomatic exchanges more urgent was a growing awareness that Charles VIII was finalising his plans. The potential trouble spot in the south-west of his realm was Roussillon, Catalan territory occupied by Louis XI but now returned to the king of Aragon without tangible benefit to the French; this act has traditionally been seen as an attempt to ensure that Ferdinand the Catholic would not interfere in Charles' Italian plans.[41] So too there were overtures to the Holy Roman Emperor, who had ancient rights in northern Italy, and with whom there were substantial past differences over control of the remnants of the former Valois duchy of Burgundy after the death in battle of Charles the Bold at Nancy (1477).

These developments, especially in the highly influential interpretation of Guicciardini, should not be allowed to mask the similarity between what was happening in 1492-94 and what had happened on many an occasion earlier in the fifteenth century: Italy once again faced a French army, though this time it was to be a royal army backed by substantially greater resources than the Angevins had ever been able to mobilise. At the time of the accession of Ferrante, a constant issue had been the presence in Italy, whether at Genoa or in the south, of *li franzisi*, the French; the need to expel them for the sake of the peace of Italy was a constant refrain of Ferrante's own letters to Francesco Sforza in Milan, and the Angevins were with some justice seen as the agents of Charles VII.

For Guicciardini, the arrival of French armies was the start of a series of calamities that transformed Italy from its 'happy state' of peace under Lorenzo and his contemporaries, into a battleground of foreign armies:

> Italy had never known such prosperity or such a desirable condition as that which it enjoyed in all tranquillity in the year 1490 and the years immediately before and after. For, all at peace and quietness, cultivated no less in the mountainous and sterile places than in the fertile regions and plains, knowing no other rule than that of its own people, Italy was not only rich in population, merchandise and wealth, but she was adorned to the highest degree by the magnificence of many princes, by the splendour of innumerable noble and beautiful cities, by the throne and majesty of religion; full

---

[41] J. Calmette, *La question des Pyrénées et la Marche d'Espagne au Moyen Age* (9th ed.,

of men most able in the administration of public affairs, and of noble minds learned in every branch of study and versed in every worthy art and skill.[42]

This is the image of Renaissance Italy which has been handed down since his day, of a Laurentian peace fostered by Florence ('no little credit was due to the industry and virtue of Lorenzo de' Medici', Guicciardini insists); since Ferrante, the duke of Milan and Lorenzo concurred in seeking peace, the internal stability of Italy was to all intents secured. The breakdown of this peace made 1494 'a most unhappy year for Italy, and truly the beginning of years of wretchedness, because it opened the way for innumerable horrible calamities which later for various reasons affected a great part of the rest of the world'.[43] Most dramatically, new forms of warfare and new attitudes to the fighting of war reached the peninsula; whereas in past times wars had cost little in blood, and had mainly consisted of tactical manoeuvres by condottiere captains, now horrible instruments arrived in Italy for the extermination of whole armies (the article in this volume by Simon Pepper expertly addresses this whole question).[44] Guicciardini romanticises the nature of combat before 1494, just as he exaggerates the degree of peace achieved in the aftermath of the Peace of Lodi of 1454; the War of Ferrara is ample testimony to the tensions that persisted within Italy in the 1480's. Yet a delicate balance had been achieved; it was also under new strains on the eve of the French invasion. Thus Pope Alexander and Ferrante fell out on the eve of the king's death over control of several castles in the Roman countryside, and factionalism within the College of Cardinals threatened to disrupt papal-Neapolitan relations; the decision by Cardinal Giuliano della Rovere, bitterest rival to the Borgias, to join the French court further complicated the pope's reactions.[45] News of French invasion plans posed a quandary for Florence; Piero de' Medici, whose hand was much less firm than that of Lorenzo, had to balance the interests of Florentine trade in France against Neapolitan demands for active support against the French. Venice too had to think hard about its stance, and, not untypically, refused to take sides despite being bombarded with pleading messages from both France and Naples; the argument for neutrality was the unsurprising one that the Turk was so serious a threat in the Balkans and in the Mediterranean (raiding, in fact, as far as Venetian territories in north-eastern Italy) that Venice could not allow herself to be sucked into peninsular rivalries.

The obvious first step in resistance against the French had to be a naval victory off Genoa which would block French access into the peninsula and

Paris, 1947).

[42] *History of Italy*, Book 1, cap. 1.

[43] *History of Italy*, Book 1, cap. 6.

[44] See the classic study by F.L. Taylor, *The art of war in Italy 1494-1529* (Cambridge, 1921, repr. London, 1993).

[45] See for this figure Christine Shaw, *Julius II. The warrior pope* (Oxford, 1993).

prevent the French from landing their field and siege artillery, much of it reportedly of types as yet unknown in Italy. Two attempts by Alfonso's brother Federigo to gain a foothold on the Genoese coast met with failure. The way was thus clear for a French army to move south; the French were at Asti in early September 1494, and nothing seemed to stand in their way as they steadily progressed southwards. It was a large army, containing many of the feared Swiss infantrymen, as well as impressive machines, and yet 'it was not the number but the calibre' of the troops that made the army so fearsome, according to Guicciardini.[46] Close discipline and effective battle tactics compounded the threat, whereas Italian troops led by mercenary captains were famed rather for their fickleness and lack of commitment to a great cause. Military might was bolstered by political successes: the French king made a courtesy call on Duke Giangaleazzo of Milan who was lying grievously ill at Pavia, either (it was said) because of immoderate sexual intercourse or because his dear uncle was poisoning him. There is in fact no reason to suppose he was murdered. In Pavia, Giangaleazzo's wife, the Neapolitan princess Isabella, threw herself in tears at the French king's feet, imploring him to show mercy to the house of Aragon; Charles was apparently much moved by the young princess' pleas, but insisted that work begun must be brought to an end.[47] In the next few days, news came that Giangaleazzo had died, leaving a small son as heir; it was not too difficult for Ludovico to persuade the ducal council to recognise himself as duke in view of the current emergency. So Ludovico had secured what he sought. In a sense, he now had little need of the French king, though his investiture by Charles with the lordship of Genoa a few weeks later was a welcome boost to his power, even if it had to be paid for handsomely in cash. Ludovico began to fall out with Charles over small territorial questions arising from control of the minor coastal towns of southern Liguria and northern Tuscany, and this growing unease, or rather sense that Charles was not an agent of Milan but a power in his own right, made Ludovico well aware that he had unleashed in Italy forces that were beyond his own control. So too in Florence Piero de' Medici was thrown into panic, and there were some skirmishes with French troops; Piero seems to have dreamed of repeating his father's success by hurrying to Naples and reinforcing the pact with the Aragonese, but he softened completely once brought into Charles' presence. As a result of exposure to Charles' potent charm, he found himself pledging 200,000 ducats as a loan towards French war expenses. Despite Florentine support for Charles, the citizens of the republic experienced a shock on discovering that Pisa, under their control for ninety years, had been regranted its liberty by the king. It was plain both that Piero de' Medici was unable to withstand Charles and that the price

---

46 *History of Italy*, Book 1, cap. 11.
47 On these events see, e.g., Cloulas, *Charles VIII*, 68-71.

paid for abandoning the Italian League was the danger that others would act as supreme arbiters of Florentine affairs. Piero was unable to hold on to power, and the Florentines managed to renegotiate terms with Charles without him, so that Pisa was simply held in gage by Charles until the end of the Neapolitan campaign. The political troubles that convulsed Florence as the Medici régime fell to pieces were to culminate in the radical reforms of Fra Girolamo Savonarola in the coming years.

Unable to hold the French away from Rome, Alfonso's son Ferrante duke of Calabria (generally known as Ferrandino) fell back with his troops, while Alexander VI also recognised that he could not withstand Charles' might. When the French king entered Rome, Alexander had to promise that the crown of Naples would eventually be his; he also handed over to him the Ottoman prince Jem, long held in detention in the west, thereby signifying that Charles must pursue the war against the Turk as soon as the affair of Naples had been settled.[48] Once the depths of winter had passed, all was ready for the final assault on Naples. Indeed, Alfonso II of Naples seemed to recognise the futility of resistance; obsessed with his past sins, he abdicated the crown, passing it on to Ferrandino (Ferrante II), and hurried in despair to Sicily, where his lived out his few remaining days behind the walls of a convent. This once famous military commander, whose experience of government stretched far back to his teens, when his father had appointed him his lieutenant during the war against Jean de Calabre, threw himself with pious passion into a life of deep religious devotion. He was well aware that he commanded fear rather than respect, and in abdicating he did not seek to hand his kingdom over to Charles but to grant his able and vigorous son a chance to win back the goodwill of his subjects, barons and townspeople alike.

Ferrandino's influence was whittled away by the mile as the French worked their way into the kingdom of Naples during February 1494. The Aragonese king proved unable to hold Capua, abandoned by the commander to whom he had entrusted this gateway into the kingdom. Retreating to Naples, Ferrandino recognised that he had no hope of withstanding the French, not just because of their might, but because of the defections which occurred day by day. He and his family, including his uncle Federigo, took ship for Ischia, hoping only that the Neapolitans would recognise before long that 'the natural arrogance of the French' (the words are Guicciardini's) would lead them some day to recall the house of Aragon.

So on 24 February 1495 Charles VIII solemnly entered Naples, having been greeted by the famed orator Giovanni Gioviano Pontano, long time adviser to the Aragonese rulers, who, like everyone else, had changed sides now that

---

[48] *At the Court of the Borgia*, 90-120. The editor comments that his promise to crown Charles king of Naples 'without bringing harm to Alfonso' was hardly achievable.

French victory seemed inevitable.[49] Violence was largely contained, with an significant exception: the Jews became the scapegoats for the misfortunes of the *Regno*, and even before the French reached Naples the Jewish quarter was sacked by local Christians. The library of the famous Jewish refugee from the court of Spain, Don Isaac Abravanel, was one sad casualty of the disorders. Indeed, as royal power weakened, it was the Jews who found themselves most exposed, since they lived in southern Italy under the willing patronage of the crown. The arrival of Jews expelled from Spain in 1492 and from Sicily in 1492-3 had exacerbated tensions, while complaints about rates of interest charged by Jewish (or indeed any other) moneylenders were legion. Charles VIII had enough understanding of the need for stability and public order to continue to protect the Jews, even though he had little experience of a people who were largely absent from France.[50] Overall, to judge from his surviving administrative acts, Charles tried to ensure that local methods of government, which had been so successful in ensuring both central control and the collection of handsome revenues, were perpetuated without major changes.[51] Guicciardini is surely very unfair when he says that Charles was content to leave the government of the south of Italy entirely to his advisers, 'who partly out of inability and partly out of avarice made a muddle of everything'.[52]

At the time of the conquest, at any rate, such problems were not yet visible. With Charles in Naples and Ferrandino in Ischia, most of the country fell away from the house of Aragon, though some coastal towns held out against the French: Tropea in Calabria and Otranto in Apulia appear to have declared for and then against the French king, though both were a long distance from Naples. Yet Charles' position was not as secure as his triumphal entry into Naples perhaps suggested; this was by far the biggest Italian state, and control of its further reaches had eluded many of his predecessors. A long stay would be necessary were the king to bond his new kingdom to the house of France. Attempts to persuade Ferrandino and his uncle (and heir apparent) Federigo to resign their claims to royal status and to hand over their extensive estates, in return for vast tracts of land in France, were met with firm but polite refusal: if God and the people of the kingdom had handed their kingdom to Charles, it was not for Ferrandino to stand in the way.[53] Charles assumed that he could solve the problems of his new kingdom by appointing a lieutenant (Gilbert de Montpensier), granting lands and office to faithful Italian allies, and then taking

---

[49] Kidwell, *Pontano*, 12-14 for the timing of Pontano's speech.

[50] N. Ferorelli, *Gli Ebrei nell'Italia meridionale dall'età romana al secolo XVIII*, ed. F. Patroni Griffi (Napoli, 1990).

[51] O. Mastrojanni, 'Sommario degli atti della cancelleria di Carlo VIII a Napoli', *Archivio storico per le province napoletane*, 20 (1895).

[52] *History of Italy*, Book 2, cap. 4.

[53] *History of Italy*, Book 2, cap. 3. This statement may, rather, reflect Guicciardini's views on the ability of men to alter their fate.

his leave. This was to underestimate first of all the residual if localised loyalty to Ferrandino, and second the growing concern of the north Italian powers that Charles' presence was generating more trouble than peace. Florence was appealing for help against the rebellious Pisans, who with some justice could complain that they had been promised liberty, and then denied it. The pope was strangely forgetful of his declared willingness to confer the kingdom of Naples on Charles; but, after all, he had said Charles could have Naples when he was Charles' somewhat unwilling host in Rome. The fall of Naples had not after all won Charles a vast number of powerful friends.

On May 20, shortly after a formal coronation in Naples and more eloquent speeches by Pontano, Charles left the *Regno* never to return. The return journey was to prove more dangerous than his descent into Italy. Old allies ganged up against him; the result of his victory had been to regenerate the Italian league, with Venice, Milan and minor Italian powers attempting to block the king's passage out of Italy. Whether this was entirely wise is a moot point. Some were then of the opinion that it was best simply to let him go over a 'silver bridge' out of Italy. When confronted by the Italian confederates at Fornovo close to the Appenines, on 6 July 1495, Charles' army acquitted itself well, and general opinion gives the French victory; but it was not so clear-cut a victory that the Italians could not claim it for themselves, nor did it change the new political reality, the abandonment by Sforza Milan of its French ally. Indeed, this was the signal for a return by the Aragonese to their south Italian lands, and Ferrandino was able to win some support from his relative and namesake Ferdinand the Catholic, king of Aragon, who supplied him with a few ships and men under the redoutable Gonzalo Fernández de Córdoba (though Ferdinand had his own ambitions in the region, and hoped at least to obtain Calabria for himself, if necessary from the French). Out of loyal bases in Calabria and Apulia, Aragonese-Neapolitan power began to expand northwards through the kingdom once again. Several Apulian towns were drawn under Venetian rule after Ferrandino pledged Trani, Brindisi, Otranto and Gallipoli to Venice in return for aid; Polignano, Mola and Monopoli were also acquired directly by Venice at this time, for the Most Serene Republic saw its chance to consolidate its hold over the shores of the Adriatic at a time when instability in southern Italy and Turkish advances in Albania and the Balkans generally threatened Venetian sea routes into the Mediterranean proper. Such concessions were worthwhile if the result was an Aragonese restoration. Ferrandino himself won praise for his energy and his bravery, though he was seen as a rash commander in the field, a criticism which was endorsed by a puzzled Gonzalo Fernández: 'he will make a decsion and later change from it, though it is good and advisable'. Nevertheless Ferrandino's career peaked in 1496 with his victorious return to Naples, after which he died still young; as with Giangaleazzo Sforza, impish observers ascribed his death to excessive sexual activity. He was succeeded by Alfonso's brother, Federigo, who counts as the last Aragonese king of Naples.

Like Ferrandino, Charles VIII only lived a few more years, dying prematurely in 1498 when he cracked his large head against a low door jamb in one of his palaces. And, like Ferrandino, he had no direct male heir, and was succeeded instead by the duke of Orléans, as King Louis XII; Louis XI had done all he could to marginalise the house of Orléans, recognising in the future Louis XII a potential challenger to royal power.[54] Louis XII in fact enlarged the conflict in Italy as a result of his claims in northern as well as southern Italy; in many ways, it was with the succession of Louis, rather than with the invasion by Charles VIII, that the fortunes of Italy began to change decisively. In some respects, though not of course its massive scale, Charles VIII's invasion bears closer comparison with those of René of Anjou than historians have allowed for; the ephemeral nature of the conquest and the lack of long-term impact on the institutional, social and economic structure of southern Italy distinguish Charles VIII's brief period of rule from the long-lasting Spanish domination of the south that began in 1502. In particular, historians have laid too much emphasis on the first French invasion of 1494-95, too little on the second which began with Louis XII's attack on Milan in 1499, in vindication of claims by the house of Orléans to the duchy which Ludovico (by 1500 a captive in French hands) had earlier won for himself by means of his subtle political skills. It has been seen that these skills were in a sense so subtle that he nearly brought disaster on himself in 1494-95. Events from 1499 onwards followed a grander pattern than those a few years before: Ferdinand the Catholic entered into the secret Treaty of Granada of November 1500, partitioning the south of Italy between the French and the Spaniards, only to abandon it when it became obvious that he could have the whole of southern Italy for himself if he confronted the French; Federigo of Naples was pensioned off, and went to live in France; the last Aragonese claimant, Cardinal Louis of Aragon, was still insisting on his suitability as ruler of Naples in the mid-sixteenth century, but events had long ago left him and his family stranded.[55] In fact, after the death of Queen Isabella of Castile in 1504, Ferdinand of Aragon diverted much of his energy into rebuilding Aragonese fortunes in the western Mediterranean.

In a sense, then, it was Ferdinand II, rather than the Aragonese house of Naples, who was the political heir to Alfonso the Magnanimous, aiming to recreate a dominion stretching from the Pyrenees across the seas and islands to the straits of Otranto. Ferdinand of Aragon differed, too, from the Aragonese

---

[54] F.J. Baumgartner, *Louis XII* (Stroud, Gloucestershire/New York, 1994) is the most recent life of this king; but see also B. Quilliet, *Louis XII père du peuple* (Paris, 1986).

[55] André Chastel, *Le cardinal Louis d'Aragon* (Paris, 1986).

kings of Naples in his resolve to purge southern Italy, as he had already purged Spain and Sicily, of Jews, though with the death of Isabella the fire sems to have gone out of his Jewish policy, and the last Jews only left Naples in 1541, long after his death. As with Alfonso, the lack of a direct heir compromised Ferdinand's many ambitions, yet the Italian and Mediterranean policies of Charles V (Carlos I of Spain) or of Francis I of France are incomprehensible without an awareness of the battle for southern Italy which had engaged princes of the house of Aragon and of the house of France since the thirteenth century.

Part I
Antecedents of the French
invasion of 1494-95

The distant origins of the Italian wars: political relations between France and Italy in the fourteenth and fifteenth centuries

Georges Peyronnet

Traditional historiography presents Charles VIII's expedition to Italy as the whim of a young King with rather vague ideas, haunted by the chivalrous visions inherited from the Middle Ages, intoxicated by the temptations of the Italian Renaissance, but incapable of understanding the true interests of France, which lay on her north-eastern borders. Such an interpretation is clearly anachronistic, dominated by the struggle which France had to sustain, first against the House of Habsburg, then against Germany, from the sixteenth century onwards. But the power of the Habsburgs was not so threatening during the reign of Charles VIII. As for the Mediterranean, it remained an important element, not only culturally and politically desirable, but also as the source of economic rivalry, even though the Portuguese were determined to find a new route to the Indies via the Atlantic, and the recent discovery of the New World by Christopher Columbus aroused only the vaguest interest.[1]

On the other hand, the attention of the French princes was always focused on Italy, ever since the Crown Lands had acquired the Mediterranean through the incorporation of Languedoc, and since the younger brother of St Louis, Charles I of Anjou, had become count of Provence through marriage in 1246. From that point onwards, Italy was often to be a theatre for French intervention.

1. The first French interventions (from the end of the thirteenth to the beginning of the fourteenth century)

Although St Louis was at first reluctant to offer full support to the papacy in its struggle against Frederick II, the south Italian threat to the papal lands refused

---

[1] For a more detailed discussion of this issue, see G. Peyronnet's 'Aux Origines des Guerres d'Italie: la lutte entre la Couronne de France et d'Aragon pour la maîtrise de la Méditerranée occidentale', *Les Cahiers de Montpellier. Forces armées et politiques de défense*, 11 (1985).

to go away after the emperor's death in 1250. Thus when two French popes offered Charles of Anjou the opportunity of conquering the Kingdom of Sicily, St Louis allowed his brother to carry out this conquest in 1266-68. Charles was authoritarian, pragmatic and ambitious. He initiated an eastern policy by buying the crown of the kingdom of Jerusalem: Frederick II had possessed it earlier, but the kingdom was destroyed by the Egyptian Mamluks in 1291. Charles was more active in the Balkans, where he prepared an expedition with the aim of re-establishing his influence in the Latin Empire of Constantinople, founded in 1204, but reconquered in 1261 by the Greeks - the Greek Orthodox, schismatics in the eyes of the Westerners.

Southern Italy thus became the French bridgehead in the Mediterranean: St Louis had died in 1270, and his son Philip III allowed himself, in effect, to be dominated by his uncle Charles. Such a situation was worrying to the Crown of Aragon, which had already conquered the Balearic Islands in 1229, and whose merchants from Barcelona were extending their interests towards North Africa and Sicily. Peter III of Aragon, known as Peter 'the Great' - and rightly so - wished to cement this Catalan East-West axis: through marriage he acquired the rights of the Hohenstaufen over the kingdom of Sicily, gaining support among the Sicilians who had suffered from the authoritarianism of Charles of Anjou; the uprising of the Sicilian Vespers (1282) chased the Angevins out of Sicily, replacing them with Aragonese rule. The house of Anjou was never able to retake the island; it had lost an important strategic position and a source of grain supply, while the Aragonese took possession of Sardinia in 1323-4. Thus the long conflict between the house of Anjou and the house of Aragon had its roots far back in the thirteenth century.

2. *French intervention takes shape in northern Italy (first half of the fourteenth century)*[2]

At first, the French monarchy only supported the house of Anjou from afar. Philip III had been defeated in the attack he had launched against Catalonia and Peter III of Aragon in the hope of helping Charles of Anjou after the Sicilian Vespers. Philip the Fair was enmeshed in his battle against Pope Boniface VIII and his dispute with the king of England. He left it to his brother, Charles of Valois, who had a rather more adventurous outlook, to reply to Boniface VIII's call for help against the Ghibellines, supporters of the empire, and to wage war in Tuscany and Sicily, but without great results. Charles' son, Philip of Valois - the future Philip VI - was again called upon for help by Pope John XXII against

---

[2] For more details on what follows, see G. Peyronnet, 'Les relations politiques entre la France et l'Italie, principalement au XIVème et dans la première moitié du XVème s.', *Le Moyen Age*, 55 (1949), 301-42 and 56 (1950), 85-113.

the Ghibellines of Lombardy: he moved into Italy, but the plots of the Visconti, lords of Milan, led him to be recalled to France. These royal interventions were facilitated by the fact that the counts of Savoy, lords of Piedmont, played an important role at the French court, and so allowed the French troops to pass through their lands.

Once he had become King, Philip VI revealed himself to be much more audacious than his predecessors with regard to Italy. He negotiated with Pope John XXII for the right to occupy Parma, Modena and Reggio Emilia, which allowed the pontiff to guarantee his domination over these cities by placing French contingents there from 1322-30. And Philip VI bought the seigneury of Lucca in 1332; for him, this was the beginning of a more far-reaching enterprise in the Italian arena, since these events took place in the same year. But he was obliged to renounce both this seigneury and his future plans, for the Hundred Years War was under way by 1340. However, he had already acquired the allegiance of the republic of Genoa against England, and he bought the Dauphiné in 1349.[3]

The Valois dynasty's attraction to Italy was even stronger after the popes had settled in Avignon in 1309, though they still sought to maintain their authority in Italy, thanks to the support of the kings of France and Naples. John the Good, son and heir to Philip VI, continued to hold back the Ghibellines, having reached an agreement with Galeazzo Visconti, lord of Milan in 1360: it was Galeazzo who advanced the ransom money for John the Good, who had been held prisoner in England since his defeat at Poitiers (1356); and Galeazzo even obtained the hand of John the Good's daughter Isabella for his son, Giangaleazzo.

Charles V, son of John the Good, concentrated his efforts on reconquering the French provinces that had been won by the English. Yet at the same time, he supported the papacy, which had returned to Rome from Avignon in 1377. Moreover, Pope Gregory XI, a native Frenchman, wished to check the ambitions of Giangaleazzo Visconti, who had become duke of Milan: in 1375, the pope called for the aid of Duke Louis I of Anjou, brother of Charles V and founder of a second House of Anjou. Louis accepted, but on condition that the pope obtain for him the title of king of Lombardy from the emperor. This plan was never carried out, as Louis I preferred to attempt to acquire Provence and the kingdom of Naples - which was under the power of the first House of Anjou - through various matrimonial negotiations which threatened the king of

---

[3] R. Cazelles, *La Société politique et la crise de la royauté sous Philippe de Valois* (Paris, 1958), 120.

Aragon, Peter IV, and which ended in an alliance with the Sardinian rebels (1377). But the rebels never enforced this agreement.[4]

3. Problems during the Great Western Schism (1378-1417)

At the end of his life, Charles V made a decision which had a great impact on relations between France and Italy. In April 1378, an Italian pope was elected, Urban VI. But his authoritarianism led a group of cardinals, a good number of whom were French, to elect another pope outside Rome in September 1378: Clement VII, who was related to the counts of Geneva. Charles V chose to recognise Clement VII.

This schism upset the whole of Europe: all of Italy recognised Urban VI, except the count of Savoy. Clement VII, quite naturally, turned towards the French monarchy, by again calling upon Louis I of Anjou, while continuing to respect the first house of Anjou which ruled in Naples. In addition, Clement VII tried to push Louis I back to northern Italy: the new pope, in 1379, promised Louis a 'Kingdom on the Adriatic' which would be carved out of the northern Church States, but which could not be joined to the kingdom of Naples.

These plans were spoiled by the fact that Clement VII had to take refuge in Avignon after being forced out of Italy. From that point on, he pressured the queen of Naples, Joanna I, to adopt Louis of Anjou, as she had no children: and she did so in 1380. The pope had been suzerain of the Kingdom 'of Sicily' since its foundation in 1130: following the death of Joanna I in 1382, Clement VII put her kingdom under the control of Louis of Anjou, but on condition that he would have no rights over any other territories belonging to the papacy. In 1381 in Rome, Urban VI had reacted by rejecting Joanna I. He placed a member of the younger branch of the house of Anjou on the throne - Charles III of Durazzo - as king 'of Sicily'. Charles seized Naples and subjugated the greater part of the kingdom: he was suspected of having Joanna I assassinated. Louis I assembled his powerful forces and went to Italy: certain Italian states gave him free passage; he waged war in the kingdom of Naples until his death in 1384.[5]

Clement VII had supported Louis of Anjou financially: but faced with the difficulties encountered by Louis, the Avignon pope turned towards northern Italy, where he had found another champion of the French. In 1387, the brother of Charles VI, Louis of Touraine (who was to become duke of Orléans in 1392), married Valentina Visconti, the daughter of Giangaleazzo, lord of Milan. One month after this marriage, Clement VII placed a large part of Romagna under

---

[4] C.-E. Labande, 'La politique méditerranéenne de Louis Ier d'Anjou et le rôle qu'y joua la Sardaigne' in *Atti del VI° Congresso Internazionale di Studi Sardi* (Cagliari, 1957), 10-23; repr. in C.-E. Labande, *Histoire de l'Europe occidentale, XIème-XIVème s.* (London, 1973).

[5] For more details, see G. Peyronnet, 'I Durazzeschi e Renato d'Angiò (1381-1442)', in *Storia di Napoli* (Naples, 1969), vol. 3, 335-436.

Louis' control. All that remained to be done was to conquer it. Moving the army by land proved to be more difficult than for Louis of Anjou, for Visconti's ambitions threatened the north of the Papal States. The sea route was safer; but the port of Genoa had to be secured.

From the twelfth century onwards, the Genoese republic had been torn apart by social factions and family feuds. This did not prevent this 'la Superba' from dominating the Mediterranean by eliminating Pisa and rivalling the Catalans. The republic had built a rich colonial empire with Corsica, several important islands in the Aegean Sea, trading posts on the western coast of Asia Minor, several islands in the Black Sea, as well as Constantinople. Such a coalition, which was economically powerful but without real political influence, aroused much envy, especially in the lord of Milan, for Genoa was the natural outlet to the sea for Lombardy. Giangaleazzo Visconti was plotting in Genoa, but a group of Genoese opponents asked for the protection of Charles VI, King of France, who reached his majority in 1392 but who went mad the very same year. The fact that the king was mad made him susceptible to contradictory influences: his wife, Isabella of Bavaria, pressured him to accept the Genoese proposals, for she was the granddaughter of the former lord of Milan, Bernabò Visconti, whom her nephew, Giangaleazzo, had had poisoned. Giangaleazzo now found the road from Milan to Genoa had been blocked. But it was still essential that the French conquer Genoa. Charles VII entrusted the military campaign to his brother Louis, who had become the duke of Orléans, since he considered Genoa the starting point in his conquest of the future Kingdom of Adria.

Giangaleazzo Visconti, brother-in-law of Louis d'Orléans, had just bought the title of duke of Milan from the Emperor (1395). And Louis had received the county of Asti as a dowry: lying between Piedmont and Lombardy, it was a good base for military operations in northern Italy. Giangaleazzo would have preferred to see Genoa governed by his son-in-law than by a representative of the king of France. However, in order to pursue his schemes in Genoa, Giangaleazzo might have perhaps preferred Louis to be satisfied with Savona, which Louis' troops had just captured in 1394: this port to the west of Genoa is the outlet of Piedmont to the sea, and had been under Genoese rule since the twelfth century. But the duke of Burgundy, Philip the Bold, uncle of Charles VI, had taken the upper hand in the government of France, with the agreement of Queen Isabella. Louis d'Orléans had to abandon Savona and Genoa (1395). The Commune of Genoa then recognised the sovereignty of Charles VI (1396). In 1401, the King sent Marshal Boucicaut to govern Genoa: he was an experienced knight, a companion of du Guesclin, and he remained governor until 1409. His administration was harsh, but by appeasing the factions his severity promoted economic prosperity in Genoa, which was then able to establish the Bank of St George, one of the most important such institutions in Italy. Thus France saw her influence in the Mediterranean become considerably extended; though she did not yet own Marseilles, she now dominated the Riviera, from Monaco to the isle of Elba, plus Corsica and the Genoese possessions in the East; Boucicaut waged war against Venice, Genoa's great rival in Cyprus, and even as far afield as Syria.

In the meantime, however, the second house of Anjou still had designs on the kingdom of Naples. Louis II of Anjou, son of Louis I, was only seven when his father died, but his lieutenants still opposed the Durazzeschi in the southern region, and ended up occupying Naples in 1387. Clement VII, in Avignon, crowned Louis king of Sicily (1389). Louis went to Naples in 1390, but the Durazzeschi continued their resistance, supported by the Roman pope, Boniface IX. And Louis saw the French deserting him more and more, as they were anxious to end the Great Schism by withdrawing their support from the pope of Avignon. Ladislas of Anjou-Durazzo, who had succeeded his father Charles III in 1386, recovered Naples in 1399. Louis II had to take refuge in Provence. Another of his attempts to gain power in central Italy, from 1409-11, was equally unsuccessful, for Louis was short of supplies and money; he returned to France where he died at Angers in 1417.

The French government then turned its attention once more towards northern Italy. It had two objectives: to thwart the ambitions of Giangaleazzo Visconti, whose dream was to found a kingdom of Italy, and to end the Great Schism. But these two goals were hindered by the rivalry between the duke of Burgundy and the duke of Orléans. Through his marriage, the former had inherited the county of Flanders, whose inhabitants supported the Roman pope; in addition, Duke Philip was pressing for another meeting of a General Council, along with the queen and the University of Paris. On the other side, Louis d'Orléans found himself alone in supporting the Avignon pope, Benedict XIII, a Spaniard and the successor of Clement VII, who had died in 1394. In 1398 Charles VI's government convinced the French Church to 'withdraw obedience' from Benedict XIII; deprived of the revenues owed to him by the French clergy, Benedict XIII was unable to support either Louis d'Orléans or Louis of Anjou.

During this time, Giangaleazzo Visconti continued to plot against France from Genoa. In addition, Charles VI's council met favourably the proposals of Florence for a treaty of alliance; in fact, Florence had just formed a coalition including several lords and cities from the Po Valley in order to prevent Giangaleazzo from gaining access to central Italy (1396). After several military reverses, a truce was agreed in 1398, but without the participation of the government of Charles VII, who was still under the influence of the queen and duke of Burgundy, both of whom were hostile to Milan. The death of Giangaleazzo in 1402 stabilised the conflict; but this was followed by a civil war in Lombardy, stirred up by the conflicting desires of the three sons of Giangaleazzo and those of the condottieri.[6]

The evolution of the Great Schism continued to influence the course of French policy in Italy. Louis d'Orléans and Louis II of Anjou continued to support Benedict XIII, the pope of Avignon. After the French clergy withdrew obedience from Benedict XIII, he found himself blockaded in Avignon by the troops of Charles VI; in 1403, the two dukes Louis helped him to escape to Provence. Benedict XIII's supporters in the French Court managed to influence the French clergy to restore allegiance to him; so Benedict returned to Avignon. War then resumed in Lombardy between Louis d'Orléans, whose troops were based in Asti, and Filippo Maria Visconti, youngest son of Giangaleazzo, who had recently prevented his rivals from succeeding to the duchy of Milan. But once again the Burgundian faction pressed Charles VI to lean towards Milan: Boucicaut was sent to Genoa to aid Visconti (1404), who was thus able to hold his ground against his adversaries; at the same time, the governor of Genoa was occupying Pisa and Livorno, which the third son of Giangaleazzo had put up for sale. Boucicaut thus kept one step ahead of the Florentines by preventing them from reaching the sea; and even though the port of Pisa was beginning to silt up, the port of Livorno constituted a potential base for France. Nevertheless, Florence succeeded in buying Pisa in 1405; but Boucicaut retained Livorno.

In Lombardy, the war continued between the the rebel condottieri and the first two sons of Giangaleazzo - the third one had died. To prevent them from carving up the duchy of Milan which he considered his birthright, Louis d'Orléans applied pressure to the Visconti through the Count of Savoy and Boucicaut (1409). But the Genoese took advantage of the departure of their governor for Lombardy to stage an uprising: Boucicaut was unable to repress this revolt and was forced to return to France in 1410. French influence in Italy was therefore diminished. Louis d'Orléans had died in 1407, assassinated by the henchmen of John the Fearless, who had been duke of Burgundy since the death of his father Philip in 1404. Louis' son Charles was then nine years old. In 1412, the elder son of Giangaleazzo was also assassinated in Milan by conspirators who recognised his younger brother Filippo Maria as duke.

French influence became weaker and weaker as the Great Schism reached its end. John the Fearless, who was then in power in France, had wanted to follow his father's policy by declaring a new withdrawal of obedience from Benedict XIII (1408). After some final diplomatic reversals, the Great Schism was resolved by the Ecumenical Council of Constance in 1414, which deposed the pretenders in 1417, and elected an Italian as pope: Martin V, who was

---

[6] For more precise details on these events, see N. Valeri, *I Capitani di ventura,* vol. 1, *Facino Cane* (Turin, s.d.), 55, and *L'Italie de la Renaissance*, ed. I. Cloulas (Paris, 1990), 29.

recognised by all of Christendom. The government of Charles VI now found itself paralysed by the civil war between the Burgundians and the Armagnacs - supporters of Charles d'Orléans, who had become the son-in-law of the High Constable Bernard d'Armagnac in 1410. The war began in 1411 and was aggravated by the Hundred Years' War in 1415: the king of England, Henry V, invaded France, destroyed Charles VI's army at Agincourt, near Calais, then took hold of Normandy. Charles d'Orléans, who had been taken prisoner at Agincourt, was not freed until 1440: his county of Asti had been disarmed. Burgundy then took sides with England after the assassination of John the Fearless by loyal supporters of the house of Orléans in 1419.

This complex period in the relations between France and Italy has disconcerted a good number of historians; one of them, who knows his subject extremely well, claims that French forays into Italy during the second half of the fourteenth century and the beginning of the fifteenth century were nothing but an expression of 'blind rivalry', lacking in foresight, between the opposing clans.[7] However, more careful researchers had already distinguished several guiding principles amid the confusion.[8] Following the adventurous policies of Philip VI of Valois, whose dream was to continue the Crusades in the East, the French monarchy supported the Avignon popes, who were also obsessed by plans for Crusades. But the vicissitudes of the Hundred Years' War hindered the action of the royal government in Italy more and more. The madness of Charles VI increased these difficulties, for the King was subject to contradictory influences. But it was the combined effort of the queen and the dukes of Burgundy which prevailed; this helped the French princes' ventures in Italy - those of Anjou, Orléans - but by controlling them and assuring a hold on Genoa and its colonies, thus thwarting a Catalan thalassocracy. In this way, the French monarchy was led to institute a policy of equilibrium towards its Italian partners; its efforts to conclude the Great Schism, by distancing itself from the Avignon popes, reinforced this tendency towards a balanced commitment.

Circumstances were different for the less interested royal princes in northern Europe than for the house of Burgundy; Charles de Valois, Louis I and Louis II of Anjou, who had a stronger hold in Italy, dreamed of founding a principality there. And when the support of the French royalty and the papacy were removed, towards the beginning of the fifteenth century, the house of

---

[7] M. De Boüard, *Les Origines des guerres d'Italie. La France et l'Italie au temps du Grand Schisme d'Occident* (Bibliothèque des Ecoles françaises d'Athènes et de Rome, 139, Paris, 1936), 17; this statement is based on A. Coville, *Les Cabochiens et l'Ordonnance de 1413* (Paris, 1888), 27 and 143.

[8] E. Jarry, *La Vie politique de Louis de France, duc d'Orléans (1372-1407)* (Paris, 1889), passim, and M. Thibaut, *Isabeau de Bavière, reine de France, la jeunesse, 1370-1405* (Paris, 1903), 39.

Anjou and the house of Orléans nevertheless continued to maintain their claims on Italy.

4. Political relations between France and Italy during the reign of Charles VII (1422-61)

a) The house of Anjou loses the kingdom of Naples

With regard to Italy, the new king was at first paralysed by the worsening of the Hundred Years' War: the Treaty of Troyes (1420) had awarded his crown to the king of England, and it was not until the intervention of Joan of Arc in 1429 that he was able to reverse the situation. During this time France lost Livorno, the only possession she had kept in Italy: Genoa sold it to Florence in 1421. In the same year, Genoa itself was conquered by the duke of Milan, who took advantage of the fact that Charles d'Orléans was in captivity to occupy the county of Asti in 1422: Charles VII, far from opposing this Milanese expansion, formed a defensive alliance with the Visconti in 1424, which allowed Charles to recruit mercenaries in Lombardy, where he purchased horses for combat whose quality was acknowledged throughout Europe.[9]

The Franco-Milanese alliance was formed for another reason: an important newcomer had arrived on the Italian scene - the king of Aragon, Alfonso V, called the Magnanimous owing to his taste for public acts of generosity. Of Castilian origin, he had inherited the crown of Aragon in 1416 after a succession crisis. Intelligent and ambitious, he understood that in order to dominate the Mediterranean his navy had to take Genoa, so he attacked Corsica in 1420. But just at that very moment, he was offered a more interesting proposition. The queen of Naples, Joanna II, sister of Ladislas of Anjou-Durazzo whom she had succeeded in 1414, moved from one favourite to another, but remained childless, and the kingdom was divided by innumerable rivalries. The French house of Anjou watched and waited: Louis II had died in 1417, but his elder son, Louis III, who was then 14 years old, took up his father's claims. In 1419 he sent emissaries to Pope Martin V, who convinced the Pope, suzerain of the kingdom of Naples, to excommunicate Joanna II by declaring that in the absence of heirs her Crown would return to Louis III. Louis III prepared an expedition to force Joanna II to accept this declaration. The queen saw no way out but to obtain the help of the king of Aragon by adopting him.

Alfonso V acted quickly: Genoa, which was still independent, supported Louis III, who had disembarked near Naples in 1420. Alfonso sent ships with

---

[9] Du Fresne de Beaucourt, *Histoire de Charles VII* (Paris, 1881-84), vol. 1, 342 and vol. 2, 341-2.

reinforcements to defend the city. He himself arrived in Naples in 1421. Louis III, who was short of funds, had to take refuge in the provinces inland. Yet Alfonso, who proved authoritarian, upset the Neapolitans, who for their part detested the Catalan entourage of their new sovereign, and began rioting. He tried in vain to hold his ground; Joanna II revoked her adoption and adopted Louis III instead (1423). The king of Aragon returned to Spain. Nevertheless, Louis III was unable to take advantage of the King of Aragon's defeat: the government of Joanna II, dominated by a new Neapolitan favourite, sent Louis III to govern Calabria, which was being threatened by Alfonso V who had set up his headquarters in Sicily. Louis III fell ill and died in 1434. Joanna II died in turn in 1435, after having made a will which recognised as her heir René of Anjou, younger brother of Louis III.

René was not ready to assume his inheritance. He was twenty-six and had fought alongside Joan of Arc. But he had then entered into a war against the Duke of Burgundy over the succession to the duchy of Lorraine. He was taken prisoner in 1431 and Philip the Good had imposed such a high ransom on him that he remained in captivity until 1437. During this time, René's wife, Isabella of Lorraine, was preparing a fleet in Provence. She had the support of the duke of Milan, Venice and the pope, all of whom were anxious at seeing Alfonso V of Aragon, recently arrived from Sicily with a large fleet and many troops, coming to attack Gaeta, an important port in the kingdom located at the very edge of the Papal State. The Genoese quickly sent a squadron to help defend Gaeta. The two fleets came face to face in front of the city; the Spanish vessels, which had too many soldiers on board, were difficult to manoeuvre: only one of them managed to escape. Alfonso V was taken prisoner with a number of Spanish and Neapolitan noblemen. Faced with this disaster, Alfonso's land army disbanded.

The Angevin cause, however, did not benefit from this Aragonese defeat. A few months after the battle came another dramatic moment. The prisoners had been taken to Milan, where the duke treated them respectfully. Alfonso V took advantage of this golden opportunity to outwit Visconti by making it plain that Milan had helped to set up a French house in Naples, which meant he had been playing into the hands of Charles VII, who was about to become reconciled with Burgundy and take the upper hand over England; Charles could then again set France's sights on Genoa and even on Milan. Convinced by these arguments, Filippo Maria released his prisoners at the end of 1435, by signing a treaty of friendship with Alfonso V. But he added a secret agreement by which Visconti promised to help Alfonso conquer the kingdom of Naples, while the king of Aragon committed himself to serve the duke by attacking the the great condottiere Francesco Sforza, traditionally an ally of the Angevins, to whom Visconti had just promised the hand of his daughter, sole heir to the duchy.

Sforza had recently carved out a principality for himself in the Marches, along the Adriatic, near the north-eastern border of the kingdom of Naples: his future father-in-law intended it to be controlled by Alfonso V.

Faced with this unexpected reversal, Isabella of Lorraine left Naples a few days after the prisoners in Milan were set free. All was not lost for Anjou, since the Genoese, furious at seeing Visconti now on the side of their Catalan rivals, had just forced out their Milanese occupiers. Isabella ruled Naples well and became very popular there. Alfonso V had returned to the kingdom at the beginning of 1436. But Pope Eugenius IV supported the Anjous; he was in dispute with the Council of Basle which was supported by Alfonso V and Filippo Maria Visconti; a pontifical army came to Isabella's aid. And René of Anjou, freed by the duke of Burgundy, amassed ships and troops in Genoa, and landed in Naples in 1437. He was given a warm welcome there: famed for his love of chivalry, he set out to please the Neapolitan people, but he was in need of money: the kingdom had been ruined by the war. Charles VII gave no aid at all. The Genoese, who wanted to be paid, sent paltry reinforcements; and Sforza, René's old ally, found himself in battle on the Po Plain in the service of Venice and Florence, against Visconti, his future father-in-law.

The king of Aragon managed to blockade Naples. In June 1442, the Aragonese were able to penetrate the city through a badly guarded underground aqueduct; after a bitter battle, René was forced to return to Provence, while Alfonso V made his way into Naples. Pope Eugenius IV recognised the *fait accompli* by conferring the investiture on the conqueror in 1443; the Pope thus gained an ally against Sforza, who was expelled from the Marches in 1443-47.

From then on, all of Southern Italy - both the mainland kingdom and Sicily - was in the hands of the Crown of Aragon, which had attained its goal: to gain commercial advantages, but mainly to control the east-west Mediterranean axis, essential to the ultimate dream of glory, winning back Jerusalem and Constantinople, conquered by the Turks in 1453. Yet the Catalans blocked the route to Venice, Genoa and France. This situation was to be the root of future conflicts.

b) Intervention by Charles VII in northern Italy

Charles VII, now at peace with Burgundy, had won back Paris and pushed the English out of Normandy and the Guyenne region; England was spent and had obtained a truce in 1444. The king of France could once again fix his sights on Italy. Charles d'Orléans, who had been freed in 1440, reclaimed his county of Asti. Filippo Maria was then at war against Venice, which sought to dominate Lombardy; the Venetian army, after a brilliant victory, arrived at the gates of Milan (1446). The duke feared being attacked from the rear; he made it known to Charles VII that he preferred to see Asti governed directly by the French monarchy, represented, for example, by the Dauphin. However, the king did not wish to abandon Charles d'Orléans; perhaps he already feared the undisguised ambition of the Dauphin Louis. Charles promised military aide to the duke of Milan if the duke withdrew his troops from Asti, which he did in 1447.

Fillipo Maria died on 13 August 1447. A serious crisis over the succession began; the Milanese declared themselves a Republic, while two pretenders, Alfonso V and Charles d'Orléans, each claimed the throne based on different wills supposedly left by the deceased; as for Sforza, he continued playing off Milan and Venice against each other. Charles d'Orléans came to Asti from France: he spent the winter of 1447-48 asking for aid. Charles VII stood down; he was preparing to win back Normandy, and the following summer the duke of Orléans had to return to France.

Yet another agitator was stirring up trouble: the Dauphin Louis. Born in 1423, alert and intelligent, he resented his father's lack of confidence in him and became embroiled in various plots; Charles VII sent him to govern the Dauphiné in 1446. Finding himself more or less in exile, Louis proved to be remarkably adept in diplomatic, economic and administrative matters, conducting his affairs in a manner that was quite independent of France. Charles VII would have liked to direct his son's sights towards Genoa. But Louis wished to work towards his own ends by plotting with the duke of Savoy to attack Milan and Genoa.[10]

These manoeuvres were nonetheless left in abeyance by the end of the Milanese crisis: after many ups and downs, Francesco Sforza was proclaimed duke by the Milanese in 1450. All that remained for him to do was to push back the Venetian army and fend off the offensive recently launched by Alfonso V, with the aid of the pope, against Florence, a long-standing ally of Sforza. Sforza was seeking an alliance with Charles VII, who concluded a treaty with him in 1452 promising military aid to the new duke; in exchange, Sforza recognised René d'Anjou's rights over the kingdom of Naples. Charles VII sent René to Lombardy with an army in 1453: but René only got involved in a few skirmishes and returned to France in 1454.

Why retreat? René's chivalrous character was out of tune with the contortions of Italian diplomacy. Moreover, the Dauphin Louis, who was responsible for supporting René, continued to plot with different partners: Savoy, Sforza, Venice, Genoa. They were mistrustful and refused the Dauphin's offers; but in any case, Florence and Milan did not wish to see the *ultramontains*

---

[10] Du Fresne de Beaucourt, 'L'Entreprise de Charles VII sur Gênes et Asti, 1445-1447', *Revue des Questions historiques*, 42 (1887), 321-52; B. De Mandrot, 'Un Projet de partage du Milanais en 1446', *Revue des questions historiques*, 44 (1883), 179-91.

gain too much ground; in 1451 Sforza had formed an alliance with Florence and Genoa to defend 'peace in Italy' against Savoy, Venice, the king of France and the dauphin. The Franco-Milanese treaty of the following year did not alter Sforza's behaviour: in 1454 he made peace with Venice and Savoy. Then, using the fall of Constantinople as a pretext to call for a crusade, and with the support of Rome, he formed the 'Peace of Lodi', which brought together Milan, Venice, Florence, Savoy, the pope and several other less important Italian states; Alfonso V ended up by giving his support, on condition that Genoa remained excluded from the Peace. The group saw itself as committed to a mutual alliance for 25 years: anyone who might violate the *status quo* in Italy would be attacked by all the members. Italy seemed forearmed against any new French invasions, and Alfonso V, king of Naples, was recognised as an Italian prince.

Alfonso, however, did not forget that he held the Crown of Aragon, whose main enemy was Genoa, which was not under the protection of the Peace of Lodi. Alfonso maintained spies in Genoa; he attacked the city in 1456. Its doge called upon France for help: in 1458 the city was placed under the protection of Charles VII, who sent them a 'royal lieutenant', Jean de Calabre, son of René of Anjou. Sforza tried in vain to use diplomacy to force both Alfonso V and Charles VII out of Genoa. Alfonso V died in 1458, leaving the kingdom of Naples to a legitimised bastard son, Ferrante, and the rest of the Crown of Aragon to John II, brother of Alfonso, who was preoccupied by problems with the Catalans, and who made a truce with the Genoese. Sforza decided to support the anti-French factions in Genoa; he obtained financial subsidies for them and arranged for King Ferrante's fleet to come to their aid. In 1461 the Genoese had revolted and forced out the French.

From 1459 onwards, however, Jean de Calabre used Genoa as a point of departure; he disembarked near Naples. Sforza, faithful to the Peace of Lodi, sent aid to Ferrante, mainly in money. As for Charles VII, he kept Jean de Calabre supplied with money, supplies and reinforcements; Jean could thus assure himself a good part of the kingdom of Naples. But Sforza countered these successes by negotiating with the Dauphin Louis, who, threatened by his father with a military expedition in Dauphiné, had taken refuge with the duke of Burgundy in 1456 and continued to plot against his father. In 1460 Louis formed a defensive alliance with Francesco Sforza; the dauphin promised to respect the Peace of Lodi: to him this meant ceasing all support to the houses of Orléans and Anjou. Charles VII, mortified by his son's behaviour, died in 1461.[11]

---

[11] For more details on this period, see G. Peyronnet, 'La politica italiana di Luigi delfino di Francia (1444-1461)', *Rivista Storica Italiana*, 64 (1952), 19-44.

5. Political relations between France and Italy during the reign of Louis XI (1461-83)[12]

a) The unsuccessful continuation of Charles VII's policies (1461-63)

Once he had become King, Louis wanted to take advantage of what he considered to be the rights of the French crown: to this end, he once again took up France's traditional policy and set his sights on Asti, Genoa and Naples, not openly though - he was too prudent - but by using the princely houses as an intermediary. He supported Jean de Calabre financially in the kingdom of Naples. But he avoided any conflicts with Francesco Sforza, with whom he remained allied by the treaty of 1460, which was also supported by the duke of Burgundy. Louis XI, however, sought to win supporters in Genoa. And the king pressured Sforza to cease giving aid to Ferrante of Naples. He used Florence to gain support for his plans: an old friend of France, Florence was effectively ruled by the great banker Cosimo de' Medici, who financed Francesco Sforza. Louis also pressured Pope Pius II to abandon Ferrante, by moderating the Gallican tendencies of the French monarchy.

Sforza would not give in, knowing that Louis XI lacked the military strength to intervene in Italy, for he had to give his attention to an Aragonese threat against Navarre. And Pope Pius II, who was hardly a friend of the French, was in no hurry to support Jean de Calabre. Sforza negotiated with Burgundy. Louis XI's affairs in Italy suffered more and more as Jean de Calabre's position grew worse: he had no rear support, as Genoa, independent again since 1461, found itself once again torn apart by factions; and Sforza continued to send aid to Ferrante. Ferrante managed to inflict a serious defeat on his rival in 1462, from which Jean never recovered; he was forced to return to Provence in 1464. This defeat of Anjou made it useless for France to attempt to reconquer Genoa. Louis XI was quickly able to adapt to this new situation.

b) Louis XI changes his policy in Italy: the Franco-Milanese Agreement and its consequences (1464-65)

In the course of 1463, Louis XI reduced his financial aid to Jean de Calabre and made overtures to Sforza to negotiate a new Franco-Milanese agreement. Sforza reacted favourably. The treaty was concluded at the end of 1463; Louis XI abandoned Genoa, which was occupied by Milanese troops in 1464. In exchange, Sforza agreed not to intervene in Savoy, where Louis XI had strengthened French influence: the King preferred to keep a bridgehead in Italy which was nearer to France, by deserting the lost cause of the house of Anjou

---

[12] See P.M. Kendall, *Louis XI* (London, 1971).

and respecting the balance of power in Italy. Louis XI was already looking forward: he sought Milan's cooperation, along with Genoa and Naples, so as to counter Venice commercially, by making use of the merchant fleet owned by the nephew of Jacques Coeur; Charles VII, on the contrary, had broken the economic ambitions of Jacques Coeur in the Mediterranean.

This new policy of the king of France was to face opposition. The first, quite clearly, were René of Anjou and his son Jean, as well as Louis d'Orléans, whose father Charles had died in 1465. The great lords joined forces with the other feudal powers in the kingdom: Burgundy, Brittany, Bourbon. The nobility was supported by the bourgeoisie and other members of the populace who had suffered from Louis XI's authoritarianism. Thus was formed the so-called 'League of the Public Weal', so named because it had the intention of enacting policies of reform. In reality, it was a coalition of incongruous interests. Nevertheless, because he was weaker than the coalition members, Louis XI asked Sforza to send an expedition to capture Burgundy from the rear: free passage through the Alps was obtained through a personal letter from the king of France to his sister Yolanda, wife of Amadeus IX, duke of Savoy: as the duke was an epileptic, control of the duchy had been entrusted to Yolanda.

Sforza sent Louis XI 3,000 cavalrymen and 1,000 foot soldiers, under the command of Galeazzo, the elder son of Duke Francesco. This was a great relief to the king, as the pressure brought to bear by the Burgundian and Breton troops had forced him to take refuge in Paris. The Milanese army came to attack the Bourbons. But the Milanese stopped there, as the King had chosen to make peace with his adversaries by granting them concessions. However, he won back almost immediately what he had conceded; moreover, he refused to modify his new policy towards Italy. A balance was thus restored in Franco-Italian relations when Francesco Sforza died in 1466. Galeazzo and his army returned to Lombardy, with the consent of Louis XI.

c) Louis XI strives to maintain the balance of power in Italy (1446-80) [13]

Galeazzo Maria Sforza acceded to the throne at the age of twenty-two. He was sensual, debauched, authoritarian, and cruel; he loved luxury; he was cultured, favouring literature and the arts. He did not lack political judgment, but it was hindered by his defects. His initial rise to power was facilitated by his mother, the wise and popular Bianca Maria Sforza. Louis XI as well protected Galeazzo at the beginning, by preventing the other states of the peninsula from taking advantage of his accession to upset the balance of power in Italy. At the same

---

[13] J. Huillard-Bréholles, 'Louis XI protecteur de la Confédération italienne', *Revue des Sociétés Savantes*, ser. 2, 5 (1861), 314-32.

time, the king of France was encouraging negotiations to arrange a marriage between Galeazzo and Bona of Savoy, daughter of the late Duke Louis I; this union was celebrated in 1468: Galeazzo became the brother-in-law of Louis XI, who extended his influence by forming an alliance between Milan, Florence and Naples in 1467; the king remained mistrustful of both Venice and the papacy.

These two powers were concerned by the great influence France had acquired. In 1468, after the humiliation suffered by Louis XI at Péronne at the hands of Charles the Bold, who had become duke of Burgundy the year before, an alliance was formed between Venice, the pope and Burgundy. Moreover, Galeazzo Sforza's mother had just died, and the duke of Milan was behaving in a more and more tyrannical fashion. In addition, Burgundy and Venice plotted together to each take a share of Milan. Galeazzo reacted by renewing his alliance with France. But the balance of power remained precarious, for Ferrante of Naples was influenced by the increasing power of his uncle, John II of Aragon, who, in 1469, had arranged for his son Ferdinand to marry Isabella, heiress to the Kingdom of Castile; Ferrante and John II signed a pact with Burgundy in 1472. Charles the Bold then seriously considered attacking Milan and Genoa, and began to recruit experienced Italian mercenaries in great numbers.[14]

Galeazzo lost confidence in Louis XI, who was in conflict with Burgundy. Even more than in 1472, after the death of Amadeus IX, duke of Savoy, Queen Yolanda found herself controlled by an anti-French faction and pressured Galeazzo to align himself with Charles the Bold, with whom he had formed an alliance in 1475; Charles promised to obtain the title of 'King of Lombardy' for him. But in 1476 Charles the Bold was twice defeated by the Swiss; Galeazzo initiated negotiations with Louis XI. In Savoy, Yolanda also abandoned Burgundy, whose Duke, furious at his defeats, had her kidnapped: but she was rescued by a detachment of troops sent by her royal brother. Galeazzo was assassinated by two young Milanese noblemen shortly after; his son, Giangaleazzo Maria, was then nine years old: the Dowager Duchess Bona of Savoy assumed the Regency; she governed wisely and renewed her alliance with France. In 1477 Charles the Bold died on a battlefield in the Lorraine region. Louis XI, once again in a position of power, signed a treaty of friendship with Venice in 1478. In the same year, Genoa took advantage of the difficulties being experienced by the Milanese to revolt and reclaim its

---

[14] R. Fubini, 'I Rapporti diplomatici tra Milano e Borgogna con particolare riguardo all'alleanza del 1475', in *Milan et les États bourguignons, deux ensembles princiers entre Moyen Age et Renaissance (XIVème-XVIème siècles)*, Publications du Centre Européen d'Études Bourguignonnes, 28 (1988), 95-114, repr. in R. Fubini, *Italia Quattrocentesca* (Florence, 1994), 327-50.

independence: but Louis XI, preoccupied in France by the succession of Burgundy, made no move to help Milan.

A new crisis again compromised the balance of power in Italy in 1478. One of the greatest guarantors of this balance of power was Lorenzo de' Medici; but the Medici had bitter rivals in Florence, the Pazzi, who plotted against them in 1478 with a nephew of Pope Sixtus IV: this pope practised nepotism and wanted to give his nephew a principality in Romagna, but this was opposed by Lorenzo, in the interests of maintaining the balance of power in Italy. The plot failed; but the pope excommunicated Lorenzo and began a war against Florence, with Naples as an ally. Louis XI acted to help Florence by threatening the pope with Milanese intervention, and by convening an Ecumenical Council. Ferrante of Naples, frightened, made peace with Florence; and Sixtus IV made peace with the Medici in 1480. The king of France had consented to a concession to Ferrante by supporting Ludovico il Moro, younger brother of Galeazzo Sforza, who had taken refuge in Naples to plot against his nephew, the young duke of Milan. In 1480, Ludovico returned to Milan where he was awarded the regency by the duchess and her Council. None of the Italian states protested. Louis XI intervened to prevent Ludovico from inflicting any ill treatment on Bona of Savoy; il Moro agreed to honour this request in principle.

d) *Louis XI controls the balance of power in Italy (1481-83)*

In 1481, a new Peace League was formed between the principal Italian states, with the participation of the king of France: it was made permanent in 1482. The superiority again enjoyed by Louis XI in the peninsula allowed a strengthening of French influence over Savoy, where the Duchess Yolanda had died in 1478, leaving a son of 13, Philibert. Louis XI gave Philibert his protection by having him taken to Touraine, to remove him from the pressures brought to bear by the Savoyard noblemen. Philibert was brought back to Savoy in 1481, but several noblemen kidnapped him and had him taken to Turin. Louis XI threatened these revolutionaries with military intervention: the king's supporters then freed Philibert, who was taken to Lyon, where he died in 1482. His younger brother Charles had inherited the duchy at the age of 14, under the protection that Louis XI exercised over him indirectly, by way of the pro-French faction.

Louis XI's influence was equally evident in a new crisis in the balance of power in Italy: the Ferrara war. It was started by Venice, which coveted the duchy of Ferrara because it controlled the mouth of the Po river. The marriage of the Duke of Ferrara and the daughter of Ferrante of Naples, rival of Venice in the Adriatic, provided the pretext for Venice. She allied herself to the pope, who had his own reasons for wanting to add Ferrara to the Papal States; war broke out in 1482. The other Italian powers supported Ferrara, in order to re-establish the balance of power. The Venetians occupied nearly all of the coveted duchy. The Pope grew anxious and deserted Venice in 1483. But Ludovico il Moro, who was still concerned about the balance of power, arranged a peace with Venice in 1484. Through his diplomats, Louis XI acted very quickly to bring about the desired result: when he died in 1483, he could be satisfied that he had maintained French influence over a pacified Italy.

The king of France had just obtained another success in the direction of Italy: the conclusion to his own advantage of the succession to Anjou-Provence. King René had died in 1480, leaving his nephew Charles du Maine as heir in his will. Charles died in 1481, bequeathing his lands to Louis XI. Now ruler of Marseille, Louis XI bought the ships of the nephew of Jacques Coeur, and formed a Mediterranean fleet flying the royal flag.[15]

Louis XI had more foresight than his predecessors, and in new directions. Rather than supporting the claims of the princely dynasties, or direct intervention by the monarchy, he had instituted a policy of arbitration aimed at maintaining the Italian powers in a state of balance, favourable to position of the French government, a policy which was designed to prevent the great princely houses, and especially Burgundy, from continuing to upset the balance of power throughout all Europe. By exercising this role of arbitrator, Louis XI heightened the prestige of the crown of France. In fact, he held in reserve the possibility of intervening more directly, for he had established a sort of protectorate over the duchy of Savoy, extending into the duchy of Asti: he could thus eventually set his sights on Milan and Genoa.

On the other hand, Louis XI favoured the expansion of commercial relations between France and Italy. France recovered fairly quickly from the destruction of the Hundred Years' War, under the impetus of a king whose lively and inquisitive mind was keenly interested by economic affairs. Italian wealth penetrated France, to the profit of businessmen of Lyons and their trade fairs licensed by Louis XI. And Louis also attracted Italian artisans skilled in silk making, Milanese armourers, engineers who were specialists in military fortifications. In the final years of his reign, Louis revealed even greater plans: after he had distanced the Neapolitan monarchy from Aragon by stirring up rivalry between Aragon and Venice, the king launched a royal merchant fleet in the Mediterranean.

All of these policies broke with the traditions inherited from the Middle Ages: pursuing the ideal of the crusades, dynastic rivalries, and so on. The 'modern' character of Louis XI's actions was a result, in great part, of his

---

[15] J. Calmette, *Le grand règne de Louis XI* (Paris, 1938), 233.

understanding of the Italians and his sympathy for them. He had got to know them during his reign in Dauphiné. He understood and spoke Italian very well. He took Italians into his service: equerries, doctors, diplomats. He enjoyed talking at length with the Italian ambassadors in his Court; all of them were astounded by his profound understanding of their country and its people. He demonstrated boundless admiration for Francesco Sforza. Like the Italian princes, he preferred to substitute for war his own subtle diplomatic manoeuvres, among them spying and bribery. Louis XI was a 'prince in the Italian style', superstitious but realistic, so embroiled in intrigues that he was often the cause of his own disappointments; and yet events such as the War of the Public Weal, demonstrated a remarkable ability to recover.

This 'pre-Machiavellian' king thus seems almost ahead of his time. In Italy, the equilibrium established by the Peace of Lodi found itself compromised on several occasions by conflicting interests or by the clash of egotistical ambitions. After the death of Louis XI, who could assume his role as sovereign arbitrator?

6. The beginnings of the reign of Charles VIII (1483-94) [16]

Louis XI left a thirteen year old son: Charles VIII. According to the wishes of the late king, the Regency was assumed by Anne, Charles' elder sister, who was ten years older than he, and her husband, Pierre de Bourbon, Lord of Beaujeu, who was forty-four years old. The couple acted in line with direction sketched out by Louis XI, with wisdom and firmness. Certain discontented subjects who felt they had been victimised by the authoritarianism of the late king wished to limit absolute royal power: the Beaujeus convened the Estates-General of 1484 and manipulated them so well that no reforms emerged. In addition, the great vassals revolted in 1485, grouped around the most powerful amongst them, François II, Duke of Brittany. In 1488 the royal army defeated the coalition, which restored peace.

François II died the same year: he was succeeded by his daughter Anne, aged 12. The Beaujeus sought to marry the heiress to Charles VIII. The Bretons resisted; Anne was married, by proxy, to Maximilian Habsburg, heir to the Holy Roman Empire, and, as son-in-law of Charles the Bold, to a large portion of the possessions of the former house of Burgundy. In the face of this growing threat, the Beaujeus started another war against Brittany, which was conquered by the royal army; Anne reluctantly decided to marry Charles VIII in 1491.

---

[16] See Y. Labande-Mailfert, *Charles VIII. Le vouloir et la destinée* (Paris, 1986).

During this period, the young king had not taken any political action. He showed himself to be a good military leader, which suited his taste for pomp. But he had inherited prudent advice from his father at the end of his life: advice which was put into practice under the guidance of the Beaujeu. After Charles VIII was married, he governed in his own way; he was already educated in the practices of war and diplomacy: contrary to what his detractors claimed, inspired by the slander of his Italian enemies, the new king of France did not have a mediocre and unstable mind.

Once his kingdom was at peace, Charles VIII began to become interested in Italy. He dreamed of leading a Crusade against the Turks, who continued to push forward towards the Balkans. The rights of France over the kingdom of Naples, inherited from the Anjous, resumed their former significance. Pope Innocent VIII, suzerain of the southern kingdom, had these rights in mind in 1490, when he approached Charles VIII to oppose Ferrante of Naples, whose authoritarianism was causing renewed tension. Once again, the balance of power in Italy was wavering: its surest guarantor, Lorenzo the Magnificent, died in 1492. Ludovico il Moro then considered the moment ripe for becoming duke of Milan by eliminating his young nephew, whose guardian he had been since 1480.

Il Moro was ambitious and secretive, with a very strong personality; he made the Court of Milan one of the most brilliant of the Renaissance. He was cultured, and knew how to rule: under him, the duchy of Milan became one of the best administered and richest states in Europe. But Ludovico was blinded by his own success: he thought he could use the young King of France to overthrow Ferrante, who had become dangerous to the balance of power in Italy. Italy would then be dominated by the duke of Milan. Ludovico had already taken Genoa in 1488, with the agreement of Charles VIII, who wished to use this great port as a base for operations against Naples. Counting on the support of former clients of the Angevins in the Kingdom of Naples, Charles decided to go ahead with the expedition. It was a personal and considered decision: the monarch had studied the matter closely: total strength, land and sea weaponry, routes, financial support. This decision was accelerated in 1494 by the death of Ferrante, and the support given to his successor, his son Alfonso II, by the new pope Alexander VI Borgia. Moreover, the king of Aragon, Ferdinand the Catholic, had been governing Spain with his wife Isabella of Castile since 1479, and they had just conquered the Kingdom of Granada in 1492. Ludovico saw the possibility of an Aragonese coalition threatening Italy; he offered Charles VIII troops and money to conquer the kingdom of Naples.[17]

---

[17] For details on the preparation for the expedition to Naples, see I. Cloulas, *Charles VIII et le mirage italien* (Paris, 1986).

As for Charles, he heavily taxed his rich kingdom to obtain two armies with a total of 40,000 men, the most powerful artillery in Europe and a fleet of over 100 ships.

As early as 1491, Charles VIII had announced his intention of exercising his rights over the kingdom of Naples. He made sure he would not be attacked from the rear by making peace on those borders. In 1491, England had been neutralised by a large subsidy. In 1493, France returned Roussillon to Spain, which John II of Aragon had mortgaged to Louis XI in order to obtain financial aid against the Catalan rebels; the Catholic Kings reimbursed Charles VIII and promised not to intervene in Italy. There now remained only one adversary, but the most dangerous: Maximilian of Habsburg, ruler of Austria, Germany and the Netherlands. Maximilian was furious that Charles VIII had rejected his daughter, to whom he was originally engaged, to marry Anne of Brittany. In 1493, the Habsburgs made peace by recovering the Artois and Franche-Comté regions, which had been his daughter's dowry.

Beneath this diplomatic and military activity many serious economic issues were brewing. In 1487, the Portuguese had reached the Cape of Good Hope. At the end of 1492, Columbus, acting on behalf of Spain, had discovered the New World, still believing it to be eastern Asia. Thus were opened new routes for the profitable imports coming from the Far East. The traditional Mediterranean route was controlled by the Turks in the east, which increased the price of many items. The ideal of the Crusades now became confused with the desire to unlock this route in order to reestablish a shorter, less expensive commercial route than via the ocean. In Europe, the increasing power of the Habsburgs, whose strength lay in their possession of the rich Netherlands, was in competition with the French economy; in addition, the French leaders were tempted to seize the wealth available in Italy, thanks to the military strength enjoyed by their monarch in light of the fact that Italy was divided by the rivalries of its princes.[18] A lobby of powerful merchants close to Charles VIII took action along these lines: it was headed by the Briçonnet family of Tours, and under the command of William, Bishop of Saint-Malô, who was to become Cardinal in 1495; this was the king's main advisor. His banker relatives were guarantors of the monarch's private expenditure: chateaux, celebrations, various gifts. As for the public finances, William Briçonnet had taken complete control over them, to the great profit of his own family.

For all these reasons, Charles VIII was attracted to Italy. He understood Italian well, like his father. And if the decision to undertake the expedition was made for personal reasons, after he had considered it for many years, a great

---

[18] P. Faure, *La Renaissance* (Paris, 3rd ed. 1961), 22; F. Catalano, in *Storia di Milano*, vol. 7 (Milan, 1956), 430.

number of his French and Italian contemporaries approved of the enterprise. At that time, Italy was perceived as the most civilised region of Europe, and rightly so, not only due to her culture and arts, but also for her economic wealth, technological advances, and administrative and diplomatic methods. To control Italy was to control Europe.[19]   And France had no intention of letting anyone else win control.   Confident of her renewed influence, France wished to bypass Louis XI's prudent policy of arbitration in order to take advantage of the instability of the balance of power in Italy.   As for the Italians, they overestimated their cultural supremacy in thinking that French intervention would be no more than a passing interlude, as it had been in the past, which they could manipulate to their advantage to re-establish their former balance of power, which would be guaranteed by a new mediator, Italian this time, as Lorenzo the Magnificent had been. This was the reasoning of Ludovico, who began to put these plans into action by having himself proclaimed duke of Milan two months after the French entered Italy, just after the death of his nephew Giangaleazzo Maria, whose son he ousted.   Charles VIII did not interfere: he needed the support of the new duke too much.

Elsewhere, the preparations for the expedition to Naples continued in a climate of intense propaganda to sway public opinion. The advance of the Turks fired up visionaries who also feared a politicised papacy whose clergy preached customs that were hardly Christian. In keeping with the medieval mentality of the populace, satirists in France and in Italy proclaimed that a French monarch sent by God would triumph in Rome by helping to reform the Church, would receive the imperial crown and would deliver Constantinople and Jerusalem.   Astrologers confirmed these predictions, based as well on spectacular signs: storms, apparitions, ghosts.   In Florence, the apocalyptic predictions of the Dominican friar Savonarola depicted the king of France as a liberating Messiah.

It was in this optimistic and rather fanatical atmosphere that on 13 March 1494, in Lyons, Charles VIII took the title of king of Jerusalem and Sicily. On the following 3 September, the French army crossed the border between the Dauphiné and Piedmont.

7. Conclusion

The expedition to Naples in 1494 was far from being a fanciful enterprise conceived by an unbalanced mind. Rather, it was a considered and conscious decision made by Charles VIII and his advisors, based on a long tradition

---

[19] J. Calmette and E. Déprez, *Les premières grandes puissances*, in *Histoire du Moyen Age*, vol. 7, part 2 (Paris, 1939), 595-6. J. Delumeau, *L'Italie de Botticelli à Bonaparte* (Paris, 1974), 53.

spanning more than two centuries; it combined dynastic claims - considered legitimate - with ideological considerations: the crusades, the return of the Byzantine Church to papal control, the reform of the Catholic Church. To these concerns were added economic ambitions: ruling the Mediterranean axis. All in all, Renaissance Italy was irresistibly attractive to the French aristocracy.

The dynastic claims were symptomatic of a traditional mentality, which regarded family lineage as an important legal consideration. In France, these claims were made by the princes of royal blood: the two houses of Anjou, the Orléans. The royal government remained in the background, unable to demonstrate a direct claim before Charles VIII, heir of the Anjou. But it supported nearly all of the ventures of the cadet royal branches, within the limits imposed by the vicissitudes of the Hundred Years' War. In this way, the kings diverted such boisterous energies away from France; at the same time, they made use of these inroads to the advantage of the monarchy. For there remained certain constant considerations within royal policy: to counter the thalassocracy of the Crown of Aragon; to retain a certain amount of control over the papacy, be it in Avignon or Rome: the Holy See was suzerain of the kingdom of Naples, but the kings of France were defenders of Gallicanism. Moreover, the French kings agreed with the popes that the crusades should be resumed. For all these reasons, a hold over the kingdom of Naples seemed useful. It was therefore necessary to use Genoa as a rear base; there had always been French partisans amongst the Genoese, the traditional opponents of Catalan commerce; Genoa was governed directly by the French monarchy on two occasions, under Charles VI and Charles VIII. And when Genoa fell to Milanese rule, on several occasions, the kings of France arranged to recruit the rulers of Milan as allies, or to have them watched, thanks to the Orléans situated in Asti, and to have the count-dukes of Savoy-Piedmont placed under a French protectorate of sorts.

Louis XI introduced a new method into this diplomacy. After several years in power, he ceased supporting the French princely houses and was contented with the role of arbitrator in Italy, which better suited his taste for intrigue, itself a result of his attraction to Italy. Having done this, he nevertheless continued to control the duchy of Savoy, the French bridgehead. In this way, he prevented the house of Burgundy from acting to conquer various Italian states. For Louis XI did not wish to disturb the balance of power in Italy which resulted from the Peace of Lodi of 1454.

Charles VIII inherited this beneficial policy. He had as allies Savoy, Florence, and Milan, which again occupied Genoa and which had put Venice out of the picture. He could place pressure on the papacy. But he wished to intervene in Naples by taking up his ancestors' claims. And the heir to Charles the Bold was Maximilian of Habsburg, ruler of the Holy Roman Empire from where he administered direct rule over the Netherlands, and holder of the imperial rights in Italy which could allow him to replace the king of France as arbitrator of the balance of power in Italy.

The French intervention of 1494, therefore, was not just a whimsical venture. On the way though, it became more like a military parade. The following year, however, Charles VIII abandoned his new kingdom and had to return to France; he had underestimated the powerful intrigues of Venice and the Spanish pope Alexander Borgia. Charles and most of his advisors, as well as his Italian supporters, were determined to prepare themselves to reconquer Naples; this was prevented by his early death in 1498. Half a century later, despite the efforts of his successors, France had lost all its Italian possessions. But the Italians did not gain from this: Ludovico il Moro, who had called the French into Italy, was taken prisoner by them in 1500 and sent to a fortress in France, at Loches, where he remained in captivity until his death in 1508. Italy then became a European battlefield, over which Spain reigned supreme, encouraging the dreams of Charles V, which were similar to the dreams of his grandfather, Maximilian, and those of Charles VIII: to reestablish imperial hegemony over Europe in order to lead the crusades. These dreams as well were dashed. The balance of power in Europe which was beginning to become established between the great states thwarted the ambitions of the house of Austria.

It was Italy that had provided the model for the balance of power in Europe. Throughout the fourteenth and fifteenth centuries, Italy had set out novel methods of war, diplomacy, administration and economics. These innovations were imitated by all of Europe. Thus the Renaissance was not only an intellectual and artistic movement originating in Italy, of which France was one of the main beneficiaries. Italy, through France, was to teach Europe how to form permanent armies with considerable fire power to face newly enhanced fortifications. Italy took the initiative in establishing permanent embassies and coded letters. The bureaucratic organisation of the State was born in Italy, as well as a more complex economy, with its logical methods and the development of accountancy and a system of credit. In brief, the Italian Renaissance established the model for political realism: *raison d'État*, from this point onwards, was to govern the behaviour of European leaders. It was this fundamental change which was germinating in 1494, when Charles VIII led his expedition into Italy.[20]

Translated by Sandra Smith

---

[20] Reference may also be made to: E. Sol, *Les Rapports de la France avec l'Italie du 12ème siècle à la fin du 1er Empire d'après la série K des Archives Nationales* (Paris, 1905); P. Mirot, 'La Politique française en Italie 1380-1422', in *Revue des Études Historiques*, 100 (1933), 493-542; B. Buser, *Die Beziehungen der Mediceer zu Frankreich in ihrem Zusammenhang mit den allgemeine Verhältnisse Italiens, 1434-1494* (Leipzig, 1879); P.M. Perret, *Histoire des relations de la France avec Venise, du 12ème siècle à l'avènement de Charles VIII* (Paris, 1896), 2 vols.; H.F. Delaborde, *L'Expédition de Charles VIII en Italie* (Paris, 1888).

The Angevin bid for Naples, 1380-1480

Alan Ryder

When in November 1459 Jean, son of René of Anjou, raised his standard on Neapolitan soil he trod in the steps of forebears who had striven unsuccessfully for three generations to make good their claim to the throne of Naples. Ultimately that claim derived from rights of conquest and papal grant secured by the French prince Charles, brother of St Louis, duke of Anjou and Provence, who in 1265 had answered a papal summons to wrest the kingdom of Sicily from the excommunicated Hohenstaufen.[1] It was reinforced in the 1370s by the eruption of simultaneous, interlocked contests for the papal and Neapolitan thrones. Charles' last direct descendant, the dissolute and childless Joanna I, chose in 1378 to recognise the anti-pope Clement VII despite the popularity which his rival, the Neapolitan Urban VI, enjoyed among her subjects.[2] Urban retaliated by calling on Charles of Durazzo, the nearest male survivor of the Angevin line in Naples, to depose her.[3] Against that onslaught Joanna turned

---

[1] Since its creation by the Normans, rulers of the 'kingdom of Sicily' (Sicily and the southern mainland) had acknowledged papal overlordship. Angevin monarchs continued to do so after the Sicilian Vespers (1282) restricted their authority to the mainland; and they continued to style themselves kings of Sicily. To avoid confusion the mainland territory is referred to in this paper as the kingdom of Naples. See C. de Frede, 'Da Carlo I d'Angiò a Giovanna I, 1263-1382,' *Storia di Napoli*, vol. 3 (Naples, 1969); E.G. Léonard, *Les Angevins de Naples* (Paris, 1954).

[2] Urban's election took place in April 1378; that of Clement followed on Neapolitan soil at Fondi in September. Soon afterwards Clement took refuge at Avignon in Joanna's duchy of Provence. W. Ullmann, *Origins of the great schism: a study in fourteenth-century ecclesiastical history* (London, 1972); N. Valois, *La France et le grand schisme d'occident* (Paris, 1896).

[3] Charles' grandfather was the third son of Charles II of Naples. Charles Martel, the second son, founded the Angevin dynasty in Hungary where in 1365 Charles of Durazzo settled at the court of his kinsman Louis the Great. Louis sustained Charles' Neapolitan ambitions and inculcated in him a bitter hostility towards Joanna whom the Hungarians held responsible for the murder of Louis' brother, her first husband. G. Peyronnet, 'I Durazzo e Renato d'Angio 1381-1442' in *Storia di Napoli*, vol. 3 (Naples, 1969).

for aid to her French Valois relative Louis, duke of Anjou, whom she adopted in 1380 as heir to her throne.[4]

There ensued a contest characteristic of many that were to recur during the following century. While Charles of Durazzo, having an army already on foot in Italy, was able to strike swiftly, murder Joanna and make himself master of the kingdom, it took Louis two years to free himself of French entanglements (his brother Charles V died in September 1380) before he marched across the Alps. The army he led was probably the most formidable French force to appear in Italy between the descent of Charles of Anjou in 1265 and the invasion of 1494, but Louis proved an indifferent general, allowed months to pass without forcing his adversary to pitched battle, and so saw his forces wither away in penury and pestilence. His own death on 21 September 1384 triggered the final dissolution of his army and support within the kingdom despite vain testamentary attempts to sustain the Angevin cause in the name of his seven-year-old son.[5] Predictably, that child remained in France, with his mother engaged in the more grateful task of establishing Angevin authority over Provence, the sole portion of Joanna's legacy left securely within their grasp.

Not long passed before the assassination of Charles of Durazzo (February 1386)[6] rekindled the spirit of faction within the kingdom of Naples to the immediate profit of the Angevin cause whose adherents quickly threw their Durazzo adversaries, headed by Charles' ten-year-old son Ladislas and his mother, on to the defensive. But not until Provence had been wholly mastered and young Louis crowned at Avignon in November 1389 could the newly-acquired naval power of southern France be mustered to transport the Angevin court and army to Italy. They reached Naples in August 1390 unscathed by the perils of an overland march, and poised for major victories in Apulia, Terra di Lavoro and Calabria. However, as with all such expeditions, within three years the initial resources of men and money had been exhausted; further and final victory demanded another massive injection. Despite some enthusiasm in France for a new expedition that would consolidate Angevin success and French prestige in Italy, all prospects of such aid were dashed by the death of Louis' chief paymaster, Pope Clement VII, in September 1394, and the hostility that ensued between France and Avignon.[7] Thenceforth Louis found himself totally

---

[4] The duchy of Anjou had passed from the Neapolitan dynasty to Charles de Valois on his marriage to a daughter of Charles II of Naples in 1290. Charles de Valois' daughter became the mother of Joanna I.

[5] See E.G. Léonard, *Histoire de Jeanne I* (Monaco-Paris, 1942). See also A. Sala, *La lotta tra Carlo III di Durazzo e Luigi I* (Naples, 1880).

[6] Having seized the Hungarian throne on the death of Louis the Great, Charles soon afterwards fell victim to a plot.

[7] Clement was succeeded in Avignon by a Spaniard, Benedict XIII. Even before Clement's death the French king had been seeking an end to the schism; after it he distanced himself from Benedict, and in July 1398 withdrew obedience. Fear of English designs in

dependent upon Neapolitan support, principally that of the Sanseverino clan and the city of Naples; support which amounted to little more than a convenient cover for domestic feuds and ambitions. If his opponents were in no better case financially and politically (both parties showered largesse wholesale on an insatiable baronage), Louis was revealing a character devoid of leadership while his rival Ladislas had begun to display that acumen and ruthlessness which were to make him the terror of Italy. Surrendering the initiative, the Angevin camp allowed itself to be hemmed in by an ever more confident enemy until little remained to it beyond the confines of the city of Naples. Louis' desperate foray into Puglia in February 1399, designed to galvanize wavering barons into action, offered instead to a demoralised capital and supporters the opportunity to make their peace with Ladislas. By July all was lost; abandoned and humiliated the Angevin prince set sail for Provence.[8]

Domestic squabbles around a disputed throne had thus far been the occasion for Angevin descents upon Naples. Ten years later it was conflict among the states of Italy that lured Louis back. Spurred by unbounded ambition, Ladislas had made himself master of Rome and much of central Italy; Florence and Siena in alarm sought safety in an alliance with his dynastic rival Louis II to whom they promised aid in winning Naples in return for Angevin support in Tuscany (26 June 1409). A new papal backer gave Louis added confidence: in place of Benedict XIII, a fugitive who could do nothing for him, he had the blessing of the pope recently elected by the Council of Pisa, Alexander V, an irreconcilable enemy of Ladislas. Alexander duly invested him with the kingdom in Pisa on 19 August 1409, the third pope to confer that elusive title![9]

It took very little time to discover that self-interest motivated Italian powers as much as it did Neapolitan barons. Once Louis had, in the role of a condottiere, combined with Attendolo Sforza and Braccio da Montone,[10] to drive Ladislas' forces from Rome (October 1409), he found his allies lukewarm over Naples. Even Alexander V, though still fulminating against Ladislas, could only urge Louis to return to Provence in search of more men and money. Still undeterred he made his way home in November 1409,[11] collected a

---

France and the insanity of Charles VI had put an end to the Italian project of 1393. In 1396 Charles signed a treaty with Florence promising French neutrality in Naples.

[8] See A. Cutolo, *Re Ladislao d'Angiò Durazzo* (Naples, 1969).

[9] In March 1403 Benedict, threatened by a French army, had fled from Avignon. Deposed by the Council of Pisa in 1409, in 1414 he settled finally under Aragonese protection at Peñiscola. The council likewise deposed the 'Roman' pope, Gregory XII, but Ladislas continued to uphold him and to occupy Rome.

[10] 'The two greatest condottiere figures of this period': M. Mallett, *Mercenaries and their masters* (London, 1974), 66.

[11] Léonard (*Les Angevins*, 481) attributes his withdrawal to anxiety that communications with France might be jeopardised by the revolt of Genoa against French overlordship (3 September 1409). Cutolo maintains that Louis' position in Rome had become untenable, and

handsome subsidy from France, and hastened back to Italy in April 1410 leaving the bulk of his fleet to follow from Marseilles. That decision cost him dear, for a month later all but one of those vessels with everything they carried fell prey to a Neapolitan fleet.[12]

Moreover his papal champion, Alexander, had died in his absence. Fortunately for Louis, John XXIII, his successor, proved an even more bitter foe of Ladislas,[13] and between them they had by September 1410 scraped together enough money to despatch an army commanded by Louis and Sforza to Rome. There the prince saw the year out in a round of religious devotions. Spring and further consultations with Pope John breathed new life into the enterprise despite the defection of Florence, and there followed a sensational victory over Ladislas at Roccasecca near Cassino (18 May 1411). Had it exploited that advantage, the Papal-Angevin army might have fallen without delay upon Naples or Gaeta. Instead Louis gave his opponent time to recover, and then, having failed in a cautious attempt to push forward, in July he fell back on Rome. With a reputation in tatters, he finally abandoned Italy and his Neapolitan dreams in August 1411.[14]

There Angevin aspirations might have ended had not Ladislas died childless in August 1414 leaving his throne to his only sister, Joanna, a widow, also childless, and at forty-five manifestly beyond the age of child-bearing. Once more the kingdom faced the dismal prospect of an uncertain succession, and once more rival parties within and without manoeuvred for advantage. Louis II might have lost heart but the French court was loathe to surrender its dynastic claims, so it readily agreed to a marriage between Joanna II and Jacques de Bourbon, count of la Marche, a distant cousin of Louis. With that alliance France had wrecked the schemes of two rivals, Benedict XIII, the last schismatic pope of the Avignon line, and Ferdinand I, the first ruler of the new Trastámara dynasty in Aragon; both had hoped to marry Joanna to Ferdinand's son Juan.[15] From Benedict there was in truth little more to fear once the Council

---

that he appeared before Alexander in Prato early in November, 'più in veste di fuggiasco che di paladino della sua autorità' (*Re Ladislao*, 389).

[12] French aid amounted to 200,000 francs. On the eight ships of the transport fleet were embarked his horses, arms, provisions, money, and most of his troops. Genoese readiness to aid Ladislas against the French played a large part in this catastrophe.

[13] Cardinal Baldassarre Cossa, elected pope by the Pisan cardinals on 17 May, had been papal legate with the army that took Rome.

[14] Sickness among his troops, lack of provisions and money, and pressure from his captains may account, as Léonard argues (*Les Angevins*, 481), for his decision to quit Rome in August. But they do not explain his failure to follow-up the victory in May which demonstrates once again that he was a captain, 'quanto altri mai inabile e titubante' (Cutolo, *Re Ladislao*, 405).

[15] Benedict had been instrumental in putting the Castilian Ferdinand on the throne of his native Aragon through his influence in the Compromise of Casp (1412) which had decided among many claimants following the extinction of the native dynasty. With Naples as a springboard, Benedict had hoped to make himself master of Rome.

of Constance had managed in November 1417 to win virtually universal recognition for Pope Martin V. Aragon on the contrary presented a formidable challenge to French claims on Naples, a challenge that had its origin in the Sicilian Vespers and had recently been strengthened by the reincorporation of Sicily into the Crown of Aragon.[16] In the time of Louis I rivalry between Anjou and Aragon had been quiescent; indeed that French prince had on several occasions solicited and received Aragonese aid in his Neapolitan adventures; and marriages had taken place between the two houses.[17] Then, around the beginning of the fifteenth century, things began to change. Aragon's forward policy in Sicily and Sardinia sharpened the commercial rivalry between Catalans and Provençals throughout the western Mediterranean.[18] Dynastic antagonism flared in 1412 when Louis II saw himself worsted by Ferdinand in the election to the vacant Aragonese throne. Subjects and rulers on both sides were therefore keenly sensitive to the implications of an impending contest for the Neapolitan crown.

What had seemed a French triumph - the marriage of Joanna to Jacques de Bourbon in 1415 - swiftly proved illusory, for that luckless noble floundered amid Neapolitan intrigue, found himself a prisoner, and was happy to flee back to France in 1418.[19] None the less Pope Martin V, once he had taken possession of Rome in September 1420, appeared keen to stabilise the kingdom of Naples by settling the succession in favour of Anjou; and that he proceeded to do by proclaiming Louis III, who had succeeded his father in April 1417, as heir presumptive to Joanna II.[20] It was not of course the first time that a pope had so disposed of the Neapolitan crown; like earlier Angevins Louis III needed to make good his title against a host of enemies. Foremost among them stood the queen's favourite, Gianni Caracciolo, who feared to lose his position as virtual master of the kingdom should Louis assume that tutelage over Joanna which the pope clearly intended. On the Angevin side, in addition to the papacy, were

---

[16] The Aragonese dynasty installed in Sicily by the Vespers (1282) came to a chaotic end with a scramble for the hand of Maria, daughter and heiress of the last king, Frederick IV, who died in 1377. Martin, grandson of the king of Aragon, won the prize, gathered an army, conquered the island in 1392, and assumed the royal title. When he died in 1409 without a legitimate heir, he left Sicily to his father, King Martin of Aragon, who incorporated it with the Crown of Aragon. So the island passed to his successor Ferdinand. See G. Fasoli, 'L'unione della Sicilia all'Aragona,' *Rivista storica italiana*, (1953).

[17] The most important was that of Louis II of Anjou to Yolande, daughter of King John of Aragon (1 December 1400).

[18] For Sicily see S.R. Epstein, *An island for itself: economic development and social change in late medieval Sicily* (Cambridge, 1992); for Sardinia, A. Boscolo, *Medioevo aragonese* (Padua, 1958); for Catalan commercial activity, M. del Treppo, *I mercanti catalani e l'espansione della corona aragonese nel secolo XV* (Naples, 1972).

[19] For the reign of Joanna II see N.F. Faraglia, *Storia della regina Joanna II d'Angiò* (Lanciano, 1904)

[20] For the political strategy adopted by Martin see P. Partner, *The papal state under Martin V* (London, 1958).

ranged France and Sforza, the ablest of Italian condottieri. Confronted with so disparate an array of forces, the foes of Anjou looked around for an ally powerful enough to redress the balance, and they found one in Alfonso V, the young king of Aragon who happened at that moment to be engaged with Genoa in a battle for control of Corsica.[21]

The emergent economic and dynastic antagonism between Aragon and Anjou had already acquired a Neapolitan focus in the marriage intrigues of 1415. Alfonso, Juan's elder brother, now grasped this renewed opportunity to lay claim to the kingdom of Naples, a prize which might guarantee him and his Catalan subjects mastery of the western Mediterranean.[22] In June 1421 he disembarked at Naples, was adopted by Joanna as her son and heir, and prepared to confront the besieging forces of Louis III and Sforza.

Although Alfonso's intervention brought Catalonia's inveterate foes, the Genoese, into the Angevin camp, the balance of forces initially favoured him for, in addition to his own large resources, he could count upon the army of Braccio da Montone and the alliance of Milan.[23] Pope Martin moreover was browbeaten into neutrality by Aragonese threats to espouse the cause of his only surviving rival, Benedict XIII. Despite this adverse turn of fortune, Louis maintained an effective blockade of Naples for some months, only to see his forces crumble when he unwisely turned his back to seek help from Rome. The Angevin menace having vanished, it immediately became evident that the Neapolitans had no further use for Alfonso. Beset by intrigue and treachery, he came to blows with the queen, was deserted by Milan, and found his own subjects unwilling to pour their wealth into so uncertain an enterprise. In October 1423 reluctantly he set sail for Spain, leaving garrisons in a few fortresses. Meanwhile Joanna II and her advisers, having experienced the masterful behaviour of Spaniards, determined that, since an heir must be designated, they could live more comfortably with Louis of Anjou, who was solemnly installed in Alfonso's place on 14 September 1423.

So ended the struggle between the houses of Durazzo and Anjou which had hitherto played a large part in frustrating the Neapolitan ambitions of the latter. Freed of all overt opposition, Louis III was able to settle confidently but discreetly into a waiting role at Joanna's side, and even to absent himself for five years to aid his overlord the king of France against England without prejudicing

---

[21] Alfonso had succeeded Ferdinand as king of Aragon in 1416. In 1420 he led an expedition to Sardinia to reassert Aragonese control over the island, and, having attained that objective, he turned his forces against Corsica. Pope Boniface VIII had invested James II of Aragon with the title to Corsica in 1297 but it had never been made good in the face of Genoese opposition. For Alfonso see A. Ryder, *Alfonso the Magnanimous* (Oxford, 1990).

[22] See del Treppo, *I mercanti catalani* and G. Pistarino, 'Genova e Barcellona: incontro e scontro di due civiltà,' *Atti del primo congresso storico Liguria-Catalogna* (Bordighera, 1974).

[23] The duke of Milan, Filippo Maria Visconti, had designs on Genoa.

his position in Naples. He returned in 1431 with fresh military laurels to keep watch over a now aged queen.

Alfonso had, it is true, in the meantime doggedly maintained the validity of his title in a long-drawn altercation with the papacy,[24] and from time to time received invitations to make it good from prominent Neapolitan nobles who began to view with dismay the prospect of a smooth succession and rejuvenated royal authority.[25] But for almost a decade he found himself occupied with problems and prospects in the Iberian peninsula, and it took ignominious failure against Castile in 1430 to rekindle Italian ambitions. Once revived they were to be pursued with quite remarkable single-mindedness from 1432, when he established his headquarters in Sicily, until the end of his life. For the moment however he could do little but canvas support among the barons in the hope of challenging Louis whenever Joanna might die.

What happened confounded all expectations, for it was Louis who succumbed to fever in November 1434, giving the queen barely time to name his brother René as heir, before she followed him to the grave in February 1435. Nor did Angevin misfortune end there: since 1431 René had been held captive by his family's bitter enemy, the duke of Burgundy, who was demanding a huge ransom.[26]

At this crucial moment the party of Anjou thus found itself leaderless. Little seemed to stand in Alfonso's way when in May 1435 he landed near Gaeta which had been selected as an easier target than the capital where Angevin sympathies ran deep. And all might have gone according to plan had not resistance in Gaeta been stiffened by a Genoese garrison. Resolved at all costs to foil the expansionist schemes of its Catalan rivals, Genoa had stepped into the contest for the Neapolitan throne as the champion of Anjou, and to such effect that, after its troops had checked Alfonso at Gaeta, its ships inflicted a devastating defeat on the Aragonese fleet off the island of Ponza (5 August 1435). They carried away prisoner the king, two of his brothers, and the pick of his Neapolitan partisans.

---

[24] When Benedict XIII died (30 May 1423) Alfonso permitted a rump conclave at Peñiscola to elect another Aragonese anti-pope, Clement VIII.

[25] The Neapolitan branch of the Orsini family initiated these overtures in outraged reaction to the installation among the nobility of their hereditary enemy, the Colonna family of Martin V. Caracciolo himself, in an elaborate strategy of double bluff, opened negotiations with Alfonso in 1430.

[26] Enmity between Anjou and Burgundy dated from 1407 when Louis II retracted the betrothal of his son to Catherine of Burgundy following the murder of the duke of Orléans by her father. It erupted into violence in 1431 over possession of Bar and Lorraine, claimed by René of Anjou in virtue of his marriage to the heiress of those duchies. René's defeat at Bulgneville (2 July 1431) delivered him into the hands of Philip of Burgundy, and the prospect that he might become king of Naples served only to inflate the size of his ransom. For René see A. Lecoy de la Marche, *Le roi René*, 2 vols. (Paris, 1875).

Angevin fortunes raised anew looked still brighter when René's wife Isabelle arrived in October 1435 to fill the place of the captive duke. But in that same month Alfonso turned the tables by persuading the duke of Milan, Genoa's overlord, not merely to set him free but to abandon his pro-French stance for an alliance designed to ensure an Aragonese victory in Naples.[27]

By February 1436 the king was installed in Gaeta - one of the first fruits garnered from the Milanese alliance - prepared to wear down his opponents in a war of attrition and manoeuvre, eschewing the rash bravura that had led to the Ponza disaster. The money needed he extracted with great ingenuity from the pockets of his subjects both Spanish and Italian. On the Angevin side the line-up of forces had a familiar air: a large number of Neapolitan barons scanning the entrails of war to identify a victor, the republic of Genoa, and Pope Eugenius IV who confirmed earlier bulls in favour of Anjou and despatched a papal army into the kingdom. René himself arrived there, financially crippled, with his eldest son Jean in May 1438, having scraped together a ransom for Burgundy and haggled long and hard with Genoa over the price of aid.[28] His engaging, debonair personality undoubtedly strengthened his cause among the capital's populace, and so helped frustrate Alfonso's many attempts to seize Naples, but as a military commander he revealed little talent and was content to leave the direction of operations in the hands of Jacobo Caldora, a self-seeking condottiere who would bestir himself only when well furnished with cash, which René could seldom supply.

This combination of Aragonese caution and Angevin penury led to an overall military stalemate; similar deadlock prevailed on the diplomatic front where Aragon and Milan failed to browbeat the pope through their support for the Council of Basle and its new anti-pope,[29] and where half-hearted French attempts at mediation came to naught. In such circumstances the advantage swung inexorably towards Alfonso: his relatively abundant supplies of cash began to lure wavering barons;[30] his steadfast determination persuaded many

---

[27] Although Aragonese naval support had helped Filippo Maria bring Genoa under his control in October 1421, relations were subsequently soured by Alfonso's demands that the duke force the Genoese to surrender Corsica to Aragon. Filippo Maria was none the less embarrassed to find himself Alfonso's captor in 1435. The abruptness of his change of front may be gauged by the fact that he signed an alliance with Anjou on 21 September and the pact with Aragon on 8 October.

[28] In January 1437 Burgundy agreed on a ransom of 400,000 écus, half to be paid after the conquest of Naples. Although the dowry of the duke of Bourbon's daughter, married to René's son, accounted for the first instalment of 100,000 écus, finding the second 100,000 still stretched Angevin resources to the limit. René had planned to spend five days in Genoa. Instead he found himself detained for two weeks until he had agreed under protest to Genoese demands.

[29] For this council see A. Black, *Council and commune: the conciliar movement and the Council of Basle* (London, 1979).

[30] René failed to extract any regular or substantial subsidies from his French possessions. Alfonso, by contrast, cajoled large amounts in cash and kind from his Spanish and Sicilian

that he must eventually triumph. One by one they transferred their allegiance, province by province he extended his sway, while René allowed himself to be ever more closely confined within Naples. From being an advantage, possession of the capital became a liability because feeding the population, one of the largest in the Mediterranean,[31] put enormous strains upon Angevin resources and began to dictate René's strategy.

The conflict came to a crisis in 1440. René had staked all on leading a midwinter foray into the Abruzzi designed to join forces with Caldora and stir him into action; when that gamble failed his confidence visibly began to wane despite renewed pledges of aid from Rome and Genoa. In August he sent his wife and children home to Provence, and took himself into the fortress of Castelnuovo, so evident was his terror of capture and further long years of imprisonment.[32] He even offered to cede the throne to his rival on condition that Alfonso, who lacked legitimate children, would adopt René's son Jean as his heir. Small wonder that the nobility began to desert in droves, and Genoa to backpedal.[33] A valiant display during the final Aragonese assault on Naples (2 June 1442) preserved his reputation for personal courage but not his kingdom which he abandoned in July.[34] Pausing in Florence to confer with Eugenius IV, he collected the bulls investing him with his lost kingdom, and with nothing more to show rejoined his family in Provence.

Once master of Naples, Alfonso embarked on a reorganization aimed at enhancing royal authority, and binding the kingdom administratively and commercially with his other states in the Crown of Aragon.[35] Politically however it was destined to preserve its independence for he arranged that the crown should pass not to Aragon but to his only son, the illegitimate Ferrante. On the wider Italian scene the Aragonese victor soon gave other states cause to reinforce earlier doubts about his further ambitions. Hegemony over Genoa and the papal states quickly emerged as primary goals, along with a readiness to coerce Florence and Venice into acquiescence. As a result the peninsula was thrown into a kaleidoscopic series of wars in which Alfonso found himself

---

subjects. See A. Ryder, 'Cloth and credit: Aragonese war finance in the mid-fifteenth century,' *War and society*, 2 (1984).

[31] Peyronnet ('I Durazzo,' *Storia di Napoli*, vol. 3, 410) estimates the population of the city in this period at 60,000.

[32] Castelnuovo, standing outside the walls of Naples, offered access to the sea, and hence an escape route. Previously René had resided in Castelcapuano within the city.

[33] A relief fleet promised by the republic early in 1441 never materialised, for Genoa was becoming reconciled to an Aragonese victory.

[34] According to a contemporary account, René fought sword in hand to stem the attack until, seeing himself in danger of being surrounded, he cried out, 'Ay dio se fosse certo essere morto non curara ma io temo essere presone': *Diurnali detti del Duca di Monteleone*, ed. N. Faraglia (Naples, 1895), 124. He then retired to Castelnuovo and escaped the following month aboard a Genoese vessel.

[35] See A. Ryder, *The kingdom of Naples under Alfonso the Magnanimous* (Oxford, 1976).

always at odds with at least one major state; in such an imbroglio the cause of Anjou could always find a voice.

As early as 1448 Florence, the current target of Alfonso's operations, began to probe René's resolution; five years later in alliance with the new duke of Milan, Francesco Sforza,[36] the republic convinced René that his services in Lombardy and Tuscany would be rewarded with aid against Naples. René accordingly bound himself, by a treaty signed in April 1453, to appear two months later with an army of at least 2400 horse. Charles VII of France, whose main interest was to restore French suzerainty over Genoa, urged him on with assurances of military assistance. And René kept his word; the end of September 1453 saw him join the Milanese army beyond the River Adda; by the middle of November he had helped clear the Venetians from most of Brescia province. But already he felt the slippery political ground of Italy moving under his feet: Florence openly refused him money and winter quarters; both his allies were secretly seeking peace. Perhaps it was in fear of imminent betrayal that he abandoned Italy in January 1454, pleading that he needed to consult Charles VII, and promising to send his son Jean in his place. The Florentine ambassador in France, on the other hand, later attributed René's departure to cowardice, while Sforza, more convincingly, found him totally absorbed by his passion for Jeanne de Laval.[37] Whatever the reasons behind it, this abrupt departure cast lasting doubt upon his mettle both as soldier and statesman. Jean, who promptly appeared to fill his father's place, had but little time to rescue something of Anjou's tarnished reputation before the warring Italian powers made peace in April 1454. They did so without consulting René, and in the subsequently formed league of Italian states blighted any future Angevin designs by pledging mutual assistance against all aggressors. A few chinks were however left in the league's defences. Of these the most important was Genoa, still the goal of Catalan ambition, and hence excluded, at Alfonso's insistence, from all guarantees. It proved a serious misjudgement for, having failed to dislodge the ruling Campofregoso faction, he drove it *in extremis* into the arms of the only available ally, France. Thereby was Anjou able to regain a

---

[36] Francesco, the son of Alfonso's inveterate adversary Muzio Attendolo Sforza, made himself master of Milan in 1450 following the death of Filippo Maria Visconti. Initially the hostility of Venice and Naples brought him into alliance with Florence against those two powers.

[37] According to Angelo Acciajuolo (Lecoy de la Marche, *Le Roi René*, vol. 2, 279) René had asked a friend to contrive that the king of France should write a letter recalling him from Italy. Learning of this by accident, Charles VII had ordered him to remain, only to find that he had already left. That news, wrote Acciajuolo, caused the king to denounce René as 'quello che haveva disfacto lo stato et honor di Franza in Ytalia'. Accusations of cowardice do not however carry conviction; more plausible is the suggestion that René, mistrustful of his Italian allies, readily succumbed to the lure of twenty-one year old Jeanne. His wife Isabelle had died in February 1453; he married Jeanne in September 1454.

footing in Italy, this time in the person of Jean who in May 1458 took possession of Genoa in the name of Charles VII.

His arrival there came at a moment propitious to the fortunes of Anjou, for a month later Alfonso died leaving Naples to his son Ferrante.[38] Like earlier adversaries of Anjou, Ferrante enjoyed the advantage of possession and the additional benefit of support from the Italian League, none of whose members responded to French blandishments to abandon him. Against him weighed first the pent-up domestic hostility to a Spanish régime which had curbed the nobility and raised taxes, secondly the bitter enmity of the Spanish pope Calixtus III who made no secret of his resolve to drive the son of his erstwhile master from the Neapolitan throne, and thirdly the determination of Genoa to rid itself of the Catalan incubus by expelling the Aragonese dynasty from Italian soil. Despite these dangers, Ferrante appeared at first secure in his kingdom: no baron dared yet raise his head, and, more importantly still, Calixtus III died in August 1458, to be succeeded by the avowedly pro-Aragonese Pius II. This pontiff, firmly rejecting René's claims to the Neapolitan crown, placed it on his rival's head in February 1459.[39]

Ferrante's domestic enemies did not lose heart because behind them stood the most powerful noble in the kingdom, Giovanni Antonio del Balzo Orsini, Prince of Taranto, who had long coveted the role of kingmaker.[40] Thanks to his barely covert machinations unrest spread among the baronage and through the provinces, most menacingly in Calabria where the demands of Antonio Centelles, stripped of his lands by Alfonso for rebellion, found support among an overtaxed population; by November 1458 much of that province had risen against the king.[41] Ferrante responded with dissimulation and compromise in the hope that he might, with support from Aragon and Milan, drive the French from Genoa and thus deprive his domestic malcontents of hopes of foreign aid before seeking a confrontation with them. Only in Calabria, where Angevin agents were already busy among the rebels, did he resort immediately to arms.

---

[38] In his will Alfonso's father had stipulated that, should Alfonso die without a legitimate heir, all the states of the Crown of Aragon must pass to his brother Juan. Only the kingdom of Naples, conquered by Alfonso and not incorporated with the Crown of Aragon, remained at his free disposal. Eugenius IV had legitimized Ferrante and declared him able to succeed to the Italian kingdom. See, *infra*, David Abulafia, 'The inception of the reign of Ferrante'.

[39] For a detailed account of the contest between Ferrante and Jean of Anjou see E. Nunziante, 'I primi anni di Ferdinando d'Aragona e l'invasione di Giovanni d'Angiò,' *Archivio storico per le province napoletane*, 17 (1892), 299-357, 564-86, 731-79; 18 (1893), 3-40, 207-46, 411-62, 563-620; 19 (1894), 37-96, 300-53, 419-44, 595-658; 20 (1895), 206-64, 442-516; 21 (1896), 265-89, 494-532; 22 (1897), 47-64, 204-40; 23 (1898), 144-210.

[40] He had sought to play that part in the Aragonese camp as long as Alfonso remained a contender for the throne, but after 1442 retired to his estates manifestly resentful that his days of power-brokering were finished. In a vain effort to placate him Alfonso had married Ferrante to the prince's favourite niece.

[41] See E. Pontieri, *La Calabria a metà del secolo XV e le rivolte di Antonio Centelles* (Naples, 1963).

Politic as such caution may have been, it gave the Prince of Taranto time to play upon wavering nobles and negotiate with Jean d'Anjou, who in March 1459 persuaded the Genoese to commission a naval expedition against Naples.

Insurgent expectations that René would champion their cause in person were quickly dashed because that prince, ever more disillusioned by his recent rebuff at the hands of the Italian powers, refused to hazard himself again. So it was his son who sailed from Genoa in October 1459 to try Angevin fortunes once more in the southern kingdom. The failure of Jean's initial attempts to land near Naples encouraged Ferrante to persevere with the suppression of Calabria, in the belief that the enemy fleet would soon be forced to withdraw. But conspiracy cut even deeper than he had imagined; and it was his own brother-in-law, the Prince of Rossano,[42] who welcomed the invaders ashore on the northern coasts of the Terra del Lavoro (16 November). Many other nobles of the region quickly followed suit; in the Abruzzi most declared for Anjou; in Puglia the cautious Prince of Taranto finally threw off the mask in January 1460. A seemingly relentless tide of defections cast gloom over the Aragonese camp and bred heady optimism among the Angevins. In truth, however, Ferrante still enjoyed important advantages: the firm backing of Pius II, Francesco Sforza, Cosimo de' Medici, and the king of Aragon; the loyalty of Spanish families planted in the kingdom by Alfonso (notably the Guevara and Davalos); and an irreducible following of Neapolitans implacably hostile to those who had embraced the Angevin cause. Jean, by contrast, having received no effective aid from France, and seeing Genoa recall its fleet in December, found himself totally dependent upon his Neapolitan supporters and condemned to follow a strategy dictated by their rivalries and ambitions. Each one of any note insisted on giving priority to the defence and advancement of his own regional interests, so making impossible any central direction or concentration of the Angevin forces; whereas Ferrante, exercising much greater authority over his followers, was able to deploy his somewhat smaller numbers as need dictated.

With Calabria subdued before Jean's arrival, Ferrante spent much of the winter securing the northern frontiers of the Terra di Lavoro to keep open the way for expected papal and Milanese aid. In the spring of 1460 he focussed his efforts upon Puglia with the object of denying the Angevins the only remaining substantial source of revenue within the kingdom: the grazing tax levied on animals brought to pasture there. Fortunately for Jean, the Prince of Taranto was still ready to act as paymaster, and in June 1460 the two joined forces to march towards Naples, while a large Genoese fleet prowled off the city. Had

---

[42] Like her brother Ferrante, Alfonso's illegitimate daughter Leonor was married into the Neapolitan baronage in an effort to attach powerful families to the Aragonese dynasty; her husband, the prince, belonged to the Ruffo clan.

they struck decisively at that moment the capital might well have fallen; instead they fell back into a defensive position, probably at Taranto's behest. That display of timidity emboldened Ferrante; buoyed up with a reinforcement of papal troops, and with news that forces promised by Francesco Sforza had at last appeared in the Abruzzi, he attempted to crush his rival in a pitched battle at Sarno (7 July 1460). Over-confidence among his men led instead to a rout which presented the Angevins with a fresh opening towards Naples, and again they failed to seize it.

Sorry though Ferrante's plight remained after Sarno, with an empty treasury and his father's fabulous jewel collection in pawn,[43] Jean had not persuaded Italy that he could win. Outside aid consequently continued to reach Ferrante on a scale that increasingly put his enemies at a hopeless disadvantage. So while August saw the Genoese sail home, in September a formidable body of Albanians, led by Alfonso's old ally Scanderbeg,[44] landed on the Apulian coast and brought the Prince of Taranto scurrying back to defend his own territory; and in the following month the arrival of an Aragonese fleet secured the western coasts. Sensing the tide had turned, opportunistic barons began making their peace with the king while room remained to bargain.

Jean now found himself forced back into the central plain of Puglia and reliant for military support upon the whim of Jacopo Piccinino, a condottiere bent on carving a fortune at anyone's expense.[45] Further disaster struck his cause on 9 March 1461 when Genoa rose in revolt and expelled the French; an attempt by his father René to retake the city having failed ingloriously in July, the main external prop of the Neapolitan enterprise collapsed.[46] Hope that the new king of France, Louis XI, might make good the loss with an aggressive policy in Italy seemed momentarily justified when he began to put pressure on Pius II and Milan; but his threats never crossed the threshold of bluster. So, as one by one the provinces fell to Ferrante, Jean with his hard core of support became marooned in central Puglia. The end came on 18 August 1462 with their defeat at the battle of Troia. 'Questa è stata quella giornata che ha messo et

---

[43] The Milanese ambassador in Naples calculated Alfonso's jewels, precious objects and tapestries to be worth four or five hundred thousand ducats (Nunziante, 'I primi anni', 18 (1893) 21, n.3). With much of his revenue lost through rebellion or concession, Ferrante was able to raise loans against these treasures.

[44] George Castriota ('Scanderbeg') had been aided by Alfonso in defending Albania against the Turks.

[45] Seeking like Francesco Sforza, his life-long foe, to make himself master of a state, Piccinino had set his eyes on papal lands. Despite some support received from Alfonso, he so mistrusted the growing affinity between Naples and Sforza's Milan that he readily embraced the Angevin cause.

[46] René's inept performance on this occasion strengthens doubts about his military competence. He failed to get his troops ashore to support the French attacking Genoa; then, having watched while they were routed, he ordered his ships to sail before many of the fugitives could struggle aboard. A large number were left to drown.

fermata la corona de questo Regno al signore Re', wrote the Milanese ambassador. The Prince of Taranto lost no time in making peace with the victor; Jean and Piccinino obtained eighteen days' grace to remove themselves by sea.

They made for the northern Abruzzi, where a knot of supporters led by Antonio Caldora still commanded some territory. Combining forces they succeeded during that winter in taking a number of towns including Sulmona, the provincial capital. But they were unable to link up with Jean's other steadfast partisan, the Prince of Rossano, in the Terra di Lavoro, so that in the summer of 1463 Ferrante had little difficulty in extinguishing resistance in both provinces. By the end of August the principal adherents of Anjou had all laid down their arms, and Jean himself was again driven to seek safe passage from the realm. He found temporary refuge in September on the island of Ischia, perhaps hoping that the Prince of Taranto might, even at this last hour, rekindle the conflict, an expectation not entirely unrealistic, had not that potentate died in November 1463. Anjou's other last hope vanished when Louis XI decided that his interests were best served by an understanding with Sforza. Nothing then remained for Jean but to leave Ischia in April 1464 and take the familiar path home through Florence with as brave a show as possible.

Jean never forgave the king of France for betraying the Angevin cause in Naples, a fault which Louis later compounded with illusory promises of aid to René and his son in their war with Ferrante's uncle, John II of Aragon.[47] They failed to understand that Louis aimed to undermine and not enhance the territorial power of French princes, and that he was not above making overtures to Ferrante behind their backs. For the victor of the Neapolitan war, however, the threat after 1464 came no longer from the Angevins but from the prospect that Provence, and with it the claims to Naples, might fall into the hands of the king of France. The death of Jean, René's only surviving son, in 1470, followed in 1473 by his grandson brought that eventuality so uncomfortably close that Ferrante was moved to offer René a handsome price for the renunciation of his claims. But to no avail; the aged duke persisted in his determination to bequeath them to his one surviving nephew, Charles, duke of Maine. When that prince died in December 1481, barely eighteen months after succeeding his uncle, Provence passed, as Ferrante had feared, to Louis XI. Thus was the way opened for the French crown to pursue the Neapolitan enterprise through ephemeral success to ultimate failure as its Angevin cousins had done through so many generations.

---

[47] The Catalans in revolt against Juan II offered the throne of Aragon to René in August 1466. The duke of Anjou accepted and sent his son Jean to Catalonia. Jean's sudden death in December 1470 precipitated the ruin of the Catalan cause, and with it René's half-hearted pretentions to another throne. The only French beneficiary in the whole episode was Louis XI who occupied the Catalan counties of Cerdagne and Roussillon.

Why had they failed? Ultimately because the kingdom of France had been unwilling or unable to devote to the undertaking the huge resources in money and men that it demanded. Angevin pretenders had consequently been reduced to over-dependence on the precarious and inadequate favours of a few Italian powers, and ultimately to the mercy of unscrupulous Neapolitan nobles. They found themselves repeatedly in the disadvantageous position of having to challenge *de facto* rulers. And in the crucial qualities of political and military leadership they all proved inferior to a distinguished line of opponents: Charles of Durazzo, Ladislas, Alfonso of Aragon, and Ferrante.

The inception of the reign of King Ferrante I of Naples: the events of summer 1458 in the light of documentation from Milan

David Abulafia

I

The opening years of the reign of Ferrante I of Naples appear at first sight to have been studied with an exhaustiveness that is not matched by existing studies of his later years; Count Emilio Nunziante's study of the first years of Ferrante published a century ago in Naples is arguably one of the longest monographs ever to be graced with the mere title of 'article', and has long been a major place of reference.[1] Yet Nunziante insisted that he was not a historian who had set out to analyse his archival material, but only a compiler of data which others would perhaps be able to utilise; this was perhaps a sign of undue modesty, yet even so the sheer scale of his enterprise makes it hard to see the wood for the trees.[2] Ernesto Pontieri's discussion of the early life of Ferrante has also done much to illuminate understanding of the bastard prince's role in the political plans of his father Alfonso the Magnanimous after the Aragonese king succeeded in

[1] E. Nunziante, 'I primi anni di Ferdinando d'Aragona e l'invasione di Giovanni d'Angiò', *Archivio storico per le province napoletane*, 17 (1892), 299-357, 564-86, 731-76; 18 (1893), 3-40, 207-46, 411-62, 563-620; 19 (1894), 37-96, 300-53, 419-44, 596-658; 20 (1895), 206-64, 442-513; 21 (1896), 265-89, 494-532; 22 (1897), 47-64, 204-40; 23 (1898), 144-210. The aim here has been to avoid repeating the essentials of Nunziante's discussion, notably his attention to the question of Genoa, and to concentrate rather on the way Ferrante pressed his case at the court of Milan and further afield.

[2] For an overview, see G. Soldi Rondinini, 'Milano, il Regno di Napoli e gli Aragonesi (secoli XIV-XV)', in *Gli Sforza a Milano e in Lombardia e i loro rapporti con gli Stati italiani ed europei (1450-1535). Convegno internazionale, Milano 18-21 maggio 1981* (Milan, 1982), 229-90, repr. in G. Soldi Rondinini, *Saggi di storia e storiografia visconteo-sforzesco* (Milan, 1984), 83-129. See also P.M. Kendall and V. Ilardi, *Dispatches with related documents of Milanese ambassadors in France and Burgundy 1450-1483*, vol. 1, *1450-1460* (Athens, Ohio, 1970).

conquering southern Italy under the nose of René of Anjou.[3] Yet it remains true
that Pontieri's preliminary studies of the reign of Ferrante were never worked
together into the full-scale study of this king's role in Italian war and diplomacy
that has always been much needed; it has been a lacuna since the humanist
Antonio Beccadelli, or Panormita, himself penned a life of the young Ferrante
which was intended to serve as the prelude to a fuller eulogy of his career as
king of Naples.[4] And one over-riding reason for this gap in the literature has
been not a lack of sources but a super-abundance of them, even after the loss of
a great proportion of the Neapolitan archives in 1943: the ambassadors' reports
and letters preserved in Milan, which were used to good effect by Nunziante,
are so detailed that at key moments the king's actions can be documented almost
by the hour.

This discussion is built out of the Milanese documentation, which has
been placed alongside another major source for the early career of King
Ferrante, the unique register of royal correspondence preserved in Paris and
published in 1912 by Messer.[5] The Paris manuscript consists of a register
Exterorum beginning with the accession of Ferrante to the Neapolitan throne,
and continuing up to February 1460. It is one of only four known registers of
this type out of a probable total of thirty-four.[6] The others only commence in
1467, and they remained in Naples. The appearance of the very earliest register
in Paris (and previously in Blois) thus prompted Messer to speculate on how it
could have arrived there: possibly among the effects of the widow of King
Federigo of Naples, who spent his last years on French soil; possibly too among
the items carried off from Naples by Charles VIII, whose wish to investigate the
foreign relationships that had sustained Ferrante in power would be
understandable.[7] In the context of this discussion, the second possibility is
particularly attractive: there is, surely, little need to insist upon the importance
of the events of 1458 as part of the essential background to those of 1494. It is
evident that the French invasion of Italy in 1494-95 grew out of a longstanding
rejection of the Aragonese claim to Naples by the house of Anjou-Provence, to
whose supposed rights Charles VIII of France was the successor. Although

---

[3] E. Pontieri, 'La giovinezza di Ferrante I d'Aragona', in *Studi in onore di Riccardo
Filangieri* (Naples, 1959), vol. 1, 531-601.

[4] *Antonii Panhormitae Liber Rerum Gestarum Ferdinandi Regis*, ed. G. Resta (Palermo,
1968). On Beccadelli, see A.F.C. Ryder, 'Antonio Beccadelli: a humanist in government', in
C.H. Clough, ed., *Cultural aspects of the Italian Renaissance. Essays in honour of Paul
Oskar Kristeller* (Manchester, 1976), 123-40.

[5] Arm.-Ad. Messer, *Le Codice Aragonese. Étude générale, publication du manuscrit de
Paris. Contribution à l'histoire des Aragonais de Naples* (Paris, 1912).

[6] For the others, see F. Trinchera, *Codice Aragonese, o sia lettere regie, ordinamenti ed
altri atti governativi de'sovrani aragonesi in Napoli, riguardanti l'amministrazione interna
del Reame e le relazioni all'estero*, 3 vols. (Naples, 1866-74).

[7] Messer, *Codice Aragonese*, LXXXIX.

Louis XI had shown some willingness to co-exist with Ferrante, even perhaps some admiration for his abilities as diplomat and despot, Louis also understood the importance of gaining what remained of René's dominions for the crown of France after the Angevin duke died; the prize he sought was Provence, but it carried with it the claim to Naples and Jerusalem, which Charles VIII took up with such enthusiasm. As the plans for an Italian invasion developed, Ferrante was still living, and the issue of his lack of right to the throne was thus of critical importance in the justification of Charles' campaign. It therefore makes sense to step back further in time to the start of Ferrante's reign, in order to see how the Aragonese court itself projected its right to the throne. This means retracing the steps taken by Nunziante in his study of the early years of King Ferrante; but, whereas Nunziante laid stress most heavily on ambassadors' reports, the intention here is to combine that documentation with the evidence provided by the letters of King Ferrante and his family preserved in the Archivio di Stato at Milan, evidence which has been passed over on the apparent assumption that it is banal and predictable; this will be set alongside the evidence of the Paris manuscript.[8] It is also proposed here to concentrate on the days immediately after the succession of Ferrante, in order to judge the expectations of king and duke between the death of King Alfonso and the election of Pope Pius II later the same year, an election that offered Ferrante the prospect of papal confirmation of his claim to the throne.

In Summer, 1458, awareness grew that King Alfonso of Aragon was seriously ill with fever.[9] This was a dangerous moment for the king to fall ill, since the struggle against the Angevin claimants for control of Genoa was now reaching a critical stage, and Genoa was long seen as the essential bridgehead for a French descent into Italy[10]; Ferrante himself at first put a brave face on events, writing in early June to the duke of Milan that the king his father would recover and was *fora de periculo*.[11] Yet the Milanese were becoming anxious that the alliance of Italian states created in the aftermath of the Peace of Lodi would not hold together in the face of what they regarded now and afterwards as the attempt of the French, *franzesi*, to set foot in Italy; there were doubts, for

---

[8] Archivio di Stato di Milano, Sforzesco Potenze Estere, busta 198 onwards. Documents referred to here are all to be found in busta or cartella 198 unless otherwise stated; references are supplied only to the *carta* number, and an asterisked number indicates that the *carta* is to be found after the numbering in the busta recommences at c*1. Italics indicate material sent in cypher, and transcribed generally from decipherments made in Milan at the time.

[9] c137: 1.6.1458, Antonio da Trezzo to the Duke of Milan: Questi di passati vene qua nouella per lettere de certi mercatanti... como la maiesta del... Re era infirma de febre.

[10] 2.6.1458: Instructio Orpheij ituri ad Classem Regiam, die II Junii 1458: Responsio prefatorum M. Capitaneorum supra classe die lune V yunii 1458. Cf. the instructions of the duke of Milan to his ambassador sent to the king of France in May 1460: *Dispatches*, 294-301.

[11] c140: Ferrante to Duke, Naples, Castelnuovo, 4.6.1458.

instance, about the reaction of the Florentines to any successes the Angevins might achieve.[12] Genoa was a particularly sensitive point, since Alfonso had sought to steer his new allies away from close discussion of the city's future when he adhered to the Italian League, in the light of Milanese claims to dominion over Genoa (claims from which he had in the past benefited to striking effect, after the battle of Ponza in 1435).[13] The presence of the Angevin army at Genoa was proof that French interests were still active in Italy; it remained an open question how far René's men were the agents of France in the north of Italy, and how far they were pursuing traditional Angevin ambitions aimed more at the south of Italy.

As the days went by it became plain that the king of Aragon was not available for audience, so that the duke of Milan's emissary, Antonio da Trezzo, was deprived of his customary ready access to the king's ear.[14] Ferrante himself wrote again, this time in his own hand, to Francesco Sforza to explain that his father was somewhat indisposed, also expressing the hope that the illness would before long be cured.[15] But Antonio da Trezzo was not deprived of access to the highest power in the land, for the duke of Calabria, that is, Ferrante, was only too glad to assure him of his goodwill towards Milan, even though Ferrante was obviously pessimistic about his father's chance of survival.[16] Indeed, the king

---

[12] c142: 5.6.58 da Trezzo to Duke, Naples: De quatro cose (se bene e recorda) ragionassero cum el prefato Duca: cioe de li facti de Zenoa: del facto de firentini per lo saluoconducto de la galeaza: del facto de Senesi, et del facto del Magnifico Astorre, de le quale cose el prefato duca dice habere consento cum la Maiesta del Re.

[13] c144-6: da Trezzo to Duke, Napoli, per vesc. Modena, 5.6.1458: Zenoua... de la quale pel Re de ragona cognosce non poterli per se caciare, poteua la Maiesta sua richiedere le potentie de Italia in aiuto suo, come quello al quale da Galici e tolta la preda sua che quantumque li capitoli de la lega dicano che niuna potentia italica se posse impazare de le cose de Zenoa, non e pero concesso al Re de franza che se la pigli et che pigliandola non gli possa far contra... *Ad questa parte el duca me ha resposto che scriua, e conforta lo vescouo ad volire rasonari de questa materia cum el papa, cum Senesi, et cum i firentini in quello modo che meglio gli pare; cum dirli lo periculo seria che francesi fermassero el pede in Italia et che ad ognuno per lo comune bene de tuta Italia spectaria de fare cio che se potesse per leuarli. Et uidere come se moue el papa et li altri disposti a questa cosa; et auisarne qua perche trouandoli disposti ad questo allora faria forsi pensiero la M.ta del Re de rechiedere le potentie Italice...*

[14] For this figure, see P. Margaroli, 'Bianca Maria e Galeazzo Maria Sforza nelle ultime lettere di Antonio da Trezzo (1467-1469)', *Archivio storico lombardo*, 111 (1985), 327-77.

[15] c148: Ferrante to Duke, 8.6.1458 (1), Naples, in Ferrante's own hand: que la Maiesta del S.R. staua alguntanto indisposto piu che solito qual fo causa e non poterli donare si presta audientia como la volenta de sua M.ta. c149 Ferrante to Duke (2), Naples, 8.6.1458: speramo tamen in dio che presto sera ad perfectissima sanitate reducta.

[16] c152: da Trezzo to Duke, 9.6.1458 (2), Naples: ragiono heri cum mi un bon pezo el prefato duca de Calabria et fra laltre cosse ce disse chel non sapeua cio che dio uolesse disponere de la dita de la Mta del Re... esso sa che el ha ad hauere bisogno de la s.v. de la qual sola fa piu stima e fundamento che de tuto el resto.

rallied, and Ferrante yet again wrote to the duke in his own hand to tell him so.[17] Da Trezzo visited the sick king, to be told that the Aragonese expected soon to report victory at Genoa over their Angevin foes.[18] On the other hand, da Trezzo was well aware that Genoa could become a flashpoint in an unnecessary conflict between Milan and Naples, and so he assured his master (in code) that Francesco Sforza need not worry about Aragonese intentions, since he doubted whether King Alfonso had the energy to pursue any gains he might achieve there.[19] It appears that Francesco Sforza had no illusions about the gravity of Alfonso's illness, for he wrote to Ferrante late in June to commiserate with the prince, and Ferrante himself, in general terms, began now to implore the duke's favour in a manner typical of his future correspondence as king of Naples.[20] There was more than enough to worry about, not merely on the Genoese front but in central Italy, where the pope was awaiting his chance to intervene in the affairs of his vassal kingdom of Naples.[21] Another live issue in central Italy was the struggle among the local warlords, Jacopo Piccinino, Federico da Montefeltro and Sigismondo Malatesta, the first of whom was anything but secure in his dominion around Assisi.

On 27 June 1458 King Alfonso died in Naples, and the next day Ferrante wrote to Milan to notify the duke not merely of his father's Christian death, but of his own accession to the throne, for he signed his letter with a vigorous and florid *Rex Ferd'* in what was to become his characteristic way, and he notified the duke that the city of Naples was standing by the house of Aragon, as would surely the entire kingdom.[22] In reality, of course, matters were not so

---

[17] c160: Ferrante [by his own hand] to Duke, 13.6.1458: sta molto bene per modo che simo fora de omne suspecto.

[18] c161-3: da Trezzo to Duke, Giugliano, 14.6.1458: me transferri a Napoli et fui cum lo Illmo S. duca de calabria... la s. sua introducendomme al lecto de la M.ta del Re... che per quanto era auisata vi scriueua la s.v. le cose de de [sic] Zenoua stanno in termine che sua M.ta ha ad sperare de reportarne aptata victoria...

[19] c161-3: da Trezzo to Duke, Giugliano, 14.6.1458: *ma quando pu seguisse per dire el vero ad v.s. non me desperaria troppo perche sel vive et obtenga la impresa de Zenoa dubito che l'habia ad mettere qualche foco in Italia per la mala dispositione che l'ha in queste di monstrato...*

[20] c206: Duke to Ferrante, 24.6.1458: [partly in the duke's hand] alla parte dela infirmita del S.mo S.re Re v.ro patre [dico] ho hauuto grandissimo despiacere et affano che magiore non poria hauere del male dela soa M.ta...; cf. c207, Ferrante to Duke, in Castello, 26.6.1458: si dio per la grande sua misericordia miraculose non ce operasse... pregando vi strictissamente che dal vostro chanto si ne bisognera el fauore vostro vogliate stare preparato.... in hoc casu vogliate consigliare et recordarui quello et quanto ad vuy paresse debian fare.

[21] c211: da Trezzo to Duke, Giugliano, 27.6.1458; see also Nunziante, vol. 17, 773: *El papa fa qualche pensero de darli impazo... quanto lettere vengono da Roma dicono chel papa parla tanto male del quanto possa dir et exulta el conte Jacomo...*

[22] c212: Ferrante to Duke, Naples, 28.6.1458: Non senza grande et inextimabile dolore de core ve notificamo la morte del Serenissimo Re Segnore et patre nostro reuerendissimo... facto tucto ordine de catolico et vero christiano... poy de la morte del quale hauemo hauuta

straightforward. Alfonso had some time earlier gained papal approval for the succession of Ferrante, despite his illegitimate birth; if anyone could set the stigma of bastardy aside, it was the pope, and if anyone could nominate a ruler for Naples it was also the pope, as the kingdom's overlord. And yet the present pontiff, Calixtus III, was only too ready to turn on his former Aragonese masters in order to show who was really in charge of the affairs of Naples. There was certainly a sense of the end of an era. Catalan officials packed their bags and wended their way back to Barcelona.[23] More significantly, the rights of Ferrante risked a challenge from Charles, prince of Viana, the disconsolate nephew of Alfonso the Magnanimous, whose difficulties with his own father, John of Navarre, were only compounded when John succeeded to Alfonso's lands in Spain and the Italian islands, leaving southern Italy as a separate dominion for Ferrante. As a legitimate member of the house of Aragon, Charles had a claim of sorts to Naples; more significantly he was actually in Naples, and he even had a small fleet with him.[24] In the event, Charles received little support; those who disliked the duke of Calabria did so primarily on the grounds that he was an Aragonese prince, and from that point of view Charles was surely in no way preferable. Ferrante was not slow to rise to this and all other challenges, sending messages throughout Italy to announce his accession; this was crucial if he were to secure the support of other members of the Italian League in his struggle against the house of Anjou.[25] He not unnaturally also took great care to keep his Aragonese uncle fully informed about events, instructing his anbassadors to Catalonia to describe in the most emphatic terms the great grief Ferrante felt at the passing of King Alfonso (itself worthy of telling in some detail).[26] Ferrante commended himself to King John of Aragon as one bound by the strictest bonds of filial affection: *com sieren de hun propri, legitim, natural, e carissimo fill seu.* He implored John's aid in presenting his case to the pope and to the College of Cardinals; he himself would do all he could to ensure that the island kingdom of Sicily retained its loyalty to the house of Aragon; it was also plain that Ferrante was offering his help in ensuring that the Prince of Viana would not trouble the king of Aragon, attributing present difficulties to *falsos reports o alguns mals altres enginys... per causar alguna gran discordia*

---

plenissima obediencia del populo de questa Cita et cussi speramo haueremo infallanter de tucto lo resto del Reame...; [cf. c218 infra].

[23] c214: da Trezzo to Duke, 28.6.1458 Giugliano: Molti catallani se partono, et credo pochi ne remarano qua.

[24] c214: da Trezzo to Duke, 28.6.1458 Giugliano: Lo s.ro principe de Nauarra, hogi cum cinque naue e uenuto sopra Castelnuouo. Cf. Nunziante, 'Primi anni', 17 (1892), 571-7.

[25] c215-6: Pietro Villacase to Bartolomeo de Recanati oratori Ill.mi dominum ducem [Medi]olani 28.6.1458 Naples: Questo signore Re mandara per tutta Italia a notificare la prefatta morte e sua assumpcione et poi deue mandare micer Matheo Malferit per tuta Italia.

[26] Messer, *Codice Aragonese*, doc. 1, 3-9, 1.7.58.

moviment e scandel. Ferrante's ambassadors were not to point the finger at Don Carlos of Viana, but they were trusted to make plain Ferrante's awareness that it was the king of Aragon rather than his son who alone could offer viable and reliable support. Ferrante was aware, therefore, of the potential difficulty of his relationship to the other lands his father had ruled; John of Aragon would not be welcome to pull rank and claim authority over him, but he too could offer John the support the Aragonese king would need in asserting his own rights within Spain and the Italian islands. And if there were any doubt about Ferrante's own intentions, it should be made clear that he

> ha pres pacificament e quiete de continent la veu, nom, titol e exercici de Rey de Sicilia, deça Far, de Hierusalem e Ongria e ha presa possessio dels castells, terres e ysles per aquell aquestades com apartenyents e annexes a ell en la dita sua accessio.

In other words, he insisted that he controlled the kingdom and there was no room for argument.[27]

Some indication of how Ferrante proposed to present himself to the world beyond his family can be found in an elegant parchment letter sent to the duke of Milan on 28 June (that is, within a day of becoming king), expressed in the best humanistic Latin; Ferrante was not slow, therefore, to press his claim, which extended not merely to the throne of 'Sicily this side of the lighthouse', that is, Naples and southern Italy, but to Jerusalem and Hungary as well:

> King of Sicily, Jerusalem and Hungary... We in fact today took the name and insignia of a king, together with the full obedience of the people of the city, and we hope in future that of all the kingdom. We know that you will first of all be saddened at the death of my father who loved you as his son and without a doubt was loved by you; thus we know that you will rejoice at the obedience and faithfulness of our people and kingdom...[28]

The new queen, Isabella di Chiaramonte, was also assigned the task of explaining more informally to the Milanese that Ferrante had been rapturously accepted as king in Naples:

> The king our most reverend husband has received the castles and has ridden through the city and was received by everyone as king and lord with great festivity and infinite happiness at this time. The cities of Terra di Lavoro and round about have raised his banner with joy and great quiet [i.e. peacefulness] and we hope things will continue to go from good to better.[29]

---

[27] The claim to control the islands is also reflected in the order to the governor of Ischia, Messer, *Codice Aragonese*, doc. 11, 24-5, 24.7.1458.

[28] c218 [parchment]: Ferrante to Duke, Naples, 28.6.1458.

[29] c222: Isabella to Duke, Nola, 30.6.1458.

But more important than these efforts to impress the duke was the hard evidence offered by da Trezzo in his reports that powerful barons had come to court to offer their support to Ferrante:

> The duke of Sora has come to offer obedience and swear fidelity to the said king for his lands and on behalf of L'Aquila, Sulmona and other lands in Abruzzo. The same has been done by Benevento and nearly all Apulia and the demesne lands. So too the prince of Rossano has come. The count of Fondi has raised the royal banner, but has not come to Naples for fear of plague, though he has sent to say he will come to Capua. The duke of Melfi and many others who hold lands in the Principality and in Basilicata have come... it seems all are most content with the condition of this new king who up to now is governing most prudently.[30]

Of course, it was rather early to praise Ferrante for prudent government; he had been on the throne only for a week. Da Trezzo's optimism even went as far as the pope, who in his view was likely to offer his support to Ferrante. In addition, he noted that the Prince of Viana had accepted defeat in his own opportunistic attempt to lay claim to the throne of Naples, and that he was about to return to Catalonia.[31]

Within Italy, forces were at work which promised to strengthen the past co-operation between Naples and Milan: the count of Urbino, Federico da Montefeltro, had reputedly written to King Ferrante to remind him (as if any reminder were needed) that Alfonso V had laid great importance on the ties between Francesco Sforza and the house of Aragon.[32] Ferrante made an approach, too, to the marquis of Mantua in the hope of assuring him that his aims were peaceful even if the pope was beginning to insist otherwise:

> We however are ready to seek his benediction, he to give his malediction; we to serve the peace of Italy, he to excite warfare we are ready to obey, he is ready for plots and ecclesiastical censure.[33]

Da Trezzo's famous enthusiasm for Ferrante was based not simply on the assumption that it was his special task to promote good relations between Naples and Milan as resident ambassador of Milan in southern Italy. Da Trezzo was also beguiled by Ferrante's own undoubted charm and plausibility, for the new king neglected few opportunities to encourage da Trezzo in his support,

---

[30] c227: da Trezzo to Duke, Giugliano, 4.7.1458 [partly in cypher].

[31] c227: da Trezzo to Duke, Giugliano, 4.7.1458 [partly in cypher].

[32] c227: da Trezzo to Duke, Giugliano, 4.7.1458 [partly in cypher]. Petroarcangello me dica chel Conte durbino ha scripto al Re uno foglio de carta recordadogli cum infinita ragione che morendo, el Re per la M.ta sua de costrigersi cum v. Ex. et chel crede che esse conte durbino mandara uno suo alla S. v. de questo. El Re non me ha dicto altro. See also Messer, *Codice Aragonese*, doc. 28, 40-41, 4.8.1458, a letter sent both to the count of Urbino and to Piccinino.

[33] Messer, *Codice Aragonese*, doc. 7, 20-22, 20.7.1458.

and to supply him with confidences and opinions which he knew would be transmitted post haste to the duke of Milan:

> Most illustrious lord, yesterday after I wrote to you I rode to Aversa, about two miles away, where the king was, and hearing I was there he at once called me and I went to his chamber where we were alone together and he told me what you have just written to him... and we discussed generally the affairs of Genoa, of Sr. Astorre and of Count Jacomo, and he said to me that he wants to take full advantage of your good disposition to him... The king sat down and invited me to sit next to him. And then he began to tell me what he has said and written to me so often: that after the king his father he acknowledged no father but your excellency.[34]

On the other hand, there was an awareness in the same interview that the pope was becoming a source of difficulty; problems loomed not just over the recognition of Ferrante's royal title, but over the attempts by the *condottiere* Jacomo Piccinino to establish for himself a coherent domain around Assisi, in the very heart of the papal states; nor was Piccinino someone to ignore when Ferrante was searching for supporters within the peninsula.[35] (Later, Ferrante was to witness the effects of failing to succour Piccinino, who turned against him and joined the Angevin armies, and was later still assassinated by Ferrante just when it appeared he had been readmitted to the king's grace). It is also apparent that Ferrante instructed his closest advisers to use their best offices in ensuring that the Milanese-Neapolitan alliance would hold firm: Diomede Carafa, man of war and of letters, intimate of Ferrante, and count of Maddaloni, managed to attract da Trezzo's attention as someone who 'ha gran creduto cum sua Maiesta et e ogni di per hauerlo magiore', and also as someone who kept underlining the fundamental importance of the warm relationship between Milan and Naples.[36] This was exactly the message da Trezzo wished to hear, and to transmit to his Milanese master. It should, however, be stressed that delays in the post meant that Francesco Sforza was still writing to Ferrante as duke of Calabria, to commiserate on Alfonso's grave illness, on 7 July 1458, in response to a letter of 26 June; the duke seems at this point to have had few illusions about the likelihood of Alfonso dying, but he also wished to assure Ferrante that he placed his faith in the continuation of an intimate relationship between the courts of Naples and Milan:

---

[34] c229: da Trezzo to Duke, Giugliano, 5.7.1458.

[35] For Piccinino's significance, see Messer, *Codice Aragonese*, doc. 4, 15, 11.7.1458; doc. 28, 40-41, 4.8.1458, doc. 37, 52, 12.8.1458; doc. 39, 55, 12.8.1458, etc.

[36] c231 da Trezzo to Duke, Giugliano, 5.7.1458; see also Messer, *Codice Aragonese*, doc. 36, 51, 11.8.1458.

> We say that your lordship must stay firm and doubt for nothing, because from our point of view we are ready and will always be ready to do all we can for the maintenance and establishment of your power and all that we can do for the pleasure, good and exaltation of your most illustrious Lordship, just as much as we do for ourselves and even for our own person, because we are and want to be perpetually united in one heart, soul and will... We are certain that you plan to rule prudently and provide for everything in such a way that you will be a worthy son and successor of such a lord and father...[37]

In another letter the duke encouraged da Trezzo to console the duke of Calabria for his father's illness:

> Comfort the most illustrious lord our brother in whatever way seems suitable. He has written us a very humane letter, very amiable, about his father's condition.[38]

It will be seen that there were suitable occasions on which to treat Ferrante as brother, and other occasions when Ferrante presented himself to Francesco Sforza as an adopted son. But for the moment Ferrante emphasized the brotherhood of the two Italian princes, writing to the duke of Milan in his own hand as follows:

> Illustrious duke, my dear brother,... the more you make known to me your wisdom the more I love you and your affairs as if they are my own...[39]

The use of familial language in the correspondence between king and duke reflected not merely family ties through marriage (notably the betrothal of Ferrante's son to Sforza's daughter), but also an image of political harmony in the peninsula. In the hands of advisers such as Diomede Carafa these images of brotherhood and fatherhood could inded be piled on top of one another:

> You are so much loved by the generality of this kingdom because of the demonstration of love you have shown this most Serene Lord King your son and brother...[40]

The king of Naples was very ready to attribute his initial successes to Francesco Sforza, writing as follows in a document preserved in the Paris codex:

> We cannot write to you how much we are happy at the singular and prudent provision you have made for the security and consolidation of our power at the beginning of our reign.[41]

This was, however, merely the prelude to an attempt to urge Francesco Sforza to work hard to resolve the problem of Genoa.

---

[37] c236, 237: Duke to da Trezzo, Milan [2 copies], 7.7.1458.
[38] c238.40 [2nd copy, 241-4]: Duke to da Trezzo, 7.7.1458.
[39] c246: Ferrante to Duke, 8.7.1458 [autograph].
[40] c*147: D. Carafa to Duke, Fontana di Chyuppo, 19.8.1458.
[41] Messer, *Codice Aragonese*, doc. 29, 41, 4.8.1458.

Ferrante was not blind to reality; however much acclaim he earned from Milan, Urbino and so on, his first need was for the support of those he claimed as his subjects, and every effort was made to secure the loyalty of the provinces from Abruzzo to Calabria; both the greater nobles and the cities had to be courted, for it was in the fastnesses of the Abruzzi (for example) that loyalty to the house of Anjou had never evaporated. He sent his agents into the frontier regions of Abruzzo and the Marche, a region critical also because of his alliances with Marchese lords such as the count of Urbino:

> And we want you to travel in the Marche and in Abruzzo because... the lords and communities of the kingdom must remain content under the rule of the most illustrious lord duke [of Calabria] as worthy and legitimate successor to his father... and because we are held and obliged to observe the universal League and because of the ties of affinity and blood that we have with his lordship.[42]

Da Trezzo was satisfied, therefore, that the kingdom had accepted Ferrante as its new ruler, and that before long Ferrante would be crowned king. Moreover, even the issue of Genoa would surely be settled in his favour with the help of the 'king of Navarre', that is, King John II of Aragon, Alfonso's brother.[43]

> Reaching such a conclusion, with the king making his kingdom so secure and peaceful, and given the good understanding with the most serene king of Navarre and the lord prince his son... and with such riches and treasure as he has found in Castelnuovo, there is no danger of trouble in this his kingdom, from this direction or that, or from the pope.

King John certainly seemed disposed to help, though on what scale remained an open question.[44]

The only possible cloud on the horizon was papal hostility, 'et che tandem questo Re remanera bono figliolo de sua Santita'. There survive in Paris the instructions to Arnau Sanç, ambassador sent to the papal court in early July, 1458.[45] Ferrante's emissary was to insist relentlessly on the *instructio paternal*

---

[42] Instructio Orfei de Ricano ituri ad Ill. Dom. Ferdinandum Ducem Calabrie per viam Aprucii, 8.7.1458.

[43] c*20: da Trezzo to Duke, Capua, 9.7.1458: molti altri Sri Citta et Terre sono venuti ad prestare obedientia al prefato S. Re... et gia gli ne sono venutj vna bona parte, se satisferia ad tutto... la M.ta del Re sera incoronata... Da Trezzo cites the king's words to him: Et hauemo mandato insieme con luy doi nostri ambassatori, che andrarano dal S.re Re De Nauarra perche dagli aiuto et fauore ala dicta Impresa, et che dal canto nostro non mancharemo de cosa alcuna per ultimare la Impresa...

[44] c*56-7: 'En Johan Rey darago de Nauarra de Sicilia de Valencia de Mallorques de Serdenya & de Corcega Comte de Barcelona duch de Atenes e de Neopatria' etc. to als magnifichs amats & fiels nostres tots & qualsevol Capitans de Naus, 18.7.1458

[45] Messer, *Codice Aragonese*, doc. 2, 10-13, 5.7.1458. See also the comments of Pope Pius II: *Secret Memoirs of a Renaissance Pope. The Commentaries of Aeneas Sylvius Piccolomini, Pius II* (ed. F.A. Gragg and L.C. Gabel (2nd ed., London, 1988), 89: 'At last Ferrante was beaten, since the pope's meaning and words were always the same'.

of Alfonso to Ferrante to be ever obedient to the Church, and in particular to the pope himself, *la qual sempre lo dit Senyor Rey don Ferrando ha ben stimada e reverida com a sa Santedat de lonch temps es certe notori*. This heavy emphasis is the surest proof that Ferrante was fully aware of the papacy's hostility. To offset such dangers, Ferrante set in train a simple but generally effective strategy, bombarding the duke of Milan with letters both formal (often enough in orators' Latin, on parchment, and so presumably for public display) and informal, written with greater passion than attention to the finer points of Italian grammar and syntax.

> The king of Sicily etc. to the most illustrious and potent duke our relative and brother. We have had some pleasure from the things that Antonio da Trezzo has told us on your behalf, and so we have referred to him when it seemed useful so to do. And in order not to be excessively prolix, we only want to say that we have such trust in you that you have seen already in our letters. We advise you that we know nothing of the pope except what we have told you by cypher, but we hope soon to have news from the castellan of Castelnuovo whom we have sent to Rome...[46]

Another aspect of this strategy was Ferrante's persistence in treating Francesco Sforza as the elder statesman whose advice and support would determine his decisions:

> The said lord king awaits day by day some news and advice from your Excellency about what it appears to you he should do, and these are the words he used with me: that your Excellency can be sure that he wants to live with you in a different way to his father's, because between his father and you there were things that made relations not as free and sincere as they should have been. In particular the said king his father had so many other kingdoms besides this one and was so powerful that he seemed to have Italy in his grasp; but with him it will not be so, because between you and him there has been no trouble but only good relations... he says he has only this realm, nor does he have it in mind to gain others, but only to confirm himself in this one and with the help and favour of yourself he hopes to live as a good neighbour with everyone.[47]

The theme of Ferrante as 'figliolo' of Francesco Sforza was accompanied by an insistence that Milan's interests and those of Naples coincided. Especially realistic in this account of Ferrante's outlook was the awareness that Ferrante was merely king of Naples, and that he would need to regulate his affairs within an entirely Italian context, whereas his father had possessed kingdoms much further afield; in other words, Ferrante would not be distracted by other obligations from his role within the Italian League. It is perhaps worth noting that the claims he bore to the Hungarian crown and to the crown of Jerusalem were already being tacitly ignored, as they would be for long stretches of his reign; even when those kingdoms were mentioned, they simply appear as

---

[46] c*38 [parchment]: Ferrante to Duke, Capua, 12.7.1458.
[47] c*45-6 [copy: *4-3]: da Trezzo to Duke, Capua, 13.7.1458 [partly in cypher].

inherited titles. It is also significant that at the end of his lengthy protestations of friendship for his other father Francesco Sforza, Ferrante referred to the trouble the pope was causing him by not recognising his right of succession; he expressed the hope that Francesco Sforza would lean on those cardinals over whom he had some influence.[48]

Florence too was a major power whose support could perhaps be won with Sforza help; Diomede Carafa tried to win da Trezzo over on this issue.[49] It was also slightly worrying, as da Trezzo noted, that the prince of Taranto and certain other great nobles had not yet come to court to acknowledge Ferrante as their king.[50] Around this time, the prince was engaged in exchanges of messages with Ferrante in late July, but they were clearly very inconclusive.[51] On the other hand Ferrante was not prepared to brook delay, and it was thought likely that Ferrante's own son Alfonso would imminently be named duke of Calabria, which was good news for Milan, in view of Alfonso's betrothal to Ippolita Sforza.[52]

It is thus hardly surprising that Ferrante was soon writing to Francesco Sforza as both his *affinis* and as his *tanquam pater noster carissime*. He insisted that his own father Alfonso had urged him in his final illness to foster the peace of Italy, as well as to live peaceably with the pope. Despite his attempt to win the pope's recognition, all he had received was abuse:

> He used opprobrious words against us, rejecting all approaches from many notables of Rome and then from our own orator...[53]

Ferrante, speaking here through the elegant prose style of Beccadelli, underlined the dangers that such an attitude posed not merely to the peace of Italy but also to the security of his own kingdom. On the smoothness of succession within the *Regno* would thus depend the whole balance of power within Italy. It was a powerful, and by and large a convincing, argument. On another occasion, Ferrante related to the duke his difficulties with the pope, but carefully juxtaposed an account of how the barons of Naples were flocking to his side; in other words, it was the pope who stood alone, while Ferrante possessed all the support he could hope for.[54] The argument was taken in a different direction

---

[48] Messer, *Codice Aragonese*, doc. 2, 12, 5.7.1458, for approaches to the cardinals; also Messer, *Codice Aragonese*, doc. 18, 29-30, 31.8.1458.

[49] *49, doc. 2, copy of *47; see too Messer, *Codice Aragonese*, doc. 19, 30-1, 1.8.1458.

[50] *50 contains a list of those nobles who did offer their support to the king, though of course many would abandon him during the subsequent First Barons' Revolt.

[51] Messer, *Codice Aragonese*, no. 8, 22, 22.7.1458.

[52] c*45-6: da Trezzo to Duke, Capua, 13.7.1458.

[53] c*92: Ferrante to Duke [parchment], in Castro Lapidum Ciuitatis Capue, 20.7.1458, drawn up by Antonio Panormita (Beccadelli).

[54] c*119: Ferrante to Duke, prope Capuam, 31.7.1458 [paper]: Rex Sicilie etc. Illustrissime et potens dux affinjs et tanquam pater carissime. Perche siate aduisato de omnj

when addressing the cardinals: Ferrante insisted that *si bellum agendum est, in Turchos pocius quam in Christianis destinandum esse.*[55]

The duke was careful to praise Ferrante when writing to him directly;[56] but he had doubts of his own when writing to Antonio da Trezzo:

> Che forma et modo ha preso la prefata Maesta in gouernare et regere el stato suo, et qualli taliani et catellani hara deputato al gouerno del stato suo.

It has to be said that in the same letter Francesco Sforza was also keen to know about Ferrante's falcons and hunting dogs; the duke's curiosity was not simply political.[57] Yet he was encouraged to hear that

---

nostro progresso como la ragione vole, licet ne rediamo certi che fin adesso hauerite sentuto omnj cosa per lectera de Antonio da trezo oratore et cancellere vostro vi notificamo como dapo che la sanctita de nostro Segnore lo papa uj mandao lo breue suo et bulla copia dele quale nuy vi hauemo mandate, li respusemo et eciam scripsemo al collegio dele Cardinali como che per le Copie eciam hauerete potuto vedere, si et eciam ficemo certo acto de appellacione dela sua bolla como che simjliter per la copia hauerete veduto, dapoy de tucto questo hauemo ordinato ambassiata ala Sanctita sua per nostra parte et deli magnati et demanjo de tucto questo regno cum amplissimo posse zo fo el ducha andria Conte de sancto Angelo, Conte Carlo de campobasso et misser Cicchoanto doctore; speramo che mostrando al papa nostri euidentissimj dricti et ragionj, si canoxere li vorra el facto nostro altramente che bene non pora succedere. Et doue che la Sanctita prefata voglia preseruare jn nostra jnjusta persecucione faremo nostro potere de non uj lassare jnjuste conculcare, et cussi constera adio et al mundo che haueremo facto nostro debito et excusacione. Ad vuy tamen non cessamo rendere jnfinjte gracie del che per uuy hauuete facto si de persuadere el papa ad volere e acceptare per bon figliolo, como al confortare li baronj et magnati de quisto Regno ala fede et obedientia nostra. Li quali baronj magnati et Sindici demanjali hogi hanno concluso generale parlamento con nuy et hauendo uj supplicato che sgrauessemo li populi de cosa che muntaua Cinquanta mjlia ducati per anno offerendonj dare de presenti Cinquanta mjla ducati; nuy per contentareli hauemo sgrauateli de ducati Cento Cinquanta mjlia annuj, e a loro maior contentamento non hauemo voluto li Cinquanta mjlia ducati per loro offerti darene de presenti, dela quale cosa so remasci si cotenti che non se poria piu dire et non dubitamo che per nuy et lo stato nostro exponerano si bisognera Mille mjgliara e volte la vita de che nuy simo restati non pocho contenti. Et laudamo deo de bene che ne fa; fin adesso hauemo hauuta plena hobediencia dela piu parte deli baronj et del demanjo, et da pochi resta hora may hauera la che de tucto a gaudium vi hauemo voluto scriujre como che ad quello che hogi may et del bene et del male nostri hauete da essere participe como che nuy vice versa jntendemo essere deli vostri. Dat/ in nostris felicibus castris prope Capuam die vltimo mensis julij M CCCC LVIIIJ. Rex Ferd'. (G. Talamanca)

[55] Messer, *Codice Aragonese*, doc. 19, 30-31, 1.8.1458.

[56] c*72: Duke to Ferrante, Milan, 22-7.1458: la Maiesta vostra esser assumpta ad la Corona regale con tanta obedientia et reuerentia et concorso de quello Reame; et che tutta dia la Mta vostra da stabilendo et pacificando le cose.

[57] Item che spesa ha ordinato in la corte sua de falconi, cani, et altre cose da piacere Et cossi de ogni altra prouisione lhabia ordinata o uero che ordinara. Item generaliter de ogni altra cosa picola, mizana, et grande, che lo prefa[ta] Mta hara ordinata, tanto in corte sa, quato fore de corte, et in quella Cita di Napoli, como altroue. La quale informatione hauuta de ogni cosa, auisare per toe littere separate, le quale non contengano altro che questo. Et sforzati de auisarui del tuto distinctamente, et col ver. Ita che non sia facta cosa alcuna, ne se faza che non ne siamo auisati...

> Le cose de quelo Reame adauano propere et stabilendosi, et senza tumulto etc; dele
> quale cose hauemo receuuto grandissimo piacere et consolatione...[58]

news optimistically despatched to him only a few days after the succession took
place. Ferrante for his part commemorated the end of the first month of his rule
with another Latin epistle to Francesco Sforza, whose apparently formulaic
character hides a more complex message: everything that Alfonso V and
Francesco Sforza had achieved together could be preserved for the future so
long as the duke of Milan remained firm in his alliance with the king of Naples.
That constant fear of the Milanese turning towards France and Provence could
never quite be dissipated.[59] Later on, in May 1460, Francesco Sforza would try
to convince the French that he had ever been a loyal servitor of the house of
Anjou; he was singing this tune partly because Ferrante's fortunes had dipped by
then.[60] Moreover, even in 1458 Ferrante was under no illusion that his internal
difficulties, notably with the Prince of Taranto, would escape the attention of da
Trezzo, and hence of Francesco Sforza; the best he could hope was that da
Trezzo would use the evidence of opposition to argue that Ferrante deserved
more, not less, support.[61]   Ferrante also presented Francesco Sforza with

---

[58] c*76-80: Duke to da Trezzo, Milan 22.7.1458.

[59] c*96: Ferrante to Duke, Naples, 27.7.1458 [parchment]: Ferdinandus dei gratia Rex
Sicilie Hyerusalem et Hungarie, Illustrissime et potens Dux Affinis et tanquam pater noster
carissime, salutem et animum ad grata paratum. Et si pro nostra affinitate ac mutua et
singulari beniuolentia prolixus scribere et accuratius vobiscum gloriosissimum patris obitum
condolere deberemus, tunc id lacrimis et merori nostro pro vestra humanitate concedetis vt
paucis in presentia agamus paucisque renunciemus eius in vltimo pene spiritu de vobis ac
vestra affinitate recordationem moriens habuisse, itaque id nobis precipue iniunxit vt
vobiscum beniuolentiam constantissime seruaremus, vosque et patri loco perpetue
haberemus, hec ille moriens. Nos itaque et grauissimi patris iussu et ex affinitate que
nobiscum est vos patris loco semper habituri sumus et amiciciam perpetuo seruaturi; hoc cum
ita sit vos iterum atque iterum rogamus vt nos mutuo ametis, ac filij loco suscipiatis
affinitatem nostram constantissime seruantes. Nos quoque operam dabimus e post hac aut
amore aut officio vincamur; pauca hec ex medijs lacrimis. Dat/ in Castello nouo Ciuitatis
nostre Neapolis die xxvij mensis Julij vj[e] Indic/ Anno dominj Mill.mo Quadringentesimo
Quinquagesimo octauo. Rex Ferd'. (T. Girifalcus).

[60] *Dispatches*, vol. 1, 300-3.

[61] c*117: da Trezzo to Duke, Capua, 31.7.1458 [partly in cypher]: Vedendo chel principe
de Taranto non da uerso questo S.mo S.re Re come era oppinione chel douesse fare, o volto
intendere da *Talamanca* sel intende la casone; el me dice che altro non glie se non chel fa de
le domande al Re, le quale sono pur assai fora del honesto, et sonno queste; primo domanda
la gubernatione de Barleta, Trani, Joueazo et Biseli, che non e a dire altro, se non volerle in
dominio perche sonno terre che importano, et confinanano con lo stato suo, come la Ex. v. sa
Secundo domanda che al Sre Yosia restituischa quelle terre che alias furono sue. Tertio: che
esso S.re principe sia restituito in Jus suum quod habebat in terra Venusij, non obstante che la
bona memoria del Re passato ne habia intitulato uel data in ducato al figliolo del duca
dandria. Quarto: che essa M.ta restituischa lo stato suo al Marchese de Cotrono. Quinto et
ultimo: chel dagha larciuescouato de Napoli, el quale al presente vaca, ad uno suo nepote, che
bene luy obteguera la confirmatione del papa.

evidence for noble and popular support in his attempts to win over the pope.[62] The news that the pope was in fact seriously ill was therefore bound to be a relief.[63] When the death of Pope Calixtus III became known, Ferrante could only react one way:

> Questo Signore Re se conforta, che non se debba creare alcuno papa, che habia verso de si quella malla dispositione, che aueua papa Calixto.[64]

Ferrante noted elsewhere that the death of Calixtus marked a crisis in the affairs of the Borgias: *som avisats perque lo Papa es mort, moss. Borja e lo Cardenal vicecanceller sen eren fugits a Hostia.*[65] On the other hand, Francesco Sforza seemed as keen to obtain pomegranate juice from the *Regno* as news of its political affairs; finding the juice was another task that was thrust on da Trezzo's shoulders now and often enough thereafter.

Ferrante's aim had always been to influence the Church by way of the cardinals, since the pope was so obdurate. Once Calixtus was dead this was

---

[62] c*128: Ferrante to Duke, Capua, 4.8.1458 [parchment]: Rex Sicilie etc. Illu.me et potentissime Dux affinis et pater noster Carissime. Vt omnium rerum nostrarum certior fiat V. ex. significamus quod congregatis de nostro mandato proceribus popularibusque huius Regnj cum eis xxvjo Julij proposuissemus quedam que nobis incumbebant simulque dolere diximus quod necessitate cohacti et summi pontificis causa non poteramus in eos illa qua decreueramus liberalitate et munificentia uti. Ipsi die quidem xxvijo decreuerunt ut ad Summum pontificem regni nomine legacionem micterent qui a quibusdam licteris per illum contra nos editis euocarent simulque ei significaretur animum omnium procerum populariumque erga nos. Statumque oratores spectabiles Carolum de Campo bascio Comitem termularum et Marinum Caraczolum Comitem Sancti angeli ad Summum pontificem ordinarunt. Postridie uero curti ut sunt nostrj staus cupidi et singuli et vniuersi quinquagintamilia ducatorum ultra illud quod Sere.mo patrj nostro soluebant soluturos se obtulerunt. Nos autem cum eorum tam propensum animum uidissemus, et quinquaginta milia ducatorum que nobis obtulerunt et quasdam collectas ad centum milia ducatorum ascedentes integre remisimus, que res adeo eis grata extitit ut omnia dura et asperrima prius pati affirment quod a nostra fide et obedientia aliquando deficere. Hec v. ex. ideo significare volujmus primum ut nihil a nobis fiat quod sibi nostris licteris non scribatur. Deinde quia ex prosperis nostris successibus neminem magis gaudere certo scimus. Dat/ in nostris felicibus Castris prope Capuam die quarto Augusti sexte Indic/ M CCC LVIIIJ. Rex Ferd'. (Antonius de auersa). Ferrante could indeed count on Sforza: according to Pope Pius II, 'Giovanni Caimo, the envoy of Francesco Sforza, duke of Milan, who was passing through Viterbo, went to see Aeneas there and in the course of conversation said he had been sent to Calixtus to tell him that it was not acceptable to Francesco that Ferrante should be deposed from his father's throne; if the pope had any such intention, he must know that the duke of Milan would be against him. When he heard this, Aeneas said, "In that message you are bringing Calixtus his death-blow!" And such was the case, for when the pope heard that Francesco did not agree with him about the kingdom, he soon fell ill of the malady from which he died.' See *Secret Memoirs*, 74-5.

[63] c*132-3: Duke to da Trezzo, 5.8.1458: el papa essere grauemente jnfirma; c*137-40, letters from da Trezzo to Duke, Teano, 8.8.1458.

[64] c*145: da Trezzo to Duke, Teano, 12.8.1458.

[65] Messer, *Codice Aragonese*, docs. 32-3, 45-6, 8.8.1458; see also Messer, *Codice Aragonese*, doc. 34, 47, 8.8.1458; doc. 40, 57, 12.8.1458.

more, not less, important, since the risk of a new pope being elected who favoured René d'Anjou could not be ignored. Ferrante wrote to the duke as follows:

> To let you know our latest news, we tell you that our ambassadors in Rome have written to say that the College of Cardinals has deliberated and has decided to admit and treat our said ambassadors as ambassadors of a king...[66]

Ferrante wrote to the titular cardinal of San Lorenzo in Damaso, expressing his fears that the election of a new pope would not occur without lengthy delays: *credimo tardaranno li Cardinali multi di ad intrare in Conclavi.*[67] News came before long that the cardinals would not receive Ferrante's ambassadors as representatives of a king, at which da Trezzo professed to marvel, though the reason was obvious enough: there were still supporters of the Angevins with whom to contend in the College of Cardinals, and, besides, any cardinal worth his salt would support the principle of papal confirmation of the royal title to Naples.[68] It was not, according to this view, for Ferrante to decide that he was king, however desirable his succession might appear. Moreover, Ferrante had reason to be worried on other fronts, since there was bad news from Catalonia of further strife between his ally King John of Aragon and Charles of Viana, and Ferrante was obviously concerned that trouble within Aragon could reduce the chances of securing Aragonese-Catalan aid against the Angevins at Genoa or elsewhere.[69]

In late August the news seemd to improve, when Ferrante heard with *summa contenteza et piacere* of the election of Enea Silvio Piccolomini to the papal throne as Pius II.[70] It was also therefore time for Ferrante to show that he took seriously the duty of clearing the papal state of the Holy See's enemies, above all Jacopo Piccinino, whose war against Sigismondo Malatesta was, he declared in a letter to the duke, causing great damage. Ferrante was content enough with his own kingdom; he did not wish Francesco Sforza or anyone else to suppose that he had ambitions beyond its borders, a point which was probably valid enough, not least when he was still seeking to gain wider recognition:

---

[66] c*154: Ferrante to Duke, prope fontem populi, 19.8.1458.

[67] Messer, *Codice Aragonese*, doc. 34, 48, 8.8.1458. See also Pius II, *Secret Memoirs*, 74, 78.

[68] Nunziante, 'Primi anni', 18 (1893), 33-40, 207-13.

[69] c*154: Ferrante to Duke, prope fontem populi, 19.8.1458; cf. b199c200 da Trezzo to Duke, Teano, 10.9.1458.

[70] *162: da Trezzo to Duke, apud fontem Populi, 20.8.1458; see also Messer, *Codice Aragonese*, docs. 52-3, 70-74, 28.8.1458.

Nam cum nostro regno quod gratia dei admirabilisque Sapientia Serenissimi genitoris nostri and satis magnum and opulentum nobis parauit, contenti simus, non id querimus ut aliorum potentiam and statum perturbemus, and sanctae matris ecclesie presertim ad cuius defensionem decreuimus in idque constantissime perseuerabimus, statum, regnum, liberos, uitam denique, ipsam omnibus discriminibus and periculis obiectare.[71]

The same letter shows that Ferrante was anxious to establish in the strongest possible terms that he had not prompted Piccinino to try to create a power base around Assisi; in other words, no pope could accuse him of collusion in attempting to erode papal power in central Italy. Perhaps it had looked that way in the past, but Ferrante could not risk friendship towards the great *condottiere*. This attitude was consistently held in other letters issued by the king; writing to the duke of Andria and to an unnamed archbishop, Ferrante willingly talked of Piccinino's occupation of lands taken from the Church against its will.[72] Ferrante was thus firmly resolved to prove to the papacy and to his Italian colleagues that he would in future work with and not against the Holy See, a promise that he well knew could determine papal consent to his succession. This was not the view of a pained Piccinino, who still imagined that his protests would evoke some sympathy from the king of Naples.[73]

In late Summer 1458 there was still much to settle. Pius II took his time before he confirmed Ferrante's right to the crown.[74] The barons kept a close eye on events further north, knowing that Jean d'Anjou, on his father René's behalf, was keen to re-establish Angevin power in southern Italy. Ferrante took four years to establish himself as king, and during that period his power at times seemed to have shrunk to almost nothing. What he did understand from the start was the need to maintain a close rapport with Milan. His protestations of eternal friendship strike a hollow note, since Francesco Sforza had also in the past been prepared to fight for the Angevins; his accession to power was at first no comfort to Alfonso of Aragon, who had his own ambitions in northern Italy. Echoes of this unhappy past are rare in Ferrante's letters to Francesco Sforza. His aim was to establish such close ties of *parentela* that he would always be able to count on Sforza support. During the First Barons' War support was

---

[71] c*163: Ferrante to Duke, apud fontem Populi, 21.8.1458 [parchment].

[72] Messer, *Codice Aragonese*, doc. 56, 76-7, 28.8.1458.

[73] c*171: Piccinino to Ferrante, ex castris inter Nuceriam et Gualdum, 28.8.1458. Cf. several letters of early September 1458: busta 199 c191: da Trezzo to Duke, Naples, 4.9.1458: le creatione de questo summo pontefice... ne anche che fosse piu beniuolo ne piu affectionato ad la Maiesta sua, como siamo auisati et certificati da misser Otho nostro ambassator ad Roma. Cf. busta 199 c194: Duke to Ferrante concerning Piccinino, Milan, 4.9.1458: Et cosi siamo certi che siano bene intese da la Sanctita de nostro Sig.re iustissimo e clementissimo, et affectionato ad la M.ta vestra et cosi da le laltre potentie de Liga... li quali tutti ne remarano ben satisfacti, como siamo nuy.

[74] Pius II, *Secret Memoirs*, 90; cf. 104, 126-7, 149-51.

tardy, and Ferrante complained that it was too little, but he also underestimated Francesco Sforza's other commitments. In the face of these pleas, Francesco Sforza's reaction was cautious and measured; but the duke was well aware that Milan lay in a strategic position from which he could exercise influence within Italy but also, to some extent, in France and Provence.

To measure the effects of these policies it is necessary to look ahead a couple of years. For it is in this context that the instructions of May 1460 to the Milanese emissary to the court of France can be understood.[75] Here Francesco Sforza sought to explain his relationship with René of Anjou in a positive light, emphasizing the earlier service he had rendered to the Angevins in southern Italy against the invading Aragonese:

> There is not a man in Italy, not one, nor a household nor a family that, by rights, should hope more ardently for the victory of King René than we and our House and our kinsmen since we have lost in serving his majesty so magnificent an estate in the Kingdom of Naples... and because we are known throughout Italy as being Angevins of old and by nature [essendo nuy per tucta Italia cognosciuti antiqui et naturalmente Anzoyni] and servants of the House of France, and consequently enemies of all their rivals and enemies.[76]

Had King René seized his advantage then he and not Alfonso of Aragon would surely have held southern Italy, but Milanese fear of both Venice and the Turk necessitated the creation of a Universal Peace within Italy. After Ferrante's accession, Milan had been quite ready, Francesco Sforza asserted, to aid the Holy See against Ferrante's 'ally' Piccinino. And when Jean de Calabre invaded southern Italy on behalf of his father René, Milan received many appeals for troops 'but we were never willing to send him any'.[77] It might be said that on this occasion Francesco Sforza protested too much. The reality was that Ferrante very early convinced Sforza of the advantages of keeping the *Franzesi* out of Genoa, northern Italy and the *Regno*. But it was also necessary to be skillful in dissembling, to cite Machiavelli.

Put simply, the Aragonese in Naples were aware how much they needed Milan. The breakdown in this relationship during the reign of Ferrante, under Galeazzo Maria and under Ludovico il Moro, thus signalled the doom of the house of Aragon.

---

[75] *Dispatches*, vol. 1, 294-319.
[76] *Dispatches*, vol. 1, 308-9.
[77] *Dispatches*, vol. 1, 312-14; cf. the editors' comments, 319.

Towards the Tragedia d'Italia: Ferrante and Galeazzo Maria Sforza, friendly enemies and hostile allies

Vincent Ilardi

In the course of tracing the origin and development of the Milanese permanent resident embassy at Naples during the second half of the fifteenth century, as part of continuing research for a forthcoming book encompassing the leading Italian states of the age, it was my intention to treat foreign affairs as sparingly as possible, consistently with the central objective of assessing the growth of the institution and the role played by its first representatives. I found this necessary, self-imposed limitation difficult to apply in the case of Naples because in reading big segments of correspondence between the two states I came to realize as never before that they contained the key for a deeper understanding of the entire diplomatic scene of fifteenth-century Italy. The troubled relations between the two sons of Francesco Sforza, Galeazzo Maria and Ludovico Maria, and Ferrante constitute in my view the fatal linear progression leading to the French invasion of Italy in 1494. This correspondence also makes it clear that Naples was the focus of intense diplomatic activity throughout this period.[1] Exposed in the Adriatic to the power of Venice and the advancing Turks, threatened in the Tyrrhenian by Genoa and the Angevins, Ferrante cultivated relations with potential allies outside Italy such as Aragon, Burgundy, and England. In fact, the king displayed in this decade much of the same European-

---

[1] No historian seems to have exploited fully this rich documentation for the history of the Italian states in the second half of the fifteenth century. The effort presented here is but a summary sketch of some key diplomatic problems affecting the two states. For a general and critical view of the diplomacy of the period, see G. Pillinini, *Il sistema degli stati italiani 1454-1494* (Venice, 1970), which highlights the constant interdependence of Italian and European affairs and contains a most extensive bibliography. Fundamental for the understanding of these issues is R. Fubini, *Italia Quattrocentesca. Politica e diplomazia nell'età di Lorenzo il Magnifico* (Milan, 1994), and his other works, which will be cited below. Here the citation of secondary publications has been kept to a minimum.

wide geopolitical acumen shown by his late mentor, Francesco Sforza. Unfortunately, Ferrante's key role throughout the second half of the century has to be pieced together from the largely biased dispatches of ambassadors at his court, mostly Milanese, because few Neapolitan diplomatic papers survived the violent events in that kingdom, including the wanton destruction of what was left by the retreating German army in 1943.[2]

On the other hand, it is ironic but not surprising that Galeazzo Maria should have proved incapable of fulfilling his inherited role as the diplomatic leader of the Italian peninsula. During his late teens both Francesco and his wife, Bianca Maria, had noticed some serious character flaws in Galeazzo reminiscent of his maternal grandfather, Filippo Maria Visconti and of some other members of that family; namely, capriciousness, irascibility, moodiness, and general intractability, sometimes masked by a disarming charm that confounded his parents because it compounded his unpredictability.[3] Barely a month before his sudden death (8 March 1466), Francesco had so become exasperated by his irresponsible behavior as the nominal leader of an expeditionary force sent to help Louis XI quell a baronial revolt (the War of the Public Weal) that he admonished his son to stop acting like a 'pucto' and behave like a man.[4] His unexpected succession at the age of 22 while he was still in France exacerbated his youthful shortcomings, which now came to include profligate spending for luxuries and mistresses, cruelty, impulsiveness and intemperate speech, misguided ambition to outdo his father especially in his pursuit of the royal crown, indecisiveness in decision making, and above all lack of balance and moderation, all of which realized the worst fears of his mother and co-ruler of the duchy. Unlike his widely admired father, whom he resembled only in his amorous escapades, he was utterly unprepared emotionally or by training to take, or even less share, the process of governing arguably the richest state in Italy with the most powerful army and the most developed diplomatic network of any state in Europe. He had never governed a

---

[2] There is no biography of Ferrante based on archival documents or even on the most recent publications. The collection of eight studies published by E. Pontieri, *Per la storia del Regno di Ferrante I d'Aragona, re di Napoli*, 2nd ed. (Naples, 1969) can hardly serve this function. On the other hand, the interplay of politics and humanism during his reign has been admirably treated by J.H. Bentley, *Politics and culture in Renaissance Naples* (Princeton, 1987).

[3] For a general treatment of Galeazzo's reign, largely based on archival documents, see F. Catalano, 'Il ducato di Milano nella politica dell'equilibrio', in *Storia di Milano*, vol. 7 (Milan, 1956), 227-309. Galeazzo's court and related internal policies have been treated in detail and with discernment by G. Lubkin, *A Renaissance court. Milan under Galeazzo Maria Sforza* (Berkeley/Los Angeles, 1994). The popular biography by C. Violini, *Galeazzo Maria Sforza,* 2nd ed. (Turin, 1943), is of little use. For a succinct but pungent and accurate analysis of his policies and character, beautifully written, see G. Lopez, *Moro! Moro!* (Milan, 1992), 41-79.

[4] Full quotation in *Dispatches with related documents of Milanese ambassadors in France*, vol. 3, ed. V. Ilardi, trans. F.J. Fata (Dekalb, Illinois, 1981), xlvii, n. 24.

province or commanded an army, and his diplomatic experience consisted only of three or four ceremonial missions exercised in various Italian states.

In addition to the ready resources at his command and the sage advice of Bianca Maria, universally respected for her piety, moderation, and wide experience in government, Galeazzo had the support of two kings, whose thrones had been been saved largely with direct aid and wise advice by Francesco Sforza. Louis XI was unstinting in his public support of the young duke not only out of gratitude for the assistance he had just received, but also to fulfill the terms of the Franco-Milanese alliance signed at the end of 1463.[5] This alliance, in fact, had signalled Louis' abandonment of his aggressive pursuit of Angevin and Orleanist dynastic claims over Naples and Milan respectively, including his own over Genoa, and the initiation of a new plan to exercise a sort of diplomatic hegemony in the peninsula with Milan serving as the leader of an alliance block comprising Savoy-Piedmont, Florence, and Naples, from which he expected to receive additional aid in his continuing struggle against his feudal barons now more than ever alienated by his new policy. Alberico Maletta, the Milanese ambassador who negotiated the alliance, perceptively underlined its revolutionary significance by writing to Francesco that 'this king now seems to be the enemy of our enemies and of those of King Ferrante; nor could there be another king of France who would suit better our purposes and those of King Ferrante'.[6] Ferrante knew this better than anyone else and never tired to profess privately and publicly his debt of gratitude for the vital role played by Francesco Sforza in the defeat of his rival to the Neapolitan throne, Duke John of Anjou, just a year earlier. Indeed, both kings, about double Galeazzo's age (Louis at 43, Ferrante at 41) were eager to reciprocate and tutor the young heir in statecraft and war just as they had been tutored by Francesco.

In Italy, Galeazzo could also count on the support of Piero de' Medici in Florence, who was firmly attached to the Sforza on whose sword he depended for his very existence as nominal leader of the republic. Even Pope Paul II, a Venetian, rejected Venice's overtures for an entente against Milan to expel the Sforza, who had halted her westward expansion into Lombardy. Aside from Venice, which soon became embroiled in her sixteen-year old (1463-79) struggle to stem the advance of the Turks from the East and was forced to assume a more defensive posture, only the duchess of Savoy, Yolande, younger sister of Louis XI, seriously threatened the security of Milan's western border until Louis intervened to squash the attempt. Like Venice, the Savoyard dukes had never become reconciled to the Sforza capture of Milan, which had

---

[5] For Louis' attitude towards the new duke, see *Dispatches*, vol. 3, xxxv-l and the documens published in that volume.

[6] Quoted with the original in *Dispatches*, vol. 3, xxxviii.

deprived the dowager Duchess of Milan, Maria of Savoy (wife of Duke Filippo Maria Visconti) of her succession rights, and to the loss of some border territory to Francesco after the Peace of Lodi. Louis XI's pro-Sforza stand, combined with his projected marriage of his sister-in-law, Bona of Savoy, with Galeazzo Maria, further fuelled the enmity of this faction-ridden but strategic state against the new royal policy.

The complexities of the Italian political-diplomatic scene, summarily recapitulated above because they are constantly reflected in the documentation to be cited below, required expert monitoring and handling on the part of Italian rulers. These complexities and animosities were fully understood by the first Sforza duke, who wished to consolidate his dynasty with the peaceful succession of Galeazzo by the conclusion of the Italian League (1455), which guaranteed the territorial integrity of the Italian states and their respective dynasties as established by the Treaty of Lodi a year earlier. This guarantee was reinforced by a double marriage alliance negotiated also in 1455 which bound the ten-year old daughter of Francesco, Ippolita, to marry the seven-year old grandson of King Alfonso of Naples, also named Alfonso, whereas Francesco's third son, the four-year old Sforza Maria, was betrothed to Alfonso's five-year old granddaughter, Leonora. (The first marriage was celebrated in 1465, the second was dissolved in 1472). With this wise bond the two new dynasties sought to protect themselves above all from the most creditable threat of their age, the respective claims of the two cadet branches of the French royal family. The Milan-Naples axis, buttressed by the financial resources of the Medici, could easily have influenced the election of friendly popes and served to keep in check any Venetian attempt to expand further in the mainland, a common fear throughout this period. With a feeble Holy Roman Empire and a still disunited Spain, the Italian state system should have been capable of deterring aggression from occasional French dynastic adventurers and even assume a more aggressive posture against the Turks. Such were the hopes and goals of the first generation after the Peace of Lodi, Alfonso and Ferrante of Naples, Pope Pius II, Cosimo de' Medici, and Francesco Sforza. Galeazzo Maria had only to stay the course abroad and moderate his appetites at home, and in all likelyhood he would have basked in the glory of being a great statesman and would have escaped the assassins' daggers ten years later.

Intellectually gifted but emotionally unstable, Galeazzo was not capable of assuming his inherited diplomatic role. From the beginning he antagonized and alienated friends and allies of Milan, gradually dissipating all the respect and good will earned by his parents and turning the duchy into an unpredictable and destabilizing power in the Italian and even in the European diplomatic game. The first inklings to the outside world of what to expect from the new ruler came from his systematic and brutal exclusion of his mother from decision making, carried out in about a year from the death of Francesco. The progress of this fateful rift has been treated by historians and biographers of Bianca Maria;[7] for us its major interest lies in the effect it had on Galeazzo's relations with Ferrante and on its related disastrous consequences in the career of the first Milanese resident ambassador in Naples, Antonio da Trezzo.

Antonio da Trezzo was the first and most informed witness from the beginning of this family drama. Already a *famiglio cavalcante* or courtier/functionary of Filippo Maria Visconti from about 1445, Antonio passed into the service of Francesco Sforza two years later, discharging various diplomatic missions, especially at Ferrara (1450-55), and finally was appointed ambassador to King Alfonso of Naples in late November of 1455, residing there for the next fifteen years. He thus holds the second longest record of continuous ambassadorial residence in one capital for the age, the longest being Nicodemo Tranchedini's residence in Florence, eighteen years. Together with Alberico Maletta, who later negotiated the Franco-Milanese alliance, he concluded the double marriage alliance with Alfonso mentioned above. During the baronial revolt and Angevin invasion of the kingdom (1459-65), his dispatches constitute the most detailed account of that struggle, in the course of which he almost lost his life. He became the main conduit of that constant flow of aid to Ferrante, financial, military, psychological, that his master was able to muster with the cooperation of Pius II and Cosimo de' Medici. Francesco Sforza, who earlier had fought in the kingdom on the side of the Angevins, knew the terrain and the actors in the drama very well and through Antonio he imparted valuable advice on strategy and tactics as well. As a result of this experience, the ambassador became one of the most intimate advisers of the king, a valuable resource for Milan as well as for Naples.[8]

As news of this mother/son struggle spread throughout Italy and beyond, Ferrante became active directly and through Antonio and his own ambassadors in Milan, Antonio and Turco Cicinello, in efforts to restore unity of purpose in a state so vital for the peace of Italy then being threatened from various quarters. There were also the pathetic appeals for aid from Bianca Maria, who literally

---

[7] W. Terni de Gregorj, *Bianca Maria Visconti, duchessa di Milano* (Bergamo, 1940), 193-209; Lubkin, *A Renaissance court*, 39-48, 53-4, and 62-5. Now the most detailed acount is by P. Margaroli, 'Bianca Maria e Galeazzo Maria Sforza nelle ultime lettere di Antonio da Trezzo (1467-1469)', *Archivio storico lombardo*, 111 (1985), 327-77, who published some of the most important correspondence on the rift by Bianca Maria, Ferrante, and Antonio da Trezzo.

[8] A great number of Antonio's dispatches were published by E. Nunziante, 'I primi anni di Ferdinando d'Aragona e l'invasione di Giovanni d'Angiò', *Archivio storico per le province napoletane*, 17-23 (1892-98). Biographical sketches by N. Raponi in *Dizionario biografico degli italiani* (Rome, 1961), vol. 3 (1961), 578-80 (hereafter DBI); L. Cerioni, *La diplomazia sforzesca nella seconda metà del Quattrocento e i suoi cifrari segreti*, vol. 1 (Rome, 1970), 243-4; and the most complete by F. Leverotti, *Diplomazia e governo dello Stato: i 'famigli cavalcanti' di Francesco Sforza (1450-1466)* (Pisa, 1992), 247-50.

feared for her personal security even in her dower city of Cremona where she had taken refuge. She returned to Milan briefly only to attend the marriage of Galeazzo with Bona of Savoy in July of 1468 and she died a month later probably of malaria, aggravated by psychological stress, but also with some suspicion of poison.[9] Until the end, she kept corresponding with Ferrante and Antonio using a special cipher, a fact that was known to Galeazzo, who resented this interference in his internal affairs. There is no doubt that this episode revealed to the king the darkest side of Galeazzo's personality and began to create doubts in his mind about the reliability of his ally. For Antonio it meant the end of his twenty-two year career at the service of the Sforza. In fear for his safety, he retained his post until the beginning of 1470 only through the intercession of Ferrante, who finally gave him a position in his court, where he remained for the rest of his life.[10]

It is important to note at this point that one of Antonio's dispatches to Galeazzo in 1467 mentioned unwittingly what was soon to become the fundamental and the most emotional cause for the permanent estrangement of the two rulers. In this dispatch Antonio expressed his pleasure that Galeazzo wished to make war against Venice if he were aided by other powers. In this context he recalled his conversation with Francesco Sforza, who pointed out that he had aided Ferrante for no other reason than to have him as an ally for future contingencies and at the opportune time for a possible expansion of the duchy's borders eastward - a clear allusion to Bergamo, Brescia, and Crema, former Visconti cities ceded to Venice with the Treaty of Lodi. And Ferrante had eagerly agreed to help him once he was well established on his throne.[11]

This conversation, if it really took place exactly as recalled by the ambassador, goes counter to what we know about the prudence and wisdom of Francesco Sforza as a statesman. The contemplated aggression would have immediately tarnished the image he cultivated as a champion of the Italian League. His finances were in shambles, being heavily in debt to Florence and the Medici Bank, and the Florentines were becoming increasingly reluctant to lend more to such an *animoso spenditore* as Cosimo de' Medici just before his death (1464) had called Francesco.[12] He also was committed to sending more

---

[9] The suspicion of poison, however, has been discounted through examination of available evidence by D. Panebianco, 'Documenti sull'ultima malattia di Bianca Maria Sforza e sulla peste del 1468', *Archivio storico lombardo*, ser. 9, 8 (1971), 372.

[10] Margaroli, 'Bianca Maria', 348-9, and Antonio to Bianca Maria, Naples, 27 April 1467, 357-60 for an illuminating dispatch about the developing antagonism between the two princes.

[11] Antonio to Bianca Maria, Naples, 9 July 1467, in Margaroli, 'Bianca Maria', 360-61.

[12] On Francesco's financial relationship with Cosimo and Florence, see my article, 'The Banker-Statesman and the Condottiere-Prince: Cosimo de' Medici and Francesco Sforza (1450-1464)', in *Florence and Milan: Comparisons and Relations*, ed. Sergio Bertelli, Nicolai Rubinstein, Craig Hugh Smyth, 2 vols (Florence, 1989), vol. 2, 229-30.

troops to Louis XI, still menaced by his barons, so as to provide a first line of defence for both Milan and Naples. Nor was Venice a secondary power to be easily vanquished without a protracted general war, carrying with it the danger of Angevin or other foreign intervention. Rather one suspects that Antonio's sudden recollection was designed (probably with the king's connivance) to moderate Galeazzo's antagonistic behavior towards Ferrante, by reminding him that the king's cooperation was essential for the recovery of the lost cities. Whereas for Francesco such a contemplated recovery might have been a wishful musing in a conversation with a trusted ambassador, for Galeazzo it became an obsession, as we shall see.

Ever vigilant Venice was well aware of Galeazzo's hostile intentions, which he did not seek to hide at any rate, and actually went on the offensive to keep her potential enemies off balance. Taking advantage of the internal weakness of Florence after the Medici succession crisis (1465-66) and the parallel internal discord in Milan, the republic unleashed in Romagna (1467) its supreme commander, Bartolomeo Colleoni, acting in collusion with the pro-Angevin Duke Borso d'Este of Modena and Florentine exiles. Venice had already publicly announced that it did not feel bound by the Italian League because Francesco Sforza had allegedly broken its terms with his acquisition of Genoa in 1464. This prompted Florence, Milan, and Naples to transform their *entente cordiale* into a formal league (17 January 1467) with a pro-forma invitation to the Pope and to Venice to join as an effort to save the spirit of the Italian League, also called *lega generale* or *lega universale*.[13]

That this spirit reflected hope rather than reality is shown by the fact that Venice reacted by contracting a separate alliance with Savoy (24 October 1467). Despite the papally imposed peace (8 May 1468) settling the Colleoni crisis, the republic also attempted to form a coalition in 1468-69 comprising the pope, Burgundy, Ferrara, Savoy, Colleoni, Florentine exiles, and the Angevins for a war against the triple alliance, designed to install the Angevins in Naples. These negotiations finally resulted in the papal-Venetian alliance of May 1469, but without the inclusion of John of Anjou and Charles of Burgundy, owing to Venice's last minute fear of unduly irritating Ferrante and Galeazzo. The anti-Ferrante stand taken by Paul II was intended to force the king to pay the yearly tribute (and its arrears) owed by kings of Naples as vassals of the Holy See, but it was also part of his general policy to enforce papal rights in the church's own lands, of which his war with the triple alliance over Roberto Malatesta's succession in Rimini (August 1469) was the most clamorous example. Paul's aggressive pursuit of his objectives had already provoked a secret agreement (5 February 1469) in which Galeazzo assured Ferrante of his aid in case of a war

---

[13] On the Colleoni crisis, see the still fundamental book by B. Belotti, *La vita di Bartolomeo Colleoni* (Bergamo, 1925), 355-410.

with the pope while the king promised him support for the recovery of Bergamo, Brescia, Crema from Venice. But three days later the duke also decided to be cautious and urged the king to postpone implementation of the agreement to a more opportune and favorable occasion. Nothing is more illustrative of the total disorientation of Italian diplomacy in the three year period following the death of Francesco Sforza than this display of moves and counter-moves, a constant ripple effect, devoid of any grand design or goal.[14]

Yet there was a glimmer of hope in 1470 that the the Italian League could be renegotiated to present a united front against the Turks, whose capture of Venice's second most valuable colony after Crete, Negroponte (12 July 1470), shocked into action the Italian powers most affected: Venice, Naples, and the Holy See.[15] Sensing the gravity of its peril, a year earlier Venice had already sent Filippo Correr to Naples with instructions to pass through various capitals to promote peace in Italy for the sake of a common effort against the Turks. In May 1470, Correr was recalled for transgressing his instructions and replaced by Bernardo Giustiniani, who came to continue the negotiations for a separate anti-Turkish alliance with the king.[16] At the same time, the news of the fall of Negroponte merely accelerated discussion in Rome of peace concerning the Rimini succession struggle, while making more pressing the renewal of the Italian League of 1455. But the direct Venetian approach to Ferrante generated suspicion in Galeazzo and the Florentines, seeing it as a manoeuvre to break up the triple alliance. This suspicion prompted both Galeazzo and Lorenzo de' Medici to send their own ambassadors to Naples to confirm the triple alliance, which had grown strained in recent months over disagreements on the settlement of the Rimini question.[17]

---

[14] For papal policy, L. von Pastor, *Storia dei papi dalla fine del Medio Evo*, trans. Angelo Mercati, vol. 2 (Rome, 1961), 347-57, 391-409; for the many diplomatic moves between 1467 and 1470, Fubini, *Italia Quattrocentesca*, 227-39 and Lorenzo de' Medici, *Lettere*, ed. R. Fubini (Florence, 1977), vol. 1, 541-6.

[15] For Paul II's Turkish policy and the European reaction to the loss of Negroponte, see Pastor, *Storia*, vol. 2, 338-46, 410-17; but the latest and most detailed account is now provided by K.M. Setton, *The Papacy and the Levant (1204-1571)*, vol. 2, *The fifteenth century* (Philadelphia, 1978), 271-313.

[16] Instructions by Doge Cristoforo Moro to Filippo Correr, 6 July 1469, Venice, Archivio di Stato (hereafter ASV), *Senato Secreta*, Reg. 24, f. 30r-30; he was recalled on 22 May 1470, f. 110r-110v; instructions to B. Giustiniani, 10 May 1470, f. 106v-107r.

[17] The strained alliance is demonstrated by the protest made to Galeazzo on the orders of Ferrante by his ambassador in Milan complaining that the duke had not respected the terms of the alliance, especially with respect to the succession of Roberto Malatesta in Rimini (17 April 1470): Milan, Archivio di Stato (hereafter ASMi), Sforzesco Potenze Estere, Napoli, cart. 218. (Hereafter this frequently used series will be cited only with the cartella box number). For the contrasting policies followed by Milan and Naples concerning the Rimini succession, which in essence signified their competing spheres of influence in Romagna, see W. Tommasoli, *Momenti e figure della politica dell'equilibrio (Federico da Montefeltro e l'impresa di Rimini)* (Urbino, 1968).

The arrival in April 1470 of the new Milanese ambassador in Naples, Giovanni Andrea Cagnola, resulted shortly after in the resumption of the resident embassy just vacated by Antonio da Trezzo. Although in December 1469 Galeazzo had instructed Antonio to continue his residency as *nostro secretario et oratore*, to satisfy Ferrante's wishes, he had ignored him since August except to press the king to prevent astrologers in the kingdom from naming Galeazzo in their horoscopes for the new year. (Astrologers and their predictions were one of the duke's constant preoccupations).[18] Relations between the two rulers had been carried out mostly through Turco Cicinello, royal ambassador in Milan.[19]

Cagnola received his instructions for a three-month mission while he was in Rome for the peace negotiations and they were general in tone. He was to assure the king of Milan's desire for peace and express hopes that the king was similarly inclined. Since he was inexperienced in dealing with Ferrante, Cagnola should listen, report, and wait for further instructions, taking care not to communicate with Antonio da Trezzo, who was to be kept totally in the dark regarding his mission. If the king expressed suspicion over the keeping of Gerardo de' Colli as Milan's ambassador in Venice, he was to reply that Galeazzo was not suspicious of the residence of a Venetian ambassador in Naples. He was to be on friendly terms with the Venetian ambassador but should take care not to let the Venetian precede him on solemn occasions. Finally he was to use the enclosed cipher to communicate important matters so that even in employing the royal couriers as far as Rome, Ferrante's officials could not intercept and read his dispatches.[20]

Cagnola entered Naples on 24 April in the company of his Florentine colleague, Otto Niccolini, and was cordially received in open audience the following day amid expressions of father-son relationship of the two rulers, although the king added that Galeazzo's actions with respect to Rimini showed more desire for war than peace.[21] As negotiations progressed and rumours about an impending Neapolitan-Venetian alliance spread, Galeazzo became more pliant concerning Rimini and on the payment of the *condotta* of the count of Urbino as supreme commander for the triple league, so as to facilitate its

---

[18] cart. 218: Galeazzo to Antonio, Vigevano, 7 December 1469, and Antonio to Galeazzo, Naples, 15 January 1470. See also Lubkin, *A Renaissance court*, 116-17 for Galeazzo's preoccupation with astrological predictions.

[19] There are virtually no dispatches by Antonio da Trezzo to Galeazzo between August and the end of December 1469, but cart. 218 (cited in preceding note) has plenty of copies of Ferrante's letters to T. Cicinello, some of which were probably intercepted.

[20] Galeazzo to Antonio Anguissola da Piacenza, treasurer general, Fontaneto, 5 April 1470, ordering him to issue a letter of exchange to Cagnola for his mission to Naples 'per tri mesi et per cavalli octo'; and instructions to Cagnola, Fontaneto and Novara, 6 April, 1470, both in cart. 218.

[21] cart. 218: Cagnola to Galeazzo, Naples, 25 April 1470.

confirmation with a clause reserving the Franco-Milanese alliance. He was also willing to renew the *lega universale* as desired by the king after the confirmation, and his position was supported by Florence.[22]

Two complications, however, delayed the conclusion of the negotiations: the admission of Venice to the triple alliance as a prelude for the inclusion of the Pope in the hoped-for renewed Italian League and the reservation of the Franco-Milanese alliance. Cagnola and Niccolini were informed by Giovanni Battista Bentivoglio, royal adviser, and by Antonello Petrucci, the influential royal secretary, that in the continuing negotiation of the alliance between Naples and Venice, Filippo Correr had agreed to a clause prohibiting the allies to attack any state in Italy except in self defence. This clause had been proposed by the king to protect Florence and Milan. Correr was recalled home for his agreement to this clause and he had just left Naples (4 June). The new Venetian ambassador, Bernardo Giustiniani, who arrived on 6 June, wanted to modify this clause by stating that a member of the alliance would be permitted to attack another state if 'provoked', a modification clearly directed against Galeazzo. Ferrante insisted that Venice join the triple league without any modification whatsoever and gave the Signoria until 25 June to reply.[23] But even if Venice were to withdraw her objection, she could not be member of a league containing a reservation for the Franco-Milanese alliance because of its separate league with the duchess of Savoy, whose freedom of action was threatened under the terms of that alliance.[24]

Nor was the reservation for the king of France acceptable to Ferrante himself because of Louis' continuing support for Duke John of Anjou's campaign to take Catalonia from his uncle, King John II of Aragon, and just at this time Genoese ships were under contract with France to attack Barcelona under the terms of the Franco-Milanese alliance.[25] As a countermove, Ferrante wanted Galeazzo to press his French ally to stop this aid or he might be forced to seek an alliance with Duke Charles the Bold of Burgundy. Moreover, the king was ready to renew the league with Florence alone if Galeazzo did not

---

[22] cart. 218: Cagnola to Galeazzo, Naples, 8, 29 May and 7 June and Galeazzo to Cagnola, Pavia, 24, 29 May, 1470. The mandate to confirm the triple alliance and renew the Italian League was enclosed in Galeazzo's letter of 29 May and bears the same date; copy in ASMi, Trattati, cart. 1535.

[23] cart. 218: Cagnola to Galeazzo, Naples, 4, 6, 10 June 1470.

[24] cart. 218: Cagnola to Galeazzo, Naples, 11 June 1470.

[25] The Catalan revolt against John of Aragon, now in its eighth year, set off a diplomatic and military struggle between France and Aragon for the control of the province in the course of which the Catalan rebels offered the crown to René of Anjou (1466), whose son, John, led the military campaigns with alternating fortunes until his death (16 December 1470), but the war continued until the re-entry of King John into Barcelona (17 October 1472). The repercussions of this conflict in Italy and its European-wide ramifications are analyzed in detail by J. Calmette, *Louis XI, Jean II et la révolution catalane (1461-1473)* (Toulouse, 1903), especially 265-384.

drop his demand, and Niccolini was willing to follow his wishes (despite his instructions to support the Milanese position) particularly because Venice now appeared to be ready to enter the league without any modifications.[26]

Galeazzo remained adamant. By return post he ordered Cagnola to tell the king in the presence of the entire court with as many people as possible, including the Venetian and Florentine ambassadors, that if Ferrante and Florence did not accept the reservation, he had been ordered to return home and make the following declaration: the duke of Milan will not agree to act dishonorably by not reserving his obligations to the king of France, *suo Signore*, so that the triple league was not renewed only because he could not and would not dishonor himself. Moreover, he could not believe that the king would want to repay in such a manner the benefits he had received from Francesco Sforza, 'who made him king and now His Majesty wants to make us a traitor'.[27] Cagnola was also instructed to take special note of the king's and the audience's reaction when he said, *Re de Franza nostro Signore*. And he was expressly ordered to add the phrase, *nostro Signore*, whenever the mentioned the king of France, especially in the presence of the Venetian ambassador. Having delivered this stinging message, the ambassador was to return home although he was given the discretion to act on these instructions according to the situation of the moment. But two days later, the duke changed his mind and ordered Cagnola to renew the triple league according to the old terms without additions or reservations unless the king insisted on reserving a place for Venice. In that case, the ambassador was likewise to insist on the reservation.[28] Clearly Galeazzo did not want Venice in the league, which also meant that he was secretly opposed to the renewal of the Italian League for reasons that became more apparent later in the year.

The above ultimatum, which was never delivered (to the relief of the bewildered ambassador)[29] shows that Galeazzo was transforming the Franco-Milanese alliance more and more from the defence mechanism against common enemies on both sides of the Alps it had been designed to be into a menacing and coercive tool to dominate the entire diplomatic scene in Italy. Yet months earlier he knew that Louis XI had advised him in the king's reply to the special Milanese ambassador, Alessandro Spinola, to preserve the triple alliance as the best means of preserving peace. Spinola had been sent to the French court in February 1470 ostensibly to inform Louis on the latest shifts in peninsular

---

[26] cart. 218: Cagnola to Galeazzo, Naples, 12 June 1470.

[27] cart. 218: Che non credevamo che la M.tà Soa devesse volere remunerare li beneficii recevuti da la bona memoria del S. nostro patre, quale lo fece Re et Soa M.tà vole farne traditore.' Galeazzo to Cagnola, Pavia, 21 June 1470.

[28] cart. 218: Galeazzo to Cagnola, Pavia, 23 June 1470.

[29] Cagnola to Cicco Simonetta, Galeazzo's chief secretary, Naples, 23 June 1470, cart. 218, in which he expressed his anxiety over the burden of these vexing negotiations.

diplomacy, and primarily to ascertain his views on these events in preparation for a series of moves he was planning in the coming months. In his long instructions, Galeazzo complained against his various enemies, including the aggressive Venetians threatening his borders, the warmonger Count Federico of Urbino who was causing trouble for him with the Pope, Ferrante, and Lorenzo over the Rimini question, and he finally mentioned Ferrante's complaint about Louis' support of John of Anjou in Catalonia. He, on the other hand, wanted peace because only four years ago he had inherited a duchy saddled with debts of more than 500,000 ducats left by his father, the payment of which was a first priority in order to stabilize his state and thus be ready for service to the king.[30] The king lauded Galeazzo's inclination towards peace, encouraged him to renew the triple alliance so that he would have the security to stabilize his throne and be able to help Louis in case of need, and urged him not to alienate Italy's most renowned commander, the count of Urbino.   In reference to Ferrante's complaint, Louis led the ambassador to understand that he was following the policy worked out with Francesco Sforza five years earlier. It was his intention not to promote the aggrandizement of John of Anjou, but only to offer sufficient aid to keep him embroiled in Catalonia so as to be less of a threat in France and in Italy.   Indeed, Ferrante, whose friendship he wished to cultivate through Galeazzo, should be grateful and should also realize that in aiding Duke John he also was protecting France's interests in the county of Roussillon.[31]

In subsequent correspondence with his resident ambassador in France, Sforza Bettini, Galeazzo tried to widen this developing rift between Louis and Ferrante. He revealed that Ferrante was about to conclude an alliance with Venice, reserving a place for Milan, and that more than once he had urged him to cut his ties to the French crown.[32] Louis at first reacted with anger saying that he had always regretted that Francesco Sforza had contracted the marriage alliance with the house of Aragon and that he could always unleash the Angevins against Ferrante; but he advised Galeazzo that he could better provide security for his state by either confirming the triple alliance or by entering a general league even if he had to renounce his alliance with France. He was confident that each of them would come to the defense of the other without any

---

[30] Spinola's instructions, Pavia, 10 February 1470, were published by J. Chmel, 'Briefe und Aktenstücke zur Geschichte der Herzoge von Mailand von 1452 bis 1512', *Notizenblatt. Beilage zum Archiv für Kunde österreichischer Geschichtsquellen*, 6 (1856), 36-38, 56-62, and 62-4 for an undated (probably late May) summary relation of his mission to Galeazzo because he had left France by 17 May and was back in Milan by May 30: Sforza Bettini, Milanese resident ambassador in France, to Galeazzo, Amboise, 17 May 1470, and Galeazzo to Bettini, Pavia, 30 May 1470, ASMi, Sforzesco Potenze Estere, Francia, cart. 537.

[31] Spinola to Galeazzo, Tours, 26 March 1470, ASMi, Sforzesco Potenze Estere, Francia, cart. 537. Roussillon, along with Cerdagne, were two Catalan border counties which Louis wished to control.

[32] Galeazzo to Sforza Bettini, Pavia, 20 May 1470, c. 537.

formal treaty.³³   And when Galeazzo notified Louis in mid June that he had decided to confirm both the triple alliance and the *lega universale*, the king rejoiced not out of love for Ferrante, in whose place he would rather have King René of Anjou, but for the sake of the duke, to whom he was obligated more than to any relative or friend, adding that 'now it was not the time to turn the world upside down'. Bettini himself, noting the king's fatherly concern towards his lord and his apparent neglect of Angevin interests, advised the duke to put personal animosity aside and conclude with Ferrante: 'taking the medicine while holding his nostrils'.³⁴

These remarkable replies show that as late as 1470 Louis still saw the stability and strength of Milan and its influence in the Italian alliance system as essential factors for a viable Franco-Milanese alliance able to help him in the coming struggle with Charles of Burgundy, despite the Peace of Peronne signed two years earlier. They also demonstrate the *Realpolitik* of a first rate statesman and the dilettantish personal approach to foreign policy of a *puto*. At the same time they reveal a weakness in the conduct of French foreign policy, which did not make use of resident ambassadors who could have alerted the king that his ally was not telling the whole truth. Louis, in fact, might have felt less fatherly towards the duke had he known that at the same time that Bettini was revealing the negotiations between Ferrante and the Venetians as an anti-French move, Galeazzo himself was making secret overtures to Venice for an alliance, a goal he had pursued secretly since the end of 1468 partly to cover his own aggressive

---

³³ After expressing his Angevin threat against Ferrante, Louis reflected that 'el non fusse el più sicuro partito del mondo et ch'el saria meglio a fare ogni cosa per tenere el Re Ferrando ne termini primi'. As Bettini pointed out that Ferrante and Venice were proposing the general league to the Pope on condition that Galeazzo terminate his alliance with France, Louis replied: 'che qualora pure sequissi intelligentia et liga particulare fra el Re Ferrando et vinitiani et che esso Re Ferrando si discostassi in tutto dal Ex.tia V. et si facessi liga generale in Italia, che li pareva che omnino la Ex.tia V. li entrasse et renuntiassi liberamente a ogni intelligentia et liga che la havessi con essa, quando altrimenti la non possessi capere in dicta liga; che più tosto voleva Sua May.tà fessi così per conservarsi lo Stato che non lo fare et metterlo a pericolo, perché conservandoselo qualche volta Sua May.tà si potria valere de essa; né per questo restaria Sua May.tà de essere continuamente prompta et presta in soa posse a ogni adiuto, favore et difensione del Ex.tia V. et suo Stato... et gli bastava el buono animo et buona intentione di quella [Galeazzo] et maxime che per adesso non achadeva a Sua May.tà darvi fatica di cosa nissuna'. Bettini to Galeazzo, Amboise, 25 May 1470, Francia, cart. 537.

³⁴ Upon hearing the news, Louis again urged Galeazzo to do all he could to please Ferrante for the sake of the triple alliance addressing these formal words to Bettini: 'Sforza, tu poy ben essere certo che noy non dicemo questo per amore né carità che portiamo ad esso Re Ferrando, che voressemo se non fosse per rispecto al duca de Milano, ch'el fosse in una rivera dece anni passati, et el Re Raynero fosse alla possessione de quello suo Reame, ma lo interesse de esso duca de Milano, ad chi siamo più obligati che al prefato Re Raynero né ad niuno altro parente o amico che habiamo, ne constringe ad darli tale ricordo, parendone ch'el non sia tempo al presente ad voltare el mondo sottosopra.' Bettini's pungent phrase: 'in summa havere questa medicina senza metterli el naso'. Bettini to Galeazzo, Amboise, 12 June 1470, Francia, cart. 537.

plans against the republic.[35] Lorenzo de' Medici himself was visibly shaken when he learned of these machinations and of earlier Milanese intrigues with Florentine exiles in Rome.[36] The renewal of the triple alliance on 8 July 1470, then, was only an alignment of the moment devoid of any true commitment to a long-range goal. Likewise the confirmation of the Italian League of 1455, negotiated in Rome on 22 December 1470, was infused with the same particularistic spirit and it was never ratified by Galeazzo and Florence, the latter acting under pressure by Milan.[37] Nevertheless the idea of the *lega universale*, though never realized as a fully operative principle as originally designed, remained a point of reference that appeared constantly in the diplomatic correspondence of the age.

The fall of Negroponte only four days after the confirmation of the triple alliance created a crisis of conscience for European rulers. The religiously correct position dictated cooperation with Venice and other states more directly menaced by Turkish advances in the Balkans. Some rulers chose instead the politically correct stance of letting the Venetians fight alone in the widespread belief that any victory against the infidel would be most advantageous to Venice, as in the past. Others, such as the Florentines and the Genoese, were not reluctant to improve their trading position in the eastern Mediterranean at the expense of Venetian losses.[38]

Most happy was the duke of Milan, who upon hearing the news began to set in motion a series of initiatives to activate his plan for the recovery of the lost cities. In mid-August 1470 he asked his French 'lord' whether next Spring was the proper time to attack Venice and whether Louis XI was willing to restrain Savoy from intervening on the side of Venice, the only aid he required.[39] The king, who only two months earlier had advised his ally to keep the peace and not try to turn the world upside down, gave an exquisitely diplomatic reply. He would be happy to see Galeazzo in possession of the lost territory, but at the present one had to have regard for God and Christianity, which would be in great peril if Venice should be forced to make a deal with the

---

[35] Galeazzo's instructions to his ambassador in Venice, Gerardo de' Colli, Pavia, 10, 11 May 1470, Venezia, cart. 355 and 1314, respectively; see also P.-M. Perret, *Histoire des relations de la France avec Venise du XIIIe siècle a l'avènement de Charles VIII*, 2 vols. (Paris, 1896), vol. 1, 540-47 for other overtures.

[36] Lorenzo, *Lettere*, vol. 1, 163-4, 177-8, n.3.

[37] For the confirmation of the Italian League, see G. Nebbia, 'La lega italica del 1455: sue vicende e sua rinnovazione nel 1470', *Archivio storico lombardo*, new ser., 4 (1939), 115-35, and Lorenzo, *Lettere*, vol. 1, 230-38.

[38] For various reactions, see Setton, *The fifteenth century*, 287-89, and P. Magistretti, 'Galeazzo Maria Sforza e la caduta di Negroponte', *Archivio storico lombardo*, ser. 2, 1 (1884), 79-120, 337-56.

[39] Galeazzo's instructions to Giovanni Arcimboldi, Sagramoro Visconti, and Antonio di Romagnano, on a special mission to the French court, Milan, 16 August 1470; and Galeazzo to Bettini, Cassano, 26 Aug. (two letters of same date), all in Francia, cart. 537.

Turks. If he were to postpone his war, God would then help him in the future to recover what was rightly his in a more 'honest' and better way. Louis could not give immediate aid because he was awaiting the outcome of the Earl of Warwick's invasion of England (9 September). If Warwick dethroned Edward IV and placed Henry VI and his Angvevin queen, Margaret, on the throne, then he would have the strength to defeat Burgundy and make Savoy toe the line. This was his advice, leaving the final decision to Galeazzo's conscience.[40]

A few days earlier Galeazzo had made a more circumspect approach to Ferrante through Cagnola, whose mission was extended indefinitely so that he acquired the status of a resident.[41] The duke charged Cagnola to tell the king that his lord would not make war against Venice without his advice and approval. Then the ambassador was to add his personal view that Galeazzo would not want any aid for the campaign except Ferrante's pledge to stop the Pope from intervening on the side of Venice and to attack him if necessary so that Ferrante could settle his own affairs with the Holy See at the same time.[42] Once again Galeazzo had to be reminded of the utter impropriety of his request made at a time when negotiations were being carried out in Rome for the renewal of the Italian League, for the sake of a united effort against the enemy of Christianity. Should Venice be attacked now, Ferrante countered, she might settle with the Turks in desperation and permit their full fury to be vented against Otranto, only '80 miles' from the Turkish-held coast across the Adriatic. The king recalled once more that at the time of the Colleoni crisis he had offered his aid for the enterprise, believing it to be a good and justified opportunity to make war on Venice, and he was willing to help in the future, but not now. And in transmitting the royal reply, the ambassador advised his master to be more secretive about his moves because the Venetians were fully aware of them.[43] Cagnola added the warning that the king, being more fearful of the Turks than he had been during his war against John of Anjou, wanted Milan's aid against them desperately and if Galeazzo did not supply it, he would ally with Venice and the pope.[44] The ambassador advised that enough aid could be supplied to allow Venice to become exhausted so that she would not pose a threat in Italy; and one could simply cut the aid if she was winning and getting

---

[40] Bettini to Galeazzo, Le Mans, 14 September 1470, Francia, cart. 537.

[41] Galeazzo to Cagnola, Pavia, 19 July 1470, cart. 219: Resta mò che vuy perseverati in far como haveti facto fin qui, perché havemo deliberato che remagnati appresso la Soa M.tà et faciati l'officio del bono et fidele ambaxatore como ne rendiamo certi fareti.

[42] Galeazzo to Cagnola, Monza, 7 August 1470, cart. 219.

[43] Cagnola to Galeazzo, Naples, 23, 26 August 1470, cart. 219; the second dispatch was published by Magistretti, 'Galeazzo Maria Sforza', 113-16.

[44] Cagnola to Cicco Simonetta, Naples, 10 October 1470, cart. 219. Cagnola asked Cicco to ponder with the duke the dilemma that in helping Naples against the Turks Galeazzo would also be helping Venice, but if he refused aid, he would lose the alliance with Ferrante.

stronger.[45] But by this time it had become obvious that hardly anyone trusted Galeazzo's pronouncements; his duplicity and aggressive intentions were generally known, and his fellow rulers drew the proper conclusions about his reliability as an ally or as a statesman who respected treaties.

Ferrante was among the first to undergo a painful reassessment of his options as he came to realize that Galeazzo's anti-Venetian obsession was weakening not only the triple alliance and its possibly helpful connection with the French monarchy, but it had shattered any hope for the renewal of the Italian League and lasting peace. Unable to control his youthful ally, he engaged in a series of initiatives aiming to manage him in such a way as to minimize the damage. These measure in turn infuriated Galeazzo, who countered with initiatives of his own designed to disrupt Ferrante's schemes in every possible way, a sort of cold war leading to intense dislike and even hatred between the two. In brief, from friendly enemies they turned into hostile allies. The diplomatic correspondence is filled with these moves and countermoves, but available space permits only discussion of a few key episodes which illustrate the clouding of political judgment by personal animosity.

On 1 January 1471 Ferrante signed a secret alliance with the new Venetian ambassador, Vittore Soranzo, one that had already been discussed for most of 1470 and which Galeazzo had tried to prevent with his own secret offers to Venice, as noted above. The fifteen-year treaty was primarily directed against the Turks, but it contained separate clauses providing for the defense of their respective states and allies in Italy, a clear allusion to Galeazzo and the Angevins.[46] The alliance also strengthened the close commercial relations between the two states in view of Venice's commercial dominance of Puglia and its ports out of which came much of its food supply.[47] Ferrante made every effort to disclose his growing feud with Galeazzo to Soranzo, and to Zaccaria Barbaro, who came to replace him in November 1471. He told them that he had

---

[45] Cagnola to C. Simonetta, Naples, 25 November 1470, cart. 219. Galeazzo, claiming that he was not bound by the terms of the Italian League of 1455 to give aid unless the Turks attacked the kingdom, vacillated between denials and agreement, without any real intention to finance the struggle against the Turks. Galeazzo to Cagnola, Vigevano, 23 October and Cagnola to Galeazzo, Naples, 3 November 1470, cart. 219.

[46] Doge Cristoforo Moro's instructions to Soranzo, 12-14, 19 October 1470, Venice, Archivio di Stato, Senato Secreta, Reg. 24, f.147v-148v, 150v-52r.

[47] For the diplomatic and commercial background of this alliance, see M. Jacoviello, 'Relazioni politiche tra Venezia e Napoli nella seconda metà del XV secolo (dai documenti dell'Archivio di Stato di Venezia)', *Archivio storico per le province napoletane*, ser. 3, 17 (1978), 67-133; M. Jacoviello, *Venezia e Napoli nel Quattrocento. Rapporti fra i due stati e altri saggi* (Naples, 1992). For Ferrante's economic policy in general, see D. Abulafia, 'The Crown and the economy under Ferrante I of Naples (1458-94)', in *City and Countryside in late medieval and early Renaissance Italy. Studies presented to Philip Jones*, ed. T. Dean and C. Wickham (London, 1990), 125-46, repr. in D. Abulafia, *Commerce and conquest in the Mediterranean, 1100-1500* (Aldershot, 1993), essay 9.

waited '20 years' for this alliance with Venice.[48] He was even more explicit with Giacomo Trotti, the ambassador of Duke Ercole d'Este of Ferrara, a client of Venice, by stating bluntly that the duke of Milan was his 'capital enemy' and that he considered as enemies all of the duke's friends.[49]

Acting on this principle and often in collaboration with King John of Aragon, another fine practitioner of geopolitics, he reached outside Italy to negotiate a web of interlocking alliances encircling Louis XI and his Italian ally, Galeazzo. The alliance with Venice was followed (1 November 1471) by one with Charles of Burgundy, at whose court he had maintained ambassadors from around 1468 to keep him informed on French and English affairs. He also kept an ambassador at the English court, Garcia Betes, for several years from about 1469, but no formal treaty of alliance was signed with England.[50] Additionally, Ferrante benefited also from the alliance system built by his uncle in Aragon; namely, Aragon and England (October 1468); Aragon and Burgundy (February 1469); and Burgundy, Aragon, and Castile (August 1471). In the last treaty Naples was formally included as an ally of both Burgundy and of Aragon and Castile.[51] And finally Ferrante settled his feud with the Holy See over the non-payment of the yearly tribute. The new Pope, Sixtus IV, renounced the payment of the tribute during Ferrante's lifetime as well as the payment of the arrears, requiring only the symbolic white horse (March 1472).[52]

---

[48] Soranzo and Barbaro to the Doge, Naples, 1 November 1471, Venice, Biblioteca Nazionale Marciana, It. VII, Cod. 398 (8170): *Dispacci di Zaccaria Barbaro, ambasciatore a Napoli, inviati alla Signoria veneta dal 1 novembre 1471 al 7 settembre 1473*, f.1a-b (pagination bears same numbers on facing pages; henceforth cited: Cod. 398). This copybook represents one of the very few sets of Venetian ambassadorial dispatches that have survived for the fifteenth century, and serves to balance the reports of the Milanese ambassadors. Barbaro received his instructions on 7 October 1471: ASV, Senato Secreta, Reg. 25, f. 63v-64v.

[49] Trotti reported to Barbaro the very words used by Ferrante: 'ch'el Ducha de Milano era suo capital inimico et che non solo Sua M.tà non lo amava, ma era inimico di tuti quelli a cui el Ducha de Milano volea bene'. Barbaro to the Doge, Naples, 5 November 1471, Cod. 398, f.4b.

[50] For Charles the Bold's Italian policy, the most detailed treatment based on archival sources is now an unpublished doctoral dissertation: R. Walsh, 'Charles the Bold, last Valois duke of Burgundy 1467-1477, and Italy', (University of Hull, 1977), 3-338, 413-57. Some of his conclusions are in his article: 'Relations between Milan and Burgundy in the period 1450-1476', in *Gli Sforza a Milano e in Lombardia e i loro rapporti con gli Stati italiani ed europei (1450-1535)* (Milan, 1982), 369-94. More accessible and still useful, however, is E. Dürr, 'Galeazzo Maria Sforza und seine Stellung zu den Burgunderkriegen. Eine Untersuchung über die südfranzösisch-italiänische Politik Karls der Kühnen', *Basler Zeitschrift für Geschichte und Altertumskunde*, 10 (1911), 259-414.

[51] A synthetic, rapid sketch of John II's diplomatic counteroffensive against Louis XI is provided by J. Vicens y Vives, 'La politique européenne du royaume d'Aragon-Catalogne sous Jean II (1458-1479)', *Annales du midi*, 65 (1953), 405-14. For details, see two of his books: *Fernando el Catolico, principe de Aragón, rey de Sicilia 1458-1478* (Madrid, 1952), especially 303-26; and *Juan II de Aragón (1398-1479): Monarquia y revolucion en la España del siglo XV* (Barcelona, 1953), 297-371.

[52] Maletta to Galeazzo, Naples, 6 March 1472, cart. 221. Cf. Pastor, *Storia*, vol. 2, 464-5.

These stunning diplomatic successes for the Aragonese cause everywhere left Galeazzo with the heavy task of mounting an offensive of his own in an effort to recover momentum and prestige. In March 1471 he paid a splendid state visit to Florence, seeking to dazzle the Florentines with his retinue of more than a thousand persons and hold his younger ally, Lorenzo, more firmly in his camp. Lorenzo, still insecure in his position during his early years in power and very concerned over the growing feud of his allies, redoubled his efforts as a mediator while the anti-Milanese faction in Florence played on the republican sensibilities shaken by such extravagant display of wealth partly created by Florentine money.[53] At the same time, Galeazzo continued throughout the year to send feelers for an alliance to Venice while assuring Ferrante that he was continually pestered by Venice for such an alliance.[54] He also consulted his lawyers on whether Ferrante was bound to help Venice in case of a Milanese attack if his treaty with the republic contained a clause reserving the triple alliance.[55] And in Naples he instructed Cagnola to overcome his gentle nature and confront Ferrante most vigorously now and in the future so that his lord's *humanità* and reverence towards the king would not be misconstrued as an admission of royal superiority or control. Above all he should find out whether Naples was obligated to defend Venice if Galeazzo were to attack her, warning of severe consequences if such a promise was made. The ambassador was to remind the king again of the benefits received from Francesco Sforza, which could not be repaid by pretending that he could be a friend of both Venice and Milan.[56] All the while Cagnola was to observe attentively the king's expression so as to gauge his true feelings, a difficult task with a ruler like Ferrante, who was a master at hiding his emotions.[57]

Although an experienced diplomat, Cagnola was by training a scholarly lawyer (doctor of both laws) and a skillful negotiator used from the beginning of Francesco's reign for negotiating and drafting treaties and adjudicating fiscal

---

[53] For Galeazzo's visit, see now R. Fubini, 'La visita a Firenze del duca di Milano nel 1471', in *Lorenzo de' Medici. Studi*, ed. Gian Carlo Garfagnini (Florence, 1992), 167-77, and Lubkin, *A Renaissance court*, 98-100. For Lorenzo's position in his early years, see G. Soranzo, 'Lorenzo il Magnifico alla morte del padre e il suo primo balzo verso la Signoria', *Archivio storico italiano*, 111 (1953), 42-77.

[54] For the feelers, see Gerardo de' Colli to Galeazzo, Venice, 30 July, 21 August, 1471, and Galeazzo to Colli, Guastalla, 10 August, and Cremona, 16 August 1471, Venezia, cart. 356. Galeazzo's denials: Galeazzo to Cagnola, Vigevano, 15 November 1470, cart. 219.

[55] Galeazzo to Odoardo de Corte and Gironimo Torto, Pavia, 13 December 1470, cart. 219.

[56] Galeazzo to Cagnola, Milan, 21 December 1470, cart. 219. As these instructions show, Galeazzo already was informed of the impending alliance between Naples and Venice and throughout its duration remained fearful of the secret clauses it might contain.

[57] On at least two occasions, Cagnola remarked on this trait of Ferrante's personality: 'questo Sig.re [Ferrante] per li parlari soy non sempre exprime ciò ha in mente' (Naples, 27 March 1471); 'é sua natura de non fare may tropo demostratione né de letici né de tristicia che li achadeno' (Naples, 31 July 1471), both in cart. 220.

disputes and border controversies.[58]   It is clear that he did not have the personality to bait Ferrante into making unguarded remarks which would reveal his intimate feelings.   Galeazzo had sensed this from the beginning of his mission, because in May 1470 Cicco Simonetta, his chief secretary, had instructed Cagnola to allow Cavalchino Guidoboni, a royal secretary, to use his cipher and couriers for secret and direct communications with Milan, especially in matters relating to Ferrante's intentions.[59]   From this time onwards Cavalchino provided confidential information directly or through Cagnola. Son of the late Antonio Guidoboni (d. 1467), former Milanese ambassador in Venice and secretary of the ducal Secret Council, Cavalchino had entered Ferrante's service around 1463 with the consent of both Francesco and later Galeazzo.[60] Claiming that he was loyal to Naples as well as Milan, he was rewarded by Galeazzo with the return of three castles confiscated for some alleged misdeed of his father.[61] Using Cicco as the intermediary, he warned that the duke had lost credibility by his numerous approaches to Venice, his intemperate remarks, and his hasty actions without much deliberation, all in marked contrast with Ferrante's practice. He believed that Ferrante's relations with Venice were such that he would defend the republic against any attack, and advised that Galeazzo should not further provoke the king and rely on the triple alliance for his security. Sensible advice which was not taken: by October 1471 Guidoboni had lost hope that a reconciliation was possible and decided to hasten his return home for health reasons, but also because he did not wish to be caught in the middle of the struggle. Remarkably frankly, he openly blamed Galeazzo for the rupture, which allowed friends of Venice at court, such as the influential councillors, Diomede Carafa, count of Maddaloni, and Orso Orsini, duke of Ascoli, to fan the flames of discord.[62] In essence Guidoboni functioned more as

---

[58] For a detailed biographical sketch of Cagnola, see F. Petrucci in *DBI*, 16 (1973), 312-14.

[59] Cicco to Cagnola, Pavia, 16 May 1470, and Cagnola to Cicco, Naples, 1 June 1470, cart. 218.

[60] Guidoboni to Galeazzo, Naples, 18 June 1471, cart. 220. In this letter he wrote that he had been in Ferrante's service for eight years and he was approaching forty. Claiming to be delicate in physique and suffering from headaches because of the bad air in Naples, and wanting to be close to his young wife, he also announced his decision to follow his doctors' advice and return to his native climate in Lombardy, for which he wanted the consent of the duke. On Antonio Guidoboni and his family, see Leverotti, *Diplomazia*, 185-9.

[61] The castles (Sarzano, Castellaro, Vulpiglino) were restored partly through the intercession of Ferrante, who called Cavalchino 'nobile et egregio, nostro secretario' in a very strong letter of recommendation to Galeazzo (Naples, 27 August 1470, cart. 219). Galeazzo took this action after he gave a written account of the *inganno* perpetrated by Antonio against him to the Neapolitan ambassador in Milan, Turco Cicinello (Galeazzo to Ferrante, Parma, 20 September 1470, cart. 219). See also Cavalchino to Galeazzo, Naples, 1 October 1470, cart. 219.

[62] 'El S. nostro [Galeazzo] al vero ha dato molte cause de la ruptura de questa amicicia': Guidoboni to Cicco, Naples, 1 August and 15 October 1471, cart. 220. The quotation is in the second dispatch.

a convenient second channel of communication than as a simple informer because the king offered to promote him and increase his salary if reconciliation were to take place.[63] But his activity aroused the suspicion of Zaccaria Barbaro, who warned the Council of Ten that Cavalchino corresponded frequently with the Neapolitan ambassador at Venice, Angelo d'Atri.[64]

Guidoboni's pessimism about the chances for reconciliation was shared by Cagnola. Both confided to Cicco that Galeazzo's bizarre behavior had made him the butt of ridicule at the Neapolitan court. He was derided for being all talk and no action, a coward who would not dare attack Venice if the king opposed him or, as the count of Maddaloni put it: he would not dare to enter Bergamo and Brescia even if their gates were left open.[65] When news reached Naples in September 1471 that Galeazzo had challenged Colleoni to personal combat, it caused much laughter that two crazy persons, a young and an old one, were going to fight each other.[66] But Ferrante took the matter seriously believing that it could disturb the peace and that it might hide a secret deal between Colleoni and Galeazzo with the former taking Bergamo and Brescia in the process. He appealed to Galeazzo directly that for the sake of his own honour and dignity, and the 'good of Italy' (*bene universale de Italia*), the duke should refrain from fighting and put state interests above private rancours.[67] This is not the first time that Ferrante mentioned the overriding aspects of state interests over private passions in the conduct of foreign policy, which is the mark of a first-rate statesman. Whether his views were conditioned by the counsel of Diomede Carafa, who at this time was writing his treatise later entitled *I doveri del principe* is not known. But the diplomatic correspondence of the age has numerous expressions of political/diplomatic realism by such

---

[63] Guidoboni to Cicco, Naples, 12 October 1471, cart. 220.

[64] Barbaro to the Consiglio X, Naples, 11 November 1471, cod. 398, f. 8a-9b: 'per ogni fante viene da Venezia ha lettere dal M.co Angelo d'Atri, ambassador regio, et costui [Cavalchino] mai dal ambassador del Ducha de Milano se parte di caxa'.

[65] Cagnola to Cicco, Naples, 15 October 1471, cart. 220: 's'el Sig.re [Galeazzo] vedesse aperte le porte de Bergomo et de Bressa, che non haviria ardire de intrarli'. Cagnola, much embarrassed by these and other remarks at court, which he refrained from mentioning with the excuse that perhaps their reporting was not part of his office, left it to Cicco to inform the duke or not as he saw fit.

[66] Cavalchino had seen a letter of Angelo d'Atri in which the ambassador was instructed by the Doge to convey the news of the challenge to Ferrante, 'a ciò possa ridere de dui pazi, uno jovene et uno vechio'. He continued that at court there was much surprise that the duke wanted to fight a *vechio pazo*. Cavalchino to Cicco, 8 September 1471, cart. 220.

[67] Ferrante to Galeazzo, Aversa, 10 Sept. 1471, cart. 220: 'perché li interessi publici se vogliono preponere a li privati'. Ferrante's expressed his suspicion about a secret collusion between Galeazzo and Colleoni to Barbaro, who assured him that Colleoni was faithful to Venice and that Galeazzo was simply making trouble so that the republic would spend money for troops. Barbaro to the Doge, Naples, 8 November 1471, Cod. 398, f. 6a-7b.

princes as Francesco Sforza and Louis XI, to cite but two contemporary examples, years before Machiavelli put quill to paper.[68] Whether Cicco had the daring to inform his lord of the above derisive remarks is not known, but Galeazzo had already decided by October that Cagnola was too gentle to deal with the Neapolitan court. Without prior notification, Cagnola was recalled and rewarded with a membership in the ducal *Consiglio di Giustizia* as a consolation prize.[69] Ferrante, who liked his style and knew that he was forced to deliver the nasty messages as instructed by Galeazzo, gave him a horse and a gold chain worth two hundred ducats at his departure on 24 November 1471.[70] Apparently he was a man of few words and his dispatches lack the vivid details that often characterized the dispatches of other ambassadors, a practice generally required by rulers.

Cagnola's recall was considered a bad omen at court particularly because his replacement, Francesco Maletta, had the reputation of being contentious and confrontational.[71] Maletta, an experienced administrator and diplomat serving from the first months of the Sforza regime, turned out to be in fact a zealous, astute, and more aggressive promoter of his master's interests.[72] Unlike

---

[68] The political realism at the Neapolitan court has recently been highlighted by Bentley, *Politics and culture,* especially 138-94.

[69] Cavalchino notified Cagnola of his recall, the news having been communicated from Milan by Turco Cicinello and was already known in Florence and Rome as well: Cavalchino to Cicco, Naples, 10 November 1471, cart. 220. Cicinello had also written that Galeazzo did not want Cavalchino to reside in the duchy, but at the royal court this was interpreted as a fiction to cover the services Cavalchino had performed for Galeazzo. For Cagnola's appointment to the Consiglio di Giustizia: Cagnola to Galeazzo, Naples, 20 November 1471, cart. 220.

[70] For the gifts: Francesco Maletta to Galeazzo, Naples, 23 November 1471, cart. 220. Ferrante gave his estimate of Cagnola to the Venetian ambassador as follows: costui é homo che sente bene et voria quiete et pace, ma conviene alguna volta dir quello vuole el S.or suo. (Barbaro to the Doge, Naples, 17 November 1471, Cod. 398, f. 13a-b).

[71] In communicating the court's reaction, Cavalchino also praised highly the work done by Cagnola: 'perché credano che el nostro Ill.mo Signore remova misser Giovanni Andrea per essere più queto et per mandare homo più animoso et de cativa natura; che in vero misser Giovanni Andrea cum destro modo né mancato de far el debito suo et se é conservato in bona opinione per potere melio cavare et fare el facto del nostro Signore. Et Soa Signoria ha habuta bona advertentia de non far mai demonstratione che habia scripto cose de mala natura, che é stato ben facto, perché li ambassatori sempre se volano tenire in bona opinione de quelli apresso a cui stano. (Cavalchino to Cicco, Naples, 10 November 1471, cart. 220). It is also interesting that a known Milanese agent in Naples, Broccardo Persico, gave this estimate of Maletta to the Venetian ambassador, emphasizing his anti-Venetian bias: homo astuto et scandaloso, più tosto apto ad far male che bene, perché el Ducha et fiorentini ve sono aperti inimici. [Broccardo] era presenti quanto uxò al Re [Ferrante] queste parole: 'Vostra M.tà doveria esser contenta questi venetiani, quali tengono el bastone suo in capo a ognuno cum la superbia et modi loro, a questo tempo apto et comodo a poterlo fare fusseno smachati per liberare Italia da questa servitù'. Barbaro to the Doge, Naples, 16 November 1471, Cod. 398, f. 12a-12b. Barbaro rightly discounted much of this information, knowing the character of the source.

[72] For Maletta's career, see Cerioni, *La diplomazia,* 1, 191, and Leverotti, *Diplomazia,* 199-201.

Cagnola, whose fact-oriented lawyer's style was evident in his dry dispatches, Maletta's vivid reports satisfied Galeazzo's crave for minutest details to the point of reporting on a choice of one of Ferrante's mistresses and on the bisexuality of the heir to the throne.[73]

Maletta's task was eased enormously by the ready cooperation of two persons with access to secret information, Duchess Ippolita Sforza of Calabria and Count Broccardo Persico. Under a scheme devised by Ippolita, Maletta was to keep her informed about Milanese affairs and under this guise she would divulge Neapolitan secrets gathered from her own sources and especially from Persico, who saw much of the secret correspondence reaching the royal court.[74] And until his return to Milan in August 1472, Guidoboni still acted as an informer though no longer working in the royal chancery.[75] With this superb access to confidential information, Galeazzo had prior knowledge of royal plans and negotiating positions. It is not clear, however, how far the king was aware of this nest of spies in his midst and if he used them for his own purposes as he had done with Guidoboni.

Ippolita's motives in jeopardizing royal interests, and her own as a future queen, are difficult to establish unless one takes at face value all her numerous expressions of devotion to her brother, whose character she knew better than anyone else, having been educated by the same tutors.[76] Her actions require

---

[73] Maletta to Galeazzo, Naples, 3 July 1472, cart. 222. In this long dispatch he described the taking of the tearful Giovannella, young daughter of Count Giacomo Caracciolo, Grand Chancellor of Naples, by Alfonso and Federico to convey to their father's quarters in Castel Novo all with the consent of her father, who was properly rewarded. Alfonso's bisexuality is revealed by Maletta in a later dispatch (Naples, 2 November 1473, cart. 225), in which he reported that Alfonso was ill and though he could moderate his diet, 'he non se può continere dal cohito, tanto feminile quanto masculo'. It is noteworthy that this information was given to Maletta by Francesco Galeota, soldier, poet, and intimate courtier of Alfonso but also a Milanese informer. On Galeota's career, see *Regis Ferdinandi Primi, Instructionum liber (10 maggio 1486-10 maggio 1488)*, ed. Luigi Volpicella (Naples, 1916), 338-39.

[74] Maletta to Galeazzo, Naples, 30, 31 December 1471, both misdated 1472 and misfiled in cart. 223.

[75] By December 1471, Guidoboni had been deprived of his office and Ippolita and Maletta asked Galeazzo to allow him to repatriate and compensate him because he was no longer useful as an informer. He would be more useful, they pointed out, as adviser on Neapolitan affairs in Milan: Maletta and Ippolita, Naples, 19 December 1471, cart. 220. But he continued to cultivate his contacts at court through the Spring of 1472, offering some valuable advice, and finally returned to Milan on 1 August: Galeazzo to Maletta, Gonzaga, 1 August 1472, cart. 222.

[76] Her devotion to her brother seems to have been genuine, according to Lubkin, *A Renaissance court*, 42: 'In all the world, the person who looked on Galeazzo most fondly was probably his sister Ippolita.' For Ippolita's education, her love of the classics and her fondness for jewelry, see, as well as the study *infra* by Evelyn Welch, A. Cutolo, 'La giovinezza di Ippolita Sforza, duchessa di Calabria', *Archivio storico per le province napoletane*, new ser., 34 (1955), 119-33, and A.M. Cesari, 'Un'orazione inedita di Ippolita Sforza e alcune lettere di Galeazzo Sforza', *Archivio storico lombardo*, new ser., 4 (1964-65), 50-64. Additional information about her can also be found in *Regis Ferdinandi Primi*, 443-4.

further investigation; for now the most likely motive seems to have been a deep resentment over the meagre pension accorded to her by Ferrante, contrary to her expectations as a princess coming from a more luxurious court, and over her abusive treatment by a husband noted for his coarseness, violent temper, and numerous extramarital affairs.[77]   Secret resentment may also have motivated Persico, who had been treacherously imprisoned by Ferrante together with Piccinino in 1465, freed in 1471, and then was appointed a royal secretary, probably in recognition of his earlier services for king Alfonso. He was a rather successful survivor with divided loyalties, having been at first a leader of the *Bracceschi* and adviser of Piccinino, and later (1464) a member of Francesco Sforza's Secret Council.[78]   Maletta thought he was trustworthy, devoted to Galeazzo, and that his information was so valuable that it could gain his lord a 'state.'[79]

The value of confidential information from the royal court became dramatically evident during the negotiations for the dissolution of the marriage of Eleonora and Sforza Maria, to be replaced by a new marriage between the eighteen-month daughter of Ippolita, Isabella, and Galeazzo's first-born, the three-year old Gian Galeazzo. The dissolution of the first marriage, contracted in 1455 and never consummated, was convenient to both.[80]   Galeazzo did not wish to give a city in appanage to his brother as the contract required, and Ferrante was particularly eager that his first-born legitimate daughter be a reigning princess by marrying Duke Ercole of Ferrara. Knowing the king's

---

[77] In thanking Galeazzo for his gift of four thousand gold ducats, whose generosity amazed the court, Ippolita confided that she was in such a great necessity that she had considered selling her jewels: Ippolita to Galeazzo, Castello Capuano, 19 February 1471, cart. 220. At the end of that year, she complained that Ferrante had broken his promise to Galeazzo to provide adequately for her since the birth of her two children: Maletta to Galeazzo, Naples, 19 December 1471, cart. 220. In an undated memorandum (probably July 1472, cart. 1248), given to Guidoboni as he was leaving for Milan, both Ippolita and Maletta requested a number of concessions for themselves and others as rewards for their services to Galeazzo, with Ippolita emphasizing adequate provision for herself. For a brief sketch of Alfonso's career and his crude and immoderately lascivious character, see *Regis Ferdinandi Primi*, 225-28. On the other hand, the daughter of Francesco and sister of Galeazzo Sforza could hardly have been shocked by extra-marital affairs, though she might have resented being the victim of them.

[78] For brief biographical sketches of Persico, see E. Lazzeroni, 'Il Consiglio Segreto o Senato Sforzesco', *Atti e memorie del terzo congresso storico lombardo* (Milan, 1939), 125, n.193, and Cerioni, *La diplomazia*, 207.

[79] In recommending the most generous rewards for Persico's extraordinary services, both Ippolita and Maletta advised Galeazzo to compensate his father, who had been forced to sell his possessions at Cremona in order to free his son from Ferrante's prison. Referring to the value of Persico's inside information, Maletta added: ogni aviso suo ve poterà guadagnare uno stato. Maletta to Galeazzo, Naples, 10 May 1472, cart. 222. It is amazing that Persico apparently remained in Ferrante's service until the end of his life, probably in 1491.

[80] The circumstances surrounding the dissolution of this marriage have been amply treated by N. Ferorelli, 'Il ducato di Bari sotto Sforza Maria Sforza e Ludovico il Moro', *Archivio storico lombardo*, ser. 5, 41 (1914), 389-433.

eagerness, Galeazzo tried to take advantage of it by insisting that the prospective bride should reside at his court by the age of three, hoping thus to make sure that Ferrante would respect the contract, suspecting that at the same time Ferrante was offering Isabella in marriage to the seven-year-old duke Filiberto of Savoy.[81] He also requested once more aid or at least Ferrante's neutrality for his ever projected war against Venice.[82]

The tense negotiations gave rise to mutual recriminations over past disagreements and to threats, in the course of which Ferrante let down his customary reserve, and angrily threatened the most serious reprisals if Galeazzo did not change course, especially with respect to his continued support of the rebels in Barcelona. The king again recalled his debt of gratitude to Francesco Sforza, which he had tried to repay in so many ways, including the elimination of the troublesome condottiere, Jacopo Piccinino, who could have threatened Galeazzo's own succession: an ambiguous admission that Piccinino's death in a Neapolitan prison in 1465 was less accidental than it had been portrayed.[83] This outburst, probably calculated, astonished Maletta and produced a compromise agreement, hammered out by the ambassador together with Ippolita, the count of Maddaloni, and other trusted advisers eager to avoid a rupture.[84] It was signed in absolute secrecy on 14 July 1472 and included a pledge by Galeazzo not to aid the rebels in Barcelona, while Ferrante bound himself by oath not to aid Venice with more than 4,000 horse and 2,000 foot if attacked by Milan during the term of the Italian League, and to aid Milan with the same number of troops after expiration of the League in 1480. Sforza Maria was allowed to keep the duchy of Bari. This agreement re-established temporarily the so-called

---

[81] On the progress of the negotiations and the shifting positions taken by Galeazzo, see especially: Instructions by Galeazzo to Turco Cicinello (Neapolitan ambassador in Milan) and Giovanni Andrea Cagnola, Pavia, 23 February 1472; Galeazzo to T. Cicinello and Cagnola, Vigevano, 21 March 1472; Maletta to Galeazzo, Naples, 31 March, 4 April 1472; Galeazzo to T. Cicinello, Cagnola, and Maletta, Milan, 11 April 1472; Cagnola, T. Cicinello, Maletta to Galeazzo, Naples, 19 April, all in cart. 221; Maletta to Galeazzo, Naples, 7 May 1472, cart. 222. For Ferrante's approach to the duchess of Savoy: Galeazzo to Maletta, Pavia, 23 May 1472, cart. 222.

[82] Galeazzo to Maletta, Pavia, 3 June 1472, cart. 222.

[83] Maletta to Galeazzo, Naples, 4 June 1472, cart. 222. In reference to Piccinino, Maletta quoted Ferrante as follows: Io levay de mezo dicto Conte et assecuray el Stato ad esso Duca Galeaz. Luy fa el contrario de quello che ha facto el patre per mi et de quello che io ho facto per luy; et sempre é stato atento, se l'é accaduta alcuna cosa che m'habi poduto nocere et darme nel cuore, l'ha facto gagliardamente. Ferrante spoke 'cum colera et turbatione assay'. Maletta added that although the king 'sia uno S. che molto cella et governa bene le passione sue, nondimeno ad questa volta s'é pur scoperto tuto et ne le resposte sue s'é portato molto colericamente et impatientemente'. For the controversial death of Piccinino and the respective roles of Ferrante and F. Sforza and related bibliography, see F. Forte, 'Atti del processo contro Jacopo Piccinino (1465)', in *Miscellanea di studi di storia in onore di A. Luzio*, 2 vols (Florence, 1933), vol. 1, 375-411.

[84] Maletta to Galeazzo, Naples, 16 June 1472 and Galeazzo to Maletta, Pavia, 20, 25, 26 June 1472, all in cart. 222.

father-son relationship; and Ferrante, in a euphoric mood after the signing, charged Maletta to write to his lord that from that day Galeazzo could rest assured that he would donate Brescia, Bergamo and Crema to him.[85]

It was an unwise promise that Galeazzo at first thought to exploit immediately, counting on his recently reorganized army; but he decided to postpone operations out of deference for Ferrante's own fears of the Turkish threat.[86] Such unusual acquiescence on the part of the duke may have been caused by other factors, including the steady deterioration of his relations with Louis XI for most of 1472, over the contested control of the government in Savoy between duchess Yolande (supported by Milan) and her brother-in-law, Philip (backed by France), royal demands for aid against Burgundy and Aragon, and Galeazzo's growing impatience with the heavy hand of French tutelage. At the end of July the Milanese ambassador, Sforza Bettini, had been dismissed by Louis, who openly admitted that he and Ferrante had been discussing an alliance and that he had in mind to propose a double marriage: the dauphin with Isabella, daughter of duke Alfonso and her brother, Ferdinand, with the king's daughter, Anne. Adding more pressure, Louis declared to the startled ambassador that Ferrante was Galeazzo's 'mortal enemy' and predicted an early rupture between the two.[87] Far more alarming, however, was Ferrante's revelation that at the end of 1471 Louis was so irritated with Galeazzo and so anxious for peace with Burgundy, that he had offered all sorts of concessions to Charles the Bold including the duchy of Milan with Genoa and Savona, to be conquered with royal help.[88] In the end, the duke was able to buy back Louis' tolerance, but not

---

[85] Maletta to Galeazzo, Naples, 14 July 1472, cart. 222: scrive al S. Duca che io cum grande amore et sincerità sonno venuto ad queste conclusione et che in questo giorno tenga per fermo ch'io gli dono Bressa, Bergamo et Crema.

[86] Galeazzo to Ferrante, Fontaneto, 23 November 1472 (*manu propria*), and Galeazzo to Antonio Cicinello (Neapolitan ambassador in Milan), [Milan], 3 January 1473, both in cart. 223.

[87] Sforza Bettini to Galeazzo, Segré, 15 July 1472, ASMi, Francia, cart. 539: con dire più volte ch'el Re Ferrando vi voleva male di morte, né dubitava punto che fra voi sequiria quistione del tutto... mi certificava ch'el Re Ferrando ve era inimico mortale. The emissary for these negotiations between Louis and Ferrante was Tommaso Taquino or Tacchini, a former Florentine merchant and one of Ferrante's advisers, acting secretely also with some support from Lorenzo de' Medici. See Maletta to Galeazzo, Naples, 1 October 1472, and Galeazzo to Maletta, Galliate, 8 October, Monza, 16 October, and Robbio, 5 November 1472, all in cart. 223.

[88] Maletta to Galeazzo, Naples, 6 November 1472, cart. 223. This secret was contained in a lost dispatch of 2 January 1472 by Ferrante's ambassador in Burgundy, Francesco Bertini, bishop of Capaccio, who was informed of this offer by Charles himself. Ferrante, without informing Galeazzo, notified Charles that he was bound to defend Milan if attacked, adding: che loro signori ultramontani se levano de mente che potentati de Italia vogliano patire essi vengano ad aquistare palmo de terreno in Italia. Shaken by this revelation, and having ascertained in the king's register that Ferrante had actualy made this reply, Maletta thanked him *cum le zenochia ad terra*, which in turn earned him a stern rebuke from his lord - he should not have placed faith in such false reports and above all no Milanese ambassador

his trust, with a gift of 50,000 ducats, which also led to the renewal of their alliance and of the infeudation of Genoa and Savona, (16 January 1473).[89] Clearly in this world of intrigue and counter intrigue, Galeazzo could not trust either Charles or Louis, and he could not risk a probable two-front war with Venice. He was also now fully aware that Ferrante was determined to settle the Angevin claims with a deal with Louis XI and take away from Milan its most powerful advantage. It was time for a reassessment of foreign policy by all the leading players, a reassement that led to a reversal of the alliance system in the next two years.

The catalyst for that reversal was the disputed succession in the kingdom of Cyprus, an island nominally under the suzerainty of the sultan of Egypt, but long contested by Venetian and Genoese merchants, with some competition by Neapolitan and Catalan traders for its rich exports of sugar, salt, and cotton. At the death of king John II of Lusignan (1458), he was succeeded by his daughter, Charlotte, wife since 1459 of Lodovico of Savoy, count of Geneva. Two years later, Charlotte was dethroned by John's illegitimate son, James, who assumed the title of king of Jerusalem, Cyprus, and Armenia as James II. He banished the Genoese and placed himself under Venetian protection with his marriage (1468) to Caterina Corner, member of a family that had long dominated the economy of the island. Seeking to balance Venetian tutelage with Neapolitan/Catalan power, the insecure king a few months before his death (6 July 1473) agreed to a marriage alliance with Ferrante with rights of succession: his illegitimate five-year-old daughter, Charla, was to marry one of Ferrante's illegitimate sons, the eleven-year-old Alfonso. But the posthumous birth (28 August) of James II's son and designated successor, who died barely a year later, frustrated and then encouraged Ferrante's plans. In the process there ensued a cascade of claims and counterclaims that would challenge the brains of a doctor of both laws, especially when other claims by Galeazzo are considered.[90]

The duke of Milan, who at first had encouraged Ferrante to press his claims so as to foment discord between Venice and Naples, decided to accept the invitation of one of the Cypriot factions and claim the throne for himself. After all he was lord of the Genoese, who had been banished from the island, and through his wife, Bona of Savoy, brother-in-law of the dispossessed,

---

should kneel before other rulers. Galeazzo to Maletta, Galliate, 28 November 1472, and Maletta's reply, Naples, 9 December 1472, both in cart. 223.

[89] For the circumstances surrounding Bettini's dismissal, see *Dispatches*, 3, xix-xxi.

[90] The struggle between Venice and Ferrante for the control of the island is now succinctly summarized by M. Jacoviello, 'L'ingerenza di Ferrante d'Aragona nella devoluzione di Cipro e l'opposizione di Venezia (1473-1489)', *Archivio storico per le province napoletane*, ser. 3, 20 (1981), 177-92, repr. in M. Jacoviello, *Venezia e Napoli*.

legitimate king and queen of Cyprus.[91] It is not clear how serious Galeazzo was in this matter, but we do know that he had royal ambitions in wanting to be appointed king of Lombardy by the emperor.[92] The rule of a rich island in the Aegean with a long royal title would certainly have satisfied his vanity and his secret craving of surpassing his father.

The Neapolitan-Venetian struggle for the control of Cyprus, often bloody, which ended with the outright annexation of the island by Venice in 1489, gave Galeazzo another opportunity to dominate the diplomatic game in Italy. On his western frontier, the duke watched closely the playing out of the duel between France and Burgundy, keeping friendly relations with both, so as to be ready to join the winning side. In the east the time had come once and for all to press Ferrante for aid in his recovery of the claimed territory, and if he refused, to secure that border through an alliance with Venice, and in the process to punish and isolate the king. He decided to pursue both objectives at the same time. In November 1473 he sent Leonardo Botta to re-establish his embassy in Venice and blame Ferrante for past bad relations between the republic and the duchy.[93]

Galeazzo's approaches to Venice provoked another serious crisis in the father-son relationship, and generated fears of a permanent rupture until the intervention of the duke of Urbino led to another secret agreement buttressed by appropriate oaths (September 1474). The agreement stipulated mutual aid in case Ferrante and Galeazzo attacked Venice to recover Cyprus and the claimed Lombard cities respectively. Counting on victory, Don Francesco (Ferrante's illegitimate son) was to be given Venetian territory on the *terraferma* east of Brescia and marry Bianca, Galeazzo's only legitimate daughter, while Antonio, illegitimate son of the count of Urbino, was to marry Chiara, illegitimate daughter of Galeazzo, and be given Colleoni's territorial possessions, plus Bergamo to be held in a feudal tie to the duke. Significantly, the agreement also generated a promise by Ferrante to increase the pension for Ippolita and promote better relations with her husband.[94] This anti-Venetian compact was

---

[91] See P. Ghinzoni, 'Galeazzo Maria Sforza e il regno di Cipro, 1473-1474', *Archivio storico lombardo*, 6 (1879), 721-45, who published several relevant dispatches by Maletta.

[92] For Galeazzo's royal aspirations and Ferrante's secret plans to impede them, see A. Cicinello to Ferrante, Milan, 27 April 1474 and Maletta to Galeazzo, Naples, 28 May 1474, both in cart. 225. This aspect of Galeazzo's ambition has been fully documented by F. Cusin, 'I rapporti tra la Lombardia e l'Impero dalla morte di Francesco Sforza all'avvento di Lodovico il Moro (1466-1480)', *Annali della R. Università degli Studi economici e commerciali di Trieste*, 6 (1934), 246-309.

[93] Galeazzo to Botta, Pavia, 29 October 1473, ASMi, Venezia, cart. 357. Ferrante was fully aware of these intrigues: Maletta to Galeazzo, Naples, 2 March 1474, and Ferrante to A. Cicinello, Naples, 21 May 1474, cart. 525.

[94] For the negotiation of this complex agreement and other details about its provisions, see Maletta to Galeazzo, Naples, 3, 5, 6, 22, 24, 30 August, and Casale del Principe, 16 September 1474 (text of Ferrante's oath); Galeazzo to Maletta, Milan, 9, 14 August, and Villanova, 3 September 1474, all in cart. 226. The influential role of the duke of Urbino at Ferrante's court has been treated most recently by C.H. Clough, 'Federico da Montefeltro and

then buttressed by a marriage alliance with King Matthias Corvinus of Hungary, whose marriage to Ferrante's daughter, Beatrice, was concluded in the same month.[95]

The rupture, however, was only postponed for less than a month after the oaths had been exchanged. In October the duke notified his ally that negotiations by Florence and Milan for an alliance with Venice were in the final stages and he could no longer stop the Florentines, who were angered by Neapolitan support of the Pope against their client, Niccolò Vitelli, in the contest for control of Città di Castello.[96] But Galeazzo explained that such an alliance, together with another contemplated attempt to confirm the Italian League, would actually serve as a screen for their secret agreement, which could be activated at the will of the king even as the terms of the alliance were being agreed upon and the treaty signed on 2 November 1474![97] Ferrante, who had discounted the possibility of such an alignment of arch enemies, reacted with anger, realizing that Lorenzo and Galeazzo had made a pact with the devil against their own interests in order to exact revenge.[98] The rupture was now complete and final, with either side blaming the other over past broken promises and secret intrigues, and vowing never to trust each other again.[99] Laying the blame entirely on the king, Galeazzo freely boasted that he had caused no end of troubles for Naples, especially the loss of Cyprus, being willing even to become

---

the kings of Naples: a study in fifteenth-century survival', *Renaissance studies*, 6 (1992), 129-63. Clough, however, does not mention this secret agreement.

[95] Maletta to Galeazzo, Naples, 4 September 1474, cart. 226.

[96] Galeazzo to Maletta, Pavia, 30 September, 1 October 1474, cart. 226. Anti-Lorenzo feelings continued to run high at the Neapolitan court, encouraged by the duke of Urbino, who repeatedly advised Ferrante to plot with Lorenzo's many enemies for his expulsion or murder: cazarlo de Fiorenza o farlo tagliare a peze (Maletta to Galeazzo, Naples, 8 July 1475, cart. 227 and earlier, Naples, 21 October 1474, cart. 226). For the general diplomatic background of the struggle for the control of Città di Castello, see Lorenzo, *Lettere*, vol. 2, 475-84.

[97] Galeazzo to Maletta, Pavia, 6, 7, 17, 24 October and Milan, 7 November 1474, cart. 226. The Florentine and Milanese positions on the negotiation of this alliance are summarized in Lorenzo, *Lettere*, vol. 2, 485-90.

[98] In a vivid dispatch, (Naples, 13 October 1474, cart. 226), Maletta described Ferrante's anger and quoted him extensively: Hora comprehendo manifestamente ch'el Duca ha facte le preterite conclusione cum me non per observarle né perch'el habia uno minimo sentimento ad recuperare may el suo, ma solamente per delegiarme et per fare mercantie de esse conclusione ad Venexia sicomo el fece de le altre per demonstrarse in tutto bono figliolo et tenero del bene de Sancto Marcho... Pegio me fa ch'el Duca me vole spazare per uno homo grossero et ignorante... suggiongendo che may non speri V. Celsitudine tirarla ad la executione de le cose iurate per queste vie indirecte, che prima ellegeria de morire.

[99] Galeazzo to Maletta, Pavia, 18, 20 October 1474 and Maletta to Galeazzo, Naples, 21 October, 12 November, and Aversa, 24 October 1474, cart. 226; Maletta to Galeazzo, Naples, 15 April, 17 May, 23 June 1475, cart. 227.

a vassal of Venice and risk the ultimate ruin of both states so as to punish Ferrante for his lack of support in the recovery of his lands.[100]

This inordinate subordination of state interests to personal animosity mainly on the part of the duke astounded the Neapolitan court. One experienced Neapolitan ambassador expressed it best when he reminded Galeazzo that, there being no logical reasons for the estrangement of the two states, such as border disputes or an ambition by one state to conquer the other, only cooperation on the basis of existing bonds of marriage and alliance would guarantee their survival and their joint hegemony over the entire peninsula.[101] The strain had also taken its toll on Maletta, who after four years at his post began to suffer from a 'nervous' disorder, and was more than happy to be recalled home in August 1475 without a replacement.[102] His Neapolitan counterpart in Milan, Antonio Cicinello, had already left his post in April, having asked to be relieved after he had endured the duke's constant volubility and harassment including the interception of his correspondence.[103] He returned with the conclusion that only God's intervention would have been able to establish a permanent reconciliation of the two rulers, a view that was shared by

---

[100] Galeazzo's position is summarised in an undated memorandum of late 1475 addressed to an unnamed person for delivery to A. Cicinello, cart. 227. He accused Ferrante of wanting to maintain the friendship of both Milan and Venice to control both: che per certo se inganna s'el se crede tenere venetiani et nui insieme et lui stare per stanga di mezo fra dui cavalli grossi et mantenirne ad questo modo... mantenghi amicicia con venetiani et con noi et che l'uno seria contrapeso ad l'altro. As a result now: venetiani non hano fede ad tutti duoi et in questo mezo fano lo facto loro et se rideno de li facti nostri. See also Galeazzo to Maletta, Pavia, 28 April, 29 May 1475, cart. 227.

[101] Giovanni Palomar, Neapolitan ambassador in Savoy, to Galeazzo, Monte Calerio, 1 July 1475, cart. 227: qui non c'é stato morti de patri né figlioli, qui non occupacioni de Stati né imbicioni de toglier l'uno le Stato de l'altro, né antiqui odii de vecinanca com'é acaduto con li predecessori di questo vostro principato. Dove se pò né deve meglio apogiar la Ex. V. e soy figlioli che in la M. de Re et converso luy e li soy?... Et conclusive cognoxerse manifestamente che l'uno sensa l'altro non poria a consequire quello che uniti tucti duy insieme poriano. Rather than heeding this advice, Galeazzo prevailed on the Duchess of Savoy to end Palomar's mission, making certain that the ambassador knew of his intervention: Galeazzo to Maletta, Pavia, 8 July 1475, cart. 227.

[102] Maletta to Galeazzo, Naples, 24 March 1475, cart. 227: io me son trovato già molti dì patire passione de nervi, la quale hora me ha lassata, ma cum molto destemperamento de stomaco unde anchora me trovo in mane de medici... On orders from Galeazzo, he had already sent back his correspondence and burned his minutes and copybooks in his possession: Maletta to Galeazzo, 9 January 1475, cart. 227. Thereafter he awaited final orders to depart, leaving behind for a month his relative, Assalito Maletta, with the pretext of settling the latter's private affairs. Maletta left Naples on 6 August: Maletta to Galeazzo, Naples, 31 July, 5 August 1475, cart. 227; Jacobo Parmisano, Francesco Maletta's secretary, to Galeazzo, Naples, 16 September 1475, cart. 227.

[103] Cicinello returned to Naples at the end of April (Maletta to Galeazzo, 3 May 1475, cart. 227), having repeatedly pleaded with the king to send another in his place (Maletta to Galeazzo, Naples, 1 March 1475, cart. 227). For examples of intercepted correspondence, see Ferrante to Cicinello and Antonio Petrucci to Cicinello, Naples, 4 July 1474, and Cicinello to Ferrante, Milan, 13 July 1474, all in cart. 225.

the entire court.[104] It is noteworthy that Ippolita, an increasingly bitter woman, actually urged her brother to work for the total diplomatic isolation of the king by pressing his allies to recall their ambassadors from Naples and dismiss the Neapolitan ambassadors from their capitals so as to plunge a 'poisoned arrow in his heart' and 'bury' him.[105]

But God seemed to intervene at last in November 1475, when both Ferrante and his heir to the throne, Alfonso, became seriously ill at the same time with tertian fever brought on possibly by malaria, and their death was feared. The court became alarmed, especially Ippolita, who quickly appealed to her brother for support should both die.[106] Galeazzo realized immediately the common danger of a succession crisis in Naples and sent his ambassador in Rome, Sacramoro da Rimini, Bishop of Piacenza, on a special mission to the Neapolitan court, while alerting his troops in Romagna and Lombardy to march south if needed.[107] This prompt solicitude generated hopes of a true reconciliation, as Ferrante and Alfonso recovered by the end of the year and thought was given to the resumption of the reciprocal embassies.[108] The matter became more pressing for the duke when Charles of Burgundy, his ally since 30 January 1475, was defeated twice by the Swiss at Grandson (2 March 1476) and at Morat (22 June), all of which generated fears alternately of a French or Burgundian invasion of Milan, with Galeazzo scrambling back to the French fold by July. It was now Ferrante's turn to offer aid in this eventuality.[109] There

---

[104] Assalito Maletta to Galeazzo, Naples, 19 August 1475, cart. 227.

[105] Maletta to Galeazzo, Naples, 29 July 1475, cart. 227. Maletta quoted Ippolita as follows: che per volere V. Ill.ma S. dare de una saicta avenenata in lo cuore de questo Re et per sepelirlo in tutto et mecterlo in uno labarinto, non possa trovare porta da usire fora, che V. S. voglia fare ogni opera che l'oratore de la Ill.ma S. de Venecia sia levato ad uno medesimo tempo col vostro, et che l'oratore suo sta a Venecia et quello sta a Fiorenza siano licenciati. Et se V. Subl.tà dovesse ben soprasedere a levarme da qui alcuni dì più, l'ha debia fare, che questo effecto sequita, che sequendo, como la liga fui el fiore de torre le doe parte de la reputatione qui, questa cosa serrà el fructo de ogni suo abisso.

[106] Ippolita to Galeazzo, Castello Capuano, 12, 14, 15, 16, 17, 18, 19 November 1475 in which she sent medical bulletins, 'hour by hour' via the Neapolitan ambassador in Rome and thence to Milan by Milanese couriers. Ippolita's letters of 12, 16, 18, 19 November were published in *Lettere inedite di Joviano Pontano in nome de' reali di Napoli*, ed. Ferdinando Gabotto (Bologna, 1893), 64-73, together with a few additional letters on this subject, 74-89. Many others remain unpublished.

[107] Galeazzo to Ippolita (*manu propria*), Galliate, 21 November, 1475, cart. 227: teneti per fermo che con lo S.re Duca predicto [Alfonso] voglio stare ad uno bene et ad uno male, et per manternerli lo Stato obediente, quieto et pacifico me mettarò in persona cum tutte le mei facultate sul tavolero senza reservo alcuno. Galeazzo sent similar letters on same day to Alfonso and Antonio Petrucci, Ferrante's secretary. See also Sacramoro to Galeazzo, Molo di Gaeta, 29 November and Caleni, 30 November, 1475, cart. 227.

[108] For the new spirit created by this emergency, see Sacramoro to Galeazzo, Naples, 4, 5, 7 December, and Terracina, 13 December 1475, cart. 227.

[109] Illustrative of Galeazzo's new attitude as he feared a French or Burgundian invasion of his duchy is his handwritten letter to Ferrante, Pavia, 11 May 1476, cart. 228: Sacra M.tà e padre mio. Per el Papa, per el Duca de Ferrara, per Laurenzo de li Medici et ancho da

could hardly be a more dramatic demonstration of the linkage of the fate of the two states as Galeazzo fell to the assassins' dagger at the end of that year while reconciliation was still being discussed.

That linkage, fully recognized and at times consciously protected by both parties, was muted mostly by Galeazzo's obsession with the recovery of the claimed cities, and in the end also by Ferrante's parallel obsession with the possession of Cyprus. Contemporaries, however, are virtually unanimous in assigning the major share of the blame to Galeazzo, who was seen as the most destabilising ruler in Italy since Filippo Maria Visconti, and totally unlike his father. I found no evidence to contradict this verdict. During this decade Ferrante mostly reacted to threats or perceived threats to his security, wholly or in part produced by his so-called Milanese ally often in cooperation with non-Italian powers, which in turn generated similar counter-intrigues and alliances with such bewildering frequency that it is difficult to keep track of them, let alone assess them, even assuming that they all have been discovered. So this seemingly uneventful decade without a major war in the peninsula is characterized by a lack of a meaningful guiding principle or vision. The vision of the Italian League was recalled at appropriate moments almost always to shame an adversary or gain a diplomatic advantage masking particularistic interests. By contrast, the principle of the general league had played some role in the thinking and in at least some of the actions of Francesco Sforza, Cosimo de' Medici, and Pius II. It appears even from this limited assessment of the diplomatic correspondence that Ferrante could have risen to their level as he tried to pose as a responsible Italian prince acting for the good of all of Italy, just as his Sforza mentor had claimed to act.[110] Even his sometime enemy, Louis XI, expressed admiration for his statecraft and wanted to imitate his administration.[111] Like Louis, commonly known as 'King Spider', Ferrante

---

Venetia ho inteso (benché ne fosse certissimo) de la optima dispositione de la M.tà V. verso de mi et Stato mio, che é vostro, quando da oltramontani se innovasse offesa alcuna alle cose de Italia, che principalmente pare seria contra lo Stato mio. Ringratio quanto so et posso la M.tà V. Quello ch'ella facesse per mi et questo mio Stato fa per se medesima, perché soa nepote gli ha ad succedere duchessa et goderlo, certificandola che in ogni bisogno del Reame suo tanto si pò valere et disponere de Galeaz, del Ducato de Milano et de tuto el Stato mio quanto del mio fratello, Duca de Calabria, suo filiolo, et del Reame suo proprio de Napole. His tone had certainly changed! The diplomatic maneuvering of the last two years, especially by Florence and Milan, is succinctly analyzed in Lorenzo, *Lettere*, vol. 2, 485-96

110 As another example of this lofty 'Italian' role Ferrante liked to assume, it is noteworthy to quote his sarcastic comment to the Florentine ambassador in Naples upon being notified of the just concluded alliance of Florence, Milan, and Venice: che assay gli piaceva questa liga facta perché, essendo luy vero italiano Re, non gli può né deve se non grandemente piacere tutte quelle cose che tendano ad la conservatione de la pace italica, quale é questa liga (Maletta to Galeazzo, Naples, 12 November 1474, cart. 226).

111 In 1475 Maletta learned that Louis XI requested Ferrante to send him four of his principal courtiers because he wanted to learn from them how Ferrante governed his state and imitate him (Maletta to Galeazzo, Naples, 29 July 1475, cart. 227).

acquired an unsavoury reputation for deception and cruelty, particularly for his actions in the second part of his reign; but in both cases it can be argued that they were forced to act like spiders in order to deflect the stings of other spiders both inside and outside their kingdoms. In addition, Ferrante had the misfortune of being flanked by two inexperienced *puti* - an insecure one in Florence, much influenced by an emotionally unstable one in Milan - both of whom impeded whatever spark of greatness was in him.[112]

This correspondence, on the other hand, offers the richest documentation I have seen to date of the constant interdependence of peninsular and European affairs. There was hardly a major move planned in Milan or Naples without reference to events within and outside Italy in a continuous balancing of moves and countermoves. The Italian states, in brief, were at the center of a constellation of European states with Burgundy, France, and Aragon constantly influencing the centre and with England, the Empire, Hungary, and the Turks affecting the balance at appropriate moments. Finally, there is also much dramatic evidence, a small portion of which is cited here for lack of space, of the personal factor in decision making. The feud between the two rulers degenerated into a personal hatred, affecting their judgment and leadership at the expense of state interests. In my view, a crisis in leadership is what conditions the history of the Italian states in the second half of the Quattrocento, just as Guicciardini later wrote. Perhaps the appearance of this commemorative volume may serve as impetus for a group of young scholars on both sides of the Atlantic to publish the diplomatic correspondence between Milan and Naples on a collaborative basis like the current publication of Lorenzo de' Medici's letters. If we can then resume the publication of the temporarily stalled edition of the correspondence between Milan and France, we could in the end have all the evidence needed to assess the validity of Guicciardini's conclusion.

---

[112] Lorenzo's achievements in statecraft for this period especially have been recently reduced to more realistic proportions and this correspondence confirms this judgment. See N. Rubinstein, 'Lorenzo de' Medici: The formation of his statecraft', and M. Mallett, 'Diplomacy and war in later fifteenth-century Italy', in *Lorenzo de' Medici: Studi*, ed. Gian Carlo Garfagnini (Florence, 1992), 41-60 and 233-56 respectively.

Between Milan and Naples: Ippolita Maria Sforza, duchess of Calabria

Evelyn S. Welch

For almost twenty-three years Ippolita Maria Sforza, daughter-in-law of King Ferrante and daughter of Duke Francesco Sforza, acted as the physical embodiment of the friendship between Milan and Naples. Yet from her arrival in 1465 to her death in 1489, the new bride strained this *amicitia* as often as she strengthened it. Ippolita Maria's marriage to Alfonso of Calabria did not prove a happy one and, although she is an often overlooked figure, her personal difficulties cannot be easily disentangled from the turbulent diplomatic relations of the period. She was, moreover, an active participant in this political and matrimonial game. She took advantage of her position to support Sforza interests and to intervene, both privately and publicly, for figures such as Lorenzo de' Medici on whose behalf she signed the treaty of 1480 reconciling Florence with Naples.

Although she could not operate in ways open to her male counterparts, Ippolita Maria was widely regarded as an astute commentator and intermediary during her lifetime. Nevertheless, her posthumous biography has become enmeshed in the ecomiastic literature which developed to praise contemporary women, a tradition which emphasized the ideals of piety, decorum and learning. In his book on illustrious women printed in Ferrara in 1497, the Augustinian humanist Giacomo Foresti singled out Ippolita Maria for the oration she delivered before Pius II during the Diet of Mantua in 1459.[1] In his compilation of female biographies, the *Gynevra delle clare donne*, Sabadino degli Arienti included Ippolita Maria along with her mother, Bianca Maria and mother-in-law, Isabelle of Chiaramonte, in his list of famous women where, again, she was

---

[1] Giacomo Filippo Foresti (Fra Bartolomeo da Bergamo), *De Plurimis claris selectisque mulieribus* (Ferrara, 1497), 159-60.

Francesco Laurana, Bust of Ippolita Maria Sforza, duchess of Calabria,
the Frick Collection, New York.

lauded for her Latin scholarship.[2] Although Sabadino also emphasised her wit and charm, he placed her firmly amongst the characteristic virtuous women of her period: chaste, religious and devoted to her family. Similarly portrait busts attributed to Francesco Laurana which are thought to represent Ippolita Maria and her sisters-in-law, Beatrice and Eleanora of Aragon, reveal a remarkably uniform type. Stripped of the polychromy which once coloured the features, we are left with demure, downcast eyes and pallid expressions.[3] These are all images of appropriate female decorum and virtue, rather than individual memorials.

Other documentation reveals a more complex and flawed picture of women's lives at the Milanese and Neapolitan courts. Ippolita Maria's role had been decided in 1455 when she was nine years of age. Her betrothal to Alfonso of Aragon's grandson, and her brother Sforza Maria's engagement to his grand-daughter, confirmed the new diplomatic axis of the 1454 Peace of Lodi.[4] In preparation for her position, she was, like most aristocratic girls of the period, taught to ride, to play musical instruments, to sing in French, to dance - a skill for which she was particularly renowned - and to read and write in both the vernacular and in Latin.[5] As the eldest daughter, she had a personal tutor, Baldo Martorelli, whose Latin grammar book written on her behalf still survives. He also had Ippolita copy out works of Cato and Cicero and write her own composition in praise of her mother, a common literary activity amongst the Sforza children. Her education was able to advance to the study of Greek partly because her marriage was delayed by the many difficulties that Ferrante faced in imposing his authority in Naples. While the queen, Isabella of Chiaramonte, sent the young girl gifts she could not promise her safety in the war-torn south.[6] Thus, as Ippolita Maria entered her late adolescence and early twenties in Milan, she was given a degree of independence, a small retinue of servants and an appropriate annual income, allowing a not always welcome maturity. Indeed, the classical training which should have ensured shared interests with

---

[2] Sabadino degli Arienti, *Gynevra de le clare donne di Joanne Sabadino de li Arienti*, ed. C. Ricci and A. Bacchi della Lega, *Scelta di curiosità letterarie*, vol. 225 (Bologna, 1888). For a discussion of Sabadino's text see P. Benson, *The Invention of the Renaissance Woman: the challenge of female independence in the literature and thought of Italy and England* (University Park, PA, 1992), 40-44.

[3] C. Damianaki-Romano, *The Female Portrait Busts of Francesco Laurana*, Ph.D. thesis, University of London (Birkbeck College, 1994).

[4] C. Canetta, 'Le sponsalie di Casa Sforza con Casa d'Aragona', *Archivio storico lombardo*, 9 (1882), 136-44 and 10 (1883), 769-82.

[5] A. Cutolo, 'La giovinezza di Ippolita Maria Sforza, Duchessa di Calabria', *Archivio storico per le province napoletane*, n.s., 34 (1953), 119-34.

[6] On the relationship between Isabelle of Chiaramonte and the Sforza see, I. Schiappoli, 'Isabella di Chiaramonte, Regina di Napoli', *Archivio storico italiano*, 9 (1940), 109-24 and B. Croce, 'Due letterine familiari di principesse italiane del Quattrocento', *Humanisme et Renaissance*, 6 (1939), 296-7.

her future husband seems to have contributed to a sense of rivalry rather than to a common partnership.

Ippolita's wedding finally took place in 1465 once Ferrante, with Sforza help, had succeeded in reimposing his authority over his rebellious barons. Sheleft Milan in the summer with a large following including her secretary and tutor, Martorelli, who would remain in her service for the next decade. But further difficulties marred her transfer, most importantly, the suspected murder of her brother-in-law, Jacopo Piccinino.[7] The bridal cortège was halted in mid-route as a symbol of Francesco Sforza's public dissociation from the Neapolitan action. The procession resumed in the autumn and on Ippolita Maria's arrival in September, Ferrante sent the couple gifts which defined their respective roles. The jewellery and a devotional image of the Virgin and Child given to the bride was, the King explained, designed to provoke fertility and ensure that Ippolita Maria was pregnant by the new year. The gifts of an image of the crucifixion and a sword believed to have belonged to the Turkish sultan were meant to encourage his son to take up arms in defence of the faith.[8]

---

[7] A. Lisini, *Le feste fatte in Napoli nel 1465 per il matrimonio de Ippolita Sforza Visconti con Alfonso, Duca di Calabria. Da lettere del tempo* (Siena, 1898).

[8] Paris, Bibliothèque Nationale, cod. ital. 1591, ff. 152-3, Agostino dei Rossi to Francesco Sforza, 15 September 1465: La Maestà del Signore Re Ferrando... ha mandato a Napoli dignissimi presenti alo Reverendissimo Monsignore Cardinale de Ravenna 'legato la' de fare ali illustrissimi signore Duca de Calabria sposo et a domina Hyppolita, duchessa sua consorte, videlicet, primo ad epsa madona, uno fermaglio grande da spala con circha xxv diamanti dentro, uno mazore in tavola per mezo. Et poy li altri partum in piacta, partim tundi, et partim tavola, tanto ben posti et ordinati circumque che may se vide la più bella et la più splendida cosa. Et è un stupore a vedere el fiamegiare che fanno quelli diamanti quando se voltano verso la luce qua po essere de precio de mille ducati et molto meglio. Item una anchoneta da comune grandezza lavorata d'oro et ornata de perle et pietre preciose con una figura de nostra donna quale tene il figliolo in collo con molti anzoli intorno che sonano, chi uno instrumento et chi un'altro de valuta ben de quatro o cinque cento ducati. Et ha scripto a prefato Monsignore Cardinale legato li dica per parte sua Beatitudine che l'accepti voluntera dicta anchona et gli habia devotione in signo de nostra donna cha ha quel suo bambino in brazo gli conceda gratia a ley anchora de havere un bel figliolo in capo del'anno. Et appresso gli ha mandato anchora dece Agnus Dei d'oro forniti de perle grosse et belle: cinque mediocri et cinque minori da potere dare a quelle sue donne secondo li gradi loro como li paria et poy uno grande bello magnifico ben ornato per la persona sua che pono ben valere circha duecento ducati et meglio.

Alo illustrissimo signore sposo haveva anchora ordinato volere mandare un'altro firmaglio molto digno con un balasso grosso et bello in mezo et altre zoie intorno. Ma perchè adire el vero non era equivalente nì di così bella vista come l'altro ha deliberato più presto retenerlo. Et inscontro de ciò gli ha mandato una copa con lo coperchio et un salarolo tutti d'oro de bona valuta. Ac etiam un'altra anchoneta pur lavorata ut supra d'oro et ornata de molto gemme con lo crucifixo et alchuni altri sancti depincti de altro precio quanto po valere quella dela prefata madona. Item una bellissima spada lavorata con oro et altre zoie, qual mando la Maestà del Re de Ungaria a donare a sua Beatitudine et se dice fu del gran Turcho. Scrivendo alo Reverendissimo legato utsupra che l'amonisca sua illustrissima signoria con quella spada essere prompta a defendere la fede de quel crucifixo che sta depincto ne l'anchoneta donategli, Et similiter, gli ha mandato anchora dece Agnus Dei et un altro grande in quella forma come e dicto desopra... Data Roma xv Septembris 1465.

At first, it seemed as though Ippolita Maria had settled easily into her assigned position and into what would become the characteristic pleasures of Neapolitan court life. She was, according to enthusiastic reports from the Milanese ambassadors, able to strike up friendships with her younger sister-in-laws and act as the court's unofficial queen. On 6 January 1466 Ippolita Maria told her mother that her husband had returned and to celebrate they had gone hunting, played ball games and had read a Spanish work together on statecraft.[9] She was pregnant by the following winter and her first-born, her son Ferrandino, was born in Castel Capuano on 26 June 1467.[10] This was followed in 1470 by the birth of a daughter, Isabella, whose betrothal to her cousin, Gian Galeazzo Maria in 1472 was meant to compensate for the divorce between Eleanora and Sforza Maria Sforza and to further cement the axis between the two courts.

But while the births, betrothals, and public signs of affection suggested that the marriage had succeeded in binding the kingdom and the duchy, problems were difficult to disguise in more immediate circles. Only a few months after Ippolita Maria's arrival, the personal difficulties - both sexual and financial - which would dominate the lengthy correspondance between Naples and Milan were already well established. The Sforza daughter refused to accept the passive, private role to which she had been assigned and quickly involved her natal family in Neapolitan court intrigues. An early indication of Ippolita Maria's determination to expand beyond the expected forms of female behaviour emerged in an announcement that she was, with the help of Martorelli, creating her own *studiolo* and collecting manuscripts, including an edition of Ptolomey's works. Her secretary insisted that this was the duchess of Calabria's own initiative,

> At the moment her ladyship is finishing a beautiful studiolo and she has announced that she wishes to study. And she begs Your Illustrious ladyship [Bianca Maria Visconti] to aid her in adorning it and to send her portraits painted on panels of yourself and her father and all her brothers and her sister. And although I too delight in medals and pictures I swear... that it was not done at my suggestion - neither the study nor the books nor the pictures. But because of this, I have taken an even greater pleasure in it and already she has announced her intentions to ask for these portraits to her husband the duke and to all these gentlemen and to the count of Maddaloni [Diomede Carafa]; therefore I beg your Ladyship to reply with good effect.[11]

---

[9] T. de Marinis, *La Biblioteca napoletana dei Re d'Aragona* (Milan, 1947-52), vol. 1, 108, n. 28.

[10] A. Cutolo, 'La nascita di Ferrandino d'Aragona', *Archivio storico per le province napoletane*, n. s. 28 (1945), 99-108.

[11] De Marinis, *La Biblioteca*, 109: Sua signoria fa al presente finire uno bello studio et dice volere studiare. Et prega vostra illustrissima signore glie voglia adiutare adornarlo et mandarli in tavolletti retratti al naturale la excellentia del Signore suo padre et vostra et de tutti li soi illustrissimi fratelli et sorella. Et benche io me dilecte de medaglie et di pictura ne giuro per l'amore che porto a l'uno et l'altro Galeazo che non fo mai mio ricordo ne de studio

Surrounded by images of her family, Ippolita Maria was able to renew her status as a Sforza daughter in a private retreat. As her marital problems grew worse, she proved equally reliant on Milanese help to enforce her status in the southern court.

It was commonly accepted, even by the Sforza themselves, that Ippolita Maria's difficulties stemmed primarily from a jealous nature and from an early refusal to accept that husbands were entitled to be sexually active and unfaithful. Although her father, brothers and father-in-law had numerous illegitimate progeny, she would not grant this licence to her husband. Already unsure of Alfonso in January 1466, she ordered one of her male servants to follow him throughout the city, causing considerable amusement amongst Alfonso's friends, who would call out, 'Go back, lord duke, that man of the Duchess is waiting for you.'[12] The duke of Calabria had the young man beaten, an insult which caused considerable diplomatic embarrasment.[13] Ippolita Maria returned her servant to Milan with tales of maltreatment, causing the immediate intervention of her mother, who was by now a widow and the effective ruler of Milan. Although the duchess of Calabria was instructed to refrain from making

---

ne de libri ne de picture. Et pero ne piglio bene maggiore et incredibile piacere et cosi de fare vostra Signoria et gia ha dicto al illustrissimo Duca suo consorte et a tutti questi gentilhomini et al Conte de Mattalone havere mandate per esse pero prega vostra signoria gline faccia resposta con effecto.

[12] Milan, Archivio di Stato, Sforzesco Potenze Estere [hereafter ASMi, SPE], cartella 216, Pietro da Landriano to Bianca Maria Visconti Sforza, 10 January 1467: Va, Signor Ducha che quello homo de la duchessa te aspetta.

[13] ASMi, SPE, Napoli, 216, Antonio da Trezzo to Bianca Maria Visconti Sforza, 9 January 1467: Veduto quanto la excellentia vostra me scrive dolendose... per la venuta de Donato che era stafero de questa illustrissima madona vostra figliola... e grandamente del affano ha preso vostra illustrissima signoria di questa cosa. De la quale vedo proprie essere seguito quello che disse ad essa vostra figliola quando cum molta instantia la pregai e supplicai non volesse mandare dicto Donato e manco scrivere; che cognosceva el secundo dì lei haria facto la pace cum el Duca suo marito e la excellentia vostra ne restaria cum affano che non me havevati bisogno de più de quello ch'io sapeva che havevati. Che cosi è proprie intervenuto. Perchè come el Duca venne furono insieme de migliore animo del mondo ne poria essere altramente. Illustrissima madona mia, elle conveniente cosa che le done amano e sel se pò dire habiano qualche gielosia di li mariti che procede da grande amore ma le cose non se vogliono pigliare in extremità. Pare chel prefato Duca vostro genero mai potesse uscire de casa da quale hora se volesse che o Donato o altri de essa Madona non gli fossero dreto, il che lui comportava malvolontieri. Non perchè gli dispiacesse che se sapesse dove andava ma gli pareva de stare in meza servitori. Delchè secondo ha poi dicto se condolse cum essa Madona e ad esso Donato più de tre volte fece dire chel non gli andasse dreto che gli faria despiacere. Esso per obedire pur gli ando e gli fo facto l'acto che luy ha referto ma non pero che gli fosse facto male ne altro depoi è seguito. Se poriano dire cose assai ma ve concludo chel Duca l'ama tanto quanto mogliere posse essere amata da marito e essa luy. Et quando esso è qua, continuamente dorme cum essa che mo sua signoria lo potesse tenere ligato esso non poria stare. Che è pur de età de anni xviii vel circa e tanto vivo chel non poria stare fermo meza hora. Sì che per fare breve conforto e prego vostra excellentia che de queste cose non ne pigli uno minimo affano perchè tra loro non è discordia che duri due hore. Da l'altro canto essa vostra figliola ha uno socero che gli porta più amore che mai alcun altro portasse ad nora e questo e tanto manifesto che non se poria dire più.

further complaints and from endangering her staff, the Milanese nobleman Pietro da Landriano was sent to Naples to explain in no uncertain terms how Alfonso's attitude towards his wife would have a direct and immediate bearing on the alliance between Milan and Naples. Those at Ferrante's court quickly tried to smooth over the friction. The resident ambassador, Antonio da Trezzo, explained that such jealousy arose from the 'great love' the couple bore each other while da Landriano himself told Bianca Maria that the incident had only arisen from the personalities of the two protaganists: 'It is true that both have erred and this comes from the fact that both are young and have great spirit.'[14] But the reported discussion with Alfonso indicated the root of the problem. The duke was adamant that his wife should obey him; Ippolita was equally adamant that she should be treated 'not as a servant but as a companion'.[15] Moreover, although Ippolita Maria finally acquiesced and accepted that she had behaved indiscreetly she wrote to her mother justifying her behaviour in terms which suggested that the issues were not resolved,

> I am very sorry that I have been the cause of any pain to your ladyship with my letters; yet I had to write for I could not conceal the things which have passed. My error was in saying that the duke did not love me and that I wished him to stay near me as he should; I am sure that it is only the pregnancy which has caused me to say this. That which your ladyship has written about not putting any of my followers in danger, I will do and at the moment there is no need to send another person down to know these things for I hope to find one here. You will know the nature of the duke from Petro, and how I conduct myself with his Lordship and that he has done the best job in the world with the duke and I have spoken thus to the King. I am sure that with time everything will fall into place... But I must object to what your Ladyship commands and orders me to do, for I swear with that love which I bear for your ladyship that I will never be able to forget the things which I wrote to you and this incident of Donato. I have been wounded in the heart and I think that it has been broken in half so great was my grief.[16]

---

[14] ASMi, SPE, Napoli, 216, Pietro da Landriano to Bianca Maria, 10 January, 1467.

[15] ASMi, SPE, Napoli, 216, Pietro da Landriano to Bianca Maria, 10 January 1467.

[16] ASMi, SPE, Napoli, 216, Ippolita Maria to Bianca Maria, 13 January 1467: Molto me rincresce che io sia stata casone de dare affano a vostra signoria con mie lettere pure per non tenere più celato le cose passate la scrisse. Mio errore fece che ove disse lo signore Duca non me amava, volse gli fare mia giunta come debitamente de fare qua certo la gravidoglia me lo fece fare. Quello che vostra signoria scrive non voglia mettere niuno de li mei a pericolo lo faro et al presente non bisogna monolare altre persone per sapere dicte cose per che spero che gli ne trovaro qua. De intendere la natura del Duca per Petro, vostra signoria sera avisata como mi diporto con sua signoria et cusi ho parlato al signore Re. Credo che col tempo se acaptala ogni cosa. La venuta de Petro me fu gratissima per intendere el bene stare de vostra signoria et ancora per parlar de questa facenda, che certo ello la pigliata per lo megliomodo del mondo con el signore Duca et ne vole parlare con el Signore Re. Ma come e possibile che non pigli despiacere come vostra signoria me comanda et me constringe, con quello scongiuro per lo amore porto a vostra signoria siando le cosse come scrisse a vostra signoria et cusi questa cosa de Donato che non me scorderò mai. Et poi me fu giunto con una ferita al core, ma credo che se apresse per mezo tanto fu el dolore mio, et sera mentre non sappia vostra signoria tenere Hippolyta Maria per quella che fu...

Given her sensitivity, Ippolita found it difficult to remain silent in the face of succeeding humiliations. By 1473, her husband's favourite mistress had joined her in Castel Capuano[17] and at the same time, her right to Martorelli's services was threatened. The Milanese ambassador warned that to punish Ippolita Maria, Alfonso was threatening to remove the secretary from his position, 'because the duke can think of nothing that will bring greater disrespect and scorn to the duchess and all this comes from their jealousy and competition.'[18] Thus despite the continuing importance of the Milan-Naples relationship, Ippolita Maria's personal situation had actually worsened. She had, in addition, been forced to change tactics after Bianca Maria's death in October 1468. The new duke of Milan had his own quarrel with her, accusing Ippolita Maria of supporting their mother and King Ferrante against him during the transition from his father's reign to his own.[19] When Ippolita Maria and her husband had travelled north to attend the duke's wedding to Bona of Savoy in 1468, Ferrante had indeed considered recalling the couple because he did not trust the Milanese atmosphere while Alfonso refused to allow his wife to be alone in Galeazzo Maria's presence. Thus, although, the duke of Milan was willing to help his sister, he let her know, in no uncertain terms, that he considered her partly responsible for the tensions which had developed.[20] Furthermore, her attempts to act on Bona Sforza's behalf in asking him whether he kept a mistress also struck an improper note.[21] His angry response was to admit the adulterous

---

[17] ASMi, SPE, Napoli, 225, Francesco Maletta to Galeazzo Maria Sforza.

[18] ASMi, SPE, Napoli, 223, Francesco Maletta to Galeazzo Maria Sforza, 10 January 1473: Ceterum. Perchè vostra celsitudine sia avisata de tuto como a debito. Questi dì el Duca de Calabria motegio de volere levare magistro Baldo da pie de madona vostra sorella, non per defecto ne mancamento d'esso magistro Baldo ma perchè el Duca sa non potere fare magior despetto ne scorno ala Duchessa de questo che tuto procede da le gare e zelosie loro. La prefata madona ne fece doglianza cum mi grandissima parendo a lei non potere aspettare magiore offesa ne ingiuria perchè havia puoy cum si datamente aprire e comunicare le sue passione e li suoy bixogni e pregare lo volesse fare intendere al Re e pregare sua Maestà non comportasse questa inquieta. Io obedi sua signoria e dal Re heli gratiosa resposta prometendome non lassare incorere tale cosa. Pur dubitandome che uno qualche dì per presto apetito che ragione non transporti el Duca me parso darne avisa a vostra illustrissima signoria la quale per lo vero aviso che dicto magistro Baldo se porta tanto bene e virtuosamente quanto dire se possa.

[19] For an analysis of the tensions between Bianca Maria and her son and the role played by Naples see, P. Margaroli, 'Bianca Maria e Galeazzo Maria Sforza nelle ultime lettere di Antonio da Trezzo', *Archivio storico lombardo*, 111 (1985), 328-77.

[20] ASMi, SPE, Napoli, 218, 1 June 1469, Instructions from Galeazzo Maria Sforza to Petro da Gallarate.

[21] ASMi, SPE, Napoli, 227, Francesco Maletta to Galeazzo Maria Sforza, 15 April 1475: La illustrissima vostra sorella m'ha comiso ch'io scriva a vostra celsitudine che parlando cum essa, el Re de questi dì gli disse, 'Non sapeti Madonna che'l Duca vostro fratello e venuto in differentia cum la Duchessa sua mogliere per casone de l'amorosa che'l tene, il che non volea comportare dicta Duchessa et esso gli ha dicto se non ve piace de stare cossi andatevene in Franza o Savoya o in uno monastero como meglio ve pare. Suggiongendo el Re, 'Se io facio alcuna cosa de questi amori non sono da essere biasmato como el Duca perchè io non ho

relationship but to taunt his sister with the fact that he treated his wife better than her husband treated her.[22]   Nonetheless, just as Ippolita's letters stressed that her brother's interests and needs were her own, his letters reassured his sister that the duke kept a careful note of all the wrongs and injustices which she had suffered.   Like his mother, he regarded the Neapolitan treatment of Ippolita Maria as a sign of the relationship between the two states.   Like his mother, Galeazzo Maria also put the practicalities of diplomacy ahead of the duchess of Calabria's personal happiness, urging her to put on a brave front.   He wrote, for example, in 1469,

> You must appear to be content with every wish and deliberation of his Majesty and not demonstrate that you are offended or discontented by that which has happened because we have said and declared that although in the past days we have seemed to be angry with you; throw away that letter for you are now our dear and much loved sister and that good and bad treatment which is allotted to you we take as if it had been done to ourself and to our own person.   We praise you for acting wisely and maturely and humanely as we are sure you will do and we do not doubt that His Majesty and the duke will treat you well.   If it should prove otherwise we wish you to send word by one of your servants, and secretly.   For have no doubt, we will do for you what any brother should do for another and the good brother towards his sister.[23]

This does not mean, however, that Galeazzo Maria was happy about the treatment Ippolita Maria received.   He provided more tangible rewards than brotherly exhortations to patience.   Alongside the formal recommendations to Ferrante that she had requested and received, Ippolita Maria acquired funds and access to patronage.   Although she was supposed to receive a monthly income

---

mogliere et luy l'ha bellissima'. Respose Madonna... 'Sacro Maestà, io non credo tale cosa perche lassamo andare che'l signore mio fratello sia costumato e modestissimo signore in una ha fama de avanzare non solamente omne cosa in tutti li signori del mondo, ma ogni privata persona, cioè è de tractare bene madona sua consorte... La prefata madonna m'ha comiso ch'io scrivo anchora a vostra sublimità et pregarlla de parte sua che per consideratione sua e de suoy figlioli quella circha la domanda del Ducha suo marito non facia senon quello che concerna la reputatione, gloria et bene vostra...

[22] ASMi, SPE, Napoli, 227, Galeazzo Maria to Francesco Maletta, 28 April 1475: Ad la illustrissima Duchessa di Calabria li dirai che la Maestà del Re ha peggio de rasonare quando el parla dela nostra amorosa et che ad lei diremo el vero che l'havimo. Ma dal altro canto fasimo talmente el debito ad la nostra illustrissima consorte che voluntari facessemo contenti sua Maestà provedesse el duca la facesse tale ad sua signoria.

[23] ASMi, SPE, cartella 218, Galeazzo Maria Sforza to Ippolita Maria 7 May 1469: Voy vogliati demostrare essere contenta sempre de ogni voluntate et deliberatione d'essa Maestà et non mostrati per quello è sequito havere alcuno sdegno ne mala contenteza perchè havemo dicto et declerato che benchè ad questi dì passati habiamo mostrato havere sdegno con voy, casciare quella lettera, tam che seti nostra cara et amata sorella et che quello bono et mal trattamento te fosse facto lo reputarimo facto ad noy proprii et ala nostra persona. Il perchè laudamo che ve sforzate portarvi savamente et maturamente et humanamente como siamo certi fareti perchè non dubitamo la Maestà del Re et lo Signor Duca vostro marito ve trattarano bene et quando altramente fosse vogliati per uno deli vostri advisarne del vero et secretamente perchè faremo per voy como debbe fare l'uno fratello con l'altro et lo bon fratello verso sorella e de questo non faceti dubio alcuno.

of 1,000 ducats from the Neapolitan court, the duchess usually led a precarious financial assistance. The first allowance had been cerimoniously handed over to Martorelli on her arrival in Naples. But future installments proved harder to enforce.[24] The clothing and jewelry of her dowry formed the security for a monotonous ritual of pawn-broking and personal loans. Originally her mother had subsidized her expenditure; after 1468, Ippolita turned increasingly to the Medici bank. In 1469, for example, the duke of Calabria wrote furiously to Piero de' Medici of his shame at his wife's defaulting on her latest debts;[25] in 1471, after much debate and a lecture on careful household management, Galeazzo Maria lent 4,000 ducats to pay her servants on the security of her jewels. The duchess wrote in gratitude that she had widely publicized this welcome help which was made up of newly minted gold coins bearing the duke of Milan's more mature features:

> Your courtier, the noble Giacomo de Sereno has arrived and has given me the 4,000 gold ducats with the head of your lordship, along with a gracious and pleasing letter about the said image, which was once thin and now is fat. In truth, because I now do not wish to sell our jewels we were in great necessity and trouble... And we immediately informed His Majesty the King, our husband and the count of Maddaloni and some other lords and gentlemen who were so congratulatory that you cannot imagine such happiness and feasting.[26]

The relief was, however, only temporary. In 1474 Ippolita Maria was forced to turn once again to the Medici, asking for 2,000 ducats from Lorenzo on 'her word of honour as a woman';[27] while in 1481, Ferrante used her jewels, along with his own and those of his queen to support the war against the Turks in Otranto. At that time, Ippolita Maria made her loyalties quite clear by warning her brother and the Florentines that Ferrante had not drawn on all his financial resources and was not in the difficulties he claimed to be.[28] In 1482, Francesco Coppola lent Ippolita money so that she could redeem her favourite jewels from

---

[24] On Ippolita Maria's financial straits and the lack of an allowance see, ASMi, SPE, Napoli, cartella 220, Francesco Maleta to Galeazzo Maria Sforza, 19 December 1471 .

[25] E. Pontieri, 'La dinastia aragonese di Napoli e la Casa de' Medici di Firenze', *Archivio storico per le province napoletane*, n.s. 26 (1940), 294-5.

[26] ASMi, SPE, Napoli, 220, Ippolita Maria to Galeazzo Maria, 19 February 1471: E gionto qui il nobile Jacomo de Sereno, camarero de vostra signoria, el quale ne ha visitato lietamente de sua parte et donatame iiii mille ducati d'oro de la testa de Vostra Sua Excellentia con una gratiosa et piacevole lettera de ditta sua imagine, prima macra et hora grassa. Invero signor mio per non trovarse da vendere nostre zoie eravamo in grandissima necessitate de dinari et affano... Pure concorendo tanto cose ad uno tratto de essere così lietamente visitate con cosi gratiosa lettera et degno presente a chiara demonstratione a tutto el mondo de lo immenso amore verso di noi... Et così havendone prestissimo advisata la Maestà del signore Re, lo illustrissimo nostro consorte, il magnifico Conte de Mattalone, et alcuni signori et gentilhomini nostri ne sonno state fatte tante congratulatione con tanta festa et alegreza che non se potria explicare.

[27] A. Berzeviczy, *Beatrice d'Aragona* (Milan, 1931), 40.

[28] *Lorenzo dei Medici. Lettere*, ed. M. Mallet, vol. 5, 497.

the Spanocchi bank - a favour which may explain her attempt to warn him of Ferrante's murderous intentions towards himself and his family.[29] In 1485, Ippolita Maria is documented as asking Lorenzo to provide her with 2,000 ducats so that she would not lose the jewels and a valuable cross which she had pawned.[30]

Cash was not the only asset she sought abroad. Although the scarce documentation makes concrete conclusions difficult, it seems that the duchess of Calabria was rarely able to reward her own courtiers through Neapolitan channels.[31] Instead, she relied heavily on the patronal networks of her natal family and those of Florence, making recommendations for jobs, positions, and court offices and arranging advantageous marriages for figures who had followed her from Milan. This background of clientage, financial instability and sexual infidelity could be repeated in almost any other Quattrocento courts. There are no signs that Ferrante and Alfonso resented the Milanese assistance which Ippolita received. Indeed, many of the letters which Giovanni Pontano signed on her behalf regard just such favours and interventions; for the more financial support she gained, the less of a demand Ippolita Maria's court made on the treasury.[32] But the tensions such requests and complaints inspired go some way to enhancing our understanding the background to the conflict between Naples and Milan which exacerbated the French invasion of 1494. Ippolita Maria's unhappiness with her husband gave an impression of disdain for the Milanese in Naples which Galeazzo Maria, in his rivalry with Ferrante, was happy to believe. Her equal determination to involve her natal family in her private woes also provided numerous opportunities both to spy on and to intervene in the affairs of the Neapolitan court. Her reliance on the Medici bank's financial help also gave Ippolita Maria an incentive to assist the Florentines whenever possible. Thus we find the duchess of Calabria working with the Milanese ambassador, Francesco Maletta, to obtain information and influence at court, and calling in the Florentine representatives to provide them with secret news whenever possible.[33] She particularly encouraged Maletta to bribe Ferrante's officials, arranging to pass on a gold collar to the wife of his

---

[29] I. Schiappoli, *Napoli Aragonese: traffici e attivita marinare* (Naples, 1972), 216 and 232.

[30] Pontieri, 'La dinastia Aragonese,' 341.

[31] I have only been able to find one documented example where Ippolita Maria was able to use her position to procure an appointment. On 9 April 1484, Ferrante gave a canonry in the church of S. Nicola di Bari to one Bartolomeo de Marinella di Bari at the request of the duchess of Calabria. But this concession probably stems from Ippolita's position as her brother Ludovico's representative in Bari. For the document see, J. Mazzoleni ed., *Regesto della cancelleria Aragonese di Napoli* (Naples, 1951), 42.

[32] F. Gabotto, *Joviano Pontano e Ippolita Sforza* (Florence, 1890) and *Lettere inedite di Joviano Pontano in nome de' Reali di Napoli* (Bologna, 1893; reprinted 1968).

[33] See for example the letters of Francesco Maletta of 5 January 1474, SPE 225 and 1 March 1475, SPE 227.

chamberlain in exchange for a pro-Milanese stance. Despite her prudishness, when the king acquired a new mistress[34] Ippolita Maria was happy to stress the close relationship she enjoyed with the young girl, suggesting she could use this friendship to gain access to royal secrets. In November 1475, when her husband and father-in-law, were seemingly both fatally ill, the need for close communication grew ever more important and Ippolita immediately turned to Milan for assistance in ensuring her son's succession. Ippolita Maria tried to make private arrangements to ensure that information and assistance could move between Rome and Milan without passing throught the official Neapolitan chanels.[35]

As she entered her thirties in the 1480's, Ippolita Maria was able to act more openly on behalf of her family interests. In 1485 she governed the duchy of Bari on behalf of her brother after an appointee proved to be incompetent,[36] and she seems to have been active in securing Ferrante's support for Ludovico Maria's regency in 1480. One of her other tasks was to acquire a wife for her younger brother, Filippo Maria. The most important public demonstration of her standing as a mature and influential court figure came in 1479 when she was able to intervene skillfully on behalf of Lorenzo de' Medici. Ippolita Maria's relationship with Lorenzo dated to 1465 when the adolescent represented his family during her wedding in Milan.[37] He then visited the Duchess briefly in 1467, and met her again in 1468 as she returned from Galeazzo Maria's wedding

[34] ASMi, SPE, Napoli, 222, Francesco Maletta to Galeazzo Maria Sforza, 3 July 1472: La Maestà del Signore Re era deliberata omne modo havere Madama Johanella sua figliola [the daughter of the Count of Brugenza] in Castellonovo et tenerla honorevolemente et fara intendere a tuto el mondo che'l havesse cara sopra omne altra cosa. Unde vedendo dicto Conte questa essere totale dispositione de sua Maestà ha deliberato compiacergli. Ma per honestare la cosa et per levare ogni macula de infamia più che se puo voleva che sua Maestà mandasse il Duca de Calabria ad rechiederla ad casa et persuadere la matre et la puta ad essere contente... Quicquid sit certissimo è chel Re è passionatissimo de questa dona, la quale veramente è la più bella damisella de Napoli al iuditio de omne persona... La prefata madona vostra sorella me dice havergli dicto el Duca chel fa venire de Levante alcune cose chel vole dare manzare ad costey per le quale may non se potera ingravidare et questo fa per duy respecti. Lo primo perche il Re non habia figlioli da Ley. L'altro e perchè natura del Re è como una sua femina ha parturito perde l'amore suo et vedendo el Duca suo patre essere destinato e sobiecto ad queste passione amorese finchel viver vole più tosto chel se golda cum questa sola che havere de nove cercarne et desiarno molte altre in le quale fusse poy maiore periculo maxime de farlo dire de sì.
[35] ASMi, SPE, Napoli, 227, Ippolita Maria wrote to Galeazzo Maria regarding the crisis on 12, 14, 16, 18, 19, 23, 27 November, 1475 while Francesco Maletta reported to Milan on 4 December, 1475.
[36] See P. Pecchiai, 'Il governo di Benedetto Castiglioni in Bari', Archivio storico lombardo, 45 (1918), 31-49. See also N. Ferorelli, 'Il Ducato di Bari sotto Sforza Maria Sforza e Ludovico il Moro', Archivio storico lombardo, 41 (1914), 389-468.
[37] A. Rochon, La jeunesse de Laurant de Medicis, 1449-1478 (Paris, 1963), 87. For the background to the relationship between Lorenzo and Milan during this period of the 1460s and 1470s see C. Bonello Uricchio, 'I rapporti fra Lorenzo il Magnifico e Galeazzo Maria Sforza negli anni 1471-1473', Archivio storico lombardo, ser. 9, 4 (1964-5), 33-49.

to Bona of Savoy. These contacts were reinforced by mutual assistance of many types. Their closeness was documented on numerous occasions during the Florentine's dramatic trip to Naples. At one moment in the negotiations, Lorenzo could not be located for further discussions because he was with the duchess of Calabria with whom, it transpired, he regularly conferred.[38] As a further sign of his confidence, Lorenzo appointed Ippolita Maria as his procurator for his affairs in the *Regno*. She was, along with Niccolo Michelozzo, Lorenzo's signatory on the peace agreement which was drawn up on 13 March 1480.[39] One of the main reasons, he stated for chosing Ippolita Maria was the efforts she had put into organising the agreement, 'because of the humanity, benignity and trustworthiness of our illustrious Lady Hypolita Maria who has made this peace and concord her own work through great industry'.[40]

It was only in this last decade of her life that Ippolita Maria's capabilities as a diplomat were finally appreciated by Ferrante and Alfonso. During the difficulties following Ludovico Maria's return to Milan in 1479 and the war against Roberto da San Severino which followed, Ferrante suggested sending Ippolita Maria home to force a reconciliation between her brother and her cousin.[41] But while her father-in-law and her husband were anxious for the trip to take place, Ippolita Maria herself seems to have prevaricated, refusing to leave unless Ludovico Maria himself demanded her help. She remained a Sforza with Sforza interests to the end.

Ippolita Maria died on 19 August 1488. Her daughter, Isabella, left Naples soon after to marry the duke of Milan who remained under Ludovico's tutelage. But this marriage which was designed to cement the allegiance between the two dynasties effectively served to destroy it. Had Ippolita Maria lived, the families would have been balanced. It was now the turn of the Aragonese to intervene on behalf of their daughter's mistreatment, an involvement which also had consequences well beyond those of personal unhappiness.[42] It has been suggested that the bust of a young woman in the Frick Collection represents Ippolita Maria Sforza after her death on the basis of an obscure allegorical relief on the base. This, it has been suggested shows scenes of sacrifice of children and the self-sacrifice of mothers taken from texts of Hyginus's tales of classical myths.[43] The scene would have been a warning

---

[38] Lorenzo de' Medici, *Lettere*, vol. 4, 446.

[39] Lorenzo de' Medici, *Lettere*, vol. 4, 327.

[40] Lorenzo de' Medici, *Lettere*, vol. 4, 327.

[41] Lorenzo de' Medici, *Lettere*, vol. 6, 241.

[42] For a discussion of whether Isabella of Aragon actually called on her father to avenge her and her son see, A. Colombo, 'Il "Grido di dolore" di Isabella d'Aragona, duchessa di Milano', *Studi di storia napoletana in onore di Michelangelo Schipa* (Naples, 1926), 331-46.

[43] O. Brendel, 'Laurana's Bust of Ippolita Sforza', *Art Quarterly*, 7 (1944), 59-62. For a more recent interpretation see *The Frick Collection. An Illustrated Catalogue* (New York, 1970), vol. 3, 9-20 and Damianaki-Romano, *Female Portrait Busts*.

against Ludovico Maria's 'sacrifice' of his nephew and niece. If this identification is accurate, it would represent Ferrante and Alfonso's final use of Ippolita Maria's image and legacy to illustrate, not the happy ties between the two territorial states, but is a warning against Ludovico's usurpation of Isabella, and Gian Galeazzo's position. Thus the legacy of such marriages, designed to create permanent understanding and mutual interests, had also succeeded in arousing anger and the potential for mutual meddling.

The politics of protection in late fifteenth-century Italy: Florence and the failed Sienese exiles' plot of May 1485

Humfrey Butters

The commune of Siena was hardly in the first rank of Italian powers in the late fifteenth century, and it might appear at first sight difficult to justify devoting an essay to the analysis of a failed attempt by Sienese exiles, mostly belonging to the *Monte dei Nove*, to return to their native city. Unsuccessful endeavours of this sort were, after all, hardly *rarae aves* in the political life of fifteenth-century Italy, and the story of this one is, at a superficial level, easily told. The exiles and Giulio Orsini with about two thousand infantry assembled in Perugia, Todi and Spoleto,[1] and some men at arms, moved on Siena in early May 1485 and were defeated by government troops at San Quirico on Monday 9 May. The exiles' force fled in various directions, the bulk of the men-at-arms retreating to the area of Transteverina, which was in the territory of the Orsini.[2] This was, therefore, no Homeric enterprise, but one ending with a whimper rather than a bang.

The episode and its background are, nonetheless, of considerable interest, not just because of what they reveal about Sienese factional struggles, but also because of the light they can be used to shed on Italian political life as a whole. Siena was indeed a modest power in the fifteenth century, both politically and economically, but it was nonetheless a desirable residence, most of all for those who were exiled from it, but by no means for them alone. The strategic position

---

[1] Archivio di Stato, Siena [hereafter ASS], Balia, 522, inserto 40: Lorenzo de' Medici to the officials of the Sienese Balia, 4 May 1485; Archivio di Stato, Florence [hereafter ASF], Otto di Pratica, Legazioni e Commissarie, 3, ff. 135v-136v, *Dieci di Balia* to Bernardo Rucellai, 6 May 1485, (for the mistaken assignment of this volume and others to the *Otto di Pratica*, see my review of *Carteggi delle magistrature dell'età repubblicana*, ed. P. Viti et al., in *English Historical Review*, 106 (1991), 447). In their letter to Rucellai the *Dieci* said that Paolo Orsini was involved as well. He may well have taken a hand in the early stages of the conspiracy, but in Guidantonio Vespucci's dispatch from Rome of 12 May (see below, n. 2), which reported the news of the Sienese exiles' defeat, the only Orsini mentioned was Giulio.

[2] ASF, Dieci di Balia, Carteggi, Responsive, 34, f. 109. Guidantonio Vespucci to the Dieci di Balia, 12 May 1485.

of the Sienese state, bordering on the dominions of Florence and on the Papal State, gave it a particular importance in the eyes of the pope and the government of Florence. King Ferrante of Naples and his son the duke of Calabria coveted it, because its possession would help them to exert influence over Tuscany as a whole, to restrain the territorial ambitions of popes and, if necessary, to mount operations against Genoa.[3] The duke had already played a significant role in its political life for a time, until the Turkish capture of Otranto had forced him to relinquish it.[4] Nor were those who dreamed of dominating Siena confined to the first rank of Italian powers: the fact that anyone seeking to overthrow the regime would be able to count on the support of at least some of the exiles, with their friends and relations within the city, enabled a much less powerful ruler like Girolamo Riario,[5] or even a *condottiere* like Roberto di Sanseverino,[6] to regard the undertaking as feasible. Even a failed attempt as dismal as that of the exiles in May 1485 may reveal much, therefore, about the relations between the principal powers of the Italian peninsula, and in particular about the intimate connexions between the domestic politics and the foreign policies of each of them. These connexions were given formal expression in the treaties of alliance, the enfeoffments and the contracts of *accomandigia* with which the powers of Italy sought, by the acquisition of allies or protectors, *raccomandati* or vassals, to strengthen themselves against their rivals, both foreign and domestic.[7]

The regime in Florence had a particularly keen interest in Siena, for it saw the maintenance of a friendly government there as essential to its own security, and was particularly anxious to prevent the Neapolitans from regaining the position in Siena that they had enjoyed prior to the capture of Otranto. Bernardo Rucellai, Florentine ambassador in Milan, compared this concern to Milan's anxiety about the future of the regime in Genoa in a letter he wrote to Lorenzo de' Medici on 3 January 1485: Ludovico Sforza, he said, was afraid that '*l re non voglia disporre di quel governo e per consequente avere commodità di innovare qui, ché pare questa Gienova sia la Siena di costoro.*'[8] Bernardo may have been recalling what the *Dieci di Balìa*, Florence's principal foreign policy magistracy, had written to him two years earlier: *chi ha animo di offendere noi et indurre turbatione nelle città et cose nostre, non ha via più*

---

[3] H.C. Butters, 'Lorenzo and Naples', in *Lorenzo il Magnifico e il suo Mondo. Convegno Internazionale di Studi*, ed. G.C. Garfagnini (Florence, 1993), 147.

[4] Butters, 'Lorenzo and Naples', 147.

[5] In a letter of 10 August 1484 to Lorenzo de' Medici Pier Filippo Pandolfini, Florentine ambassador and commissioner-general in Milan and the camp of the League, reported Ludovico Sforza's suspicion that if Riario failed in his plan to capture Faenza, he would assist the exiles to return to Siena (ASF, Archivio Mediceo Avanti il Principato, 48, no. 20).

[6] See below.

[7] G. Soranzo, 'Collegati, raccomandati, aderenti negli stati italiani dei secoli xiv e xv', *Archivio storico italiano*, 99 (1941), 3-35; T. Dean, *Land and Power in late medieval Ferrara. The rule of the Este 1350-1450* (Cambridge, 1988), 74-91, 166-78.

[8] ASF, Archivio Mediceo avanti il Principato, 48, no. 279.

facile et più accomodata che pel mezzo di Siena.[9] One good reason for the *Dieci*'s comment was the Sienese occupation of Florentine places in the Chianti. The places taken by the Neapolitans in the course of the Pazzi war, such as Poggibonsi and Colle Val d'Elsa, were handed back a year after the settlement of 13 March 1480 that ended the conflict;[10] but those acquired by the Sienese, Castellina, Monte Domenici and San Polo, were not returned until 15 June 1483.[11] The capture and retention of these places by the Sienese constituted a grave loss of face for the regime in Florence, and its recovery of them was made possible by the split in Sienese politics between the *Noveschi* and their opponents. In June 1482 the pro-Neapolitan *Noveschi* regime was overthrown,[12] a major factor in its downfall being the general resentment in Siena caused by its willingness to reach an agreement with Florence about the return of the places in the Chianti.[13] To the Florentine government the reason for the removal of the *Noveschi* regime mattered less than the practical question of how to induce its successor to be as ready as it had been to hand back the three places. Lorenzo was careful to maintain contacts with *Noveschi* exiles such as Jacopo Petrucci,[14] and when at the end of January 1483 a group of *Noveschi* headed by Luzio Bellanti, Aldello Piccolomini and Niccolò Spinelli seized the border *castello* of Montereggioni, they appealed to Florence for help.[15] By withdrawing the favour that it had initially shown towards this enterprise,[16] by other demonstrations of support for the regime of the *popolo* in its confrontation with the *Noveschi* exiles, and by making clear how that regime could show its appreciation for a policy that could be abandoned if it went unrewarded, the

---

[9] ASF, Dieci di Balia, Legazioni e Commissarie, 5, f. 61v-62r. Dieci di Balia to Bernardo Rucellai, 21 April 1483. This and most of the other references to Sienese-Florentine relations in the years 1482 and 1483 contained in this essay I owe to the kindness of Professor Michael Mallett, who allowed me to see relevant parts of the typescript of his commentary on Lorenzo de' Medici's letters in the period 1482-84. Professor Mallett's edition of and commentary on Lorenzo's letters in those years will appear as volume seven of the edition of Lorenzo's letters that is being produced under the auspices of the Istituto Nazionale di Studi sul Rinascimento in Florence and the general editorship of Professor Nicolai Rubinstein.

[10] Butters, 'Lorenzo and Naples', 147.

[11] A. Allegretti, *Diari delle cose sanesi del suo tempo*, L. Muratori, *Rerum Italicarum Scriptores*, 23 (Milan, 1733), col. 814.

[12] E. Casanova, 'I tumulti del giugno 1482 a Siena e alcuni brevi di Sisto IV', *Miscellanea storica senese*, 2 (1894), 3-13.

[13] Lorenzo de' Medici, *Lettere*, vol. 6, ed. M.E. Mallett, (Florence, 1990), 317-18, n. 7.

[14] *Protocolli del Carteggio di Lorenzo il Magnifico per gli anni 1473-74, 1477-92*, ed. M. del Piazzo (Florence, 1956), 196.

[15] ASS, Balia, 404, f. 3v. Officials of the *Balia* of Siena to the *Otto di Pratica*, 1 February 1483; *eidem* to the Sienese ambassadors in Rome, 1 February; ASF, Dieci, Carteggi, Responsive, 26, f. 71; the Florentine castellans in Colle Val d'Elsa to the *Dieci*, 1 February.

[16] ASF, Dieci di Balia, Legazioni e Commissarie, 5, f. 203r-204r; Milan, Archivio di Stato [hereafter ASMi], Sforzesco Potenze Estere [SPE], Firenze, cartella 306, Malatesta Sacramoro to the Duke of Milan, 15 February 1483.

Florentine government was finally able to secure the cession of the places in the Chianti. On 14 June 1483, one day before their return, Florence and Siena signed a twenty-five year alliance.[17] The chronicler Allegretti bitterly criticised the members of the Sienese government for being prepared to harm their *patria* in order to monopolise power and keep their political opponents in exile;[18] but from a Florentine point of view the domestic unpopularity of the new regime had its advantages. Faced with opposition within the city and outside it the governors of Siena would be all the more dependent on the support of their new Florentine ally, and would not be tempted either to put themselves under the protection of Naples, since the Regno was home to many *Noveschi* exiles, nor to attempt to regain the places that they had ceded to Florence.

Its alliance with Florence brought the regime of the *popolo* in Siena many benefits. On 11 May 1484 the two governments demonstrated the warmth of their friendship by jointly hiring the military services of Jacopo Appiano, Lord of Piombino;[19] and in the negotiations that led to the peace of Bagnolo, which ended the Ferrara war, the Florentines made it clear to the other parties that they considered the security of the Sienese regime as a vital interest of theirs. On 1 August, for example, the *Dieci di Balia* wrote to Pier Filippo Pandolfini, Florentine ambassador and commissioner- general in Milan and the camp of the League, that with regard to the affairs of the government of Siena, *harai somma advertentia che si aconcino in modo che restino sicuri et liberi, non che da ogni pericolo, ma da suspitione di pericolo.*[20] Thanks to Florentine diplomatic pressure Siena was given two months by the peace of Bagnolo to become a party to it.[21] Lorenzo was on good terms with leading members of the regime, and in particular with Cristofano Guidocci, Paolo di Gherardo and Andrea Piccolomini.[22]

The closeness of the relationship between the Florentine and Sienese régimes explains why Lorenzo was sharply critical of Siena's decision to send an embassy to Venice at the end of September 1484, before the terms of Bagnolo had been fully complied with.[23] He was afraid of the damage Florence's reputation would suffer if her protégé sought to establish a special relationship with Venice, or gave the impression that she was trying to do so. The problem was not a trifling one, for it could not be denied that the financial and military resources of Venice were greater than those of Florence, and the war of Ferrara had shown that Venice could take on Milan and Florence, the

---

[17] ASF, Dieci di Balia, Deliberazioni, Condotte, Stanziamenti, 24, f. 27r-28r.

[18] *Diari*, cols. 814-15.

[19] ASF, Dieci di Balia, Deliberazioni, Condotte, Stanziamenti, 27, f. 118r-122r.

[20] ASF, Otto di Pratica, Legazioni e Commissarie, 3, f. 84r.

[21] *Codex Italiae Diplomaticus*, ed. J.C. Lünig, 3 (Frankfurt and Leipzig, 1732), col. 134.

[22] Florence, Biblioteca Nazionale, MS Palatino 552, f. 65r: Lorenzo de' Medici to Piero de' Medici, 26 November 1484.

[23] ASS, Balia, 520, inserto 28. R. Richi to Balia of Siena, 30 September 1485.

pope and the king of Naples, and still emerge from her conflict with them with the substantial gain of the Polesine of Rovigo.[24] From the point of view of a weak regime like that of Siena Venetian protection might seem infinitely more valuable than that offered by Florence, particularly as the Sienese were aware that the major powers of Italy would take a similar view. Why, therefore, was Florentine protection worth having?

Part of the answer to this question is contained, paradoxically, in an argument deployed by Bernardo Rucellai, Florence's ambassador in Milan, to persuade Ludovico Sforza, first, that he should allow the destruction of his relative Girolamo Riario, ruler of Imola and a *protégé* of Milan's, whose involvement in the Pazzi conspiracy had made him the object of Lorenzo's enduring, though often concealed, hatred;[25] and, secondly, that he should not put all his trust in his recently established alliance with Venice. Ludovico should consider, Rucellai said, what he could hope for from Florence, for although she was not one of the leading powers of Italy, no one was as loyal as she was. Venice, by contrast, was powerful enough to be an unreliable ally.[26] Rucellai's case was designed to persuade the ruler of a state far more formidable than Florence, but it might as well have been devised to convince the Sienese. It was not just Florence's financial resources, it was her relative military weakness, her need for the loyalty of the Sienese regime and her dependence on the support of the Milanese government, that could make her seem a reliable protector of the one, a faithful and serviceable ally of the other. Lorenzo used a memorable image when seeking to impress upon Richo Richi, Sienese ambassador to Venice, how important it was that Siena not jeopardize its relationship with Florence and with him by an overly sedulous courtship of the Venetians: *dirovvi uno motto che poco fa usò con me una mia figliolina di tre anni in circa che, scendendo la schala di chasa insieme, mi disse: Lorenzo, guardiate che non chadiate; et io le risposi: perché lo dici?; rispose Perché facendo male a voi, faria male a me ancora.*[27] The moral was clear: if Siena's foreign policy damaged Florence, Florence would be less able to help Siena. Richi got the point, and in a subsequent letter to Lorenzo from Venice he not merely confessed that his own safety and that of the regime depended on Lorenzo's authority and well-being, but considered it prudent to give Lorenzo a report of his discussions with the Venetians.[28]

---

[24] L. Simeoni, *Le Signorie* (Milan, 1950), vol. 1, 554.

[25] N. Rubinstein, 'Lorenzo de' Medici: the formation of his statecraft', *Lorenzo de' Medici, Studi*, ed. G. C. Garfagnini (Florence, 1992), 54.

[26] ASF, Archivio Mediceo avanti il Principato, 48, no. 268. B. Rucellai to Lorenzo de' Medici, 1 December 1484.

[27] ASS, Balia, 520, inserto 28. R. Richi to the Balia of Siena, 30 September 1484,

[28] H.C. Butters, 'Politics and Diplomacy in Late Quattrocento Italy: the Case of the Barons' War (1485-1486)', in *Florence and Italy. Renaissance Studies in Honour of Nicolai Rubinstein*, eds. P. Denley and C. Elam (London, 1988), 16.

But it would be distinctly paradoxical - however, for that very reason, attractive - to argue that the popular regime's principal reason for valuing its alliance with Florence was that the latter belonged to the second division of Italian states; and it would equally wrong to be content with Rucellai's modest evaluation of Florence's position in the league table of Italian power politics, accurate as it undoubtedly was as a judgment on the city's military capacity. For one thing, Rucellai himself did not leave his deliverance unqualified, drawing Ludovico Sforza's attention to the strength that Florence derived from the fact that, as the ambassador put it to Lorenzo in a subsequent letter, *le intrate vostre essere quelle che volavate voi medesimi, quali si exporrebbono sempre per questo stato, come altre volte s'erono exposte.*[29] But Florence's resources as a protector were not simply fiscal; her alliance with Milan and Naples, both of whom might otherwise have been tempted to secure a regime in Siena more favourable to themselves, gave her a special standing; and at this juncture both states had two good reasons for not emperilling their relationship with her. In the period after Bagnolo both Ludovico Sforza and King Ferrante, at the head of governments exhausted by the costs of the war of Ferrara, were trying to restore their authority and deal with substantial domestic opposition.[30] Neither, moreoever, trusted the other. Ferrante thought Ludovico's warm relationship with Venice after the Ferrara war extremely menacing and suspected that Ludovico was aiming to supplant his nephew, Duke Gian Galeazzo, as formal ruler of Milan.[31] This would have been a considerable blow to Ferrante and his son the duke of Calabria, since Gian Galeazzo had been betrothed since 1472 to the duke's daughter Isabella.[32] One of the Milanese nobles of whom Ludovico was most afraid, the castellan, Filippo degli Eustachi, had urged the duke of Calabria to send Isabella to Milan, clearly hoping that this would force Ludovico to act with more circumspection.[33] In addition to these tensions between them there was the struggle in which Ludovico and Ferrante were engaged for influence over Genoa, to which allusion has already been made.[34] These sources of antagonism between the two men made them compete for the friendship of Lorenzo and Florence. On paper and in normal times the revenues and military capacity of the Florentine state were considerably inferior to those of Milan or Naples; but the ability of Ludovico and Ferrante to raise money or assemble armies was crucially dependent on the nature of their relationship with

---

[29] ASF, Archivio Mediceo avanti il Principato, 48, no. 268. B. Rucellai to Lorenzo, 1 December 1484.

[30] Butters, 'Politics and Diplomacy', 15-16, 19-21.

[31] Butters, 'Lorenzo and Naples', 148-9.

[32] Lorenzo de' Medici, *Lettere*, vol. 1, ed. R. Fubini (Florence, 1977), 430.

[33] ASF, Archivio Mediceo avanti il Principato, 48, no. 44. P.F. Pandolfini to Lorenzo, 11 September 1484.

[34] See above.

the great nobles of the states they governed, and in 1484 and 1485 they both had far more to fear from domestic opposition than the Medici regime did.

These considerations help to explain why when the Sienese exiles launched their abortive attack on the Sienese dominions in May 1485, they did not dispose of more impressive forces. The kingdom of Naples was a haven for Sienese exiles, but those of them who were involved in the attempt do not appear to have received much assistance from Ferrante: Giovanni Lanfredini, Florentine ambassador in Naples, reported at the end of May 1485 that the king and the duke of Calabria had not supported the Sienese exiles, even though they favoured them in every other way with offices and other sorts of patronage. Ferrante and his son, the ambassador explained, had not backed the exiles' enterprise, because they were playing a waiting game at the moment, and also because the king's debts were so great that he had a horror of any expenditure.[35] Guido Antonio Vespucci, ambassador in Rome, who claimed to have been watching the Neapolitan ambassador like a hawk, said that he found Ferrante keen to prevent the exiles' *impresa*, and had seen letters from him to this effect urging that the pope be persuaded to join Naples in offering men and money to the Sienese regime. Vespucci said that he was inclined to believe the king, not because of the assurances of the Neapolitan ambassador, nor because of Ferrante's letters, but because he did not think it was expedient for the king at present to attempt anything counter to Florentine interests. Vespucci, whose years of diplomatic service had clearly given him a hard carapace, concluded his remarks on the subject by observing that nowadays no trust was to be had in what was said or written to one, nor in friendship, nor in *fede data*, but only in that which one judged *facci compagno et che si vede con facti*.[36]

Ludovico Sforza, for his own reasons, was able to render the Sienese regime and its Florentine protector an equally signal service by denying the exiles the formidable assistance of the *condottiere* Roberto di Sanseverino. The peace of Bagnolo had laid down that by far the largest contribution to the cost of Roberto's *condotta* should be borne by Milan and Venice,[37] and it was of them that he asked for permission to assist the exiles, some of whom were his relatives, in their attempt to return to Siena. Ludovico, who found the *condottiere* an expensive and dangerous employee, had no intention of allowing him to become more powerful, particularly at the expense of the Medici regime, so he gave Roberto his consent, but secretly persuaded the Venetians to deny

[35] Florence, Biblioteca Nazionale, 'Copialettere', II, v, 18, f. 10r. G. Lanfredini to Lorenzo de' Medici, 28 May 1485.

[36] ASF, Dieci di Balia, Carteggi, Responsive, 34, f. 93v. G.A. Vespucci to the Dieci di Balia, 8 May 1485.

[37] *Codex*, ed. Lünig, 3 col. 130.

him theirs.[38] One advantage of this episode from Ludovico's point of view was that it gave him an opportunity to test the strength of the clandestine alliance he had with Venice; and it was probably her willingness to accede to his request and refuse Roberto's that gave Ludovico the confidence not long afterwards to trick the *condottiere* into conspiring against him, thus providing the justification Ludovico needed to dismiss him from his service and strip him of his fiefs in the Milanese dominions.[39]

The help that Florence's allies gave it was not the only reason the Sienese regime had for being grateful to its protector. As soon as the Florentine government heard that the exiles were preparing to attack Siena, it began to arrange for the assembly and dispatch of military assistance. A letter of 6 May from Pier Filippo Pandolfini to Lorenzo, who was at the baths at Bagno a Morbo, described some of the measures that had been taken: letters had been sent to Montepulciano, Foiano, Monte Sansavino and Cortona ordering the local Florentine officials in these towns to raise a force of conscript infantry by commanding each household to provide one man. These troops were to prevent the exiles and their soldiers from passing through Florentine territory and, more generally, to do whatever the Sienese *Balia* instructed them to do. One hundred men-at-arms under Ranuccio Farnese were assigned to the defence of Siena, and an advance party of twenty-five of them with Ranuccio was to set off immediately. The remaining fifty men-at-arms of his company were to hold themselves in readiness.[40] As a special token of his regard for the Sienese regime Lorenzo sent Leonardo di Alfonso, a Spanish infantry commander who had been commanding his bodyguard while he was at the baths. These troops did not arrive in time to help the forces of the Sienese government at the battle of San Quirico, for Ranuccio Farnese did not reach Siena till 11 May,[41] and Lorenzo's letter to the Sienese *Balia*, announcing that Leonardo di Alfonso was on his way, was dated 12 May.[42] But the news that they were going to arrive may well have influenced the exiles' decision to disband their forces instead of attempting another attack; and, indeed, it is highly likely that the principal military aim of their enterprise had been to defeat the troops of the Sienese government and enter Siena before Florentine reinforcements could reach the city.

---

[38] ASF, Archivio Mediceo avanti il Principato, 51, no. 304. B. Rucellai to Lionardo and Francesco Spina and company in Pisa, 19 April 1485 (a letter to Lorenzo de' Medici disguised as a commercial letter). For Venice's, repeated, refusal to accede to the *condottiere's* request, see A[rchivio di] S[tato,] V[enezia], Senatus Secreta, 32, f. 134r (26 February 1485), 139r-v (5 April 1485).

[39] R. Palmarocchi, *La politica italiana di Lorenzo de' Medici* (Florence, 1933), 27-33, 249-65).

[40] ASF, Archivio Mediceo avanti il Principato, 26, no. 365.

[41] Allegretti, *Diari*, col. 818.

[42] ASS, Balia, 523, inserto 22.

But protection rarely comes without costs, and in the case of Florence's the price that the Sienese régime had to pay was giving a Genoese pope, Innocent VIII, and his Savonese counsellor Giuliano della Rovere a powerful incentive, in addition to those that they already had, for favouring the cause of its opponents. After Innocent's election in the previous year Guido Antonio Vespucci had warned the Dieci that the new pope was a keen supporter of the Genoese regime, and a close friend of the Sienese exiles. One reason, to which Vespucci referred in his letter, for Giovanni Battista Cibò's attitude towards the politics of Siena was that when he had been in the city in 1483, having been sent there with a mission to produce an accord between the factions, some of the *Noveschi* were killed and defenestrated by their political opponents, despite previous assurances that violence of this sort would not occur. He had left the city in fury.[43] Vespucci made a veiled allusion to this episode in a letter to the *Dieci* of 3 May 1485.[44] Since, despite their natural sympathies, Innocent and Giuliano della Rovere had been able to do little to help Genoa in her struggle with Florence over Pietrasanta and Sarzana, and in particular to prevent the fall of Pietrasanta in the previous year,[45] the pope had good reason to favour a change of government in Siena that would help his native city by weakening Florence.[46] At the very least he could hope that she would be more accommodating in peace negotiations with Genoa that he was sponsoring at the time.[47] But although it is easy to identify the advantages that Innocent would have derived from the successful execution of the exiles' scheme, it is less easy, though not impossible, to find evidence that he was actively involved in it. This may simply testify to the pope's skill as a dissimulator; for if he was privy to the plot, he would hardly have wanted this fact to be generally known, since he was trying at the same time to persuade the Florentines to accept him as a peacemaker in their conflict with the Genoese; and Milan and Naples, moreover, might well have been prompted to exact retribution for the damage caused to their ally. The problem of discovering what part Innocent played in the crisis is exacerbated, moreover, by the fact that he was ill at the time. On 8 May Vespucci complained, in a letter to the *Dieci di Balia*, that he had had but one audience with Innocent since the onset of the pope's illness.[48]

Whatever else the exiles might have hoped for from Innocent, it could not, therefore, have been overt military assistance. But covert aid was another matter. Innocent certainly knew about the negotiations that led to an agreement

---

[43] ASF, Dieci di Balia, Carteggi, Responsive, 32, f. 103v, 31 August 1484; Allegretti, *Diari*, cols. 813-14.

[44] ASF, Dieci di Balia, Carteggi, Responsive 34, f. 82v.

[45] Butters, 'Florence and Naples', 148.

[46] A point Vespucci made in his letter of 3 May (see above, n. 44).

[47] Palmarocchi, *La Politica*, 12-13.

[48] ASF, Dieci di Balia, Carteggi, Responsive, 34, f. 93v.

between some of the exiles and the *condottiere* Roberto di Sanseverino. In a letter of 16 April the *Dieci di Balia* informed their ambassador in Milan, Bernardo Rucellai, that a cardinal had acted as intermediary between the exiles and the *condottiere*,[49] and in an encoded *polizza* that they sent with the letter they revealed that the cardinal in question was Giuliano della Rovere.[50] At this stage of his pontificate Innocent had no more intimate or influential a counsellor than della Rovere,[51] and it is difficult to believe that in a matter of such importance the cardinal would have acted without consulting his master. But it is not clear how far the pope approved of the exiles using Sanseverino to encompass their aims; for in the letter approved by the Venetian Senate on 26 February that was sent to Sanseverino, seeking to persuade him not to ride south to help the exiles, who had offered him the lordship of the city, one of the points made was that Innocent was already heavily involved in the exiles' schemes, and had already ordered a good number of troops to be assigned to assist them.[52] The Venetians, anxious not to lose Sanseverino's services or put at risk their alliance with Milan, were obviously keen to deploy any argument that would dissuade the *condottiere* from joining the exiles, but this does not prove that their information was unreliable. It may well be, therefore, that before Sanseverino made it clear that he was interested, Innocent had agreed to provide secret military assistance for the exiles. Venice's veto put an end to Roberto's involvement,[53] which had not,in any case, met with the approval of all the exiles.[54]

It is not clear whether either Innocent or Giuliano della Rovere played a direct part in bringing the Orsini and the exiles together; but they may well have let it be known that they approved of the association and its objective. Once the enterprise was launched, Innocent did everything he could to convince the Florentine ambassador that he disapproved of it, going so far as to command the governor of Sutri and the Vice-Legate of the Patrimony at Viterbo to arrest the forces of the Sienese exiles and to send off an equerry with letters patent ordering that they be denied passage. But it is significant that these measures did not impress the Florentine ambassador Vespucci, who remarked to the *Dieci di Balia* that the pope's briefs would do as little good as those he had often seen Sixtus IV issue in similar circumstances, and pointed out that when the Sienese ambassador had asked the pope to write to Virginio and Giulio Orsini, Innocent had pretended not to understand. Even a papal proclamation of 1 May, which

---

[49] ASF, Otto di Pratica, Legazioni e Commissarie, 3, f. 128v.

[50] ASF, Otto di Pratica, Legazioni e Commissarie, 3, f. 129v.

[51] Butters, 'Politics and Diplomacy', 18-19.

[52] ASV, Senatus Secreta, 32, f. 134 r.

[53] ASF, Dieci, Carteggi, Responsive, 34, f. 29. B. Rucellai to the *Dieci di Balia*, 17 April 1485.

[54] ASF, Dieci, Carteggi, Responsive, 34: G.A. Vespucci to the *Dieci di Balia* (undated but written shortly after 22 April), f. 49.

ordered all troops not employed by the Church to leave Rome and the Papal State forthwith, failed to convince Vespucci of the pope's good faith, for his comment on it was: *la qual cosa non pare punto fuor di proposito per dare colore che non si adombri se fanterie o gente d'arme si partissino di qua.*[55] It is true that Giulio Orsini and his men were held at Bolsena and many of the exiles were arrested at Viterbo;[56] but the same letter in which Vespucci reported these encouraging developments contained the disheartening news that the exiles, with the exception of messer Cino Cinughi, had been released, and that Giulio Orsini had escaped with the help of a secretary at Bolsena. Vespucci was led to deduce that Innocent was indeed supporting the exiles, as they claimed, or at least that the pope had been fooled by those around him.[57] It is true that after the collapse of the enterprise the pope informed Vespucci that he had two of the ringleaders, messer Cino Cinughi and messer Ludovico Martinozzi under arrest, that he was about to arrest a third, Niccolò Borghesi, and that he was going to have them interrogated under torture, if necessary in the presence of the Florentine and Sienese ambassadors.[58] But the men were released shortly afterwards.[59] Vespucci's comment, made before he had learnt of the release of the three Sienese, that *donec queste differentie genovese non sono assettate, non credo si possi fare fondamento alchuno in parole che venghino di qui,*[60] seems amply justified.

While the Sienese regime might have accepted with some resignation the pope's support for the exiles' plot, it must have been disappointed that its protector, Lorenzo, had not been able to prevent Giulio Orsini from helping them, given the fact that Lorenzo's wife was an Orsini. From the pope's point of view the Sienese exiles' decision to turn to the Orsini had the advantage, as Guido Antonio Vespucci saw clearly, that it made it easy for him to deny that he had given them his consent, *non essendo li Orsini né suoi benivoli, né suoi soldati.*[61] For the Orsini, involvement in an undertaking that they had good reasons for supposing the pope supported offered the prospect of a return to papal favour, or at least of a notable increase in their influence and connections. Even for Virginio, who eventually decided, under severe Florentine pressure, not to participate, and who tried to prevent Giulio from doing so,[62] these were

---

[55] The same to the same, 4 May 1485, ASF, Dieci, Carteggi, Responsive, 34, f. 86.

[56] The same to the same, 8 May 1485, ASF, Dieci, Carteggi, Responsive, 34, f. 93.

[57] ASF, Dieci, Carteggi, Responsive, 34, f. 93v.

[58] The same to the same, 14 May 1485, ASF, Dieci, Carteggi, Responsive, 34, f. 115.

[59] S. Tizio, *Historiarum Senensium*, ASF, Dieci, Carteggi, Responsive, 34BAV, Mss. Chigiani, G, II, 36, f. 101r.

[60] G.A. Vespucci to the *Dieci di Balia*, 14 May 1485, loc. cit.ASF, Dieci, Carteggi, Responsive, 34, f. 115.

[61] The same to the same, 3 May 1485, ASF, Dieci, Carteggi, Responsive, 34, f. 83.

[62] Bartolomeo Ugolini to the *Dieci di Balia*, 8 May 1485, ASF, Dieci, Carteggi, Responsive, 34, f. 92.

serious considerations, that might well have overridden his feelings of obligation to his *parente* Lorenzo. During the pontificate of Sixtus IV, after all, this relationship had not prevented Virginio from serving the pope, even during the Pazzi war, and establishing a rapport with Lorenzo's enemy, Girolamo Riario.[63] Goro Gheri, who managed the Medici regime for Lorenzo duke of Urbino in the early sixteenth century, and who was obsessed with the fragility of the relationship of *parentado*,[64] would not have been surprised.

The final point of interest about the exiles' attempt is how seriously Florence and Lorenzo took it. Despite the fact that the exiles' force was a relatively small one, and despite the fact that neither Milan nor Naples were supporting the coup, the Sienese ambassador in Florence, Tommaso Biringucci, was bombarded with questions about the state of opinion in Siena. He had to make a determined effort to persuade leading members of the regime that the citizens of Siena were totally united and that the government was taking the appropriate measures for the defence of the city: *in ne la quale materia molto mi extesi, perché avevo veduto che di questo dubitavano, non che collegialiter mai me ne parlassero li Signori Dieci, ma da molti particulari, et de' primi, n'ero stato domandato, et le prime parole erano: Come la fate dentro? Sete voi uniti? Intendetevi voi bene? et simili parole.'*[65] Lorenzo had written to the Sienese Balia that since two thousand infantry were insufficient to take Siena, the key to surmounting the crisis was civic unity;[66] and it may well be that the modest size of the exiles' force was itself considered a cause for concern, on the grounds that if they thought it adequate for their purposes, this must mean that they were confident of support within Siena itself. This was certainly an impression that the exiles themselves were keen to foster. One is reminded of Keynes's famous comparison between investing in the economy and a competition to predict the result of a beauty contest, in which each competitor has to select not the contestant he considers the most beautiful, but the one that he thinks majority opinion will vote for; since everyone is making the same calculation, the winner will be the person for whom average opinion expects average opinion to vote.[67] In other words, if enough people were persuaded that the exiles' undertaking had enough support to be successful, it would be.

But there was an equal and opposite danger. Fearful that the *popolo* of Siena would not take the coup attempt seriously enough, the *Dieci di Balia*

---

[63] C. Shaw, 'Lorenzo de' Medici and Virginio Orsini', *Florence and Italy*, 34.

[64] H.C. Butters, *Governors and Government in early sixteenth-century Florence, 1502-1519* (Oxford, 1985), 284.

[65] ASS, Balia, 522, inserto 34.T Biringucci to the Sienese *Balia*, 28 April 1485.

[66] ASS, Balia, 522, inserto 40: Lorenzo de' Medici to the Officials of the Sienese *Balia*, 4 May 1485.

[67] For a witty and incisive discussion of Keynes's analogy, see M. Hollis, *The Cunning of Reason* (Cambridge, 1987), 102.

actually advised the Sienese government to conceal the fact that Sanseverino was no longer supporting the exiles, arguing that if the citizenry of Siena thought he still was, it would be easier for the government to raise money and troops.[68]

This was, in fact, an enterprise of whose outcome no one could be certain until it was over. Richo Richi made this quite clear in a post mortem report to Lorenzo: the coup attempt, he said, had been a very good thing for the regimes of Florence and Siena, *perché noi per li effetti habbiamo intesa la dispositione et drento a la città et de li subditi nostri, la quale non può essere più opposita a li usciti.*[69] In his letter to the *Dieci di Balia* of 12 May, which reported the news of the exiles' defeat, the Florentine ambassador Vespucci judged that the exiles would launch no more attacks that year, since they had little cash, and were unlikely to get more, *essendo questa la tertia impresa che hanno facta, et tutte riuscite a un modo.*[70] Two years later the *Noveschi* exiles were back in Siena.[71] It would be nice to think that Lorenzo's lines on the fugacity of human pleasures reflected something of his experience of Italian politics, of whose vicissitudes he was so well aware: Quant' è bella giovinezza, che si fugge tuttavia! Chi vuol essere lieto, sia: di doman non c'è certezza.[72]

---

[68] T. Biringucci to the Sienese *Balia*, 27 April 1485, ASS, Balia, 522, inserto 31.

[69] ASF, Archivio Mediceo avanti il Principato, 26, no. 387, 18 May 1485.

[70] ASF, Dieci di Balia, Carteggi, Responsive, 34, f. 109.

[71] Allegretti, *Diari*, col. 821.

[72] Lorenzo de' Medici, *Canzona di Bacco*, in *Opere*, ed. L. Cavalli (Naples, 1970), 583.

Personalities and pressures: Italian involvement in the French invasion of 1494

Michael Mallett

That the 'crisi d'Italia' in 1494 and the following years was the result of the weakness of the Italian states and the rivalries amongst them, has been a historiographical commonplace since the accounts of Paolo Giovio and Francesco Guicciardini. Ludovico Sforza and Pope Alexander VI have usually been identified as the principal villains; but the vacillation of Florence, the self-serving neutrality of Venice and the blandishments of Neapolitan exiles and dissident Italian cardinals have also been identified in a general condemnation of the Italian political world. The military captains took as much, if not more, of the blame as the political elites, but they at least were confronted with an apparently invincible military juggernaut in fleeing before which they could find some justification.[1]

Nowadays we are well aware of the need to balance this view of a one-sided military confrontation, and of Italian responsibility for their own fate. Against the self-seeking invitations and encouragements of Italy's political leaders we set the long term dynastic and strategic developments outside Italy, the whims and enthusiasms of Charles VIII of France, the individual interests and ambitions of his advisers, the appeal of the crusade, and last but not least the lure of Italy. The whole episode is set rightly in the context of French policy towards Italy throughout the century, and of rapidly emerging Franco-Spanish confrontation for dominance of the Mediterranean. 1492, the year in which Charles VIII's *impresa* began to emerge as reality, was the year of the final

---

[1] For the classic almost contemporary accounts, see Paolo Giovio, *Pauli Iovii... historiarum sui temporis tomi duo*, I (Florence, 1550) and see Francesco Guicciardini, *Storia d'Italia*, book 1, caps. 1-11. The major subsequent contributions are G. Canestrini et A. Desjardins, *Négociations diplomatiques de la France avec la Toscane*, vol. 1 (Paris, 1859), H.F. Delaborde, *L'expédition de Charles VIII en Italie. Histoire diplomatique et militaire* (Paris, 1888) and P. Negri, 'Studi sulla crisi italiana alla fine del secolo XV', *Archivio storico lombardo*, 50 (1923), and 51 (1924). Two recent studies of Charles VIII are also useful: Y. Labande-Mailfert, *Charles VIII et son milieu, 1470-98: la jeunesse au pouvoir* (Paris, 1975) and A. Denis, *Charles VIII et les italiens* (Geneva, 1979).

reconquest of Granada, with all that that implied for the release of Spanish energies, as well as the year of the deaths of Lorenzo the Magnificent and Pope Innocent VIII, events to which Guicciardini attached so much importance.

Nevertheless, it is not inappropriate, in view of the work that has been done recently on later fifteenth-century Italian politics, to re-evaluate the Italian role in the preparation and prospects of the French invasion. The judgement will still be an interim judgement as the work of editing and commenting on the letters of Lorenzo de' Medici, which is throwing so much new light on the Italian political scene of the second half of the century, is still far from complete; the last crucial years of Lorenzo's life, the moment of his greatest influence as an Italian statesman, remain largely unexplored. But centenaries cannot wait to be celebrated and 1994 is a good moment for a reassessment.[2]

Where should an investigation of the factors behind the French invasion of Italy in 1494 start? Angevin claims to the crown of Naples had been supported by the French kings since the consolidation of Aragonese rule in the Regno in 1442. Italian states had repeatedly appealed to France for help in their internecine wars. French armies had been involved in Italy in 1453 and the early 1460s, and were to be again in the 1480s. However, the early 1480s were something of a turning point with the passing of the Angevin claims to Naples to the French crown following the deaths of René of Anjou and Charles of Maine, and with the accession of Charles VIII in 1483. Charles inherited not only the new claims but also an emerging understanding with Milan, born out of mutual concern about the threats of Charles the Bold of Burgundy, and out of Ludovico Sforza's anxiety to stifle Orleanist claims to Milan and royal concern about his displacement of the Duchess Bona. However, it was more the young Charles' own ambitions to win fame as Italian prince and crusader which seemed to hasten matters on. These ambitions were fuelled by Etienne de Vesc, his tutor, who encouraged Neapolitan humanists in exile at the French court to investigate the validity of the Angevin claims, and by an Angevin-Provençal faction at court.[3]

The ambitions were also encouraged by a series of pleas for French intervention in Italy in the 1480's. In early 1484 the Venetian ambassador,

---

[2] *Lettere di Lorenzo de' Medici*, ed. R. Fubini, N. Rubinstein and M.E. Mallett, vols. 1-6 (1449-82) (Florence, 1977-90), vol. 7 (1482-84) forthcoming in 1995. Other recent works which illuminate Italian politics in the years before the French invasion are: Istituto Treccani, *Storia di Milano*, 7 (Milan, 1956); R. Fubini, *Italia Quattrocentesca. Politica e diplomazia nell'età di Lorenzo il Magnifico* (Milan, 1994); *Gli Sforza a Milano e in Lombardia e i loro rapporti con gli stati italiani ed europei (1450-1534)*, Atti del convegno internazionale (Milan, 1982); C. De Frede, *L'impresa di Napoli di Carlo VIII; commento ai primi due libri della 'Storia d' Italia' del Guicciardini* (Naples, 1982); E. Pontieri, *Per la storia del regno di Ferrante I d' Aragona, re di Napoli* (Naples, 1947).

[3] E. Pontieri, 'Napoletani alla corte di Carlo VIII', in his *Per la storia del regno di Ferrante I* and Labande-Mailfert, *Charles VIII*, 174.

Antonio Loredan, was urging Charles to intervene in the War of Ferrara against Milan.[4] In 1486, during the Barons' War, plans were afoot in Rome to call in the French to overthrow both Sforza and King Ferrante.[5] In 1489 Innocent VIII declared Ferrante deposed on 11 September, and sent Antonio Flores and Lionello Chieregato to France to invite Charles to occupy Naples.[6] The 'playing of the French card' was becoming an increasingly popular device of Italian politics and it proved moderately effective. Ludovico Sforza did suddenly move towards peace in 1484, for a variety of reasons, one of which was a fear of stirrings in France. Ferrante did come to terms with the papacy, and eventually move in late 1491 towards a formal reconciliation.

It was indeed in late 1491 that there was a speeding up of the tempo in the events that led up to the invasion. By November of that year negotiations were under way for an entente between Ferrante and Innocent VIII. Piero Nasi, the Florentine ambassador in Naples, reported on these at length to Lorenzo de' Medici who had clearly expressed worries about the rumours of the negotiations which he had heard. Nasi noted that Ferrante was mainly concerned about his isolation which he felt was being contrived by Ludovico Sforza as part of Sforza's long-term plan to supplant his ailing nephew, duke Gian Galeazzo, and the duke's Neapolitan bride. It is also clear from Nasi's dispatch that Naples was at this time extremely dependent on Florence for reliable news from France.[7] Lorenzo, jealous perhaps for his own influence at the papal court, sent his secretaries, Niccolò Michelozzi and Antonio della Valle, to Rome and Naples to watch events. Their reports confirmed the new alliance which was concluded in late January 1492 and drew attention to the role of Alfonso of Calabria and Gian Giacomo Trivulzio, now in exile from Milan and serving Naples, in promoting it. Trivulzio was said to be 'mostrando a Sua Maestà il pericolo al quale è esposta per i successi di Francia, restando il Papa di mala volontà verso di lei'.[8]

Rumours of the impending alliance had also reached Milan where Ludovico Sforza was about to welcome a French embassy sent to renew the long-term understanding between the two states. The talk was of Genoa being restored to Milanese control in return for some restoration of territory by Milan

---

[4] *Lettere di Lorenzo de' Medici*, vol. 7 (forthcoming), lett. 681 and 684, 21 and 24 luglio, 1484.

[5] Mantua, Archivio di Stato [hereafter ASMa], Archivio Gonzaga [AG], 847, cc. 513-14: G.P. Arrivabene to Francesco Gonzaga, 15 March 1486.

[6] P. Luc, 'Un appel du pape Innocent VIII au roi du France (1489)', *Mélanges d'archéologie et d'histoire de l'École française de Rome*, 16 (1939), 332-55.

[7] Florence, Archivio di Stato (ASF), Repubblica: Signoria, Dieci e Otto, 26, cc. 90r-94r: P. Nasi to Lorenzo de' Medici, 17 Nov. 1491.

[8] ASF, Archivio mediceo avanti il principato [MAP], LX, 1: Antonio della Valle to Lorenzo de' Medici, 8 Jan. 1492.

to Montferrat and Milanese military help to Charles VIII in his confrontation with Maximilian. The ambassadors watching these negotiations in Milan in January 1492, Pier Filippo Pandolfini for Florence and Giacomo Trotti for Ferrara, made no reference in their reports to any potential or planned threat to Naples, although there was talk of Neapolitan agents in France seeking to obstruct the Franco-Milanese entente.[9] Trotti commented on Ludovico's pleasure at the successful conclusion of the negotiations with France in late January and hinted darkly that within a year Ludovico would be Duke of Milan somehow.[10] Meanwhile a grand reciprocal embassy to France was being planned to be led by Gian Francesco di Sanseverino, the Count of Caiazzo. The instructions to this embassy, issued on 21 February 1492, spoke of offering all the resources of the Milanese Duchy to Charles VIII to help against his enemies, particularly in Italy.[11]

The Count of Caiazzo's embassy arrived in Paris on 26 March 1492 and was received with great honour. With him went Girolamo Tuttavilla, courtier-soldier and bastard son of the late cardinal Estouteville, and Carlo da Barbiano, Count of Belgioioso, who was to remain in France as resident ambassador for the next year.[12] It is hard to judge the impact of this embassy on the events that were to follow two years later. Obviously contacts were made with key figures at the French court, and Caiazzo and his brother Galeazzo were to be prime movers on the Milanese side. But there was clearly no open discussion at this stage of a French invasion supported by Milan, and indeed the embassy left on 5 May somewhat disappointed with their reception.[13] At this point Charles was still embroiled with the encircling alliance of Maximilian, England and Spain against him and still preoccupied with the problem of Anne of Brittany.

During the course of this embassy, Lorenzo de' Medici died on 8 April. The passing of the political leader who had, over the years, done much to hold together the triple alliance of Naples, Florence and Milan, has often been seen as a key factor in the impending crisis. However, Lorenzo's role as the mediator between Milan and Naples seems to have been increasingly ineffective in the later years. He himself became more involved in developing influence at the

---

[9] For Pandolfini's dispatches, see ASF, Repubblica, Otto di Pratica, Responsive, 8. Jan.-Feb. 1492. Those of Giacomo Trotti to Ferrara are in Modena, Archivio di Stato [ASMo], Archivio Segreto Estense [ASE], Ambasciatori, Milano, 7.

[10] ASMo, ASE, Ambasciatori, Milano, 7, c. 25: Giacomo Trotti to Ercole d'Este, 24 Jan. 1492.

[11] Milan, Archivio di Stato [ASMi], Sforzesco, Potenze Estere [SPE], Francia, cartella 549: 21 Feb. 1492.

[12] ASMi, SPE, Francia, 549: Gian Francesco di Sanseverino to duke of Milan, 29 Mar. 1492. See also Labande-Mailfert, *Charles VIII*, 213-14 and Delaborde, *L'expédition de Charles VIII*, 236-50.

[13] ASMi, SPE, Francia, 550: Gian Francesco di Sanseverino to duke of Milan, 5 May 1492.

papal court and seemed to be losing the confidence of Ludovico Sforza. He watched as the papal-Neapolitan entente developed but the Milanese ambassadors in Florence in late 1491 and early 1492, Giovan Angelo Talenti and Gian Stefano Castiglioni, made few comments on Lorenzo's attitudes and actions, which was in marked contrast to Milanese reporting of a few years earlier. Lorenzo was, of course, in failing health by this time and frequently out of Florence in one of his villas or at spas. It is impossible to speculate, given the changing circumstances, on what influence he might have had on subsequent events had he lived through 1493 and 1494.[14]

When Innocent VIII conducted the investiture of the prince of Capua, Ferrante's grandson, in June 1492 as a part of the new papal-Neapolitan alliance, the French ambassadors in Rome lodged a formal protest; but Ferrante 'mostrava tenere pocho conto, stimando che simili cose non procedessino dalla mente di quello Re ma da qualche ingegno sophistico che li è intorno'.[15] At this point the most obvious 'ingegno sophistico' close to Charles VIII was the exiled Neapolitan baron, Antonello di Sanseverino, Prince of Salerno. Sanseverino, the leader of the baronial revolt in 1485-86, had gone into exile in early 1487 and in June 1489 had arrived at the French court with a substantial entourage of relatives and supporters.[16] Charles VIII, temporarily preoccupied, gave them pensions and estates in Burgundy while Philippe de Commynes commented: 'Thus these above-mentioned barons came to France, where they were well received but poorly endowed with goods... One day they were full of hope and the next day the opposite'. This no doubt aptly described the position of these exiles in 1489-90, but does less than credit to their later role in the events of the *impresa*.[17]

It was in February 1490, at the moment of the peace of Frankfurt between Charles VIII and Maximilian, that Antonello di Sanseverino appeared again at the French court at Moulins with maps and plans. His proposals for an invasion of Naples were listened to by two marshals of France, and by Etienne de Vesc. According to the report of the papal envoy the talk was essentially practical: about the type of army needed, the siting of rivers and castles, the problems of

---

[14] For the dispatches of Talenti and Castiglioni, see ASMi, SPE, Firenze, 937 passim. For confirmation of this view of Lorenzo's declining influence, see Negri 'La crisi italiana', vol. 1, 13.

[15] He 'showed little concern, believing that such things did not proceed from the mind of the king, but from some pedantic genius close to him': ASF, Repubblica, Otto di Pratica, Responsive, 8, cc. 330r-332r: Niccolò Michelozzi to the Otto di Praktica, 16 June 1492. A copy of the instructions to the French orators in Rome is to be found in ASMa, AG 849, c. 16.

[16] Labande-Mailfert, *Charles VIII*, 191-2. Now see also R. Colapietra, *I Sanseverini di Salerno: mito e realtà del barone ribelle* (Salerno, 1985), 45-80.

[17] Philippe de Commynes, *Mémoires*, ed. J. Calmette, vol. 3 (Paris, 1925), 11.

supply, etc.[18] This was the kind of expertise that a man like Sanseverino could provide; his estates, now forfeited, lay along the west coast of the Regno, an obvious entry point for an invading force. Ten days after this meeting Charles again called for investigation of his claims to Naples, and embarked on two long visits to Marseilles to consider the question of the preparation of a fleet.[19] From this moment onwards Antonello di Sanseverino remained at court, close to Etienne de Vesc, who was to be the principal proponent of the Neapolitan enterprise, but distrusted by Guillaume Briconnet, bishop of St Malô and financial controller, who was said to be suspicious of all Italians.[20]

The death of Innocent VIII and the dramatic and unexpected election of Rodrigo Borgia as Alexander VI on 11 August 1492 was for many observers the decisive twist to events. Despite the fact that Innocent had himself at least twice appealed to France to intervene in Italian affairs, and that his Ligurian antagonism to Milan had played a significant part in arousing Ludovico's fears of isolation, it was his Spanish successor who has often been seen as the real disturber of the balance of power in Italy. Whether it was through direct encouragement to Charles VIII to intervene in early 1493, or through undue hesitation over the King's demands for investiture of Naples, or through taking unnecessary offence over the affair of the Cibò castles, or indeed through creating the League of St Mark in April 1493 and thus upsetting the balance of power, it was Alexander who became the scapegoat.[21] But Alexander, despite his nationality which in itself made him an unlikely ally of the French, had been part of the Italian political scene for forty years and played according to the same rules as Ludovico Sforza and King Ferrante. He had no interest in a permanent French presence in Naples but was perfectly prepared to threaten Ferrante with a French intervention if Naples continued to seek to destabilise the Papal State by intrigues with the leading barons.[22]

The affair of the Cibò castles, identified by Guicciardini as the little seed from which great consequences grow, was indeed one of the main preoccupations of Italian diplomats and statesmen during the winter of 1492-93.[23] It led to a new alignment in the League of St Mark of the Pope, Milan and Venice against Naples and Florence. However, the effect of these

---

[18] Luc, 'Un appel du Pape', 344-5.

[19] Labande-Mailfert, *Charles VIII*, 192-3.

[20] Ibid. 198, 201, 212.

[21] Negri 'La crisi italiana', vol. 1, 42 ff. See also G. Pepe, *La politica dei Borgia* (Naples, 1945), 35-50.

[22] Pontieri, *Per la storia del regno di Ferrante I*, 287-325 questions King Ferrante's involvement in the Cibò castles affair, but Antonio Stanga's reports from Naples to the Duke of Milan (ASMi, SPE, Napoli, 250: 30 Oct. 1492 and 16 November 1492) leave little room for doubt. See also M.E. Mallett, *The Borgias: the rise and fall of a Renaissance dynasty* (London, 1969), 124-8 for a reassessment of Alexander's diplomacy.

[23] Guicciardini, *Storia d' Italia*, book 1, cap. 3.

developments, and particularly of the success of Ascanio Sforza in controlling the 1492 papal election, was actually to reduce the fears of Ludovico Sforza. His one consistent concern was to strengthen his position in Milan and ultimately supplant his nephew as duke. Possible allies in this aim ranged from Maximilian through the Pope and Venice to Charles VIII; the main thing for him to avoid was isolation in the face of the inevitable hostility of the Aragonese dynasty in Naples. The new influence which he exercised in Rome through his brother Ascanio as Vice-Chancellor, and the new support obtained through the League of St Mark, together with the successful negotiations for the marriage of Bianca Sforza to Maximilian, made him a good deal less interested in French support for the time being. Angelo Niccolini, the Florentine ambassador in Milan in September 1492, commented on Ludovico's new found confidence, and Piero Guiccardini, who replaced Niccolini early in the following year, found little interest in Milan about French affairs or French intentions until June 1493.[24] Even then, faced by clear indications of a new French resolve to press on with an invasion, Ludovico's initial response was one of alarm. It was only towards the end of 1493, when Alexander became reconciled with Ferrante, that Ludovico reactivated his pro-French policy.

Ludovico Sforza was encouraged in this long period of relative disregard of French affairs by the reports of Carlo da Barbiano from the French court. 'Le cose de Franza sono uno chaos, né mai si può venire a conchiusione di cosa alcuna' wrote Ludovico's ambassador on 2 February 1493.[25] However, a few days later he followed up this report with the news that, despite all his preoccupations with his enemies, Charles was not prepared to listen to anything 'che non li parà vada da directo a condure la impresa di Napoli'.[26] Charles' personal determination became more apparent in May as negotiations with Maximilian moved towards a satisfactory conclusion at Senlis. Even before the treaty was published on 23 May Charles had set up a special commission to consider the affairs of Italy; Etienne de Vesc and Briconnet led the commission along with Marshal d'Esquerdes and Commynes, both well versed in Italian affairs, and Antonello di Sanseverino. At this point, according to many observers, Sanseverino began to play a big role in the preparations for the invasion.[27]

Meanwhile in Milan Piero Guicciardini was writing already on 15 May, with the Franco-Imperial treaty signed but not yet published, commenting on its

[24] ASF, MAP, LXXIV, 48 and 52: A. Niccolini to Piero de' Medici, 20 Aug. 1492 and 2 Sept. 1492. Guicciardini's dispatches to the Otto di Pratica are in ASF, Repubblica: Signoria, Dieci e Otto, 28, cc. 76 ff.

[25] ASMi, SPE, Francia, 550: Carlo da Barbiano to duke of Milan, 2 Feb. 1493.

[26] ASMi, SPE, Francia, 550: Carlo da Barbiano to duke of Milan, 24 Feb. 1493.

[27] Canestrini & Desjardins, *Négociations*, 223-4; Negri, 'La crisi italiana', 94; Labande-Mailfert, *Charles VIII*, 234.

implications for Italian affairs.[28] On 30 May Ercole d'Este wrote a strong letter of warning through his ambassador in Naples to his father in law, King Ferrante, outlining the dangerous implications of French diplomacy.[29] Finally on 4 June Carlo da Barbiano returned in disguise to the Milanese court, having ridden the 600 miles from Senlis in ten days. He carried a personal letter from Charles VIII to Ludovico 'per cosa importante a questo stato'.[30] At this point it is clear that it was Charles who was asking for Ludovico's help and making offers to him which he was finding it hard to resist. Piero Guicciardini reported Ludovico as saying: 'che gli'è venuto il tempo che tutta Italia harà a mandare allui perché remedii ad queste cose che si veggono aparechiare. Perché quando lui le lasciassi andare, e il duca di Ferrara, M. Giovanni Bentivogli, signore di Pesero, e gli altri daranno il passo in modo che loro potranno andare con la lancia in sulla coscia fin in sul Tronto'.[31] Peron de Baschi was in fact on his way to seek support for the French invasion throughout Italy and Guicciardini remarked somberly that if the Cibò castles affair had been settled two months earlier this would never have happened. Here, in the letters of his father, we can see the origins of Francesco Guicciardini's preoccupation with the castles.[32]

The mission of Peron de Baschi revealed the uncertainties of the Italian states: Ludovico hesitated and sought advice, Florence prevaricated and sent an embassy to France to seek to delay the expedition, Alexander VI temporised but moved closer to Naples, and Venice was non-committal but indicated that it was unlikely to act either for or against the French.[33] More strongly discouraging responses would undoubtedly have had a considerable effect on attitudes in France where there was already profound scepticism about the whole venture. Francesco della Casa, sent to France by Florence in June 1493, wrote in August to Piero de' Medici: 'Io non vi fo per questa altro giudizio di queste cose di Napoli che io mi abbia fatto per le altre. Parmi abbiate più da stimare le parole e le pratiche di tal cosa che li effetti, i quali mi pare impossibile che mai possino succedere. E ogni signore e uomo di giudizio di qua è in tale opinione'.[34]

---

[28] ASF, Repubblica: Signoria, Dieci, Otto, 28, c. 100r: P. Guicciardini to the Otto di Pratica, 15 May 1493.

[29] Negri, 'La crisi italiana', 90-91.

[30] ASF, Repubblica: Signoria, Dieci, Otto, 28, c. 103r: P. Guicciardini to the Otto di Pratica, 8 June 1493. Negri, 94 on the basis of a document in ASMi, SPE, Francia 550 (10 June) suggests that the ride took only six days.

[31] 'The time has arrived when all of Italy will have to come to him to deal with the situation that is emerging; because if he lets them past, the duke of Ferrara, messer G. Bentivoglio, the lord of Pesaro and the others will allow free passage so that they will be able to reach the Tronto with lances at rest': ASF, Repubblica: Signoria, Dieci, Otto, 28, cc. 105v-107v: P. Guicciardini to Otto di Pratica, 29 June 1493.

[32] Ibid, 22 June 1493.

[33] Delaborde, *L'expédition de Charles VIII*, 276-83.

[34] Canestrini and Desjardins, *Négociations*, vol. 1, 237.

In Naples rapid mobilisation in response to the League of St Mark in the early summer gave some justification to those who recognised the potential strength of Naples, but in fact King Ferrante showed little sign of alarm about French intentions until the autumn. On 19 September Antonio Stanga, the Milanese ambassador in Naples, reported that the King was beginning to get very concerned and was sending envoys in all directions to inspect troops and ships.[35] In November he sent special ambassadors to the other Italian states 'per intendere come queste cose di Francia sieno intese et obviare iuxta sua possa a ogni scandolo potessi nascere et turbare non solum lo stato suo, ma la quiete d'Italia'.[36] At this stage, in late 1493, it would have been a rash prophet to predict with any confidence that the invasion would actually take place in the following year.

Charles VIII's dependence on Ludovico Sforza's support and advice was emphasised in a long dispatch from Carlo da Barbiano on 27 November 1493: 'Signore mio, veramente questo Re è uno de li più boni et amorevoli re che sia al mondo et ha quella fede nell' Excellentia Vostra che'l ha in lui medesimo, et che questa sia vero ha deliberato, parendo a Vostra Signoria, de venire a la impresa lui in persona, et de meterse tuto in mano di quella, et questo fa che dice cognoscere che cum lo consiglio de Vostra Signoria conquistarà in breve lo reame.'[37] The Milanese ambassador can scarcely be regarded as the most reliable of witnesses to the influence of his own master, but it is clear that Milanese involvement in the preparations for the invasion increased sharply from about this moment. Ludovico, already alarmed by the reconciliation between Alexander VI and Ferrante which had taken place in the autumn and by the obvious signs of Neapolitan mobilisation, was further agitated by the news of the death of Ferrante in late January 1494 and the succession to the throne of Naples of his aggressive son, Alfonso of Calabria, the father of the hapless duchess of Milan. Once again he found himself isolated in Italy, accused of fomenting a French invasion, and threatened by the most bellicose of Italian princes. On 5 March 1494 the new Florentine ambassador in Milan, Piero Alamanni, reported on Ludovico's reaction to abuse heaped on him by a

[35] ASMi, SPE, Napoli 251: Antonio Stanga to duke of Milan, 19 Sept., 1493.

[36] 'To discover how this French business is being taken and to offset as far as possible any threat that might emerge and disrupt not only his own state, but also the peace of Italy': ASF, Repubblica, Otto di Pratica, Responsive, 9, c. 94v-v: Dionigi Pucci from Naples to the Otto di Pratica, 16 Nov. 1493 (this letter is dated 1492 but Pucci was not in Naples in November 1492 and the letter clearly fits into the context of November 1493).

[37] 'My Lord. Truly this King is one of the best and most friendly in the world, and has that faith in Your Excellency that he has in himself. Because of this he has decided to come himself on this expedition, if you agree, and place himself in your hands, and he does this, he says, because he knows that with your counsel he will quickly conquer the kingdom (of Naples)': ASMi, SPE, Francia, 551: Carlo da Barbiano from Tours to duke of Milan, 27 Nov. 1493.

Neapolitan mission returning from France: 'narrandoci che havea sopratenuta questa impresa già uno anno, et che lui non n'era stato el motore, ma statone invitato; et poi veduto e modi serano tenuti in Italia per alchuni era vera l'havea sollicitato. Et che tiene per cosa certa che l'andrà in ogni modo innanzi et affermativamente lo replicò'.[38]

News of the death of Ferrante on 28 January reached France in seven days and gave a great boost to the preparations for the expedition.[39] With the throne of Naples vacant Charles could advance his claims with greater purpose; the unpopularity of Alfonso with the Neapolitan barons was notorious; now was the moment for Alexander VI to declare himself and deprive the Aragonese dynasty of the investiture. Peron de Baschi was soon on his way to Rome once more, but Alexander had no intention of promoting such a change of dynasty in Naples and firmly declared his support for Alfonso.[40]

Alexander's stand gave a new twist to the avowed French motives for the invasion; reform of the Church and deposition of a corrupt and simoniacal pope became a part of the rhetoric.[41] This was eventually to bring a new and powerful Italian ally on to the French side in the person of Cardinal Giuliano della Rovere, but initially it did little to bring greater unity or decision to the preparations. Ludovico Sforza was distrusted by many of Charles' advisers, and the Orleanists pressed strongly for an attack on Milan as the obvious starting point for the enterprise.[42] The preparation of both fleet and army was held up by shortage of funds. Carlo da Barbiana reported that the prince of Orange who was an opponent of the king's plans, 'credo per essere motto dedito a li soi piaceri et non se vorria partire de Franza', was insisting on a great increase in the size of the proposed expedition to balance the scale of Neapolitan preparations; 'parendoli che cum questa propositione le cose se potesseno o dilatare o rompere, o per la grande spesa o per el manchamento de victualie'.[43] Ferrarese observers in France with Don Ferrante the son of Ercole d'Este, who

---

[38] 'Telling us that he had held up this expedition for over a year, and that he was not the originator but had been invited; however having seen the methods of some in Italy it was true that he had encouraged it. Now he was certain that it would go ahead and forcefully repeated this': ASF. Repubblica, Otto di Pratica, Responsive 9, cc. 433r-434r: Piero Alamanni to the Otto di Pratica, 5 March 1494.

[39] ASMo, ASE, Ambasciatori, Francia, 1, n. 16: Belardo Caracciolo from Tours to Ercole d'Este, 4 Feb. 1494.

[40] Delaborde, *L'Expédition de Charles VIII*, 322-3.

[41] ASMi, SPE, Francia 553: Galeazzo di Sanseverino from Macon to Ludovico Sforza, 13 June 1494.

[42] The widespread distrust of Ludovico Sforza at the French court was picked up by a number of ambassadors; see particularly Carlo da Barbiano to the duke of Milan, 29 Nov. and 1 Dec. 1493 (ASMi, SPE, Francia, 551) and Belardo Caracciolo to Ercole d'Este, 8 July 1494 (ASMo, ASE, Ambasciatori, Francia, 1, n. 42).

[43] ASMi, SPE, Francia, 552: Carlo da Barbiano from Lyons to the duke of Milan, 26 Mar. 1494.

was in attendance at the French court in this period, gave the same impression of totally divided counsels at this time.[44] Carlo da Barbiano on 6 March reported a conversation with the king about whether Charles should himself lead the expedition; the king, he said, was determined to go 'vedendo che la più parte del regno suo non era disposita a questa impresa et sapendo che como parlaria di andarli in persona niuno li contradiria più ....'.[45]

At this point, in the early spring of 1494, it is hard to escape the impression that Italian influences, whether those of Antonello di Sanseverino on the one hand or the Milanese envoys on the other, were strong. Camillo Pandone, an experienced diplomat who was part of the returning Neapolitan embassy to France which passed through Milan in March 1494, emphasised the crucial role of Antonello,[46] and Francesco della Casa writing earlier from France confirmed that Charles' Italian affairs were in the hands of the prince of Salerno.[47] In April Galeazzo di Sanseverino, another of the sons of the great condottiere Roberto, future son-in-law of Ludovico Sforza, and noted jouster and courtier, arrived at Lyons to strengthen the Milanese mission.[48] His letters in the subsequent weeks give a vivid, if no doubt prejudiced, account of the delays caused by the divisions at the French court. He remonstrated with the King about the lack of action, and commented on the very limited discussion which Charles allowed at the meetings of his Council.[49] He noted the temporary disenchantment of Guillaume Briconnet, concerned only to obtain a cardinal's hat, and the consequent disorder in the finances.[50] Meanwhile discussions about who should command the army were delayed and taxes were not being paid.[51] Carlo da Barbiano was to write after Galeazzo's return to Milan in June: 'la venuta qui de la Signoria Sua è stata di qualità et così a tempo che quando la fosse manchata la impresa saria o ruinata o posta in extremo periculo'.[52] Once again it is hard to take entirely at face value the comments of one Milanese envoy about another. But the evidence of Francesco della Casa, and indeed of

---

[44] 'Seeing that the greater part of his kingdom was opposed to this expedition, and knowing that if he spoke of going himself no-one would continue to contradict him': ASMo, ASE, Ambasciatori, Francia, 1, n. 32: Belardo Caracciolo to Ercole d'Este, 7 Apr. 1494.

[45] ASMi, SPE, Francia, 552: Carlo da Barbiano, from Lyons to duke of Milan, 6 Mar. 1494.

[46] Piero Alamanni to the Otto di Pratica, 5 Mar. 1494, cit.

[47] ASMi, SPE, Francia, 551: Maffeo Pirovano from Ste. Madeleine to the duke of Milan, 3 Aug. 1493. See also Canestrini and Desjardins, *Négociations*, vol. 1, 227-9, 231, 243 and 264 for Francesco della Casa's reports on Antonello's influence.

[48] ASMi, SPE, Francia, 552: Carlo da Barbiano to the Duke of Milan, 16 Apr. 1494.

[49] ASMi, SPE, Francia, 552: Galeazzo di Sanseverino to the Duke of Milan, 27 Apr. 1494.

[50] ASMi, SPE, Francia, 553: Galeazzo di Sanseverino to Ludovico Sforza, 21 May 1494.

[51] ASMi, SPE, Francia, 553: Galeazzo di Sanseverino to Ludovico Sforza, 6 June 1494.

[52] ASMi, SPE, Francia, 554: Carlo da Barbiano to Ludovico Sforza, 3 July 1494.

Commynes, confirms the impression of disorder and disunity in the French preparations, even if they throw little light on how the problems were resolved.[53]

A further intervention came with the arrival in Lyons on 1 June of Giuliano della Rovere.[54] The powerful cardinal who had controlled papal affairs during the pontificate of Innocent VIII and then temporarily attached himself to the Aragonese cause, was well known in France following a series of legations in the 1480's. His fierce rivalry with Rodrigo Borgia, and the new alliance between the Pope and Naples, now led him to take the side of the French and his arrival in Provence was much heralded. Antonello di Sanseverino, a relative by marriage, went to meet him and conduct him to the court at Lyons.[55] His influence on Charles and the preparations from this moment on was undoubtedly great; Belardo Caracciolo, the leading Ferrarese courtier in the entourage of Ferrante d'Este, commented on 8 July on a visit of Charles VIII to the lodgings of Giuliano 'quale da una grande botta a questa facenda per essere homo risoluto et parlare cum il Re di Franza chiaramente...'[56]

Undoubtedly a new urgency was given to the preparations in June and July. While money began finally to come in and Charles VIII's advisers were coaxed into line, Ludovico's anxieties increased as the Neapolitan fleet put to sea to launch an attack on Genoa and King Alfonso advanced his army into the Romagna.[57] With Neapolitan mobilisation moving much more rapidly than that of France, there seemed to be a real danger of Milan coming under attack before the French were ready to move forward. Carlo da Barbiano, still in Lyons with the King on 17 July, wrote in desperation of a new delay as he urged Charles to set the date for his departure, 'vedendo io che suo Maestà voleva temporezare questa partita et che cognosceva era solo per lo amore di una giovane sua inamorata'. Carlo's report continued that he had said frankly to the King that having pressed on with the *impresa* 'contra tuta Franza... quello che non havevano possuto fare tuti gli signori di Franza de rompere la impresa lo farà una femina'. It appeared that the opponents of the expedition 'havevano proponuta questa femina a la Maestà Sua solo per ruinare l'impresa come sommamente desideravano', and that the girl had instructions not to give way to the king in order to create the delay.[58]

While many of the troops and commanders were already assembling in Piedmont and Genoa, Charles VIII finally left Grenoble to join his army on 29

---

[53] Commynes, *Memoires*, vol. 3, 30-34.

[54] ASMi, SPE, Francia, 553: Galeazzo di Sanseverino to Ludovico Sforza, 1 June 1494.

[55] Canestrini and Desjardins, *Négociations*, vol. 1, 229, 301, 303.

[56] ASMo, ASE, Ambascatori, Francia 1, 6, n. 41: Belardo Caracciolo from Lyons to Ercole d'Este, 8 July 1494.

[57] Ludovico's growing fears about the threat from Naples were alluded to by Carlo da Barbiano in his dispatches of 13 Apr. and 25 July 1494 (ASMi, SPE, Francia, 552 and 554).

[58] ASMi, SPE, Francia, 554: Carlo da Barbiano to Ludovico Sforza, 17 July 1494.

August.[59] The summer was almost over; the army and fleet which had been assembled were substantially smaller than had been hoped; the support services were in chaos; no one knew how much help could be expected in Italy from Milan, Ferrara, the Colonna, and others who were thought to be favourably inclined. All this suggests that Italian optimism that the invasion would not materialise that year was not entirely misplaced. They underestimated Charles' own determination and the loyalty which the French king could command when he was determined. However, to what extent this determination was stimulated and encouraged by Italian influences around the King is very difficult to assess. So many of the sources for these events are Italian, written for Italian audiences and often seeking deliberately to emphasize Italian influence. The apparent absence of good sources of information on the French side, both administrative and descriptive, remains the main barrier to any definitive reassessment of the preparations for the 1494 *impresa*.

However, one is always struck when studying late fifteenth-century politics by the difficulties involved in generating *action*. On both sides of the Alps there seemed to be an increasing conflict between 'men of action' and a sort of lethargic consensus, which was at the heart of the Machiavellian message. Vested interests, factional rivalries, personal jealousies, other preoccupations including fast-growing leisure pursuits, slow communications, lack of cash, all militated against *action*. Discussion, rhetoric, bargaining, temporisation, prevailed. It was precisely because they longed for action and to some extent avoided sinking new roots and taking on new interests that political exile groups and individuals seemed to exercise great influence in this period. Antonello di Sanseverino and Giuliano della Rovere in France and Gian Giacomo Trivulzio in Naples filled that role, perhaps, more influentially than has been allowed.

---

[59] ASMi, SPE, Francia, 554: Maffeo Trivigli to Ludovico Sforza, 29 Aug. 1494.

Court and household in Ferrara, 1494*

Trevor Dean

One of the problems in study of the princely court is to establish the contours and character of court personnel.[1] For the Este court at Ferrara there exist numerous series of financial records that help us to do this.[2] Two of these series are the *Bolletta dei salariati* and the *Memoriale del soldo*. These have often been used in the past, but only to ascertain the presence of specific individuals (such as the architect Biagio Rossetti) or of specific groups (such as musicians).[3] The aim here is to study one year's list as a whole. First the character of the document must be established. The *Bolletta* and the *Memoriale* were different in scope, layout and purpose. Broadly speaking, the *Bolletta* tends to list those who served the prince, while the *Memoriale* listed those who serviced the court. Thus the *Bolletta* includes judicial counsellors, ambassadors, accountants, notaries, and officials both major and minor; while the *Memoriale* includes the palace staff of guards, footmen, cooks, falconers, stable-lads and muleteers. Few appear in both lists (about two dozen in 1494, including for example, Biagio Rossetti). Secondly, where the *Bolletta* is organised by name, with most individuals being given a double-page spread on which both debits and credits were entered, the *Memoriale* is a day-to-day 'journal' of payments, with each individual identified by name and number. Thirdly, the type of payment recorded seems to be different: the *Memoriale* appears to list cash payments actually made; the *Bolletta* lists assignments and debts as well.

* I wish to thank the Leverhulme Trust for a research grant which enabled me to conduct the archival research on which this paper is based.
    [1] J. Larner, 'Europe of the courts', *Journal of Modern History*, 55 (1983), 680; R.J. Knecht, 'La corte di Francia nel XVI secolo', in: *La 'familia' del principe e famiglia aristocratica*, ed. C. Mozzarelli (Rome, 1988), 225-6.
    [2] For survey, see P. Sitta, 'Saggio sulle istituzioni finanziarie del ducato estense nei secoli XV e XVI', *Atti della Deputazione ferrarese di storia patria*, 3 (1891), 122-30, 197-203.
    [3] L. Lockwood, *Music in Renaissance Ferrara 1400-1505* (Oxford 1984), 182-3 and Appendix.

The *Bolletta* is the more complex of the two registers. Its purpose is clear enough: to record financial transactions of all sorts with officials and servants, listing in double-entry form assignments, payments in coin and kind, debts and credits. Because payments of salaries were often in arrears, the register shifts, towards the end, to dealing with past, not current, officials, covering mainly moneys due in 1493, and paid in 1495. The register for 1494 contains about 260 names of current officials and servants, starting with six members of the Este family, and working through ambassadors, counsellors, secretary and chancery staff, financial accountants and controllers, court paymasters and doormen, to estate stewards and captains of forts and garrisons. Mixed in with these are cooks, squires, dispensers, cellarmen, chaplains, riders, and groups of women. Some of these more personal servants are noted to be those of the duke's son, Alfonso d'Este, or his wife Anna Sforza.[4]

The aim here, however, is to examine the *Memoriale* for 1494, as it gives a clearer and fuller picture of the court and household: officials operative in other parts of the city or the state do not have to be abstracted. Of the 530 names receiving payments in 1494, the occupations are noted for over three hundred. We should not assume that all these people lived at court or worked only for the court, but almost all groups involved in sustaining court life are represented here:[5] the gentlemen who provided companionship; the soldiers employed for purposes of security (mounted archers, men-at-arms, castle garrison);[6] those who provided transport (muleteers, stable-hands, carters, riders and horse-breakers),[7] food and meals (cellarmen, cooks, table-layers, bakers, dispensers)[8] and clothing (tailors, second-hand clothes dealers).[9] Princely recreation is represented in the falconers, bird-keepers and huntsmen,[10] in the trumpeters, singers and pipers.[11] Other occupations recorded include those of doorman, footman, builder, banker, stationer and secretary.[12] The keepers of various ducal possessions or stores seem also to be indicated.[13] For the large

---

[4] Modena, Archivio di Stato [hereafter ASMo], Archivio Segreto Estense, Camera ducale, Bolletta dei salariati, 12: members of Alfonso's household are recorded on f. 79-89; 'Zoanne de Voltolina fachino de Anna' on f. 123.

[5] Cf. the five functions of the court in W. Paravicini, 'Structure et fonctionnement de la cour bourguignonne au XVe siècle', in *Milano e Borgogna: due stati principeschi tra Medioevo e Rinascimento*, ed. J-M. Cauchies and G. Chittolini (Rome, 1990), 67-8.

[6] Nos. 2-26, 108-9, 114-67, 259.

[7] Nos. 16, 104-5, 107, 109-12, 116, 124, 132, 134, 135-6, 138, 142-3, 149, 157, 164-5, 170, 172, 183, 195, 248, 274, 297, 310-11, 321, 335.

[8] Nos. 62, 95, 106-7, 113-14, 168-9, 173, 194, 205, 278.

[9] Nos. 215, 225-7, 277.

[10] Nos. 28-40, 104, 116, 130, 166, 226-7, 307.

[11] Nos. 4, 40-53, 223, 249, 283, 297, 321, 323.

[12] Nos. 26-7, 59, 68, 84, 96-7, 100, 105-6, 113, 119, 137, 140, 147-8, 155, 186, 205, 214, 217, 220, 256, 265, 287, 304.

[13] Nos. 65, 67, 104, 116, 124, 150, 206, 259.

numbers whose occupation is not recorded, other documents may aid identification: Biagio da Birago (no. 73) was Ercole's stable-master,[14] Lodovico Fiaschi (64) his *maestro di camera*,[15] Moschino (82) his buffoon,[16] Filippo Bonlei (57) his sensechal,[17] and so on. The *Memoriale* does not give a complete picture of the court: the *Bolletta* for the same year records further court-staff such as 'maestro Sancto da Milano pistore di la corte', Francesco Gualengo 'provededore generale de la corte', and 'Zanone fachino scudelaro in corte', as well as having a double page for the 'Capella de la gloriosissima Madona S. Maria de Corte' and its chaplain.[18] And it is the *Bolletta*, rather than the *Memoriale*, that records payments due to women.[19] But the *Memoriale* does give a very full picture, providing the names of over 500 individuals who were present at court. The aim in this paper is to analyse this list (reproduced in the Appendix) for significant light it can throw on Ercole d'Este's position and role in the events of 1494-95.

Only a minority of these names (144 out of 530) include a place name, indicative of origin in the near or more distant past. The origins of another eighty-seven are easily identifiable by family name. Unsurprisingly, those from Ferrara dominate (sixty-four). They include members of families long established in the local elite (the Ariosti [62, 63], Boccamaiori [68], Contrari [258], Costabili [74, 89, 151, 202], Trotti [11, 12, 55, 73] and Turchi [59]), as well as more recent arrivals (the Bevilacqua [63, 318, 325, 354], Calcagnini [40], Condulmer [103, 202], dal Sagrato [64, 93, 236] and dalla Sale [66, 69, 211]). Ercole thus seems to have included both sides of the deep factional division said to have opened up in Ferrarese political society in the 1480s: neither side had apparently managed to exclude the other from ducal service. Members of the Ferrarese *notabilité* and business class too are found (2, 55, 57, 58, 69, 84, 91, 114, 139, 214, 226, 238). There are also significant numbers from other parts of the Este state, especially members of the aristocratic and patrician families of Modena (thus the Boschetti [92], Carandini [224], Cesi

---

[14] *Diario ferrarese dall'anno 1409 sino al 1502*, ed. G. Pardi, (Rerum italicarum scriptores, 2nd edn., 24/7) 236.

[15] Bernardino Zambotti, *Diario ferrarese dall'anno 1476 sino al 1504*, ed. G. Pardi, (Rerum italicarum scriptores, 2nd edn, 24/7) 20.

[16] Zambotti, *Diario*, 7; M. Catalano, 'Messer Moschino. (Beoni e buffoni ai tempi di Ludovico Ariosto)', *Giornale storico della letteratura italiana*, 88 (1926), 1-36.

[17] *Diario ferrarese*, 220. Cf. *Art and Life at the Court of Ercole I d'Este. The 'De triumphis religionis' of Giovanni Sabadino degli Arienti*, ed. W.L. Gundersheimer (Geneva, 1972), 113, whose misreading of Bonleo as Bolco led him to claim that 'no information is currently available on Socio Bolco'.

[18] *Bolletta dei salariati*, 12, ff. 50, 54, 57, 59.

[19] *Bolletta*, 12, ff. 117, 118, 119, 120, 149 ('Madonna Bartolamia za lavandara dela Illustrissima Madonna Anna [Sforza]'), 150, 174, 176, 183 ('Madonna Sufferentia una dele servente'), 185 ('Catelina lavandara'), 190, 191, 192. The only woman in the Memoriale is Lucrezia di Rinaldo d'Este, no. 98.

[83], Tassoni [81, 94, 95, 213] and perhaps Rangoni [161]). Other Modenesi are also recorded (6, 13, 16, 70, 143, 173, 300). However, from a city that was deeply divided towards the end of the fifteenth century, with extensive feuding among its leading families, this representation at court seems rather thin. Even thinner was Reggian aristocratic presence. Two of the major urban families are represented (the Zoboli [58, 201] and Fontanella [158]), as well as other individuals (10, 121, 194, 294), but none of the Bebio or Manfredi, for example. From the provinces of Modena and Reggio came some servants and soldiers, from Carpi (173, 227), Finale (118, 149), Nonantola (140, 199, 238), Correggio (11, 21, 150) and Campogaiano (23). But from outside these central territories, there was merely a trickle of men from the old Este heartland of the Polesine di Rovigo and southern Padovano (4, 118, 245). The Polesine had been occupied by Venice since 1482, and Venetian attempts to cut its social and economic ties with Ferrara had obviously had some effect.[20] And from Ercole's territories in the Romagna, we find only a small handful of men-at-arms from Lugo (65, 119, 122, 127), outnumbered by those from parts of the Romagna not ruled by the duke of Ferrara (7, 24, 79, 115, 119, 128). The role of the court in acting as an agent of integration of élites, drawn from the various constituent parts of the regional state, would thus seem to be limited. However, Ercole may have struck a balance, or series of balances, that two of his contemporary rulers fatally failed to do: Galeazzo Maria Sforza, who was unable to attract the Milanese nobility to attend his court in any numbers;[21] and Guidobaldo da Montefeltro, whose overloading of the court with foreigners alienated local support.[22] Did maintenance of this balance - between Ferrarese factions, between Ferrarese and non-Ferrarese, between subjects and foreigners - contribute in the turbulent years to come to the survival of the Este lordships?

However, while the court's openness preserved its legitimacy, it also increased its potential for storing and reviving past grievances. For the Este court, in the manner of all courts, offered a home to a number of significant exiles from other states, victims of political errors and disasters of one kind and another. Ercole Varano (77), cousin of the lord of Camerino, had been living in

---

[20] T. Dean, 'After the War of Ferrara: Relations between Venice and Ercole d'Este, 1484-1505', in *War, Culture and Society in Renaissance Venice. Essays in honour of John Hale*, ed. D.S. Chambers, C.H. Clough and M.E. Mallett (London, 1993), 93. Cf. the stronger presence of men from this area earlier in the century: T. Dean, *Land and Power in late medieval Ferrara: The Rule of the Este, 1350-1450* (Cambridge, 1987), 103-4; T. Dean, 'Notes on the Ferrarese court in the later Middle Ages', *Renaissance Studies*, 3 (1989), 363.

[21] G. Chittolini, 'Di alcuni aspetti della crisi dello stato sforzeco', in *Milano e Borgogna*.

[22] C. Clough, 'La "familia" del duca Guidubaldo da Montefeltro ed il *Cortegiano*', in *'Familia' del principe*, 340-41.

exile in Ferrara since the 1460s.[23]   Pietro Giorgio Lampugnano (57) had possibly come to Ferrara in the wake of his kinsman's assassination of Galeazzo Maria Sforza.[24] Sigismondo Cantelmo (86), former duke of Sora, and Francesco da Ortona (85), were barons of the kingdom of Naples, expelled by King Ferrante, apparently for pro-Angevin sympathies following the Aragonese-Angevin contest for the kingdom in the 1450s.[25] Such men were ready to be released into the swirl of events in the 1490s.   Ercole Varano challenged his cousin's lordship in 1493.   Sigismondo Cantelmo and Francesco da Ortona left Ferrara in January 1495, 'summoned by the king of France', 'in order to return home and recover their property'.[26] Sigismondo was present at Charles VIII's crowned progress through Naples in May 1495 and reported on it to Ercole d'Este.[27]   He took part in both Charles VIII's and Louis XII's Neapolitan campaigns, organising a pro-French conspiracy from Sora in 1496.[28] His hopes, however, died with the great French defeat at Garigliano in 1503, and he returned to his exiled life in Ferrara, where he died in 1519.[29] Also released into the warfare of the period were a number of the soldiers recorded in these lists: thirty of Ercole's mounted archers, for example, died at Fornovo, including Giampaolo Pochintesta (165).[30] Though Ercole himself proclaimed a stance of neutrality in 1495, he allowed his subjects and courtiers to fight and die in the service of others.

The geographical origin of those from outside the Este state also reveals a significant pattern. Very few came from Tuscany (mainly musicians: 44, 45, 111, 176, 249), and only slightly more from the Veneto (4, 60, 82, 88, 108, 115, 160, 161, 220).   The distinctive pattern of origin lies in those coming from Lombardy and from the kingdom of Naples. There were men from Milan itself (78, 117, 195), and even more from Pavia (107, 109, 116, 147, 217, 229). And

---

[23] J.E. Law, 'City, court and contado in Camerino, c. 1500', in *City and Countryside in late medieval and Renaissance Italy*, ed. T. Dean and C. Wickham (London, 1990), 171; Gundersheimer, *Art and Life*, 112.

[24] See in general, V. Ilardi, 'The assassination of Galeazzo Maria Sforza', in *Violence and Civil Disorder in Italian Cities 1200-1500*, ed. L. Martines (Berkeley, 1972). Pietro Giorgio is not recorded in the partial genealogy in F. Raffaelli, 'Familglia Lampugnani di Milano', *Giornale araldico*, 1 (1873-4), 229-34.

[25] R. Patitucci d'Alifera Patitario, 'Il "Missere Paduano" del codice aragonese e relazioni tra Ferrara e Napoli nel XV secolo', in *Atti del congresso internazionale di studi sull'età aragonese* (Bari, 1968), 436-7.

[26] *Diario ferrarese*, 138.

[27] C. Foucard, 'Proposta di pubblicazione di carteggio diplomatico 1492-94-95', *Archivio storico per le province napoletane*, 4 (1879), 797-9.

[28] R. Filangieri, *Una congiura di baroni nel castello d'Isola in vista di una seconda spedizione di Carlo VIII (5 agosto 1496)* (Naples, 1942).

[29] T. Ascari, 'Cantelmo, Sigismondo', in *Dizionario biografico degli italiani*, 18, 277-9, s.v.

[30] *Diario ferrarese*, 159.

there were men from all other points of the Sforza dominion: Alessandria (131), Asti (29), Birago (73), Caravaggio (109, 128, 171), Cremona (120, 287), Genoa (52), Lodi (21, 48), Novara (3), Parma (120, 123, 152) and Varese (145), as well as obscurely titled 'lombardi' (32, 55, 87, 240). From the kingdom of Naples, there were, as we have seen Sigismondo Cantelmo and Francesco da Ortona. Along with them was a whole group of soldiers from Ortona (18, 20, 25, 117, 140, 152, 153, 155, 160: were they all Francesco's relatives?). In addition, we find men from Capua, Naples, Taranto, Trani and 'the kingdom' (75, 113, 159, 163, 274) as well as a trio of 'Spaniards' (14, 47, 86). Ercole of course had long associations with the Aragonese dynasty in Naples: he had spent over a dozen years of his youth in King Alfonso's court, he had married Eleonora d'Aragona in 1473, he had drawn on Aragonese military support in his disastrous war with Venice in the 1480s. Nor were those links suddenly liquidated with Eleonora's death in 1493: in the following years, he was still arranging marriages and providing dowries for women who had been in Eleonora's household.[31] Ercole's contacts with the Sforza had been just as close:[32] Lodovico Sforza was married to Beatrice d'Este, and Ercole's son Alfonso had married Anna Sforza in 1491. His personal contacts with Lodovico were frequent: he visited Vigevano in this year (309). In 1494, Ercole tentatively followed Sforza into support for Charles VIII. The numerical prominence of Lombards and southerners at Ercole's court was thus the natural result of decades of close association of these rulers, as servants were circulated among them by recommendation,[33] and as safe homes were found for political exiles.

The character of Ercole's court in 1494 can further be gauged by comparing it with the list of stipendiaries for 1488.[34] This register contains all the same occupational categories, but total numbers are much lower (around 290). Part of this difference is accounted for by the aggregation into one entry ('Spesa del nostro Illustrissimo signore') of sixty-five servants among falconers, birdkeepers, muleteers, stable-hands and personal servants. However, the total number still remains some 150 lower than in 1494. There seems to have been little expansion in the number of soldiers in 1494, despite the engagement towards the end of the year of Orsino Orsini (206). The main expansion came

---

[31] Ferrara, Archivio di Stato [hereafter ASFe], Archivio notarile, Ferrara, no. 195 (Bartolomeo Goggi), *pacco* 6, 18 Dec. 1497, 18 Jan. and 22 Jan. 1498.

[32] P. Negri, 'Le missioni di Pandolfo Collenuccio a Papa Alessandro VI (1494-1498)', *Archivio della società romana di storia patria*, 33 (1910), 336-7, 351-9.

[33] Este servants also went to Naples: in 1488 Ercole responded to Federico d'Aragona's request for 'uno homo de quisti nostri de qua bene pratico et experto in livellare terreni et fare conducti de aqua per redure a cultura certi soi loci palustri': ASMo, Cancelleria, Leggi e decreti, reg. C 10, f. 322.

[34] ASMo, Camera ducale, Memoriale del soldo, 10.

in two areas: the falconers (thirty-three in 1494, eight in 1488),[35] and in those recorded merely as *salariati* or without any occupational description (there are fifty-five of these in 1488, over a hundred in 1494: nos. 54-103). Ercole seems to have responded to the growing uncertainties of 1494 by increasing the number of his stipendiaries, much as happened at other courts at times of danger and conflict.[36] How the character of court personnel further changed in response to the French invasions would be well worth further investigation.

---

[35] In April 1494 Charles VIII wrote thanking Ercole for the gift of two falcons, and sought to keep one of Ercole's two falconer-envoys in his own service: *Lettres di Charles VIII*, ed. P. Pélicier, 5 vols. (Paris, 1898), vol. 4, 48.

[36] Knecht, 'La corte di Francia', p. 230.

Appendix

This list has been constructed from *Memoriale del soldo* register 17, in which recipients of payments are listed by name and number. In this year the numbers obviously referred to a pre-existing list, and were not (as in 1488) a running sequence. Many recipients were also assigned second or third numbers in the course of the year. The reason for this is not immediately apparent, though in some cases the different numbers refer to different accounts ('per conto proprio', 'per conto di famii de stala'), while in others the number was altered when location of the payment office was changed (e.g. Modena instead of Ferrara). All of these repetitions have been omitted, and this accounts for most of the gaps in the numerical sequence in the second half of the list. All original spellings have been retained (e.g. for Bartolomeo, Scipione, Sigismondo, Taddeo, and so on), with the exception of occasional apostrophes introduced for comprehension.

2. Guizardo Riminaldi salariato[1]
3. Batain da Novara balestriero
    Nicola di Marchetto balestriero
4. Jacomo da Este dito Stocho balestriero
    Jacheto cantore
    Zoane dal Miarin balestriero
5. Zoane/Jani da la rocha balestriero
    Stefano sardo balestriero
6. Thadio magno balestriero
    Piero da Modena balestriero
7. Zachagnin Pezonin balestriero
    Thomaxo da Rimine balestriero
8. Thoxo[?] de Guizardo balestriero
    Valentin balestriero
10. Lorenzo Saladin balestriero

---

[1] Captain of Ercole's mounted archers throughout the 1480s and 1490s, he was sent with one hundred archers to aid the king of France against invasion of the duchy of Milan in 1503: Zambotti, *Diario*, 180, 347; *Diario ferrarese*, 115, 129.

Alberto da Rezo balestriero
11. Matthio da Corezo balestriero
    Zorzo di Lodovigo Trotti balestriero
12. Gaschon balestriero
    Sisemondo de Pollo Antonio [Trotti] balestriero
13. Gregoro todesco balestriero
    Lorenzo Vidella balestriero
    Gratia da Modena balestriero
14. Jacomo spagnolo balestriero
15. Jacomo Grasalion
    Francesco tamborin balestriero
16. Zoanebatista dito Romagnollo balestriero
    Silvestro da Modena dito el Franzoso balestriero
    Piero di Baldanza mulatiero
    Zoanebatista de Messer Cosmico balestriero [see no. 82]
17. Janello balestriero
    Marsilio dal Bondeno balestriero
18. Lorenzo di Messer Francesco da Ortona balestriero
19. Gabriele trovaluso
    Zoane Pezinino capo di balestrieri
20. Andrea da Ortona balestriero
    Marcho da Ortona balestriero
21. Rizo da Corizo
    Jacomo del Griego da Lodi balestriero
    Domenego Albanexe balestriero
22. Il Rizetto balestriero
    Franzin balestriero
23. Stefano Conversan salariato
    Thomaxo da Campogaian balestriero
24. Zachagnin schiavon balestriero
    Lazaro da Rimino balestriero
25. Thodeschin da Sanginone [?] balestriero
    Valente balestriero
26. Jacomo da Carpi balestriero
    Todeschin grande stafiero
27. Todeschin pezenino stafiero
28. Zoane Francesco dela paula falconiero
    Lionello Recetta
29. Jacomin d'Asti falconiero
30. Costa falconiero
    Lucha de Zirlo falconiero

      Zoane Spadaza falconiero
31.   Baldisera del bruni
      Lucha di Boldrin
      Zoane schacho falconiero
32.   Jacomo da Viato falconiero
      Piero Guazante falconiero
      Zoane de Tomaso [?]
      Domenego di Zoane lombardo falconiero
33.   Rizo Bivilaqua
      Romagnolo falconiero
34.   Tartaia falconiero
      Girolamo da la roxa falconiero
      Rizo de Magon [?] falconiero
      Rosso gaiardo falconiero
35.   Zorzo de Messer Sisemondo Cantelmo [see no. 86]
      Rizo del conte Lorenzo
      Michele dala barba falconiero
      Francesco de Messer Sepion
36.   Chiaveta falconiero
      Zoane Maria Maganza falconiero
37.   Zorzo vechio falconiero
      Albertazo balestriero falconiero
38.   Jacomo trovaluso falconiero
      Bernardin de Peschaduri falconiero
39.   Jacomo del brun falconiero
      Gelfo falconiero
      Vicino falconiero
40.   Lodovigo de Messer Teophylo [Calcagnini] falconiero
      Maestro Piero trombon
      Gobo falconiero
41.   Zoane trombon
      Gregoro de Alamagna pifaro
      Michiele pifaro
42.   Lodovigo da Bologna pifaro
      Carlo da Bologna pifaro
43.   Sajo trombetta[2]
      Raganello trombetta
44.   Bernardin d'Asisi trombeta
      Lucido trombeta

---

[2] Lockwood appears to have missed this group of trumpeters, claiming that they were not listed in 1494, with the exception of Raganello: *Music in Ferrara*, 325-6.

Stefano da Montepulzan trombeta
45. Francesco trombeta da Montepulzan
Piero Antonio trombeta
46. Antonio trombeta
Zilio trombeta
47. Bernardin da Colornio
Zammartin cantore
Pedros cantore
Bortelamio spagnollo cantore
48. Cornellio cantore
fra Zoanefrancesco da Lodi cantore
fra Zoane soprano
49. Mathio da Parise cantore
50. Girardo cantore
fra Jacomo d'Alba cantore
51. don Piero Carion capelan
Zoane vivias/vimas cantore
Maestro Domenego organista
don Hieronymo da la Frasina
52. Urban da Zenova tenorista
Rainaldo dal chitarin
53. Andrea da la violla
Zampollo da la violla
Guielmo da Franza tamborin
54. Antonello di Anzolin
Lodovigo del brun salariato
Pietro Antonio dai Cari salariato
55. Niccolo Trotti salariato
Hieronymo Bellaia salariato
Zoane lombardo salariato
56. Lionello de Folco salariato
Thomaxo Caraza [Caracciolo?] salariato
Filippo Bonlei dito Socio salariato[3]
57. Lodovigo dai Cari
Marcheto Piovan salariato
Piero Zorzo Lampugnano salariato[4]
58. Zoane Valengo [Gualengo?] salariato[5]

---

[3] M. Catalano, *Vita di Ludovico Ariosto*, 2 vols. (Geneva, 1930) vol. 1, 111; M. Catalano, 'Messer Moschino', 24-5.

[4] Catalano, *Ludovico Ariosto*, vol. 1, 147.

[5] Later Ercole's seneschal: *Diario ferrarese*, 220.

Zebelin di Zoboli salariato[6]
59. Aldrovandin Turcho
Hector Belinziero canzeliero[7]
60. Biaxio del Bailo[8]
Francesco da Vicenza dai morari[?]
61. Bortelamio bagatella
Messer Gregoro Zampante [da Lucca][9]
62. Rainaldo Ariosto salariato
Maestro Sperandio da Mantoa[10]
Modenino credenziero
63. Francesco da Castello[11]
Antonio deli Ariosti per suo conto proprio
Antonio Bivilaqua salariato
64. Lodovigo di Fiescho salariato
Sabastian dito Putin salariato
Rainaldo dal Sagrato salariato
65. Francesco da l'argento
Simon da Lugo
Zamjacomo da la tore
66. Conte Alberto da la Sale salariato
Camillo Strozzi
Jacomo da l'arpa salariato
67. Janiculo da selva capitanio a la Porta de lion
Agnello saltarello salariato
Bernardin da la tapezaria
Jacomo Tassun Capitanio de Castello
68. Zoane sora canzeliero
Lodovigo di Buchamaiuri
69. Lodovigo di Mazon salariato
Francesco di Lardi salariato
Zoane Maria da la Sale
70. Maestro Gasparin da Modena intaiadore

---

[6] One of the *cortexani* winning a joust-prize in 1481: Zambotti, *Diario*, 95.

[7] G. Bertoni, *L'Orlando furioso e la Rinascenza in Ferrara* (Modena, 1919), 296-7.

[8] Ercole's 'familiare' sent with a gift of tents and 'pavilions' to Charles VIII in October 1494: *Lettres de Charles VIII*, vol. 4, 339-40.

[9] Captain of Justice in Ferrara, 1490-96: *Diario ferrarese*, 182-6.

[10] Is this the medallist whom Venturi claimed was not recorded in Este registers of the 1490s (A. Venturi, 'Sperandio da Mantova', *Archivio storico dell'arte*, 1 (1888), 395)?

[11] Ercole's physician, knighted by him in 1487 (Zambotti, *Diario*, 183), later hated 'universaliter' by the Ferrarese people, 'per esserli contra in ogni cossa, et per rodere lui' (*Diario ferrarese*, 265). And see Bertoni, *L'Orlando furioso*, 196, 262; Catalano, *Ludovico Ariosto*, vol. 1, 111.

Zoane del Contugo
71. Zordan pinzeta salariato[12]
72. Sepion da Este salariato
    Rivaben di Rivaben salariato
73. Biaxio da Birago[13]
    Conte Hercule di Trotti salariato
74. Antonio di Costabili salariato[14]
    Zilio/Verzilio di Nobili
75. Sisemondo da Trani salariato
    Luchin da Corte salariato[15]
76. Messer Alberigo da San Severin salariato[16]
77. Signore Hercule da Camarin salariato[17]
78. Gasparo Visconte salariato[18]
    Zoane Antonio del conte da Millan salariato
79. Lodovigo Zangarin salariato
    Messer Pandolfo da Pisaro[19]
80. Barun dale Carte salariato[20]
    Lodovigo da Mantoa salariato
81. Daniel Tassun salariato
    Bernardin de Piamunti salariato
82. Moschin Magnanino salariato
    Cosmico da Padoa[21]

---

[12] 'Jordano Pinceta aulico': ASMo, Notai camerali ferraresi, no. 52, f. 112 (26 Oct. 1500).

[13] Ercole's 'maestro da stalla' sent posthaste to the king of France in Asti in 1499: *Diario ferrarese*, 236.

[14] Ambassador in Milan in 1499: *Diario ferrarese*, 231.

[15] 'iurisperito domino Luchino de Curte syndico camere et ducale cancelliere': ASMo, Notai camerali ferraresi, no. 52, f. 27 (22 Mar. 1497).

[16] He married a daughter of Sigismondo d'Este, and was later one of the commanders of Alfonso d'Este's brigade defending the Sforza in Milan: Zambotti, *Diario*, 218, 233, 282-3.

[17] Knighted by Ercole d'Este in 1487: Zambotti, *Diario*, 183.

[18] Catalano, *Ludovico Ariosto*, vol. 1, 300; Bertoni, *L'Orlando furioso*, 171; A. Luzio and R. Renier, 'La coltura e le relazioni letterarie di Isabella d'Este Gonzaga', *Giornale storico della letteratura italiana*, 36 (1900), 327-8. I have not seen R. Renier, *Gasparo Visconte* (Milan, 1886).

[19] This is Pandolfo Collenuccio, Ercole's ambassador in the 1490s to Pope Alexander VI and to Emperor Maximilian, and later Captain of Justice in Ferrara (1500): *Diario ferrarese*, 194, 252; Negri, 'Le missioni di Pandolfo Collenuccio'; E. Melfi, 'Collenuccio, Pandolfo', *Dizionario biografico degli italiani*, vol. 27, 1-4, s.v.

[20] Catalano, *Ludovico Ariosto*, vol. 1, 70, 110, 341; Catalano, 'Messer Moschino', 22-3.

[21] G. Bertoni, *L'Orlando furioso e la Rinascenza a Ferrara* (Modena, 1919), 10, 36, 294; G. Bertoni, *La biblioteca estense e la coltura ferrarese al tempo del duca Ercole I* (1471-1505) (Turin, 1903), 130, 153, 155-6, 161, 181.

83. Zanun Pasqualetto[22]
    Francesco da Cesi salariato
84. Filippo Maria di Pizolbechari salariato[23]
    Francesco di Pizolbechari
    Tebaldo canzeliero[24]
85. Messer Francesco da Ortona salariato
    Gasparo da Basilicapetri
86. Maestro Alovise spagnollo maestro da curami
    Messer Sisemondo Cantelmo salariato
    Siviero canzeliero
    Zoane pincharo salariato[25]
87. Piero Griego
    Sisemondo di Zoane lombardo
88. Tuodio da Trivise salariato
    Jacomo del Vendegin
89. Camillo di Costabili salariato[26]
    Antonio da la popa dito Rexan salariato
    Zoane Maria balbo
    fra Rexan
90. Giamfrancesco
91. Agostino da Villa salariato[27]
    Cosimo di Lardi
92. Al becharo di Pizolbechari
    Alberto Buschetto
93. Nicolo da Fulgiano salariato
    Aldrovandin da Sagra [Sagrato]
    Patachio salariato[28]
94. Hieronymo Tassun salariato
    Nicolo dal Caprillo salariato
    Annibal Scotto dicto Baraffo salariato

---

[22] 'ducale familiare et magistro super avibus ducalibus': ASMo, Notai camerali ferraresi, no. 52, f. 47 (22 Sept. 1498). Recorded in 1499 as a 'curiale', and in 1501 as one 'facto richo da x anni in qua': *Diario ferrarese*, 220, 276.

[23] Bertoni, *L'Orlando furioso*, 174-5.

[24] Bertoni, *L'Orlando furioso*, 290-2, 300.

[25] Bertoni, *L'Orlando furioso*, 36, 307-8.

[26] Ercole's envoy in 1497 to release to Ludovico Sforza the Castelletto di Genova, which Ercole had held as pledge of Ludovico's observance of treaty with the king of France: Zambotti, *Diario*, 276.

[27] Later ambassador to Charles VIII in Naples: Zambotti, *Diario*, 84.

[28] To 'Zoane Baptista di Gati dicto Patachio nostro cortigiano', Ercole betrothed his wife's former 'domicella', the Florentine Isabella di Simone di Diotesalvi Neroni, in 1498: ASFe, Archivio notarile, Ferrara, no. 195 (Bartolomeo Goggi), *pacco* 6, 22 Jan. 1498.

95. Messer Julio Tassun salariato[29]
    Mazucho soto canevaro
    Ugo Pangaia
96. Suppino salariato
    Zoane Corezo canzeliero
97. Gasparin de l'angelo
    Bertolamio de Mambri
    Antonio da Bugo
    Gianfora scudelaro
98. Madonna Lucretia di Messer Rainaldo da Este
    Antonio Forzate salariato
    Ruberto del vescho
99. Zoane de Tibaldo panatiero
100. Guido canevaro
    Lorenzo scudelaro
101. Nicolo da Porto salariato
102. Messer Pietro Antonio da Morcadello
103. Messer Lodovigo Condulmiero
    Lodovigo da Castello
104. Paulo mulatiero
    Zoane da la Guardaroba
    Zoane tartagno dai servixii
    Gualtiero mulatiero
    Justo mulatiero
    Zenovese dai cani
105. Antonio grande stafiero
    Giara mulatiero
    Zangarin barbiero
106. Fortuniero stafiero
    Thomaxo cogo
107. Zanun imbandidore
    Francesco da Pavia caratiero
108. Jacomo da Modena fante in Castello
    Nicolo fornaro da Padoa fante in Castello
109. Maestro Pollo recamadore
    Domenego Marescotto fante in Castello
    Pollo da Caravazo fante in Castello
    Agostin da Parma caratiero

---

[29] A. Frizzi, *Memorie per la storia di Ferrara*, 2nd edn., 5 vols. (Ferrara, 1847-8), vol. 4, 157.

110. Bernardin del cazadore mulatiero
     Nicolo mulatiero
     Michiele da la Savena
111. Zoane Campana caratiero
     Janigo Albanexe
     Bortelamio da Cutigliano mulatiero
112. Lusignano mulatiero
     Nardello mulatiero
     Piero Scarpa da Chioza panteraio
113. Maestro Antonio del Mezanega cogo
     Pollo cogo
     Francesco da Taranto stafiero
114. Betochio cogo
     Botom imbandidore
     Hercule de Avenanti homo d'arme
115. Scaramuza da Faenza homo d'arme
     Girolamo del Contugo
     Ruffino dal Castelazo homo d'arme
     Lorenzin da Trivise homo d'arme
116. Zamtonne dai barbari
     Bonivignudo dai oxelli
     Pollo da Pavia homo d'arme
117. Donino di Tognolino homo d'arme
     Alexandro da Ortona homo d'arme
     Zoane Ambroxo da Millan homo d'arme
118. Biaxio da Rovigo homo d'arme
     Il fra dal Finale salariato homo d'arme
119. Bortello stafiero
     Zanin da Lugo homo d'arme
     Marchion da Faenza homo d'arme
120. Pedrin da Parma homo d'arme
     Jacomo dal Castelazo
     Moreleto da Cremona
     Nicolo Terzo
121. Jacomo de Guarnello
     Saldazo da Rezo
122. Zorzo da Canossa homo d'arme
     Francesco da Lugo
     Barun di Guidun [Guidoni?]
123. Mathio da San Martin homo d'arme
     Michiel da Brienza

Andrea da Parma
124. Maestro Zuliano da le mule
Filippo babilon in Regio
Jacomo di Paso
125. Boldrin capo de una squadra
Zoane de Ruzo da Castello
Domenego marchese
127. Pietro Antonio di Rainaldi da Lugo homo d'arme
Francesco di Rafanelli conduto per falconiero sino adi
primo de zenaio
Maestro Colla balestriero
128. Franceschin da Caravazo homo d'arme
Guielmo da Faenza homo d'arme
Girolamo da Runchi homo d'arme
129. Agnello Saltarello per conto di famii da stala
Tarquino homo d'arme
130. Nicolo di Zanin oxeladore
131. Alexandrin d'Alexandria
Alexandro Cavaza homo d'arme
Zamberlan homo d'arme
132. Rugiero mulatiero
Schiavetto homo d'arme
Bernardin mulatiero
133. Sisimondo fantin homo d'arme
Mongren villan homo d'arme
Morello da Bersello [Brescello]
134. Prins de Cesarii homo d'arme
Magiero mulatiero
135. Piero da Cocore homo d'arme
Todeschin domadore
Pelegrin da Castellonovo homo d'arme
136. Zanin mulatiero
137. Zoane Francesco Pazaia homo d'arme
Jason portonaro
138. Zorzo caratiero
139. Mathio da Ferara homo d'arme
Superbo di Superbi homo d'arme
140. Ruberto da Ortona homo d'arme
Maestro Lazaro fante in Castello
Piero Alovise portonaro
Nicolo da Nonantola fante in Castello

142. Modenese homo d'arme
     Ramponzelo domadore
     Zoane del Modenin
     Francesco Franchin
143. Lio dal'olio caratiero
     Piero da Modena cavalchadore
     Alexandro da Porto fante in Castello
144. Catelan de Meziaprilli
     Francesco del Tura fante
     Lionello del Tura fante in Castello
145. Zulian da Cusiago homo d'arme
     fra da Varexe homo d'arme
     Zoane Francesco dito Fritella
146. Zoane vergello fante in Castello
     Jacomo da Ferara homo d'arme
147. Zoane Maria stafiero
     Biaxio Maria da Pavia
148. Andrea da la mata stafiero
     Christofalo dito Zevalo dai servixii
     Christofalo Mainardo fante
149. Castelan dal Finale homo d'arme
     Sgatya cavalchadore
150. Sisemondo del Zingano
     Zamdona da Corezo
     Batista dai pardi
151. Alberto Costabili homo d'arme
     Lodovigo brugnan fante in Castello
152. Bianchin da Parma homo d'arme
     Alovise di Messer Francesco da Ortona homo d'arme [see
     no. 86]
153. Julio da Ortona
     Christoforo bracischo homo d'arme
154. Alberto carnesala[ta]
155. Bernardin da Ortona homo d'arme
     Rustigello stafiero
156. Jacopetto da Corneto homo d'arme
     Il priete de la Freda salariato
157. Hercule de Moreto salariato
     Spagnollo caratiero
158. Antonio magno homo d'arme
     Zoanefrancesco Fontanela homo d'arme

Castilgiano dai servixii
159. Girolamo pavon homo d'arme
Ulivero del reame
160. Maestro Rigo bombardiero
Rainero da Ortona homo d'arme
Francesco da Trivixe homo d'arme
161. Mathio del Rangon homo d'arme
Pelegrin da Vicenza homo d'arme
163. Bomdonato da Capua homo d'arme
164. Francesco pichiato fante in Castello
Michaele caratiero
165. Zampaolo Pochintesta
Zoane de Mariotto mulatiero
Zoane de Pordone mulatiero
166. Zoane Capitella cazadore
Nicolo Zestaro/Costaro fante in Castello
167. Antonio Zestarello [Cistarello?] homo d'arme
Gardazo spagnollo
168. Antonio dala Fontana canevaro
Vicenzo soto cogo
169. Cabriel de Maestro Antonio cogo
170. Balzan mulatiero
171. Zampiero da Caravazo fante in Castello
172. Togno mulatiero
Antonio da San Cassan mulatiero
173. Baldisera da Modena fante in Castello
Nicolo Stabelini salariato
Maestro Antonio da Carpi cogo
174. Antonio Maria de Pandaxe
Cambio homo d'arme
Agnello da la Freda stradiotto
175. Cesare Marinetto balestriero
176. Thomaso da Pistoia
178. Rosso trombeta
179. Nicolo di Bianchi
Lodovigo bixo
181. Zoane Antonio di Suzi dito Bubino
Marcho dele Cremonexe balestriero
182. Maestro Alexandro biondo fornaxaro
183. Antonio deli Ariosti per conto di famii da stala
Antonio da Mantoa famio da stala

Bom famio da stala
186. Francesco Dalaro banchiero
187. Alo Illustrissimo Signore nostro
188. Bonavintura da Mosto salariato
189. Conte Hercule Ruscha
Carlo cantarin homo d'arme
190. Francesco Purin
191. Baptista de Ziliollo
192. Messer Sigismondo da Este
li fachini de Maestro Sperandio
193. Alo Illustrissimo nostro Signore per conto del fito di
Torelli
194. Berto da Regio frutarolo
Lodovigo da la cavaleria
195. Illustrissimi Vicenzo e fratelli di Messer Nicolo da Este[30]
195. Dona da Milla per conto di famii da stala
Orlando Palavisin salariato[31]
196. Fiorio del Moro
Antonio Maria Boion salariato
199. Antonio del Dainese
Lionello Brati da Nonantola balestriero
202. Zoane de Messer Lodovigo Condolmiero
Jacomo e fratelli di Rigizi dal Bondeno
Lanzalotto di Costabili
204. Pilgio da Mantua
205. Maestro Antonio da Cremona recamadore
Maestro Moreleto speziale
206. Maestro Zorzo dale fette
Messer Ursino di Ursini conduto sino adi primo di ginaio
Zoane Casotto per nome de Andrea de Zoboli
207. Sisimondo de Peschaduri
210. Zamhieronymo marchese
211. Messer Sisimondo Salimbeni
Sepion da la Sale
213. Christofalo de Tassoni
214. Andrea de Libanore

---

[30] Presumably Niccolo di Leonello, on whose attempted overthrow of Ercole in 1476, see A. Cappelli, 'Niccolo di Lionello d'Este', *Atti e memorie della Deputazione di storia patria per le provincie modenesi*, 5 (1868).

[31] Was this the 'zovene di Palavesini da Milano', a 'scudiero' in Este service, who was hit in the ducal chamber by Ercole Trotti (no. 73) in 1496, and returned for that reason to Milan (*Diario ferrarese*, 181)?

Rigo da San Vidalle banchiero
215. Maestro Biaxio Rossetto
Il Negro strazarollo
217. Bertolamio da Pavia cartolario
220. Bertolamio da Verona banchiero
Antonio da San Canasedo
222. Mathio dal Caprille
223. Daniele trombeta conducto sino al primo di marzo
Lucha da Checho da Roncagallo
224. Zoane Baptista Carandin
225. Bortelamio Malvizo/Maluzo strazarolo
Cabriele marchese
226. Girolamo Braxavola drapiero
Jacomo da San Vidale
Zoane Maria Maganza falconiero
Maestro Zampiero sarto salariato
227. Villano conducto per falconiero sino adi primo di zenaio
Jacomo da Bersello [Brescello]
Tarabin chi atende a lignari
Maestro Francesco da Carpi sarto
228. Fini d'Ariano
Nascimbene Mainardo
Baptista Zaninello
229. Lodovigo Sozo
Messer Luchin da Pavia
230. Baptista da la Farina
235. Spexa del fontecho
Abram ebreo[32]
236. Conte Lodovigo dal Sagra salariato
237. Piero di Piglari da Vicenza
238. Lunardo fondore da lat.
Alexandro da San Vidalle
Lionello Mestonini da Nonantola
240. Bortelamio lombardin
243. Baldisera Cadinello
245. Francesco dal'Abadia
248. Zoane da Peschiera famio da stalla
249. don Michiele fiorentin conducto per cantore soprano

---

[32] Catalano, *Ludovico Ariosto*, vol. 1, 182.

251. Uno amico secreto[33]
256. Bernardin fornaro tolto per portonaro sino a di primo di marzo
258. Conte Ugozon di Contrari[34]
259. Maestro Lorenzo da le corazine
     Hercule piapan homo d'arme
262. Batista Batain
263. Zoane fachin a legnaro salariato
265. Maestro Michaele da Porto marangon
274. Alberto da la pena
     Zoane Alovise da Napolli cavalchadore
277. Azomo[?] sarto
278. Bom orevexe conducto per balestriero sino a di primo de luio
     Zampiero panatiero/imbandidore
283. Jachotin conduto per cantore
287. Maestro Jacomo da Cremona muradore
288. Piero Jacomo scudelaro tolto ... de logo di Lorenzo scudelaro [no. 100]
294. Zoane Maria da Rezo fante in Castello
296. Ulivero Gaiardo balestriero [=159?]
297. Bachio/Bajo trombeta
     Maestro Bol... selaro
     Jacomo da Ferara homo d'arme
300. Lodovigo da Modena fante in Castello
301. Jacomo del Bailo conducto sino al primo de luio
304. Batista di Rainaldo muradore
307. Girolamo Codoso falconiero
309. A lo Illustrissimo nostro Signore a lo heremita de Santa Biancha; [Ditto] a una povera amore dei; [Ditto] a piu preti che diseno misse in Vigoevano
310. Il fiorentino [?] famio da stala
311. Lodovigo mulatiero
315. Bernardin Zestarello [Cistarello?]
318. Antonio Pelegrin de Bomnadali dal Bondeno
     Messer Bonifacio Bivilaqua
321. Galante mulatiero
     Teodotto mulatiero
     Gregoro pifaro

---

[33] Possibly Venetian: Dean, 'After the War of Ferrara', 81-2.
[34] 'primo gentilhomo et subdito del duca' in 1498: *Diario ferrarese*, 207.

323. Maestro Zoane de Argentina organista
325. Lionello Griffo balestriero
     Lodovigo de Messer Bonifacio balestriero [see no. 318]
327. Turino [?] balestriero
328. Thomaxo dai porzi
335. Francesco mulatiero tolto sino a di 15 di agosto
338. Piero biondo conduto sin a di primo de luio
340. Janello balestriero
345. Girolamo da Ferrara fante in Castello
     Minoto tolto sino a di 28 di ottobre
     Filippo di Amaduri stafiero

Part II

The French invasion of 1494-95

The Romagna campaign of 1494:
a significant military encounter

Cecil H. Clough

In Baldassare Castiglione's *The Book of the Courtier* (the second draft transcribed 1520-21, as in the final version), it was given to Count Ludovico Canossa to stress the importance of the literature of Antiquity for the courtier, whose 'principal and true profession... must be arms'.[1] Canossa echoed the theoretical view of Italian humanists who regarded Classical Antiquity as the model to adopt, a model which in the fifteenth century in some measure was consciously manifest in warfare on the Italian peninsula. Vespasiano da Bisticci's life of Federico da Montefeltro, written by 1498, emphasized that the latter's military reputation was a direct consequence of his classical studies: 'the Duke wrought the greater part of his martial deeds by ancient and modern example; from the ancients by his study of history...'.[2] The recommendation to learn warfare from the ancients is most vividly portrayed in a miniature by Giovanni Pietro Birago, dated about 1490, depicting the successful condottiere Francesco Sforza, who gained the duchy of Milan by military means, listening attentively to such classical commanders as Hannibal, Scipio and Caesar (fig. 1).[3] Canossa knew his claim had come to be seen as very flawed, for the French were victorious, yet as he admitted had little interest in letters, classical or otherwise; Canossa was forced to concede contrariwise that for all their knowledge of them 'the Italians have shown little worth in arms for some time',

---

[1] For the courtier's profession see B. Castiglione, *La seconda redazione del 'Cortegiano'*, ed. G. Ghinassi (Florence, 1968), Bk. I, xx, 28, and for the date of the second draft see C.H. Clough, *The Duchy of Urbino in the Renaissance* (London, 1981), item XVI, 24. The same passage is in the final version, see B. Castiglione, *Il Libro del Cortegiano*, ed. B. Maier (Turin, 3rd ed. rev., 1981), 112; trans. C. Singleton (Garden City, NY, 1959), 32. For the importance of letters see note 4 below.

[2] V. da Bisticci, *Le vite*, ed. A. Greco (Florence, 2 vols., 1970-76), vol. 1, 379, cf. 399; trans. W.G. and E. Waters (London, 1926), 99, cf. 105.

[3] Florence, Uffizi, one of nine cut-out miniatures, numbers 4423-30 and 843, see *Arte Lombarda dai Visconti agli Sforza* (Exhibition Catalogue) (Milan, 1958), 141-2, item 453, plate CLXXVIII.

Giovanni Pietro Birago (attributed), Francesco Sforza listening to classical generals; a cut-out miniature, c.1490, Uffizi, Florence.

presumably meaning at least since 1494. He did not elaborate, concluding: 'it is better to pass over in silence what cannot be remembered without pain'.[4]

Contemporary Italians were conscious that they fought by their own 'Italian' rules, which supposedly could find justification from classical models. These rules meant that a condottiere commander waited for the opposing general to make the first move; battle was rare and usually occurred after a formal challenge given and accepted, when each side judged victory was certain, usually because of a presumed military superiority. As the Florentine Luca Landucci wrote in his chronicle under 1 August 1478: 'The rule for our Italian soldiers seems to be this: "You pillage there and we will pillage here; there is no need for us to approach too close to one another." They often let a fort be bombarded for several days, without attempting to succour it'.[5] Such tactics ensured more pay and less risk for the military involved, as well as giving time for the political masters of the opposed forces to agree terms. Landucci reflected: 'we require to be taught by the Ultramontanes how to make war.'[6] What he had in mind was 'Continental' fighting, which consisted of surprise attacks, giving no quarter, and violence against non-combatants. Early in September 1494 in the Romagna campaign there was an occasion when the herald of the Milanese commander in league with the French proclaimed to the opposing Neapolitan general that for his part the fighting would be by 'Italian' rules, not 'a gorgia', an allusion to Plato's *Gorgias*, which denied morality and natural justice.[7]

In the fifteenth century French romances were popular reading for men in the Italian courts because French chivalry was believed to derive from the warfare of antiquity; for the Italian nobility the French man-at-arms, who epitomized chivalry, represented the living tradition of classical fighting. Yet it was appreciated that the French army as a fighting force was neither chivalric nor did it abide by Italian rules of warfare, but sought to overcome by might and terror. From the very first major encounter during the invasion of the Italian peninsula in 1494 the French army fought the 'continental' way and was

---

[4] Castiglione, *La seconda redazione*, 57-9; the same sentiments are in the final version, 163-6; trans. Singleton, 68-70. The contemporary Italian view of Charles VIII was that he was a warrior but uncultured, see C. De Frede, '"Più simile a mostro che a uomo": la bruttezza e l'incultura di Carlo VIII', *Bibliothèque d'Humanisme et Renaissance*, 44 (1982), 582-4.

[5] L. Landucci, *Diario fiorentino dal 1450 al 1516*, ed. I. del Badia (Florence, 1883), 24-5; trans. A. de R. Jervis (London, 1927), 22.

[6] *Landucci*, 25; Jervis, 22.

[7] B. Dovizi, *Epistolario*, ed. G.L. Moncallero, 2 vols. (Florence, 1955-65), vol. 1, 99, letter dated 9 September 1494 to Piero de' Medici. The distinction in fighting methods was made, for instance, by the near-contemporary historian F. Guicciardini, *Storia d'Italia*, ed. C. Panigada, 5 vols. (Bari, 1929), cap. 73-4; by such recent historians as J.S.C. Bridge, *A History of France from the Death of Louis XI*, 5 vols. (Oxford, 1920-36), vol. 2, 118-19, and Anne Denis, *Charles VIII et les Italiens: Histoire et Mythe* (Geneva, 1979), 87-8.

victorious.[8] Marino Sanuto's contemporary history was concerned exclusively with the initial French invasion, while Francesco Guicciardini and Paolo Giovio, near-contemporaries, covered the first and subsequent Italian wars. All three, like more recent scholars in the field, have sought to explain the overwhelming success of the foreign invaders, focusing either on the *malaise* of the Italian military, or on the lack of political unity on the Italian peninsula.[9]

The purpose of this study is to examine one campaign related to the French invasion of 1494: that in the Romagna, which began in July and culminated in the French sack of Mordano on 20 October. It has been neglected by historians of the Italian wars, who either have not considered it coherently as a campaign, or dismiss it in a few sentences, often on the basis of factual errors; their lead has been followed by other historians of the period.[10] Here what is provided is a miniature rather than the large canvas, and an unfinished miniature at that, as further research is needed to fill in some details. At the centre are military circumstances, though in the background are the political issues and the resulting diplomacy. The miniature itself is used to bring into relief the nature of Italian military ineptitude.

To make sense of the Romagna campaign it must be set in the context of the preparatory phase of the French invasion of 1494. An issue of importance was whether Charles VIII, king of France, would come to promote his claim to

---

[8] For the Italian nobility's attitude to the French man-at-arms and chivalry see C.H. Clough, 'Love and War in the Veneto', in *War, Culture and Society in Renaissance Venice*, ed. D.S. Chambers, C.H. Clough and M. E. Mallett (London, 1993), 108-9; for the belief that chivalry derived from Classical times see C. H. Clough, 'Chivalry and Magnificence in the Golden Age of the Italian Renaissance', in *Chivalry in the Renaissance*, ed. S. Anglo (Woodbridge, 1990), 38-9.

[9] M. Sanuto, *La spedizione di Carlo VIII in Italia*, ed. R. Fulin (Venice, 1873-83) (supplement to *Archivio veneto*, series 1, 5-6, 9-23), 63-70, 71-83, 92-8 (a chronicle based on official dispatches and on letters sent to Venice); Guicciardini, *Storia d'Italia*, xiv, I, 58-60, 85-6 (entirely lacks dates and is disjointed); P. Giovio, 'Historiarum', 3 vols. (ed. D. Visconti and T.C.P. Zimmermann), vol. 1 (1957), in P. Giovio, *Opera* (Rome, 1956 - in progress), 3, Bk. I, 32, 37-9, Bk. II, 46 (drawing on Dovizi's letters to Piero de' Medici, when he was able to consult material subsequently lost, cf. Dovizi's *Epistolario*; trans. L. Domenichi (Venice, 'Al Segno della Concordia', 2 parts, 1608), vol. 1, Bk. I, 32, 37-40, Bk. II, 48-50. More recent work includes that of L. von Ranke, *History of the Latin and Teutonic Nations (1494-1514)*, trans. G.R. Dennis (London, 1909), 6 (only two sentences relate); H.-F. Delaborde, *L'expédition de Charles VIII en Italie* (Paris, 1888), 369-70, 372, 384-5, 430-31; Bridge, *A History of France*, vol. 2, 126-9, 143, 154-5 (disjointed and poorly documented); P. Pieri, *Rinascimento e la crisi militare italiana* (2nd ed., Turin, 1952), 236-7, 329-31 (poorly documented); Y. Labande-Mailfert, *Charles VIII et son milieu (1470-1498)* (Paris, 1975), 259-60, 271, 280, 285-6 (disjointed and poorly documented); I. Cloulas, *Charles VIII et le mirage italien* (Paris, 1986), 60-61 (very brief and essentially erroneous).

[10] The exception is G.L. Moncallero, 'Documenti inediti sulla guerra di Romagna', in *Rinascimento*, 4 (1953), 233-61, 5 (1954), 45-79, 6 (1955), 3-74 (which draws heavily on Dovizi's *Epistolario*). For the histories of the wars see note 9 above; for a history in this area cf. L. Pastor, *The History of the Popes*, 40 vols., London, 1891-1953), vol. 5, ed. F.I. Antrobus (1898), 430-31.

the kingdom of Naples by military means, as he had threatened. In 1493 there were doubts that Charles would ever invade. This meant that King Ferrante's preparations, both tangible and diplomatic, were modest, in part because they might prove unnecessary expense (and the kingdom's resources were limited), in part because by too much activity King Ferrante could stimulate a French invasion as a reaction.[11] Ferrante died suddenly on 25 January 1494, to be succeeded by his son, Alfonso II, a cultured man who had behind him a long career as a military commander. Initially he took much the same line as his father had concerning military preparations, though his hatred of Ludovico Sforza meant that no last-minute agreement was likely, something King Ferrante had been working towards. For instance, on 15 February Bernardo Dovizi wrote from Naples to Piero de' Medici in Florence to report that Alfonso did not believe invasion would come, or fear it if it did.[12] As it became clearer that Charles would invade, so increasingly the kingdom of Naples' resources were channelled into the requirements of warfare. Niccolò Orsini, a highly rated, if elderly, condottiere general, was given his *condotta* in Neapolitan service on 7 February; other generals and captains were recruited subsequently.[13] In January 1494 a contract was agreed for a new defensive system for Naples, 60,000 ducats being levied as tax to build it, with work commencing in October. In April, to strengthen the Tyrrhenian coast from French naval attack, the construction of two new forts near Baia in the Bay of Pozzuoli was in progress as in late August, was the strengthening of coastline fortifications of Calabria and Puglia.[14] In early August, however, the French king and his main army still had not reached the Italian peninsula and Alfonso claimed the danger was averted for the year, it being too late in the season to embark French troops: after July the Mediterranean was deemed dangerous for galleys to navigate.[15]

Charles VIII was determined on invasion, and the necessary short-term arrangements were made on his behalf while he resided mainly in Lyons from March to late July; for example, a letter from Louis, duke of Orléans, reached

---

[11] Cf. Pieri, *Il Rinascimento e la crisi militare italiana*, 325.

[12] For Ferrante's death see G.A. Summonte, *Dell'historia della Città e Regno di Napoli*, 4 vols. (Naples, 1675), vol. 3, 481. For Alfonso II's culture see G.L. Hersey, *Alfonso II and the Artistic Renewal of Naples*, 1485-1495 (New Haven, CT., 1969), and E. Pèrcopo, 'La vita di G. Pontano', in *Archivio storico per le province napoletane*, 41 (1936), 192-3. For the letter of 15 February see Dovizi, *Epistolario*, 43.

[13] Labande-Mailfert, *Charles VIII*, 229-30 (no source).

[14] For the defences of Naples see Hersey, *Alfonso II and the Artistic Renewal*, 88-9; for the coastline defences see I. Mazzoleni, 'Gli apprestamenti difensivi dei castelli di Calabria ultra', *Archivio storico per le province napoletane*, n.s. 30 (1947), 132-44, and cf. Summonte, *Dell' historia della Città e Regno di Napoli*, vol. 3, 495.

[15] Labande-Mailfert, *Charles VIII*, 230. The 'Autumn voyage' for pilgrims from Venice to Jaffa ceased about 1450 because storms rendered it unpopular, cf. M.M. Newett, *Canon Pietro Casola's Pilgrimage to Jerusalem in the year 1494* (Manchester, 1907), 78, 92.

his fief of Asti on 17 April advising the Astigiani to prepare to welcome the monarch and to provide lodging for his army.[16] On 29 July Charles took a boat to Vienne, where he assumed command of his army for its crossing of the Alps by Mount Genèvre; Turin, in the duchy of Savoy, was reached on 5 September and Asti four days later. After illness, Charles left Asti in early October and began the march south with the main body of his troops.[17] In Lyons the monarch had been visited on 1 June by Cardinal Giuliano della Rovere, who stressed the importance of Genoa for the success of the invasion. This port, and the Ligurian territory it controlled, had been occupied for the Sforza of Milan in August 1487. In 1493 Ludovico Sforza, seeking investiture of Genoa from the French monarch, had agreed that the French fleet could enjoy its harbour facilities; from April the following year ships, from galleys to large vessels, began to assemble there, where others were being built to the French king's specifications. Ships were required to convey supplies for the army and seemingly the French fleet was envisaged as defending the supply route from Marseilles; subsequently it was intended to use it to attack Naples by sea in co-ordination with the French army.[18] Cardinal Della Rovere appears to have warned of an imminent Neapolitan attack on the port of Genoa, and shortly after his visit Milanese troops and Swiss under Antoine de Bessey (*bailli* of Dijon) were sent to strengthen its defences.[19] Ludovico Sforza's object in facilitating the landing of the French army at Genoa presumably was that the rest of the duchy of Milan would not be touched as it passed south to Naples - this hope proved mistaken.

King Alfonso did indeed determine to strike the first military blow against French invasion plans by sending the Neapolitan fleet carrying a force of infantry to occupy Genoa. Archbishop Fregoso and some Genoese exiled by the Sforza encouraged Alfonso to believe that as soon as his fleet arrived there would be a revolt against Milanese rule within the city. On 22 June a strong Neapolitan fleet with some Neapolitan infantry on board under Federigo, prince

---

[16] For Charles' residence in Lyons see the testimony of his letters, Charles VIII, *Lettres*, ed. P. Pélicier, 5 vols. (Paris, 1898-1905), vol. 4 (1903), 23 onwards, the source for Labande-Mailfert, *Charles VIII*, 267-8. F. Gabotto, *La vita in Asti al tempo di Gian Giorgio Alione* (Asti, 1899), 12-14.

[17] For Charles taking a boat to Vienne see Charles VIII, *Lettres*, vol. 4, 80-81; for the king reaching Turin, his illness in Asti and departure for the south see Labande-Mailfert, *Charles VIII*, 278-83; for his arrival at Asti see Delaborde, *L'expédition de Charles VIII*, 399.

[18] C. Shaw, *Julius II: The Warrior Pope* (Oxford, 1993), 96-7. For Sforza seeking the investiture of Genoa see P. de Commynes, *Lettres et négociations*, ed. J.M.B.C. Kervyn de Lettenhove, 3 vols. (Brussels, 1867-74), vol. 2, 97. For the fleet in Genoa see the 'Instructions', 4 May 1494 issued by Charles in P. de Commynes, *Mémoires*, ed. L.N.E. Dupont, 3 vols. (Paris, 1840-47), vol. 3, 370-75, doc. XL, and cf. Labande-Mailfert, *Charles VIII*, 243 and C. Kidwell, *Marullus: Soldier Poet of the Renaissance* (London, 1989), 210-11.

[19] Delaborde, *L'expédition de Charles VIII*, 384; cf. Labande-Mailfert, *Charles VIII*, 218, where it is suggested the cardinal divulged the enemy's secrets to the king.

of Altamura, the king's brother, sailed from Naples, reaching safe anchorage in Livorno (the Florentine port conceded for use by Piero de' Medici, who was allied to the Neapolitan monarch, and where presumably a force of Sienese mercenaries was embarked). After an attempt on Genoa by sea on about 13 July was abandoned because of the arrival of the French fleet, the Neapolitan vessels sailed southwards to near Florentine-held Sarzana, landing some 400 troops at Portovenere (near La Spezia) on 14 July. In seeking to take the town this force was so vigorously repulsed that it re-embarked after five days, the fleet thereafter returning to Naples.[20] King Alfonso had not formally declared war, presumably because he deemed his offensive justified in the face of French threats and preparations, and because his ambassador had been ordered from the court of the French king on 14 January 1494. Furthermore, Count Caiazzo, whose fief was in the kingdom, had been summoned to Naples (though had declined), Ludovico Sforza had been deprived forthwith of his duchy of Bari, and by 12 June the king had recalled his ambassadors from Milan; the Milanese ambassadors to the Neapolitan court had left.[21] Hence the stage had already been set for war.

Given Alfonso's notions on the dangers inherent in sailing the Mediterranean after July his authorisation of a second attempt on Genoa marked the monarch's awareness that Charles VIII with his army actually was crossing the Alps. In late August the Neapolitan fleet again sailed towards Genoa, and on about 5 September a force of 4,000 infantry with some Genoese exiles were landed at the unfortified village of Rapallo, some thirty miles south of Genoa. With the arrival of the French fleet, well-armed with cannon, the Neapolitan vessels withdrew, being carried south off Sestri Levante by contrary winds. Meanwhile on 8 September the flagship of the French fleet bombarded the Neapolitan infantry behind its earth ramparts; a land-force from Genoa joined with the Swiss from the French vessels to assault the invaders from front and rear, resulting in heavy casualties for the Neapolitans; the Swiss even

---

[20] For Pontano urging the expedition see J.H. Bentley, *Politics and Culture in Renaissance Naples* (Princeton, NJ, 1987), 192 (the letter's date 11 July appears erroneous). Notar Giacomo, *Cronaca di Napoli*, ed. P. Garzilli (Naples, 1845), and G. Passero, *Storie in forma di giornali*, ed. M.M. Vecchioni (Naples, 1785), 62-3 (a critical edition of this compilation is much needed) for the naval expedition; cf. Delaborde, *L'expédition de Charles VIII*, 369, 384-5 (without distinguishing two naval expeditions, and Pieri, *Il Rinascimento e la crisi militare italiana*, 325-6, and by Labande-Mailfert, *Charles VIII*, 274. For the force of mercenaries see F. Guicciardini, *Storia d'Italia*, ed. C. Panigada, 5 vols. (Bari, 1929), I, Bk. I, chap. viii, 57: 'per soldave insino al numero di Quattromila fauti, ne' porti somesi...'; cf. Delaborde, 369 errs in giving 5,000 from this source. For news of the defeat in a letter of 20 July see C. de' Rosmini, *Dell'istoria intorno alle militari imprese e alla vita di C. J. Trivulzio*, 2 vols. (Milan, 1815), vol. 2, 202, doc. 32.

[21] Delaborde, *L'expédition de Charles VIII*, 299-300, 368-9; cf. Labande-Mailfert, *Charles VIII*, 274, who misunderstands with 'Sans déclaration d'hostilité, Frédéric... a tenté, le 16 [juillet] un coup de main sur Gênes...'

slaughtered the wounded and sacked Rapallo, a foretaste of warfare not according to Italian rules.[22]

The two Neapolitan strikes by sea were ambitious, intended to deprive the French of their naval base on the peninsula, and also to enable the Neapolitan forces themselves to use it in order to attack the duchy of Milan from the west. The strike was envisaged as one thrust of a pincer movement, and initially was brought to bear following the withdrawal of the Neapolitan ambassador from Milan in early June. Simultaneously with the first sea assault on Genoa, the advance guard of a Neapolitan land-force was moving into position to attack the Parma region in the south of the duchy of Milan by way of the Via Emilia. This latter offensive deteriorated into the stalemate of the Romagna campaign. Had it been correctly timed and successful the pincer movement might have brought about Ludovico Sforza's overthrow by popular revolt within the duchy of Milan. Certainly when in late August 1494 the duke of Calabria appealed to Caterina Sforza, he claimed the intention of his army was to restore her half-brother, Giangaleazzo, as ruler of the duchy of Milan.[23]   Who devised the pincer movement remains uncertain, but probably both King Ferrante and his son had a hand in it. There is possible evidence that preparations were under way in 1493, when Ferrante ordered the construction of galleys, perhaps for the attack on Genoa; in that year he made secret alliances with the pope and Piero de' Medici; their permission was vital for the passage northwards of the land force. The testimony, though, is not conclusive, as these measures may not have originated specifically with the pincer movement. Even so it was reported on 8 February 1494 from Amboise to Ludovico Sforza, that King Ferrante (whose death was not then known there) intended to block the threatened French advance towards his kingdom by sending a Neapolitan force to the Romagna.[24]

Ferrandino, duke of Calabria, was sent with some 240 cavalry by his father, Alfonso, initially to spear-head the eventual land attack on the duchy. His force left from the Terra del Lavoro north of Naples, reaching somewhere in the

---

[22] Delaborde, *L'expédition de Charles VIII*, 400-8; Pieri, *Il Rinascimento e la crisi militare italiana*, 327-8, and Labande-Mailfert, *Charles VIII*, 279 (and see there note 395 for a view opposed to Pieri regarding the importance of cannon fire). Giovio, trans. Domenichi, vol. 1, Bk. I, 34-7 wrongly indicates that the Rapallo landing followed immediately that at Portovenere. For a letter with news of the defeat, dated Rapallo, 8 September, see De' Rosmini, *Dell'istoria... di G. J. Trivulzio*, vol. 2, 202, doc. 33. Charles VIII, *Lettres*, vol. 4, 89-93, no. DCCC. For the Swiss killing the wounded and sacking Rapallo see Giovio, Bk. I, 36-7, perhaps from Sanuto, *La spedizione di Carlo VIII*, 84.

[23] A. Bernardi, 'Cronache forlivesi', ed. G. Mazzatinti in *Monumenti istorici pertinenti alle provincie della Romagna*, series 3: *Cronache, Deputazione di Storia Patria*, 2 vols. (Bologna, 1895-97), vol. 1, part 2, 13; E. Pèrcopo, 'La vita di G. Pontano', 197.

[24] Bridge, *A History of France*, vol. 2, 126-7, states categorically the scheme was devised by Ferrante and inherited by his son, but gives no evidence. For the building of the galleys see Labande-Mailfert, *Charles VIII*, 230. For the secret alliances see Labande-Mailfert, *Charles VIII*, 229, without a source, and see Delaborde, *L'expédition de Charles VIII*, 341 for an accord of 1 April 1494.

Abruzzi by 2 July; it was encamped outside Cesena by 19 July, and perhaps its route was Avezzano, L'Aquilà, Rieti, Terni, Foligno, Perugia, Città di Castello, San Sepolcro, thence across the Appenines to Bagno and Mercato.[25] On 5 August the duke rode to the locality of San Sepolcro to rendezvous with Piero de' Medici. The secret discussions, extended over four days, concerned the promise made by Piero to send troops and money for the Neapolitan force intent on advancing against the duchy of Milan. King Alfonso had already met the pope on 14 July at the Orsini stronghold of Vicovaro, near Tivoli, when the secret alliance of 3 August 1493 was renewed; seemingly at secret sessions over three days the pope agreed to fund a contingent to be recruited to fight alongside the Neapolitan land force. The pope had taken possession of Ostia but fearing the intentions of the Colonna, and concerned about likely dissension in the Campagna as a French army approached, he requested the immediate military support of King Alfonso, who had been invested with his kingdom by him. Originally the plan had been for the entire Neapolitan army to advance north under King Alfonso; he, however, to satisfy the pope, by late July had detached 30 squadrons of men-at-arms, over whom he remained in command, to be stationed at Tagliacozzo, some 116 miles east of Rome. Moreover Gentile Virginio Orsini, who was appointed Grand Constable on 7 May, with 200 men-at-arms and some light cavalry was sent to the Campagna to overawe the Colonna.[26] As a result the duke of Calabria was given command of the army to march north, with the assistance of tried condottiere generals, notably Niccolò Orsini, Giangiacomo Trivulzio and Bartolomeo Alviano.[27] In effect, too, the fighting force of some 650 men-at-arms and 2,500 light horse was denied the Romagna army at a crucial time. This was probably the decisive factor in the army's failure to reach the duchy of Milan, since in August with depleted strength it was in no position to persuade by a show of might such cities as Forlì, Imola and Bologna that it was in their best interest to grant it passage through their territories. By the time the Neapolitan army was anything like

---

[25] For the force in the Abruzzi see C. Kidwell, *Pontano: Poet and Prime Minister* (London, 1991), 245; for its size as '4... squadre' see Bernardi, 'Cronache forlivesi', vol. 1, part 2, 11, which also provides the date of arrival at Cesena. The likely route is on the basis of Giovio, trans., vol. 1, Bk. I, 32. This advance force is not mentioned by Delaborde, *L'expédition de Charles VIII*, 395. Kidwell, *Marullus*, 215, mentions the Neapolitan force advancing up the Adriatic coast to the Romagna, without a source.

[26] For the meeting between the duke and Piero see Sanuto, *La spedizione di Carlo VIII*, 67, the source for Delaborde, *L'expédition de Charles VIII*, 369-70, the source for Pastor, *The History of the Popes*, 430 and for Bridge, *A History of France*, vol. 2, 127-8; that the meeting was for 3 days is indicated by Summonte, *Dell'historia della Città... di Napoli*, vol. 3, 496. For the secret alliance see note 24 above, and for the appointment of the Constable see Labande-Mailfert, *Charles VIII*, 230, without a source. For the pope obtaining Ostia on 24 May see Pastor, *The History of the Popes*, vol. 5, 424-5, and Shaw, *Julius II*, 97 without a source.

[27] L. Cobelli, 'Cronache forlivesi', ed. G. Carducci, E. Fanti and F. Guarini, in *Monumenti istorici*, ser. 3 (Bologna, 1874), 356; Dovizi, *Epistolario*, 89 for Alviano.

Adriano Fiorentino, Ferrandino duke of Calabria and his devices; medal, after
26 January 1494 and before 23 January 1495: Bargello, Florence.

strong enough, an enemy force had arrived nearby. Indeed Ludovico Sforza had sent Gasparo (Fracasso) Sanseverino with three hundred cavalry (including men-at-arms) to the Sforza fief of Cotignola in the first week of July, even before the duke of Calabria's advance party reached Cesena, and as will be seen this force steadily increased in size over the following two months.[28]

In the years immediately prior to 1494 Charles VIII had negotiated with foreign powers to enable him with some security to leave France with a large army. Early in 1494, when final preparations were under way, the king sent envoys to seek safe-passage and provisions for his force as it moved south down the peninsula towards Naples.[29] Already in 1493 King Ferrante, aware of the French diplomatic moves, had sought to strengthen accords with the pope and with Piero de' Medici.[30] These were to prove inadequate in terms of the Romagna campaign. In July 1494, as the French invasion was under way, the pope's insistence on protection had serious consequences for the Neapolitan land attack, as has been indicated.[31] Piero, for his part, was to hold the Florentine frontier against any force sent by Ludovico Sforza, so as to ensure that the Neapolitan army would not be outflanked as it moved along the Via Emilia. The request made on 4 May 1494 by the French envoys (among them Bernard Stuart d'Aubigny) that Florence grant passage and supplies to the French army as it advanced towards the kingdom of Naples was answered two days later. The special ties with France were recognized, but the Republic could not breach the alliance with Naples promoted by Louis XI of France. This reply resulted in Charles VIII dismissing the Florentine ambassadors from his court in order to put pressure on the Florentine government. On 28 June the French envoys returned and the Florentine response delivered on 14 July was as before, though by then Aubigny, on the orders of his sovereign, had left Florence to raise troops in the duchy of Milan. Already in late June the Neapolitan fleet had been allowed to harbour in the Florentine port of Livorno, where Piero visited it, and early in September Piero committed Florence unequivocally to the cause of Naples by sending troops to join the army of the duke of Calabria in the Romagna.[32]

---

[28] Letter of 7 July from L. de' Medici to the Otto di Pratica, Florence, relating to Sanseverino's transit to Cotignola with 300 men through the territory of Faenza without permission, see G. Donati, *La fine della Signoria dei Manfredi di Faenza* (Turin, 1938), 90-91; cf. also the letter of 9 July from Cotignola mentioned by V. Adami, *Il carteggio di un capitano di ventura: Gasparo San Severino* (Venice, 1930), 13.

[29] For the negotiations see Delaborde, *L'expédition de Charles VIII*, 358-67, and Labande-Mailfert, *Charles VIII*, 227-9; for particular requests for passage and provisions see below at notes 32, 39, 43, 48.

[30] See note 24 above.

[31] See the text above note 26.

[32] Delaborde, *L'expédition de Charles VIII*, 364, 367; F. Cordero, *Savonarola*, 3 vols. (Bari, 1986-88), vol. 1, 294-7; G. Guidi, *Ciò che accadde al tempo della Signoria di novembre-dicembre in Firenze, l'anno 1494* (Florence, 1988), 14-15.

The Neapolitan army's projected route along the Via Emilia involved passage through the territory of Faenza, and while this was a papal vicariate the ruling dynasty of the Manfredi enjoyed Florentine protection. After the assassination of Galeotto Manfredi in 1488 Lorenzo de' Medici had frustrated Ludovico Sforza's attempts to extend his influence in the Romagna by ensuring the succession of Astorre III; Piero de' Medici was informed of all developments in Faenza by his own secret agent.[33] On the Adriatic coast to the north of the Via Emilia was the territory of Ravenna, controlled by Venice. The Republic's declared neutrality in the face of the French invasion was pithily reported by the Florentine ambassador in Venice, writing to Piero on 5 August: 'the policy is to wait and see' whatever would be in the Republic's best interests. Moreover, fearful of troops of the opposed armies pillaging in the territory of Ravenna, the Republic sent her own forces to protect the frontier.[34]

Immediately to the west and north of Ravenna was territory held by Ercole d'Este, duke of Ferrara and duke of Modena, and this represented an unresolved problem for Neapolitan advance along the Via Emilia. Ercole held the duchy of Ferrara as a papal vicariate, Modena as an imperial fief; Maximilian, king of the Romans, had renewed investiture on 24 April 1494.[35] On 30 November 1493 the proxy marriage had taken place between Bianca Maria, sister of Duke Giangaleazzo Sforza, and Maximilian.[36] In 1473 Ercole d'Este had married Eleonora, King Ferrante's daughter, who died on 11 October 1493.[37] The couple's daughter, Beatrice, had married Ludovico Sforza on 17 January 1491, and five days later Alfonso, Duke Ercole's heir, married Anna Sforza, daughter of Duke Galeazzo Sforza. Against this background of marriage connections and personal considerations Ercole naturally took refuge in claiming neutrality.[38] After the visit of the French envoy on 24-26 April Ercole granted passage through his duchies to forces of Charles VIII's army, and provisions at a fair price, maintaining this promise despite a papal brief of 25 August ordering him as papal vicar of Ferrara not to do so.[39] On 5 June Ercole

---

[33] The issues are documented by Donati, *La fine della Signoria dei Manfredi*, cf. also G.B. Picotti, 'Caterina Sforza e la Romagna alla calata di Carlo VIII', in *Atti del convegno di studi per il V centenario della nascita di Caterina Sforza* (published in *Atti e Memorie della Deputazione di Storia Patria per le provincie di Romagna*, series 5, 15-16, 1967) (Bologna, 1967), 176.

[34] Delaborde, *L'expédition de Charles VIII*, 372.

[35] A. Frizzi, *Memorie per la storia di Ferrara*, ed. C. Laderchi, 5 vols. (2nd ed., Ferrara, 1847-48), vol. 4 (1848), 176.

[36] C. M. Ady, *A History of Milan under the Sforza* (London, 1907), 148-9.

[37] L. Chiappini, 'Eleonora d'Aragona', in *Atti e memorie della Deputazione di Storia Patria*, n.s. 16 (1956), 95, and as a monograph (Rovigo, 1956), with the same pagination.

[38] J. Cartwright, *Beatrice d'Este* (London, 1899), 65, 70.

[39] For the late-April visit see Frizzi, *Memorie per la storia di Ferrara*, vol. 4, 176; Delaborde, *L'expédition de Charles VIII*, 362 and E.G. Gardner, *Dukes and Poets at Ferrara* (London, 1904), 250; for the brief see Picotti, 'Caterina Sforza', 177 without a source.

conferred with Giovanni Bentivoglio, 'first citizen' of Bologna, when Bentivoglio agreed to follow Ercole's example.[40] Piero de' Medici, preoccupied with the accord with Naples and the advent of the French envoys on a second occasion, on 26 June sent envoys to Bentivoglio in an effort to persuade him not to concede passage, but to no avail. On 19 August the pope issued a brief ordering Bentivoglio not to harbour Milanese troops and another on 2 September forbidding him giving passage to the French forces.[41]

Bologna was the key to the Via Emilia, as both protagonists were aware. Charles VIII at Chambéry (the capital of Savoy) in August, just prior to crossing the Alps, was reported as recognizing this, as King Alfonso certainly did on 9 October, when the Romagna campaign had been at stalemate for over two months.[42] In April 1494 Bentivoglio's reply to the French request for passage and supplies had been non-committal though, as mentioned, in early June he was swayed by Ercole d'Este to grant the request.[43] Bentivoglio was married to a Sforza and owed much to his connection with the family; in 1493 he was appointed Governor-General of the Milanese armies, a post he retained in 1494 (but because of arrears of pay he excused himself from active service).[44] From his correspondence of 1494 it is evident that he was aware of the dangers to the entire peninsula of a French invasion, yet self-interest rather than statesmanship prevailed. Seemingly he allowed himself to be won over by Ercole so as to have a bargaining counter with the pope, from whom he ardently sought a cardinal's hat for his son Antongaleazzo; when on the pope's list of 27 October his son's name did appear, it was too late to influence in any way the Romagna campaign.[45] Bentivoglio's eldest son, Annibale, had a *condotta* with Florence, and Piero calculatedly put him in command of the Florentine contingent sent to assist the Neapolitan army in the Romagna; Bentivoglio carefully avoided showing his son and the latter's force any favour, presumably in part because he did not want to weaken pressure on the pope in his bid for the cardinal's hat.[46] On 3 November Annibale and his contingent left for Florence under the terms of

[40] Frizzi, *Memorie per la storia di Ferrara*, vol. 4, 176.

[41] Frizzi, vol. 4, 176, for the meeting on 26 June; for Pontano sent by the king of Naples for a meeting see C.M. Ady, *The Bentivoglio of Bologna* (Oxford, 1937), 112. For the brief see Pastor, *The History of the Popes*, 431 note.

[42] Ady, *The Bentivoglio of Bologna*, 111.

[43] For the non-committal initial reply see G.B. Picotti, 'La neutralità bolognese nella discesa di Carlo VIII', in *Atti e Memorie della Deputazione di Storia Patria per le provincie di Romagna*, series 4, 9 (1919), 176-8. Cf. also Labande-Mailfert, *Charles VIII*, 286 n. 406, citing P.A. Berselli, *L'atteggiamento di Bologna durante la calata di Carlo VIII*, which I have been unable to trace.

[44] Ady, *The Bentivoglio of Bologna*, 111-12.

[45] Ady, *The Bentivoglio of Bologna*, 114.

[46] Ady, *The Bentivoglio of Bologna*. 115-16.

that city's submission to Charles VIII as arranged by Piero de' Medici, who on 9 November left Florence for exile.[47]

On 15 April 1494 Ludovico Sforza wrote to his niece Caterina Sforza, who ruled the papal vicariates of Imola and Forlì as regent for her sons. He informed her that the king of France was coming to dispossess King Alfonso of the kingdom of Naples by military means, and he sought her assurance that she would allow passage to the French and allied army, through the territories she controlled and sell it provisions. Her reply appears lost, but was probably non-committal.[48] On 30 June Cardinal Raffaello Riario, her deceased husband's nephew, visited her to seek to align her with the pope and Naples, as the Neapolitan land-force was being formed and its route was to be the Via Emilia. She gave him no assurances, claiming neutrality.[49] Two days previously Ludovico Sforza had written to state that he knew she had contact with King Alfonso; this she admitted in her reply of 1 July, saying that she had to do the best she could, since he had sent her no tangible assistance.[50] On 30 July the cardinal returned again seeking to influence her in favour of the Neapolitan allies, including the pope, whose vicariates her sons held.[51] To counter this Ludovico Sforza sent his envoy on 8 August, offering her eldest son a Milanese *condotta*.[52] In the past Ludovico Sforza had provided her some protection if only out of self-interest, but she also enjoyed cordial relations with the Medici; Lorenzo had supported her in several clashes of interest with neighbouring states in the Romagna, and in 1489 had helped promote the marriage of her daughter Bianca to Astorre III Manfredi of Faenza.[53] Her situation was analogous to that of Giovanni Bentivoglio, since she had connections with both sides and her territories, like Bologna, straddled the route likely to be taken by the opposed armies, and to concede passage to one would surely earn the enmity of the other. Procrastination was the safest policy until it was clearer which force was the more powerful. Ludovico Sforza, aware of these issues, on 13 August had decided not to waste time but wrote to tell her that he had ordered

---

[47] For the departure of Annibale Bentivoglio see note 86; for Piero de' Medici see Delaborde, *L'expédition de Charles VIII*, 434-9, 443-4, Guidi, *Ciò che accadde*, 16-17, 34-8, Cordero, *Savonarola*, 303, 310-12.

[48] P. D. Pasolini, *Caterina Sforza*, 3 vols. (Rome, 1893), vol. 3, 203, doc. 514 (synopsis).

[49] E. Breisach, *Caterina Sforza: A Renaissance Virago* (Chicago, 1967), 153, 312 n.3.

[50] Pasolini, *Caterina Sforza*, vol. 3, 208-9, doc. 525.

[51] *Ibid.*, vol. 3, 210 doc. 530 (synopsis); Bernardi, 'Cronache forlivesi', vol. 1, part 2, 12.

[52] Pasolini, *Caterina Sforza*, vol. 3, 210-11, doc. 531.

[53] For relations with Ludovico Sforza see Breisach, *Caterina Sforza*, 141-4, and for relations with Lorenzo de' Medici see Donati, *La fine della Signoria dei Manfredi*, 40-43, and for both see also P. Zama, 'Caterina Sforza e gli ultimi Manfredi Signori di Faenza (1488-1500)', in *Atti del convegno di studi per il V centenario della nascita di Caterina Sforza*, 123-34.

Count Caiazzo and his forces to occupy her territories.[54] This did not mean the force could enter her walled towns, and since there was the Neapolitan army nearby, it drove Caterina to look to that as a counter to maintain her interests.

Historians of late have tended to put emphasis on the procrastinations and vacillations of both Caterina Sforza and Giovanni Bentivoglio, judging these individuals as the prime cause of the Neapolitan army's failure in the Romagna campaign.[55] This neglects the military situation. It has been indicated above that the duke of Calabria's advance-force of cavalry reached Cesena on 19 July and that previously in the first week of that month Ludovico Sforza had sent a force of cavalry to Cotignola.[56] To reiterate the point already made: the stalemate in the Romagna developed because the duke of Calabria was unable to establish quickly enough a sufficiently powerful army to overawe the rulers of the Romagna, and pass through their states, before the arrival of the enemy in sufficient strength to deter the rulers from granting passage. Having said that, it is also true that the Neapolitan army was too slow in reaching sufficient strength to warrant its advance towards the duchy of Milan. This latter aspect, hitherto overlooked, will now be examined. First the strength of the force under the duke of Calabria as it fluctuated between mid-July and late October will be considered, then that of the army under Count Caiazzo and Bernard Stuart d'Aubigny for much the same period. Thereafter the interaction between the two forces will be analysed briefly.

The strength of the two opposed forces cannot be given precisely but, as the vagaries in the statistics appear broadly true for both, comparison seems possible. In most instances muster rolls do not exist, and contemporary figures from other sources are subject to notable variations.[57] Detachments of troops came and went continually. Moreover, terminology is a problem, as a term may have been used loosely and inconsistently. Here for the Italians a *squadra* is taken to comprise the normal 20 *lanze*; however, according to Dovizi writing on 4 September to Piero de' Medici, many squadrons in the Aragonese camp had as

---

[54] Pasolini, *Caterina Sforza*, vol. 3, 212, doc. 532 (synopsis), for the document's location see Breisach, *Caterina Sforza*, 313 n. 13.

[55] Cf. Bridge, *A History of France*, vol. 2, 128 referring to events before 8 August 1494: 'Ferrantino moved forward slowly, and presently found his progress stopped entirely by continued difficulties with regard to Imola, Forlì and Bologna'; Pieri, *Il Rinascimento e la crisi militare italiana*, 326: [the Neapolitan forces remained inactive] 'sia perché bisognose di reordinamento, sia perché incerte del contegno di Caterina Sforza a Forlì e di Annibale [*sic* for Giovanni] Bentivoglio a Bologna'. The contemporary Cobelli, 'Cronache forlivesi', 356, stated categorically that it was Caterina Sforza who delayed the advance of the two forces, and this is paraphrased by Pasolini, *Caterina Sforza*, vol. 1, 336.

[56] See above, note 28.

[57] An example is given below to illustrate this in the text at note 84.

many as 30, and a few not 20.[58] By 1490 on the Italian peninsula the formation known as a *lanza*, or lance, usually meant four mounted men: one was a man-at-arms in heavy armour; there was his page with a change of horse and spare arms, and two more lightly armed men bore lances as the man-at-arm's bodyguard.[59] In a squadron of 20 lances broadly speaking there were 60 fighting men, of whom 20 were heavily armed and 40 more lightly armed, and the two together formed the cavalry. Here reference to a specific number of 'men-at-arms' is usually taken to refer to lances; in battle formation, though, the heavily armed usually formed a corps and most likely the 'men-at-arms' specified meant precisely that. There was also light cavalry comprising among others Levantine *stradioti*, as well as mounted crossbow-men (who also had a javelin) and mounted archers.[60] Often, but not invariably, in the case of the French a lance consisted of six men, of whom two were heavily armed and four more lightly armed; however generally two servants were included in the statistics, and in this case the force of lances was reduced effectively as a fighting force by a third. Here it is assumed that a French lance had twice the number of heavily armed men as the Italian, and two lightly armed mounted soldiers. Since usually it is not specified whether Italian sources adopted six or four when referring to a French lance, figures provided here for the French are taken essentially from French sources, those for the Italians from Italian ones. Whenever possible statistics as to the strength of the forces are taken from letters, official bulletins and similar lists rather than from chronicles. Whatever the source, the information may have been consciously distorted, quite apart from merely being inaccurate, but by and large the figures given in chronicles appear reported guesses. The same official and semi-official sources for the Romagna campaign provide details of the movements of the two forces, and of skirmishes between the two.[61]

---

[58] For the normal 20 lances (often termed 'men-at-arms') in a *squadra* see Dovizi, *Epistolario*, 107, and for the variations in actuality see 95; cf. Delaborde, *L'expédition de Charles VIII*, 395 n.3, where the term 'men-at-arms' is used incorrectly.

[59] For the *lanza* see M.E. Mallett and J.R. Hale, *The Military Organization of a Renaissance State: Venice c.1400 to 1617* (Cambridge, 1984), 70-72, 367; Delaborde, *L'expédition de Charles VIII*, 324 notes 3 and 4 citing two contemporary sources. Pieri, *Il Rinascimento e la crisi militare italiana*, appears to calculate the Italian lance as an effective fighting force of 4, which over-estimates by a quarter, cf. 331: '70 squadre, ossia 1400 lance (5600 cavalli)'.

[60] For mounted crossbow-men see Mallett and Hale, *Military Organization*, 71-2.

[61] F. Lot, *Recherches sur les effectifs des armées françaises des Guerres d'Italie aux Guerres de Religion, 1494-1562* (Paris, 1962), 16-7 for the French lance comprising 6 men, of whom 2 were men-at-arms, 2 mounted archers, 2 servants (an *écuyer* or varlet and a page) and see pp. 15-21 for a consideration of the problems involved in interpreting the evidence concerning the size of the French army; Delaborde, *L'expédition de Charles VIII*, 324 n. 3 cites a contemporary source for the lance comprising 6 men, but mistakenly assumes this was an effective fighting force; Labande-Mailfert, *Charles VIII*, 257 n. 355 states the number should be 3 men for a lance, which distorts in the other direction.

The advance-force under the duke of Calabria at Cesena by 19 July consisted of some 240 cavalry.[62] The main force of Neapolitan cavalry reached camp there before 10 August. Emilia Pio, familiar from Castiglione's *Courtier* and related by marriage to Count Caiazzo, commander of the Milanese force in the Romagna, wrote a letter on 10 August to her brother, joint-ruler of Carpi, providing the details he requested of the Neapolitan force; she sent a man specifically to the camp to get them.[63] In total there were 2,480 cavalry, of whom 560 were men-at-arms, and there were 200 infantry, her letter mentioned 25 *contestabili* seeking to recruit companies of infantry in the Romagna and the Marches for a muster on 16 August. The infantry in the duke's force was not from the kingdom but locally recruited and on short-term contracts, for it was assumed fighting would cease with the winter season from early November at the latest. The letter mentioned a further 26 squadrons of lances expected to arrive by the muster date, as was a papal contingent - some of this latter was still awaited a month later.[64] She concluded by writing that eventually there would be 80 squadrons of men-at-arms. In the event recruitment proved slow. When on 2 September Dovizi reached camp near Cesena (presumably as agreed at the meeting between Piero de' Medici and the duke of Calabria near Borgo Sansepolcro in early August), he reported to Piero that there were 55 squadrons of men-at-arms, perhaps reaching 70 within days (the squadrons including some 500 mounted crossbow-men) and 100 *stradioti*; there were 1,000 infantry (soon to be 3,000) and 500 foot-soldiers with crossbows under the duke of Urbino, engaged on a renewable fifteen-day contract.[65] On 4 September part of the promised Florentine force, whose absence embarrassed Dovizi, reached Forlì

---

[62] See note 25 above.

[63] De' Rosmini, *Dell'istoria di G.J. Trivulzio*, vol. 2, 202-3 doc. 34; for Emilia Pio's marriage connection with the Sanseverino family see C.H. Clough, 'Caterina Sforza, Gasparo Sanseverino e *Il Cortegiano* del Castiglione' in *Atti del convegno di studi per il V centenario della nascita di Caterina Sforza,* 188-9. Her husband was Count Antonio da Montefeltro, Duke Guidobaldo's half-brother; she was writing from the fief of Sant'Agata Feltria (held by Agostino Fregoso, who had married Gentile, half-sister of Duke Guidobaldo). The town was near the Neapolitan encampment.

[64] Dovizi, *Epistolario*, 95, 99.

[65] For the meeting near Borgo Sansepolcro see the text above at note 26. Dovizi, *Epistolario*, 82, 88 (the latter corrects the previous reference to the duke of Urbino's crossbow-men as being mounted). Duke Guidobaldo was under arms by 12 August and reached Pennabili on 14 August; see Sanuto, *La spedizione di Carlo VIII*, 67. Apparently the duke's *condotta* was from King Alfonso and for 200 men-at-arms with the annual pay of 24,000 ducats (presumably Neapolitan ducats); see J. Dennistoun, *Memoirs of the Dukes of Urbino*, 3 vols. (London, 1851), vol. 1, 334, without a source. According to Sanuto on 14 August he had 4 squadrons (the implication is lances), and a further 10 were to join him; this would have been 280 lances, or an effective fighting force of 840 cavalry, of whom 280 were men-at-arms. Hence the 500 crossbow-men mentioned by Dovizi appear to relate to a separate *condotta*.

and comprised Annibale Bentivoglio's 10 squadrons of men-at-arms.[66] Infantry captains with soldiers arrived to offer their services; these included Dionigi and Vincenzo Naldi of Brisghella in the Val di Lamone above Faenza, briefly in camp from about 18 September, and Ramazotto with a force of 600 infantry had arrived by 11 September.[67] Probably Pietro dal Monte's infantry, paid for by Florence, had arrived by 15 September, bringing the entire strength of the infantry in camp at that time to some 4,000.[68] Giovanni Sforza and Giampaolo Baglioni with 9 squadrons of men-at-arms, part of the papal contingent, were expected on 12 September.[69] It had taken some two months to increase the force's size from 240 cavalry to 4,200 cavalry and 4,000 infantry. Figures for the artillery do not exist, but by 2 October Dovizi judged there was plenty.[70] When on 2 September Dovizi had first reached camp the strategy had been explained to him: the duke of Calabria had anticipated that he would advance against the duchy of Milan with a force of some 14,000 men, but could not dare do so with less than 10,000. Quite apart from difficulties with poor weather and supplies, at no stage did he have this strength, and this was the fundamental reason for the delay in advancing.[71] By mid-September, when the peak was reached, troops were complaining because they had not been paid or provided with provisions; an infantry force was detached to assist with the garrisoning of Caterina Sforza's fortresses. News of the defeat at Rapallo so reduced morale that some troops were unwilling to fight, not being assured of victory.[72] It is worth remarking that enormous requirements of food for men and horses of the two camps caused grave problems for the Romagna and increasing hostility

---

[66] Dovizi, *Epistolario*, 82, 84, 88, 93, 96, 98, 104; cf. Bernardi, 'Cronache forlivesi', vol. 1, part 2, 14, which perhaps indicates the same day for Annibale's arrival in Forlì, but gives only 'about 6 squadrons'.

[67] Dovizi, *Epistolario*, 83, 105, 116, 129, 132, cf. 218. Donati, *La fine della Signoria dei Manfredi*, 92.

[68] For the strength of the infantry in camp on 15 September see Dovizi, *Epistolario*, 107; see 88 for 1,000 from Florence, perhaps dal Monte's force, since he certainly was there on 29 September, see 143.

[69] Dovizi, 99, 105, 149; for papal briefs of 22 and 29 July summoning Giovanni Sforza to arms, see Pastor, *The History of the Popes*, vol. 5, 431 note.

[70] Dovizi, *Epistolario*, 147: 'per la molta artigleria che ci è et viene, di mano in mano...'

[71] For the strategy see 83, letter of 2 September; for rains and consequently mud see 82, 92, 147 and Sanuto, *La spedizione di Carlo VIII*, 95. Some provisions were sent from the kingdom by sea, see Dovizi, 92, Sanuto, 94, but most was provided locally, see Dovizi, 96, 166, Sanuto, 79.

[72] For the need for money and the dissatisfaction of troops see Dovizi, *Epistolario*, 105, 143, 192; the problem was not limited to the Neapolitan force, but was true on occasion in the Milanese camp, see Sanuto, *La spedizione di Carlo VIII*, 76; the French troops appear to have been well paid, see same source. There were celebrations in the Franco-Milanese camp to celebrate the victory at Rapallo, see Dovizi, 109, letter of 15 September. For the refusal of Neapolitan forces to fight see Labande-Mailfert, *Charles VIII*, 280. For forces sent to Bubbano, Mordano and Bagnara see Dovizi, 186, letter of 11 Otober and for Mordano see the text below at note 84.

from the local population. Pillaging by troops brought famine particularly to the towns. Until its retreat in late October the Neapolitan army enjoyed a much better reputation in this regard than the opposing force, and certainly the duke of Calabria had sought to maintain strict discipline and ensure provisions were paid for.[73]

Ludovico Sforza, aware of the arrival near Cesena of the advance force of cavalry under the duke of Calabria, on 27 July appointed Count Caiazzo commander of the Milanese force to counter the new threat by going to the Romagna; his brother Gasparo Sanseverino with 300 cavalry, who had been sent to Cotignola early in the month, was to assist him.[74] Count Caiazzo left Milan on 28 July, and on his way south recruited infantry. By 2 August Caiazzo's force had passed through the territory of Ercole d'Este, where on its way to encamp near Bologna it grossly maltreated peasants, presumably by pillaging.[75] By then the combined force of the two Sanseverino brothers was some 900 'men-at-arms' (supposedly 225 heavily armed and 450 lightly armed cavalry), to be joined later by 3,000 infantry, probably some of whom were Swiss.[76] Charles VIII writing from Lyons on 1 July ordered Bernard Stuart d'Aubigny, then his ambassador in Florence, to put himself at the head of a French force (presumably landed at Genoa) under the orders of Ludovico Sforza.[77] The latter sent him with his troops to reinforce the Milanese force in the Romagna under Count Caiazzo who apparently remained supreme commander, at least initially. By 23 August d'Aubigny had reached Parma; his force's arrival in camp on 29 August was recorded in a letter to Ludovico Sforza, where it was indicated as comprising sixty to seventy 'men-at-arms'

---

[73] For scarcity of food in Faenza, for instance, see Donati, *La fine della Signoria dei Manfredi*, 93. For the Neapolitan force normally paying for provisions see Pasolini, *Caterina Sforza*, vol. 1, 340 n.1, Bernardi, 'Cronache forlivesi', vol. 1, part 2, 14 for Caterina selling the force food and 16 for its general good conduct in this regard, though both sides fired standing crops. The Neapolitans and Milanese pillaged the territory of Ravenna, see Sanuto, *La spedizione di Carlo VIII*, 78 and Bernardi, 23. The Neapolitan army did pillage when it began to withdraw but less than was expected, see Cobelli, 'Cronache forlivesi', 358-9. There was a dearth of provisions in the French camp, at least initially, see De' Rosmini, *Dell'istoria di C. J. Trivulzio*, vol. 2, 204 doc. 39 and 40; cf. Dovizi, *Epistolario*, 108, 130.

[74] For Caiazzo as commander see Sanuto, *La spedizione di Carlo VIII*, 54; for Gasparo see the text above at note 28.

[75] For Caiazzo's departure from Milan and his recruiting forces see Pieri, *Il Rinascimento e la crisi militare italiana*, 226, without a source; for his troops pillaging the Ferrarese see Gardner, *Dukes and Poets in Ferrara*, 250, citing a letter of 2 August.

[76] For 600 Italian 'men-at-arms' see Giovio, trans. Domenichi, vol. 1, Bk. I, 38; Commynes, *Mémoires*, vol. 2, 334 gives 500, perhaps the source for Gardner, *Dukes and Poets at Ferrara*, 250. The letter of 2 August cited by Gardner referred to other forces as being expected to arrive; Giovio specified 3,000 'soldati vecchi' (meaning experienced) infantry with Count Caiazzo; Sanuto, *La spedizione di Carlo VIII*, 68 mentioned 1,500 infantry present by 18 August. Charles VIII, *Lettres*, vol. 4, 73-4, letter of 1 July refers to Swiss infantry reaching the duchy of Milan.

[77] Charles VIII, *Lettres*, vol. 4, 73-4.

(which I suppose in this case to be French lances: 120 heavily armed and 120 lighter armed cavalry), some 220 mounted crossbow-men under Antoine de Ville, lord of Domjulien, 60 mounted (Scots) archers, 40 *stradioti*.[78] When the main French army had crossed the Alps a force of 400 lances and mounted archers under Gilbert, count of Montpensier, was detached and sent to support the troops in the Romagna, though in the event it remained near Parma until 20 October, when Montpensier took his troops across the Cisa pass into Tuscany.[79] Gasparo Sanseverino wrote from Parma on 22 and 23 September concerning the recruitment of 200 men-at-arms; 10 Milanese squadrons reached camp in early October and the infantry with the Franco-Milanese force in the Romagna likewise steadily increased from September. On 2 October Dovizi estimated the opposing force numbered some 9,000 to 10,000 men, about the same as that of the Neapolitan army when he had first arrived in camp a month before. The Franco-Milanese force had 18 or perhaps 22 pieces of artillery.[80]

On the basis of the above information in early August the duke of Calabria's cavalry was some 2,180 against the Milanese 675, but his infantry was but 200 as against 3,000. A month later after the arrival of d'Aubigny's troops, the Neapolitan army comprised some 3,900 cavalry and 1,500 infantry against 1,230 mounted troops of various kinds and 3,000 infantry. By mid-September the numerical odds in favour of the Neapolitan army had increased to almost two to one. Given the latter's considerable superiority of some three to one cavalry it is not surprising that the Franco-Milanese force encamped

---

[78] As in previous note; and cf. Cobelli, 'Cronache forlivesi', 356, who implies this. For d'Aubigny and his force at Parma see Ady, *Milan under the Sforza*, 151; for its arrival in camp on 29 August see De' Rosmini, *Dell'istoria... di G. J. Trivulzio...*, vol. 2, 203-4 doc. 37, 38; Bernardi, 'Cronache forlivesi', vol. 1, part 2, 12 provides 27 August. For the size of the force see De' Rosmini, vol. 2, 204 doc. 38 (Commynes, *Mémoires*, vol. 2, 346 gives 150 to 200 men-at-arms and an unspecified number of Swiss).

[79] Adami, *Il carteggio di un capitano*, 13, 51-3, letters 35 to 38. Delaborde, *L'expédition de Charles VIII*, 430; Labande-Mailfert, *Charles VIII*, 287.

[80] For Gasparo Sanseverino recruiting see Adami, *Carteggio di un capitano*, 52-3, letters 37, 38. For the arrival of 10 Milanese squadrons see Dovizi, *Epistolario*, 150; for infantry joining the camp see Dovizi, 175 and Sanuto, *La spedizione di Carlo VIII*, 82, 92. For the estimate of 2 October see Dovizi, 149, and for the increase in size thereafter Dovizi, 180. For the artillery see the *Bulletin*, assigned to early November, reprinted in Lot, *Recherches sur les effectifs des armées françaises*, 194, but cf. Labande-Mailfert, *Charles VIII*, 260 n.360 for 22 pieces. The maximum strength of the Franco-Milanese army in the Romagna is difficult to estimate. Labande-Mailfert, 259 appears to depend on the numbers in the *Bulletin*, but misreads them; for instance she gives '2,400 cavaliers' for the 1,200 'lances ytaliennes' with Aubigny (as against French lance) with 1,200 men-at-arms, but effective cavalry 3,600. This latter, with her figure of 1,600 mounted crossbow-men (arrived at by adding all the rest of the forces of the *Bulletin*) gives 5,200 rather than her figure of 5,100; cf. Lot, 18, and that of Delaborde, *L'expédition de Charles VIII*, 395. While Dovizi's estimate of 2 October may exaggerate, that of the *Bulletin*, seemingly of November, appears to me to under-estimate. It appears significant that Dovizi's confidence in the outcome waned as the strength of the enemy increased, until on 27 September (135) he confessed the Neapolitan army might either have to withdraw or strengthen the encampment for fear that it would be attacked.

behind ditches in boggy terrain.[81] It is equally understandable why the Franco-Milanese refused the challenge to battle, remaining behind entrenchments protected by cannons.[82] Thereafter the Neapolitan army gave way to inertia: money was lacking, provisions failed; news of the defeat at Rapallo and of Charles VIII's arrival at Asti with a large army (he reached Pavia on 14 October) further demoralised it. The news considerably encouraged the enemy, whose troop-numbers steadily increased until there was almost parity with the Neapolitan camp. From late September Neapolitan advance against the duchy of Milan was impossible unless the Franco-Milanese army in the Romagna could be entirely routed, and by then that force lacked the will to fight.[83]

The sack of Mordano marked the Franco-Milanese force's seizure of the initiative with comparable numbers; since it did so effectively the result was the end of the campaign. On 19 October a force of 2,000 infantry, comprising 300 Milanese, 300 Swiss, 200 Scots, 1,000 French archers, supported by artillery (the chronicler of Forlì, Bernardi, thought a force of 14,000) advanced to Mordano in the territory of Imola. This fortress was defended according to Bernardi by a force of 200 (the French *Bulletin* claimed 1,500), half being from the duke of Calabria's army, the rest paid for by Caterina Sforza, and it was packed with the inhabitants of the place and its neighbourhood. The army of the duke of Calabria was some seven miles distant yet, when requested, made no move to assist the besieged. The following day Gasparo Sanseverino sought surrender on honourable terms. This was refused and Sanseverino gave dire warning that no mercy would be shown to the defenders as the French fought like 'mad dogs'. After a three-hour bombardment by cannon the wall was breached and the force entered, most within being slaughtered.[84] On 25 October

---

[81] Dovizi, *Epistolario*, 111.

[82] Dovizi, 111; seemingly another challenge was made on 29 August: see Pieri, *Il Rinascimento e la crisi militare italiana*, 330 n. 2 (where the date of 19 August in Sanuto, *La spedizione di Carlo VIII*, 82 is corrected). Cf. also the commanders who were with the duke of Calabria (apart from Pitigliano) urging battle; see Giovio, trans. Domenichi, vol. 1, bk. 1, 39-40; Sanuto, 77-8 indicates the challenge to battle of 16-17 September, and 79 again on 21 September.

[83] For the defeat at Rapallo see the text above at note 72; for the king reaching Asti see the text above at note 17, and for him reaching Pavia see Labande-Mailfert, *Charles VIII*, 284.

[84] For the size of the Franco-Milanese force see the *Bulletin*, reprinted in Lot, *Recherches sur les effectifs des armées françaises*, 194; for the defenders see Bernardi, 'Cronache forlivesi', vol. 1, part 2, 17-19, and cf. the *Bulletin* in Lot, 193. Labande-Mailfert, *Charles VIII*, 286 follows the *Bulletin*; Pieri, *Il Rinascimento e la crisi militare italiana*, 330-1 gives few defenders, following Bernardi. The attack and fall of Mordano was on 20 October (not 19 as in Labande-Mailfert) and see Bernardi, where Sanseverino's demand for surrender is indicated, and also see Cobelli, 'Cronache forlivesi', 358 (under 27 October), Sanuto, *La spedizione di Carlo VIII*, 95-6; cf. Briesach, *Caterina Sforza*, 156. For Caterina's request for help see Pasolini, *Caterina Sforza*, vol. 3, 218-19, 221, doc. 546, 547. The duke of Calabria was encamped under the walls of Imola; the *Bulletin* gives the distance as 'due petites lieues', followed by Labande-Mailfert. For Pieri, 331, there was nothing new in the encounter in

Caterina Sforza agreed terms with the Franco-Milanese army.[85]   Thereafter condottieri captains, including some of those sent by the pope, sought licence to leave the Neapolitan camp, and the Florentine contingent was recalled. On 30 October the Neapolitan force withdrew to Cesena, where it remained until 26 November, when the withdrawal south began.[86]

Initially the duke of Calabria's force had insufficient strength to attack the duchy of Milan. By mid-August it was strong enough to have obtained passage along the Via Emilia, but was still under strength for an attack on the duchy of Milan. Then, too, Count Caiazzo's force could not be ignored, as it was likely to attack the rear of the Neapolitan army should it advance. Stalemate while both sides sought to increase their strengths was the inevitable consequence, and it was at this stage that the understandable procrastinations of Giovanni Bentivoglio and Caterina Sforza came into play. By late August it was probably too late anyway, since Charles VIII with his main army was crossing the Alps. From the Neapolitan point of view the basic weakness of the campaign was that from the very start the force had insufficient troops to undertake the expected thrust into the duchy of Milan.

Machiavelli's *Florentine History* provides the well-known caricature of mercenaries engaged in fighting in 1440, when according to Machiavelli at the battle of Anghiari the two opposing forces fought some four hours, and the only man of importance to die did so in consequence of falling off his horse.[87] The soldiers of the Neapolitan army in the Romagna campaign were mercenaries. It was the Milanese commander Caiazzo, likewise a mercenary, who in early September undertook to fight by Italian rules.[88]   By mid-October the Ultramontanes in the Franco-Milanese force were sufficiently in evidence to fight *a gorgia* at Mordano. Machiavelli, like Landucci, was well aware of the

---

terms of artillery, or tactics, simply Franco-Milanese superiority in numbers and greater cruelty than usual in the sack.

[85] Pasolini, *Caterina Sforza*, vol. 3, 222-3, doc. 552 (synopsis); Briesach, *Caterina Sforza*, 157.

[86] The Neapolitan army withdrew to Cesena on 30 October, see Cobelli, 'Cronache forlivesi', 359, and only retreated towards Rome on 26 November, see Bernardi, 'Cronache forlivesi', vol. 1, part 2, 35; when it reached Rome on 10 December it supposedly comprised 55 squadrons of cavalry and 500 infantry, see Delaborde, *L'expédition de Charles VIII*, 286, which errs giving 8 October for the withdrawal towards Rimini and Urbino. Giovanni Gonzaga and his force asked permission to leave on 25 October, see Delaborde, 432, and for Gonzaga's *condotta* see Sanuto, *La spedizione di Carlo VIII*, 97. Annibale Bentivoglio left shortly after the move to Cesena, see Bernardi, vol. 1, part 2, 22, cf. Ady, *The Bentivoglio of Bologna*, 117 stating he was recalled and left on 3 November, without a source. For the duke of Urbino and Giovanni Sforza asking to leave see B. Baldi, *Della vita e de' fatti di Guidobaldo I da Montefeltro*, ed. C. de' Rosmini, 2 vols. (Milan, 1821), vol. 1, 1324. Dovizi was recalled shortly after 25 October, see Dovizi, *Epistolario*, 235-7, letter LXXXI.

[87] N. Machiavelli, 'Istorie fiorentine', in *Tutte le opere*, ed. G. Mazzoni and M. Casella (Florence, 1929), bk. 5, section 33, 528; N. Machiavelli, *The Chief Works*, trans. A. Gilbert, 3 vols. (Durham, NC, 1965), vol. 3, 1279-80.

[88] See the text above at note 7.

Mordano: engraving of 1830

Ultramontanes' success in fighting, and went into the causes as Canossa did not, roundly blaming mercenaries and, by implication, the Italian rules of fighting. His professed solution would have won Canossa's approval, as he urged imitation both of the strategies of the generals of Antiquity and of the classical techniques of warfare, ignoring that these were the very sources of inspiration for such successful mercenary leaders as Francesco Sforza and Federico da Montefeltro.[89] There was a difference: the Roman soldier, Machiavelli believed, was a citizen, fighting for his country, a model of sobriety and discipline, unlike the contemporary mercenary.[90] Yet the duke of Calabria, who had been tutored by the humanist Gabriele Altilio, sought to conduct his camp and campaign on classical lines.[91] Initially his encampment had strict discipline and prostitutes were confined to a locality outside camp (however eventually to while away dull moments the duke on occasion left camp to visit his mistress).[92] Dovizi stressed how admirably turned out the troops were, and how alert the camp guards.[93] The duke's strategy, for which he had the support of three Italian generals who were distinguished mercenaries, was conceived as a set-battle, much as that fought in 1453 is described by the marquis of Mantua in a letter to his wife.[94] The duke of Calabria preferred the Italian way of fighting, man-at-arms against man-at-arms, as lauded by Luigi da Porto in his *Lettere storiche*, written about 1522, and by Castiglione in his Book of the Courtier.[95] Quite apart from the Milanese contingent in the Romagna, the French army there included Bernard Stuart d'Aubigny with Scots who were foreign mercenaries as well as a sizeable company of Swiss, all from beyond the Alps.[96] Hence it was

---

[89] Machiavelli, 'Arte della Guerra', in *Tutte le opere*, bk. 1, 270-71; trans. vol. 2, 573-6. The issues are considered by M.E. Mallett, *Mercenaries and their Masters* (London, 1974), 231-60, with a somewhat different emphasis to that proposed in this paper.

[90] Machiavelli, 'Arte della Guerra', bk. 1, 271-83; trans. 576-83.

[91] For the tutor, G. Altilio of Caggiano (province of Salerno) see J.H. Bentley, *Politics and Culture in Renaissance Naples* (Princeton, NJ, 1987), 192, and M.E. Cosenza, *Dictionary of the Italian Humanists, 1300-1800*, 6 vols. (Boston, MA, 1962-67), vol. 5, 18 nos. 62, 63a.

[92] For discipline in camp and a *bordello* outside see Dovizi, *Epistolario*, 91, letter of 3 September. For the mistress of the duke of Calabria, Caterina, daughter of Giorgio Gonzaga of Novellara, see Dovizi, 155-60, letter of 4 October; for her see Dovizi, 161 n.1, 86 n.1. She had been the mistress of Piero de' Medici and was to be of Charles VIII, cf. Picotti, 'Caterina Sforza e la Romagna', 182-3, and C. De Frede, '"Più simile a mostro che a uomo"', *Bibliothèque d'Humanisme et Renaissance*, 44 (1982), 571.

[93] For the troops so alert a false call to arms was made see Dovizi, *Epistolario*, vol. 1, 98; for the well-turned out force see 91 (the duke of Urbino's men), 98 in general 'vi dico che troviamo questo esercito essere una bella cosa'.

[94] For the challenges to battle see the text above at note 82. For the letter of the marquis see C.H. Clough, 'Love and War in the Veneto', in *War, Culture and Society in Renaissance Venice*, ed. D.S. Chambers, C.H. Clough, and M.E. Mallett (London, 1993), 108-9.

[95] For Luigi da Porto and Castiglione see Clough, 'Love and War'. For challenges to combat man to man in the Romagna campaign see Dovizi, *Epistolario*, 152, 179, Sanuto, *La spedizione di Carlo VIII*, cited in note 9, 78.

[96] For Scots and Swiss at Mordano, for instance, see the text above at note 84.

not so much that Italian military ineptitude lay in the employment of mercenaries, as Machiavelli claimed.[97]   Leaving aside the obvious lack of political unity on the peninsula and the self-interest that took its place, the issue was that the French army was not trammelled by the imitation of supposed classical models and the associated chivalry; the French fought to win at all costs with utter ruthlessness.[98] For the French warfare was something other than a spectacle in the form of a diverting echo of Antiquity.

[97] This point is made by Mallett, *Mercenaries and their Masters*, 208-11, 231-2.

[98] Witness the butchery at Rapallo, Fivizzano and Mordano. It might be argued that the French were more brutal since they were operating in 'hostile' territory, so with a different outlook on cruelty to civilians and devastation, cf. Mallett, *Mercenaries and their Masters*, 191-2.

Francesco II Gonzaga, marquis of Mantua, 'Liberator of Italy'

David Chambers

Charles VIII's descent upon Italy was described by contemporaries in cosmic terms as a conflagration or a deluge, but its political effects varied widely in Italy, and were not always negative, even if there were fatal upheavals in Florence and Naples. At Mantua, for instance, a north Italian *signoria* of second rank, the outcome was positively beneficial to the regime. This was owing to the fame which Marquis Francesco Gonzaga managed to obtain as the victorious commander in the Battle of Fornovo on 6 July 1495. What follows below is less about the military aspects of that event than its domestic and promotional importance for the Mantuan ruler, and is largely based upon letters surviving in the Gonzaga archives.[1]

By 1494 Mantua had barely emerged from the time of troubles which began ten years' earlier with Francesco's succession as an orphan of seventeen, and the conclusion of the War of Ferrara in the Peace of Bagnolo, which had assigned some Gonzaga dominions to Venice. Francesco's title as Marquis had not been confirmed for almost a year, and the stability of the regime was strained by the attitude towards his succession of Francesco's three paternal uncles (Gianfrancesco, Rodolfo and Ludovico Gonzaga) and their resentment at his subjection to an uncle by marriage who had gained the former Marquis's deathbed blessing. Francesco Secco d'Aragona, a senior military figure of formidable physique, husband to a bastard daughter of Marquis Ludovico Gonzaga, was potentially the Ludovico il Moro of Mantua, though his arbitrary powers and mastery over the immature and over-trusting heir, and the semi-disgrace in 1487 of the three uncles for alleged conspiracy, need not detain us here; by 1491 the dominance of Secco had come to an end with his flight to

---

[1] Archivio di Stato, Mantua, Archivio Gonzaga, abbreviated below as AG. Unfortunately, when this paper was being prepared in the summer of 1994 it was not possible to inspect the series 'Lettere originali dei Gonzaga' for the relevant period since buste 2109-11 were under repair: but many of these letters are duplicated in registers, and much relevant correspondence is filed in other series.

FRANCESCO II GONZAGA, FOURTH
MARQUESS OF MANTUA 1484-1519
SPERANDIO ITALIAN C.1425-C.1504
A868.131A

Francesco II Gonzaga, fourth marquis of Mantua;
medal by Sperandio, National Gallery of Art, Washington DC: obverse.

Naples, and his trial and condemnation *in absentia*.[2] Naples, and his trial and condemnation *in absentia*. The scandal of Secco's downfall had greatly shocked the young marquis, who admitted to his sister Chiara that it had affected him like a bereavement and made him physically ill.[3] Francesco was not in a strong position; he had, unlike the disgraced Francesco Secco, no outstanding military experience, and in March 1489 when he had passed from the service of Milan to that of Venice, his bargaining position was not strong and he had had to confirm the territorial losses to his new employer.[4]

On the other hand, Francesco's personal and diplomatic rating may have begun to rise after February 1490 when his forthright wife Isabella d'Este arrived in Mantua; indeed she may have played a crucial part in the overthrowal of Secco, whose excessive control over her husband's correspondence and decision-making must have been humiliating.[5] Even if her first pregnancy in 1492 did not end with a male heir, Isabella, a grand-daughter of King Ferrante of Naples, was a great asset to Francesco. She was not, however, much use or probably much concerned about one of his most serious problems: lack of ready cash and heavy spending commitments on building and other forms of display. For instance, in May 1492 there was a series of tournaments and an elaborate military review for which the *massaro* of Mantua was ordered to supply all money in hand.[6] Salaries were not paid and even the podestà and other judges protested and declared they could not work for nothing.[7] Perhaps as a symptom of the strains upon administration, an increase in crime was reported in December 1492.[8] But as the storm clouds gathered over Italy after Lorenzo de' Medici's death and the old entente between Milan and Naples collapsed, one of the most serious problems of the Mantuan regime remained Francesco's sheer lack of distinction, and particularly his slight record in the military tradition of his father, grandfather and great-grandfather.

As the possibility of a French invasion, encouraged by Ludovico il Moro, began to loom, an appalling dilemma faced Francesco Gonzaga. He was contracted to Venice, which was so far warily uncommitted, but he still had strong motives to maintain good relations with the Duchy of Milan, not least

---

[2] See in general L. Mazzoldi, *Mantova. La Storia*, vol. 2 (Mantua, 1961), 77-108; F. Secco d'Aragona, 'Francesco Secco, i Gonzaga e Paolo Erba', *Archivio storico lombardo*, 83 (1956), 210-61; G. Coniglio, 'La politica di Francesco Gonzaga nell'opera di un immigrato meridionale: Iacopo Probo d'Atri', *Archivio storico lombardo*, 88 (1961), 131-67 (on Secco, esp. 132-4).

[3] Letter of 3 December 1491 (AG b. 2905 lib. 142, f. 19r-20r).

[4] Mazzoldi, *La Storia*, vol. 2, 79, summarises the contract (30,000 ducats annually in peacetime, 40,000 ducats in war).

[5] Mazzoldi, *La Storia*, 119 n. 27.

[6] Mazzoldi, *La Storia*, vol. 2, 127 n.12.

[7] AG b. 2904, lib. 141, ff. 45, 47; Coniglio, 'Politica di Francesco Gonzaga', 137 n.ll.

[8] Giovan Battista de Castello to Marquis F. Gonzaga, 7 December 1492 (AG b. 2441).

Francesco II Gonzaga, fourth marquis of Mantua;
medal by Sperandio, National Gallery of Art, Washington DC: reverse.

because of the marriage of his wife's sister Beatrice to Ludovico, its *de facto* ruler. On all sides he had family connections. His mother-in-law, Eleanora d'Aragona, was a daughter of King Ferrante of Naples and sister of Alfonso of Calabria; Isabella was therefore a first cousin of her namesake, wife of the unfortunate Giangaleazzo Sforza, the titular duke of Milan. On the other hand, Francesco's elder sister, Chiara, was married to Gilbert de Montpensier, a leading figure in the entourage of Charles VIII. Should the worst happen, in which direction should he jump? After Ferrante's death in January 1494, the throne of Naples had passed to Alfonso duke of Calabria, a former military colleague of Francesco's father, and Jacobo Probo d'Atri, the trusted Neapolitan secretary who later immortalised Francesco's deeds in a chronicle, characterised the marquis as Alfonso's only friend in Italy.[9] The Milanese ambassador in Venice even reported that Francesco was going to Naples to arrange military assistance, whereas in fact he had merely been invited to the coronation.[10] However, in April 1494, a prestigious French delegation, headed by d'Aubigny and Pérron de Baschi, had visited Mantua; according to the account of it Francesco himself sent to Isabella at Ferrara on 23 April, they had offered him tempting military office and reinstatement in the lands lost previously to Venice, in exchange for free passage through Mantuan territory with supplies which would be paid for.[11] A detail hitherto overlooked, which appears in a letter of the secretary Antimaco, is that d'Aubigny demanded that the delegation should be received in Mantegna's 'Painted Room' (*Camera degli Sposi*).[12] Francesco turned down these offers in view of his obligations to Venice, but he may well have felt uneasy about closing all doors. In fact his agents would closely monitor the progress of the invading army: already Alessandro Arrivabene had affirmed from Milan that its coming was a certainty;[13] and a correspondence ensued with his brother-in-law Montpensier, who wrote rather patronisingly from Lyons on 26 April that he thought Francesco must be aware

---

[9] Jacopo Probo ed. E. Visconti, 'Croniche del Marchese di Mantova', ser. 1, 6 (1879), 38-68 (at 42), and 333-56, 500-13.

[10] A. Segre, 'Lodovico Sforza, detto il Moro, e la Republica di Venezia dall'autunno 1494 alla primavera 1495', *Archivio storico lombardo*, ser. 3, 18 (1902), 249-317 (at 265).

[11] Letter of 23 April 1494 addressed from Marmirolo (AG b. 2961 lib. 3 f. 8r-8v), quoted in A. Luzio and R. Renier, 'Francesco Gonzaga alla battaglia di Fornovo (1495) secondo i documenti mantovani', *Archivio storico italiano*, 5th series, 6 (1890), (repr. Mantua, 1976, different pagination) 205-46. A letter in French announcing this embassy was signed by Charles VIII at Vienne, 17 March 1494 (AG b. 626).

[12] Antimaco to Isabella, 22 April 1494: '...son alogiati ale camere bianche de sopra e de sotto, tanto bene apparate che non se li poteria giongere. Hano voluto audientia in castello nela camera depincta et per quanto ho potuto comprehendere, rimangono satisfactissimi in ogni cosa' (AG b. 2446 c. 611).

[13] Letter of 26 March 1494: 'qui se affirma pure la venuta de' francosi' (AG b. 1630).

of the expedition and that leading Italian princes were supporting it,[14] and with more Gallic condescension wrote from Aosta on 20 September to tell his brother-in-law that Charles VIII had appointed him his lieutenant-general.[15] Montpensier wrote again from Parma (the invading forces' nearest point of approach to Mantua), where Isabella d'Este had herself sighted some French cavalry in August,[16] and Giacomo Probo wrote from that city on 27 September that he had paid respects to the king of France, who was dismayed to learn that Giovanni Gonzaga (the marquis's brother) had actually gone to serve the king of Naples.[17] But the most regular information was provided by the Mantuan agent Ghivizzano who accompanied the army.[18]

As Charles VIII proceeded on his triumphant way in the winter of 1494-5, provoking the fall of the Medici régime in Florence in November and of the throne of Naples in February, Francesco's feet grew colder still. While he had bluffed in October in asking his agent at Venice, Jacopo Probo, to request permission to attack the French should they enter his territory,[19] he tried to maintain good relations with Charles VIII through his sister Chiara, who came to stay in Mantua in December.[20] With or without Francesco's knowledge and consent, already a close relative, a son (probably Ludovico) of his uncle Gianfrancesco, lord of Bozzolo, and a follower of Francesco Secco, had joined Charles VIII.[21] On the other hand, Isabella d'Este, already distressed by the deaths of her mother Eleonora and grandfather Ferrante, was almost incredulous at the news from Naples, and the fall from power in rapid succession of her uncle Alfonso and her cousin Ferrandino; she mingled grief with an almost Machiavellian sagacity, writing from Milan: 'this should be a lesson to all the lords and potentates of the world, to put more trust in the hearts of their subjects than in fortresses, treasure and men at arms, because the discontent of subjects makes for a worse sort of war than that with an enemy on the field of battle'.[22]

---

[14] 'Je croy que estes assez adverti de l'entreprise que le Roy a fait pour le recouvrement de son royaume de Napples et pareillement des principaulx d'Ytali, qui se sont venus joyeulx... por le servir de tout leur pouvoir' (AG b. 626).

[15] 'il a pleu au Roy me faire son lieutenant-general a ce voyage de Naples' (ibid).

[16] AG b. 2991 lib. 4 f. 88v, cited by A. Luzio and R. Renier, 'Delle relazioni di Isabella d'Este Gonzaga con Ludovico e Beatrice Sforza', *Archivio storico lombardo*, 17 (1890), 393.

[17] AG b. 1367.

[18] E.g. his letters from Milan, Parma, Florence (AG b. 1630, 1367, 1102).

[19] Letter of 19 October 1494 cited by Coniglio 'Politica di Francesco Gonzaga', 142-3.

[20] Coniglio, 146. Francesco wrote about her coming to Jacopo Probo on 21 November 1494, commenting that 'del paese suo di Franza vengono novamente tanti franzozi uno stupore' (AG, b. 2906 lib. 153 f. 65v).

[21] Giorgio Brognolo reported this in a letter of 6 September 1495, by which time the renegade had returned home repentant, as one might have expected by then (AG b. 2961 lib. 4a, f. 87v).

[22] Luzio and Renier, 'Delle relazioni', 622-3 (letter of 28 February 1495 in AG b. 2992 lib. 5, f. 18v-19r). On 1 March she was still exclaiming that such events were 'an unheard-of thing' (ibid., f. 19v).

When the League of Venice was formed in April 1495[23] Francesco had at last come out on the side of his wife's rather than his sister's relations, and he now held a more formal military title from the Doge - that of governor-general. On 11 June he announced to the Doge that, in the name of God and St George, he was setting off to seek battle with the French accompanied by his uncle Rodolfo Gonzaga.[24] Francesco boasted to his wife on 2 July, not without reason, of the immense size and potential of the army he had assembled,[25] and with the near prospect of a major battle with the northward-bound French army, his clerical brother Sigismondo and Isabella d'Este, left in control of Mantuan affairs, responded to his call for prayers and intercessory masses from all the clergy; Isabella even sent him an *agnus dei*, said to contain a fragment of the True Cross, to wear around his neck.[26] Isabella urged him on the eve of battle to be prudent and not to act at all without 'mature consideration' (not very realistic advice to a soldier in the field) and on the very morning of battle wrote that she was praying for his victory.[27] All this was against what seems to have been a tense background in Mantua, where government officials were exasperated by the reckless expenditure on military purposes and lack of money for domestic commitments.[28] The serving podestà later complained that since March or April he and his officials had been hardly paid anything because of the diversion of funds to meet the marquis' needs.[29] Meanwhile, because of the high price of cereals there were reports of bread riots, though these were officially denied. Surprise was expressed that any rumours of disorder should have reached the marquis at all.[30] Even so, Isabella d'Este acknowledged that she had had one

---

[23] Coniglio, 147. A. Portioli, *La lega contro Carlo VIII* (Mantua, 1876), published the letter from Francesco's ambassador in Venice, Antonio Salimbeni, 12 April 1495, who attended the proclamation of the League in the Senate and subsequent celebrations, including allegorical processions.

[24] AG b. 2961 reg. 4a, f. 1: '...col nome de Dio e de Sancto Zorzo melevr col S. Rodulpho'. This suggests that the date of 21 June on the letter of appointment given by Jacopo Probo in his 'Croniche', 43-4, is wrong.

[25] '.. retrovandose noi il più potente et magno exercito che gran tempo fa e forse mai ad questa età fosse visto...': Luzio and Renier, 215.

[26] Marquis F. Gonzaga to Sigismondo, 30 June 1495 (AG b. 2961 reg. 4, f. 19v-20r); Isabella to Francesco, 2 July 1495 (AG b. 2992 lib. 5, f. 50v-51r), quoted by Luzio and Renier, 214.

[27] Isabella to Marquis F. Gonzaga, 5-6 July (AG b. 2992 lib. 5, f. 51r-53r).

[28] e.g. Baldassare Soardi's letters of 17 and 19 June complaining of the lack of funds to pay the numerous painters working at the castle of Gonzaga since the marquis went on campaign (AG b. 2447 cc. 307, 308). Isabella d'Este reported difficulty in getting local communities to pay their tax levies for sappers (AG b. 2992 lib. 5, f. 47v-48r). The *Magistri Intratarum*, desperate for cash, proposed demanding advance payment of the levy for August from the Jewish community (AG b. 2447 c. 331).

[29] Cesare Valentini to Marquis F. Gonzaga, Mantua, 17 September 1495: '...li salari di li ultimi sei mesi ne haveà tochò asai picola summa... per havere ad supplire a li bisogni del prefato signore che se ritrovava a campo' (AG b. 2441).

[30] Letter of Baldassare Soardi and Antonio Gonzaga, 1 July 1495 (AG b. 2447 c. 433).

trouble-maker put in prison ('as an example to others') for daring to say there was no bread on sale in the piazza,[31] and she admitted a few days later that offensive graffiti had appeared on the walls.[32]

Fornovo changed everything. The version of events Francesco sent to Isabella, to the Doge of Venice, to Gian Carlo Scalona, Mantuan ambassador in Venice and to many others, indeed the version which the Venetian provveditori also sent home, was soon diffused throughout Italy.[33] That he had fought fiercely[34] - with at least one and perhaps more horses killed under him - is hardly in doubt, nor surprising, since his survival as a ruler depended on his performance: the threat of Francesco Secco's presence in the French army would not have been lost on him. Francesco Gonzaga's sheer brutality is well testified, including the order to give no quarter, on pain of death, but simply to kill 'for the glory of the Latin name'.[35] Even the death in battle of his uncle Rodolfo, that veteran of the Burgundian wars of the 1460s, may have been an indirect stroke of fortune, since it left Francesco in a stronger position as the family hero. With a certain lack of tact, he had kept his sister Chiara, Montpensier's wife, informed of his preparations and quest for honour and victory; on 12 July he even wrote to say he was sure she must be delighted by the news of his successs at Fornovo.[36] On 16 July, in a letter to his other sister, Elisabetta duchess of Urbino, he wrote that he had given birth to the liberation and liberty of Italy.[37] As was pointed out long ago, in the days and weeks after the battle Francesco seems to have become more and more convinced by his own legend that he had vindicated Italian honour, liberty and glory. No doubt his self-esteem was even more inflated upon the arrival of Commines to express Charles VIII's wish to make him 'il primo homo de Italia'.[38] On 27 July, announcing his promotion to the supreme rank of Captain General of the Venetian Republic, Francesco boasted to his wife that such an honour, which included a cash bonusfor Isabella, had never been conferred on any of his predecessors.[39]

Others were not slow to add their written tributes. Already on 7 July, Alessandro De Baesio, one of the marquis's companions-in-arms, wrote to Isabella from Parma that 'since Hector of Troy no-one has ever done what he did on horseback. I believe he killed ten men. His immortal fame is assured.'[40]

---

[31] Isabella to Marquis F. Gonzaga, 30 June 1495 (AG b. 2992 lib. 5, f. 49r-50r).

[32] Ibid. f. 52v.

[33] Luzio and Renier, 214-15; 'Croniche', 48.

[34] 'quello che noi facessimo cum la persona nostra assai è noto' he wrote to Isabella on 7 July (Luzio and Renier, 221).

[35] 'Croniche', 50. On Secco at Fornovo see F. Guicciardini, *Storia d'Italia*, book 2, cap. 9.

[36] AG, b. 2961 lib. 4 f. 30.

[37] 'havendo parturito la liberatione et libertà de Italia... non possemo e non ringratiare Dio' (Luzio and Renier, 224).

[38] Luzio and Renier, 224-5; 'Croniche', 51.

[39] AG b. 2961 lib. 4a ff. 39v-40r; 'Croniche', 58-9.

[40] AG b. 1367, cited (without reference) in Luzio and Renier, 220, n. 5.

(The Hector parallel seems to have caught on quite widely; Pietro Duodo, the Venetian provveditore, also called Francesco 'a modern Hector').[41] Benedetto Capilupi wrote on 11 July, 'privately in this city we mourn the dead, but publicly we congratulate ourselves and rejoice that you are safe and sound with honour.'[42] On 17 July Ermolao Bardolino, a former podestà of Mantua and now one of the council, wrote emphatically that no one else of the *patria italica* had had the courage to confront and pit himself against the French.[43] On the same day, Zirone Agnelli, a scion of one of Mantua's oldest families, assured the marquis that no Roman or Greek, not even Julius Caesar or Alexander the Great, had ever equalled his achievements.[44] On 30 July Capilupi assured him that the rejoicing of his subjects quite outdid the bitter sorrow of so many deaths,[45] while the archpriest of the cathedral, Stefano Guidotti, congratulated him as 'liberator della nostra Italia' from the oppression of French barbarians.[46] No attention was drawn to the fact that the Marquis's own brother-in-law was a leader of the barbarian hordes, or to the paradox that the prize prisoner, the bastard of Bourbon, chamberlain to Charles VIII, who had been taken prisoner at Fornovo and brought to Mantua, was treated with much honour and released on 26 September.[47] The only ironical note came from Floriano Dolfo in Bologna, replying to one of the marquis' self-glorifying accounts of the conflict in which the French were designated as barbarians (notwithstanding the fact that the notoriously savage stradiots were on the allied side); he pointed out that all eye-witnesses had reported more Italians were slain than French, but perhaps the Marquis's pioneer corps (*exploratori*) might be excused on account of the difficulty in distinguishing 'Latin' from barbarian corpses since nearly all of the slain were naked and mutilated; he advised the marquis to be less foolhardy in future and not to expose himself to such dangers.[48] Francesco seems to have missed the point, writing to Dolfo on 12 July that if many had died on the allied side at least they had died gloriously in a noble cause.[49] Maybe the idea of the barbarian enemy was exploited to help drown sorrow, but it did not convince everyone in Mantua; Isabella d'Este herself recognised its transparency, and even issued a proclamation on 16 July forbidding Mantuans to insult or attack Frenchmen in the city - owing to Chiara Gonzaga's presence there were quite a

---

[41] Luzio and Renier, 232 n. 3, citing Malipiero, 362.

[42] AG b. 2447; Mazzoldi, 105-6, n. 129.

[43] AG b. 2447 c. 181.

[44] AG b. 2447 c. 192.

[45] Mazzoldi, 105-6 n. 129.

[46] AG b. 2447 c. 370.

[47] Luzio and Renier, 220-21, n. 5.

[48] Luzio and Renier, 228-9.

[49] AG b. 2961 lib. 4a f. 24v-25r.

number of them - 'these Frenchmen being just as dear to us as our own Italians'.[50]

Nevertheless the triumphal theme was well and truly launched. One vernacular contribution in verse, by Antonio Tebaldeo, was allegedly sent from Bologna only two days after the battle; it stressed sorrow for the deaths of Rodolfo Gonzaga and others, and aroused the Marquis's terse comment that they had died gloriously for the liberty of Italy;[51] more pleasing, no doubt, was a sentiment of the Paduan Antonio di Conti who rejoiced to see the 'black eagle' (the imperial emblem on the Gonzaga arms) on its ivory field bearing the honour of Italy.[52] Congratulations upon Francesco's promotion to be Captain General of Venice were no less fulsome; Benedetto Tosabezzi wrote that that his glory had won immortal fame not only for himself but also for his subjects.[53]

A discordant note was struck by Baldassare Soardi, whose son-in-law Giovanni Maria Gonzaga (husband of Baldassare's daughter Costanza) had been killed in the fighting. On 8 Jul he wrote of his desperate grief at seeing the coffin containing the body of Giovan Maria, and on 12 July referred also to the death of Rodolfo Gonzaga; on 30 July he was still bewailing so many 'atrocious deaths'.[54]

For a year or two Francesco basked in this flattery, based on the glorious legend which he had done so much himself to trumpet. He was credited with more heroic activity besieging the duke of Orleans at Novara in August and September 1495. Isabella sent him playing-cards to relieve the tedium and also family news, even a make-believe letter from their two-year old daughter Leonora, emboldening him to expel the French and liberate Italy from the barbarians,[55] but according to Jacopo Probo d'Atri Francesco was far from inactive; he rode around so energetically that he became ill.[56] In spite of all this, and pejorative references to Charles VIII as 'the enemy king' ('Il re inimico') in letters, no small degree of ambiguity remained in Francesco's relations with the other side. Charles, who had sent a courteous letter, significantly, in Italian, from Turin on 17 August, concerning the return of his album of semi-

---

[50] 'non havendo mancho chari essi francesi come l'ha li taliani proprii' (AG, b. 2038-9, fasc. 8, f. 20v).

[51] Luzio and Renier, 238-9.

[52] AG b. 2447 f. 14 (in a letter of 26 August). On these and other verses, both Latin and vernacular, see Luzio and Renier, 236-44. The culmination was Battista Spagnoli's *Trophaeum Francisci Gonzagae libri quinque*, printed in his *Tertius et ultimus Tomus Poematum* (Paris 1513).

[53] AG b. 2447 c. 40.

[54] AG b. 2447 c. 315. See also R. Signorini, 'Baldassare Soardi dedicatorio della "Vita" di Vittorino da Feltre del Platina', in A. Campana and P.M. Masotti, eds., *Bartolomeo Sacchi il Platina* (Padua 1986), 153-208 (at 173-9).

[55] Luzio and Renier, 244-5.

[56] 'Croniche', 66-7.

pornographic drawings and various holy relics lost on the battlefield,[57] was only too eager to receive Francesco in person. In spite of disapproval from Venice Francesco accepted the invitation in early October.[58]

For many weeks urged by Isabella to return to Mantua - on 13 September 1495 she assured Francesco that 'tutto el popolo' awaited him[59] - the Marquis arrived back in Mantua in November, and then proceeded to Venice for a reception so triumphal that he described it to Isabella as 'like a plenary indulgence'.[60] Perhaps it was at this time that he commissioned the medal from Sperandio which commemorates his victory at Fornovo. As well as Francesco's portrait on the obverse, it shows on the reverse the Marquis surrounded by fellow-warriors in armour (including the backview of a dwarf on horseback, reminiscent of the one on Pisanello's medal of Francesco's great grandfather and namesake) with the inscription 'For the restored liberty of Italy.'[61]

On 26 February 1496 he set forth again from Mantua, with a new commission from Venice to mop up areas of pro-French resistance in the south (in spite of the fact that his brother-in-law Montpensier remained at Naples as Charles VIII's vicar).[62] While he was on his journey south, it was announced that the papal honour of the Golden Rose was to be conferred on the marquis; at first he even had the temerity to tell his ambassador in Rome he would not go there for this or for any other empty ceremony (*ficta demonstratione*) unless his brother Sigismondo was made a cardinal; on advice from Venice, however, he changed his itinerary, leaving Fano to travel overland to Rome.[63] The military campaign, in Molise and Apulia, was not outstanding, though it was characterised by some violent sackings of small towns which Francesco blithely justified to his wife, in letters which were otherwise more taken up with his travel experiences.[64] Francesco was no Napoleon and complained ceaselessly of the material hardships of military life, eagerly awaiting the consignments of cheese and salami which Isabella sent from Mantua. 'Many years will pass before I again leave Mantua', he complained on May 22:[65] The campaign was ended by a thirty-day truce with Montpensier, signed on 21 July, while

---

[57] Luzio and Renier, 235-6 (AG b. 626).

[58] Luzio and Renier, 28-9; letter from Doge Agostino Barbarigo to Francesco, 12 October 1495 (b. 1423).

[59] AG b. 2992 lib. 5, f. 86r.

[60] 'Croniche', 352-3; letter of Francesco to Isabella, 9 November 1495 (AG b. 2961 lib. 4a, f. 146r-7r).

[61] C. Hill, *A Corpus of Medals of the Italian Renaissance before Cellini* (London, 1930), no. 400. N.B. See medal by Sperandio, p. 218 above.

[62] G. Coniglio, 'Francesco Gonzaga e la guerra contro i francesi nel regno di Napoli', *Samnium*, 34 (1961), 192-209 (at 192).

[63] Coniglio, 'F. Gonzaga e la guerra', 194n. The ceremony is described in a letter to Isabella d'Este, 28 March 1496 (AG b. 2907 lib. 155, ff. 52v-53r).

[64] Coniglio, 'F. Gonzaga e la guerra', 195.

[65] Coniglio, 'F. Gonzaga e la guerra', 195.

Francesco himself struggled against a combined force of syphilis, typhoid and malaria.[66] Montpensier wrote to his Gonzaga brother-in-law on 26 July a personal letter, mainly expressing thoughts about his wife, Chiara.[67]

To most Mantuans the details of this campaign would have been unfamiliar and distant; in the meantime, there was plenty of leeway left in the Fornovo factor. The business of Mantuan government in Francesco's absence had devolved largely upon his wife but also upon his brother, protonotary Sigismondo Gonzaga, who had continued to exploit the intercessionary aspect of Francesco's victory, claiming that it signified favour and reward from the Madonna and those saints to whom the marquis had dedicated himself. As is well known there was a new surge of Mantuan mariolatry with the founding of the chapel on the site of the house of the Jew Daniele of Nursia (demolished on the insistence of Sigismondo and the fanatics who had his ear). Mantegna's huge altarpiece was first commissioned with instructions from Sigismondo in agreement with the absentee marquis's council. The first instruction was to include with Francesco on the right of the spectator his brothers (Sigismondo himself and Giovanni) but not, strange to say, their deceased uncle Rodolfo and his wife on the other side;): the second version removed the others and placed Francesco directly under the care of St Michael and St George.[68] Barely ready in time,[69] it was carried through huge crowds on the first anniversary of Fornovo, 6 July 1496, when masses were celebrated at the new chapel, named the Madonna della Vittoria, and prayers were offered to the Madonna for Francesco's safe return with new victories. Francesco himself was not of course present for the occasion; from Antella in distant Apulia he wrote on 8 July that he remembered it was a year since his great victory 'against the enemy King of France; God knows how deeply it upsets me that there is nothing relevant I can do...'[70] He received in return a rather reproachful note from Baldassare Soardi, pointing out that he had only remembered two days after the event,[71] though in fact the requiem masses for Rodolfo and Giovanmaria Gonzaga had been held a week earlier, to coincide with the greater influx of people into Mantua for the races on the vigil of the *festa* of St Peter.[72]

---

[66] Coniglio, 'F. Gonzaga e la guerra', 193-6.

[67] AG b. 626.

[68] R. Lightbown, *Mantegna* (Oxford 1986), 178-9.

[69] Antimaco mentions that it was 'de recenti picta' in his letter of 7 July 1496; he describes the procession of the previous day; so do Sigismondo Gonzaga and Isabella d'Este in letters of 6 and 10 July (A. Portioli, 'La chiesa e la Madonna della Vittoria di A. Mantegna in Mantova', *Archivio storico lombardo*, 10 (1883), 448-73 (at 467-8); P. Kristeller, *Andrea Mantegna* (Berlin, 1902) Dokumente nos. 140-42, 561-3.

[70] Coniglio, 208.

[71] Letter of 26 July 1496 (AG b. 2449 c. 114).

[72] Letter from Isabella d'Este, 30 June 1495 (b. 2992 lib. 7, f. 59v-60r).

Francesco finally arrived back in Mantua on 21 November 1496, after another triumphal if rather funereal visit to Venice,[73] for he was now in mourning not only for Ferrandino II of Naples (for whom a requiem mass had been celebrated in Mantua six days earlier)[74] but also for his uncle Gianfrancesco Gonzaga and his brother-in-law Gilbert de Montpensier. It cannot be said that Francesco managed to personify the honour of Italy for long; his opportunism in 1499, when Louis XII's army allied to Venice, swept Sforza Milan off the map, and during the League of Cambrai War in 1509, when in turn Venice's dominions were overwhelmed, hardly evoked Italic glory, since on both occasions he chose the side of the foreigners. But his authority in Mantua and his status throughout Italy had been fixed indelibly by Fornovo; paradoxically one of the main beneficiaries from the invasion and withdrawal of Charles VIII, he was neither the first nor the last political figure to manufacture and thrive upon the idea of being Italy's liberator.

---

[73] Marin Sanuto, ed. R. Fulin etc., *Diarii*, vol. 1 (Venice 1879), cols. 383-4.
[74] Sanuto, *Diarii*, col. 385.

Political and cultural implications of secret diplomacy: Commynes and Ferrara in the light of unpublished documents

Joël Blanchard

Night time in Venice, May 1495. A man in disguise was stealthily leaving the Benedictine Abbey of San Giorgio Maggiore, on the island of the same name situated at the mouth of the Giudecca canal. This used to be the dwelling place of foreign ambassadors, entertained *honorifice* by the Signoria ('a spexe de San Marco'). One needed a *barca* to get there. It was not the first time that this man was walking, at night, through the city of the doges in order to meet important representatives of international diplomacy. That particular night, he met the ambassador from Ferrara, a skillful and energetic agent ('de ingenio'). Our *stravestito* man (we are not told what sort of disguise he had chosen on that night) was Commynes - a character the Italians knew well. He had been spotted and shadowed by the henchmen of the Signoria long ago, but so far his movements had not given rise to much emotion in Venice. As a matter of fact, the city of the doges was full of excitement since that night of 1 April when the League was signed; diplomats from all over Europe and from the Levant were staying there at the same time, organising many more or less unofficial contacts and exchanges. But at that very moment, the situation was considered serious enough by the Milanese ambassador in Venice for him to report to his chancery about the *sinistre pratiche* of Commynes.[1]

This was the beginning of one of the most extraordinary episodes in the diplomatic career of Commynes, an episode so far uncommented upon by critics

---

[1] Archivio di Stato di Milan, Sforzesco Potenze Estere [hereafter ASMi, SPE], Venezia, b. 383 (Antonio Trivulzio, Bernardo Visconti and Taddeo Vimercati to Sforza, 4th May 1495, extracts in A. Segre, 'I prodomi della ritirata di Carlo VIII, re di Francia, da Napoli', *Archivio storico italiano*, 5th ser., 33 (1904), 351.

for lack of documents. Even a witness as important as Marin Sanudo, a Venetian, usually well informed about all the events taking place in his City, recognised he had no inside information on an adventure which proved to be so momentous for the diplomatic, political and cultural history of the *impresa*.[2]

A corpus of about fifteen unpublished letters, addressed to Ercole d'Este by the Ferrarese ambassador to the French court, is now available which clarifies the progress of a diplomatic adventure in which the main actors of Italian and French politics were involved.[3] At the centre of these negociations, of this *pratica* to use the Italian expression of the time, stood Commynes. The letters of his Italian counterparts mentioned him, described him at length in action, insisted on the part he played as a vigorous negotiator, a skilful schemer, and, for the Italians, the inevitable go-between with the French court. In a moment when resentment and frustration drove everyone to the most drastic solutions, Commynes together with Ferrara and its agents displayed an accomplished diplomatic skill, acting behind the scenes to avert the risks of war and to ward off threatening storms from the king. In this paper we intend to investigate the reasons for the convergence between Commynes and the city-state of Ferrara: however small, Ferrara occupied an outstanding and decisive position in the Italian diplomatic game. This convergence was to be long-lasting since the *pratiche* of Commynes and Ercole d'Este, duke of Ferrara, developed during the greatest part of the *impresa*, i.e. from May to November 1495.

This body of diplomatic documents is exceptional. In their letters secret agents used to report Commynes' confidential remarks. Commynes would express himself freely on the personality of the main political actors of his time and on the political and cultural implications of a conflict which he analyzed from the inside. Thus, the relaxed tone of intimate conversations, secret and familiar, free from the decorum and devices of official reports, is restored to us. These letters are all the more precious for it. These asides, these quick glances may appear as a sort of draft of the meditation on the 'conditions and natures' to which the memorialist was accustomed to giving a paramount importance and which we find also, sometimes with the same ring, the same cast of mind, in his *Mémoires*. Last, but not least, what comes out of these texts is the strong concordance between Commynes and his Italian counterparts: another proof, and a glaring one too, that the diplomatic correspondence of the time is an

---

[2] Marin Sanudo, *La spedizione di Carlo VIII in Italia*, ed. R. Fulin (Venice, 1873), 380: 'Et a dì 9 ditto expedite uno so orator a esso Re, chiamato domino Antonio di Constabeli kav., el qual partite molto celeramente, andando verso Fiorenza. La cagione perché non se intese; ma è da judicar tramasse qual cossa insieme....' See also Sanudo, *Spedizione*, 401.

[3] Archivio di Stato, Modena, Archivio Segreto Estense, Carteggio Ambasciatori [hereafter ASMo, ASE, Amb.], Francia, b. 1.

essential documentation requiring close study from the historian who tries to analyse and understand the political and literary behaviour of the period.

1. Commynes and Ferrara: common and converging interests

Whereas during the night of the 1st of April 1495, in Venice, the most important Italian states formed a league with foreign countries, other states of the peninsula, smaller ones, endeavoured to stay apart from this vast defensive coalition against the invader. The dukedom of Ferrara was one of those. The situation of Ferrara on the Italian political scene was indeed a very peculiar one and this needs comment. Ercole d'Este intended well by staying outside the League. This open independence had given rise to some astonishment and made some neighbours, especially Venice, very suspicious; but finally they had tolerated it, without too much hostility towards this little state which was asserting its intention to have its own way. Among the reasons adduced for the League, a clause had been arranged providing for the possibility of any state adhering to the coalition.[4] Thus, Ercole d'Este could join the confederates at any moment.

The reasons for this manifestation of independence were addressed by the duke himself in several letters sent to Iacomo Troto, his ambassador to the duke of Milan. First, the inhabitants of Ferrara entertained strong anti-Venetian feelings: there was an old hatred between them dating back to the war of Ferrara and Venice, at the end of which Venice occupied and kept the Polesine of Rovigo - a low and swampy but extremely fertile plain lying between the Adige and the Po - which formerly belonged to the dukedom and was now in the hands of Venice. In his *Mémoires* (Book 7, cap. 3) Commynes recalls the circumstances of this war which took place about twelve years before the Italian expedition.[5] It had left severe scars in the minds of the people of Ferrara, enough to explain their reluctance to enter into a coalition with former enemies.[6]

Their wish to stay out of military clashes was based on various geopolitical, historical, psychological and military considerations. All seem to belong to a well structured and coherent doctrine in which Ercole d'Este was a firm believer. He was determined by his concern for a negotiated solution. He

---

[4] 'Et quanto sia per reservarli il loco de intrare in queste lege per uno de li capi etc.; Sua Excellentia me ha resposto che de questo Vostra Signoria non se dia penssero perché l'harà ogni bon respecto al facto vostro quando serà bisogno, et che li pare che recordiati saviamente a stare cussì...' (I. Trotto to Ercole, 27 March 1495 (1), ASMo, ASE, Amb., Milano, b. 9.).

[5] Philippe de Commynes, *Mémoires*, ed. J. Calmette, 3 vols. (Paris 1924-5) [hereafter *Mémoires*], vol. 3, 18; and again, vol. 3, 230.

[6] Other middle-sized States like Bologna were not as steadfast. Bologna did not resist the commands of the confederates very long and offered allegiance very soon after the League was signed. Sanudo delighted in underlining the difference between the two small States in order to expose Ferrara. But Sanudo was a Venetian!

refused to *experimentare la fortuna* and to jeopardize his State, 'perché le cosse de la fortuna sono molto pericolose'.[7] This sentence keeps recurring like a leitmotiv in all the letters the duke addressed to his ambassadors.[8] This prudent attitude he had already displayed, before the League was signed, when warning his son-in-law, Sforza, against the risks of a confederation with other States.

Remaining thus neutral was difficult. On all occasions it compelled the duke to *simulare et temporegiare*[9] and to give tokens of good faith on all sides. For instance, since his younger son Ferdinando was committed on the French side, his elder son, Alfonso, was sent to the service of his son-in-law, the duke of Milan.[10] Because of this tendency to hedge the duke of Ferrara was exposed to the criticism of his neighbours. The confederates, mostly the Venetians, accused him of fishing in troubled waters. Sanudo echoed these rumours, all of which were ill-founded. The duke of Ferrara and his subjects were accused of being too favourable to the French.[11] But the duke of Ferrara's refusal to commit himself could also give the opportunity and the framework for a mediation between the conflicting powers;[12] this was an argument the duke used to maintain his neutrality. And in the end so he appeared to public opinion, as a man of compromise, a *homo di mezzo*.[13]

This exceptional stand of Ferrara on the Italian political scene, this non-commitment, attracted men sharing the same sort of interests toward the city.

---

[7] A. Costabile to Ercole, 15 June 1495 (1) (ASMo, ASE, Amb. Francia, b. 1).

[8] Ercole to I. Trotto, 2, 5, 9 June 1495 (ASMo, ASE, Amb., Milano, b. 10).

[9] Ercole must 'anche simulare et temporegiare col re de Franza et fingere de stare neutrale... per le quale ragione vostra Sublimità se doveva governare molto saviamente' (I. Trotto to Ercole, 23 June 1495 (ASMo, ASE, Amb., Milano, b. 9). Same wish to temporize with the duke of Milan.

[10] On hearing the League had been signed in Venice, he had his subjects kindle bonfires and go on processions, but he did not explain the reasons for these improvised manifestations to them.

[11] Antonio Costabile to Ercole, 15 June 1495 (1) (ASMo, ASE, Amb., Francia, b. 1): 'munsigniore de Argientun suiunse che non crede che nesuno francoso anuntia da amore (sic) vostra Excellentia, et che tuta Ferara è frantiosa, digandoli che quando Sua Signoria intrò a Ferara li puti cridavano *Frantia, Frantia*...'; see also Bernardino Prosperi to Ercole, 10 June (ASMo, ASE, Amb., Francia, b. 1). The fact that Ferrara was so well-disposed towards the French was underlined by several witnesses: Taddeo Vimercati to Sforza, 18 June 1495 (ASMi, SPE, Venezia, 383); Taddeo Vimercati to Sforza, 5 July (ASMi, SPE, Venezia, b. 384): '[Ercole] ha cativo animo et è inclinato al re de Franza...'.

[12] The duke of Ferrara mentioned the idea several times, in particular in a letter to I. Trotto (24th March 1495 (1), ASMo, ASE, Amb., Milano, b. 10): '...mai sì, quando il paresse a la Sua Signoria che havessemo a starsene cussì de mezo senza intrare per adesso in dicta liga, forsi per poterse lei per questo modo servirse meglio del mezo nostro a qualche suo proposito, seremo nonché contenti di quello che piacerà alla Sua Excellentia, purché per epsa ce sia promesso che a nui né al stato nostro non serà dato molestia, et che poteremo stare sicuri, et poteria essere che a Sua Excellentia non dispaceria questa propositione, attento ch'el nostro intrare in epsa liga poteria portare pocho fructo a li colligati, et stando cussi neutrali accaderia forsi al prefato signor Duca a valerse meglio de nui...'.

[13] *Diarium Ferrariense*, in *Rerum italicarum scriptores*, ed. L.A. Muratori (Milan, 1738), vol. 34, col. 307.

The first contacts between Commynes and Ferrara dated back to April 1495 when the Frenchman, as we saw, had many secret meetings, in Venice with Guidoni Aldobrandino, the Ferrarese ambassador.[14] Commynes left from Venice on 30 May bound for Ferrara.[15] The relationships between France and the dukedom were hearty and friendly. Ferdinando's presence alongside Charles VIII, the warm welcome of a population favourable to the French, made the beginning of a *praticha* easier.[16] In a letter to Sforza, Taddeo Vimercati gave an account of this welcome; the Milanese ambassador alluded to the rumours concerning the current negotiations between Ercole and the French.[17] It was during these conversations between Commynes and Ercole that the project of a mediation between the duke of Milan and Charles VIII developed - a mediation allowing the latter to return to France unhampered. The content of the discussions between Commynes and the duke of Ferrara is known to us thanks to a letter dated 2 June and addressed by Ercole to Messer Iacomo, his ambassador to Milan.[18] Let us give a brief account of it.

---

[14] The first contacts between Commynes and Ferrara had taken place much earlier. In December 1483 - January 1484, Commynes received the ambassadors of the duke of Ferrara in Lyons. Ten years later, in December 1493, it was Commynes again who was in charge of welcoming don Ferdinando on his entering Amboise (Sigismondo Cantelmo and Giulio Tassoni to the duke of Ferrara, 8 December 1493, ASMo, ASE, Amb., Francia, b. 1).

[15] Through the texts - those of Bembo in particular - we get the image of a man surprised, even shattered by the signature of the League. In fact, Commynes suspected it and had warned the king about it. Immediately after, he asked that the necessary defensive measures should be taken to face this threatening League. Unlike what is generally believed, Charles VIII had been warned by Commynes even before the Venetian ambassadors had given an official confirmation of it (ASMi, SPE, Napoli, b. 253, [April 1495]: 'Summario [de lettere...]: Lettere de 4 del conte de Caiacia per le quale declara l'aviso dato da monsignore de Argentono al re de la lega, afirmandola per facta, quantunche a luy non li fosse anchora communicata per la Signoria...'). From that moment, Commynes reacted very quickly and engaged in great activity, but, as the Venetians refused to cooperate in spite of the arrival of the French envoy in Venice, sent to explain the French position, Commynes turned to Ferrara to promote the negotiated solution he planned.

[16] Commynes was very warmly welcome in Ferrara. Antonio Vicecomes to Sforza, 2 June 1495 (ASMi, SPE, Ferrara, b. 335): 'Her sera gionse qua Monsignore d'Argenton, quale è stato ad Venetia per oratore del Re de Franza, et insieme era uno secretario de la Maestà Sua, quale pare fuosse andato a levarlo per retornare da quella. Questo Illustrissimo signore Duca li andò incontra, et cum soni de trombe et piferi li ha accompagnati sino in la corte sua et poi in la camera dove li ha facti allogiare. Questa matina, essendo loro andati da la Excellentia Sua in el zerdino de la quondam bona memoria de la Illustrissima Madama, dove habita, epsa li ha accompagnati in la capella ducale et ivi ha facto celebrare la messa cum solemnitate. Dopo disnare, facendo spazare et annetare tutte le contrate, primo li ha accompagnati ad vedere le fosse nove et el barco suo, et poi la citade: le quale cose hanno facto murmurare asai che sia alla voglia del prefato Re contra la serenissima lega, et tanto più che dominica proxima passata l'Excellentia Sua mandò Bernardino Prospero da don Ferdinando suo fiolo...'. If Commynes devoted only a few words to the welcome he received in Ferrara, it was probably to avoid being repetitive of his previous account of his being welcome in Venice to which he devoted several pages.

[17] Antonio Vicecomes to Sforza, 2 June 1495, ASMi, SPE, Ferrara, b. 335.

[18] Ercole to I. Trotto, 2 June 1495, ASMo, ASE, Amb., Milano, b. 10.

Commynes recalls the intention of the French king of going to France without harming anybody. He resorts alternately to reassurances and to threats. The French would go through central Lombardy, marching clear of the towns where the confederates would have gathered.[19] They would be provided with fresh supplies to make this passage easier. In exchange for that, the king would guarantee the duke of Milan's safety. But 'quando li venga facto obstaculo on datoli impedimento, lo usarà la forza et experimentarà la fortuna'.[20] The adversaries of Charles VIII are mistaken, goes on Commynes, in thinking the king is deprived of means. Indeed, on the way out, the *impresa* started out deplorably badly prepared, but now these times are over and since the king

> è in Italia et ch'el vole ritornare in Franza, le cose andarano ad un altro modo, concludendo in fine che sua Maestà haverà tanta gente et dinari quanto la vorà, et che se la lassasse fare el Duca de Borbon et a li altri che sono in Francia, se vederiano cose maravegliose...[21]

Commynes found a benevolent ear in the duke of Ferrara who was aware of the dangers of war arising from the League. Just after the signature of the League, Sforza, his son-in-law, had launched an *impresa* against the duke of Orléans who was preparing for war in Asti. In a sort of rough copy of this same letter of 2 June, Ercole warned Sforza against the terrible risks he was running in this test of strength; he recalled the threats uttered by Commynes against the duke of Milan.[22] He advised prudence to Sforza. He used military but also psychological arguments. Ercole underlined how risky it would be for the duke of Milan to attack an army on its way home because an army thus cornered by necessity is always more dangerous for its enemy ('sòle essere molto periculoso obstare a gente che siano conducte a tale necessità' [23]).

To this main argument he added other considerations likely to convince Sforza of rejoining Commynes's plan allowing free passage to the king. All

---

[19] 'Il me respose che a questo li era rimedio et se poteva provedere opportunamente al tutto; perché la Excellentia de quello Signor Duca poterà mettere dentro de le citade et terre per dove se haverà a passare le gente d'arme et soldati suoi et de la signoria de Venetia, et Sua Maestà passaria de fuori via col suo exercito, et che a questo modo seria proviso al passare del Signor Re et a la secureza del prefato Signor Duca...' (Ercole to I. Trotto, 2 June 1495, ASMo, ASE, Amb., Milano, b. 10.).

[20] Ercole to I. Trotto, 2 June 1495, ASMo, ASE, Amb., Milano, b. 10.

[21] Ercole to I. Trotto, 2 June 1495, ASMo, ASE, Amb., Milano, b. 10.

[22] These were the very words of Commynes (*queste formale parole*) reported by Ercole in his letter 'che veramente come quello che sempre è stato affectionato a Sua Excellentia li rencresceva molto che la se ritrovasse in questi fastidii et spese, et che de libera che la era la si è facta schiava de altri, et maxime de chi naturalmente li sono inimici, et deinde volendo il prefato monsignore dimonstrare la possanza del suo Signore Re, el ne dixe che in Hasti sino a quest' hora vi sono circa septecento homini d'arme, et ch'el Duca de Borbon ne havea preparati et li mandava in dicto loco altri milleduecento homini d'arme, et che epso monsignore de Borbon ne haveria mandato il doppio più...' (Ercole to I. Trotto, 2 June 1495, ASMo, ASE, Amb., Milano, b. 10.).

[23] Ercole to I. Trotto, 2 June 1495, ASMo, ASE, Amb., Milano, b. 10.

these alluded to the institutional, political and economic frailty of the duke of Milan in those days. So the latter would be well advised to accept the proposition made to him. These pieces of advice given by Ercole to Sforza were repeated in a letter dated 5 June and addressed to Trotto.[24] Three days later, Ercole received a letter from Sforza in which the latter expressed his interest in the proposition made by his father-in-law.[25] Thus was the process of the *pratica* initiated. The beginning of the negotiation was completed by the sending of Antonio Costabile to the king.

2. Pressure groups and power struggles: 'Gioveni' and 'Antiqui'

Commynes left Ferrara on 3 June. He stopped in Bologna[26] then rode on towards Florence where he was received *privatamente*.[27] Costabile rejoined him there on 11 June. During the following days Costabile met Commynes then the king or certain important lords of the court for unofficial talks which lasted about ten days in the different staying places of Commynes and of the king: Commynes and Costabile met in Florence; Costabile and Commynes met up with the king in Siena, then in the *campo fiorentino* near Florence, in Pisa and finally in Lucca. There Costabile left the court after the negotiations were broken off.

The mission of Costabile was indeed a remarkable episode in the secret diplomacy of the fifteenth century. Let us underline a few aspects which are all the more interesting, given the lack of previous appreciation of his skills. Reading Sanudo, we get the impression that the secret was well kept since he does not know what was in the *pratica* (*nescio qua de causa*); he simply says that the *orator* of Ferrara (Costabile) went away *'molto celeramente, andando*

---

[24] Et volemo che de novo faciati intendere a Sua Excellentia che, quanto più li pensamo, più ne pare che sia da fare dicto effecto et non volere tentare la fortuna, considerato che il Re in persona ritorna a casa et ha cum sé li soi baroni et soldati fidelissimi, li quali al tutto hanno deliberato de passare on de morire, et è cosa periculosa ad opponerse ad epsi, perché spesse volte se è visto fare cose stupende a quelli che sono constrecti a tale necessità (Ercole to I. Trotto, 5 June 1495, ASMo, ASE, Amb., Milano, b. 10).

[25] Ercole to I. Trotto, 8 June 1495, ASMo, ASE, Amb., Milano, b. 10.

[26] Commynes's route is well known to us: he stayed in Ferrara on the 2nd and 3rd of June 'per riposarsi un pocho, perché prima lo andare in barcha lo havea fastidito, et lo havere di poi cavalchato per la via de Padua lo havea alquanto molestato et faticato; zobìa se partirà de qui et andarà al viaggio suo verso Bologna...' (Ercole to I. Trotto, 2 June 1495, ASMo, ASE, Amb., Milano, b. 10). In Bologna, Commynes must have met Giovanni Bentivoglio, but the results were probably *frustatoria*, because the stand of Bologna towards the French was not ambiguous: Bentivoglio positively refused to let the French pass through his land; see Manfredo Manfredi to Ercole, 15 June 1495, ASMo, ASE, Amb., Firenze, b. 9.

[27] Questa matina è gionto qua monsignore de Argentono, li è andato incontra Ioanne di Piero Francesco et duy altri citadini privatamente; pur la signoria l'ha allogiato a casa di uno citadino... (Giovan Stefano Castiglione (ambassador from Milan to Florence) to Sforza, 7 June 1495, ASMo, ASE, Amb., Milano, b. 9).

verso Fiorenza', but *'la cagione perché non se intese'*.[28] In the letters addressed by Costabile to Ercole, the name of Commynes appears in cipher (one of the rare instances when we can spot his name thus hidden); or else when the name is not ciphered according to a secret and confidential code, Commynes is alluded to as *questo amicho*, or *l'amicho de la Vostra Signoria* (Ercole). The secret was implied by the confidential nature of the *pratica*. First and foremost, the mediators wanted to avoid leaks which might elicit violent reactions from the confederates against Sforza and Ercole on the one hand, and on the other hand, violent reactions at court against Commynes from the advocates of a military solution. But there was also a more technical reason pertaining to the diplomatic habits of the time. Why did Commynes, the *dicto amico,* prefer not to be mentioned by name? He himself explained that it was then hardly admitted that an important negotiation might be carried on by a single person:

> Arivato in casa de munsigniore de Argientun Sua Signioria me se fece incuntro con molte scuse, digandome che io li perdonase se Sua Signioria mandava per me, perché lo faceva per non me parlare a la presentia d'altri, a ciò che como se fano ne le corte non se potese dire che lui volese essere quello che volese menare questa praticha solo; li resposi che io non poteva avere magiore gratia da sua signior<i>a che parlarli in sua chasa, et che io el pregava che di quanto io stava qua fusse cuntento che se parlasimo una volta, et cusì fu ordinato.[29]

So the asides of Commynes to Aloysius Becchetto, the apostolic nuncio, and to the Ferrarese ambassador whom he met in Venice, brought about indignant reactions from the other ambassadors. But it seems Commynes was used to such ways. Commynes was accustomed to act *motu proprio*, with the more or less official approval of the authorities, of the king or of his representatives; he was a specialist in delicate if not impossible missions. There we have one of the fascinating aspects of Commynes's diplomacy, which we already mentioned elsewhere:[30] the use of masks, of stratagems and tricks, the will to put people off the scent. Commynes had become an expert in secret diplomacy and his consummate artistry aroused the suspicions of the Italian authorities who were past masters in the same art and were well aware that the *consuete arte et astucie* of the Frenchman were dangerous.[31]

This *pratica* of Costabile and Commynes developed in difficult circumstances because of the strong reluctance which they encountered in both camps, with Sforza as well as with the entourage of Charles VIII. The hazards of the *pratica* are linked to the influence of pressure groups in both camps, opposing the advocates of war to those who favoured negotiation. Costabile

---

[28] Sanudo, *La spedizione,* 380.

[29] A. Costabile to Ercole, 15 June 1495 (2) (ASMo, ASE, Amb., Francia, b. 1).

[30] J. Blanchard, *Commynes et les Italiens. Lettres inédites du mémorialiste* (Paris, 1993), 11-24.

[31] Signoria to the proveditors, 8 July 1495, ASV, Sen. Secret. XXXV, f° 152v°.

addressed about fifteen letters to the duke of Ferrara which enable us to have a pretty good idea of the atmosphere which prevailed at the court of France during the first fortnight of June 1495: a decisive moment during the return from Naples.

Among the important men at court, in June 1495, we find Saint-Malo whose opinion was particularly valued by the king, but things were changing and the king was falling more and more under the influence of *quilli camberlani gioveni* who wanted to fight with the confederates, mainly Sforza. In this group of young chamberlains are to be ranked Trivulzio, Gié and Foi. They often were keen supporters of the duke of Orléans and *per mostarse animosi, sempre li* (to the king) *parlano gaiardamente.*[32]

The announcement that the League had been signed justified this warlike passion. After a first moment of relative indifference, French opinion, shocked by the information transmitted by Commynes, had quickly enough realised the obstacles the French might meet on their way back home. Opinion was divided: some wishing to fight against the confederates, others favouring a peaceful solution. Moreover there was a natural tendency of the French always, according to Commynes, to *incalarse quando se li oferise.*[33]

The latter tendency expressed itself loudly when the news of the capture of Novara by the duke of Orléans reached the court. Opinion flared up in favour of the young duke and all the repressed rancours were released. Did not Sforza attack a sick man (*amalato*)?[34] Did he not fail to keep his promises? Did he not insult the king, even calling him *naimo* (dwarf)?[35] These were heavy blunders, from a psychological as well as from a tactical point of view, which were to keep deep resentment against the duke of Milan alive.

Among the most active supporters of warlike passion was Trivulzio: a schemer, a renegade who, in Naples, had forsaken the side of Sforza to enter Charles VIII's service, partly out of vexation and partly out of interest.[36] These bellicose characters even forced on the king the idea 'che bandisca publicamente

---

[32] Et più tosto se cunsilgia cun quilli camberlani gioveni de li fati de la guera che cun niuno de li altri, et che loro per mostarse animosi sempre li parlano gaiardamente... (A. Costabile to Ercole, 15 June 1495 (1), ASMo, ASE, Amb., Francia, b. 1).

[33] A. Costabile to Ercole, 15 June 1495 (1), ASMo, ASE, Amb., Francia, b. 1.

[34] Digandome che discortesia è stata la sua di volere tore la sua vila a munsigniore de Orliens essendoli dentro amalato... (A. Costabile to Ercole, 15 June 1495 (1), ASMo, ASE, Amb., Francia, b. 1).

[35] A. Costabile to Ercole, 22 July 1495 (ASMo, ASE, Amb., Milano, b. 11). Commynes was more moderate (et si petit homme de corps ne fut jamais que ledit roy... [*Mémoires*, III, 258]). For further evidence of the Italian grotesque representation of Charles VIII, see C. de Frede, 'Più simile è mostro ch'è uomo. La bruttezza e l'incultura di Carlo VIII nella rappresentazione degli Italiani del Rinascimento', *Bibliothèque d'Humanisme et Renaissance*, 44 (1982), 545-85.

[36] Sunto certo che lui cerchi de perturbare questa cossa (la praticha) quanto el pò (A. Costabile to Ercole, 15 June 1495 (2), ASMo, ASE, Amb., Francia, b. 1; in this letter Trivulzio explained why he went over to Charles VIII).

la guera cuntra al Ducha de Milano, et àno fato cometere una litera ad uno Ruberteto secretario de la magistà regia, la cumtinentia de la quale lui non me ave voluto dire';[37] at the last moment, because of Commynes' entreaties, the king refused to send this declaration of war. Commynes had much trouble imposing his views; youth prevailed:

> In quista corte li sono diferenti animi: li sono de quelli che sono parciali de Munsigniore d'Orliens, de quelli che parlano solamente per le particularità loro, et de quelli che tendino solamente a l'utile et honore de la Magistà Regia, ma se ave da fare cum signiore giovene, in modo che li più de quisti signiori sapi et antiqui asai se strengieno et se retirano.[38]

No doubt it was Commynes who was aimed at by the words *sapi et antiqui asai*. And indeed his task was difficult for several reasons. First because Commynes who had been staying in Venice for nine months had been away from court for a long period during which things had changed.[39] At court people still had a conservative image of him, that of an opponent to the *impresa*, almost that of a coward:

> et àme dito che avendo pure scrito prima quasi in questi toni, li fu scrito che se lui aveva pavura, se andase a rescundere, in modo che per questa causa non andava se non li fusse scrito.[40]

Suspicion towards him was fostered by the partisans of Orléans. Commynes bitterly resented this sign of mistrust because lui 'stete uno ano im persone (= *presone*, i.e. prigione) per le cosse de Munsigniore d'Orliens cum suo grandisimo dano'.[41] Yet his thinly veiled animosity against Orléans was based on his analysis fundamentally diverging from that of the young supporters of the duke, and this accounts for the severe judgment Commynes passed on him: he lacks experience; he is *uno ardito signiore*,[42] but according to La Trémoille (a supporter of peace, like Commynes), the duke 'non è tropo homo

---

[37] A. Costabile to Ercole, 16 June 1495 (ASMo, ASE, Amb., Francia, b. 1).

[38] A. Costabile to Ercole, 21 June 1495 (ASMo, ASE, Amb., Francia, b. 1).

[39] [Commynes] diseme che el Re era giovene, et che aveva retorvate le cosse molto mutate (A. Costabile to Ercole, 15 June 1495 (1), ASMo, ASE, Amb., Francia, b. 1).

[40] A. Costabile to Ercole, 11 June 1495 (ASMo, ASE, Amb., Francia, b. 1).

[41] A. Costabile to Ercole, 21 June 1495 (ASMo, ASE, Amb., Francia, b. 1). The reference is to what took place during the *Guerre Folle* in which Commynes compromised himself in siding with the duke of Orléans. See *Mémoires*, vol. 3, 314: Quant j'euz couché une nuyt à Amboyse, allay devers ce roy nouveau [Louis XII], de qui j'avoye aussi esté privé que nulle autre personne, et pour luy avoye esté en tous mes troubles et pertes...

[42] A. Costabile to Ercole, 11 June 1495, ASMo, ASE, Amb., Francia, b. 1. See also A. Costabile to Ercole, 15 June 1495 (2), ASMo, ASE, Amb., Francia, 1: Me ave dito munsigni<o>re de Argientun che stima che in ogni modo se abia a fare fate d'arme, perché eso munsigniore d'Orliens è molto ardito et più tosto che re tenuto, et ave secho giente de arme valente più tosto che homeni de governo.

praticho di guera',[43] hence jeopardizing the king in Lombardy when launching into an adventurous and warlike policy.[44]

To counter the radical positions of the opposite party, Commynes could rely on the king. Charles VIII acknowledged the privileged part he played in the settlement of Italian affairs:

> el Re à comandato che non se parli de niuna cossa che io non sia dimandato, de le cosse de Italia spetialmente, et amè dito el tuto.[45]

But the king had a weak, easily influenced mind. So Commynes endeavoured to find favourable ground on which he could press his advantage home. Charles VIII shared his point of view on the duke of Orléans : he disapproved of his dangerous personal initiatives. The capture of Novara did not please him at all:

> per quanto intendo da questo amicho [= Commynes] di Vostra Ex.tia, a la Magistà del Re non li è piac<i>uto questa presa di Novara, et pure che Sua Magistà avesse abuto passo non curava de altro...[46]

Charles ironically commented upon the expansionist views of his cousin, worried about the feeble reaction of Sforza[47] and, as if to cancel out the disastrous effects of this bellicose tendency, asked Commynes to carry on with the process of the *pratica*.[48] At the same time, he signified his trust by promising 'che mai più lo trarrà suspitione alcuna per le cosse de Munsigniore d'Orliens'.[49]

In his plan to impose negotiations, Commynes could also rely on some people at court who upheld his ideas. Among them were La Trémoille, Pienes

---

[43] A. Costabile to Ercole, 18 June 1495 (ASMo, ASE, Amb., Francia, b. 1).

[44] The impulsiveness was the very opposite of the political intelligence needed to take advantages by skilful practices of the benefits drawn from a military victory (*Mémoires,* vol. 3, 159).

[45] A. Costabile to Ercole, 15 June 1495 (1) (ASMo, ASE, Amb., Francia, b. 1).

[46] A. Costabile to Ercole, 21 June 1495 (ASMo, ASE, Amb., Francia, b. 1).

[47] Ma me ave dito [Commynes] che mai la magistà regia li respose a proposito, et che sempre se voltava a lui digandolo: *L' èt una gran giosa che cusì tosto el ducha de Milano se lasi pigliare,* et replicando quilli de munsigniore d'Orliens cusì essere la verità, Sua Maistà li respose bene et di ben essere cuntento et alegro: *Questo lo farà guarire la febre quartana!,* poi se voltò verso lui digando: *Ill èt una gran giosa che el Duca de Milano se lasa perdere cusì,* mostrando Sua Maistà non tropo se ne alegrare... (A. Costabile to Ercole, 15 June 1495 (2), ASMo, ASE, Amb., Francia, b. 1).

[48] Commynes was skilfully testing the king's dispositions towards the *pratica* when he asked if the Ferrarese ambassador was to be sent home: se non li voliti atendere, seria bene a lasarlo andare, dice [Commynes]. Li respose [Charles VIII]: No, non volgio, ve prego li fatiati charetie et el teniati qua anchora cun mi, mostrando non refutare la praticha. (A. Costabile to Ercole, 15 June 1495 (2), ASMo, ASE, Amb., Francia, b. 1).

[49] A. Costabile to Ercole, 21 June 1495 (ASMo, ASE, Amb., Francia, b. 1).

and the Prince of Orange. They were supporters of the *pratica*.[50] Behind the scenes, Commynes took skilful advantage of this swing which either estranged the king from him or brought him back to him. But Commynes and Costabile found it hard to fight against the radical positions of a French party favourable to war and strengthened by the military and verbal outbidding of their Italian opponents. For at the court of the duke of Milan too there was a party of war, namely the Sanseverini, Messer Galeazzo and Count Carlo di Belgioioso.[51] The duke of Milan, like the king, had a fickle, easily influenced mind, and immediately after the League was signed, he had been under pressure from his most extreme subjects and was now a prisoner of war logic. Moreover he was under pressure from the confederate States, in particular the Spanish ambassador in Milan, as well as the Venetians who stopped temporising, and adopted a more offensive attitude.

As Costabile expressed it very aptly, for things to go more smoothly, some sort of gesture would have been necessary from both sides: on the French side, 'le cosse non fusseno cussì grasse... come le se fanno'; on the Milanese side, 'volendosse un pocho humiliare quello Illustrissimo Signore Duca de Milano, se poteriano forsi legiermente adaptare le cose'.[52] But constant outbidding made any agreement impossible. Circumstances made things even more difficult, for instance the French attempts to overthrow the authority of Milan in Genoa during the negotiations, or the consequences of the fall of Novara. These events only nurtured mistrust on both sides. Finally, Costabile had to admit that in spite of Commynes's efforts and the inveterate optimism of the diplomat who never ceased to hope for a negotiated solution, things were not taking the turn he wished. However, after considering the ultimate French propositions transmitted by Costabile and Ercole to Sforza, the duke of Milan decided to break off the *pratica* and, on 17 June, he asked the duke of Ferrara to recall his ambassador.[53]

---

[50] Et se bene a Fiorentia ve disse che el marescal de Gie seria contrario a questa praticha, niente di meno [Commynes] me ave dito che li pare bene fato che se atenda a pasare cun concordia, et el simile munsigniore de Pientia et munsigniore de la Tramogia, el quale è tuto di vostra Excellentia, como ve scrisi.... (A. Costabile to Ercole, 15 June 1495 (1) (ASMo, ASE, Amb., Francia, b. 1).

[51] Recordandove che la Maistà Sua sempre diceva che el Ducha de Milano era el più sapio signiore del mundo et amavalo como patre, ma per Dio à 'buto gran torto cuntra la regia Maistà, perché li ave molto bene atesso tuto quello li pormese del fato di Gienua, et meser Galeatio et el cunte Carlo di Bello Zoioso sono stati gran causa di queste diferentie... (A. Costabile to Ercole, 15 June 1495 (1) (ASMo, ASE, Amb., Francia, b. 1).

[52] Ercole to I. Trotto, 19 June 1495 (ASMo, ASE, Amb., Milano, b. 10). These are almost the very words of the letter of Antonio Costabile to Ercole (16 June 1495, ASMo, ASE, Francia, b. 1) which are reported here by the duke to his ambassador in Milan.

[53] Ercole to I. Trotto, 20 June 1495 (ASMo, ASE, Amb., Milano, b. 10): the duke of Ferrara acknowledged a letter from Trotto (dated Milan, 17 June) in which the latter informed him that Sforza did not intend to pursue the *pratica*: Ercole informed Costabile and asked him to take leave of the king.

3. *The profound Italian influence on Commynes's diplomacy: political and cultural interplay*

What we have just related here is an unknown and forgotten episode in the history of Commynes, an episode bringing to the fore the essential part played by Commynes in the numerous plans for a negotiated solution during Charles VIII's return to France. And, above all, it is an episode which brings out the personality of the man of politics who, whether denigrated or valued, was never indifferent to the protagonists of French and Italian politics, Charles VIII, Ercole d'Este, Sforza, Pietro de' Medici, Lorenzo de' Medici. Commynes was an outstanding character in the context of the Italian expedition, all the more so because of his political and diplomatic stand. He was opposed to the warlike passion of a younger generation of politicians in the entourage of the king and obstinately, tenaciously, proposed a negotiated solution with the Italians.

This will to maintain diplomatic negotiations even, sometimes, in a clearly hostile atmosphere was a constant characteristic of his political process. In his *Mémoires*, Commynes mentioned it again: he advised young princes always to keep the door open to negotiations by sending ambassadors, even in the most desperate situations:

> Encores me semble que, quant la guerre seroit jà commancée, si ne doit-l'on rompre nulle praticque ne ouverture que on face de paix, car on ne scet l' heure que on a affaire, mais les entretenir toutes et ouyr tous messaiges faisans les choses dessusdictez et faire faire bon guet quelz gens yroient parler à eulx, qui seroient envoyéz tant de jour que de nuyct, mais le plus secrettement que l'on peült. Et pour ung messaige ou embassadeur qu'ilz m'envoyeroient, je leur en envoyeroie deux; et, encores qu'ilz s'en ennuyassent, disans que on n'y renvoyast plus, si y vouldroys-je renvoyer quant j'en auroye opportunité et le moyen...[54]

Commynes shared with the duke of Ferrara this confidence in the power of diplomacy, and indeed the fact that Sforza refused to go on with the *pratica* was not the end of the conciliatory schemes attempted by Ercole and Commynes together. We may surmise, even if documents concerning the period from July to October 1495 are less numerous, that this mainly secret activity never stopped. Before and after Fornovo, the *praticques d'appointement* started again, initiated by Commynes, probably in close collaboration with Ercole and in spite of the opposition he met at court.[55] The

---

[54] *Mémoires*, vol. 3, 219-220.

[55] On the eve of Fornovo (6 July 1495) final conciliatory endeavours were made (I. Trotto to Ercole, 5 July, ASMO, Milano, b. 9). The presence in the French camp of a *stravestito* (disguised) envoy of the duke of Ferrara (probably Costabile) was reported. The *pratiche* started again after Fornovo. Costabile mentioned his being in the French camp in letters dated 10 July (A. Costabile to Ercole, ASMo, ASE, Amb., Francia, b. 1). There he had a long conversation with Commynes (restai a parlamento cum munsigniore de Argientum de la praticha nostra...) and was given an audience by the king. The French asked him to go to the camp of the League, though he had no formal order from the duke of Ferrara (A. Costabile to

Ercole, 10 July 1495, ASMO, ASE, Amb., Francia, b. 1). There he had an interview with the count of Caiazzo who took it upon himself to accept the compromise proposed by the French under conditions which Costabile already deemed unacceptable: hostages were required in exchange for free passage (A. Costabile to Ercole, ASMO, ASE, Amb., Francia, b. 1). It seems many letters were exchanged between Commynes, Charles VIII and Ercole, which were carried by A. Costabile and Bernardino Prosperi who had remained with the French king after Costabile had gone (Bernardino Prosperi to Ercole, 10 July 1495, ASMo, ASE, Amb., Francia, b. 1; Ercole to I. Trotto, 14 July, ASMo, Minutario cronologico, b. 4). In this tight game, I. Trotto, the ambassador of Ercole to Sforza, played, of course, a decisive part. It is through him that we have information on the contacts Costabile had with the French. The duke of Milan proved very reluctant and Ercole laid the responsibility for the slowness and interruptions at his door, so that the French king should not think he had been *ingannato* by the duke of Ferrara (Ercole to Costabile, 14 July 1495 (1), ASMo, ASE, Amb., Milano, b. 11). Costabile travelled again, *incognito* and *stravestito*: his presence in the French camp was reported before 20 July (I. Trotto to Ercole, 21 July 1495, ASMo, ASE, Amb., Milano, b. 9; Costabile to Ercole, 22 July 1495, ASMo, ASE, Amb., Milano, b. 11). On 21 July, Costabile was with Sforza again (Costabile to Ercole, 22 July 1495, ASMO, ASE, Amb., Milano, b. 11). How many times Costabile went back and forth between the French and the Milanese camp during this short period is not exactly known; however, underground negotiation was going on alongside the official procedures, sometimes several of the protagonists being completely unaware of it. Commynes played, of course, a leading part in these *pratiche*.

Negotiations started again at the beginning of September initiated by Commynes, probably once more in close collaboration with Ercole. We may even surmise that between the two men contacts were never interrupted. Commynes was sent to Casale in the first days of September to settle the problems of succession brought about by the death of the marchioness of Montferrat and to make sure of the support or at least of the neutrality of the men in charge of the marquisate. There he carried on with his *praticques d'appointement*, in spite of the opposition he met in the court itself, in particular the opposition of the cardinal of Saint-Malo. It was in Casale that Commynes started the negotiations with Giacomo Suardo, the ambassador of the League, sent on 28 August 1495 in order to 'faire doleance de la mort de ladite marquise, et cestuy-là et moy entrasmes en parolles d'appoincter ces deux ostz sans combatre' (*Mémoires*, vol. 3, 226). It was in Casale, too, that Commynes took upon himself to write to the two Venetian *provveditori*, Luca Pisani and Marco Trevisano. And finally, it was from Casale that, through Costantino Arnito, he informed the duke of Milano of his desire to discuss peace with one of his agents.

No doubt these initiatives reviving the dormant process of peace-making were elaborated with the agreement of the duke of Ferrara or of his representatives. Most certainly it was at the entreaties of Ercole and of his envoy Iacomo Trotto that Sforza, on 12 September, sent instructions to Giulio Cattaneo about the discussions to which Commynes had invited him. The letters sent by the duke of Ferrara to his ambassador in Milan bespeak the strong encouragement Ercole had addressed to his son-in-law to make him 'voglia cum ogni studio e diligentia attendere a lo accordo et pace cum il prefato re..., etiam se li altri soi confederati non li volesseno attendere...' (Ercole to I. Trotto, 19 September 1495, ASMo, ASE, Amb., Milano, b. 10. See also in ASMo, ASE, Amb., Milano, b. 10 the letters dated 17, 21, 22 September, 1 October). According to the opinion expressed by Ercole, it was a question of survival for the duke of Milan and the action of the duke of Ferrara was decisive in this process. The details of the negotiations about the treatise of Vercelli are well known. We know them through Commynes himself. The character of Count Albertino Boschetti appears clearly in the *Mémoires*. He was the special envoy of the duke of Ferrara and played, together with Commynes, an essential part. We also know that the duke of Ferrara himself came to the camp in order to accelerate the process of peace-making. Moreover, he was a party to the agreement which granted him the *castello* of Genoa for two years. He was therefore a guarantor for the agreement. The Venetians bore the same hatred to Ercole, to

particulars of the negotiations about the treatise of Verceil during the autumn of 1495 are well known, thanks to Commynes himself. The name of Count Albertino Boschetti is mentioned prominently in the *Mémoires*.[56] With Commynes, the special envoy of the duke of Ferrara played an essential part.[57]

If Commynes and Ferrara took concerted action it was because, in this affair, they made the same analysis and shared the same values, among which a concern for 'non tentare la fortuna'. This *fortuna* consisted in resorting to mere violence with all its hazards and risks: 'era periculoso assai combatere cum desperati e cum necessitati...'.[58] Ercole, like Commynes, took the geo-political and military realities of his time into account; this consciousness led both of them to choose the less risky way and to extol its advantages to other people. This concern for usefulness prompted the duke of Ferrara to give his son-in-law so many warnings. Had he acted in another way, 'non ne haveria ni utile ni beneficio veruno, et se metteria a periculo il stato et la persona de suo cognato...'.[59] And this is why Commynes and he initiated this *pratique* which allowed Charles VIII to come back to France through Lombardy while protecting the interests of all.

Thus we can draw a parallel between Commynes and Ercole. Each of them had a moderating influence on the person he was trying to guide, Charles VIII in the former and Sforza in the latter case. The same desire inspired Commynes and Ercole, a wish to rectify the dangerous political behaviour of men unable to take on the government of a State in a particularly risky moment of history. On the one hand the duke of Ferrara tempered Sforza's *ombrosità*, his pathological anxiety which led him, in his decisions, to follow the advice of Messer Ambrogio Varese da Rosate his astrologer,[60] his excessive fear stemming from his being unsure of his political legitimacy and inducing him to listen to the last piece of advice; on the other hand, Commynes corrected the

---

Count Albertino and to Commynes, furious as they were that Sforza should have signed an agreement with the French without them and even against them. Kervyn de Lettenhove, *Lettres et négociations de Philippe de Commynes*, 3 vols. (Bruxelles, 1867-74; repr. Geneva, 1972), vol. 2, 201 n2, mistook Count Albertino Boschetti for Aloysius Bechetto, the apostolic nuncio who was then in Venice and whom Commynes met a few days before his departure. Same mistake on 228.

[56] *Mémoires*, vol. 3, 229-30.

[57] To express his gratitude to Count Albertino Boschetti who had been very active in the elaboration of the treatise, Charles VIII bestowed on him the fiefs of Civitate and of Rodi in Apulia. See P. Balan, *Storia d'Italia* (Modena, 1877), vol. 5, 359. This was an acknowledgment of the prominent part played by Ferrara in this negotiation.

[58] Ercole [to Guido Aldobrandino ?], 18 July 1495 (ASMo, ASE, Amb., Venezia, b. 9).

[59] I. Trotto to Ercole, 23 June 1495, ASMo, ASE, Amb., Milano, b. 9.

[60] Sforza followed the advice of his astrologer for every act of public life : for instance, the Milanese ambassador, the bishop of Como and Francesco Bernardino Visconti set out for Venice *domane ch' è Domenicha ad hore xviii per puncto de astrologia* (I. Trotto to Ercole, 21 February 1495, ASMo, ASE, Amb., Milano, b. 9).

easily influenced character of Charles VIII who was haunted by the same fears as his Italian cousin:

> Ma bene me à dito munsigniore d'Argienton che la natura sua [of Charles VIII] è la matina essere d'um volere, la sira d'una altra, segundo se li remfrescano le nove, et che talle nove poteriano venire che la cossa serà fata, et anche talle che non bisogniaria stare più in pratiche.[61]

But we cannot draw the parallel any further, for compared to the case of Sforza that of Charles VIII presents still another problem: that of generation. Charles VIII was bullied by pressure groups that did not treat him with consideration and did not even respect the royal office; confronted with those, Commynes, who was a man of experience but already an aged man, *se va retirando*.[62] The vision of the court we obtain from Costabile's letters suggests the precarious situation of a young prince badly advised and completely wrapped up in *una frotta* of fiery young men eager to fight, impulsive and addicted to the pleasures of jousting and violent games:

> Aveva una frota de soi gientilhomeni gioveni intorno, cun li quali tanto dimestamente burlava che me pareva una cossa da farse li homeni sciavi et semtia [without] alcuno rispeto per sua Magistà exponerse ad ogni gran periculo multe volte...[63]

The king, in the midst of a circle which made of him a *schiavo* (slave), was losing even his dignity and majesty. This striking image is to be found in the Italian correspondence, it is also one of the most remarkable images in the *Mémoires*.[64] Indeed Commynes's experience was made of a stuff into which the mutability and precariousness of princes was woven. The situation of June 1495 to which the memorialist devoted great attention was for him a perfect illustration of these moments of crisis during which the prince was staking his all. Princes, like the duke of Ferrara, who make a point of jeopardising neither their person nor their State are able to overcome such crises.[65] This corresponds

---

[61] A. Costabile to Ercole, 15 June 1495 (2) (ASMo, ASE, Amb., Francia, b. 1).

[62] Se adatariano le cosse, masimamente avendose questo amicho, el quale va a bono camino, et non per altro, se non perché li pare che le cosse del Re andariano melgio cusì, recordando a Vostra Excellentia che già ave prencipio asai et è giamato dal Re in tutte queste cosse, ma lui se va retirando, perché in questa corte li camberlani fano el tuto, et non li voriano vedere niuno... (A. Costabile to Ercole, 16 June 1495 (ASMo, ASE, Amb., Francia, b. 1).

[63] A. Costabile to Ercole, 20 June 1495 (ASMo, ASE, Francia, b. 1). Commynes noted in his *Mémoires* this generation gap between *gioveni* and *antiqui* or *vecchi* and expressed his reluctance concerning the risky initiatives of the *gioveni*. For a study of this conflict in another context, see R.C. Trexler, *Public Life in Renaissance Florence* (New York, 1980), 387-8.

[64] J. Blanchard, 'L'histoire commynienne: pragmatique et mémoire dans l'ordre politique', *Annales: Economies, Sociétés, Civilisations* (1991), 1071-105.

[65] *Mémoires*, vol. 1, 60, 108, 121, 250; vol. 2, 10, 242; this was Louis XI's point of view, who estoit si heureux ('lucky') en tous ses affaires, tant qu'il sembloit que toutes choses

to an entirely Italian definition of wisdom which may run counter to a certain conception of honour, as illustrated by the tournaments and other violent and disorderly games which were a training for war, and which Commynes and Costabile equally denounced to the court as vain and dangerous. These had been the memorialist's convictions for long; they were decisively strengthened during the spring of 1495 when, returning from his mission in Venice he discovered the pitiful scene of a king being manipulated by his entourage, sharing the pleasures of his young friends without discretion, and, in a way, abdicating his authority.

Thus in the correspondence which we have just discovered, it was the main ideology of the *Mémoires* which was already foreshadowed. Through the common interests of Commynes and Ferrara, we can see how deep was the influence of Italy upon Commynes. Italy certainly was for him an incomparable field of experience. There Commynes was initiated or confirmed in his opinions about politics. His political consciousness and ideas were elaborated there through his encounters with the strong personalities he met and his observation of the balance of power which was developing there. This Italy of 1495 to which he devoted a large part of his *Mémoires* was unquestionably an intense moment in his experience. It had a great impact on his behaviour, his diplomatic practice and even his language, and forged a new and original political vision at the dawn of modern times. It is no longer possible to be unaware of the influence of Italy on political or literary activities, and particularly on the making of Commynes' thought and on the composition of the *Mémoires*. This forgotten episode of the relationships between Commynes and Ferrara appears as manifest proof of that influence.

---

allassent à son plaisir; mais aussi son sens aydoit bien à luy faire venir ceste heur, car il ne mectoit riens en hazard et ne vouloit pour riens les batailles: aussy ceste-cy n'estoit point de son commandement. (*Mémoires*, vol. 2, 277) ; see also *Mémoires*, vol. 1, 121: Par quoy on doit bien craindre de se mectre au hazard d'une bataille qui n'y est contrainct et, si force est que on y vienne, mectre avant le coup toutes les doubtes dont on se peult adviser.

The Roman barons and the French descent into Italy

Christine Shaw

To those planning and making preparations for the French descent into Italy, and to those preparing to oppose it, securing the services of the Roman barons appeared to be of prime importance. As *condottieri*, as the possessors of estates well-endowed with fortresses which encircled Rome and extended down to the Neapolitan border, and as leaders of the Guelf and Ghibelline factions in Rome and the surrounding provinces of the Papal States, the barons, it was believed, held the keys to the defence not only of Rome but of the kingdom of Naples as well. They and their estates could constitute either forward bastions of defence for the kingdom, or crucial stepping-stones to ease the advance of the French. Both sides considered that the support of one or other of the two leading clans, the Orsini or the Colonna, was also an essential instrument in their efforts to secure the adherence of the pope. The barons, well aware of the value placed on their services, were able to command large and valuable *condotte*, but they had to make careful political calculations about the risks they would run if war came with the French to the region around Rome.

Even before he became troubled by serious anxiety about the prospect of a French invasion of his kingdom, Ferrante, confronted by the continuing hostility of Pope Innocent VIII after the end of the Barons' War in 1486, had aimed to gather at least the leading Roman barons into his service. His primary concern was to have first call on Virginio Orsini, one of the two most senior *condottieri* in his family, and holder of far more extensive estates than his cousin and rival, Niccolo Orsini da Pitigliano.[1] Virginio had been in Ferrante's pay, as governor-general of the league of Florence, Milan and Naples formed in 1485 to support Ferrante in the Barons' War. This *condotta* had been renewed,

---

[1] For the rivalry between Virginio and Niccolo, see Christine Shaw, 'Lorenzo de' Medici and Niccolo Orsini', in *Lorenzo de' Medici*: Studi, ed. Gian Carlo Garfagnini (Florence, 1992), 257-79.

with some difficulty, in 1487, but by 1489 its rationale had all but disappeared. Despite increasingly close personal and political links with Lorenzo de' Medici, Virginio could not hope to obtain the size of *condotta* he desired from Florence alone, so he was ready to accept one from Ferrante, with the title of Captain General. Even before this was concluded, Ferrante had wanted Virginio to come to his lands in the Papal States 'to curb the insolence of the pope'.[2] The following year, Ferrante took on the two up-and-coming *condottieri* of the Colonna family, the cousins Prospero and Fabrizio; some diplomacy was needed to get them to agree to be under Virginio's command and Virginio to accept them. Other *condottieri* had to be dismissed so that Ferrante could afford to pay the Colonna.

If Ferrante felt more secure with both Orsini and Colonna in his service, Innocent gave no indication he felt threatened; his reconciliation with the king in early 1492 was not prompted by fears that the barons would be used against him. As Innocent lay dying later that year, and Ferrante ordered Virginio, Prospero and Fabrizio to move to Rome, there were fears that the king wanted to force the cardinals to elect a successor of his choice, but the barons had been instructed to act with discretion. Ferrante hoped to influence the College of Cardinals by winning their goodwill, sending the barons to help keep order in Rome, and to be at the command of the College. Virginio and the Colonna declared they were ready, if need be, to defend the liberty of the Church with their lands and their lives.[3] When Virginio went before the College to tell them of his commission from the king, he added, on his own behalf, 'that he and all the Orsini would behave as good and faithful subjects of Holy Church, and were ready to risk their lives and their estates for its state and liberty, out of respect for their homeland; and because the House of Orsini had received countless benefits from the Church, they were bound to do this, without regard for any others.'[4]

The new pope, Alexander VI, was not convinced. When Virginio bought Anguillara and Cerveteri from Franceschetto Cibo, the son of Innocent VIII, only a few weeks after Alexander's election, the new pope saw in this transaction a deliberate attempt by Ferrante to increase the already considerable power of his commander in the area north of Rome. In fact, Ferrante was almost certainly not concerned in arranging this transaction at all, but Alexander refused to accept his protestations. By harping on Virginio's connections with the king, the pope turned the purchase of these lands into the basis of a

---

[2] Florence, Archivio di Stato [hereafter ASF], Otto di Pratica, Responsive, b. 6, c. 439: Piero Vittorini, 19 June 1489, Naples.

[3] ASF, Otto di Pratica, Responsive, b. 8, c. 380: Filippo Valori, 26 July 1492, Rome.

[4] Johannes Burckhardt, *Diarium sive rerum urbanarum commentarii* (1483-1506), ed. L. Thuasne, 3 vols (Paris, 1883-5), vol. 2, 575-6: Filippo Valori to Otto di Pratica of Florence, 1 Aug. 1492, Rome.

diplomatic crisis, involving all the major states of Italy. Ferrante and Piero de' Medici were in league to exalt the power of the Roman barons so that they could bend the pope to their will, Alexander claimed.[5] When he negotiated with Venice and Milan about forming a new league, he said, it was the need for security against the barons that was constraining him to do so.[6] As Virginio was on good terms with the Colonna, and both were in Ferrante's pay, he maintained that he felt besieged in Rome.[7] He began to try to win over the Colonna, offering to make Prospero captain of the Church, and to give the rich abbey of Subiaco to a member of the family, according to Prospero himself.[8] He also wrote to Charles VIII, inviting him to invade the kingdom of Naples.

As the threat of a French invasion gathered substance, Ferrante became more concerned about the hostility of the pope and did much to help bring about a settlement of the dispute over Anguillara and Cerveteri in August 1493. Even when this problem had been disposed of, he remained anxious that Alexander was trying to win over the Colonna, and he summoned Prospero and Fabrizio Colonna and Antonello Savelli, their close ally and a *condottiere* of growing reputation, to Naples. There were contradictory reports on the frame of mind in which they returned from Naples. One correspondent wrote to Ludovico Sforza that they were not too happy, while a Mantuan agent told Francesco Gonzaga that they had been made much of by the king and were well content with him.[9] A month later, the Mantuan agent gave a reason to substantiate his account. Fabrizio Colonna, he wrote, had been given a subvention by the king to improve his fortifications at Marino, the first major fortress on the road to Naples from Rome, and sent him munitions; Antonello Savelli was receiving similar help for Albano, and Giuliano della Rovere, Cardinal San Pietro ad Vincula, for Ostia and Grottaferrata.[10] The news of such preparations would have strengthened the hand of Cardinal Ascanio Sforza, as he urged on Alexander the advantages he could derive from a French invasion: the punishment of Virginio Orsini and San Pietro ad Vincula,[11] the opportunity to endow his family with the barons' lands.

---

[5] Paolo Negri, 'Studi dulla crisi italiana alla fine del secolo XV', *Archivio Storico Lombardo*, 51 (1924), 122: Stefano Taverna to Lodovico Sforza, 16 Feb. 1493, Rome.

[6] Burckhardt, *Diarium*, ed. Thuasne, vol. 2, p. 639: Filippo Valori to Otto di Pratica of Florence, 9 Mar. 1493, Rome.

[7] ASF, Otto di Pratica, Responsive, b. 9, c. 301: Filippo Valori, 19 March 1493, Rome.

[8] Rome, Archivio Capitolino, Archivio Orsini, series I [hereafter AOrsini], b. 102, c. 601: Bartolomeo da Bracciano to Virginio Orsini, received 30 Apr. 1493, Rome.

[9] Milan, Archivio di Stato, Sforzesco Potenze Estere [hereafter ASMi, SPE], Roma, b. 107: Bartolomeo Saliceto to Lodovico Sforza, 14 Nov. 1493, 'Balnea Regio'; Mantua, Archivio di Stato, Archivio Gonzaga [hereafter ASMa, AG], b. 849, c. 345: Gianlucido Cattaneo to Francesco Gonzaga, 6 Nov. 1493, Rome.

[10] ASMa, AG, b. 849, cc. 348-9: Gianlucido Cattaneo to Francesco Gonzaga, 4 Dec. 1493, Rome.

[11] For the quarrel between Alexander and San Pietro ad Vincula, see Christine Shaw, *Julius II: The Warrior Pope* (Oxford, 1993), 81-92.

One of the last letters Ferrante dictated before his death expressed his anxiety about the effect this advice might have on the pope.[12]

Ferrante's death made both the Colonna and the Orsini take stock of their position. Ferrante had been a master to whom it had been difficult to feel loyal; his son Alfonso was even harder to trust. He had had a reputation for being generous to his soldiers, and for being popular with them, but his record as a military commander was chequered, and included at least one episode, in 1486 during the Barons' War, when he had deserted his men near Rome and fled north to take refuge at Pitigliano. His flight had been precipitated by the reconciliation of one branch of the Orsini, the Monterotondo, to the pope, but the others had remained loyal to the league of Florence, Milan and Naples, and it had been the Orsini who rescued his troops after he deserted them. More worrying, perhaps, than the doubts this episode must have raised in the minds of the Orsini as to Alfonso's qualities as a commander, was his deserved reputation for hostility to the barons of the kingdom of Naples. His declared intention of cutting the barons down to size had been one of the major causes of the revolt by the Sanseverino and their allies in 1485. Both the Orsini and the Colonna held estates in the kingdom.

On 4 February 1494 several members of the Orsini family (Cardinal Gianbattista, Virginio, Niccolo da Pitigliano, Giulio, Roberto, Archbishop of Florence and Organtino) spent all day together at an inn between Monterotondo and Fiano, discussing what their attitude to Alfonso should be. It was thought that Virginio and the Cardinal were trying to persuade Niccolo, who had held a *condotta* from the pope, to serve Alfonso, while he insisted he would prefer to serve either Florence or Venice. Niccolo was said to be included in a general obligation entered into by the Orsini after the Barons' War, that they would not attack Ferrante and would side with him when he was under attack; Niccolo maintained that he was not obliged to serve in person, but only that his estates in Naples (he was count of Nola) should not be used against the king.[13] Before Ferrante's death, the Neapolitan ambassadors in Rome had put a different interpretation on this agreement with the king - they had told the pope that all the Orsini, if the French moved against the kingdom of Naples, were obliged to take up arms for the king, an obligation specified in the terms by which they held their lands there.[14] While most of the Orsini decided to continue to support the Aragonese dynasty of Naples, the Colonna were deciding they would not do so. Their obligation to serve Naples expired on the death of Ferrante, as Ascanio Sforza was quick to remind Prospero Colonna. Prospero replied that

---

[12] ASMi, SPE, Roma, b. 108: Ascanio to Lodovico, 6 Jan. 1494, Rome; *Codice Aragonese*, ed. Francesco Trinchera, 2 vols, (Naples, 1866-70), vol. 2, ii, 421-31: Ferrante to Luigi de' Paladini, 17 Jan. 1494, Naples.

[13] ASMi, SPE, Roma, b. 108: Stefano Taverna to Lodovico Sforza, 5 Feb. 1494, Rome.

[14] ASMi, SPE, Roma, b. 108: Stefano Taverna to Lodovico Sforza, 6 Jan. 1494, Rome.

they were glad to be free of their commitment to Naples, and to be able to accept other offers without danger to their honour or their property.[15]

The Colonna were in demand, especially Prospero. Alexander had been angling for them for several months, although his commitment to spending money on them which might be used to pay a *condotta* for his son, the duke of Gandia, was considered by Ascanio to be uncertain. The French, too, had weighed the advantages of hiring them. Alfonso was said to be ready to do anything to get them; but the Sforza were also quite determined to have Prospero at least, preferably sharing his *condotta* with Alexander. The Colonna, exploiting the fact that they were in such demand, pitched their terms high: too high, Ascanio felt, worrying that they would put Alexander off the idea of joining in the *condotta* for Prospero. Ascanio placed great emphasis on Prospero's position as head of his family, and head of his faction: if they had Prospero in their service, both Ascanio and Alexander could feel safe in Rome, he argued. If Alexander did not have any of the major Roman barons in his service, Ascanio feared, he might be tempted to swing over to support Alfonso. The pope, however, was alert to the advantages of having the head of the Colonna faction in his service, and a joint papal-Milanese *condotta* for Prospero was agreed in early March 1494.[16]

There was a delay in the despatch of the mandate for the *condotta* from Milan, and the Milanese ambassador in Rome spelled out to Lodovico the importance of not allowing Prospero to be tempted away by Alfonso. Nothing was more crucial, he argued, particularly as Alexander seemed to be coming to terms with Alfonso and Florence. If Alfonso gave a *condotta* to Prospero, alone, or jointly with the pope, the king would become master of Rome, there would be an end to all hopes of winning back the pope, and Cardinal San Pietro ad Vincula could return safely to Rome, rendering Ascanio's position untenable. If Alfonso won Prospero, the king and his Florentine allies would be assured of influence over this and future popes; if Milan had Prospero, the king and Florence could never be certain of the pope.[17] Lodovico sent the mandate, but, as so often, money was not so readily available. In the end, Ascanio paid Prospero's *prestanza*, together with an additional 2,000 ducats from his own resources. Lodovico was waiting for money from France to pay the Milanese share; he had told Charles that Prospero had been hired for France. Charles congratulated him on having contrived so cleverly to have the pope pick up half of the bill.[18] Prospero himself did not know of this arrangement. As far as he was concerned, his *condotta* was with Milan.

Ascanio had even more need than before of Prospero's support, because by the end of March Alexander had openly sided with Alfonso. Alfonso had

---

[15] ASMi, SPE, Roma, b. 108: Ascanio Sforza to Lodovico Sforza, 28 Jan. 1494, Rome.

[16] ASMi, SPE, Roma, b. 108: Stefano Taverna to Lodovico Sforza, 14 Feb. 1494, Rome; Ascanio to Lodovico, 1 Mar. 1494, Rome; Stefano Taverna to Lodovico, 2 Mar. 1494, Rome.

[17] ASMi, SPE, Roma, b. 108: Stefano Taverna to Lodovico Sforza, 18 Mar. 1494, Rome.

[18] ASMi, SPE, b. 552, Carlo Barbiano to Lodovico Sforza, 3 Mar. 1494, 'Rhoane'.

been very anxious to be invested with the kingdom by Alexander, and the pope tried to exploit this by setting a very high price, both financially - he wanted payment for the investiture of up to 200,000 ducats, and an annual census of nearly 50,000 ducats - and in endowments for his children: for Juan, duke of Gandia, alone he wanted one of the two major baronial estates of Naples, the principate of Salerno or that of Bisignano. After hard bargaining, he was persuaded to make more reasonable terms, but still succeeded in gaining lands, titles, offices and benefices for three sons. In return Alfonso secured the investiture, and agreement that one of Alexander's sons, Jofrè, whose marriage to Alfonso's illegitimate daughter Sancia had been arranged in July 1493, should settle with his bride in Naples.

Virginio Orsini, now Great Constable of Naples, had been one of those negotiating with the pope for Alfonso, who had been concerned that Virginio should not be too generous in making offers on his behalf.[19] In the following months, Virginio would be an important intermediary between the pope and the king, and Alexander would become anxious to keep him in the Papal States, assigning him a central role in plans for the defence of Rome. He was also one of several envoys sent repeatedly to Ostia on behalf of the king, to try to persuade the reluctant Cardinal San Pietro ad Vincula to return to Rome. A guarantee of the cardinal's safety had been one of the terms agreed between the pope and the king, although the pope's promise that no reprisals would be taken against Vincula had been conditional on his behaving as a good cardinal should.[20] Vincula was justifiably reluctant to put himself in Alexander's power, and chose instead to depart for France, leaving his fortresses at Ostia and Grottaferrata in the custody of Fabrizio Colonna.

While the French and the Sforza had been suggesting Vincula should go to France for some time, he appears to have chosen his moment to leave without consulting them.[21] It left Ascanio Sforza and Prospero Colonna in a difficult position, and the Orsini were quick to fuel the pope's suspicions against them. Alexander told Virginio's son, Carlo, that he was sure Ascanio and Prospero were behind Vincula's flight, and said he looked to Alfonso and the Orsini for help. He wanted Virginio, Niccolo and Giulio Orsini to come to Rome, and ordered Carlo to stay and to bring his troops into the city.[22] Niccolo and Giulio came quickly, and after a long discussion with Alexander, it was decided troops should be sent under their command to take Ostia.

Ascanio and Ludovico Sforza were in a quandary. Vincula had sent to Prospero to say he was leaving his lands in the custody of the Colonna, who

---

[19] AOrsini, b. 102, c. 696: Antonello Sinibaldo and Marco to Virginio Orsini, 5 Mar. 1494, Naples.

[20] Ut bonum cardinalem decet: agreement between Alexander and Alfonso, 28 Mar. 1494, in Peter de Roo, *Materials for a history of Pope Alexander VI, his relatives and his times*, 5 vols. (Bruges, 1924), vol. 4, 505.

[21] For the lead-up to his departure, see Shaw, *Julius II*, 92-4.

[22] AOrsini, b. 102, c.745: Angelo Leonino and Carlo Orsini to Virginio Orsini, 24 Apr. 1494, Rome.

were to be guided by Ascanio's orders concerning them.[23] The Sforza did not consider the time was yet ripe for Ascanio openly to break with the pope by leaving Rome without permission, or for the *condottieri* they were recruiting in the Papal States openly to act in support of French interests. They could not, therefore, encourage the Colonna to defy the pope at this juncture. The best Ludovico could suggest was that Fabrizio be given a *condotta* by the pope and Milan, and that if Alexander was urged by Alfonso or Virginio to attack Fabrizio, he should be warned that Fabrizio was holding the fortresses on behalf of one who had gone to serve the king of France, and that it would be unwise for Alexander to antagonize Charles, or, by weakening the Colonna, to make the Orsini masters of Rome.[24]

Prospero Colonna, who was, after all, in the service of the pope, was ordered to join the troops laying siege to Ostia. At first he agreed, but then he refused, saying that he did not want to serve under Niccolo Orsini. At length he go, undertaking to try to persuade Fabrizio to surrender Ostia and Grottaferrata. Fabrizio was not so close to the Sforza as Prospero was; his close connection with San Pietro ad Vincula (he and Vincula's brother, Giovanni della Rovere, had married sisters, the daughters of Federico da Montefeltro, duke of Urbino) was enough in itself to make him slightly suspect in their eyes. The Sforza had been debating for months whether or not to offer him a *condotta*, but at the time of the Ostia crisis, Fabrizio was still in the service of Alfonso. He was not ready to provoke an attack on his lands by the pope for the sake of keeping Ostia at the disposal of the French, but he was ready to bargain hard to retain Grottaferrata, which was in the middle of his own lands. Alexander was eventually brought to agree to this, and Prospero and Fabrizio negotiated the surrender of Ostia by Vincula's castellan to the pope on 23 May. Ludovico commented to Ascanio that he was sure that the Colonna had done what they had to secure themselves and their friends and he could not blame them for this, but he had to remark that Ostia had been well-supplied to withstand a siege and French preparations to send reinforcements were well under way: the loss of Ostia would be a setback for the French expedition.[25]

Even before the surrender of Ostia, Ascanio and Ludovico had been trying to resolve the problem of how they could hold on to the *condottieri* they had been hiring in the Papal States for themselves and for France, when there was still no sign that the French would be coming to Italy that year. Ascanio, Ludovico and the French were all alive to the benefits of having at their disposal a number of barons with estates that were contiguous, or at least close enough so that they could help one another if necessary, and Ludovico stressed the

---

[23] ASMi, SPE, Roma, b.109: Ascanio to Lodovico, 24 Apr. 1494, Rome.
[24] ASMi, SPE, Roma, b. 109: Lodovico Sforza to Stefano Taverna, 1 May 1494, Vigevano.
[25] ASMi, SPE, Roma, b. 110: Lodovico to Ascanio, ? June 1494

importance of choosing those with estates strong enough to be capable of putting up some resistance to an attack by Alexander or Alfonso. If the pope and king took hostages from the barons, or some other guarantee that they would not serve the king of France, the *condotte* would be useless.[26] Ascanio, mindful of his own position, was more aware than was his brother of the dilemma confronting the barons, particularly Prospero Colonna and Antonello Savelli, whose *condotte* were with the pope as well as Milan. Prospero would not be pleased, Ascanio said, when he learned that the Milanese portion of his *condotta* was just a front and that really he was in the employment of France.[27] Ludovico professed to appreciate the problem, but his prime anxiety was that whoever might nominally be the employer of Prospero and Antonello, the French should pay for them. Even if they were to be paid by France, Ascanio replied, the *condottieri* wanted their *condotte* to be in the name of Milan. In his negotiations with Fabrizio Colonna, Fabrizio had expressly said that he wanted his estates to be under the protection of Milan. Ludovico had demurred, but Ascanio was sure they could not have Fabrizio unless they promised him protection. Prospero, too, had been speaking to Ascanio of his need for protection if he was to break with the pope. They could not expect the barons to risk their estates without this insurance.[28] In fact, none of the barons was willing to act openly in support of France until the French fleet was off the shores of the Papal States and the French army was approaching; and neither the French nor Ludovico were willing to pay out much money until the barons were prepared to declare themselves.

After Ascanio finally left Rome at the end of June, taking refuge on the lands of the Colonna and their allies to the south of the city, Alexander increased the pressure on the Colonna to declare their allegiance. He wanted to have Prospero either in his service alone, or to share his *condotta* with Alfonso; Prospero kept away from Rome, ignoring Alexander's summonses to come to see him. Fabrizio's position was, in its way, as difficult as that of Prospero. He still held a *condotta* from Alfonso, and the king was ordering him to go to the kingdom to take his part in the preparations for defence. He and Prospero had evidently had long discussions about what he should do. He said he wanted to serve Milan and France, but did not want to show his hand before the French came. He would delay his departure for Naples for as long as possible, but if he had to leave before the French came, he would leave his lands in the Papal States in Prospero's hands; if Prospero were attacked, he would come to his defence. What they hoped to achieve, one way or another, was to force the pope

---

[26] ASMi, SPE, Roma, b. 109: Lodovico to Ascanio, 22 May 1494, Vigevano.
[27] ASMi, SPE, Roma, b. 109: Ascanio to Lodovico, 12 May 1494, Rome.
[28] ASMi, SPE, Roma, b. 109: Ascanio to Lodovico, 28 May 1494, Rome.

either to go over to join Milan and France, or at least to prevent him giving further help to Alfonso.[29]

Alexander, who had been persuaded that the French would not be coming to Italy that year, and that if they did come, he and Alfonso and Florence would have enough troops together to be more than a match for them, was inclined to attack the Colonna. It was said he wanted their estates for his children, although he claimed that Alfonso and Virginio were urging him on. Virginio Orsini favoured the idea of attacking them, but did not want to go to Naples to speak to the king about the matter, because he knew Alfonso did not. Alfonso still had hopes of keeping Fabrizio, and was keen to try to win over Prospero as well, so he was not willing to join an attack on their lands. Alexander was obliged to negotiate, and set out the terms he wanted: Cardinals Savelli and Colonna and Prospero and Fabrizio Colonna should pledge their estates and benefices as security that they would not use their estates against the pope or the king; Prospero Colonna and Antonello Savelli should serve the pope with his share of their troops under the joint *condotte* with Milan, though they would not have to serve in person; they could serve with the Milanese portion of their *condotte* against anyone except the pope; once they had raised their troops from their estates they could not return to them until the war was over; Fabrizio was to serve the king in person, and Cardinals Savelli and Colonna were to reside in Rome.[30] To gain time, the Colonna and Ascanio spun out the negotiations. By the beginning of August, Alexander had given up, and was again pressing Alfonso to attack, thinking he saw an opportunity to win the Colonna estates for his family at Alfonso's expense. The king, however, still nourished hopes of winning the Colonna over, and now had more pressing business in hand as the French army at last advanced into northern Italy. The Colonna were willing to bide their time until the French came nearer.

By mid-September, they were ready to move. Fabrizio had finally abandoned the pretence of serving Alfonso and accepted a *condotta* from France in early September.[31] On 18 September, Prospero, with French help, took Ostia by a trick, and occupied it for San Pietro ad Vincula. The move took Ascanio and Stefano Taverna, the Milanese ambassador, who were at Prospero's *castello* of Genazzano, by surprise. Nothing could be of greater help in advancing the French enterprise, they thought, but at the same time they were aware that nothing could be more disturbing to Alexander, and they were concerned that he would hold the Milanese responsible and take reprisals against them.[32] The pope was indeed dismayed by the news of the loss of Ostia, and talked of leaving Rome for Orvieto, but he was then persuaded that the French fleet

---

[29] ASMi, SPE, Roma, b. 110: Ascanio to Lodovico, 21 June 1494, Rome.
[30] ASMi, SPE, Roma, b. 110: Stefano Taverna to Lodovico, 11 July 1494, Rome.
[31] ASF, Otto di Pratica, Responsive, b. 10, c. 145: Antonio da Colle, 11 Sept. 1494, Rome.
[32] ASMi, SPE, Roma, b. 111: Stefano Taverna to Lodovico, 18 Sept. 1494, Genazzano.

would not be coming south that year, and determined to attack the supporters of France and Milan, above all the Colonna.

As soon as he had heard of the fall of Ostia, Alexander had summoned Virginio to Rome. Although Virginio was Great Constable of Naples and figured large in Alfonso's plans for the defence of his kingdom, Alexander appears to have felt that he had first claim on Virginio. In the note he made of points to discuss with Virginio before the meeting he had with Alfonso at Virginio's fortress of Vicovaro in mid-July, Alexander specified he wanted Virginio's troops to stay around Rome, and Virginio himself to be in Rome.[33] If he were to keep his ally, the king had little option but to try to adapt his plans to the pope's personal agenda. After the fall of Ostia, this meant attacking the Colonna, even though it hindered him from sending reinforcements to his son, Ferrandino, duke of Calabria, who was commanding the Neapolitan forces confronting the French and Milanese troops in the Romagna. For Alfonso himself, attacking the Colonna was not a high priority. He heard that they were short of money and dissatisfied with Ascanio, and he believed that if Alexander were not so anxious to have their lands for his own children, an agreement could be reached with the Colonna within days.[34]

Once the idea of a direct assault on Ostia had been rejected, Alfonso wanted Virginio to besiege Nettuno, a Colonna harbour on the coast which could be useful to the French, while Alexander wanted him to stay near Rome. Neither the king nor the pope stuck to any plan for long, however. While Alfonso dithered at Terracina, and Alexander dithered in Rome, Virginio became increasingly undecided and discontented himself. Meanwhile, Lodovico's support for Charles was wavering. In mid-November, he recalled the Milanese troops supporting the French in Tuscany and the Romagna, and instructed Ascanio to call off the Colonna:[35] even though Prospero and Fabrizio Colonna, with Antonello Savelli, were included in a list he had sent to his envoy to Charles of the *condottieri* he had hired for the French.[36]

By late November, Ascanio was anxious that if the unlooked-for success of the French continued, and Alexander were forced to come to terms with the king, his rival San Pietro ad Vincula would be triumphant; for his part, Alexander was pinning his hopes of extricating himself from his difficulties on

[33] Giuliano Gasca Queirazza, *Gli scritti autografi di Alessandro VI nell' 'Archivium Arcis'* (Torino 1959), 15-16.

[34] *Négociations diplomatiques de la France avec la Toscane*, ed. A. Desjardins and G. Canestrini, 6 vols (*Documents inédits sur l'histoire de France*, Paris, 1859-86), vol. 1, 464, 477: Filippo Valori to Piero de' Medici, 13, 20 Oct. 1494, Terracina.

[35] A. Segre, 'Lodovico Sforza, detto il Moro, e la Repubblica di Venezia dall'autunno 1494 alla primavera 1495', *Archivio Storico Lombardo*, ser. 3, 18 (1902), 293.

[36] ASMi, SPE, Roma, b. 554: Lodovico to Carlo Barbiano, 3 Oct. 1494, Vigevano.

Ascanio.[37] He began using Ascanio as an intermediary in negotiations with Charles, with the aim of inducing the king to pass peacefully through the Papal States. Ascanio arrived back in Rome for discussions with Alexander on 2 December. One of the assurances the pope wanted was that the Colonna would protect him if Charles attacked him.[38] Ascanio overplayed his hand: among the demands he made of Alexander was that he should have a personal veto over future creations of cardinals. On 10 December Alexander arrested him and Prospero Colonna, who had also come to Rome. Prospero was soon released, having agreed terms with Alexander for a joint *condotta* with him and Alfonso, and possibly with Milan too, though this would be kept secret.[39] Prospero was to induce Cardinal Giovanni Colonna to reside in Rome, and he was to go to Ostia and induce Fabrizio to surrender the fortress to the pope and accept the new *condotta*. He went to Ostia, but while he was there, on 25 December, Cardinal San Pietro ad Vincula arrived with some French troops. Vincula was under instructions from Charles to keep the Colonna in the service of France,[40] and this he did. That same day, Ascanio was released, at the insistence of Charles who was in the final stages of arranging his own entry into Rome, and the Duke of Calabria was forced to leave Rome, with the blessing of the pope, to make his way back to the kingdom of Naples.

While Alexander had been negotiating with Charles, the Orsini had made their own approaches to him. In late November, an Orsini envoy spoke to the king in Florence, trying to bring about a reconciliation between Charles and the Orsini, leading on to an agreement between Charles and Alfonso. This negotiation was not being kept from the knowledge of the pope, because the Orsini envoy sent a message from Charles to Alexander.[41] It may have been this man to whom Alexander was referring when he rebuked Cardinal Orsini for being too precipitate in sending 'that bishop'; by that time Alexander was holding talks with Ascanio, and an Orsini agent in Rome feared he was preparing to shift responsibility on to the Orsini for letting Alfonso down.[42] It was particularly difficult at this point to read Alexander's intentions, and it

---

[37] P. Negri, 'Le missioni di Pandolfo Collenuccio a Papa Alessandro VI (1494-1498)', *Archivio della R. Società Romana di Storia Patria*, 33 (1910), 429-30: Pandolfo Collenuccio to Ercole d'Este, 30 Nov. 1494, Rome.

[38] Queirazza, *Gli scritti autografi*, 30-31.

[39] Alexander's draft terms show that he wanted the Colonna condotta to be paid one-third by him, one-third by Alfonso and one-third by Milan, with Milan's participation being kept secret. The terms as announced in consistory on 18 December, according to Sanudo, were that Alfonso should pay two-thirds and Alexander one-third: Queirazza, *Gli scritti autografi*, 16-18; Marino Sanudo, *La spedizione di Carlo VIII in Italia*, ed. Rinaldo Fulin (Venice, 1873), 154-5.

[40] ASMi, SPE, Roma, b. 111: Stefano Taverna to Lodovico, 22 Dec. 1494, Bracciano.

[41] AOrsini, b. 102, c. 619: ? (signature illegible) to Virginio Orsini, 27 Nov. 1494, Florence.

[42] AOrsini, b. 102, c. 640: Angelo Leonino to Virginio Orsini, 4 Dec. 1494, Rome.

would have been easy for the Orsini to give credence to the idea that he would be prepared to sacrifice them to help save himself. They would also know - few were in a better position than Virginio to know - how irresolute Alfonso was. He had been contemplating abandoning his kingdom for months, gathering his valuables together to take with him, and leaving his troops unpaid. That Virginio should give instructions, only a day or so after he would have received the report from his agent in Rome, that Charles should be allowed to pass through his lands unopposed and that the French should be given supplies from them, was not, in the circumstances, surprising. This action has often been condemned, but to have done anything else would in fact have been quixotic. If he had ordered his vassals to resist the advance of the French, he would have risked bringing about the deaths of many of his men and their families, and the destruction of their property and his own, while it was very unlikely that he would have inspired either Alexander or Alfonso to heroic resistance in their turn. He decided to save his men and his property in the Papal States, and went to fulfil his obligations to Alfonso by going to serve him in person at the head of his troops, leaving his son Carlo to see his instructions were carried out. The other Orsini followed his example, and their estates, too, were to be at the disposal of the French.

The French were glad of the supplies they received from the Orsini lands, and Charles made Virginio's castle at Bracciano his base for several days, but it could not be argued that the action of the Orsini made a significant difference to the outcome of the French invasion of Naples. Alfonso's subjects were not ready to sacrifice themselves for him and he was not prepared to stay to confront the French. After Alfonso abdicated in favour of his son Ferrandino and fled to Sicily, the withdrawal of Virginio and Niccolo Orsini to Niccolo's county of Nola, in the last desperate days of Ferrandino's attempt to rally some resistance to the French in February 1495, was scarcely heroic. Nevertheless, according to their own account, they had waited until they saw that Ferrandino's cause was hopeless, and had been released from his service before they approached the French.[43] Taken prisoner by the French, they were promised a pardon, but Charles refused to let them go, in case they were taken into service by the new league that was being formed against him.

Prospero Colonna was one of those who stood surety for the safety of the Orsini when they came to Naples. There had been so little fighting that the Colonna had not had much opportunity to prove their worth as *condottieri* to the French, after all the trouble that had been taken to hire them. They had helped keep Alfonso and Alexander anxious and undecided in the autumn, and had helped to take Ostia for the French, but they had not been called upon to do much else. Prospero took advantage of the passage of the French army from

---

[43] Segre, 'Lodovico Sforza', *Archivio Storico Lombardo*, ser. 3, 20 (1903), 407-8.

Rome to the Neapolitan border to turn French troops and artillery against the castles of the Conti, factional rivals with whom he had a dispute over some lands, and was given the captured territories by the king. After that, there had been little fighting in which he and Fabrizio could show their mettle.

It is somewhat ironic, after all the planning and the plotting and the negotiations that had gone on among the Sforza and the pope, the French and the Aragonese kings of Naples, to secure the services of the Colonna and the Orsini, how little, in the end, the barons were called upon to do. But this is just one element of the greater irony of how, after all the years of planning and anticipation of the French invasion, Charles was able, with such ease, to ride through Italy to enforce his claim to the kingdom of Naples.

Castles and cannon in the Naples campaign of 1494-95

Simon Pepper

The campaign of 1494-95 which took the French army of Charles VIII to Naples and back to the battlefields of Fornovo and Novara has long been seen as a watershed in military as well as in European history. Not least amongst the military changes was the impact made on Italian fortifications by the improved French artillery on its first major expedition south of the Alps, and the revolution in the speed and tactics of siege warfare which these events were seen to have highlighted. Francesco Guicciardini was not the only near contemporary author to have noted the watershed, but his analysis has been so frequently quoted that it has assumed enormous authority. The technical superiority of the new weapons, the skills of the gunners and the logistical efficiency of the French siege train all feature in one of the best known of Guicciardini's passages:

> The French brought a much handier engine made of brass, called Cannon, which they charged with heavy, iron balls, smaller without comparison than those of stone made use of hitherto, and drove them on carriages with horses, not with oxen, as was the custom in Italy; and they were attended by such clever men, and on such instruments appointed for the purpose that they almost ever kept pace with the army. They were planted against the walls of a town with such speed, the space between each shot was so little, and the balls flew so quick, and were impelled with such force, that as much execution was done in a few hours, as formerly, in Italy, in the like number of days. These, rather diabolical than human instruments, were used not only in sieges, but also in the field, and were mixed with others of a smaller size. Such artillery rendered Charles's army very formidable to all Italy.[1]

Paolo Giovio described the French siege train as it passed through Rome in January 1495, giving further details of the guns themselves which brought up the rear of the procession. Controlled by riders using voice commands as well

---

[1] Francesco Guicciardini, *The History of Italy*, trans. Chevalier Austin Parke Goddard (London, 1754), vol.1, 148-9.

as harness, the horse teams were driven fast enough to keep pace with marching cavalry.

> Above all what caused astonishment and impressed everyone was more than thirty-six guns on carriages, which were drawn by horses at incredible speed over both level and uneven ground. The biggest of these, eight feet in length and 6,000 pounds of bronze in weight, were called cannon and threw an iron ball as big as a man's head. After the cannon came the culverins, half as long again but with a smaller barrel and ball. The falcons followed - some bigger than others but in the same proportions [as the culverins] - the smallest of which threw a ball the size of an apple or orange.[2]

The improvements in late fifteenth century French artillery turned on the use of iron cannon balls, which allowed smaller projectiles to achieve the same destructive impact as much larger stone shot, which in turn allowed the size and weight of the guns themselves to be reduced. The introduction of trunnions - lugs cast into the barrel at the point of balance - allowed the French artillerists to mount their guns permanently on wheeled carriages from which they could be brought quickly into action, trained easily on to different targets, and elevated or depressed about the point of balance.[3] It is tempting to over-emphasise the novelty[4] as well as the mobility and efficiency of the modernised French artillery, but there can be little doubt about the many improvements that it offered over the previous generation of immensely heavy and often gigantic bombards, which fired stone shot from flatbed mountings, needed to be transported (sometimes in two or three separate parts) on large carts, and were not easily moved once placed on the ground in their firing position. However, to evaluate the performance of the artillery in 1494-95 it is necessary to ask some basic questions about the operations of the *anno terribile*. What was the French strategy for the transport and use of artillery? How many guns did Charles VIII bring south for the Naples campaign? Were they as effective and as fast-moving as the contemporary historians would have us believe? What of

---

[2] Paolo Giovio, *Dell'Istoria del suo tempo di Mons. Paolo Giovio da Como, Vescovo de Nocera* (tradotta per M. Lodovico Domenichi, Firenze, 1555), 54-5. Author's translation into English. Illustrations of the French artillery bands show each pair of horses with a rider astride the horse (like 19th century field artillery) and Giovio points out that 'i cavalli postivi sotto incitati dalle sforze & dalle voci...'

[3] Illustrations of pre-1490s artillery do show other guns mounted on two-wheeled carts, which could of course be used in action in certain circumstances. But the trunnion suspension system allowed the gun trail to be set firmly on the ground where it could be traversed left and right, while the gun itself could be fine-tuned for elevation (which might have to be done between each shot as a heavy gun dug itself into the ground with the movement of the recoil). The French guns, we are told, were kept loaded on the march.

[4] M.E. Mallett and J.R. Hale, *The Military Organisation of a Renaissance State: Venice c.1400 to 1617* (Cambridge, 1984), 83-5 show that prior to the French invasion Venice was also involved in the development of lighter, more mobile guns in the 1480s and early 1490s, often employing foreign (implicitly northern artillery experts for this purpose), and experimenting *inter alia* with shrapnel balls.

their targets, the fortresses? Were these forts as old-fashioned and inadequate as a simple reading of standard accounts would suggest? So much has been based on the relatively brief analysis of Guicciardini and the figures suggested in Giovio's description that a review of these aspects of the campaign is overdue.

This paper sets out to provide such a review within a narrative of the French march to Naples, the minor sieges *en route*, and the two important sieges of Naples in 1495. Sometimes narrative can obscure analysis. The reader is urged to recall the questions set out in the previous paragraph and - to anticipate my conclusions - to retain at all times a healthy scepticism for the more strident claims advanced for new weapon technology.

I

The original French plan was based on a sea-borne campaign against Naples. The French fleet would operate from Genoa, which had been held by Ludovico Sforza since 1487 and had been conceded by him to France as a harbour in 1493. From here the fleet would carry much of the army and its siege artillery most of the way towards the objectives in southern Italy.[5] Vestiges of this original scheme survived in the actual operations of 1494-95, although the troop strengths were increased very considerably as the invasion approached.[6] Even with additional vessels chartered from Genoa the carrying capacity of the fleet available to the French would probably have proved insufficient for an invasion which, by the summer of 1494, seemed likely to meet determined resistance.[7]

Large sections of the walls of Naples had been refortified since 1484, and the Castel Nuovo, the principal stronghold in the capital, had been extensively strengthened throughout the second half of the 15th century.[8] Work began in

---

[5] Commines, *The Memoirs of Philip de Commines, Lord of Argenton* (ed. Scoble, 2 vols, London, 1855-56), vol. 2, bk 7, cap. 5.

[6] Ferdinand Lot, *Recherches sur les effectifs des armées françaises* (Paris, 1962), 16.

[7] H-Francois Delaborde, *L'Expédition de Charles VIII en Italie. Histoire diplomatique et militaire* (Paris, 1888), 327 for the provision of 50 galleys, 24 round ships (*navires*) and 12 galions from various ports in the north as well as the Mediterranean.

[8] Most of the Eastern section had been rebuilt between 1484 and 1488 in solid masonry between 5 and 7 metres thick, with semi-circular towers, although 'innocent of those deep ravelins, high scarps and vaulted casemates in the design of which Alfonso's later architects were to be innovators'. For the walls see: George L. Hersey, *Alfonso II and the Artistic Renewal of Naples 1485-1495*, New Haven and London, 1969, chapters 4 and 6, especially 48; L. De la Ville sur-Yllon, 'Le mura e le porte di Napoli', *Napoli Nobilissima*, 12 (1903), 49-56; and Giovanni Sepe, *La Murazione aragonese di Napoli. Studi di restituzione* (Naples, 1942); and most recently Michael S. A. Dechert, 'The Military Architecture of Francesco di Giorgio in Southern Italy', *Journal of the Society of Architectural Historians*, 49, 2 (June 1990), 161-80 which also contains interesting material on the Calabrian and Puglian schemes. An excellent recent overview is by Nicholas Adams, 'L'architettura militare di Francesco di Giorgio', in Francesco Paolo Fiore and Manfredo Tafuri (eds.), *Francesco di Giorgio*

September 1494 on a new fortress at Baia to defend the port and bay of Pozzuoli, a potential invasion site just to the west of Naples.[9] From late 1492 Don Cesare, the second of King Ferrante I's eight natural sons, had been coordinating the refurbishment of the southern fortresses against the Turkish threat. In August 1494 this programme was accelerated in Calabria and Puglia, as well as in the northern approaches where Alfonso II himself took charge of preparations, indicating a policy of defence in considerable depth throughout the *Regno*.[10] It was clear by the summer of 1494 that any French armada would be opposed by a substantial Aragonese naval force which represented a real threat to an operation relying too heavily on fleet transport.

In the event, it was the Aragonese who made the first moves in an aggressive strategy which recalled the 'forward' defence policy of Alfonso I in the middle years of the century.[11] An Aragonese land force was despatched to the Romagna under Ferrante, duke of Calabria (Alfonso II's eldest son, and soon to become King Ferrandino) to oppose the anticipated offensives by causing a revolt in the duchy of Milan and attempting to take Genoa. Ferrandino was supported by an able soldier and Milanese rebel, Giangiacomo Trivulzio. The outcome of Ferrandino's campaign in the Romagna is described in detail by Cecil Clough in another article in this volume. It ended in defeat on 20 October 1494, when the French and Milanese stormed the fortified town of Mordano killing many of the defenders and inhabitants in the first of a series of massacres which were to send shock waves throughout Italy.[12] Mordano was lost within a few miles of Ferrante's force, which failed to intervene to save the town, despite pleas for support. A few days later, after the capitulation of Florence gave the French unopposed access to Tuscany, the Aragonese began to withdraw, first to the Marche, then to Rome, and eventually back to the borders of Naples in the face of superior French tactics and aggression.[13]

---

architetto (Siena, 1993), 126-62, an exhibition catalogue which contains other useful entries on individual fortresses by the Sienese master.

[9] Ferraiolo, *Una Cronaca Napoletana figurata del Quattrocento*, ed. Riccardo Filangieri, (Naples, 1956), cap.63.

[10] Jole Mazzoleni, 'Gli apprestamenti difensivi dei castelli di Calabria ultra alla fine del Regno Aragonese (1494-1495)', *Archivio storico per le province napoletane* (hereafter *ASPN*), 69 (1947), 132-44.

[11] Alan Ryder, *The Kingdom of Naples under Alfonso the Magnanimous: the making of a modern state* (Oxford, 1976), 259.

[12] For the actions at Mordano on 19-20 October 1494, see Sanuto, *Spedizione*, 95-96; Bernardi, *Cronache forlivesi*, 1, parte 2 (1896), 18 and L. Cobelli, *Cronache forlivesi* (Bologna, 1874), 357-8. I am grateful to Cecil Clough for the references to Bernardi and Cobelli, and for his assessment of the town of Mordano as a strong place, with thick walls and a wet ditch, with the only weakness being the gate where the French eventually forced an entry.

[13] Delaborde, 428 and following.

The Aragonese fleet commanded by Don Federigo, brother of Alfonso II, had sailed from Naples towards Liguria on 22 June. Federigo's fleet comprised at least thirty-five light galleys and eighteen *navi*, plus many smaller vessels amounting to perhaps as many as 96 sail.[14] It carried 3,000 foot from Naples and another 5,000 from Siena - Alfonso's ally from the Tuscan War of the 1478-80 - and was said to have been well equipped with artillery.[15] The French and Milanese, however, secured their grip on Genoa in August and repulsed the Aragonese fleet off Rapallo on 8 September 1494. These moves were later to be seen by Guicciardini as the first decisive engagements of the Italian Wars.

French control of Genoa was vital because the port remained an essential part of the plan to transport their famously-mobile heavy artillery siege train by sea. With Genoa in French hands, the big guns were moved into Italy in two stages: from Marseilles to Genoa, and from Genoa to La Spezia, where they were landed in time to meet the main elements of Charles VIII's Grand Army of Italy as it debouched from the Appenine pass that led from Lombardy to the northern Tuscan seaboard.

The march of the main French force from Asti (which Charles VIII left on 6 October), via Pavia (14-17 October), Piacenza (23 October), Fornovo (25 October), Pontremoli (28 October) to Sarzana (30 October) was achieved without the heavy artillery. Moreover, the main infantry units kept up a much steadier and slower pace than the King, whose movements - those given above - are recorded in the daily diary of André de la Vigne, secretary to Anne of Brittany. The King and his court dallied for four days at Pavia and five days at Piacenza for what the diarist called 'acclamations, triomphes & magnificences comme incroyables'.[16] Pride moved de la Vigne to explain away a full six days of inactivity before Sarzana 'tant pour le respect de la feste de la Toussaint, que pour donner temps aux Troupes lassées & fatiguées de se rafraîchir & reprendre haleine; & aussi pour donner quelque repos aux malades'.[17] The army probably was tired, and many were no doubt sick. More importantly, it was stuck in front

---

[14] Notar Giacomo, *Cronica di Napoli di Notar Giacomo*, ed. Paolo Garzilli (Naples, 1845), 185 gives 'galere 30, galiune 4, arbatose 3, nave 4 (named), barze 30', in all 96 sail. Passero agrees on the total 96 sail, but provides a different breakdown. Giuliano Passero, *Giornali*, ed. Vincenso Maria Altobelli et al. (Naples, 1785), 62-3 for the naval operations.

[15] For the artillery: Passero, 59: 'In questo anno 1494 le lavorano con gran furia allo farcinale de Napoli 45. galere, et 4. galiune molto grosse, e 4 scorpiune, che queste quattro galiune, et quattro scorpiune portano quattro bombarde per uno che menano ducento libre di petra per una, et cosi sta in ordine questa armata...'

[16] André de la Vigne (a.k.a. Le Vergier d'Honneur), 'Extrait de l'Histoire du Voyage de Naples du Roy Charles VIII, mise par escrit, en forme de iournal de son exprés vouloir & commandement par ADLV, Secretaire d'Anne de Bretagne, Reyne de France', in Guillaume de Jaligny, *Histoire de Charles VIII*, ed. Godefroy (Paris, 1684), 116.

[17] de la Vigne, 116.

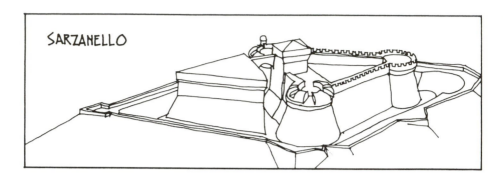

SARZANELLO

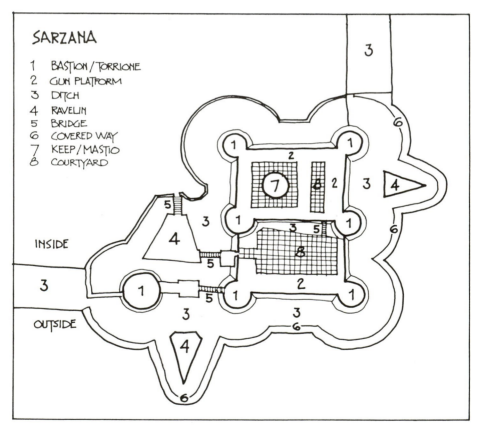

SARZANA

1 BASTION / TORRIONE
2 GUN PLATFORM
3 DITCH
4 RAVELIN
5 BRIDGE
6 COVERED WAY
7 KEEP / MASTIO
8 COURTYARD

INSIDE

OUTSIDE

of the newly built Florentine fortresses at Sarzana and Sarzanello, where the early French attacks had been repulsed.

Sarzana had been taken back from Genoa by Florence at the end of the War of 1484-87. The walls and towers had been badly damaged in the fighting and, shortly after its capture on 22 June 1487, the Otto di Practica gave orders for the town's re-fortification - together with Sarzanello - 'either in its former state or in another form'. The chief designers were Francione and La Cecca.[18] Most of the Florentine early efforts were concentrated on the radical reconstruction of the citadel of Sarzana, which had been built originally by the Pisans and was known as the Fortezza Firmafede, or the citadel. Works on the citadel were completed in 1492 and, by the time the French appeared in October 1494, Sarzanello also was almost complete and, as it proved, defensible.

By the standards of the 1490s, Sarzana was a strong place. The citadel on the north east corner of the town was surrounded by deep, wide ditches. Its scarped main walls were thick enough to support a continuous wide gun platform which connected the round corner 'bastions', allowing defensive artillery to be mounted and moved easily around the walls between the bastions, which were built at the same level as the curtains. Triangular outworks, already known here as *rivellini*, were placed in the ditch between the round bastions, providing some protection for the curtains and serving as advanced fire-bases for guns which swept the approaches to the ditch. Another triangular ravelin served as an island for the two drawbridges that led into the citadel from the town. Inside the citadel further ditches and bridges divided the outer from the inner wards, and provided security for the keep and its central circular tower.

The steep hill overlooking Sarzana was occupied by the unusual triangular fortress of Sarzanello.[19] Three round corner bastions, similar to those

---

[18] Franco Buselli, *Documenti sulla edificazione della fortezza di Sarzana, 1487-1492* (Florence, 1970), 42-5 for La Cecca and 67-78 for Francione.

[19] Carlo Promis, *Sarzanello* (1845).

Opposite: **The Florentine frontier forts: Sarzana and Sarzanello**
Above: **Sarzanello in its completed form, early sixteenth century**. (Re-drawn by the author from an air photograph.) The fortifications which faced the French in 1494 probably consisted only of the works bounded by the three circular towers and the square, roofed keep. The large triangular ravelin (seen here to the left) was probably designed by the Florentines but completed by the Genoese, and the thickened, curved parapet on the nearest round tower was probably also a sixteenth century improvement although some turn of the century fortifications show similar features.
Below: **Sarzana, the Fortezza Firmafede and its outworks**. (Re-drawn by the author from reproductions of early survey drawings.) The main fortress survives as a prison, but the ditches and outworks shown standing in them are no longer to be seen. If the outworks formed part of the completed fortress which faced the French in 1494, Sarzana would provide an early built example of systematised free-standing triangular ditchworks, all of which are efficiently flanked by gun positions in the adjacent round towers.

of Sarzana's citadel, and a gigantic triangular ravelin gave the completed fortress a diamond or lozenge-shaped plan. The ravelin was a later addition, completed in 1502 after the town had again changed hands, but probably built to an earlier Florentine plan. Even without the ravelin, the triangular fortress was a formidable stronghold because of its commanding site and the immensely deep ditch surrounding it.

Guicciardini tells us that the French attacks on Sarzanello were making no headway when the treaty negotiated by Piero de' Medici brought action to a halt, gave the French free passage through northern Tuscany, and enabled Charles VIII to enter Florence on 17 November 1494 as a conqueror. This was a diplomatic victory for the French, hastened by pressure on Florence from the storming and brutal sack of Fivizzano on 26 October[20] and the capture of two dozen more of their smaller frontier fortresses and villages. The key modern positions of Sarzana and Sarzanello had not been taken by force.[21] Indeed, what might be called Guicciardini's *Blitzkrieg* thesis lacks a good example of a modern fortress shot away by the guns of 1494-95. Philippe de Commines clearly felt that Sarzana, threatening the narrow coastal plain, was the major obstacle to the French advance. He also appreciated what might so easily have been the predicament of the French army stuck before Sarzana in winter, with snow on the bare hills and few supplies save those shipped in by a fleet which was still vulnerable to Aragonese naval forces.

Florence was cowed into support and entertained the king from 17 to 29 November 1494. Siena was in no position to oppose the French and, as elements of Charles' army moved towards Rome in late November and December, the internal divisions of the Church States provided as many friends as enemies. The Colonna had declared for France as early as June, had sheltered the French cardinals at Nettuno, and in August had seized the coastal fortress at Ostia, thus dominating the Tiber estuary and Rome's port. To the north of Rome the Orsini now opened their castle at Bracciano to Charles. Ferrante and Trivulzio had extracted what was left of their broken Aragonese expeditionary force from the Romagna and had fallen back on Rome, entering the city on 10 December.[22] However, here there was no serious thought of defence, although at this time the French armies were still dispersed widely across central Italy and the main French siege train did not leave Pisa until 24

---

[20] Delaborde, *Expédition*, 433, who notes that here the French seem not to have been the principle culprits in the massacre. He quotes Parenti, fol.57v: opera de vicini nostri di Fosdinovo pie che de Franzesi...

[21] Sanuto, *La Spedizione di Carlo VIII in Italia raccontata da Marino Sanuto il Giovane*, ed. Rinaldo Fulin (Venice, 1883), 105-6 for details of the twenty-four positions captured in the Fiorentino in October 1494.

[22] Delaborde, *Expédition*, 499.

November.[23] Ferrandino marched out of the Porta San Sebastiano on the last day of 1494, as the French came in through the Porta del Popolo 'headed by the King, armed, lance on thigh, as he had entered into Florence'.[24] Pope Alexander took refuge in the Castel Sant'Angelo and was only persuaded to come out for negotiations when some of the guns which had been paraded through Rome in Charles VIII's formal entry procession were placed threateningly in front of the papal fortress.

Almost a month was spent in Rome before King Charles set off for the Colonna town of Marino, near Grottaferrata. The artillery had gone ahead with the advanced guard, although sadly we are not told how much of a head-start the guns had been given. Once again, the king's well documented progress seems to have leap-frogged with that of the artillery train and its escort. The French advanced in separate columns; one moving along the coast from Nettuno, another somewhat over-extended in its attempt to seize L'Aquila, with the main force spread out over more than fifty miles on the line taken by the king. Charles VIII spent four days at Velletri (30 January to 2 February 1495) followed by one night at Valmontone (3 February), two nights at Ferentino (4 and 5 February) and five days at Veroli (6 to 10 February). Bad weather may have contributed to the slow movement.[25] The return journey with a smaller army and fewer guns followed much the same route from Naples to Rome but took only thirteen days at the end of May 1495.[26] The first part of the February march, however, was against an as yet undefeated enemy and was broken by two further siege actions.

Montefortino, near Valmontone, was stormed and sacked on 31 January, apparently without the use of artillery.[27] The place was the fief of Iacomo Visconti who had at first declared for Charles and then switched sides, and the satisfaction with which the normally moderate de la Vigne reports the massacre of the garrison suggests a reprisal. Among the few survivors in the *rocca* were the count's two little sons, who were held for ransom because of their father's perfidy.[28]

The attack on Monte San Giovanni on 9 February began as a straightforward military operation against a strong and well garrisoned position on high ground threatening the road leading to the Neapolitan frontier at Monte Cassino. When the French heralds who had been sent forward to summons the place to surrender returned without their noses and ears, the siege was pressed

---

[23] Delaborde, *Expédition*, 475, n.2 citing Portovenere, 290.

[24] As Guicciardini remarks.

[25] Itinerary in de la Vigne, 128.

[26] de la Vigne, 149-50.

[27] Sanuto, 207, says the town was taken by force with great cruelty 'killing as many as they found' but the *rocca* surrendered at discretion when the artillery was planted.

[28] de la Vigne, 128.

with an urgency and bitterness not seen before, even at the massacres of Mordano, Fivizzano and Monte Fortino.[29]   After a seven to eight hour bombardment, a small breach was made in the wall and under the eyes of the King the dismounted *gendarmerie* fought their way into the castle against a desperate defence.[30] No quarter was given and 'the carnage was one of the most horrible ever seen' as the bodies of the defenders were thrown into the ditch in their hundreds. By the French account, fully one thousand defenders died in the castle and the town.[31]

The massacre at Monte San Giovanni contributed to the collapse of the already crumbling Aragonese defence. The French expected stiff fighting for San Germano, its three castles and the fortified monastery on the heights of Monte Cassino.[32] The Pass of Cancello, which by-passed Monte Cassino, was reported to be blocked by field fortifications and entanglements of felled trees.[33] If the Aragonese were to make a stand, it had to be here.[34] But all of these positions were abandoned as Ferrandino left hurriedly for Naples, where King Alfonso II abdicated in his favour and fled to Sicily. Fortresses and cities everywhere opened their gates to the French as nobles and citizens hastened to make their peace with a new master. For Charles VIII and his court, the last few days of the march to Naples became a triumph. San Germano and the Monte Cassino group of fortifications were occupied on 12 February, Calvi on 17 February, Capua on 18 February and Aversa on 19 February. All received him 'avec toute la magnificence possible' and by 21 February Charles enjoyed the pleasures of Poggio Reale's villa and park while preparing for his formal entry to Naples on 22 February 1495.[35]

---

[29] Sanuto, 209, says the heralds were hanged as well as mutilated, and (reporting the Venetian ambassadors' letters) says the French lost only ten dead and twenty-five wounded for the 700 men, women and children killed in the town and castle. Giovio 65 says only that 'fecero quasi ingiuria a una trombetta Francese' which had greatly inflamed 'gli animi di quella nation superba, perche in Francia stimano cosa mal fatta il fare ingiuria a una trombetta, ch'essi chaimano Araldo...' Many of the 300 garrison managed to escape, he adds, leaving unarmed civilians to bear the brunt of the reprisals. De la Vigne, 129 glosses over the insult to the heralds but stresses the bad character of the garrison, 'composé de plusieurs gens ramassaez des diverses nations, scavoir des voleurs & bannis pour la pluspart, determinez & resolus à toutes sortes d'extremitez...'.

[30] Commines, vol. 2, 160.

[31] de la Vigne, 130.

[32] de la Vigne, 130: 'Sainct Germain est le clef & le passage qu'il faut necessairement auoir pour pouvoir entrer dans le Royaume...'

[33] Giovio, 61-2.

[34] Commines, bk 7, cap 16: 'This was the place for him to fight or not at all...'

[35] de la Vigne, 131-2 for the approach to Naples, with a graphic description of Poggio Reale and its park.

Naples and its fortifications

Page following:
Late fifteenth-century Naples viewed from the sea. Drawing by the author, based on part of the Tavola Strozzi, excluding ships, people and minor buildings.

A: Castel Dell'Uovo, B: Palace of the Prince of Aragon, C: Santa Croce, D: Santa Trinita and its walled precinct, E: Parco (note height of the fortified retaining walls on the seaward side), F: Fosso della Giostra (probably blocked by a cross-wall further into the ditch, leaving the small landing beach shown here open to the sea), G: Torre di San Vincenzio (with its dock forming an outer fortification), H: Castel Nuovo, J: Cittadella, outer gate and bridge, K: Piazza Nuova, L: Arsenale, M: Molo Grande (note the high breakwater and the much lower quays on the harbour side on which the Aragonese were able to shelter from fire from the Castelnuovo during the second siege of 1495), N: Inner Harbour, O: part of the Molo Piccolo, sheltering the arsenal basin, P: Castel Sant'Elmo and the Certosa di San Martino, Q: unidentified medieval works, possibly indicating the line of the defences under construction on the eve of the French invasion.

Opposite following page:

　　Above: Castelnuovo and its fortifications, c.1494

　　Below: Naples, c.1494

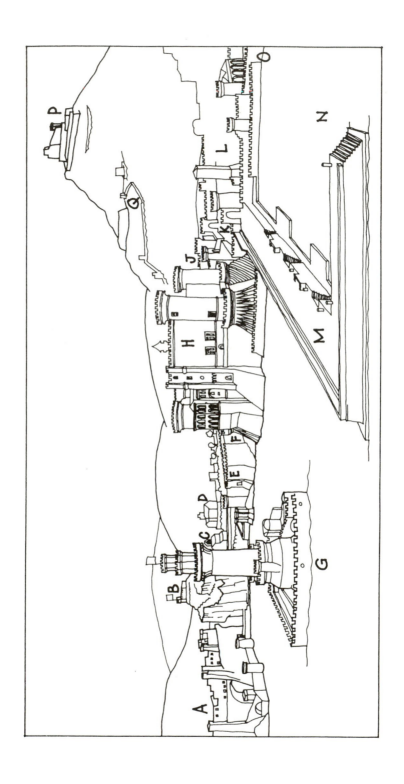

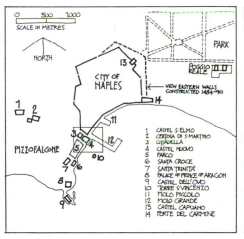

1 CASTEL S.ELMO
2 CERTOSA DI S.MARTINO
3 CITTADELLA
4 CASTEL NUOVO
5 PARCO
6 SANTA CROCE
7 SANTA TRINITÀ
8 PALACE OF PRINCE OF ARAGON
9 CASTEL DELL'OVO
10 TORRE S.VINCENZO
11 MOLO PICCOLO
12 MOLO GRANDE
13 CASTEL CAPUANO
14 PORTE DEL CARMINE

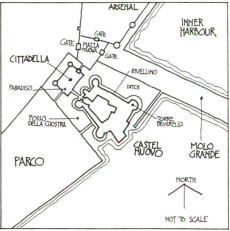

The Aragonese loyalists now held only the three sea-side fortresses of Naples: the Castel Nuovo overlooking the harbour and its mole; the Castel dell'Ovo on its island crag joined to the land only by its high bridgeworks; and the Torre di San Vincenzo on a reef in the bay between the two bigger castles. The Castel Capuana, already largely a civil residence just inside the northern Porta Capuana, and the Forte del Carmine, the enlarged gate complex guarding the east end of the city walls, had both been abandoned; as had a number of fortified monasteries and small castles outside the walls on the southwestern heights of Pizzofalcone. By far the most important French objective was the Castel Nuovo which effectively closed the harbour and the *molo grande* with its guns. Guns from the castle also commanded much of the town.

II

The core of the Castel Nuovo was medieval. The central keep with its irregular quadrangle and cylindrical corner towers had been built originally in the late-thirteenth century, and substantially rebuilt on the same plan in the early-fifteenth century. The corner towers and much of the curtains had been reconstructed once again in the middle years of the century following the castle's capture in 1442 by Alfonso V of Aragon and I of Naples at the end of his war of succession against René of Anjou. The Aragonese rebuilding programme was largely complete by 1451, although the outer skin of *piperno* and the elaborate projecting *merlatura* around the tops of the towers remained to be finished during the 1450s, and the decorated portal - the so-called Aragonese Arch - which illustrated Alfonso's triumphal procession was not completed until the late 1460s.[36]

Alfonso's rebuilding of the 1440s retained the traditional high profile of the keep and its embellishments. During the 1450s a double gallery was added to the upper curtains (the lengths of wall between the towers), possibly to provide additional protected firing positions for crossbowmen. It was a distinctively Spanish contribution which was almost certainly the work of Guglielmo Sagrera from Ciutat de Mallorca (the modern Palma), an architect

---

[36] Riccardo Filangieri is the principal historian of the Castel Nuovo, see his 'La Cittadella Aragonese e il recinto bastionate di Castel Nuovo', *Atti della Accademia Pontaniana*, 59 (1929), 49-73; 'Rassegna critica delle fonti per la storia di Castel Nuovo: Parte Prima, Il castello angioino', *ASPN*, 61 (1936), 251-323; 'Rassegna critica... Parte Seconda: Il castello aragonese', *ASPN*, 62 (1937), 267-333; 'Rassegna critica... Parte Terza: Opere di compimento e di restauro durante il periodo aragonese', *ASPN*, 63 (1938), 258-342; which describe the evolution of the Castel Nuovo with all of the documentary sources. Filangieri's *Castel Nuovo Reggia Angioina-Aragonese di Napoli* (Naples, 1934) summarises the text of the *ASPN* articles without the academic references. George Hersey, *The Aragonese Arch at Naples* (New Haven, CN, 1973) deals in detail with the famous portal.

who directed works from 1452 to 1454 and was succeeded in this post by his cousin Giovanni Sagrera, and Giovanni's son, Giacomo.[37]

The Sagrera family were probably also responsible for the thickening of the lower walls during the 1460s with a broad platform running around the base of the keep on the three landward-facing sides.[38] Decorated with fluted and spiral-pattern masonry, this platform was the principal modern feature of the Castel Nuovo. It was known misleadingly at Naples as the *rivellino* and provided firing positions for a large number of guns, delivering more or less horizontal fire onto the approaches to the castle. It too was provided with an elaborate *merlatura* to protect the gunners from small arms fire and arrows. Later in the century, as the threat from gunpowder artillery became more serious, a number of vaulted bomb-proof shelters, or *casamatte*, were added to the *rivellino* to provide more substantial cover.[39] A number of *casamatte* were also built on the floor of the deep ditch that surrounded the keep. Filangieri believed them to have been added shortly before the French invasion.[40] The ditch-level *casamatte* seem to have been reached from the outer wall of the ditch and were practically impossible to hit with cannon.[41]

Filangieri, writing before the destruction of the Neapolitan archive in World War II, attributed most of this later work to Antonio Marchesi da Settignano (sometimes called Antonio Fiorentino) who served the Aragonese kings almost continuously before, during and after the war of 1494-95.[42] The celebrated military architect Francesco di Giorgio Martini of Siena, who also worked in Naples before the war, served with the Aragonese during the second siege of 1495 (see below) and again briefly after the expulsion of the French.[43] There is a strong wish on the part of art historians to identify Francesco's hand in the design of the pre-siege works, particularly the casamatte, which are a distinctive feature of many of the fortification designs illustrated in his treatise.[44] The only documentary evidence for his direct involvement is the testimony of Ferraiolo, whose *Cronica figurata* (edited by Filangieri in 1956) credits

---

[37] Filangieri, 'Rassegna', 2, 280-81.

[38] Filangieri, 'Rassegna', 2, 280-81.

[39] Filangieri, 'Rassegna', 3, 266.

[40] Filangieri, 'Rassegna', 3, 266, 268-9.

[41] See below: the defenders of the ditch-level casamatte were killed or captured when the cittadella was overrun in the final days of the second siege of 1495, presumably because they were unable to escape into the main castle keep, as would have been possible if they had been reached from the inner side of the ditch.

[42] Filangieri, 'Rassegna', 3, 273 and following.

[43] Dechert, 'The Military Architecture of Francesco di Giorgio in Southern Italy', 161-80 provides the best recent account.

[44] Francesco di Giorgio Martini, *Trattati di architettura, ingegneria e arte militare* (ed. Corrado Maltese Livia Maltese Degrassi, 2 vols., Milan, 1967), vol. 2, tavole 245-9, 268, 292 for views of casamatte in the ditches and on the upper works of fortifications.

Francesco with last-minute pre-war designs for a rebuilt castle of Sant'Elmo, as well as the casamatte of the Castel Nuovo.[45]

The casamatte do not, of course, appear in the best view of the late-fifteenth-century Castel Nuovo, the panorama of Naples known as the Tavola Strozzi which probably dates from the mid-1460s.[46] Drawn from a vantage

---

[45] Ferraiolo, caps. 62-63, 112-14: 'Un messere Francisco, senese, tavolario della Maistà del sig. re Alfonso et mastro zufficiente de adificie, in ditto anno 1495, a dì XIII de innaro, XIII indicione, la Maistà del sig. Re fece bottare in terra le doie turre che stevano sopre la porta dello castiello de Sant'Eramo; quale fece bottare per lo ditto consiglio de messere Francisco, perchè Sua Maestà voleva fare uno castiello lo più bella che mai in Talia fosse. Et fo prencipiate dallo mese de sottiembro de ditto annon, et in quisso tiempo la Maistà del sig. Re fece fare la bastia sopra Baia, per defencione de Vaia; lo quale ei una bella cosa, con quelle case matte e defese bene ordinate.// Et in quisto ditto anno [1494] dello mese de ottubro la ditta Maistà del sig. Re fece fare una bastia chiamata casa matta allo ponte dello fusso dello Castiello Novo, appiede la torre de Viviriello; et se ditta casa matta fosse stata sconputo [compiuta], sarria stata la disfacione de questa citate in ditta guerra.// In ditto anno 1495, alli XIIII de innaro la Maistà del sig. re Alfonso ditto ut supra ingigniao a fare fare fusse et innante fusse et case matte attuorno lo Castiello Novo, et alla citatella puro defese per reparo dello ditto Castiello. Quale fece de gran cose et de grande repare, perchè Sua Maistà se credeva de tenerese assaie et de no intravenire a quello che intravenne.' Details of the works to Sant'Elmo are not known, but Sanuto confirms that frantic efforts on ditches and walls was taking place in the winter of 1494-95 'quale abbrazavano tutto el monte de San Martino sina al Castel novo', *Spedizione*, 121. When Filangieri edited Ferraiolo he modified his earlier views to place Francesco di Giorgio himself in Naples in January 1495, with a scheme for S. Elmo which *may* have formed the basis for the much later sixteenth-century reconstruction of that fortress (which was actually supervised by Scriva for the Spanish Viceroys) and with the construction of additional *casematte* around the Castelnuovo and the *Cittadella*. Ferraiolo's statement, however, hardly sustains Hersey's conclusion: 'In other words, Alfonso began the erection... at the Castel Nuovo of the low, thrusting bastions, or torrioni, topped with vaulted gun chambers that distinguish the new type of fortification.' (*Alfonso II*, 90). Still less does it 'make it certain that Francesco di Giorgio created the plans for the new western defenses and that he began building them during the reign of Alfonso II' (90-91 and n.47) Francesco may well have proposed a plan for the refortification of the western approaches, including a substantial second modernisation of the Castel Nuovo by the addition of an outer *enceinte* of ramparts and *torrioni* around the three landward faces of the castle. Such plans may have been similar to those actually carried out in the early sixteenth century and illustrated in Francisco de Hollanda's well known view of 1539/40. But this is by no means *certain* and Nicholas Adams rightly points out that the upper works, in particular the *merlatura* shown in Hollanda's view, are quite unlike anything in Francesco di Giorgio's *oeuvre* (Adams, 'L'architettura militare', 144). Ferraiolo's quite explicit testimony only serves to confirm Francesco's involvement in the starting of more *casamatte*, in addition to the one already started in October 1494 'at the foot of the tower of Viviriello' (where it may have blocked the partly-open, sea end of the ditch, or contributed to the fortification of the landward end of Molo Grande, see plan). What happened to Francesco's proposals after this war and into the next century will continue to perplex his many admirers, but need not confuse our p;icture of events in 1494-95.

[46] This painting was discovered in the Casa Strozzi, in Florence, and is now in the Museo di San Martino, Naples. It was first thought to show the arrival of Lorenzo the Magnificent at Naples in 1479, as he attempted to negotiate an end to the Tuscan War by private diplomacy. Later it was thought to be the Naval Triumph of Ferrante I after his victory at the Battle of Ischia (1464). Filangieri identifies it as the seven galleys and the two dismasted *fuste* captured from Carlo de Torellas by Bernardo Villamarina, the Aragonese admiral. Its date is

point offshore, or possibly from the end of the *molo grande*, the Tavola exposes the rivellino and its decorative masonry, and indicates the battlemented wall closing the sea end of the ditch. The other important works on the inland side of the castle are largely obscured but battlemented walls, a bridge and its gate tower can be glimpsed to the right. In many ways these outworks were the most important features in the two sieges of 1495.

Outside the ditch to the north-west of the main keep was a fortified enclosure, or barbican, about 70 metres wide across its frontage, and 65 metres deep. A double gate system controlled access through the barbican to an open space known at Naples as the *piazza* which separated the castle from the town and the arsenal. The barbican complex was known in Naples, confusingly but consistently, as the *cittadella*. It contained a large artillery shed, magazines, armoury, guard houses and at the southern end a small walled garden with a loggia elevated on a platform, the *Paradiso*. The *cittadella* was fortified with round towers at its two outer corners and was, in effect, an island entirely surrounded by deep ditches.[47]

To the south, separated from the castle and its barbican by the so-called Fosso della Giostra (from the jousts and tournaments sometimes held in it) and reached by bridges from both the castle and the barbican, were the main royal gardens, or *Parco*.[48] This was a walled enclosure containing plantations, casinos, fountains and the famous aviary with its parrots:[49] the lions lived in the ditch.[50] Although not specifically fortified, the Parco was raised on a platform to give security, privacy and fine views across the city and the bay towards the Castel dell'Ovo and the offshore Torre di San Vincenzo. Fine views, of course, were also potential fields of fire.

III

The French bombardment of the Castel Nuovo began without delay on 22 February, the day of Charles VIII's formal entry into Naples. The French put up gallows within view of the garrison to support their threat to hang all of them if they did not surrender, a threat which produced a defiant salvo in reply. One

---

still disputed. Spinazzola dates it to some 20 years after 1464 because it does not show the lantern on the mole which was demolished in the 1480s. The artist may simply have left out the lantern for compositional reasons (it would have obscured the Castel Nuovo and its new building works). Filangieri leans towards a date close to 1464 when Filippo Strozzi himself was in Naples and could have acquired or been given the painting. See Filangieri, 'Rassegna', 2, 293, n1.

[47] Filangieri, 'Rassegna', 2, 271, 278, 291-2.

[48] Filangieri, 'Rassegna', 3, 271-2.

[49] Sanuto, 238-9 describes the *Parco* after its capture by the French; see also Filangieri, *Castel Nuovo*, 307-8.

[50] Filangieri, 'Rassegna', 1, 284.

report suggests that as many as 70 heavy guns were available to the French for a continual bombardment[51] and that these were placed in the 'piazza che guarda verso la città' as well as the Parco. Passero, a local observer, gives the much lower figure of thirty pieces in four batteries shooting from the arsenal, the mole, from positions opposite Santo Spirito and from the Parco 'che non si può affacciare una mosca dallo castiello'.[52] The French kept up their bombardment night and day, firing on fixed lines in the darkness.[53]

The bombardment continued until 26 February when the dismounted *gendarmerie* carried the walls of the *cittadella* in a fierce assault and briefly occupied the advanced work, where they destroyed some guns and burnt some timber defences before being forced to retire by fire from the keep which overlooked the works from its towers, curtain and probably the *rivellino* too.[54] At this point there was a parley, apparently initiated by the French,[55] but no agreement for surrender could be reached and the bombardment resumed for the period 26 February to 2 March, when another parley took place. It was now agreed that the castle would surrender unless relief had arrived by 7 March.[56] Hostages were given by the defenders. When time ran out, however, yet another bombardment had to be delivered. An ammunition explosion in one of the towers finally drove the shocked survivors to surrender against a background of panic, mutiny by the German-speaking Swiss of the garrison, and French threats against the hostages for the defenders' breach of the earlier accord.[57] It is not clear whether the ammunition explosion was accidental or caused by the French bombardment.

When the Castel Nuovo surrendered a second bombardment had already begun against the Castel dell'Ovo on 4 March. It continued with only brief interruptions until the castle, by now much damaged and surrounded by dead fish floating in the sea, was surrendered on 13 March.[58] The Torre di San Vicenzo had surrendered the day before.

The first siege of 1495 was perhaps not quite the classic victory of new guns over old fortifications that first appears. It had certainly taken much

---

[51] Sanuto, 234 almost certainly means to suggest heavy artillery when he adds 'tirati da X in 12 cavalli', although some accounts give bigger horse teams for the heaviest guns. Delaborde, 559 says 66 guns.

[52] Passero, 68.

[53] Giovio, 69: 'Percioche i Francesi hauendo una uolta piatato l'artiglierie, & drizzate ò liuello, scaricauano ancor di mira le palle al buio in quei luoghi doue essi hauenano disegnato.'

[54] Sanuto, 241-2. The height of the *cittadella* is not known. Probably it did not obstruct the rivellino, but other accounts suggest that it prevented French shot from hitting all but the uppermost works, which bespeaks considerable height.

[55] Sanuto, 242.

[56] Sanuto, 230; de la Vigne, 134.

[57] Giovio, 69-70.

[58] de la Vigne, 135-8.

longer than the two days promised by a French gunner sent to spy out the Castel Nuovo just before the invasion.[59] The final surrender of the Castel Nuovo had been prompted by the breakdown of discipline in the exhausted garrison, who began to fight amongst themselves in the aftermath of an explosion which had killed and dismembered many victims and left others, horribly burnt, screaming for help and 'running like madmen throughout the castle'.[60] Moreover, Sanuto reports that the French bombardment of the Castel Nuovo was not as effective as might be thought because the *cittadella* was shielding most of the castle below the merli, and it was only possible to bombard the castle from one side, the *Parco*.[61] The assaults on the *cittadella* were launched because the bombardment was getting nowhere and, if the Venetian is right, it was the French who decided to parley. Sanuto also mentions the difficulties of the French gunners, who were taking casualties and running short of iron balls as well as powder, which forced them to send to the ships at Ostia for more ammunition.[62] Nowhere is it suggested that the fortifications of the Castel Nuovo were less than adequate. Indeed, Sanuto remarks that after ten days of bombardment only the windows and the *merlatura* had been destroyed, so strong were the walls.[63] Elsewhere, the same author indicates that repairs were needed on the broken bridge[64] (presumably the main bridge into the *cittadella*) and in the *cittadella* itself where French incendiaries had ruined part of the walls (presumably timber revetments, or palisades constructed to impede those scaling the ramparts).[65] The *cittadella* was essentially little more than a broad platform planted in front of the Castel Nuovo, shielding it and providing a spacious advanced base for the mounting of defensive artillery. It worked. In the second siege of 1495 the French were to show that a resolute defence of the same fortifications would yield one of the longer defences of the late fifteenth-century.

---

[59] 'Un cannonier, envoyé comme espion à Naples, affirme sur sa tête qu'en deux jour il prend le Castel Nuovo; certes les Français sont vantards par nature, mais Francesco della casa et autres Florentines, qui ont vu les pièces de leurs yeux, en racontent des choses à faire frémir.' Cited by Philippe Contamine, 'L'artillerie royale française à la veille des Guerres d'Italie," *Annales de Bretagne*, 71, 2 (1964), 223 who cites Canestrini and Desjardins, who cite J. S. C. Bridge, *A History of France from the Death of Louis XI*, vol. 2, 112.

[60] Giovio, 69.

[61] Sanuto, 241-2 and 249-30.

[62] Sanuto, 246-7.

[63] Sanuto, 250: essendo sta bombardato *solum* 10 zorni, nè fu rotto altro che le merladure et fenestre, tanto era forte di muraglie... See also 244.

[64] Sanuto, 259: [Re] comandò fusse riconzato dove le bombarde havia fatto danno, et *maxime* el ponte el qual era roto.

[65] Sanuto, 242: et con fuoghi artificiadi ruinò qualche parte de diffe muraglie...

IV

Charles VIII left Naples on 20 May 1495, with most of his army and a somewhat reduced artillery train. After their unexpected escape from the massed Italian forces of the Holy League at Fornovo on 6 July, the main French force - minus much of their baggage train - managed to reach safety in Asti by a further eight forced marches. By this time the French garrison which had been left behind in Naples was already under siege by the Aragonese forces of King Ferrante II, and a Neapolitan population which had turned against the French invaders as quickly as they had welcomed them. The French had lost the city of Naples on 6 and 7 July as the people rose in support of Ferrandino's return from Calabria, quickly abandoning their efforts to hold - much less retake - the narrow lanes of the old city against the local Neapolitan street-fighters.[66] Although surprised by the rapid turn of events, the French recovered themselves quickly and were clearly much better prepared to defend the city's strongholds in July 1495 than their Aragonese opponents had been in February and March.

The earlier siege had seen the Aragonese isolated in the Castel Nuovo, the Castel dell'Ovo and the Torre di San Vincenzo. In July the French fell back on a continuous, or near continuous, line of fortifications along the shore which included the Castel Nuovo, the royal gardens or *Parco*, the convent of Santa Croce and the neighbouring church of Santa Trinità,[67] the Castel dell'Uovo and the offshore Torre di San Vincenzo. Giovio also lists what he calls the Castello di Pizzofalcone, on the heights overlooking the Castel dell'Ovo.[68] Sanuto includes the Castel Sant'Elmo as a separate item, that is, a second fortified position on Pizzofalcone, presumably on the site later occupied by the extant Fortezza Sant'Elmo.[69] The Castello di Pizzofalcone was probably the fortified

---

[66] Giovio, bk. 3, 112-16 gives an excellent account of the uprising and the street-fighting tactics of the Neapolitans: barrels half-filled with stones were rolled noisily towards the French horses; carts had been placed in the streets to give cover to those fighting the French with 'scoppietti, & saette, ma molto più con pietre ...' and, following the loss of the streets, Pescara had trenches dug around the areas defended by the French, closing the street openings with earth-filled gabbions, and knocking through the party walls of houses to allow movement under cover and the secret emplacement of artillery. Some aspects of this operation were clearly well planned.

[67] I am most grateful to Professor Alan Ryder of Bristol University and to Professoressa Teresa Colletta of the Federico II University of Naples for their assistance in locating Santa Croce and the Trinità, both of which are now under the exedra of the Piazza Plebiscito. Alan Ryder tells me that Santa Croce was in danger of falling into the sea in the 15th century and must then, therefore, have been very close to the shoreline. For the topography of medieval and Renaissance Naples see the invaluable paper by Teresa Colletta, 'Napoli: la cartografia pre-catastale', *Storia della città*, 34-5 (1985), 5-180, particularly 23 and tavola 2 on page 26.

[68] Giovio, 116.

[69] Sanuto, 501. Pizza (sic) Falcon et un monasterio di Santa Croce, a modo di forteza et Castel Santo Elmo...

Palace of the Prince of Aragon, on the edge of the cliff just above the Castel dell'Ovo.

This chain of fortified positions allowed Montpensier's 6,000 French troops in Naples to reinforce threatened sectors, and to keep most of the bay between the Castel Nuovo and the Castel dell'Ovo as a relatively safe anchorage for the ships which represented their lifeline in and out of the besieged city. Pizzofalcone was vital. Once lost, it would have been only a matter of time for the Aragonese to fight their way down into the French-held monasteries of Santa Croce and Santa Trinità, isolating the Castel dell'Ovo and closing the anchorage. The second siege of July to November 1495 saw bitter fighting for control of the high ground on Pizzofalcone, as well as in the 'front line' - a butcher's shambles of rotting horseflesh[70] - which ran between the cittadella of the Castel Nuovo and the buildings on the city side of the piazza.

The battle to protect the French fleet was also intense. As soon as the town was theirs, the Aragonese placed guns on the small mole and in the burnt-out arsenal, shooting across the inner harbour and forcing the French to move their ships from moorings inside the *molo grande* to the bay between the Castel Nuovo and Castel dell'Ovo. The *molo grande* was then captured in an amphibious assault on 23 July, and the Aragonese managed to install culverins in the lighthouse which could reach some of the French vessels in their new anchorage,[71] sinking a number of them with long range fire, and later attempting to drive them out of shelter with fireships.[72] The French responded with a series of major sorties along the mole on the 19, 20 and 21 September and knocked out the Aragonese gun positions there with a bombardment from the Castel Nuovo.[73]

Operations against Santa Croce, now 'more a fortress than a monastery', began on 15 August,[74] but the Aragonese petitioned the pope for consent to batter the place and, at the same time, sought to borrow extra guns from Rome.[75] The fortress of Pizzofalcone came under fire on 27 August, and by 20 September the walls had been flattened: 'it seems that it had never been a castle, only the bare stone remains'.[76] But the French defenders held out in the ruins,

---

[70] Giovio, 115-16 points out that the seven French positions were congested with the 6,000 men of Montpensier's garrison. Although provisions were plentiful the large number of horses represented a real feeding problem. The less useful beasts were driven into no-man's-land where they, plus the daring Neapolitans who attempted to seize them, were shot down: essi cogliendo loro di mira con l'artiglierie, gli ammazzavano come per giuco'.

[71] Giovio, 117-18; Sanuto, 531.

[72] Sanuto, 592-3; Notar Giacomo, 193-4 gives the date of 3 September for the fireship attack.

[73] Sanuto, 592-5.

[74] Sanuto, 576.

[75] Sanuto, 595.

[76] Sanuto, 539 and 595.

digging trenches where the guns could not reach them, protected by the deep ditch. At Pizzofalcone and Santa Croce the French conducted an aggressive defence, sallying out in strength to assault the Aragonese.[77] The Castel Nuovo replied vigorously to the fire from the Aragonese siege batteries which had to be well concealed in the ruins of the buildings at the edge of the piazza, and protected by heavy shutters which would be raised only briefly for a shot.[78] The French were evidently no longer short of ammunition for by the end of July as many as 4,000 rounds had been fired into the city.[79] Nor had they abandoned hope of relief, for d'Aubigny - now serving as French Viceroy of Calabria - had recaptured Salerno, defeated a force sent out from Naples, and by early October was only eight miles from the city with 8,000 men, when King Ferrandino took 21,000 men from the various sieges in the city and forced d'Aubigny back to the south.[80] Ferrante, however, was sufficiently concerned about the eventual outcome to offer the French terms and on 4 October 1495 a treaty was signed for surrender 'by appointment' within 50 days unless Naples was relieved.[81]

The treaty of 4 October was no more effective than that negotiated in February when roles had been reversed, although Montpensier and a number of other senior officers took advantage of it to leave Naples to join d'Aubigny: an action which was denounced as a breach of faith by the Aragonese, but which obviously put pressure on them to finish the siege.[82]

On 13 November a major assault on the *cittadella* was repulsed with heavy losses when the attackers, having gained a foothold on the upper works, were stopped by inner defences and came under heavy fire from the keep.[83] Other measures were clearly needed. Indeed, work had already begun on 9 November on the excavation of a mine shaft beneath the *cittadella*.[84] The siege

---

[77] Guillaume de Villeneuve, 'Mémoires de Guillaume de Villeneuve, commençant en 1494 et finissant en 1497, contenant la Conquête du Royaume de Naples par Charles VIII, et la manière dont les Français cu furent chassès', in M. Petitot, *Collection Complète des Mémoires relatifs a l'Histoire de France* (Paris, 1826), vol. 14, 265-6.

[78] Giovio, 119.

[79] Gallo, 15: lo Castiello tirò più di 4000 colpi et non ammazzò si non otto e tirava prete di 9 palmi di giro, et di peso più di rotola cinquanta. Passero, 79: dipoi detti franzisi ordinaro certe palumbarde grosse quali incomenzano a tirare per la terra donde che per questo li Napoletani stavano con molto paura: pensate che menavano pietre che pesava quattro cantara l'una, e questo faceano con certe artigliere, che le chiamavano li mortali [mortars]. Ma come volse Iddio, & la Vergine Maria, & Santi patroni de Napoli questa artiglieria mai fece male a persona alcuna.

[80] Sanuto, 633-4.

[81] Sanuto, 631-2; Notar Giacomo, 196.

[82] Delaborde, *Expédition*, 676; Sanuto, 631.

[83] Sanuto, 643; Passero, 88 mentions the French use of 'pignate di polvere' (grenades) in fighting off the assaults on the *Cittadella*.

[84] Ferraiolo, cap. 133, 198-9. Other sources suggest the mine was started after the failure of the attack on 13 November. Whether it started on 9 or 13 November, it was excavated very quickly and the shaft could not have been very long. See also John Bury, 'The Early

of the Castel Nuovo effectively ended on 27 November 1495 when the Aragonese exploded what may have been the first gunpowder mine in the history of modern warfare, possibly devised by Francesco di Giorgio Martini (who is widely believed to be the figure described by Giovio as the 'Etruscan Narcissus, inventor of marvellous contrivances').[85] A shaft was excavated from the ditch in front of the *cittadella*, propped and filled with explosive. A diversionary attack was then started to bring the French defenders to their action stations on the walls. The mine was then sprung: 'Suddenly with a horrible crash the entire wall was uprooted from its foundations, with fearful slaughter of the French that were above.'[86]

Giacomo Gallo, the Neapolitan diarist, provides the most detailed account of the explosion. The mine was placed under the front wall of the *cittadella*, the stones and earth settling after the explosion to form a slope up which the Aragonese stormed to capture all of the works inside the cittadella and the Paradiso. The bridges over the ditch were also destroyed, cutting off many defenders in the *cittadella*, some of whom died jumping into the ditch as they tried to escape. Simultaneous attacks were launched against the *casamatte* in the ditch, the defenders of which died, 'unable to get back to the inner castle because all of the bridges were broken'. This suggests that the casemates were accessed from the *cittadella* side of the main ditch. Guillaume de Villeneuve, an experienced soldier who saw the attack as a prisoner of the Aragonese, confirms the essential details and comments on the loss of the *cittadella* which was, 'the *boulevart* and the main strength of the castle'.[87] Short of food, the defenders of the main castle surrendered on 8 December 1495.[88] The Torre di San Vincenzo had already surrendered on 29 November. What remained of the other French positions in Naples surrendered shortly afterwards, except for the Castel dell'Ovo which held out until 17 February 1496.[89]

By then the main theatre of action had shifted elsewhere in the *Regno* to a seemingly endless series of small sieges as Ferrandino, aided by Venice and Aragon, imposed his authority on 'rebel' fortresses and towns, and attempted to corner Montpensier in the Terra del Lavoro, d'Aubigny in Calabria and Gratien

---

History of the Explosive Mine', *Fort*, 10 (1982), 23-30 and Simon Pepper, 'The Underground Siege', 31-8.

[85] Giovio, 120-21: Narcisso Toscano, machinatore d'opere meravigliose, & sopra tutto grande artefice di far mine, offerse il suo ingegno à Ferrando in gettare à terra le mura della Cittadella.' Passero, 90, loyally credits it to 'quillo vaso di sapientia don Federico che havea fatto una cava sotto la citadella'; Gallo, 20: 'lo Signore Re fe' fare una tagliata alle mura della Cittadella.' Ferraiolo, who has credited Francesco with other works, says nothing to help us here.

[86] Giovio, 120-21.

[87] Petitot, vol. 14, 295-6.

[88] Sanuto, 644; Passero, 90; Feltrio, 296; Guarino, 223-4.

[89] Feltrio, 296.

de Guerre in the Abruzzi. Only Gratien de Guerre was still free when the Treaty of 18 January 1497 brought the conflict in this theatre to an end.[90]

V

Although no one knows the exact number of guns used by the armies of Charles VIII in Italy, some very large figures are quoted. These range from the 'trente-six cannons attelés' reported by De la Pilorgerie (quoting Giovio's account of the Roman entry parade, to which all other types of gun in the procession would have to be added)[91], to the '700 pièces de dimensions prodigeuses' quoted by Delaborde as an example of exaggeration[92] or the 100 siege pieces and 25,000 draught horses reported to the Marquis of Mantua just before the opening of the campaign.[93] Leaving aside the question of deliberate disinformation - which in the context of 1494 should not perhaps be ignored - there is a real problem of definition rising from the inability of non-specialists to distinguish properly between different types of gun. Cannon, culverins and bombards all had meanings as classes of weapons, but as often as not were used indiscriminately as synonyms for any big guns.[94] Some simple descriptions and definitions are to be found in Appendix A.

When Paolo Giovio reported the formal processional entry of Charles VIII and his army into Rome in January 1495 he listed more than 36 carriage-mounted guns, the biggest of which were the cannon throwing an iron ball 'as big as a man's head'.[95] No precise breakdown is given for the culverins and falcons also described in the French siege train, and a number of authors (following Pilorgerie) have assumed that Giovio's figure of 36 refers only to the full-sized cannon. Because of this ambiguity it is worth looking elsewhere for confirmation or further clues to the number and types of guns employed in 1494-95.

---

[90] Delaborde, *L'Expédition*, 676-82 for the last year of the war. Montpensier was finally cornered and forced to surrender at Atella. He was harshly treated because of his supposed breach of the Naples truce and imprisoned in the unhealthy malarial conditions of Pozzuoli, where he died with most of his men. D'Aubigny was eventually forced to yield to Gonzalvo da Córdoba at Groppoli, but later was returned to France.

[91] J. De la Pilorgerie, *Campagnes et Bulletins de la Grande Armée d'Italie commandée par Charles VIII, 1494-1495* (Nantes/Paris, 1866), 115.

[92] Delaborde, *L'Expédition*, 326.

[93] Delaborde, *L'Expédition*, 327.

[94] Commines's comment at the crossing of the Appenines is pertinent: 'such great guns had never been seen till then; for those with which Duke Galeas had passed that way were but four falconets, which perhaps weighed five hundred pounds a-piece, and yet the people regarded them with infinite wonder': vol. 2, 197.

[95] Giovio, 54-5.

The first French campaign *Bulletin* dated November 1494[96] described the situation in October and itemised the guns then with d'Aubigny's army in the Romagna: three Cannon Serpentine (the biggest), three culverins and twelve small falcons, all supervised by Jean de la Grange, one of the two Maîtres d'Artillerie with the French armies in Italy.[97] The same *Bulletin* mentions Montpensier who was by then with the advanced elements in Tuscany and shortly to be supplied by sea with 'une bonne bende d'artillerye' comprising nine Cannon Serpentines, four culverins and forty falcons. The total of twelve canon is still far short of the thirty-six big guns believed by many to have headed the artillery train in Rome. However, the two siege trains did not combine. The two armies joined in Tuscany for the march to Rome, but d'Aubigny had been ordered to leave his artillery in the Romagna because of the difficulty of taking it over the Appenine passes and in the hope that it would be moved to the *Regno* by sea.[98] In February 1495 Commines was still trying to negotiate its shipment by the Venetians from Castelcaro.[99] Since Venice was by then about to to join the anti-French coalition and later to assist the Aragonese in clearing the French out of Puglia, it seems highly unlikely that the French saw these particular guns again.

However, if Giovio's figure of 'more than 36 guns' is taken to describe all of the French artillery in the Roman parade, it sits quite comfortably beside other sources. The November *Bulletin* is confirmed by a Venetian intelligence report from the end of December 1494 listing the French guns in some detail. With the king of France himself ('a la guardia sua') were six carriage-mounted falconi of 1,000 lb., firing eight pound bullets. With his army (that is, with Montpensier) he had twenty carriage-mounted falconi, and eight 'serpentini: et cannon di peso de 7 miara' shooting fifty pound iron rounds. In addition there was '*Item* colovrine 12 di lunghezza pie 4, trazeva lire 32 di ferro", which must mean 4 x 12-foot long culverins, firing thirty-two 32 pound iron shot. In total forty *carrette*, or carriage-mounted guns (I make the total thirty-eight).[100]

The November 1494 *Bulletin* and Sanuto's December 1494 intelligence tally very closely, giving Montpensier and Charles eight or nine cannon (very close agreement), four culverins (complete accord), and forty falcons (in the *Bulletin*) or 6 + 20 falcons and eight serpentini giving a total of thirty-four small

[96] De la Pilorgerie, 84-9, also reproduced in Lot, 193-4.

[97] Biography in Contamine, 'L'artillerie', 233.

[98] Delaborde, *L'expédition*, 486-7.

[99] Sanuto, 211. This must be Castrocaro Terme, some 12 km south west of Forli, by the foothills of the Appenines.

[100] Sanuto, 127. In the same report Sanuto records twenty-two carriage-mounted guns still at Castelcaro: '12 falconi, 5 cortaldi and 5 colovrine' belonging to the king [Charles VIII] and in the charge of 'Basileo da la Scola vicentino e el gran maestro di l'artigliaria dil Roy...' These were presumably the guns left behind at Castelcaro by d'Aubigny.

guns (in Sanuto). Giovio's 'more than thirty-six guns' is securely bracketed and it seems safe to dismiss any reading of thirty-six cannon *qua* Cannon, which would represent an enormous siege train even by the mid-sixteenth century.[101] The proportion of different types of big gun in Charles VIII's Italian artillery train (eight or nine cannon and four culverin) also matches the numbers and proportions of the cannon to culverins in the other French artillery bands on the eve of the Italian wars, although Charles VIII had very many more small guns in his 1494 campaign.[102]

Once the French took Naples, the picture becomes more confused because there the French captured what was perhaps one of the larger collections of artillery in Italian hands.[103] Four big guns were discovered buried in a monastery in Naples during the first siege, recovered and added to the French batteries.[104] When the French entered the Castel Nuovo in March 1494 they found enormous supplies of guns and ammunition in the fortress magazines, including 'one room full of culverins, supplied with bullets... without number'.[105] These were probably 'light' culverins, and it may be that some of the 200 *coulevrines moyennes* which appear for the first time in the *Bulletin* listing the guns taken with Charles VIII's army for its return to France were removed from the Castel Nuovo. Other guns captured in the Castel Nuovo were known to have been shipped back to France between March and May 1495.[106] Even so, the Castel Nuovo itself clearly remained well furnished with guns and ammunition. Throughout the summer of 1495 the French defenders gave back as good as they received, bombarding much of the city of Naples, causing little loss of life but a good deal of property damage. On 16 July the diarist, Jacomo Gallo, recorded a stone of forty *rotola* which passed through two walls of his room. Gallo counted over 4,000 shots from the castle into the

---

[101] Simon Pepper and Nicholas Adams, *Firearms and Fortifications: Military Architecture and Siege Warfare in Sixteenth Century Siena* (Chicago, 1986), 11-12.

[102] Contamine, 'L'Artillerie', *passim*.

[103] Ryder, 279-82 for Alfonso I's artillery. For later fifteenth century artillery see Filangieri, 'Rassegna', 2, 233.

[104] Sanuto, 246: a uno monasterio, chiamato le Madalene, in la città, era sta scose 4 bombarde grosse per Aragonesi sotto terra, et quelle mandò a tuor et fece fiantar per bombarder el castello.

[105] de la Vigne, 143.

[106] Antonello Coniger, 'Recoglimento de' più scartafi fatto per me Antonello Coniger de certe Coronache moderne & intiche de più cose... in questa Provincia di Terra d'Otranto...', in A.A. Pelliccia, *Raccolta di varie croniche, diari, ed altri opuscoli cosi Italiani, come Latini appartenenti alla storia del Regno di Napoli* (Napoli, 1782), vol. 5, 30: '1495. Die 21. Februarij... mandò in paris le porte da metallo del Castello novo e la maggior parte delle pombarde grandi'. (The famous bronze gates were later recovered when the ship was taken off Rapallo.) Sanuto, 229, says that the Aragonese had removed 'molte bombarde' in ships before the fall of Naples, but in the *munitione* were still 'X bombarde grande di metallo, tra le qual do grandissimi passavolanti... in un'altra parte assa' bombarde di ferro, da fortezze et galee'. (238)

town by July, some of them over nine *palmi* in circumference and weighing as much as fifty *rotola*.[107] These details suggest that the missiles were captured big stone balls, rather than the iron balls which were the preferred projectile in the modern French guns, *pace* Guicciardini, but which had run short during the bombardments of February and March.

On the French return from Naples in May 1495 the main force took with them six Cannon Serpentines, two Gross Culverins, twenty-four falcons and 200 culverines moyennes.[108] From the numbers given in the *Bulletin* these last were evidently light pieces. But the six Cannon Serpentines and two Gross Culverins are sufficiently close to the numbers of big guns that went through Rome on the march south, that they could very well represent most of Charles VIII's mobile siege train, minus any losses they had suffered from fractures or enemy action during the first siege of Naples. Given the rate of loss recorded elsewhere in the period, it would have been surprising if two or three cannon and two culverins had not been damaged in action, blown up or rendered unusable by pressure fractures in the course of heavy bombardment.[109]

For the epic crossing of the Appenine passes on the way to Fornovo, Commines reports that the Swiss infantry manhandled fourteen 'great guns' which the king refused to break up, a common expedient for the movement of heavy artillery at the time, whereby guns were smashed into smaller chunks of metal and then re-cast at their destination.[110] Commines is specific on the number and relates at length the efforts of the German-speaking Swiss infantry, who made up for their lack of discipline at the sack of Pontremoli by manhandling the heavy guns over the passes, urged on by the oratory of La Tremouille. This suggests that the eight big guns taken from Naples had been supplemented by another six heavy weapons collected from Pisa, or the fortresses between Pisa and Sarzana where French garrisons had been left on the way south.

What emerges from this brief analysis is a picture, albeit frustratingly incomplete, of a much smaller French artillery train than might be supposed from the more exaggerated accounts of the invasion. Certainly the number of the biggest siege pieces needs to be revised downwards from the figures

---

[107] Gallo, 20.

[108] Pilorgerie, 277; Lot, 195.

[109] Pepper and Adams, 103.

[110] Commines, 199-200: 'Our train consisted of fourteen extraordinary great guns... Many advised the King, for the expedition's sake, to break up his great guns, but he would by no means consent to it'. The Turks made a general practice of re-casting their guns in the Balkans campaigns of the late fifteenth century, because of the difficulty of moving large weapons over long distances and mountainous terrain. See Simon Pepper, 'Fortress and Fleet: the defence of Venice's mainland Greek colonies in the late fifteenth century', in David S. Chambers, Cecil H. Clough and Michael E. Mallett, *War, Culture and Society in Renaissance Venice. Essays in Honour of John Hale* (London, 1993), 43 and n45.

suggested by some readings of Giovio's celebrated account of Charles VIII's entry into Rome.

Charles VIII's artillery impressed most contemporary Italians, and may well have stimulated new fortification construction, such as that started by the Duke of Ferrara in the summer of 1496.[111] It stimulated Venice immediately to order the new guns and to engage one of their own subjects, Basileo de la Scola, who had been employed by Charles VIII in 1494 to supervise their manufacture.[112] Even before the Castel Nuovo had been retaken in the second siege of 1495, the Aragonese had begun to cast iron balls in the Naples arsenal.[113] Frederick Taylor may have been right to claim that the 'immediate result of the conquest of Naples was a general disbelief in the power of fortresses to withstand the new heavy siege guns'.[114] But it is clearly wrong simply to report de la Vigne's bombastic claim that the 'twin citadels of Naples were so overawed by the preliminary havoc wrought by the French siege train that they surrendered without waiting for the final assault'.[115] The actual performance of the artillery against the many fortifications attacked in 1494-95 bears more critical attention than has been possible here. Monte San Giovanni probably fell to the guns, but the breach was said to be very narrow (and one account mentions a small gateway broken open). Mordano, by one account, was taken when a chance ball broke the drawbridge chain, bringing down the bridge and allowing a group of French to rush the gate.[116] Another version has Mordano overwhelmed by French troops using scaling ladders from the ditch.[117] None of these is a clear cut victory for cannon firepower. Sarzana and Sarzanello, the most modern fortresses to confront the French in 1494, resisted

---

[111] *Diario Ferrarese* 10 May and 10 August 1496, cited by F. L. Taylor, *The Art of War in Italy, 1494-1529* (Cambridge, 1921), 136.

[112] Sanuto, *Diarii*, vol. 1, col. 146 (Maggio 1496): 'Ancora fo principiato dar far alcune artegliarie da bombardar come fanno le bombarde grosse, le qual vien menate su charete al costume et modo usano le francesi. Sono longe quasi pasavolanti, ma grosse. Trazano ballote di peso di 1.6 in 12 l'una, et sempre sta su dicti cari. Et e da saper era in questa terra Basilio da la Scola vicentino, era stato col re di Franza sora le artigliarie, et cussi fo cominzato a far et gitar dicte artigliarie in Canarejo pezi 100 et mandato dicto basilio con lettere per le terre nostre ad tuor legname et far li cari, li qualli a Padova si lavoravano.' Later in the same year 100 'passavolanti, fati novamenti in questa terra per Paolo da Veniexia et ordinate per Basilio da la Scola vicentino, era stato a le artellarie di re di Franza...' were tested at the Lido, col. 375 (November 1496). Basilio was then paid a monthly salary of 12 ducats. After many years of Venetian service, Basileo deserted back to the French during the Battle of Agnadello: Mallett and Hale, 87.

[113] Ferraiolo, 204: 'A dì XXII del ditto mese de noviembro et anno ditto 1495 se incigniaro a fare le palle de fierro, che non gienne foro fatte maye in questa terra. Et facenosse allo Tarcinale, per le bonbarde.'

[114] Taylor, *Art of War*, 94.

[115] Taylor, *Art of War*, 95.

[116] Giovio, vol. 1, 48.

[117] Sanuto, 95.

initial bombardment and the French were evidently eager to avoid a serious siege here if at all possible. Commines described the citadel of Sarzana as 'extremely well fortified' when it was left in the custody of the Count of Roussy shortly before Fornovo.[118] At the first siege of the Castel dell'Ovo, the already demoralised and by then isolated defenders were bombarded into submission. The decisive event in the first siege of the Castel Nuovo seems to have been the magazine explosion. The towering upper works of the castle keep were damaged, of course, but the main outer defences of the cittadella were not breached. The French defenders of the same works held out for almost five months in the second siege of 1495 against a bombardment which, if not as powerful as that of the French, was not to be underestimated. It was the gunpowder mine which finally caused the loss of the cittadella and ditch, and brought about the surrender of the Castel Nuovo in November 1495.

The moral and shock effect of saturation bombardment from a large number of relatively light guns was evidently considerable. The speed with which the French brought their guns into action and kept up a rapid fire represented a novel and frightening experience for troops unused to northern warfare. That the 1494-95 campaign represented a watershed in the conduct of war was appreciated very quickly by contemporaries, but it was French efficiency in the handling of their artillery arm, and their general ruthlessness and determination which proved decisive in the short period of time which was needed for the Italians to adapt their own defensive techniques. A relatively small number of big guns, and a larger number of small ones, made an impact out of all proportion to their real ability to destroy fortresses.

---

[118] Commines, vol. 2, 192.

Appendix: Late fifteenth and early sixteenth-century artillery types

Bombards came in all shapes and sizes. The biggest and heaviest were often made in two or even three sections, transported separately and screwed together on site. The breech section was often separate, and cast with much thicker walls so as to withstand the high pressures of detonation. Shorter bombards were cast in one piece by the end of the fifteenth-century, but the wide barrel (for a big stone ball) and the smaller breech chamber remained characteristic features and eventually evolved into mortars.

The full 'cannon of battery' as it was sometimes later called became standardised as a relatively short-fat muzzle-loader, cast in one piece in bronze about eight to ten feet long, weighing 6,000 to 8,000 pounds and firing something in the region of fifty pound iron shot. The French clearly had some such pieces in 1494, for Giovio specifies eight feet length and a fifty pound iron shot for the biggest guns in Charles VIII's siege train.

Full-sized culverins (also known as *passavolanti* in Italy) were longer single-casting bronze guns with barrels 12-15 feet in length; generally somewhat slimmer than cannon, and firing a smaller iron ball of 30 to 40 pounds weight. They were popular with gunners for long range fire. This was not because of their length - which gave them no real advantage in this respect - but because the strength of the casting in a long-barrelled gun cast breech down in a pit (i.e. under greater pressure at the breech) allowed them to be more fully charged than the cannon, which as a type did not enjoy such a reputation for reliability.[1]

There were other very much smaller calibre culverins in circulation which shared the same long-thin proportions. The culverin *moyenne* was mentioned from time to time in documents from 1494-95 and, from the numbers involved, was clearly very small. Falcons (and their close equivalent, spingards) were amongst the smallest guns to be employed in siege batteries, but useful as accurate sniping weapons against enemy gunners and in other anti-personnel

---

[1] John Francis Guilmartin Jr, *Gunpowder and Galleys: Changing Technology and Mediterranean Warfare at Sea in the Sixteenth Century* (Cambridge, 1974), 284-91, discusses this phenomenon in detail. The book is an important source on early artillery in general.

roles. The smaller falcons usually fired lead bullets to give the projectile extra weight in circumstances where penetration of masonry was not a factor.

Serpentines were a class of long, thin weapons - hence the name. They could be big or small, which makes them a source of considerable potential confusion. Sanuto[2] uses them as synonyms for cannon, but elsewhere reports an order placed by the French in Milan at the beginning of August 1494 for the manufacture of no less than '100 artegliarie a modo serpentine; messe sopra di carrette tirate da un solo cavallo per mando in campo in Parmesana'.[3] Cannon serpentine, however, were long versions of the fifty pounders, and thus very big siege pieces. Basilisc was another term sometimes employed for what might be called the 'stretched' cannon.

---

[2] *Spedizione*, 559
[3] Sanuto, 70-71.

Venice, the French invasion and the Apulian ports

Carol Kidwell

Although in 1495-96 Venice did more than any Italian state to free Italy of foreign invaders she was, nevertheless, not entirely blameless for their presence. In 1483 and in 1484, when she was deserted by the pope on whose behalf, ostensibly, she was waging war against Ferrara, Naples and Milan, she had urged the Duke of Lorraine, whom she sometimes employed as a condottiere, to assert the Angevin claim to Naples and the Duke of Orleans to press his to Milan.[1] Then, when the French threat from Charles VIII, to whom the Angevin claim had reverted, became palpable, Venice proclaimed her neutrality.[2] As Ludovico il Moro told Charles VIII when they met in Asti in 1494, there are three major powers in Italy, the papacy, Milan and Venice. The first two support you and Venice will not budge. Your success is assured.[3]

The French had tried to buy Venetian support for their Neapolitan enterprise by offering the doge the Apulian ports of Brindisi and Otranto, an

[1] *Diarium Ferrariense,* Rerum Italicarum Scriptores, 24 (Milan, 1738), 269; S. Romanin, *Storia documentata di Venezia,* 4, part 4 (Venice, 1856), 415; Armand Baschet, *La diplomatie vénitienne,* (Paris, 1862), 302; H. François Delaborde, *L'expédition de Charles VIII en Italie* (Paris, 1888), 168: Francesco Ercole, *Da Carlo VIII a Carlo V* (Florence, 1932), 40; Ernesto Pontieri, *L'età dell'equilibrio politico in Italia (1454-1494)* (Naples, 1962), 311, 313; Gaetano Cozzi and Michael Knapton, *La repubblica di Venezia nell'età moderna dalla guerra di Chioggia al 1517* (Torino, 1986), 73; Michele Jacoviello, *Venezia e Napoli nel Quattrocento* (Naples, 1992), 69.

[2] Pietro Bembo, *Istoria viniziana* (Milan, 1978), 91-2, 100-1; Philippe de Commynes, *Mémoires,* ed. B. de Mandrot, 2 (Paris, 1903), 214n1; Marino Sanuto, *La spedizione di Carlo VIII in Italia,* ed. Rinaldo Fulin (Venice, 1883), 56; Girolamo Priuli, *I diarii,* ed. Arturo Segre, Rerum Italicarum Scriptores, 24, part 3, vol. 1 (Città di Castello, 1912), 4; Arturo Segre, 'Ludovico Sforza, detto il Moro, e la repubblica di Venezia dall'autunno 1494 alla primavera 1495', *Archivio Storico Lombardo,* ser. 3, 18, ann. 29 (Milan, 1902), 257, 276.

[3] Philippe de Commynes, *Lettres et négotiations,* ed. H. Kerwyn de Lettenhove, 2 (Brussels, 1867), 104 and *Mémoires,* 2, 144.

offer which Barbarigo had shrewdly declined.[4] Venice would, however, remain neutral as long as Venetian territory was unharmed[5] and would even victual French forces if they passed through the Republic.[6] Venice did, nevertheless, take precautions, alerting her fleet, posting guards in places judged vulnerable, raising taxes, hiring mercenaries.[7] Thus, when fears grew throughout Italy that Charles aimed at the conquest of the whole of the peninsula[8] and Venice had, on 31 March 1495, organised the defensive League of St. Mark,[9] she was in a position to strike. As a maritime power she struck first and most successfully at sea and began her action against those very ports which the French had offered her in 1494.[10]

At the beginning of April 1495 Venice ordered the fleet from Corfù to Saseno (modern Sazan), an island off the Albanian coast opposite Otranto, then instructed the Captain General to cruise along the Apulian coast encouraging those ports still in Aragonese hands to hold out against the French.[11] The Venetians were fêted in Brindisi and Otranto but scrupulously instructed the population to remain loyal to Ferrante II, refused to allow them to raise the Lion of St Mark and did not offer any help against the besieging French.[12] They were there as morale builders only. By June, however, Charles VIII had given

---

[4] Pietro Bembo, *Historiae venetae* in: *Degl'istorici delle cose veneziane i quali hanno scritto per pubblico decreto*, 2 (Venice, 1718), 41; Commynes, *Lettres*, 2, 110, *Mémoires*, 2, 205n4, 213; Domenico Malipiero, 'Annali', *Archivio Storico Italiano*, 7 (Florence, 1843), 447 quotes Geronimo Donato's 1496 apology for Venice which states that Charles VIII had promised Venice all of Apulia and the rest of the Adriatic coast of the Kingdom in return for assistance on land and sea; Delaborde, *Expédition*, 415.

[5] Bembo, *Istoria*, 91-2, 100-1; Priuli, *Diarii*, 4.

[6] Commynes, *Mémoires*, 2, 206.

[7] Sanuto, *Spedizione*, 60-62; Malipiero, *Annali*, 321; Priuli, *Diarii*, 10; Commynes, *Lettres*, 2, 148-9; Marco Guazzo, *Historie... ove se contengono la venuta, e partita d'Italia di Carlo Ottavo re di Francia* (Venice, 1547), 18r-v. Although Guazzo plagiarised Sanuto's unpublished account of the French invasion Sanuto's editor, Fulin, 5n1, believes he is worth reading. Guazzo omits details that he considers unimportant or uninteresting.

[8] Bembo, *Istoria*, 118-19; Commynes, *Mémoires*, 2, 214-15, *Lettres*, 2, 106-7; Priuli, *Diarii*, 19; Delaborde, *Expédition*, 481, 528, 530, 533; Fernand Braudel, *The Mediterranean and the Mediterranean world in the age of Philip II* (London, 1992), 460.

[9] Bembo, *Istoria*, 118-19; Malipiero, *Annali*, 333-4; Sanuto, *Spedizione*, 219-20, 269-71, 283-5; Priuli, *Diarii*, 19; Commynes, *Mémoires*, 2, 216-23 and *Lettres*, 2, lxxxviii, 150, 152, 155, 168-9; Guazzo, *Historie*, 109r-110r, 121v-123r; Delaborde, *Expédition*, 590-91; Segre, 'Ludovico', continuation, *Archivio Storico Lombardo*, ser. 3, vol. 20, ann. 30 (Milan 1903), 40-48, 370, 392; Jacoviello, *Venezia*, 140-41, 146, 148.

[10] See note 4. This offer was repeated by Commynes in November 1495, Malipiero, *Annali*, 406.

[11] Bembo, *Historia*, 77; Malipiero, *Annali*, 339; Commynes, *Lettres*, 2, 180-83, 183-7; Guazzo, *Historie*, 125v-126r, 129v-130r; G. Guerrieri, *Le relazioni tra Venezia e Terra d'Otranto fino al 1530* (Trani, 1903), 97; Arturo Segre, 'I prodromi della ritirata di Carlo VIII, re di Francia, da Napoli', *Archivio Storico Italiano*, 34 (Torino, 1904), 363-5; Vito Vitale, *Trani dagli Angioini agli Spagnuoli*, 320-21; Jacoviello, *Venezia*, 153.

[12] Bembo, *Historia*, 77; Malipiero, *Annali*, 339; Guazzo, *Historie*, 130r, 150r, 165v-166r; Guerrieri, *Relazioni*, 97-8; Vitale, *Trani*, 321.

Venice reason to abandon her formal neutrality. The French had attacked and plundered Toscanella, a papal possession, and captured Novara, a city belonging to the duchy of Milan.[13] By the terms of the League of St Mark Venice was committed to avenge aggression against her allies. On 13 June 1495 the Venetian fleet was ordered to attack French positions in Apulia.[14]

The Captain General, Antonio Grimani, who was already on station 'by the rocks of Brindisi',[15] (Isola S. Andrea?), sailed up the coast to French-held Monopoli with twenty galleys and a ship carrying military supplies.[16] On 30 June he and the representative of the Venetian government, the Proveditore, Girolamo Contarini, decided to set fire to some olive groves and a wheat field outside Monopoli to see if the city would surrender. Then they put *stratioti* and seamen ashore, who raided the countryside up to the city gates. There was some fighting, but no offer of negotiation from the French. The next day, 1 July, they decided to attack. Artillery from the ships was answered by cannon from the walls, arrows and projectiles flew.[17] One of the Venetian captains was killed. Then ladders were brought up and Grimani offered 100 ducats to the first man to scale the wall, 50 to the second and 25 to the third and promised the victors the spoils of the city. Fighting was fierce, with 500 Venetians killed. The streets, piazza and houses ran with blood. The situation got out of hand. No respect was shown to church or the civilian population. Ladies of quality were stripped to their shifts and fled, hair streaming, to the bishop's palace, clutching their children.

Grimani personally stopped the rape of Monopoli. With knife in hand he forced the men back to the ships. He sent a surgeon to treat the wounded. He made attacks on person or property a capital offence. The women could return home safely. He distributed biscuits, the mainstay of the Venetian fleet, and the next day flour from the French stores. The Venetian flag was raised, a provisional governor appointed until an official one could be sent out from Venice and the city was exempted from taxation for ten years. A force of 100 *stratioti*, the governor's armed ship and four galleys were left to guard

---

[13] Malipiero, *Annali*, 448-50; Priuli, *Diarii*, 24; Giovanni Italo Cassandro, 'Contributi alla storia della dominazione veneta in Puglia', *Archivio Veneto*, ser. 5, 17 (Venice, 1935), 3. Commynes in his letter to Charles VIII of the second week of April 1495, *Lettres*, 2, 181, had warned him that if he did anything Venice would land men in Apulia.

[14] Bembo, *Historia*, 78; Cassandro, 'Contributi', 4.

[15] Cassandro, 'Contributi', 4n2 quoting *Sen. Secr.* 35, c122.

[16] Bembo, *Historia*, 78; Guazzo, *Historie*, 184v; Guerrieri, *Relazioni*, 99-100.

[17] Frederic C. Lane, 'Naval actions and fleet organization 1499-1502', in J.R. Hale, ed., *Renaissance Venice* (London, 1974), 163, states that Contarini showed a realisation of the importance of shipboard cannon in Apulia in 1495. In *Venice. A Maritime Republic* (Baltimore, MD, 1973), 40, Lane says that Venice was expert at siege operations, using masts of ships as siege towers and spars as launching pads for a descent on enemy walls.

Monopoli. The fleet remained for a few days to reassure the population.[18] Contarini reported the sack of Monopoli to the doge in full detail.[19] The Signoria was horrified and ordered Grimani, henceforth, to conquer the French in Apulia by peaceful means.[20]

In fact two neighbouring towns, Polignano and Mola, surrendered immediately. On 2 July the bishop of Polignano brought chickens and preserved meats (*salumi*) to the Venetians in Monopoli and requested aid against the French at Conversano who were harassing his people. Grimani appointed a governor and sent 135 *stratioti*, the light-armed swift horsemen whom Venice recruited in Greece and Albania, to Polignano. They skirmished that day with the French from Conversano.[21] Mola also begged for a governor.[22] As Venetian ships sailed up the coast Trani and Barletta immediately raised the Lion of St Mark, but were instructed by Grimani to fly the flag of Aragon.[23] Ferrante II had now entered Naples (6 July 1495) and the Kingdom was technically in the hands of its legal ruler. The Senate ordered the fleet back to Corfù,[24] then, at royal and papal request, sent ships directly to Naples to help Ferrante.[25] Venice held on to Monopoli, Polignano and Mola, however, as conquests from the French.[26]

Soon Ferrante II realised that he did not have the resources to drive the French out of the Kingdom. He appealed to Venice. In return for a loan of 200,000 ducats he offered Venice the ports of Trani, Brindisi and Otranto to exploit until the debt was repaid.[27] The agreement was countersigned by the

---

[18] For accounts of the sack of Monopoli see Bembo, *Historia*, 77-8 and *Istoria*, 160-63; Malipiero, *Annali*, 362, 372-6, 399; Priuli, *Diarii*, 29; Sanuto, *Spedizione*, 493-5; Guazzo, *Historie*, 184v-7v; Vitale, *Trani*, 322-4.

[19] The letter is quoted in Malipiero, *Annali*, 372-6.

[20] Vitale, *Trani*, 324-5.

[21] Malipiero, *Annali*, 375; Priuli, *Diarii*, 29n7; Sanuto, *Spedizione*, 497-8; Guazzo, Historie, 187v-188r; Vitale, *Trani*, 323.

[22] Malipiero, *Annali*, 489; Guerrieri, *Relazioni*, 99-100; Vitale, *Trani*, 323; Cassandro, 'Contributi', 4.

[23] Malipiero, *Annali*, 380-81; Vitale, *Trani*, 326-7; Guerrieri, *Relazioni*, 101-2.

[24] Bembo, *Istoria*, 164; Cassandro, 'Contributi', 4n8 quoting *Sen. Secr.* 35, c147.

[25] Malipiero, *Annali*, 381; Sanuto, *Spedizione*, 633-5; Priuli, *Diarii*, 38; Guazzo, *Historie*, 231v; Cassandro, 'Contributi', 5.

[26] Cassandro, 'Contributi', 4n8 quoting *Sen. Secr.* 35, c147 and 13-14.

[27] Negotiations began as early as November 1495, Bembo, *Istoria*, 173-4; Commynes, *Mémoires*, 2, 345n2; Malipiero, *Annali*, 408, 418, 419-22 (agreement quoted), 424; Priuli, *Diarii*, 43-5; Sanuto, *Diarii* 1, 6r, 9, 11, 12-15 (treaty quoted); Giuliano Passero, *Historie* (Naples, 1785), 91-2; A. Zambler and Francesco Carabellese, *Le relazioni commerciali fra la Puglia e la republica di Venezia dal secolo X al XV*, 2 vols. (Trani, 1897-8), vol. 2, 103; Guerrieri, *Relazioni*, 103-5; Vitale, *Trani*, 330-31; Michele Jacoviello, 'Sui traffici veneziani nel Mezzogiorno d'Italia durante la seconda metà del secolo XV', *Atti dell'Accademia Pontaniana*, n.s., 35 (Naples, 1986), 179 and *Venezia*, 117. The agreement was not signed until 21 January 1496. For Venetian military aid in the kingdom see Malipiero, *Annali*, 432-3, 471; Sanuto, *Diarii*, 1, 11-12, 348; Passero, *Historie*, 95; Giacomo Gallo, *Diurnali*, ed.

pope as feudal overlord of the Kingdom of Naples.[28]   Through her political astuteness and her correct conduct Venice had now acquired, legitimately, what she had craved for half a millennium. She quickly appointed administrators and garrisons for the three cities.[29]

Apulia had always been Venice's chief source of grain and remained so even after her fifteenth century expansion on the mainland.[30] To safeguard her food supply Venice had regularly intervened in the upheavals in Apulia, seeking advantageous concessions from the various rulers, Byzantine, Ostrogothic, Lombard, Norman, Swabian, Angevin, Aragonese,[31] suppressing piracy in the Adriatic[32] and defending Christian interests against Saracens and Turks.[33] Her fortunes fluctuated in the face of Pisan and Florentine competition[34] but from the tenth century Venice had flourishing commercial centres in Apulia,[35] by the twelfth an Arab geographer could describe the Adriatic as the Gulf of Venice[36] and by the mid-thirteenth century Venice had a permanent consulate in Trani to look after the affairs of her resident merchant families.[37]

Scipione Volpicella (Naples, 1846), 27; Commynes, *Mémoires*, 2, 345n2, 346-9; *Croniche del Marchese di Mantova*, ed. C. Visconti, *Archivio Storico Lombardo*, 6 (Milan, 1879), 354, 500-12.

[28] Malipiero, *Annali*, 424; Vitale, *Trani*, 331. Venice, knowing that she was envied and hated by the whole of Italy, insisted that the preamble and conclusion of the treaty state that she acted under pressure from the pope and Ferrante II and for the good of Italy, Cassandro, 'Contributi', 6.

[29] Malipiero, *Annali*, 423; Guerrieri, *Relazioni*, 111.

[30] Nicola Nicolini, 'Il consolato generale veneto nel Regno di Napoli', *Archivio storico per le province napoletane*, n.s., 13, 52 (Naples, 1927), 65; Jacoviello, 'Traffici', 159; Braudel, *Mediterranean*, 423.

[31] Carabellese, *Relazioni commerciali*, vol. 1, 6, 7, 8, 14, 15, 16-17; Zambler and Carabellese, *Relazioni*, vol. 2, 12, 14, 20, 31ff, 61-2, 87-8, 91, 94; Gellio Cassi, *Il mare adriatico* (Milan, 1915), 212; Vitale, *Trani*, 272, 288; N. Nicolini, 'Consolato', 62; Pontieri, *Equilibrio*, 212-3; Lane, *Venice*, 68; Michele Jacoviello, 'Venezia e l'avvento di Alfonso il Magnanimo al Regno di Napoli', *Atti dell'Accademia Pontaniana*, n.s., 34 (Naples, 1985), 116, 'Traffici', 161, 164-5, 171-6 and *Venezia*, 51; David Abulafia, 'Venice and the Kingdom of Naples in the last years of Robert the Wise', in David Abulafia, *Italy, Sicily and the Mediterranean 1100-1400* (London, 1987), essay XI, 186.

[32] Romanin, *Storia*, 4, 448-9; Lane, *Venice*, 68, 76-7.

[33] Carabellese, *Relazioni*, 6; Zambler and Carabellese, *Relazioni*, 9; Pontieri, *Equilibrio*, 292; Lane, *Venice*, 27.

[34] Carabellese, *Relazioni*, 16; Zambler and Carabellese, *Relazioni*, 35, 39; Abulafia, 'Venice', 194-5.

[35] N. Nicolini, 'Consolato', 61; Jacoviello, 'Traffici', 159n1 mentions Venetian traders established in the Duchy of Benevento as early as 835.

[36] William J. Bouwsma, *Venice and the defense of republican liberty* (Berkeley/Los Angeles, 1968), 68; Michel Mollat, Philippe Braunstein, Jean Claude Hocquet, 'Réflexions sur l'expansion vénitienne en Méditerranée', in: A. Pertusi, *Venezia e il Levante fino al secolo XV*, 1 (Florence, 1973), 520. The Adriatic was referred to as the Gulf of Venice on some maps as late as the beginning of the nineteenth century, see *La Puglia e il mare*, ed. Cosimo Damiano Fonseca (Milan, 1984), maps on 34, 35, 36-7, 43, 51, 63.

[37] Fausto Nicolini, 'L'origine della ambasiata veneta in Napoli', in *Studi di storia napoletana in onore di Michelangelo Schipa* (Naples, 1926), 249.

From Trani Venice imported wheat, barley, millet, rye, wine, oil, vegetables, almonds, saltpetre and salt.[38] To Trani she exported not only the products of her trade with the east, spices, precious stones, silks and damasks, but also fine woollens from London, rough fustians, metals and timber from her Germanic hinterland, and her own textiles, glass and high-quality crystal.[39] She also traded in Bari, Brindisi, Gallipoli and Taranto, whence her merchants covered the rest of Apulia, Basilicata and Calabria, and participated in fairs in Barletta, Molfetta, Lucera and Lecce.[40]

Venetian families in Apulia did business worth hundreds of thousands of ducats per annum. The gold ducat was legal tender, though most accounts were settled by letters of exchange paid in Trani.[41] This level of trade, together with favourable tax regimes conceded over the centuries by the various ruling powers, had created a great deal of wealth for Venice at the expense of local traders.[42] During the high Middle Ages ships from Barletta, Trani, Bari and Brindisi had transported pilgrims and crusaders to the Holy Land and had done business in Constantinople, Cyprus and Alexandria[43] but Venice had gradually throttled this trade and was now the commercial mistress of the Adriatic. This was a position which Venice was eager to consolidate by introducing good government as soon as Trani, Brindisi and Otranto were hers.

In February 1496 elections were held in the Venetian Senate for the governorships of the three treaty cities. The candidate who received the most votes was assigned to Trani, the second one to Otranto and the third to Brindisi. The terms were of two years' duration with salaries of 600 ducats per annum for Trani and 500 each for Otranto and Brindisi. The governors, called Rectors or Proveditori, were required to take up their posts within a fortnight of appointment.

The Rector was head of the administration and had overall responsibility, through various agents, for justice, commerce, taxation, defence and the implementation of instructions from central government.[44] He was judge in criminal cases, except in the most serious instances, those subject to penalties of banishment or death, which had to be referred to Venice.[45] So did charges

---

[38] Roberto Cessi, *La repubblica di Venezia e il problema adriatico* (Naples, 1953), 57; Jacoviello, 'Traffici', 159 and *Venezia* 44, 95. Antonio Battistella, 'Il Dominio del Golfo', *Nuovo Archivio Veneto*, 35 (Venice, 1918), 13-15.

[39] Jacoviello, *Venezia*, 94; Braudel, *Mediterranean*, 229.

[40] Jacoviello, 'Traffici', 163 and *Venezia*, 98.

[41] Jacoviello, 'Traffici', 166 and *Venezia*, 97, 98; Vitale, *Trani*, 529; Alfonso Leone, 'Il versante adriatico del Regno nell'ultimo quarto del secolo XV: Trani, 1484-1488', *Archivio storico per le provincie napoletane*, ser. 3, 20 (1981), 221-2.

[42] Zambler and Carabellese, *Relazioni*, 40.

[43] Cassi, *Adriatico*, 211-12, 258; Zambler and Carabellese, *Relazioni*, 4-5, 123.

[44] Cassandro, 'Contributi', 15-18.

[45] Cassandro, 'Contributi', 21.

against local Venetian officials.[46] According to the treaty consigning the three cities to Venetian rule the law which the Rector had to apply was that of the kingdom of Naples,[47] but appeals were to Venice not Naples. The Rector could also act as arbitrator in civil cases and heard civil appeals from the judge of first instance, called the Vicario, also a Venetian appointment. There were two other legal functionaries to assist the Rector and Vicario, a Cancelliere or clerk of the court, and an administrator called the Cavallaro.[48] Civil law was that of the local community. The people of the Apulian cities had produced their own customary law based on Roman law, Lombard usage and that of the other Germanic peoples who had settled the region[49] and Venice, as was her wont, upheld it.[50] She was always wary of upsetting local traditions. In addition Trani had its own maritime law, the *Ordinamenta Maris*, supposedly dating back to 1063.[51]

The Rector was head of the local Chamber of Commerce[52] and was responsible for the imposition and collection of taxes by the Chamberlain, who was usually also the Saliniero in charge of the salt pans and the distribution of salt in specified quantities to Apulian cities. He was elected in the Venetian Senate and, in addition to his salary, received 2% of the taxes he collected to encourage him to keep exact records. There was also a Customs Officer in each city who collected duties on merchandise and was assisted by an accountant and a number of clerks. He and the accountant were chosen by the Rector with their appointments confirmed by the central government.[53]

Finally there was a Castellan, also elected in the Venetian Senate, and a galley captain chosen by the Rector in consultation with the local people since he had to recruit his oarsmen locally.[54] The Castellan was a Venetian patrician, as were other senior members of government. During his two-year term of office he was forbidden to leave the castle except in extraordinary circumstances and then only after he had received the Rector's permission and was able to provide a substitute, also a Venetian nobleman, who enjoyed the Rector's confidence. The punishment for disobedience was severe, even capital. The Castellan was paid little, and out of local funds. If his salary was seriously

[46] Cassandro, 'Contributi', 22.
[47] Vitale, *Trani*, 353.
[48] Cassandro, 'Contributi', 21.
[49] Zambler and Carabellese, *Relazioni*, 6.
[50] Cassandro, 'Contributi', 39.
[51] Luigi Genuardi, 'Commercio e diritto marittimo in Napoli nei secoli XIII, XIV e XV', in *Studi di storia napoletana in onore di Michelangelo Schipa* (Naples, 1926), 123; Cosimo Damiano Fonseca, 'Gli 'Ordinamenta et consuetudo maris' di Trani', in: Puglia, ed. Fonseca, 267-76, discusses the scholarship and supports the traditional date.
[52] Cassandro, 'Contributi', 25.
[53] Cassandro, 'Contributi, 32-3.
[54] Cassandro, 'Contributi', 30.

in arrears because the city he was guarding had had a bad year, he could apply to a richer city for payment. Thus in one year the city of Monopoli paid the castellans of both Brindisi and Otranto, as well as the mercenaries serving under them. The Castellan owed obedience to the Rector who transmitted orders from central government.[55]

Mercenaries were stationed in each city for the guard and defence of the walls and the maintenance of public order. Those assigned to the castle were allowed out only two at a time and during daylight, with the Castellan's permission. They were not allowed out at night. They were under the command of a constable and various corporals and were paid out of local funds. Generally mercenaries could not be recruited from among local people and close relations could not serve together in the garrison for security reasons and good order.[56]

There was also a local government which functioned under the Rector. Trani had a council of sixty members, one third of whom were nobles, one third merchants and one third ordinary citizens, with an executive committee of six *priori*, two from each group, who were in office for six months and could not be immediately re-elected. The council elected a mayor or *sindaco* annually, a treasurer, a judicial officer (*mastro giurato*) and procurators. These officials could not be re-elected without a two-year interval between appointments. A decision of the council required a two-thirds majority and the minority must yield to the wishes of the majority. Although the Rector presided at council meetings he was not allowed to propose candidates for office or otherwise interfere in the elections.[57] The whole system of government was akin to that of Venice, but it did entail an even greater degree of personal involvement in a population estimated at about 6,000.[58]

The officials sent out from Venice were not eligible for another administrative post during a period corresponding to the time that they had served abroad, and could not have the same appointment before four years had passed.[59] Considering that these posts were not well paid, but rather a form of compulsory national service for the nobility, this restriction was really a relief and allowed the nobleman to return to the real business of life, which was making money. Moreover, in an unusual application of *noblesse oblige* the salaries of these officials were heavily taxed, up to 50% in times of need, and

[55] Cassandro, 'Contributi', 23-6.

[56] Cassandro, 'Contributi', 27-9.

[57] Cassandro, 'Contributi', 41; Vitale, *Trani*, 349, 471, 473-4. Vito Vitale, 'Un particolare ignorato di storia pugliese. Neofiti e mercanti', *Studi... in onore di M. Schipa*, 237-8 and passim, argues that most of the *mercanti* were *neofiti*, i.e., Christian converts from Judaism, and that the two terms were virtually synonymous.

[58] Vitale, *Trani*, 577.

[59] Cassandro, 'Contributi', 18.

late payment of tax incurred a 4% fine. Genuine employees, however, and the garrison were exempt from taxation.[60]

During his term of office the Rector had to keep a *Libro rosso*, a Red Book, containing an account of his appointment and arrival at his post, his instructions, his proclamations, civil acts, court cases heard, both criminal and civil, the incomings and outgoings of the city, including capital expenditure, in short, a full record of his administration.[61] We find the Rector of Trani reporting that he had to spend money on the port. It was so silted up that whereas a galley had previously been able to come in, now not even a gondola could make way. The pier and the tower were also ruined and had to be rebuilt.[62]

To ensure that the Rector fulfilled his instructions to provide mild, humane and just government Venice sent out two commissioners to check on every aspect of administration, to listen to complaints and to hear petitions. The commissioners made an impressive body, each one accompanied by four servants, two notaries from the ducal chancellery, one accountant with his servant and one cook. They were paid 800 gold ducats each, considerably more than any of the Rectors, their salaries being met half by Venice and half by the governments which they were investigating.[63]

In 1498 commissioners visited Trani, Mola, Polignano, Monopoli, Brindisi and Otranto.[64] One of their surprising findings at Trani was that the guards of the gates had filled in the moats and cultivated them for their own use, thereby damaging the defences of the city and depriving citizens of their ancient right to pasture animals there.[65] On that visitation there was much comment about exploitation of the Jews.[66] In 1499 there were complaints that the mercenaries left the castle at night and engaged in smuggling and damaged the countryside. The commissioners ordered that the city gate by the castle be closed. The trouble continued. On 18 April 1500 the Council of Ten in Venice decided that the two small city gates towards the sea should be walled in, though in such a way that they could be reopened if necessary, because they were not only dangerous for defence but facilitated smuggling. The only gate left open should be the one towards the land.[67] In 1498 the commissioners at Trani also forbade the giving of presents to officials. Offenders would be fined

---

[60] Cassandro, 'Contributi', 18n9, 20n3, 44.
[61] Cassandro, 'Contributi', 20.
[62] Zambler and Carabellese, *Relazioni*, 107; Vitale, *Trani*, 355.
[63] Cassandro, 'Contributi', 35-6.
[64] Vitale, *Trani*, 346; Cassandro, 'Contributi', 34-6.
[65] Vitale, *Trani*, 349.
[66] Vitale, *Trani*, 346ff.
[67] Vitale, *Trani*, 349, 365.

200 ducats, as would recipients.[68] This was a heavy fine, equivalent to more than the average annual pre-tax salary of a Venetian official.[69] Bribery was definitely not to be countenanced. In more serious offences the commissioners were very severe. On 1 August 1502, on the basis of their report, the Council of Ten ordered the Rector of Brindisi to present himself with his two sons at the prison in Venice. The case against them had been carefully prepared and they were tried and sentenced on 11 November 1502.[70] Less important cases within the competence of the local authorities, but which the commissioners felt had been incorrectly judged, were referred back to the relevant courts in Venice.[71]

Venice had conquered Monopoli, Polignano and Mola from the French and received Trani, Brindisi and Otranto from Ferrante II as security for a loan, but Taranto presented the Venetians with a problem. An immensely strong fortified port, it was held by the French. In September and October 1495 Don Federigo, the king's uncle, had tried to capture it with the help of Venetian *stratioti*.[72] He failed.[73] Taranto was, however, later besieged by the Aragonese with the promise of Spanish help.[74] In September 1496 the people of Taranto then sent an ambassador to the Venetian Rector in Monopoli offering the city to Venice. Taranto wanted nothing further to do with the Aragonese. It was Venice or the Turks.[75]

The Venetian Senate discussed their dilemma. If they accepted the city they would be breaking the promise they had made to Ferrante II that they would not take any additional territory in the Kingdom.[76] If they did not, the Turks might arrive in Italy. On 7 October 1496 Ferrante II died. There were those who argued that this freed Venice.[77] On 9 October Taranto raised the Lion of St Mark in four places in the city, including the castle.[78] The French castellan hoped that Venice would pay his salary arrears![79] The Tarentini sent ambassadors to all the princes of Italy proclaiming their new allegiance.[80] At the same time the government of Taranto sent a letter to the Venetian Rector at Brindisi stating that the text of an agreement between Ferrante II and Charles

---

[68] Vitale, *Trani*, 350.

[69] Cassandro, 'Contributi', 20-21 gives information on salaries.

[70] Cassandro, 'Contributi', 38-9.

[71] Cassandro, 'Contributi', 35-6.

[72] Priuli, *Diarii*, 38. For the Venetian contribution see Grimani's letter of 27 September 1495, Sanuto, *Spedizione*, 635.

[73] Sanuto, *Spedizione*, 636, 638; Guazzo, *Historie*, 232r.

[74] Guazzo, *Historie*, 125ff.

[75] Malipiero, *Annali*, 470.

[76] Malipiero, *Annali*, 421; Guerrieri, *Relazioni*, 106, 126.

[77] Guerrieri, *Relazioni*, 131; Andrea Navagero, *Historia Veneta ab origine urbis usque ad annum MCDXCVIII*, Rerum Italicarum Scriptores, 23 (Milan, 1733), 1208.

[78] Malipiero, *Annali*, 474; Guerrieri, *Relazioni*, 129.

[79] 12,000 ducats, Guerrieri, *Relazioni*, 129.

[80] Malipiero, *Annali*, 478; Guerrieri, *Relazioni*, 130.

VIII's viceroy, Montpensier, had come into their hands. Among other things it stated that this city, along with its castles, is granted its liberty and can make a free choice of its future. In these circumstances it has considered various contemporary powers as possible rulers and, with mature counsel, has unanimously decided to give itself to Venice. It has raised the Venetian flag and there have been celebrations throughout the city.[81]

On 3 November ambassadors from Taranto arrived in Venice, three Frenchmen and two Tarentini. They addressed the Senate the following day. The Senate carefully considered their pleas.[82] It informed the new king, Federigo III, about what was going on and sent him copies of the letters from the Tarentini.[83] It consulted its allies in the League of St Mark, Milan and Spain.[84] On 15 November the doge said that he was against accepting Taranto. On 19 November the Senate summoned the ambassadors and told them that Venice could not accept Taranto because of their pact with Ferrante II. They would, however, try to bring about a reconciliation with Federigo III and win their pardon.[85]

News arrived from Corfù that a Turkish fleet had sailed from Constantinople.[86] Knowing that Taranto had sent a messenger to Valona to summon the Turks the Senate decided to send the Head of the Council of Ten, Zancani, to Taranto to compel the city to submit to Federigo III. Don Cesare d'Aragona, Federigo's bastard brother, was camped with an army near the city. Zancani was to persuade the French castellan to hand over the fortresses to him in the presence of a representative of Federigo III and should see to it that the city, suffering near famine because of the siege, was victualled. If Taranto refused to yield peacefully Zancani was to capture the city and hand it over to the Aragonese. He should bring in food supplies from Monopoli whose Rector would have received them from Corfù. Finally, if the Tarentini absolutely refused to pledge allegiance to Federigo and persisted with their threats to give the city to the Turks, Zancani was to take it in the name of Venice and restore it to the king later. Venice would pay the French castellan, who should hand over the fortresses and his arms, then depart with his men.[87] Although Zancani

---

[81] Malipiero, *Annali*, 475-6.

[82] Malipiero, *Annali*, 478; Priuli, *Diarii*, 61 refers to the French captain and two leading citizens; Guerrieri, *Relazioni*, 133.

[83] Guerrieri, *Relazioni*, 131-2.

[84] Guerrieri, *Relazioni*, 134-6.

[85] Guerrieri, *Relazioni*, 137. Priuli, *Diarii*, 61; Bembo, *Istoria*, 191-4. Venice had already been presented with this problem and had taken a similar decision when Aquila, of ever-shifting allegiance, had offered herself in 1495: Malipiero, *Annali*, 338. Unfortunately Venice was not so wise in dealing with Pisa.

[86] Guerrieri, *Relazioni*, 138.

[87] Priuli, *Diarii*, 61; Malipiero, *Annali*, 479, 483; Guerrieri, *Relazioni*, 138-42. Navagero, *Historia*, 1209, has a slightly different version.

himself did not go his substitute, Zorzi Franco, tried to implement the Senate's decision.[88]

Between November and January Taranto tried to give itself to Venice.[89] Although Federigo said that he was pleased that Venice might take Taranto to save it from the Turks,[90] the doge and Senate resisted temptation. Despite pleas from military commanders to keep cities bought with Venetian blood and to secure ports on her trade routes[91] Venice felt that the occupation of Taranto would provoke problems with the pope, the feudal overlord of the Kingdom, who was adept at energising military intervention on his behalf. It was also likely to provoke a reaction from powerful and expansionist Spain, already in Sicily and with an army under the Gran Capitan in southern Italy.[92] Finally, under unremitting Venetian pressure, on 4 Feb. 1497, Taranto returned to obedience to Federigo III. It was the very day when a Turkish ambassador arrived to take possession.[93]

Venetian policy regarding Taranto was realistic and far-sighted. In the three treaty cities of Trani, Brindisi and Otranto Venice tried to introduce good government and win the affections of the local population. Unfortunately the times were hardly propitious. Encouraged by Ludovico il Moro, Federigo III of Naples and the Emperor Maximilian, who all envied and feared Venice for varying reasons and even offered to contribute to their expenses,[94] the Turks attacked Venetian possessions in Greece and the Balkans. After her successes against the French in 1495-96 Venice had reduced her fleet from thirty-five galleys to about thirteen, thereby losing her maritime supremacy.[95] The Turks with a stronger fleet, better ships and more evolved artillery tactics captured the Venetian fortresses of Modon, Coron and Navarino in the Peloponnese, Lepanto on the Gulf of Corinth and Durazzo in Albania. They also raided Dalmatia and Friuli, carrying off people and animals.[96] Naturally enough the Apulian ports

---

[88] Priuli, *Diarii*, 61; Malipiero, *Annali*, 483; Navagero, *Historia*, 1209.

[89] Priuli, *Diarii*, 61.

[90] Malipiero, *Annali*, 476; Navagero, *Historia*, 1208; Guerrieri, *Relazioni*, 146. At other times Federigo said that he would rather lose his whole kingdom than let the Venetians have Taranto.

[91] Malipiero, *Annali*, 365, 375; Cassandro, 'Contributi', 4.

[92] Malipiero, *Annali*, 365; Vitale, *Trani*, 337; Guerrieri, Relazioni, 150.

[93] Malipiero, *Annali*, 484.

[94] Priuli, *Diarii*, 97, 131; *Diario Ferrarese*, 365-6; Vitale, *Trani*, 363, 367; V.J. Parry, 'The Ottoman Empire (1481-1520)', in *New Cambridge Modern History*, vol. 1, 403; Guerrieri, *Relazioni*, 168; Lane, 'Naval actions', 148.

[95] Lane, 'Naval actions', 148. In addition many of the galleys which had been long at sea, were in poor condition and the crews were suffering severely from the French disease, Marino Sanuto [Girolamo Priuli], *De bello gallico*, Rerum Italicarum Scriptores, 24 (Milan, 1738), 74.

[96] Priuli, *Diarii*, 132, 203, 206; *Diario Ferrarese*, 365; Vitale, *Trani*, 367; Parry, 'Ottoman Empire', 402-4; J.R. Hale, 'International relations in the west: diplomacy and war', *New*

were expected to contribute to the war. They armed galleys[97] and Trani supplied biscuits, not always of the best quality,[98] to the fleet stationed in Corfù. But trade was badly disrupted[99] and the population, like Venetian citizens at home, was heavily taxed to pay for the war, as heavily taxed as they had been under the Aragonese.[100]

There were other problems. Federigo, eager to get back his ports without repaying the debt, and therefore intent on weakening Venice, refused to allow citizens of the kingdom to enlist in Venetian galleys, restricted the sale of grain to merchants in Trani, placing a heavy export tax on it and prohibited the sale of saltpetre needed for making gunpowder.[101] In these hard times there were anti-Venetian uprisings in the cities.[102]

The end of the Turkish war (1501) was followed immediately by the invasion of the kingdom of Naples by French and Spanish armies, the overthrow of Federigo III, who had even offered Taranto and Lecce to the Turks in an attempt to get their support,[103] and the division of the Kingdom between the two occupying powers (1501). In the inevitable war that followed between the French and Spanish occupiers the Spanish eventually triumphed and, in January 1504, the kingdom of Naples became part of the Spanish empire. But during those three turbulent years the ports had suffered grievously.

In 1502 the French had reoccupied most of Apulia and were besieging the Spanish in Barletta.[104] Venice tried to maintain the neutrality of the ports but she did not have sufficient forces in Apulia to give them adequate protection.[105] The French complained to the Senate that Venice gave money to the Spanish. The Senate replied that it was not the state but individual merchants, who were free men. The French complained that Trani supplied besieged Barletta with grain. The doge denied it. There was a shortage of grain in Apulia and Venice had had to import it from Sicily.[106] Then the Spanish ambassador complained that the Rector of Trani was anti-Spanish. The doge denied it. Trani was neutral and the population had stood on the walls watching French and Spanish fighting outside and had not intervened.[107]

Cambridge Modern History, vol. 1, 265; Lane, 'Naval actions', 146, 162, 164; Lane, *Venice*, 242.

[97] Sanuto, *Diarii*, 4, 279.
[98] Sanuto, *Diarii*, 4, 1584.
[99] Vitale, *Trani*, 311.
[100] Cassandro, 'Contributi', 45; Vitale, *Trani*, 307, 311.
[101] Vitale, *Trani*, 356, 357, 359, 361, 362; Cassandro, 'Contributi', 46.
[102] Zambler and Carabellese, *Relazioni*, 106.
[103] Vitale, *Trani*, 363.
[104] Vitale, *Trani*, 379.
[105] Vitale, *Trani*, 384, 388.
[106] Sanuto, *Diarii*, 4, 339, 558.
[107] Sanuto, *Diarii*, 4, 473.

Soon complaints reached the Senate from Trani of the ill-treatment of its citizens by both the French and Spanish who intercepted grain shipments and pillaged the countryside, driving off herds.[108] There was a serious food shortage and great poverty. Trade was ruined. By the time the war ended at the beginning of 1504 Trani was half-depopulated, Monopoli in great misery, the troops unpaid and suffering.[109]

Venice was never able to restore the prosperity of the ports. In 1509 they were returned to the kingdom of Naples. Ferdinand the Catholic, its new ruler, paid the debt incurred by Ferrante II, which the pope had legitimated.[110] In 1528-29 Venice held the ports again, then surrendered them at the Peace of Bologna. She left no permanent legacy in Apulia.

---

[108] Sanuto, *Diarii*, 4, 620, 626, 627, 728-9, 763, 771-2; Vitale, Trani, 384ff.

[109] Vitale, *Trani*, 381-3, 389-90.

[110] Cassandro, 'Contributi', 14. Priuli, *Diarii*, 62, states that in addition to the loan to Ferrante II Federigo III owed Venice 300,000 ducats for her assistance in the reconquest of the Kingdom through her provision of men-at-arms and ships.

Part III
Reaction and effects

'Il semble que ce soit là un vrai Paradis terrestre': Charles VIII's conquest of Naples and the French Renaissance

A. V. Antonovics

Charles VIII's Italian expedition of 1494/5 has traditionally been regarded as a great turning point in French cultural history. It was perhaps Jules Michelet, the nineteenth-century Romantic historian, who first vividly presented the classic picture of a boorish French nobility awestruck by the beauties of Renaissance Italy.[1] The theme was taken up later, for English readers, in the influential volume by W.H. Ward on *Renaissance Architecture in France*:

> The French invasions gave an opportunity for large numbers of men of all classes to see with their own eyes the triumphs of an alien culture. Italy received them in her gayest mood and most festive attire. In the first few months the French army passed from fête to fête. Natural beauties and marvels of art were unrolled before them in an ever-shifting pageant... What wonder that eyes accustomed to the narrow and muddy alleys of French cities with their crowded gables, the grim blank walls of feudal keeps, the grey stone and the darkened timber of the north, should be dazzled at the sight of sunbathed piazzas and colonnades, paved streets lined with palaces which glowed with marble and frescoes. Or that airy villas among terraced gardens, set with fountains and statues, orange trees and vine pergolas, should seem of more than earthly beauty to their new northern owners... Italy was henceforth the promised land, the home of all delights of mind and sense; and it became the ambition of every French gentleman to reproduce at home the palaces and gardens of Italy, and to people them with paintings, statuary, and marble fountains... It was to soldiers that France owed the greatest impetus towards the Renaissance, for the campaigns gave thousands of Frenchmen, from kings downwards, an opportunity of seeing and admiring Italian art.[2]

---

[1] J. Michelet, *Oeuvres Complètes*, vol. 7, *Histoire de France au seizième siècle: Renaissance et Reformation*, ed. P. Villaneix (Paris, 1978).

[2] W.H. Ward, *Renaissance Architecture in France* (2nd ed., New York, 1976), 3-4.

The stimulus of the Italian Renaissance has been seen by many historians as all the more necessary in late fifteenth-century France because of the decline and disintegration of its native medieval heritage: the later Middle Ages being viewed as a period of cultural exhaustion in the visual arts and intellectual activity. This interpretation was summed up in Arthur Tilley's *Dawn of the French Renaissance*, where he set out to show why 'France was now ready for the Renaissance'.[3]

Not all art historians, of course, have succumbed to this interpretation. In the later nineteenth century, Louis Courajod, curator of the sculpture collection of the Louvre in Paris, reacted against the thesis of profound Italian influences on French culture. Indeed he argued that Italy owed more to northern Europe than vice versa. For Courajod French Renaissance art arose first as a spontaneous national development, related to the development of a strong monarchy and new aristocracy and a new merchant and legal class. It was from an interaction of Flemish influences adopted in northern France about the middle of the fourteenth century that 'the general movement from which emerged the definitive style of the Renaissance, including the style of the Italian Renaissance' arose. The influence of clasical art as such was only of secondary importance, influential only after 'the Italian consciousness was enlightened by the emancipating counsels of naturalism'. Italian art indeed lagged behind that of the north until in fifteenth century Italy 'art at last entered the current of ideas which France and Flanders had brought to birth'. Without the Hundred Years' War, civil war and foreign occupation, Courajod believed that a spontaneous northern Renaissance already under way, including that of the Valois courts, could have effected the cultural conquest of Europe.[4]

While these arguments about national cultural leadership have a fascination, they are arguably misconceived. Perhaps different areas of cultural activity have different chronologies. In the field of music, for example, northern Europe had little to learn from Italy and Italian rulers recruited intensely for French and Flemish musicians. Or it may be that there were experts from particular regions in particular traditional skills who were in demand internationally: workers in marble, makers of wooden or stuccoed ceilings, marquetry or various kinds of ceramics might be examples. The military engineers or manufacturers of specialised armour are a further category.

---

[3] A. Tilley, *The Dawn of the French Renaissance* (Cambridge, 1911), 591.
[4] Courajod's views are set out especially in his *Leçons professées a l'École du Louvre (1887-1896)*, ed. H. Lemmonnier and A. Michel, vol. 2, *Origines de la Renaissance* (Paris, 1901). Further on Courajod, see W.K. Ferguson, *The Renaissance in Historical Thought* (Cambridge, MA, 1948), 316-19; F. Haskell, *History and Its Images* (New Haven/London, 1993), 442-5, 465. *Dictionnaire de Biographie Francaise*, 'Courajod, L-C-L.' (Roman d'Amat), s.v.

The greatest obstacle to clear historical thought in these areas are *a priori* assumptions made that tend to oust conclusions founded on evidence. The artistic links between France and Italy during the Renaissance remain to be fully explored; and how much there is still to discover is only just emerging from detailed archival work.[5] Too often historians have started with assumptions of how the French in Italy must have reacted to their surroundings, rather than demonstrating from the records how they did, in fact, react. Influences are not to be assumed.

What, for example, did the King, his nobles and ordinary soldiers see and admire in Italy? What did they bring back with them? What did they commission and why? The ordinary soldiers, even those of some rank, by and large had other things to think about in Italy than looking at works of art. We have remarkable testimony of their preoccupations in an extensive correspondence that survives from their stay in Naples early in 1495.[6] Far from everything in Italy impressed them. Charles VIII himself wrote of the air of Naples that it was 'bad and hot, difficult to endure'. One soldier, witnessing the royal entry into the city, found it all 'tedious, but do not wonder at it, for I was on foot and overcome by the most unquenchable thirst'.[7] The wines Commynes described as 'sour and our men did not like this'.[8] Nor were the women any more pleasing or accessible. One correspondent lamented how the beautiful women were kept out of sight: 'one never sees them at all, which makes us quite ill. As for me I have no hostess who is not aged over sixty'. Admittedly he was writing to his wife and no doubt wished to reassure her, but the theme was common.[9] For those soldiers who did have sexual adventures, there loomed the dreadful prospect of *le mal de Naples*, the scourge of syphilis, so graphically described by contemporaries. What most soldiers looked for was to be paid on time, to gather some loot and get back home as quickly as possible. There were many things to attend to: Tanneguy de la Gambertière wrote from Naples to his brother to advise on a sluice to divert water from a local stream to his castle and its surrounding meadows.[10] As the delays to Charles VIII's return grew, so did the complaints. 'We shall leave tomorrow, tomorrow and tomorrow and tomorrow never comes', wrote one soldier. And what they brought back home

---

[5] See, for example, the new research on Francis I's artistic patronage summarised now in R.J. Knecht, *Renaissance warrior and patron: the reign of Francis I* (Cambridge, 1994).

[6] A. Cutolo, 'Nuovi documenti francesi sulla impresa di Carlo VIII', *Archivio storico per le province napoletane*, 63 (1938),183-257. See also on newsletters from Italy, J.P. Seguin, 'La découverte de l'Italie par les soldats de Charles VIII', *Gazette des Beaux-Arts*, 6:50, 127.

[7] Cutolo, *Nuovo documenti*, 226.

[8] *The Memoirs of Philippe de Commynes*, ed. S. Kinser, transl. I. Cazeaux (Columbia, South Carolina), vol. 2, 456.

[9] Cutolo, *Nuovi documenti*, 234-5.

[10] Cutolo, *Nuovi documenti*, 250-51.

were not, except rarely, works of art. Jacques de Puyelamand packed a trunk to be shipped to Lyons and picked up by his girlfriend, Catherine Chauvet: 'a hundred livres of linen and a case full of small trinkets [petites follies]'. He did not seem too optimistic that they would arrive safely: 'but if they were to be lost, it would not be a great loss'.[11] Jean Lapostolle brought back for his wife some oil from the shrine of St Nicholas of Bari in Apulia 'which is good against every disease'.[12] Another companion of Charles VIII returned from Naples with white mulberry plants for his parish.

Only a few tantalising references to an interest in the artistic fashions of Italy appear in this correspondence. Jacques du Puyclamand wrote to Jean Robertet, secretary to the duchess of Bourbon at Moulins,[13] that 'he had secured for him some good ancient medallions [medailles anticques]'.[14] Louis de Poncher asked that the building that he had started before his departure be completed in the manner that he would have wished had he been back home; seemingly, there was no hint of changes required to account for Italian models.[15]

Among the few works of art known to have been brought back from Italy by persons about the king was the mosaic of the Virgin and Child with two angels, by David Ghirlandaio, given by Jean de Gannay to the church of St Merri in Paris and now in the Musée de Cluny.[16] A good deal of the French booty was indeed lost on route back from Naples, a major part at Fornovo and other items in the naval encounter near Rapallo in 1495.[17] In 1497, the French Cardinal, Jean de Bilhères, bishop of Lombez and abbot of St Denis, and frequent royal envoy to Rome, commissioned Michelangelo's Pietà, now in St Peter's, Rome.[18] Labande-Mailfert doubts if a commission of this importance,

---

[11] Cutolo, Nuovi documenti, 218.

[12] Cutolo, Nuovi documenti, 244.

[13] For Jean Robertet, G. Robertet, Les Robertet au XVIe siècle (Paris, 1888); C.M. Zsuppan, 'Jean Robertet's life and career', Bibliothèque d'Humanisme et Renaissance, 31 (1969), 333-42.

[14] Cutolo, Nuovi documenti, 232.

[15] Cutolo, Nuovi documenti, 248: 'Je vous prie qui vous plaist faire parachever mon bastiment en maniere qui puisse estre paracheve quant nous serons par dela'.

[16] E. De Ganay, Un Chancelier de France sous Louis XII: Jean de Ganay (Paris, 1932). The mosaic at Paris is signed and dated in 1496. For workshops of mosaic artists in Renaissance Florence, M. Wackernagel, The World of the Florentine Renaissance Artist, trans. A. Luchs (Princeton, 1981), 35, 183, 185.

[17] On Fornovo, A. Benedetti, Diario de bello carolino, ed. and trans. D.M. Schullian (New York, 1956), Commynes, ed. Kinser, vol. 2, 533 on Rapallo; for the loss of booty from Naples, L. Volpicella, Le porte di Castelnuovo e il bottino di Carlo VIII (Naples, 1921) = Napoli nobilissima, 2nd ser., 1 (1920), 153-60.

[18] On the patron, C. Samaran, Jean de Bilhères-Lagraulas, cardinal de Saint-Denis (Paris, 1921). On his links with the medallist and historian, Giovanni di Candida, J. Porcher', Jean de Candida et le cardinal de Saint-Denis', Mélanges d'archéologie et d'histoire, 39 (1921-22), 319-26. For the commission, K. Weil-Garris Brandt, 'Michelangelo's Pietà for the Capella del Re di Francia', in Il se rendit en Italie. Études offertes à André Chastel (Rome/Paris,

designed for the chapel of the kings of France, could have been made without Charles VIII's personal knowledge or approval, but documentary evidence on this is lacking.[19] How directly this is related to the French expedition is again problematical.

The cardinal of St Denis is but one example of a continuous story of diplomatic and ecclesiastical links with the Italian peninsula in this period, which included notable art patrons such as Cardinal Guillaume d'Estouteville.

What of the visual impact of Italy upon French minds? The case of Philippe de Commynes is both puzzling and perhaps intructive. A specialist diplomat and counsellor on Italian affairs as well as historian of the expedition, his frequent contacts with Florence and other areas of Italy seem to have had limited cultural impact.[20] The *Mémoires* of Commynes alluded rarely to the artistic monuments of Italy during his account of the invasion. He mentioned the tomb of Giangaleazzo Visconti at the Certosa of Pavia: 'this beautiful church, all of fine marble, and in truth the finest that I have ever seen'.[21] In Florence he showed concern for the plunder by the mob of the Medici palace and its collection of jewels, cameos and medallions.[22] When in Venice, in 1495, Commynes noted 'the most adorned and well furnished churches' that he had seen. He judged the Grand Canal 'the most beautiful street in the whole world and the one with the most beautiful buildings', and described in detail the large and high houses 'made of fine stone... and all painted', their facades of white marble, and the 'rich mantlepieces of cut marble, gilded bedsteads, and the painted and gilded screens, and very fine furniture inside'. The Doge's Palace, again with its 'well-cut marble and richly gilded rooms' left him equally impressed and above all the mosaic chapel of San Marco and its treasury, with 'twelve or fourteen large diamonds... one weighs seven hundred carats and the other eight hundred'.[23] Commynes seems as out of his depth in matters cultural as arguably he was in diplomacy.

What of the king, Charles VIII? The best known comments are those made in the letter of 28 March 1495 from Naples to the duke of Bourbon, in

---

1987), 77; M. Hirst, 'Michelangelo, Carrara and the marble for the Cardinal's Pietà', *Burlington Magazine*, 127 (1985), 154-7.

[19] Labande-Mailfert, *Charles VIII et son milieu (1470-1498). La jeunesse au pouvoir* (Paris, 1975), 504.

[20] For his biography, J. Dufournet, *La vie de Philippe de Commynes* (Paris, 1969). For his contacts with Italy, J. Blanchard, *Commynes et les Italiens* (Paris, 1993).

[21] *Commynes*, ed. S. Kinser and trans. I. Cazeaux, 465. On a later description of Pavia by a Frenchman see J. Snow-Smith, 'Pasquier Le Moyne's 1515 Account of Art and War in Northern Italy: a translation of his diary from le couronnement'. *Studies in Iconography*, 5 (1979), 173-234.

[22] *Commynes*, ed. Kinser, vol. 2, 471. The precise fate of this collection is a matter of some controversy.

[23] *Commynes*, ed. Kinser, vol. 2, 489-92.

charge at home during Charles VIII's absence. These record the king's initial response to what he had seen at Naples:

> Moreover, you could not believe the beautiful gardens that I possess in this city, for by my faith it seems that there is nothing lacking except Adam and Eve to make them into an earthly paradise so beautiful as they are and full of all fine and excellent things, as I hope to tell you about, when I next see you. I have also found here some very fine painters; I will send them to you in order to paint for you the most beautiful ceilings [planchers] possible. The ceilings of Beauce, Lyons and other places in France do not in any way approach the beauty and richness of those here; that is why I shall gather some of them together and bring them with me, and have some made at Amboise.[24]

We shall see how far the king's intentions were fulfilled later.

One tantalising aspect of the artistic impact of the expedition is the reference to one of the king's painters in Italy to be found in the letter sent by Charles VIII to the duke of Milan some months after the battle of Fornovo:

> My cousin, I have found that my physician, master Theodore, lost on the day of Fornovo, certain medical books which were taken by one or other of the people who were on your side. There were also lost numerous paintings of diverse shapes and devices which one of my painters had drawn and portrayed on which there were certain cities and castles, quatres marines[25] and still other novelties from over there [nouvelles choses de par-dela], and apparently the registers and papers which relate to my expense accounts.[26]

He went on to request help for their safe return. In a separate letter to the marquis of Mantua, Charles VIII acknowledged: 'I have received from your herald, your letter together with certain drawings which were lost by one of my painters and which were recovered among your soldiers, for which I am most grateful.'[27]

Is it possible to identify this 'king's painter'? There seem to be two front-running candidates. Jean Bourdichon, the best known painter at the French Court under Charles VIII, began in the service of Louis XI and was called *peintre du roi* by 1484. He was first and foremost a painter of miniatures.[28] Art historians have speculated on a possible visit by Bourdichon

---

[24] *Lettres de Charles VIII*, ed. P. Pelicier, vol. 4, 187-88.

[25] Four marines: one scholar translates as marine paintings, but could they be maps of coasts or harbours?

[26] *Lettres de Charles VIII*, vol. 4, 259-60.

[27] *Lettres de Charles VIII*, vol. 4, 321-2 (7 Dec. 1495).

[28] There is a very large scattered literature on Bourdichon. E. Male, 'Jean Bourdichon et son atelier', *Gazette des Beaux Arts* (1904), 441-57; J. Guignard, 'Quelques oeuvres de l'atelier de Bourdichon conservés en Italie', *Mélanges d'archéologie et d'histoire*, 56 (1939); McGibbon, *Jean Bourdichon* (privately printed, 1933); R.Fiot, *Jean Bourdichon et Saint Francois de Paule* (Tours, 1961); J. Ehrmann, 'Un portrait inédit de Charles VIII par Jean Bourdichon', *Bulletin de la Société Antiquaires de France* (1978-9), 265-72 (not a convincing attribution).

to Italy, perhaps even before the French expedition of 1494, possibly to the court of Ferrante of Naples. This is based largely on the identification of his hand in a panel painting, a triptych at Naples.[29] There is much better evidence for his role in painting banners, harnesses and costumes for men-at-arms at the time that the expedition was in preparation. For Louis of Orléans, for example, Bourdichon made eight banners with the duke's arms on one side and those of Milan on the other. The large payment of 252 l.t. suggests that it was a luxurious item.[30]

Perhaps a stronger case can be made for Jean Perreal, although anyone who appears in the records as 'Jean de Paris' was bound to create problems for historians. Only recently has the study of the documents allowed one to distinguish more clearly a Jean de Paris, who probably moved from the household of Charlotte of Savoy to work for Pierre de Bourbon, lord of Beaujeu, from another Jean de Paris, who is first known from the town accounts of Lyons.[31] The problem, however, remains of fitting known paintings or miniatures to Perreal's oeuvre, despite his great reputation among contemporaries.[32] Perreal is not recorded as *valet de Chambre* or *peintre du roi* before 1495. It is quite possible that he did accompany the king on his expedition into Italy and indeed there is a reference - yes, 'Jean de Paris'! - in the Naples soldiers' correspondence previously mentioned.[33]

Another cryptic allusion to Charles VIII's artistic taste is to be found in Vasari's *Life* of the Florentine architect, Giuliano da Sangallo. The story is recounted of the presentation to the French king at Lyons by Cardinal Giuliano della Rovere, legate at Avignon, of 'the model of a palace made for him by Giuliano [da Sangallo], a very richly decorated work, with spacious apartments capable of accommodating all the court... and the king was so delighted that he rewarded the architect liberally, praising him loudly, and heartily thanking the Cardinal'.[34]

---

[29] J.Dupont, 'Un triptyque de Jean Bourdichon au Musée de Naples', *Monuments et Mémoires E. Piot*, 35 (1935-36), 179-88.

[30] Fiot, *Jean Bourdichon*, 51.

[31] P. Pradel, 'Les autographes de Jean Perreal', *Bibliothèque de l'École des Chartes*, 121 (1963), 132-86; C. Sterling, 'Une peinture certaine de Perreal enfin retrouvée', *L'Oeil*, 103/104 (1963), 2-15, 64-5.

[32] For a tortuous but ultimately unconvincing attempt to identify the Maitre de Moulins as Jean Perreal, see M. Huillet d'Istria, *La Peinture française de la fin du Moyen Age (1480-1530). De l'art gothique à la première Renaissance. Le Maitre de Moulins* (Paris,1961). An important critique in A. Chatelet, 'A Plea for the Master of Moulins', *Burlington Magazine*, 104 (1962), 517-24.

[33] A. Cutolo, 'Nuovi documenti', 210. He was said to be in the entourage of Charles Le Coq, *président des généraux des monnaies*.

[34] G. Vasari, *Lives* (Everyman's Library, London, 1927), vol. 2, 216.

Unfortunately, while we know that Giuliano da Sangallo was active in Provence somewhere between 1494 and 1496, when details are known of his itinerary, no evidence has come to light that points to royal patronage at this time or later.[35]

The major monument that reflects the artistic impact of the expedition to Naples is the castle at Amboise. There Charles VIII began what Commynes described as:

> the most august and magnificent building that any prince had undertaken for one hundred years before... He had brought his artificers (as his carvers, painters, and such like) from Italy, so that the whole fabric seemed the enterprise of a young prince who had no thought of dying so soon: for he collected whatever was commended to him either in France, Italy, or Flanders.[36]

Unfortunately, beyond this striking testimony to the eclectic artistic influences on the French court at the time, Commynes tells us little further about the layout of the building. Because of the successive demolitions and alterations that the castle has undergone, it is not easy to be certain about what was completed during the king's lifetime. Only a general picture can be pieced together from the fragmentary accounts and later drawings that survive.[37]

Nor can one be much clearer about how far it was the sight of various palaces in Italy that inspired the king or led him to make any significant modifications to the existing buildings. It is above all Poggioreale, a few miles outside Naples, that seem to have impressed Charles VIII and possibly led him

---

[35] From a considerable modern literature one may consult S. Borsi, *Giuliano da Sangallo. I disegni di architettura e dell'antico* (Rome,1985) and, as a foretaste of forthcoming larger study of his palace-designs and building, L. Pellechia, 'Reconstructing the Greek House: Giuliano da Sangallo's Villa for the Medici in Florence', *Journal of the Society of Architectural Historians*, 52 (1993), 323-38, which refers to other palace-plans of the architect. E. Muntz, 'Giuliano da San Gallo et les Monuments Antiques du Midi de la France au XVe siècle', *Mémoires de la Société Nationale des Antiquaires de France*, 45 (1994), prints an itinerary by the architect in southern France from April-May 1496, accompanied by his patron Cardinal Giuliano della Rovere.

[36] *Commynes*, ed.Kinser, vol. 2, 589

[37] For drawings, see D. Thomson, ed. Jacques Androuet du Cerceau, *Les Plus Excellents Batiments de France* (Paris, 1988). In general from the extensive literature on Amboise L. Bosseboeuf, *Amboise, le château, la ville et le canton* (Tours, 1897); J. Melet-Sanson, *Le château d'Amboise* (Paris, 1973); J. Melet-Sanson, 'La ville d'Amboise au XVe siècle', *Bulletin de la Société Archéologique de Touraine* (1974), 263-9. On Charles VIII's emblems at Amboise, Y. Labande-Mailfert, 'L'épée dite flamboyante de Charles VIII', *Bulletin monumental*, 108 (1950), 91-101. An important recent contribution is E. Thomas, 'Les logis royaux d'Amboise', *Gazette des Beaux-Arts* (1994), 44. The main buildings accounts so far printed are C.L. de Grandmaison, *Compte de la construction du chateau royal d'Amboise (1495-96)* (Paris, 1912); C. de Grandmaison, 'Compotus particularis pagamenti oramentorum et aliorum utensilium castri Ambasie', *Bulletin de la Société archéologique de Touraine*, 1 (Tours, 1866-70), 253-304; A. de Spont, 'Documents relatifs a la reconstruction du château royale d'Amboise', *Correspondance historique et archéologique*, 1 (1894), 367-72. A useful general introduction in English is I. Dunlop, *The Chateaux of the Loire* (London, 1969).

to emulate their beauty and richness, including the splendour of their gardens.[38]
The chronicler of Charles VIII's expedition, André de la Vigne, was almost at a
loss for words to describe Poggioreale:

> such that the fine words of master Alain Chartier, the skill of master Jean de Meun,
> and the hand of Fouquet could not sufficiently tell of it, describe it or paint it. It is
> situated as far from the city as is Plessis from Tours, and from the gate to the city as
> far as the villa, one approaches it by wide paths and avenues set on all sides. It is
> surrounded by orange-trees and by rosemary and other fruit trees both in winter and
> summer in such great quantity that one cannot estimate it. The gardens are enclosed
> by brick walls, and are so beautiful that I could not in one lifetime describe them to
> you. Around the villa are beautiful fountains, the trees full of birds of all kinds and
> more exotic than you could imagine. On the other side there is a fine park where
> there are large animals in abundance, a warren of rabbits and hares, another of
> pheasants, of partridges, and it seems that everything is there fashioned for human
> pleasure.[39]

In areas of France such as the Loire valley, under the guidance of such figures
as René of Anjou, increasingly elaborate standards of comfort and decoration
had already been introduced, but Amboise was intended to outshine such prior
initiatives.[40]

Charles VIII had to work with an existing fairly restricted site and to
extend building work already began. We know that the work had gained new
momentum even before Charles VIII's Italian expedition of 1494. Important
testimony comes from the Florentine envoy in France in the autumn of 1493,
Gentile Becchi, who reported:

> He begins to make designs of walls; and he had shown to us his model [modello] for a
> castle that he is building at Amboise, which he wishes to make into a city, bringing a
> fountain there; and continually he is making walls there.[41]

From the end of Louis XI's reign can be dated the building of the brick oratory
of Sainte-Blaise, to which was later added the chapel proper, with its famous
bas-relief on the tympanum of the vision of St Hubert. The main work on the
chapel seems to have been completed by 1493 and reflects the powerful Flemish
influences on French art at the time.[42]

---

[38] On Poggioreale, A. Blunt, *Neapolitan Baroque and Rococo Architecture* (London,
1975), 12-14; G.L. Hersey, *Alfonso II and the Artistic renewal of Naples* (New Haven, 1969),
60, citing earlier literature at 60 n.9.

[39] André de la Vigne, *Le Voyage de Naples*, ed. A. Slerca (Milan, 1981), 248-9.

[40] Angevin castles: N. Coulet, A. Planche, F. Robin, *Le Roi René: Le prince, le mécène, le
mythe* (Aix-en-Provence, 1982).

[41] *Négociations diplomatiques de la France avec la Toscane*, ed., G. Canestrini and A.
Desjardins (Paris, 1859), vol. 1, 339-40.

[42] Chapel of St Blaise, P. Vitry, *Michel Colombe et la sculpture francaise de son temps*
(Paris, 1901), 242-6.

The building accounts provide a fuller record of work during these years, as well as details on the furnishings supplied by various merchants and *tapissiers*. The master mason was Colin Biart, who was involved in so much castle-building of this period at Le Verger, Blois and Gaillon.[43] He received a lower salary than the king's painter, Antoine Bryant, in charge of the decoration of the main rooms and galleries. The names in the accounts of 1495/6 are very predominantly French. It is largely northern tapestries that serve as decorations such as a tapestry ceiling *de menue verdure* and three curtains of taffeta sustained by buckles. However, in 1496 two men were paid 20d. for moving 'the tapestry brought from Naples' from one room to another.

There exist two key documents on the impact of the Neapolitan expedition. First, the reference to a special convoy that was embarked at Pisa for Provence, bringing to Lyons in December 1495 and to Amboise shortly thereafter, the bronze doors of Castel Nuovo (apparently of French workmanship) and the great window of the Annunziata. The extraordinary weight of this convoy - some 87,000 1. - was due mainly to the block of porphyry and various marbles to be used for the decoration of the gardens and of which no further details are known. To the *têtes de Naples*, housed in the Queen's apartments, must be added some 130 tapestries, 172 carpets and 39 hangings in painted and gilded leather as well as quantities of furniture (beds, chests, cupboards) ivories, *tableaux de mosaique*, of alabaster, amber and various items of jewellery.[44]

The second document is the list of workmen and craftsmen (*ouvriers et gens de mestier*) - 21 in number, if one excludes the Greek scholar John Lascaris - brought back from Italy by the king 'pour edifier et faire ouvraiges a son devis et plaisir, à la mode d'Italie'.[45] This document can be supplemented by a more recently published payment, dating from 25 November 1495, from Jean de Chandiou, *maire d'hôtel* of Charles VIII to the receiver-general in Normandy for part of 1,500 l.t. advanced

> for having maintained for some time a certain number of special persons [gens officiers] whom the said king made come from Naples, as makers of harnesses? [hardes], decorators [deviseurs] of buildings, goldsmiths and several others, and to bring them to Amboise.[46]

---

[43] F. Leseur, 'Colin Biart, maitre maçon de la Renaissance', *Gazette des Beaux-Arts*, (1929), 210-31.

[44] L. Lalanne, 'Transport d'oeuvres d'art de Naples au château d'Amboise en 1495', *Archives de l'art français*, (1853), 94.

[45] M. Fillon, 'Ouvriers italiens employés par Charles VIII', *Archives de l'art français*, 1 (1851), 273-6. A. de Montaiglon, 'État des gages des ouvriers italiens employés par Charles VIII', *Archives de l'art français*, 1 (1851-2), 94-122; P. Lesueur, 'Les Italiens à Amboise au debut de la Renaissance', *Bulletin de la Société de l'Histoire de l'Art Français* (1929), 7-11.

[46] Lesueur, 'Les italiens à Amboise'.

It consists of a very miscellaneous group of skills and professions, including dressmakers (master Silvestro Abbast 'faiseur d'abillements de dames a l'ytallienne de toutes sortes'; Jacques de Dyanno 'faiseur de journades' - women's tunics - and his companion Henard de San Severio; Pantaleone Come (Conti?), 'ouvrier de broderures'; a furrier; a maker of perfumes, Paolo de Oliveri, together with his wife 'ouvriers de chemises a la facon de Cathelogne'. In addition, there was an organ-maker, also termed a priest [*prebstre*],[47] one Joannes de Granna, and a keeper of parrots, Jérome Nigre.[48] An engineer from Naples, Luca Beisjeame (Vigeno or Legiano?) was designated as 'inventeur subtil a faire couver et naistre poulletz', seemingly an expert in hatching chickens.[49] Perhaps of more interest to the art historian are the specialist craftsmen in various types of decorative work. Bernardino de Brissia (Brecsia?) was 'ouvrier de planchers et menuisier de toutes couleurs' (a worker of ceilings and other types of woodwork and marquetry).[50] Alfonso Damasso, 'tourneur darbalestre' (a turner of alabaster?), was returning to Naples 'querir sa femme'. (Girolamo Solobrini (Solobrino d Forli?) was famed for his work in terracotta and it is known that a special furnace was built for him at Amboise.) A leading sculptor, 'maistre ouvrier de maconnerie', at an annual salary of 240 l.t., was Girolamo Pachiarotti ('Passerot'), later employed in the making of the tomb of Duke Francis II of Brittany at Nantes and, at Gaillon, for Georges d'Amboise under Louis XII.[51]

The entry concerning Fra Giocondo has given rise to the most speculation - 'a frere Jehan Jocoundus deviseur de batimens trente ducatsz de carlins par mois'. It has been said of Fra Giocondo, in an important article seeking to clarify his identity, 'si è molto fantasticato e molto si fantastica': a Franciscan who has alleged to have been at any one time an engineer, a philologist, epigrapher, sculptor, theologian, architect.[52] Not all these attributes will stand

---

[47] On organ-making at Naples, A.W. Atlas, *Music at the Aragonese Court of Naples* (Cambridge, 1985), 31, 42, 101, 106, 136. This figure is not among the organ-builders at the Aragonese court in the 1470's listed in Atlas, 42. A more specific study is G. Ceci, 'Maestri organari a Napoli dal XV al XVIII secolo', *Scritti storici* (Naples, 1931), 1-10, who mentions a Giovanni Donadio di Mormanno as active in 1493.

[48] For Renaissance interest in keeping parrots, H. Diener, 'Die Camera papagalli im Palast des Papstes', *Archiv fur Kulturgeschichte*, 49 (1967), 43-97.

[49] Luca Vigeno, see Labande-Mailfert, 503 n.

[50] Marquetry and woodwork: a useful general survey F. Hamilton Jackson, *Intarsia and Marquetry* (London,1903).

[51] On the tomb of Francis II, P. Pradel, *Michel Colombe* (Paris, 1953), 44. For his role at Gaillon, E. Chirol, *Un premier foyer de la Renaissance: le château de Gaillon* (Rouen, 1952). P. Lesueur, 'Remarques sur Jerome Pacherot et le Chateau de Gaillon', *Bulletin de l'histoire de la Société de l'Art français* (1937), 67-87.

[52] L. Ciapponi, 'Appunti per una biografia di Giovanni Giocondo da Verona', *Italia medioevale e umanistica*, 4 (1961), 131-58. From a further extensive literature, R. Brenzoni,

examination, (he was neither a sculptor or a theologian) but he did end his long and varied career as being jointly nominated with Raphael and Giuliano da San Gallo on 1 August 1514 as architect of St Peter's. He was almost certainly at Naples when Charles VIII was there and was to remain in France after the king's return for some ten years and to promote Italian influences not only in architecture but also in humanist scholarship.[53] His interest in hydraulic engineering is well attested - not only in his pioneering efforts to stop Venice sinking - but also by his edition of Frontinus' *De Acquis urbis Romanae*. Indeed he has been rather felicitiously dubbed by W.H. Adams in his book on *The French Garden* as 'the plumber-humanist'.[54] He later lectured on Vitruvius, lectures that were attended by Guillaume Budé at Paris in 1502. It was probably the same influence that led Geoffroy Tory in 1512 to publish in France an edition of Alberti's treatise on architecture, giving further stimulus to the study of classical buildings.

In view of the large collection of architectural drawings associated with Fra Giocondo, it is natural that it should have been suggested that he may have had some role in the general design of Amboise and perhaps other contemporary French châteaux. Florimond Robertet, French royal secretary to monarchs from Charles VIII to Francis I and an important figure in the spread of Italianate fashions in French art, recorded in an inventory of 1532 that his castle at Bury was designed by 'l'architect italien... le quel excellent maistre depuis qu'il en est retourne a Rome trouver Sanct-Père le Pape qui le demande pour continuer les beaux travaux du Vatican', which seems to fit what we know of Fra Giocondo.[55] Beyond this at the moment one can only speculate.

Another architect, Domenico da Cortona (called il Boccadoro) was also listed as a 'faiseur de chasteaux et menuisier de toutes ouvrages de menuiserie'. Again, he was probably above all a specialist woodcarver, although it is known that he was a pupil of Giuliano da San Gallo and possibly had some interest in architecture and military engineering. Very little record of his activity has come to light from the reign of Charles VIII, but later he has been associated with rebuilding the Pont Notre-Dame (Pont Neuf) after its collapse in 1499 and worked on the château of Blois. More speculatively he may have had some part

---

Fra Giocondo veronese (Florence, 1960); P. Lesueur, 'Fra Giocondo en France', *Bulletin de la Société de l'histoire de l'art français* (1931), 115-44.

[53] V. Juren, 'Fra Giacomo Giocondo et le debut des etudes vitruviennes en France', *Rinascimento*, 2nd ser., 14 (1974), 102-16; L.I. Ciapponi, 'Fra Giocondo da Verona and his edition of Vitruvius', *Journal of the Warburg and Courtauld Institutes*, 47 (1984), 72-90.

[54] W.H. Adams, *The French Garden 1500-1800* (London, 1979), 13.

[55] C.A. Mayer, 'Florimond Robertet: Italianisme et Renaissance française', *Mélanges à la mémoire de Franco Simone* (Geneva, 1983), vol. 4, 135-49.

in the design of the Hôtel de Ville at Paris during his long stay in France into the reign of Francis I.[56]

Lastly, one must mention Charles VIII's Italian gardener, Pacello da Mercogliano, another person seemingly with a clerical background.[57] It is likely that he laid out the gardens very much on the pattern of Poggioreale, within a large rectangular plot divided into compartments with plum, pear, cherry and orange trees. A covered and painted gallery constructed to the north to give additional shelter probably dated from Louis XII and parallels similar galleries known elsewhere, for example, at Gaillon. Pacello is recorded as working at Blois, Bury and Gaillon in later years.

Exactly how Italian Renaissance gardens differed from French ones is a difficult question to answer. The authorities seem to be a shade confused.[58] Eugenio Battisti's splendidly entitled article 'Natura Artificiosa to Natura Artificialis' is helpful especially in suggesting many basic continuities:

> The Gothic-type garden survived for a long time, with minor changes resulting from the parallel evolution of architecture and furniture. The seats became marble, with painted decoration; the arbors acquired supporting columns, like a cloister; but maintained their medieval covering, in the form of a barrel vault, and an elaborate wooden or iron framework. The central part of the garden became a setting for a pavilion in the form of a classical round temple or a pool as in Roman villas. [The transformation] occurs not in the garden itself, but in the overall layout of the palace or villa, and in the relationship between garden and landscape.[59]

In the absence of surviving gardens from this period and our dependence on partial descriptions and later drawings, the question will remain difficult to resolve. When and where Italianate fashions first appeared in French garden design is equally mysterious - the gardens of the castles of René of Anjou in Provence probably predate Amboise.[60] There is also record of Pacello's involvement in a scheme for bringing water from the Amasse into the château

---

[56] Domenico Bernabei detto Boccadoro (or Becalor, Becaliz) da Cortona. For a sketch of his career and bibliography see *Dizionario Biografico degli Italiani*, 9 (1967), cols. 127-9. On later project for the Hotel de Ville at Paris, L. Beltrami, *L'Hôtel de Ville di Parigi e l'architetto Domenico da Cortona* (Rome, 1882); H. Stein, 'Boccador et l'Hôtel de Ville de Paris', *Bulletin de la Société de l'Histoire de l'art français*, 31 (1904), 123-36. D. Thomson, *Renaissance Paris* (London, 1984), 75, 199 n.7.

[57] P. Lesueur, 'Pacello da Mercogliano et les jardins d'Amboise, Blois et Gaillon', *Bulletin de la Société de l'histoire de l'art français* (1935), 90-117; G. Mombelli, 'Pacello da Mercogliano, architetto giardiniere nel periodo del Rinascimento (+1533)', *Samnium*, 49 (1976), 61-76.

[58] Comito, *The Idea of the Garden in Renaissance Italy* (Hassocks, Sussex, 1979). C. Lazzaro, *The Italian Renaissance Garden* (New Haven/London, 1990) provides general guidance and a rich bibliography.

[59] D.R. Coffin, ed., *The Italian Garden* (First Dumbarton Oaks Colloquium on the History of Landscape Architecture) (Washington, DC, 1972),1-36.

[60] Gardens in castles of René of Anjou, N. Coulet et al., *Le Roi René*, 95': 'en Anjou-Provence, l'embellissement des jardins devient l'un des soucis majeurs'.

by some mechanical means.[61]   Hydraulic engineering projects of various kinds were known at Naples itself particularly during the period of 'artistic renewal' under Alfonso II.[62]   Italian expertise in many areas of such engineering enterprises is well attested during the Renaissance. Whether this precludes native French involvement is not so clear.[63]

The sculptor Guido Mazzoni, or 'messieur Pagueny' as he was known, was also at Amboise, according to an entry in the accounts for July-September 1496, but nothing is known in detail of his work before the tomb of Charles VIII.[64]   An Italian contemporary noted: 'inter pretiosa atque opima Neapolitani spolia in galliam est deportatus'.[65]   Charles VIII could have seen Mazzoni's Lamentation group in the monastic church of S. Maria di Monteoliveto (known now as S. Anna dei Lombardi), which was probably completed a few years before the French conquest, but there is no clear evidence.[66]   In France Mazzoni was paid at a rate of 50 ducats per month, the highest paid of all the artists brought north.   He is characterised in the document that records his salary as *painctre et enlumineur*, something that has puzzled some scholars, as nothing is known of his activity other than a sculptor.   It may, however, simply refer to the fact that much of his sculpture was coloured (including the tomb of Charles VIII) and the bronze sometimes gilded.[67]   A document granting to him and his male heirs knightly rank and an heraldic device, as well as the rights and privileges of a French subject, also survives from October 1496.[68]

The overall importance of this list of craftsmen for French art has been variously assessed.   Violet-le-Duc thought that the artists that did come to France from Italy were those of second rank.   It is true, perhaps, that the *atelier d'Amboise* cannot match the *atelier de Fontainbleau* under Francis I, but there is no reason to believe that the craftsmen whom Charles VIII brought to France were lacking in ability or competence.   In certain specialised aspects of decoration, such as terracotta, and marquetry and woodwork of various types, Italian skills were clearly especially prized by contemporaries.   They had long

---

[61] Fra Giocondo translated Frontinus's *De acquis urbis Romanae*. On Leonardo da Vinci's diagram of a water conduit built by Fra Giaconodo in the gardens of the castle at Blois, C. Pedretti, *Leonardo da Vinci. The Royal Palace at Romorantin* (Cambridge, Mass., 1972), 104, 146, 313, 325 and fig. 146.

[62] See Hersey, *Alfonso II*.

[63] W.B. Parsons, *Engineers and Engineering in the Renaissance* (Cambridge, MA, 1939; repr. 1969), esp. pt. 5, Hydraulic Engineers.

[64] T. Verdon, *The Art of Guido Mazzoni* (New York, 1978).

[65] Quotation in Verdon, 120.

[66] G.L. Hersey, *Alfonso II*, 118-24.   But there was already a strong French tradition, W. Forsyth, *The Entombment of Christ: French Sculptures of the Fifteenth and Sixteenth Centuries* (Cambridge, MA, 1970).

[67] Verdon, *Guido Mazzoni*, 131-2.

[68] Verdon, *Guido Mazzoni*, 272-6.

been used in France. The Italian decorators worked side by side with French craftsmen and the evidence is insufficient to distinguish clearly the work of one group from another.

Historians are sometimes inclined to assume the artistic and intellectual sophistication of Renaissance rulers. 'Hunting, dogs, birds and horses' is how the Florentine envoy, Gentile Becchi, summed up the king's main interests. Another envoy describes his pleasure at receiving a gift of falcons.[69] Among the books that survive are Guillaume Tardif's *Art of Falconry* including a prefatory letter to Charles VIII in the vellum copy:

> At your command all that I could find necessary and valid for the art of falconry and hunting, I have set down for you in a small book. And to divert your royal Majesty from his great affairs of state I have translated as chastely as I could the Facetiae of Poggio. And having regard not only for your honest bodily pleasure but also to the good of your soul I have composed and set in order a small volume of Hours... Included in this Book of Hours are the seven Psalms which I have translated from the Latin and almost in as few words as in the Latin. And the obscurities and difficulties I have by a word or a few words explained and set out.[70]

By no stretch of the imagination could Charles VIII be described as a scholar monarch or someone with a sophisticted literary or artistic tastes. His personal library consisted almost exclusively of conventional religious and devotional works, together with certain classics of chivalric literature. His appreciation of the visual arts was no more advanced. While in Italy he clearly spent more time visiting shrines and relic collections than searching out masterpieces of Renaissance art.[71] While, as we have seen, he did respond enthusiastically to some aspects of Italian workmanship and fashion and subsequently made moves to incorporating the new *all'antica* decorative motifs in his building at Amboise, these were merely grafted on to existing flamboyant Gothic conventions. Overall Charles VIII's expedition to conquer Naples was as limited in its results culturally as it was politically.

---

[69] Gift of falcons: *Négocations diplomatiques*, vol. 1, 239-40.

[70] G. Tardif, E. Beltran, 'L'humaniste Guillaume Tardif', *Bibliothèque d'Humanisme et Renaissance*, 48 (1986), 7-39.

[71] On visits to relics, *Voyage de Naples*, ed. A. Slerca, 192 (tabernacle at Piacenza); 227 (Santa Rosa at Viterbo); 232 (round of shrines in Rome) 261 (Naples, feast of S. Gennaro); 273-4 (procession of Holy Sacrament at Poggibonsi).

Institutional and social continuities in the kingdom of Naples between 1443 and 1528

Eleni Sakellariou

In 1443 Alfonso V of Aragon conquered the throne of the kingdom of Naples, which was contested between him and René of Anjou-Provence.[1] The settlement of an Aragonese King in Naples divided the barons (the term commonly used in Neapolitan historiography for the tenants-in-chief) and the demesnial towns into one party that supported the deposed Angevin dynasty, and another, loyal to the Aragonese and, later, to the Spanish cause. The Angevin party rebelled against the Aragonese twice in the fifteenth century, and during that time many Neapolitan barons invited the king of France to restore the Angevin dynasty in Southern Italy.[2] The rapid conquest of Charles VIII and the unconditioned retreat of Alfonso II and Ferrante II (commonly known as Ferrandino) in 1495 may have been related to the fact that the Aragonese kings of Naples did not have the support of many of their barons.[3] In 1496 the Aragonese dynasty was restored in Naples, but in November 1500, with the treaty of Granada, the kings of France and Spain agreed to share the kingdom of

---

[1] Alfonso and René had been adopted by Joanna II, last Angevin ruler of Naples, as her successors to the throne: N.F. Faraglia, *Storia della regina Giovanna d'Angiò* (Lanciano, 1904); Faraglia, *Storia della lotta tra Alfonso V d'Aragona e Renato d'Angiò* (Lanciano, 1908); E. Pontieri, 'Alfonso V d'Aragona nel quadro della politica italiana del suo tempo', in E. Pontieri, *Divagazioni storiche e storiografiche, prima serie* (Naples, 1960), 223-39; A. Ryder, *The kingdom of Naples under Alfonso the Magnanimous. The Making of a Modern State* (Oxford, 1976), 23-6.

[2] Y. Labande-Mailfert, *Charles VIII et son milieu (1470-1498). La jeunesse au pouvoir* (Paris, 1975), 174-5, 191-3, 196-209; A. Denis, *Charles VIII et les Italiens. Histoire et Mythe* (Geneva, 1979), 9-10, 33-4; for a more popularised narrative, Y. Labande Mailfert, *Charles VIII. Le vouloir et la destinée* (Paris, 1986); I. Cloulas, *Charles VIII et le mirage italien* (Paris, 1986).

[3] B. Croce, *Storia del Regno di Napoli* (Bari, 1924; fourth revised ed., Bari, 1953; new ed. with a note by G. Galasso, Milan, 1992), 132-3; C. De Frede, 'Alfonso II d'Aragona e la difesa del Regno di Napoli nel 1494', *Archivio storico per le province napoletane* [from now on *A.S.P.N.*], 99 (1981), 193-219.

Naples between them.[4] The two allies soon clashed, and by 1504 Spain had conquered Southern Italy for herself.[5] The Neapolitan Angevin party remained active for many years after that, and meanwhile Spain and France were at war over Italy a number of times (1512-13, 1521-26, 1527-29, 1536-38, 1542-44). Although the final peace between Spain and France was signed at Cateau-Cambrésis in 1559,[6] the last dangerous French attack against the kingdom of Naples was the expedition of Odin de Foix, viscount of Lautrec, and his defeat in 1528 coincided with the final retreat from resistance of the Angevin party under the impact of an autarchic, centralising Spanish government.[7] The upper limit of the present paper will be 1443, when Alfonso V of Aragon conquered Naples, deposed the Angevin dynasty, and brought the region into the sphere of influence of Aragon and, later, Spain; the lower limit, 1528, when the resistance of the Angevin party was finally subdued and Spanish rule in Southern Italy was asserted. The aim will be to outline the nature of central authority in Southern Italy in this period, and to assess to what extent it contributed to the formation of an institutional framework; when the present state of research permits it, the interaction between this institutional setting and society will also be analysed. The pattern that will emerge is one of institutional continuity; nevertheless, in the long run, social change did occur.

In these years, Europe witnessed profound mutations. At a time of the emergence of big monarchies with a renewed structure and the continuous availability of funds based on the administration of tax revenues and of extensive territories by a new group of bureaucrats, the Italian 'city-states' with their successful and largely opportunist élites of entrepreneurs, or even the territorial states into which many communes evolved, did not seem to have a future. 'National states' like France and Spain were the new protagonists.[8] The Italian expedition of Charles VIII in 1494-95 revealed the weakness of the precarious system of equilibrium achieved in Italy after the peace of Lodi in 1454.[9] After 1495, Italy became the territory where the antagonism between

---

[4] L. Volpicella, *Federigo d'Aragona e la fine del Regno di Napoli nel 1501* (Naples, 1908); P. Pieri, *Il Rinascimento e la crisi militare italiana* (Turin, 1952), 377-98; C. Vivanti, 'La storia politica e sociale. Dall'avvenimento delle signorie all'Italia spagnola', in *Storia d'Italia*, vol. 2, part 1 (Turin, 1974), 354-5.

[5] Croce, *Storia*, 134-7; E. Pontieri, *Le lotte per il predominio in Europa e la fine della "libertà" d'Italia (1494-1530)* (Naples, 1961), 157-64; Vivanti, 'La storia politica e sociale', 355.

[6] Vivanti, 'La storia politica e sociale', 383.

[7] L. Santoro, *La spedizione di Lautrec nel Regno di Napoli*, ed. T. Pedìo (Galatina, 1972): Santoro, a Calabrian noble and supporter of the French, wrote his memoirs in the middle of the sixteenth century; Croce, *Storia*, 138-42.

[8] J.H. Elliott, *Imperial Spain 1469-1716* (London, 1963), 65-72; Vivanti, 'La storia politica e sociale', 377.

[9] R. Cessi, 'La "lega italica" e la sua funzione storica nella seconda metà del secolo XV', *Atti dell'Istituto Veneto di scienze lettere ed arti, parte seconda, classe di scienze morali e lettere,* 102 (1942-43), 99-176; Denis, *Charles VIII,* 13-18; M. Mallett, 'Diplomacy and War

France and Spain developed: its possession was a source of revenues (because the peninsula was a rich land), as well as of prestige for its ruler.[10] In the conflict for control over Italy, Spain prevailed over France: Southern Italy was annexed to the Spanish state in 1504, and Milan in 1535. In the first three decades of the sixteenth century, then, the kingdom of Naples was of particular importance to Spain, because it was her only secure basis in mainland Italy. It provided the Iberian peninsula with grain and the Spanish and, later, imperial troops in Lombardy, where the war with France continued at intervals, with men and money (mainly from increasing tax exactions). After the integration of Milan into the Spanish empire, Spanish strategic interests moved towards the North, partly because Spain was absorbed in the wars of the Low Countries; but Southern Italy continued to be the most important supplier of victuals, men and funds in Europe after Castile, and was thus the cornerstone of Spanish possessions in Italy; until 1535 the Viceroy of Naples was considered to be the chief Spanish office holder in the peninsula.[11] The region also preserved a degree of autonomy, because what linked it to the Spanish Empire was legitimate dynastic continuity (Ferdinand of Aragon was the cousin of Frederick III, better known as Federigo, the last Aragonese king of Naples), and also because when incorporating new territories (mainly by dynastic alliances), the Spanish Empire showed respect for the institutions of each one of them and allowed a certain degree of self-government (in giving shape to its Empire, the unified Spanish state followed the example of the medieval Crown of Aragon).[12]

In recent years, the tendency to stress the continuity between the Aragonese and the Spanish period, despite the political breach caused by the loss of independence, has been gaining ground in Neapolitan historiography.[13]

---

in Later Fifteenth-Century Italy', *Proceedings of the British Academy*, 67 (1981), 267-88; R. Fubini, 'Lega italica e "politica dell'equilibrio" all'avvento di Lorenzo de' Medici al potere', *Rivista Storica Italiana*, 105 (1993), 373-410.

[10] G. Galasso, 'La crisi italiana e il sistema politico europeo nella prima metà del secolo XVI', *Atti dell'Accademia di scienze morali e politiche in Napoli*, 72 (1961), 101-38; on the importance of territorial expansion and military success for the early modern, 'absolutist' European states, 'Introduction', in *Absolutism in Seventeenth-Century Europe* ed. J. Miller, (London, 1990), 5-6.

[11] T. Pedìo, 'Gli Spagnoli alla conquista dell'Italia', in: Pedìo, *Napoli e Spagna nella prima metà del Cinquecento* (Bari, 1971), 116; Vivanti, 'La storia politica e sociale', 385-94; G. Galasso, *Il Mezzogiorno nella storia d'Italia* (Florence, 1977), 174-80; Galasso, 'Trends and Problems in Neapolitan History in the Age of Charles V', in *Good Government in Spanish Naples*, ed. A. Calabria and J.A. Marino (New York, 1990: translation of the 1965 version, with added bibliography), 31, n. 57.

[12] On the 'constitutionalism' of the Crown of Aragon, Elliott, *Imperial Spain*, 72, 157-8; A. Ryder, 'The Evolution of Imperial Government in Naples under Alfonso V of Aragon', in *Europe in the late Middle Ages*, ed. J.R. Hale, J.R.L. Highfield, B. Smalley (London, 1965), 332; G. Galasso, *Potere e istituzioni in Italia* (Turin, 1974), 92.

[13] G. Delille, *Famille et propriété dans le royaume de Naples (XVe-XIXe siècles)* (Rome-Paris, 1985) on society; J.A. Marino, *Pastoral economics in the kingdom of Naples* (Baltimore-London, 1988) on the sheep Custom House of Puglia; A. Bulgarelli Lukacs,

Similarities are particularly strong in the first decades of the sixteenth century, when Italy was the centre of interest of Spanish external policy, since the colonies in America and war in the Low Countries had not yet removed Spain's attention from the Mediterranean; until the death of Ferdinand the Catholic in 1516, the kingdom of Naples was directly linked to his hereditary Crown, that of Aragon, which guaranteed the preservation of local institutions to the States that were integrated into its 'confederation'.[14]

In the second half of the fifteenth century, Western European states witnessed the increase of their rulers' power and a more precise definition of their social hierarchies.[15] Alfonso's rule in the kingdom of Naples coincided to a large extent with this simple model: it was Alfonso who laid the foundations of what would evolve into the Neapolitan version of the modern state during the period of Spanish rule; faithful to the Catalan-Aragonese tradition, Alfonso maintained the autonomy of the kingdom (he did not even try to unify politically and administratively the kingdom of Naples and Sicily, despite the historical precedent[16]), introduced innovations to already existing structures and tried to assert royal authority by way of a policy of consensus with local society.[17] The union with the states of the Crown of Aragon was advantageous to the kingdom of Naples in many respects: it did not degrade the kingdom to the status of an annexed, semi-autonomous province; on the contrary, the choice of Naples by Alfonso as his customary residence upgraded the city to the temporary centre of the Crown of Aragon. In addition, the fact that a strong monarch who could rely on substantial support from outside the kingdom settled

L'imposta diretta nel Regno di Napoli in età moderna (Milan, 1993) on direct taxation, all of whom start their analysis with the ascent of Alfonso to the throne in 1443 and pursue it until at least the end of the eighteenth century.

[14] On the personal, not institutional-administrative union of the Crowns of Aragon and Castile under Ferdinand and Isabella, F. Soldevila, Història de Catalunya, vol. 2 (Barcelona, 1962), 775-86; Elliott, Imperial Spain, 65-74; J.N. Hillgarth, The Spanish Kingdoms, 1250-1516, vol. 2 (Oxford, 1978), 613-14; on the pluralist inclinations of the Crown of Aragon, M.V. Gomez Mampaso, 'Contribución al estudio de los titulos adoptados por los reyes Catolicos', Boletín de la Real Academia de la Historia, 169 (1972), 630-31.

[15] B. Guenée, States and Rulers in Later Medieval Europe (Oxford, 1985), 207-8; on developments in Sicily in the period examined by Guenée, P. Corrao, Governare un Regno. Potere, società e istituzioni in Sicilia fra Trecento e Quattrocento (Naples, 1991).

[16] C. Giardina, 'Unione personale o unione reale tra Sicilia e Aragona e tra Sicilia e Napoli durante il regno di Alfonso il Magnanimo', in: Atti dell Congresso Internazionale di studi sull'età Aragonese (Bari, 1968), 191-225; E. Pontieri, 'Dinastia, Regno e Capitale nel Mezzogiorno Aragonese', in: Storia di Napoli, vol. 4, part 1 (Naples, 1974), 30; Ryder, The kingdom of Naples, 32; E. Pispisa, Regnum Sicilie. La polemica sulla intitolazione (Palermo, 1988), 6-14; G. Galasso, Il Regno di Napoli. Il Mezzogiorno angioino e aragonese (1266-1494) (Storia d'Italia diretta da G. Galasso, vol. 15, part 1, Turin, 1992), 1-4.

[17] Italian scholars are more moderate than Ryder, The kingdom of Naples, 367, in judging Alfonso's reforms as a 'revolution in government', without ignoring, though, the innovative character of his interventions: Galasso, Il Regno di Napoli, 732-34, 736. On the policy of consensus, A. Musi, 'Stato e stratificazioni nel Regno di Napoli (XVI-XVIII secolo)', Clio, 29 (1993), 191.

in Naples overruled the balance of power between central authority and ruling groups in the region.[18] Thanks to this favourable condition, Alfonso introduced his reforms that laid the foundations of the early modern state in Naples. His policy aimed at the improvement of the efficiency of imperfectly functioning institutions, at the rationalisation of central administration and the curtailment of the excessive political power that the barons had assumed during the rule of the last Angevins; he achieved that by reforming the seven Great Offices, the highest institution of Angevin administration, of Norman-Swabian origin, traditionally an apanage of the barons, and by showing preference to government by councils, which often replaced single officials with great authority concentrated in their hands; many members of the new councils were of non noble origin.

The Great Chancellor, responsible for the stipulation of royal acts, was one of the seven Great Officials; Alfonso reorganised the Chancery according to its Catalan-Aragonese equivalent, since it was responsible for royal acts concerning not only the kingdom of Naples, but the other states of the Crown as well. In doing that, he revealed his tendency to transfer the actual functions of the Great Offices from the titular holders to delegates, and to transform them into honorary titles (the Great Offices had already lost much of their authority, but not their prestige, under the Angevins): in Alfonso's Chancery a regent Vice-Chancellor usually signed the acts in the place of the Chancellor. The members of the Chancery were of Catalan-Aragonese origin in their majority; Neapolitans appeared in its lower ranks only in the last years of his reign.[19]

In their acts of government the Angevin kings sought the advice of their *Consiglieri Collaterali*, who formed an informal royal council that replaced the Norman-Swabian *Magna Curia*. Alfonso did not abolish the *Consiglieri Collaterali* (who would give their name to the Government Council of Spanish Naples),[20] but because he was the ruler of other states as well, he felt free to form different groups of councillors for different problems.[21] Gradually though, he gave shape to a supreme royal council, which became known as the *Sacro Regio Consiglio*.[22] That council was reformed in 1449, when its function as a supreme court of appeal and first instance with jurisdiction in all the states of

---

[18] Pontieri, 'Dinastia, Regno e Capitale', 30; Galasso, *Il Regno di Napoli*, 733-4.

[19] R. Moscati, 'Nella burocrazia centrale di Alfonso d'Aragona: le cariche generali', in *Miscellanea in onore di Roberto Cessi*, vol. 1 (Rome, 1958), 368-72; J. Mazzoleni, *Il "Codice Chigi". Un registro della Cancelleria di Alfonso I d'Aragona re di Napoli per gli anni 1451-1453* (Naples, 1965), XI-XII; Pontieri, 'Dinastia, Regno e Capitale', 43-4, 51.

[20] M.L. Capograssi Barbini, 'Note sul Consiglio Collaterale del Regno di Napoli', *Samnium*, 38 (1965), 207-12, 217.

[21] Ryder, *The kingdom of Naples*, 94-123.

[22] On its origins, G.I. Cassandro, 'Sulle origini del sacro consiglio Napoletano', in *Studi in onore di Riccardo Filangieri*, vol. 2 (Naples, 1959), 1-17; B. Ferrante, *Frammento del Registro "Curie Summarie"* (Fonti Aragonesi, vol. 8, Naples, 1971), 32, n. 16.

Alfonso was established.[23] What is important to our argument is that in the reformed council of 1449 all the regular non-legal councillors were excluded and it was established that its permanent nucleus was to consist of persons trained in jurisprudence (Catalans and Sicilians as well as Neapolitans in the years of Alfonso): it was the Neapolitan nobility that was affected by the reform, since, although later on Neapolitan nobles were again admitted as ordinary councillors, political authority remained in the hands of the jurists of the permanent nucleus. The council decided upon petitions presented by the subjects; traditionally the Protonotary, one of the seven Great Officials, was responsible for the presentation of petitions to the king. It now followed that his office degenerated into a routine bureaucratic task and his jurisdictions were assumed by the council.[24]

The *Mastro Giustiziere* (the Great Justiciar), another of the seven Great Officials, shared the fate of the Chancellor and the Protonotary: on a lower level of justice (with respect to that of the *Sacro Regio Consiglio*), Alfonso put an end to the confusion of jurisdiction between two Angevin tribunals, the Court of the *Mastro Giustiziere* and that of the *Vicaria*, by integrating the former into the latter. Thus the *Mastro Giustiziere* was deprived of his authority: nominally he was President of an extended council of justice, the reformed *Gran Corte della Vicaria;* but actual authority was in the hands of a regent, who acted as his delegate.[25]

In the Angevin period, fiscal and financial administration was under the control of two institutions, the *Camera della Sommaria*, responsible for the verification of accounts, and the Court of the *Maestri Razionali*, responsible for minor issues; in practice their jurisdictions were overlapping and confused. Alfonso resolved the problem of disorder by unifying the two Courts within the Sommaria, without abolishing the *Maestri Razionali*, usually of noble origin, who now became subordinated to the Presidents of the *Sommaria*, men with an education in jurisprudence, but not necessarily of distinguished origin.[26] He appointed to the presidency of that supreme financial court the *Gran Camerario*, another of the seven Great Officials; but again his office developed into an honorary title, since actual jurisdiction was transferred to a delegate.[27] The reformed *Regia Camera della Sommaria* was not a new institution: the

---

[23] Text of the edict of the reform in: N. Toppi, *De origine tribunalium urbis Neapolis,* vol. 2 (Naples, 1659), 440-44; R. Pescione, *Corti di giustizia nell'Italia meridionale* (Milan-Rome-Florence, 1924), 210-15.

[24] Pontieri, 'Dinastia, Regno e Capitale', 48-9, 51; Ryder, *The kingdom of Naples,* 112-16; Galasso, *Il Regno di Napoli,* 734-5.

[25] G.I. Cassandro, *Lineamenti del diritto pubblico nel Regno di Napoli citra Farum sotto gli Aragonesi* (Bari, 1934), 75; Pontieri, 'Dinastia, Regno e Capitale', 50; Galasso, *Il Regno di Napoli,* 736.

[26] The text of Alfonso's reform (1450) in Toppi, *De origine tribunalium,* vol. 1, 259-62.

[27] Pontieri, 'Dinastia, Regno e Capitale', 50; Ryder, *The kingdom of Naples,* 169-70.

Maestri Razionali had their origins in Norman-Swabian times, while the *Sommaria* itself gained importance already under the last Angevins; but Alfonso's intervention endowed it with great efficiency. The *Sommaria* of the Aragonese period had jurisdiction upon all affairs that pertained to the Royal Patrimony (lands, tax exactions, tolls, monopolies) and also upon feudal cases of a financial nature. Thanks to its ample jurisdiction, this supreme financial court became a powerful instrument of centralisation, and its various dependents spread over the provinces of the kingdom claiming back for the state prerogatives usurped by local potentates.[28]

Another 'reform' with some significance to our argument was the revival of the institution of the General Parliament. The Neapolitan Parliament had its origin in the Norman-Swabian period, but under the Angevins it degenerated into a rarely convoked assembly of barons (the clergy, freed from taxation, did not attend, and demesne representation decayed). The Neapolitan Parliament had limited functions: it did not have legislative power, and the ruler could summon and dismiss it at will, and determine what matters should be brought before it. But according to the Constitutions of the kingdom only a General Parliament could grant extraordinary taxation to the ruler, although this function had fallen into disuse; and theoretically its representatives echoed the subjects' reaction to royal policies. Alfonso revived the institution by summoning it frequently (eight times during his reign) and by restoring its representative character (he encouraged the representatives of the demesne to participate), although he obviously did not wish to grant it greater authority, like those of its Catalan counterparts. It was under Alfonso that the function of the early modern Neapolitan Parliament was established: the government would negotiate with the representatives of the barons and the cities the concession of tax exactions in return for royal graces in the form of privileges.[29]

Alfonso's intervention in the administrative system of the kingdom did not drastically change its form, but contributed to the increase of its efficiency (and better administration also meant a greater degree of centralisation and of control over the provinces). The function and jurisdiction of offices were

---

[28] R. Delle Donne, *Per la storia di una magistratura del Regno di Napoli: la Regia Camera della Sommaria. Studi e documenti* (Doctoral thesis, Università degli Studi di Napoli, 1985-88), vol. 1, 119-47; R. Delle Donne, 'Alle origini della regia Camera della Sommaria', *Rassegna Storica Salernitana, n.s.*, 8 (1991), 25-61.

[29] P. Gentile, 'Finanze e parlamenti nel Regno di Napoli dal 1450 al 1457', *A.S.P.N.*, 38 (1913), 185-223; Gentile, 'Lo stato napoletano sotto Alfonso I d'Aragona', *A.S.P.N.*, n.s., 23 (1937), 5-10; A. Marongiù,'Il Parlamento baronale del Regno di Napoli del 1443', *Samnium*, 23 (1950), 5-20; Pontieri, 'Dinastia, Regno e Capitale', 38-40; Ryder, *The kingdom of Naples*, 124-35; G. D'Agostino, *Parlamento e società nel Regno di Napoli, secoli XV-XVII* (Naples, 1979), 139-59; and the bitter comments of G.M. Galanti, *Nuova descrizione storica e geografica delle Sicilie*, vol. 1 (Naples, 1786), 155-6: 'Sotto di lui [Alfonso] s'introdusse un uso che divenne poi l'unica occupazione del governo: questo fu di conceder grazie per ottener donativi...'.

redefined on a more rational basis: the seven Great Offices, which were an apanage of the higher nobility and had established a 'ministerial' (in the medieval sense of offering service to the king) relationship between these officials and the king, were transformed into honorary titles (a process already set in motion in the Angevin period), and their jurisdiction devolved to delegates or to councils consisting of many members, where preference was shown to men with a degree in law and not necessarily of noble origin. This policy aimed at, and to some extent resulted in, the creation of a more 'impersonal' relation between the king and the administrative organisation, and in the foundation of a group of bureaucrats that recruited its members from various social groups (not only the feudal nobility, but also the urban patriciate and the upper levels of the *bourgeoisie*, on condition that they had the necessary training). The roots of the 'robe nobility' (*nobiltà di toga*) that shared political authority with the Spanish government in early modern Naples must be sought in the second half of the fifteenth century. As the social basis of this developing ruling group became broader, the barons lost part of their traditional political power.[30]

These comments could be misleading: if Alfonso put the kingdom of Naples on a track that would eventually lead it to a certain degree of 'modernisation', in the middle of the fifteenth century it was still far from modernised. Alfonso's action was limited by his effort to consolidate his personal rule and his dynasty by way of compromising with the most powerful social group in the kingdom, the feudal nobility.[31] Alfonso may well have deprived its members of part of their political authority; but on the social and economic level he compromised greatly.[32] In February-March 1443, the first General Parliament of his reign (in which only barons participated) conceded to Alfonso recognition of his illegitimate son Ferrante as his successor in the kingdom of Naples. In return, Alfonso conceded to the barons the *mero e misto imperio*, jurisdiction over their vassals in their feudal possessions.[33] In this way Neapolitan fiefs were transformed into 'feudal states', in which royal officials had limited rights to intervene (although Alfonso encouraged them to do so).[34]

---

[30] Pontieri, 'Dinastia, Regno e Capitale', 46, 50-53; Ryder, *The kingdom of Naples*, 47-8, 58; Galasso, *Il Regno di Napoli*, 740-41, 744.

[31] Pontieri, 'Dinastia, Regno e Capitale', 32-40.

[32] A similar policy towards the high nobility was adopted by Ferdinand and Isabella in Spain: Elliott, *Imperial Spain*, 99-103.

[33] Text of the proceedings of the Parliament in: N. De Bottis (ed.), *Privilegii et Capitoli, con altre gratie concesse alla fidelissima Città di Napoli et Regno* (Venice, 1588; first, very rare edition, Naples, 1524), f. 2v-6r of the 1588 edition.

[34] On the origins of 'feudal states' in Southern Italy, G.M. Monti, 'I grandi domini feudali del Regno di Sicilia o soggetti ai suoi sovrani', in G.M. Monti, *Dai Normanni agli Aragonesi*, Trani, 1936, 147-95, especially 149-50, 184-7; On 'feudal states' in Sicily, H. Bresc, *Un monde méditerranéen. Économie et société en Sicile, 1300-1450*, vol. 2 (Rome/Palermo, 1986), 875-901.

The fact that the last Angevin kings often ceded the *mero e misto imperio*, although always on a personal basis and only for life, does not minimise the importance of Alfonso's concession, which now became generalised and applicable to all cases. It is true that Neapolitan jurisprudence still conceived the fief as a possession ceded *quoad demanium* and not *quoad dominium*, and that Alfonso felt powerful enough to claim that, despite its generalised character, the *mero e misto imperio* was ceded at his *beneplacitum;*[35] but the effect of this policy was reduced by his effort to achieve a consensus with the powerful barons.[36]

Later rulers of Southern Italy tried to found their authority on a consensus with local society too; but Alfonso more than the rest limited his action almost exclusively to the nobility, and showed less interest in the relation of the Crown to the communes (demesnial and feudal) and the *popolo*.[37] As far as the communes were concerned, after the conquest and the confiscation of lands of his enemies, Alfonso had the opportunity to strengthen the royal demesne (to which only 134 of the 1550 settlements of Southern Italy belonged);[38] but his own policy of winning over the Neapolitan nobility by generous grants of land and planting trusted Spaniards among them had prevented him from that; indeed, Alfonso has been accused of having increased the number of enfeoffed lands.[39] In addition, by conceding a baronial petition at the 1456 Parliament, he continued the policy of his predecessors of permitting the barons to nominate the communal officials in feudal towns.[40] While Alfonso allowed the increase of baronial authority over feudal communes, he also enhanced central authority control in the demesne: the *capitani*, officials appointed by the king, were his representatives in the demesnial towns.[41] In the communes themselves he did

---

[35] Ryder, *The kingdom of Naples*, 49-53; Galasso, *Il Regno di Napoli*, 742-5.

[36] Pontieri, 'Dinastia, Regno e Capitale', 34-7, 41-2.

[37] *Popolo* is the term used in the documents for the *bourgeoisie*, both in Naples and in other towns. In Naples in particular, already since the time of Robert of Anjou, this social group was divided into *popolo grasso*, consisting of men of affairs, merchants, free professionals, civil servants, small landowners, major manufacturers; and *popolo minuto*, the mass of small shopkeepers and artisans, workers and labourers: G.I. Cassandro, 'Il comune meridionale nell'età aragonese', in *Atti del Congresso sull'età aragonese*, 161; M. Schipa, 'Contese sociali napoletane nel medioevo', *A.S.P.N.*, 32 (1907), 366, doc. 2 (dated 1339); Schipa, 'Il popolo di Napoli dal 1495 al 1522 (curiosità storiche)', *A.S.P.N.*, 34 (1909), 293, 705; G. D'Agostino, 'Il Mezzogiorno aragonese', in *Storia di Napoli*, vol. 4, part 1 (Naples, 1974), 278.

[38] C. Foucard, 'Fonti di storia napoletana nell'Archivio di Stato di Modena', *A.S.P.N.*, 2 (1877), 741-6; Gentile, 'Lo stato napoletano', 47; Pontieri, 'Dinastia, Regno e Capitale', 59; Ryder, *The kingdom of Naples*, 317.

[39] F. Calasso, *La legislazione statutaria nell'Italia meridionale* (Rome, 1929), 231; E. Pontieri, *Il comune dell'Aquila nel declino del Medioevo* (L' Aquila, 1978), 92.

[40] Ryder, *The kingdom of Naples*, 318, 339.

[41] G.I. Cassandro, *Le pergamene della Biblioteca Comunale di Barletta (1186-1507)* (Codice Diplomatico Barese, nuova serie, vol. 15, Trani, 1938), XVII-XXIV; Ryder, *The kingdom of Naples*, 331-43.

not prevent oligarchic tendencies (common in cities of central and Northern Italy at the same time[42]): it was then that the municipal representatives started being elected not by an assembly of all the citizens, but by a narrower council.[43] Before coming to any conclusions about the oligarchic tendencies of Alfonso, it must be stressed that a prerequisite for the appointment of even elected municipal officials was royal consent, and that in general Alfonso's social policies were affected by his desire to enhance royal control. For that purpose, in Catalonia he supported the *remensa* peasants in the countryside and the merchants, members of professions and artisans in Barcelona against the ruling oligarchy that had traditionally caused him trouble by questioning royal prerogatives and by reacting to his autocratic, centralised way of government. In Southern Italy, where the power of the barons was too conspicuous to be ignored, he preferred to concentrate his efforts on fostering an alliance with them. In all cases he offered his support on condition that this would reinforce royal control.[44]

Alfonso's policy towards Naples also reveals his inclination to compromise primarily with the nobility. In the late Middle Ages Neapolitan municipal life was organised around the *Seggi*. Originally the *Seggi* were the buildings in which the inhabitants of a district of Naples would gather and discuss their common problems. With time the word came to mean the district itself, although its territorial limits were not well defined. In Alfonso's time there were six *Seggi* in Naples, five controlled by the urban nobility, and one by the *popolo*. The *Seggio del popolo* did not correspond to a territorial circumscription, but had jurisdiction over the *popolo* of the entire city. Each *Seggio* had rights of self administration; but that of the *popolo* did not have the right to participate in the highest level of municipal administration, the *Tribunale di San Lorenzo*, at which only the representatives of the five noble *Seggi* could attend, with one vote for each *Seggio*. In moments of crisis though, not rare during the rule of the last Angevins, the six *Seggi* would come to an understanding, and the entire municipal organisation of Naples, including the *popolani,* would assume extraordinary political prerogatives.[45] With Alfonso

---

[42] E. Fasano Guarini (ed.), *Potere e società negli stati regionali italiani del '500 e '600* (Bologna, 1978), 10, 19-20.

[43] Cassandro, *Pergamene di Barletta*, XXXIV; Cassandro, *Storia di una terra del Mezzogiorno. Atena Lucana e i suoi statuti* (Rome, 1946), 35-6; Cassandro, 'Il comune meridionale', 152-3.

[44] T.N. Bisson, *The Medieval Crown of Aragon. A Short History* (Oxford, 1986), 140-47; A Ryder, *Alfonso the Magnanimous, King of Aragon, Naples and Sicily, 1396-1458* (Oxford, 1990), 381-92.

[45] C. Tutini, *Dell'origine e fundatione de' Seggi di Napoli* (Naples, 1644); M. Schipa, 'Contese sociali napoletane nel medioevo', *A.S.P.N.*, 31 (1906), 396-402, 609-22; 32 (1907), 68-123, 344-59, 513-86, 757-74; E. Gothein, *Il Rinascimento nell'Italia meridionale* (translated and annotated by T. Persico) (Florence, 1915), 31-62; Schipa, 'Nobili e popolani

royal authority became stable and the moments of crisis lapsed; faithful to his decision not to intervene in already existing institutions, Alfonso did not sanction the extraordinary political powers of the *Seggio del popolo:* not only did he not grant the *popolo* representation in the *Tribunale di San Lorenzo;* he also gave certain offices which, like the *maestri giustizieri della zecca,* had been the apanage of the *popolani,* to members of the urban nobility.[46] This may seem to be a contradiction of other actions of the king, which favoured the creation of a group of bureaucrats on a wide social basis; but Alfonso encouraged the social ascent of the members of the *popolo grasso* not by promoting their own social group, but by assimilating them to the nobility of the *Seggi:* it was then that the *popolano* families of the Coppola and the Miroballo became members of the noble *Seggi* of Porto and Portanova by royal grace.[47] The banker Giovanni Miroballo was one of the Presidents of the Sommaria since 1448 and participated in the king's council.[48]

Finally, Alfonso compromised the formation of a local ruling group by appointing Catalans to many offices, thus alienating the affection of his new subjects. With that he also contradicted his own decision to make his natural son Ferrante his successor to a truly independent kingdom of Naples;[49] but it was precisely with Ferrante that some of the contradictions of Alfonso's government were toned down. According to literary sources of the time, one of the first measures of the new king after his father's death on 27 June 1458 was to send the majority of the Catalans home, a measure long desired by Neapolitans.[50] Despite the fact that with Ferrante I the kingdom of Naples was separated from the states of the Crown of Aragon and returned to independence, his reign is a continuation of his father's government with respect to many issues.

Ferrante brought little change to the administrative system as this had been organised by Alfonso. Naturally, after the separation from the Crown of Aragon, the Neapolitan Chancery and the *Sacro Regio Consiglio* had jurisdiction only on Neapolitan issues. With an edict of 1477 Ferrante brought to completion the process of transformation of the *Sacro Regio Consiglio* into a supreme Court of Justice, whereas for government counselling he relied on the

---

in Napoli nel medioevo in rapporto all'amministrazione municipale', *Archivio storico italiano,* 83 (1925), 24-7, 33-42; Pontieri, 'Dinastia, Regno e Capitale', 73-7.

[46] Schipa, 'Contese sociali', 781-97; Schipa, 'Nobili e popolani', 225-27; Pontieri, 'Dinastia, Regno e Capitale', 78-81.

[47] Schipa, 'Contese sociali', 796-7.

[48] Ryder, *The kingdom of Naples,* 100, 101, 120, 198.

[49] The choice of Ferrante as his heir in Naples meant that he did not envisage a permanent bond between the Spanish and Italian mainlands: Ryder, *Alfonso the Magnanimous,* 365.

[50] An apocryphal tradition presents this measure as deathbed advice of Alfonso to his son: B. Croce, *La Spagna nella vita italiana durante la Rinascenza* (Bari, 1917), 54-6; Pontieri, 'Dinastia, Regno e Capitale', 194; Ryder, *The kingdom of Naples,* 49; C. Foucard, 'Proposta fatta dalla corte Estense ad Alfonso I re di Napoli', *A.S.P.N.,* 4 (1879), 714.

Consiglieri Collaterali.[51] The departure of the Catalans and their replacement with Neapolitan and Italian bureaucrats has been mentioned; for the rest, with a number of edicts Ferrante defined with precision the jurisdiction of officials and the function of the renewed administrative apparatus.[52] Where Ferrante left the stamp of his personal rule was in his social and economic policy. The present analysis will be occupied with his social conduct.

Like Alfonso, Ferrante concentrated his efforts on building a solid basis for the establishment of royal authority in the kingdom; and like his father, he focused his attention on the most powerful social group, the feudal nobility. But conditions in the kingdom forced Ferrante to diverge from Alfonso's consistent policy of consensus towards the barons: the independent kingdom could not automatically rely on the immediate support of the Crown of Aragon, as was the case in the years of Alfonso,[53] and the barons took advantage of the situation in order to gain back their lost political prerogatives.[54] During his long government Ferrante had to suppress two open rebellions of the barons against him, one at the beginning of his reign, in 1459-64, and one after the Turkish occupation of the city of Otranto (1480-81) and other military events in Italy, in 1485-86.[55] The violent suppression especially of the second revolt, which left a deep impression on his contemporaries,[56] leads to some important conclusions about his policy in general. It has been argued that Ferrante was not fully aware of the significance of his conflict, as king, against a rebellious baronage, and that would explain his brutal revenge against his personal enemies; also that his concept of the monarchy was still largely feudal: the sovereign and the barons should co-operate harmoniously; their relationship should be based on the unconditional loyalty of the feudatory, since his authority depended on the benevolent concession of the king; it was the part of the king to correct the flaws of the system and to preserve its balance: and this was perhaps the only

---

[51] Pontieri, 'Dinastia, Regno e Capitale', 49; G. Coniglio, *Consulte e bilanci del Viceregno di Napoli dal 1507 al 1533* (Rome, 1983), 17.

[52] B. Altimari, *Pragmaticae, edicta, decreta regiaeque sanctiones Regni Neapolitani*, 3 vols. (Naples, 1682), vol. 1, 28-32 (De actuariis, scribis et eorum salario, 1469-77); 259-60 (De commissariis et executoribus, 1490); vol. 2, 708-9 (De muneribus officialium, 1490); 729-31 (De notariis, 1477); 807-8 (De officio baiuli, 1477); 847 (on the Vicaria, 1481); 927-9 (on the Sommaria, 1482); vol. 3, 1374-5 (De trigesimis et salario officialium, 1471).

[53] Although both John II and Ferdinand of Aragon adhered to a policy of alliance with Ferrante, quite often their support was more of a diplomatic than of a military nature: Hillgarth, *The Spanish Kingdoms*, vol. 2, 546-47.

[54] D'Agostino, 'Il Mezzogiorno aragonese', 237.

[55] E. Pontieri, *L'età dell'equilibrio politico in Italia (1454-1494)* (Naples, n.d. but 1962), 113-47, 245-75; Pontieri, *La Calabria a metà del secolo XV e le rivolte di Antonio Centelles* (Naples, 1963), 218-30; Galasso, *Il Regno di Napoli*, 629-63, 699-709.

[56] J.H. Bentley, *Politics and Culture in Renaissance Naples* (Princeton, 1988), 21-34; Galasso, *Il Regno di Napoli,* 663-65; the main old account of the second revolt is the sixteenth-century one by C. Porzio, *La congiura de' baroni nel Regno di Napoli contra il re Ferdinando Primo* (Naples, 1958 and other editions).

clearly absolutist tendency in such a theory.[57] From this perspective, Ferrante's anti-feudal activity was not a conscious policy, but consisted of spontaneous decisions in favour of what he thought to be the well-being of the kingdom. This approach could also explain the effort of Ferrante to compromise with the barons in the central years of his reign.[58]

However, irrespective of the degree of his awareness, Ferrante's consistent effort to curtail the political power of the barons to the advantage of royal authority cannot be denied. It was during his reign, in 1463, that the greatest feudal 'state', that of Giovanni Antonio del Balzo Orsini in Terra d'Otranto, devolved to the state.[59] After the suppression of the rebellion of 1485-86, Ferrante proceeded to confiscations as well.[60] Aiming perhaps at the creation of an alternative social group on which he could rely, the king tried to change the consistency of the traditional baronage by inserting new members among its ranks; he made it possible for others to acquire feudal possessions by allowing large-scale alienations by sale; he offered his support to the lesser nobility both in the capital and in the provinces, by ceding to its members fiefs and titles as well as offices in the state bureaucracy.[61] In the provinces he showed interest in the development of the demesnial communes, in order to create a counterbalance to the power of the barons: although he kept municipal administration under state control, he left a great degree of initiative to the communes in social and economic matters. This policy is best expressed in the increasing number of privileges and graces ceded to the communes by Ferrante: just for the years 1490-93 at least 86 such privileges have survived.[62]

---

[57] Doctrine expressed by G.G. Pontano, 'De obedientia', in Pontano, *Opera omnia soluta oratione composita*, vol. 1 (Venice, 1518), 32; G. Vitale, 'Le rivolte di Giovanni Caracciolo, duca di Melfi, e di Giacomo Caracciolo, conte di Avellino, contro Ferrante I d'Aragona' *A.S.P.N.*, 3rd ser., 84-5 (1966-67), 8; on Pontano and his treatise 'De obedientia', Bentley, *Politics and Culture*, 182-94, 202-3.

[58] Vitale, 'Le rivolte', 29; D'Agostino, 'Il Mezzogiorno aragonese', 244.

[59] This occurred after the death of Orsini, for which Ferrante has been suspected: E. Pontieri, 'La Puglia nel quadro della Monarchia degli Aragonesi di Napoli', in *Atti del Congresso sull'età aragonese*, 33-4; on the 'state' of the del Balzo Orsini: M.A. Visceglia, *Territorio feudo e potere locale. Terra d'Otranto tra medioevo ed età moderna* (Naples, 1988), 167-81.

[60] Galasso, *Il Regno di Napoli*, 714; but see the reservations of M. Del Treppo, 'Il Regno aragonese', in *Storia del Mezzogiorno*, ed. G. Galasso, R. Romeo, vol. 4 (Rome-Naples, 1986), 126-8, also mentioned by Galasso.

[61] E. Nunziante, 'I primi anni di Ferdinando d'Aragona e l'invasione di Giovanni d'Angiò', *A.S.P.N.*, 18 (1893), 459-62.; Pontieri, 'La Puglia', 35-6; D'Agostino, 'Il Mezzogiorno aragonese', 246-7; Galasso, *Il Regno di Napoli*, 746-7.

[62] Pontieri, 'La Puglia', 31, 38-9, 43-4; Cassandro, *Pergamene di Barletta*, XXXV-XL; Cassandro, 'Il Comune meridionale', 160-64; D'Agostino, 'Il Mezzogiorno aragonese', 244; Galasso, *Il Regno di Napoli*, 751-2; privileges published in F. Trinchera, *Codice Aragonese*, vol. 3 (Naples, 1874); on the decline of municipal political prerogatives as a parallel phenomenon to state centralisation, G. D'Agostino, *Per una storia di Napoli capitale* (Naples, 1988), 17-20; on the importance of the concession of privileges to towns, S.R. Epstein, 'Governo centrale e comunità locali nella Sicilia tardomedievale: le fonti capitolari (1282-

Ferrante scored the greatest success of his struggle against the political power of the barons in his effort to build a centralised, rational, bureaucratic state.[63] The renewed administrative system secured control over the provinces; the change in the character of the feudal nobility thanks to the commercialisation of fiefs and to social ascent via the acquisition of public offices has already been discussed.[64] Ferrante went one step further by laying the foundation of what would develop into a local ruling group. Fundamental in this process was the role of Naples. During the reign of Ferrante, the city entered upon the process of its transformation from a medieval commune into the capital city of an early modern state. The relative mobility encouraged by Ferrante in the ranks of the feudal nobility permitted the overlapping of that group with the group that had administrative control at the highest level of the city, the urban patriciate distributed in the five noble *Seggi*. This urban patriciate, reinforced by feudal elements (and into which, exceptionally, distinguished members of the *popolo grasso* could be integrated) zealously preserved control of the administration of the city and started acquiring the characteristics of a closed 'caste'. In addition, and most importantly, thanks to continuous negotiations with the king, this social group assumed part of the political authority that had been taken away from the traditional baronage: since social ascent was possible also through appointment to public offices, the urban patriciate manned the administrative system, thus coalescing to a great extent as a ruling group.[65] The fact that only the Neapolitan urban patriciate assumed this role was a result of the increasing importance of Naples as a pole of population and resource attraction in Southern Italy.[66] Ferrante encouraged this process also with the reform of the University of Naples, which now provided training for the new bureaucrats.[67] The roots of the consensus between the monarchy

---

1499)', in *Atti e comunicazioni del XIV Congresso di Storia della Corona d'Aragona* (in fact, *pre-atti*), vol. 5 (Cagliari, 1990), 403-38.

[63] D'Agostino, 'Il Mezzogiorno aragonese', 245; Galasso, *Il Regno di Napoli,* 681.

[64] On the short duration of the life of baronial families see Gothein, *Il Rinascimento,* 5.

[65] The most easily accessible source on these aspects of Neapolitan history is the collection of graces ceded to the city: De Bottis, *Privilegii et Capitoli,* 14r-15r (1466); 16r-19r (1476: for correct date, D'Agostino, 'Il Mezzogiorno aragonese', 306, n. 22); 15v-16v (1481); also the edict *De immunitate Neapolitanorum* (1479) in Altimari, *Pragmaticae,* vol. 2, 517-18; see the suggestive analysis of D'Agostino, 'Il Mezzogiorno aragonese', 245-60; D'Agostino, *La capitale ambigua. Napoli dal 1458 al 1580* (Naples, 1979), 8-12, 18-90.

[66] On Neapolitan demographic and urban histoy B. Capasso, 'Sulla circoscrizione civile ed ecclesiastica e sulla popolazione della città di Napoli dalla fine del secolo XIII fino al 1809. Ricerche e documenti', *Atti dell'Accademia Pontaniana,* 15 (1883), 99-225; C. De Seta, *Storia della città di Napoli dalle origini al Settecento* (Bari, 1973), 125-234; C. Petraccone, *Napoli dal '500 al '800. Problemi di storia demografica e sociale* (Naples, 1974), 3-53; F. Russo, 'La murazione aragonese di Napoli: il limite di un'era', *A.S.P.N.,* 103 (1985), 87-120.

[67] R. Filangieri, 'L'età aragonese', in: *Storia dell'Università di Napoli* (Naples, 1924), 153-99; M.G. Castellano Lanzara, 'Origine della stampa a Napoli e Biblioteche dello Stato nelle due Sicilie', in *Studi Filangieri,* vol. 2, 97. Students were urged to study in Naples and not to go abroad: Altimari, *Pragmaticae,* vol. 3, 1327 (De scholaribus doctorantibus, 1486)

and a local ruling group with a relatively wide social basis, which allowed the consolidation of Spanish rule in the sixteenth century, are to be found here.[68] The weakness of this process, which compromised its outcome in the long term, must be sought in the fact that institutional developments were not accompanied by an equal degree of economic evolution. As a result of the fact that, with the exception of the larger cities, the greatest part of the territory and of the population of the kingdom of Naples was under feudal control, a unified domestic market that would promote inter-regional integration and would be able to profit from the existence of a strong centralised government did not emerge. Despite the effort of central authority to suppress the political autonomy of the feudal nobility, its economic and social power persisted throughout the late Middle Ages and the early modern period.[69] The immediate outcome of the effort of Ferrante was also conditioned by the political breach caused by the French invasion of 1495 and the years of instability until integration in the Spanish state in 1504.[70]

Ferrante I died on 25 January 1494 and was succeeded by his son Alfonso II. Alfonso ruled for less than one year: on 22 January 1495, and while the king of France Charles VIII was in Rome preparing his march to Naples, he abdicated in favour of his son Ferrante II (commonly known as Ferrandino); but Ferrandino as well, together with his family and the pro-Aragonese nobility had to retreat to Ischia, Sicily or Calabria when Charles VIII entered Naples on 22 February. Charles stayed in Naples only until the 20th of May, but his short-lasting government left interesting traces.[71] The fact that he appointed almost

---

[68] D'Agostino, 'Il Mezzogiorno aragonese', 247. This ruling group will be identified with a local 'robe nobility' by scholars of early modern Neapolitan history; see what follows.

[69] S.R. Epstein, *An island for itself. Economic development and social change in late medieval Sicily* (Cambridge, 1992), 402-12; T. Astarita, *The Continuity of Feudal Power. The Caracciolo di Brienza in Spanish Naples* (Cambridge, 1992), 233. On Ferrante's economic initiatives, see David Abulafia, 'The Crown and the economy under Ferrante I of Naples (1458-1494)', in *City and Countryside in late medieval and early Renaissance Italy. Studies presented to Philip Jones*, ed. T. Dean and C. Wickham (London, 1990), 125-46, repr. in D. Abulafia, *Commerce and conquest in the Mediterranean, 1100-1500* (Aldershot, 1993), essay IX.

[70] Pontieri, 'La Puglia', 23; Galasso, *Il Regno di Napoli*, 682, 742.

[71] For an account of those events, Labande-Mailfert, *Charles VIII et son milieu*, 327-40; Labande-Mailfert, *Charles VIII. Le vouloir et la destinée*, 281-98; and the following sources: M. Sanudo, *La spedizione di Carlo VIII in Italia* (Venice, 1873); E.O. Mastroianni, 'Sommario degli atti della Cancelleria di Carlo VIII a Napoli', *A.S.P.N.*, 20 (1895), 48-63, 265-82, 517-42, 563-97; E. Pèrcopo, 'Per l'entrata solenne di Carlo VIII in Napoli', in *Studi in onore di Michelangelo Schipa* (Naples, 1926), 347-52; E. Pontieri, 'Napoletani alla Corte di Carlo VIII. Giovanni di Candida e due suoi compendi di Storia del Regno di Napoli', *A.S.P.N.*, n.s., 24 (1938), 127-82; A. Cutolo, 'Nuovi documenti francesi sulla impresa di Carlo VIII', *A.S.P.N.*, n.s., 24 (1938), 183-258; R. Filangieri, *Una cronaca napoletana figurata del Quattrocento* (Naples, 1956); I did not have access to C. De Frede, *L'impresa di Napoli di Carlo VIII, commento ai primi due libri della "Storia d' Italia" del Guicciardini* (Naples, 1982).

exclusively Frenchmen to the most important administrative offices (in the lower offices Neapolitans preserved their pre-eminence) is not surprising.[72] What the Angevin nobles, who had actually invited Charles to conquer the kingdom, most probably did not expect was that when distributing lands, revenues and titles to those who had helped him, Charles was careful not to abuse property rights of the supporters of the Aragonese cause, towards whom he observed a policy of conciliation (just as Alfonso the Magnanimous had done after his own victory over half a century earlier).[73] Even more remarkably, Charles modified the composition of the highest representative institution of the commune of Naples, the *Tribunale di San Lorenzo*, and gave more space to the *popolo* in the administration of the city. On 6 March Charles expressed his gratitude to Naples, without the support of which he would not have been able to conquer the kingdom, and he resolved that fifty state offices would be ceded to Neapolitans, ten of which would be reserved for members of the *popolo*.[74] On 2 April he confirmed all the privileges and statutes of the corporations of the merchants and manufacturers of woollen and silk textiles, first ceded by Ferrante and Alfonso.[75] On many occasions Charles, accustomed to the substantial influence of the *bourgeoisie* in France, expressed his surprise at the absence of political representation of the Neapolitan *popolo*. Shortly before his departure from Naples, and possibly because he was in need of a loan which, indeed, in the end was provided by wealthy members of the *popolo grasso*, Charles authorised the *Seggio* of the *popolo* to organise its own administration and to choose a place where its members could meet and discuss; also to elect a representative (*Eletto*), who would from then on take part in the decision making institution of the *Tribunale di San Lorenzo*, an exclusive apanage of the *Eletti* of the five noble *Seggi* until then.[76] The king's concessions were confirmed after his departure, on 17 June, by his viceroy Gilbert de Montpensier, to the disappointment of the nobility. The participation of the *Eletto* of the *popolo* was established: at least in financial matters, a decision could be reached only if the *Eletto* of the *popolo* agreed with at least four noble *Eletti*.[77]

The reforms of Charles were the fruit of a long term evolution. The concession of fifty offices to Neapolitans is in agreement with the process of

---

[72] Labande-Mailfert, *Charles VIII et son milieu*, 350-53.

[73] D'Agostino, 'Il Mezzogiorno aragonese', 270-72.

[74] Sanudo, *La spedizione di Carlo,* 248; Schipa, 'Contese sociali', *A.S.P.N.,* 33 (1908), 91, n. 2; Labande-Mailfert, *Charles VIII. Le vouloir et la destinée,* 313.

[75] Mastroianni, 'Sommario degli atti', 525; D'Agostino, 'Il Mezzogiorno aragonese', 270-71.

[76] Schipa, 'Contese sociali', *A.S.P.N.,* 33 (1908), 85-102, from a little known contemporary chronicle.

[77] Text in Schipa, 'Contese sociali', *A.S.P.N.,* 33 (1908), 124-6; see also Schipa, 'Il popolo', 294-7.

partial identification of the patriciate of Naples with the ruling group of the kingdom.[78] The reservation of ten of those offices for the *popolo* sanctioned the participation of the *popolo grasso* in the same group, which had already been encouraged by Alfonso (although the first Aragonese king preferred to assimilate them to the patriciate rather than recognising the importance of their own status). Even before Charles, the *popolo* enjoyed self-administration for affairs internal to their *Seggio;* what they were deprived of was representation in the *Tribunale di San Lorenzo*, which deliberated for the entire commune, although on two or three occasions at least, in the last years of Angevin rule, the *popolo* assumed extraordinary prerogatives, in co-operation with the nobility. What Charles did, then, was to give an ordinary character to this representation.[79] Although the influence of the *Eletto* of the *popolo* in decision making was curtailed later on, he did not lose his right of participation in the *Tribunale di San Lorenzo*. Charles stayed in Naples for less than three months, but his reform lasted for over three centuries.

On 7 July 1495 Ferrandino returned to Naples and to his throne, thanks to military aid from Spain and to the support of the pro-Aragonese *popolo* of Naples. The nobles, traditionally favourable to the French, preferred to move away from the city, also because a plague epidemic soon broke out. Thanks to the absence of the nobles and the benevolence of Ferrandino, the *popolo* assumed control of the situation in Naples and improved their political position:[80] on 28 June 1496, Ferrandino confirmed a petition (divided into twenty one articles) presented only by the *popolo* of Naples.[81] The text of the petition reflects the division of the Neapolitan people into *popolo grasso* and *popolo minuto*. Social and economic conditions in the second half of the fifteenth century (Naples was a big market of distribution for rural products and a place of concentration of manufacturing activities, as well as the centre of bureaucracy and administrative control) gave the lead to the *popolo grasso*: the elected representatives of the people came from this group; one of its aims was equal participation of both burgesses and nobles in municipal offices and in the state bureaucracy;[82] the petition of 28 June sought both confirmation of the rights of representation of the *Eletto* of the *popolo*, and preference for

---

[78] On the promotion of Naples as capital city of the kingdom, see also the privilege ceded by Charles on 6 May 1495 in Mastroianni, 'Sommario degli atti', 577-9.

[79] This process had been suspended by Alfonso and Ferrante; see also the comments of D'Agostino, 'Il Mezzogiorno aragonese', 310, n. 55.

[80] Schipa, 'Il popolo', 292-305; D'Agostino, 'Il Mezzogiorno aragonese', 275-8; Labande Mailfert, *Charles VIII. Le vouloir et la destinée*, 369-71; on division of nobles into 'Angevin' and 'Aragonese' in those years, M. Sanudo, *I diarii*, vol. 1 (Venice, 1879), col. 225-6 (20 June 1496).

[81] Published in Schipa, 'Il popolo', 311-18; see also G. Racioppi, 'La capitolazione di Atella', *A.S.P.N.*, 16 (1891), 863-70.

[82] D'Agostino, 'Il Mezzogiorno aragonese', 278.

Neapolitan 'doctori et altri citatini' in appointment to public offices in the city and in the kingdom.[83]

Popular control of the commune of Naples came to an end with the death of Ferrandino on 5 October 1496.   The new king, Frederick (Federigo) of Taranto, one of the younger sons of Ferrante I, was known for his aristocratic inclinations.   The barons, whose authority had not recovered after the suppression of the rebellion of 1485-86, saw in Federico an opportunity to reaffirm their social and political pre-eminence; but after the years of political instability which followed the death of Ferrante, during which state control over the provinces became weak and, consequently, the capital city assumed particular importance, the objective of the barons could be achieved only if the predominant role of Naples was accepted.   In other words it had to be accepted that the interests of the feudal nobility and of the urban patriciate of the *Seggi* coincided at least in part.[84]   Federigo encouraged the tendencies of those two social groups, as well as the effort of the *popolo grasso* at equal representation in city and state offices,[85] hoping perhaps that in this way he could promote the widening of the social basis of political power in the kingdom and the achievement of consensus.   In reality though, and despite the fact that the tendency of the barons to identify their interests with those of the capital city is an indication of centralisation, the understanding among the three social groups was still dictated by individualistic motives and was not linked to sentiments of loyalty to the king or the dynasty; nor was this institutional evolution accompanied by equally important economic developments that would guarantee a greater degree of consistency in the action of some of the social groups involved.[86]   In addition, some of the acts of Federigo were tactless and provoked the alienation of, at least, the *popolo* of Naples: such was the case

---

[83]   Articles VIII, XI-XIV, XVII-XVIII of the petition.

[84]   The rapprochement of the feudal and the urban aristocracy in the effort for the promotion of the capital would become a common theme of later developments in Naples. See G. Galasso, *Napoli spagnola dopo Masaniello,* 2 vols (Florence, 1982), first published as Galasso, 'Napoli nel Viceregno spagnolo dal 1648 al 1696', in *Storia di Napoli,* vol. 6, part 1 (Naples, 1970), 1-400 (especially 161-77, 241-323), and Galasso, 'Napoli nel Viceregno spagnolo 1696-1707', in *Storia di Napoli,* vol. 7 (Naples, 1972), 1-346 (especially 105-285).

[85] This effort of coming together is reflected in a petition that was presented by 'la Cita et Universita de Napoli et soi Gentilhomini et Citatini populari et Baroni del Regno collegati alla prefata Universita', and confirmed by Federigo on 23 October 1496: De Bottis, *Privilegii et Capitoli,* 22v.

[86] The closing up of the *Seggi* into well defined and difficult to penetrate 'castes', a process that officially started in 1500, can be seen as a result of this situation.   D'Agostino, 'Il Mezzogiorno aragonese', 292-3, observes: 'The appropriation of a leading role by the urban patriciate of the *Seggi*... needed to be sanctioned...'; if the economic role of this group was less important than its political influence, this sanction could only be achieved in a formal way, with an official codification, a definition of the prerogatives of the group and of its rules of membership.   The formation of aristocratic, difficult to penetrate 'castes' is a common process in early modern Italy: C. Donati, *L'idea di nobiltà in Italia, secoli XIV-XVIII* (Bari, 1988), 36-44, 52-80.

with his edict of 17 July 1498, with which he tried to regulate the relations between the nobles and the *popolo* of Naples, although he ended up seriously limiting the rights of self administration and representation of the latter to the advantage of the former and of the king himself.[87] Federigo was acting under diplomatic and, later, military pressure from France and Spain, which did not give up their expansionist intentions with respect to the kingdom; despite his errors, it is to his credit that he sought support for his authority in consensus among the leading social forces.

The distinction between the 'Angevin' nobility and the 'Aragonese' *popolo* of Naples became obvious again with the events of 1501-03. In July 1501 Federigo ceded Naples to the king of France, Louis XII, as was provided by the treaty of Granada. The French found support among the nobles; but as the Spanish army gradually came closer, the *popolo*, faithful to the Aragonese cause, saw in the general of Ferdinand the Catholic Gonzalo Fernández de Córdoba the restorer of the Aragonese dynasty, and opened the doors of the city to him. The period of the *Viceregno* started with the broadly diffused conviction that Spanish rule was not far from legitimate. The first representative of Spanish authority in Naples was Gonzalo himself. Increasing difficulties in Castile and in Naples convinced Ferdinand of the usefulness of visiting Naples. His stay lasted for seven months (from November 1506 to June 1507), and nourished the hope that he, like Alfonso, might choose Naples as his residence; but Ferdinand returned to Spain after a period of short and energetic rule. The first Viceroy after him was Giovanni d'Aragona, count of Ripacorsa (1507-09), a mediocre governor. He was succeeded by Ramón de Cardona, count of Albento (of Catalan origin). During his long rule (1509-22) Cardona gained the affection of the Neapolitans; but after the death of Ferdinand on 22 January 1516, the policy of the Viceroy in Naples did not agree with the instructions from the Court of the new king of Spain Charles I (later Emperor Charles V): the kingdom entered a long period of crisis. Cardona died on 10 March 1522, and was succeeded by Charles de Lannoy, a member of the nobility of the Low Countries. In 1523 Lannoy was called to the leadership of the imperial troops fighting against the French in Lombardy; he died in May 1527, when the French army of Lautrec had already invaded the kingdom. The expedition of Lautrec culminated in the siege of Naples, and meanwhile the 'Angevin' barons turned their back on the Spanish régime and opened the doors of the kingdom to the French army. Lautrec was finally defeated in July-August

---

[87] De Bottis, *Privilegii et Capitoli*, 28v-29v; also published in Coniglio, *Consulte e bilanci*, 63 67, doc. 1; from now on decisions in the *Tribunale di San Lorenzo* could be taken by absolute majority; and the king would appoint the captains of the 29 *piazze* (territorial divisions) of the *popolo*. Also F. Imperato, *Discorso politico intorno al reggimento delle piazze della città di Napoli* (Naples, 1604); Schipa, 'Il popolo', 478-89; D'Agostino, 'Il Mezzogiorno aragonese', 280-89.

1528, and that was the last dangerous 'revolt' of the Angevin barons against Spanish rule in Naples: the leader of the Spanish army and acting Viceroy of Naples, Philibert de Chalon prince of Orange, punished the rebels harshly.[88]

Faithful to the Catalan-Aragonese tradition, Ferdinand respected the institutions of the kingdom;[89] the few changes in the administrative system were dictated by the modification of its political status: having lost its independence, it became part of a composite state, the king of which did not reside in Naples. Spanish government in the kingdom took its final form after the short visit of Ferdinand. The king of Spain was represented in Naples by a Viceroy, an office of Catalan-Aragonese origin that resolved the problem of royal absenteeism in the medieval Crown of Aragon first, and then in the early modern Spanish Empire.[90] The Viceroy ruled together with the *Consiglio Collaterale*, a government council that in Naples assumed greater authority beside the Viceroy than similar councils with respect to the Viceroys in other Spanish states.[91] The function of the *Consiglio* was primarily consultative, but it also had some authority to carry out decisions and decrees; in addition, under extraordinary circumstances (death, absence), it could replace the Viceroy. The prevailing opinion is that the *Consiglio Collaterale* was shaped by Ferdinand during his stay in Naples. In it were integrated the functions of the councillors of previous kings in their double capacity as *Consiglieri Collaterali* and *Regi Auditori*, and of the Chancery (the *Sacro Regio Consiglio* continued to function independently as a supreme tribunal).[92] Problems that could not be resolved by the Viceroy and his Council were addressed to the king of Spain via the Council of Aragon, responsible for the states that were attached to the Crown of Aragon (in 1555 the Council of Italy, a special council for the Italian States of Spain, Milan, Naples and Sicily, replaced the Council of Aragon).[93] The aim of Ferdinand was to create a 'professional' government council, some of whose members were not drawn from the feudal nobility, but were men educated in jurisprudence and qualified for government action; however, it took some time for the composition and the name of the *Consiglio Collaterale* to be established. In a list of salaries paid in the kingdom of Naples, dated 1514, the members of the *Consiglio* were listed under the heading *Conseglio regale;* three ordinary councillors (chosen

---

[88] Schipa, 'Il popolo', 490-94, 676; E. Pontieri, 'Ferdinando il Cattolico e i regni di Napoli e di Sicilia nella storiografia italiana dell'ultimo cinquantennio', in Pontieri, *Divagazioni,* 339-50; G. D'Agostino, 'Il governo spagnolo nell'Italia meridionale', in *Storia di Napoli*, vol. 5, part 1 (Naples, 1972), 3-45; D'Agostino, *La capitale ambigua*, 182-93.

[89] Galasso, 'Trends and Problems', 19.

[90] Soldevila, *Història,* vol. 2, 682-5; Elliott, *Imperial Spain,* 18-19, 72; Ryder, 'Imperial Government', 332-3, 335-9.

[91] Capograssi Barbini, 'Consiglio Collaterale', *Samnium,* 38 (1965), 227.

[92] Capograssi Barbini, 'Consiglio Collaterale', 212, 226-8; Coniglio, *Consulte e bilanci,* 21, 49-51.

[93] Capograssi Barbini, 'Consiglio Collaterale', 220-21.

among the barons), two regents of the Chancery and a secretary (members of the urban patriciate or of the *popolo*) were named.[94] In state budgets of 1530-31 the Council appeared as *regio Collaterale Consiglio*, and the number of the regents of the Chancery had risen to four. Meanwhile, other persons had acquired the right to participate in the Council, although they were not among the ordinary councillors.[95] Those persons were probably ceded the right of participation (and a not negligible salary) during the troubled government of the prince of Orange, as a reward for their military contribution to the final victory over the French in 1527-28.[96] They did not necessarily have the appropriate qualifications for participation in the government (for example, a degree in law), and they belonged to what could be called a 'sword nobility' (*nobiltà di spada*). They were removed in 1531 in a reform of the council which was part of a reorganisation desired by Charles V and aiming at the reinforcement of the authority of the Viceroy and his Council and of the juridical and financial courts in the kingdom. Their removal was a victory of the 'robe nobility', from the members of which came the regents of the Chancery and the majority of the officials of the Sommaria, the Vicaria and other institutions of central administration.[97] It also proved the state's determination to remove political authority from the feudal nobility.

The last comments raise the issue of the tension between the emerging robe and sword nobility, which became obvious in the first years of Spanish rule. With the Spanish conquest the kingdom of Naples became part of a powerful political entity, and the relative authority of the barons suddenly seemed to be lessened. Very much the same happened when Alfonso conquered Naples in 1443; what was new now was that Spanish rule tried to achieve a consensus not only with the barons, as was Alfonso's political inclination, but with all the elements that participated in the local ruling group under formation. Showing respect towards existing conditions in the kingdom, Ferdinand avoided challenging the social and economic pre-eminence of the barons, although he continued the policy of reducing their political power, which had been initiated by the Aragonese;[98] since excessive baronial power could place at risk the preservation of the conquest, Ferdinand developed mechanisms of counterbalance and control: he inserted Parliament into the structure of the state as a permanent institution of negotiation (even though this negotiation was formalised and inflexible) between the central authority and the orders

---

[94] Coniglio, *Consulte e bilanci*, 221, doc. 17.

[95] Coniglio, *Consulte e bilanci*, 419, doc. 40; 465-66, doc. 44.

[96] Coniglio, *Consulte e bilanci*, 19-21, 37.

[97] G. Coniglio, *Aspetti della società meridionale nel secolo XVI* (Naples, 1978), 32; R. Pilati, 'Togati e dialettica degli "status" a Napoli: il Collaterale nel 1532', *A.S.P.N.*, 103 (1985), 139-47.

[98] D'Agostino, 'Il governo spagnolo', 9-11; Galasso, 'Trends and Problems', 29, 30.

represented in it: Naples, the barons and the demesnial cities.[99] He promoted the role of Naples as a capital city with extraordinary influence on the rest of the country, and the participation of its ruling group in State administration.[100] He also ceded a privilege to the *popolo* of Naples, with which he amended Federico's unfavourable sentence of 1498.[101]

The results of Ferdinand's policy became obvious already in the first years of Cardona's government. The court of the Viceroy in Naples, with its glamour, the offices in institutions of central administration residing in the capital and the titles and favours that it could offer, became a pole of attraction not only for the city's patriciate, but also for the provincial feudal nobility. The training offered at the University, increasingly less humanist and more juridical, gave, at least in theory, equal opportunities of participation in political action both to the aristocracy (urban and feudal) and to the *popolo grasso*. A 'robe nobility' was slowly being formed, the origins of which can be traced back to the years of Ferrante I: its point of convergence was state administration.[102] This development is obvious in a report on the government of the kingdom, composed by Luca Russo, *Eletto* of the *popolo*, in 1508, at the request of Ferdinand. After a brief description of the main administrative institutions, Russo provided lists of the members of the upper social groups and of the government. Most of the barons held offices in the army, and only some of them were councillors: this group then could be partly identified with a 'sword nobility'. Russo praised the members of the noble *Seggi* for their good education; many of them participated in the administration not only as councillors, but also as bureaucrats of high rank. Then Russo provided a list of the doctors of law that lived in Naples, lists of the doctors of law that held public offices, and of the members of the *popolo* that either held offices or were, according to his judgement, suitable for appointment in the government or in the army. In the lists of the law graduates the urban patriciate had the lead, but many members of the *popolo* were also included.[103] The precondition for membership in this 'robe nobility' was obviously a degree in law and a bureaucratic office. Friction between these social groups did exist: the members of the 'robe nobility' had started to develop a mentality that differed in many

---

[99] During his reign, the Parliament was convoked four times (1504, 1507, 1508, 1511): G. Grimaldi, *Istoria delle leggi e magistrati del Regno di Napoli*, vol. 5 (Naples, 1767), 110, 132-204, 234-5; D'Agostino, *Parlamento e società*, 163-200.

[100] This is already obvious in the privilege ceded to Naples by Ferdinand in Segovia on 5 October 1505: De Bottis, *Privilegii et Capitoli*, 39r-50r.

[101] De Bottis, *Privilegii et Capitoli*, 62r-66r; F. Imperato, *Privilegi, Capituli e Gratie concesse al fedelissimo populo Napolitano, et alla sua Piazza... ristampa con molte... additioni* (Naples, 1624; first ed. 1598), 8-9; Schipa, 'Il popolo', 680-85; D'Agostino, 'Il governo spagnolo', 12.

[102] D'Agostino, 'Il governo spagnolo', 18-20.

[103] Coniglio, *Consulte e bilanci*, 94-110, doc. 4.

respects from that, more traditional, of the 'sword nobility';[104] in addition, the noble *Seggi* tried to assume the exclusive character of a caste, in an effort to protect their ranks from invaders that came from the provincial feudal nobility or even from the *popolo grasso*.[105] However, the policy of the central authority with respect to the distribution of offices was a factor of convergence.

On the other hand, during the years of Cardona, the pre-eminence of Naples in the kingdom and of the aristocracy in the ruling group is well represented in the function of the Parliament: in it, precedence was given to Naples among the representatives of the kingdom, and the *Sindico*, the President of the *Tribunale di San Lorenzo,* always under aristocratic control, was the President of the Parliament.[106] Charged with such a degree of administrative, social and economic importance, Naples was destined to become the major pole of population attraction in Southern Italy. It must be stressed that from the beginning, high population density in Naples was characterised by massive poverty and parasitism.[107] The origins of hyper-centralised, overpopulated Naples may arguably be sought in those years.

After the death of Ferdinand in 1516, Cardona was confirmed in his office; but now the policy of the Spanish court and that of the Neapolitan government diverged. Cardona was faithful to Ferdinand's doctrine that local institutions should be respected and had an intimate knowledge of Neapolitan conditions; under the influence of the gradual 'castilianisation' of his court, Charles V developed a more 'absolutist' concept of his relation with his subjects: he wished to achieve a greater degree of subordination and of control by central authority over his dominions, and this demanded a certain limitation of the initiatives that local ruling groups had assumed under Ferdinand. In addition,

---

[104] There is an increasing literature on this issue. Older works, best represented by R. Villari, *La rivolta antispagnola a Napoli. Le origini (1585-1647)* (Bari, 1967; there is a recent English translation, by J. Newell and J.A. Marino: Villari, *The Revolt of Naples*, Cambridge, 1993, based on the fifth, unaltered Italian edition of 1987) and texts of G. Galasso such as 'Spagna e Mezzogiorno' in Galasso, *Il Mezzogiorno*, 162-208, conceive Neapolitan society as divided into classes conflicting with each other, rather than in mutually penetrating groups; the latter is the new prevailing approach: with special reference to the robe nobility: V.I. Comparato, *Uffici e società a Napoli (1600-1647). Aspetti dell'ideologia del magistrato nell'età moderna* (Florence, 1974), 31-8; P.L. Rovito, *Respublica dei togati. Giuristi e società nella Napoli del '600* (Naples, 1981); R. Mantelli, *Burocrazia e finanze pubbliche nel Regno di Napoli a metà del Cinquecento* (Naples, 1981); Mantelli, *Il pubblico impiego nell'economia del Regno di Napoli* (Naples, 1986); A. Musi, 'La venalità degli uffici in Principato Citra. Contributo allo studio del sistema dell'amministrazione periferica in età spagnola', *Rassegna Storica Salernitana, n.s.,* 3 (1986), 77-91; on the mentality of the sword nobility, A. Musi, *Finanze e politica nella Napoli del '600: Bartolomeo d'Aquino* (Naples, 1976), 51-4; on the robe nobility and its mentality, Pilati, 'Togati e dialettica degli "status"', 120-27, 150-56; on the feudal nobility, Astarita, *Continuity of Feudal Power*, 202-7.

[105] D'Agostino, 'Il governo spagnolo', 15.

[106] G. De Blasiis, 'De precedentia nobilium sedilium in onoribus et dignitatibus occurentibus Universitati Neapolis', *A.S.P.N.,* 2 (1877), 546-53.

[107] Schipa, 'Il popolo', 700-3; Galasso, 'Trends and Problems', 49-50.

the immense military effort and financial aid that his imperial plans requested could be met only with increased fiscal pressure on his possessions (including Castile).[108]

The tension between the Neapolitan government and the Spanish Court was expressed in a report that the secretary of Charles, Mercurino da Gattinara, sent to him from Calais in October 1521.[109] Gattinara accused Cardona and his councillors of having disobeyed imperial orders with reference to extraordinary funds needed in the Spanish Court, of having used other funds, that were also to be sent to the Court, for local needs or, even worse, for useless expenditures, and of having neglected the application of justice in the kingdom, causing dissatisfaction among the subjects; but the kingdom's problems could hardly be traced, as in Gattinara's diagnosis, merely to the corruption and the personal ambitions of Cardona and his administrators. The truth is that the Neapolitans tried to evade Spain's continual requests for money; that the nobility almost monopolised the administration of justice, especially in the provinces; and that the demesnial towns lived under constant fear of their sale to the nobility, a practice from which the Spanish government did not shrink when trying to meet its financial needs.[110] Furthermore, the inhabitants of the kingdom resented having to carry out orders issued without full knowledge of local conditions (which the Aragonese instead had always kept in mind), and to contend with the Court's insensitivity to needs which could be vital and urgent to the kingdom. Under increasingly heavy financial and fiscal pressure, the nobility, one of the privileged social orders, came to embody what could still be called the kingdom's separatist consciousness, which was expressed as support for the French. Among the unprivileged groups discontent came to the surface as anti-feudal revolts and banditry in the provinces[111] and social unrest in the cities.[112] Between Naples and Charles' Court, Cardona found himself always further removed from the latter. In accordance with his stance he allowed, against his will, the revival (the last occasion for a long time) of the kingdom's autonomist spirit and centrifugal social forces.[113]

The tension was relieved with Cardona's death in 1522; but Charles' plan to suppress autonomist tendencies and make sure that his orders were carried out quickly and efficiently by subjecting the local ruling groups to the power of

---

[108] On fiscal pressure in Castile, Elliott, *Imperial Spain,* 191-203.

[109] Published in K. Lanz, *Actenstücke und Briefe zur Geschichte Kaiser Karl V aus dem k.k. Haus-, Hof- und Staats Archive zu Wien* (Vienna, 1853), 401-18.

[110] For a recent, sober evaluation of this issue, F. Del Vecchio, 'La vendita delle terre demaniali nel Regno di Napoli dal 1628 al 1648', *A.S.P.N.,* 103 (1985), 163-211.

[111] C. De Frede, 'Rivolte antifeudali nel Mezzogiorno d'Italia durante il Cinquecento', in *Studi in onore di Amintore Fanfani,* vol. 5 (Milan, 1962), 3-42.

[112] A. Lepre, *Storia del Mezzogiorno d'Italia,* vol. 1 (Naples, 1986), 204-9.

[113] D'Agostino, 'Il governo spagnolo', 29-36; Galasso, 'Trends and Problems', 24-31.

law and continuing fiscal pressure had to be postponed.[114] Cardona's successor Charles de Lannoy was benevolent towards Neapolitan affairs; in addition, military events required immediate attention. In 1523 Spain was at war with France again, and Lannoy was called to the leadership of the imperial troops in Lombardy. He died in May 1527, when the French troops of Lautrec had already invaded the kingdom and it had become clear in Naples that the loyalty of the barons to Spain was not at all to be taken for granted. The defeat of the French in 1528 put an end to the illusions of the anti-Spanish faction. The new Viceroy, the prince of Orange, severely punished the 'rebels', with the intention of striking a blow against the old feudal system and of collecting money for the troops, as well as of rewarding those who contributed to the final victory.[115] Nevertheless, with the return of peace, Charles' centralising plans for a more direct and effective linkage between the imperial government and the court of Naples could be implemented at last. The man who undertook this task was the new Viceroy Don Pedro Alvarez de Toledo (1532-53). During his government the consensus between the (foreign) monarchy and the, now loyal, ruling groups would be restored and consolidated, at least until the revolt of Masaniello (1647-48).[116]

The creation of a to a large extent 'modern', state in Southern Italy in the Spanish period was achieved thanks to the implementation of a consensus between the (foreign) monarchy and local social groups. This process had been inaugurated by the Aragonese kings of Naples, but Spanish rule pursued it in a more consistent way, seeking compromise on three levels: with Naples, capital of the kingdom; with the leading social forces; with an effort to keep a balance between the fiscal system and private finance.[117]

The result of this compromise was the formation, already in the first half of the sixteenth century, of a local ruling group with a broadened social basis, which shared power with the central (Spanish) authority. Indeed, this group included members of the feudal nobility, of the urban patriciate and of the upper

---

[114] On the early modern concept, prevailing in Castile, that the 'absolute' power of the king was something that operated within the limits of the law on behalf of the common good, and on the increasing needs of the 'fiscal-military' (or, for other historians, absolutist) state, I.A.A. Thompson, 'Castile', in Miller (ed.), *Absolutism*, 71-6, 96-7; Miller, 'Introduction', 7, 13-14; see also *Origini dello Stato. Processi di formazione statale in Italia fra medioevo ed età moderna,* ed. P. Schiera (Bologna, 1994).

[115] Schipa, 'Il popolo', 690-91; D'Agostino, 'Il governo spagnolo', 35-45; Galasso, 'Trends and Problems', 32-41; also the list, dated 1531, of the confiscated possessions of the rebels, published by N. Cortese, 'Feudi e feudatari napoletani della prima metà del cinquecento', *A.S.P.N.,* n.s., 15 (1929), 28-150; 16 (1930), 41-102.

[116] Villari, *Rivolta antispagnola,* 11-29 (although he identifies the ruling group with the feudal nobility).

[117] Marino, *Pastoral Economics,* 1-11; Musi, 'Stato e stratificazioni', 191, 194-5. Although this paper is not concerned with economic and financial matters, a brief reference to this issue needs to be made here.

levels of the *popolo*. Those social groups had diverging, if not antagonistic interests, but the state managed to secure their co-operation in the sharing of the administrative apparatus by coming to an understanding with each one of them separately. The integration of the barons in the administration led to their transformation from political potentates (this is what they were in the last decades of Angevin rule) into factors of social and economic power.[118] In recompense, the monarchy fully recognised their rights of jurisdiction in their 'feudal states', and confirmed the hereditary transmission of fiefs.[119] On the other hand, the state favoured a greater mobility in the ranks of the traditional baronage, perhaps, among other reasons, because it wished to blunt its character of a closed caste, and for that reason it encouraged the commercialisation of fiefs (a practice that became common in the last years of Angevin rule, and an adopted policy of the Aragonese kings).[120] The large scale confiscations and alienations of fiefs as a means of suppression of French sympathies among the barons by the prince of Orange after the defeat of Lautrec in 1528 sanctioned this practice. Apart from the possibility of acquiring feudal possessions, the urban patriciate and the upper middle group could aim at social ascent by obtaining a degree in jurisprudence (at the University of Naples, which had been reformed for that purpose by Ferrante I in 1465), which was a prerequisite for appointment to administrative offices. Lower offices were more easily accessible by this group of jurists, and they were the springboard for higher titles. In addition, although salaries were small, the administration of a public office left an important margin for the receipt of favour in the Court and the gathering of wealth in ways that were not always orthodox; and wealth permitted the acquisition of fiefs. It is true that such practices, as well as the venality of offices, led to the invasion of the system by corruption; but the overlapping of public and private interests, patron-client relations and parasitism were common characteristics in other bureaucratic apparatuses of the early modern period too.[121] In addition, the state achieved a consensus not of course with the rural population in the provinces or the *popolo minuto* in Naples, who actually bore the greatest part of the increasing fiscal burden, but with the not negligible (even in terms of numbers) group of bureaucrats.[122]

---

[118] Similar evolution in Spain: Elliott, *Imperial Spain*, 99-106.

[119] A. Cernigliaro, *Sovranità e feudo nel Regno di Napoli 1505-1557*, vol. 1 (Naples, 1983), 157-67; Cernigliaro, 'Giurisdizione baronale e prassi delle avocazioni nel Cinquecento napoletano', *A.S.P.N.*, 104 (1986), 240-41.

[120] Galasso, *Il Regno di Napoli*, 742-43, 747; Musi, 'Stato e stratificazione', 206-7.

[121] Elliott, *Imperial Spain*, 170-72; also J. Leschassier, 'La maladie de la France', in Leschassier, *Le recueil des excellens et libres discours sur l'estat present de la France* (Paris, 1606), part 7, 1-45, and K.W. Swart, *Sale of offices in the seventeenth century* (The Hague, 1949).

[122] Musi, 'Stato e stratificazioni', 209.

Special reference must be made to the consensus achieved between the capital and central administration. In return for support for the Spanish cause even in very difficult moments (1503, 1527-28), Naples had its degree of self-government increased, and secured the participation of its highest municipal institution, the *Tribunale di San Lorenzo*, in state administration. In that way Spanish rule established an important prerequisite of centralisation, whereas the city saw its ruling group, composed of members of the urban patriciate, of the provincial feudal aristocracy and of the *popolo grasso,* being promoted to one of the main components of the ruling group of the kingdom. The foundations of this evolution, which would be one of the constants of the long period of Spanish rule in the kingdom of Naples, were laid by the Aragonese kings: they revitalised the centralising tradition of the kingdom without injecting radical innovations into its social and institutional tissue.

Machiavelli, *italianità* and the French invasion of 1494

David Laven

Of Niccolò Machiavelli's life before his appointment to the Florentine chancery in 1498 we are extremely ignorant. A little is known of his education, chiefly from the diaries kept by his father, Bernardo, for the period 1474-1487. Otherwise not much has been added to our knowledge of his early years since Villari remarked prophetically that they would 'perhaps always... remain involved in obscurity'.[1] It is not surprising, given the scant sources for his first twenty-eight years, that historians seeking to explain the origins of Machiavelli's ideas have dwelt on those sections of his biography for which evidence is plentiful: his practical experiences in politics as a diplomat and administrator after the fall of Savonarola; his period in the political wilderness after the Spanish restoration of Medici power in 1512; his close contacts with the humanist circle of Cosimo Rucellai and the Orti Oricellari; his tardy rehabilitation into public life by Clement VII. The only general exception to this understandable reluctance to treat Machiavelli's early life has been a widespread readiness to assert the influence of the humanist milieu in which

---

[1] P. Villari, *The Life and times of Niccolò Machiavelli* trans. L. Villari (4th impression, London, n.d.), 218.

On our ignorance of Machiavelli's life before 1498 see especially J.N. Stephens and H.C. Butters, 'Notes and documents: new light on Machiavelli', *English Historical Review*, 97 (1982), 54-69. See especially 54-5. Stephens and Butters reproduce two documents relating to Machiavelli's 'lost years' dating from 1494 and 1497 respectively. However, neither is of any great interest. For an addition of Bernardo Machiavelli's diary, see C. Olschki (ed.), *Libro di ricordi* (Florence, 1954). S. Anglo, *Machiavelli: a dissection* (London, 1969), 13-14 argues that this is an over-used source, but also provides an accessible account of what we know of Machiavelli's early career. The standard biography of Machiavelli remains, however, R. Ridolfi, *Vita di Niccolò Machiavelli* (Rome, 1954), published in a translation by C. Grayson as *The life of Niccolò Machiavelli* (London, 1963).

In *Il giovane Machiavelli banchiere con Berto Berti a Roma* (Florence, 1973), D. Maffei suggested that Machiavelli had worked as a banker's apprentice in Rome after 1489. This was rapidly disproved in M. Martelli, *L'altro Niccolò di Bernardo Machiavelli* (Quaderni di Rinascimento, 1975).

young Niccolò was raised.[2] There is in fact - paternal diaries notwithstanding - little hard evidence of the actual nature of his studies; but from what is known of fifteenth-century Florence in general, and of Bernardo's tastes and station in particular, it is possible to surmise with some confidence the sort of schooling that Machiavelli received. In contrast, besides some conjecture regarding the likelihood of Machiavelli's continuing his studies at university under Marcello Adriani, the period between 1487 and 1498 is largely ignored. Yet there is a danger inherent in neglecting Machiavelli's 'lost years'. While it is pointless to speculate on what he was doing for most of his twenties, there can be no doubt from what he wrote later in his life that the events of the 1490s, prior to his elevation to government office, played a pivotal part in shaping his political outlook, and that an examination of his response to the French invasion of 1494 in particular is especially important to understanding his thinking.

Of course, Charles VIII's invasion of 1494 was not quite the striking breach with the past suggested by the famous opening paragraphs of Guicciardini's *Storia d'Italia*. It has long been customary to point to the tradition of foreign interference in Italian affairs, and to the many precedents, even within the fifteenth century, for French involvement in the peninsula. Contemporaries certainly recognised this fact, and Machiavelli himself, as we shall see, was careful to acknowledge it in his *Istorie fiorentine*. Moreover, the Peace of Lodi by no means initiated an interlude of idyllic calm between the Milanese and the Italian Wars as has sometimes been suggested. Indeed, it has become a commonplace to decry and deride the treaty. Even at its inception, Alfonso I insisted on special conditions for his adherence which exempted Naples from respecting Genoese territory and shipping. In the forty years that followed land-hungry *condottieri*, grasping popes, rebellious barons, and expansionist doges - not to mention the Sultan - ensured that the peninsula experienced its fair share of war and conflict.[3] Nor was the 1494 invasion marked by the overwhelming military superiority sometimes attributed to Charles VIII's forces. As Michael Mallett showed, 'the French army, when fully assembled, was the largest army that had been seen in Europe for more than a century... much of its strength was rapidly dispersed in garrisons, and the army actually in the field rarely outnumbered the Italians opposed to it'; the artillery, so vividly described by Guicciardini, spent more time at sea than on land, and was 'scarcely used', while the fabled Swiss infantry were not only far fewer in

---

[2] See, for example, Q. Skinner, *Machiavelli* (Oxford, 1981), 3-6.
[3] See, for example, D. Hay and J. Law, *Italy in the age of the Renaissance 1380-1530* (London, 1989), 151-64 and G. Mattingly, *Renaissance diplomacy* (Boston, 1955) 78-86. For Guicciardini's famous account of Italy before 1494 see F. Guicciardini, *Storia d'Italia*, ed. E. Mazzali, 3 vols (1988), vol. 1, 3-5.

number than Charles's Gascon crossbowmen, but also 'played no part in the campaign'.[4]

While we must be careful not to over-estimate the military might of Charles or the novelty of his expedition, it is equally important not to under-estimate the dramatic impact of the invasion on Machiavelli and his fellow Italians. Alexander VI remarked (and many - Commynes and Machiavelli included - repeated) that the French had conquered Italy with a 'piece of chalk'.[5] It was in this that the real significance of Charles VIII's descent lay: for the dramatic and ignominious collapse of the peninsula revealed not the remarkable might of France - after all many sections of France's nobility were openly hostile to the project, and even the king's most sanguine supporters had failed to predict so easy a victory[6] - but the intrinsic military and political weaknesses of the Italians. 1494 did not signal the pre-eminence of France, but the bankruptcy of Italy. It was Italian princes who had foolishly invited the foreigner to settle their differences, it was the peninsula's élites that had neglected martial virtues for luxury and the arts, it was Italian citizens who had permitted the hire of *condottieri* in place of the traditional militias. In short, it was Italian decadence that enabled the *oltramontani* to dictate their political future, or, at least, so it seemed by the early sixteenth century when Machiavelli began to pen his most famous works of history and politics. It is in this sense that 1494 is of its greatest import in Machiavelli's writings: for it is seen as *the* turning point in the history of modern Italy, the opening of an era of incessant conflict and of foreign ascendancy that 'stank in the nostrils of everyone'.[7]

Even the most cursory reading of *Il Principe* or *I Discorsi, Dell'arte della guerra,* or, name notwithstanding, the *Istorie fiorentine* makes it abundantly clear that Machiavelli always retained an acute awareness of the broader Italian perspective. However, the significance of 1494 was not merely that it brutally

---

[4] M. Mallett, *Mercenaries and their masters. Warfare in Renaissance Italy* (London, 1974), 238-40. For a rather old-fashioned but nonetheless clear account of the campaign of 1494 and its aftermath see P. Pieri, *Il Rinascimento e la crisi militare italiano* (Turin, 1952), 320-98.

[5] Commynes applies the phrase specifically to the Kingdom of Naples: 'For aside from the castle of Naples, there was no other place which stopped the king for one single day; and, as Pope Alexander [VI] who reigns today has said, the French went there with spurs of wood and chalk in the hands of their commissarial agents to mark up their lodgings, without further trouble.' S. Kinser (ed.), *The Memoirs of Philippe de Commynes,* trans. I. Cazeaux 2 vols (Columbia, S. Carolina, 1969 & 1973), vol. 2, 478. Machiavelli is both more general and more laconic: 'onde che a Carlo re di Francia fu licito pigliare la Italia col gesso'. A. Panella (ed.), *Niccolò Machiavelli: Opere,* 2 vols (Milan-Rome, 1938-39), vol. 2, *Scritti politici,* 47.

[6] Y. Labande-Mailfert, *Charles VIII et son milieu (1470-1498). La jeunesse au pouvoir* (Paris, 1975), 219-31.

[7] The observation comes from the final 'Exhortation' at the end of *Il Principe.* N. Machiavelli, *Opere,* vol. 2, 95.

revealed the weaknesses of Italy. For if the French invasion ushered in a period of foreign domination and political strife throughout the states of Italy, Machiavelli's own Republic of Florence was no exception to this general trend: the events of 1494 brought to an end the sixty-year old Medici hegemony, and initiated a phase in the city's history which was to be marked by sudden and often violent changes in government, accompanied by a striking reduction in its independence of political action. It was in the services of this humbled Florentine state, against a background of domestic flux, and military and diplomatic impotence, that Machiavelli's ideas on the practice of politics would develop. Consequently when we examine Machiavelli's response to the invasion we must approach it from two albeit closely related angles: the Florentine and the Italian. Likewise we must also remember that in all his extant works Machiavelli is writing of the events of 1494 with hindsight. Alas, we are unlikely ever to discover how he viewed the invasion when it actually occurred.

Unfortunately Machiavelli has nowhere left a detailed account of 1494 to compare with that of his friend Guicciardini. Certainly his correspondence, including the so-called *Legazioni*, offers little. With one important exception - the often neglected *Decennale primo* - it is necessary to concentrate any investigation of his response to 1494 on his best-known works. Even these have their limitations. The most useful is *Il Principe* to which we must return later. Less revealing are the *Discorsi* and the *Arte della guerra*, which both draw more heavily on classical examples and make very few *direct* references to the French invasion, although, as we shall see, this does not rule them out as a worthwhile source. Finally, there are the *Istorie fiorentine*.

At first glance the *Istorie fiorentine* might seem to be of limited value for the obvious reason that they conclude with the death of Lorenzo the Magnificent in 1492. Written between 1520 and 1525, the *Istorie* constitute Machiavelli's last important literary enterprise. As Felix Gilbert suggested Machiavelli probably had no great desire to produce a major work of history, but felt it politic to accept a commission from a figure so powerful as Cardinal Giulio de' Medici, the future Clement VII.[8] Doubtless Machiavelli shied away from addressing the actual fall of his new found patrons; after all Giulio would probably not have welcomed an account of the ignominious capitulation and exile of his cousin Piero: hence the conclusion in 1492. Nevertheless, the *Istorie* are still extremely revealing. It is no coincidence that the closing lines clearly refer to the disaster to come in 1494: deprived of the wisdom and counsel of Lorenzo, Italy lacked a leader capable of curbing Lodovico Sforza's

---

[8] F. Gilbert, *Machiavelli and Guicciardini. Politics and history in sixteenth-century Florence* (New York, 1965), 236-7.

ambitions; on Lorenzo's death the seeds of Italy's ruin began to germinate.[9] But while Machiavelli ends on this gloomy note of imminent barbarian invasion, brought about by the stupidity and arrogance of the Duke of Milan, there are plenty of warnings earlier in the text of the likely consequences of Italian decadence. In Machiavelli's opinion the plight of both Florence and Italy in the years from Charles's invasion until his own death in 1527 could be attributed to the marked absence of political and martial *virtù* among modern Italians. But he also held that the origins of this corruption could be traced back to earlier periods of Italian history. In this sense the *Istorie* are both self-consciously teleological and a vehicle for the author's ideological hobby-horses, with Machiavelli seeking constantly to identify the causes of Italy's eventual humiliation. In the introductory passage to Book Five, for example, Machiavelli carefully emphasises the longer-term, fifteenth-century origins of the defeat of 1494, particularly identifying the 'perverse' methods of military organisation, as well as the corrupting influence of Italy's degenerate ruling houses.[10] He also studiedly demonstrates the way in which Italian affairs had often been determined by the fortunes of more powerful neighbours. This is particularly well illustrated in his description of the inability of Louis XI to assist Jean d'Anjou's designs on Genoa and Naples in 1464: it was quite clear to Machiavelli that it was not Italian strength which had prevented the French king from dictating the future of these Italian states, but rather the domestic threat posed by Charles, Count of Charolais, the future Charles the Bold of Burgundy, and François II, Duke of Brittany.[11] However, Machiavelli did not see these characteristics as peculiarly fifteenth-century phenomena. Certainly the origins of Italian martial decline are traced back to the fourteenth century and earlier, with Machiavelli writing at the conclusion of Book One:

> In short they [Italy's military men] reduced war to such baseness that any pedestrian captain, in whom the merest scintilla of ancient *virtù* had reappeared, would have reviled them - to the amazement of all Italy which in its folly honoured them.

---

[9] N. Machiavelli, *Opere*, vol. 1, *Scritti storici e letterari. Lettere familiari*, 516.

[10] 'Tanto che quella virtú, che per una lunga pace si soleva nelle altre provincie spegnere, fu dalla viltá di quelle in Italia spenta, come chiaramente si potrá cognoscere per quello che da noi sará da il 1435 al '94 discritto: dove si vedrá come alla fine si aperse di nuovo la via a' barbari, e riposesi la Italia nella servitú di quelli.' N. Machiavelli, *Opere*, vol. 1, 281-2.

At the beginning of Book Six Machiavelli again laments the 'perverso modo di milizia' of the Italian rulers during the Milanese Wars: 341-2. It is noteworthy, however, that he is at pains in all his works to stress that there is nothing intrinsically weak about the Italian fighting man. Indeed, he emphasises at the end of *Il Principe* that in single combat Italians are often far superior to other Europeans, while in both the *Arte della guerra* and the *Discorsi* it is made abundantly clear that the creation of effective fighting men is not dependent on national characteristics, but rather on good laws and institutions, and the appropriate manipulation of religion. With these discipline and valour can readily be developed.

[11] N. Machiavelli, *Opere*, vol. 1, 413.

> Therefore, my history will be full of these slothful princes and of these most degraded warriors.[12]

Machiavelli keeps his promise. Throughout the work he picks up on the military inadequacies of Italy's princes and the *condottieri* they employed, in sharp contrast with the virtues of the Florentine militia, which he liked to show both as victorious on the battlefield and as a shield against would-be tyrants.[13] Machiavelli is especially critical of the use of foreign mercenaries: at the start of Book Three, for example, we find him inveighing against both the Avignon Papacy and the Emperor for using 'Inghilesi, Tedeschi e Brettoni' to maintain their authority in the peninsula.[14] But it is not just in its criticism of mercenaries that this passage is typical of the position adopted throughout the *Istorie*. That Machiavelli chooses to attack influences from outside Italy in general, and lambasts the Papacy in particular is also characteristic.[15]

The recurrent themes of the *Istorie* echo those that Machiavelli had already developed while penning his other major works in the period 1513-20. Perhaps the most obvious example is the way in which in all three works we are time and again exposed to Machiavelli's almost obsessional contempt for mercenaries, and his impassioned advocacy of a citizen militia supposedly modelled on the legions of republican Rome. It is scarcely a surprise that this subject gets its fullest treatment in the *Arte della guerra*. The only one of Machiavelli's political writings to have been published in his life time,[16] it is today probably the least read. That it is now so neglected in large part reflects the fact that it is boring: the text consists of a fictional dialogue in which the interlocutors discuss military manoeuvres and evolutions, the selection and training of conscripts, the correct arrangement of camps, the deployment of scouts, the virtues of different types of weaponry, and so on. Nevertheless, the *Arte della guerra* does provide arresting insights into Machiavelli's thought in general and his response to 1494 in particular.[17]

---

[12] N. Machiavelli, *Opere*, vol. 1, 104.

[13] For two typical expressions in the *Istorie* of Machiavelli's firmly-held belief in the *virtù* of the Florentine militia see his description of the 'Martinella', and his account of the relief of Prato from Castruccio Castracani: N. Machiavelli, *Opere*, vol. 1, 112-13 and 142.

[14] N. Machiavelli, *Opere*, vol. 1, 176.

[15] Machiavelli is careful to identify the Papacy - in the guise of Urban IV - as responsible for inviting Charles of Anjou into Italy, to seize the kingdom of Naples, and in so doing create the basis for later French claims on Italian territory. N. Machiavelli, *Opere*, vol. 1, 82.

[16] Published in 1521, the *Arte della guerra* was the only major work by Machiavelli to be printed under his own name during his lifetime. However, a plagiarised Latin translation of *Il Principe* was published by Agostino Nifo in 1523.

[17] If the *Arte della guerra* is probably now the least studied of Machiavelli's works it would be foolish to underestimate its historical significance. Machiavelli himself seems to have considered it among his most important works, and not only was it the first to appear in print, but besides the 1521 and 1529 Florentine editions, six more were published in Italy

Until the seventh and final book, Charles VIII's invasion is mentioned only twice, on both occasions as little more than an aside: the first is in reference to the growing tendency to employ Swiss or 'German' style infantry in the aftermath of 1494,[18] the second to changes in the design of Italian fortification as a legacy of the Charles's use of artillery.[19] However, the closing pages of the work make explicit the enormous significance that Machiavelli attached to the French invasion. The defeats of 1494 are presented clearly as the direct consequence of the failure of Italy's princes to concentrate on maintaining disciplined forces drawn from their own citizenry. Indeed, while acknowledging the short-comings of modern Italian soldiers, Machiavelli quite specifically exonerates them from blame. Italian defeat must be seen as solely the responsibility of Italy's rulers.

> It is not the people that are to blame, but their princes, who have been rightly punished for their stupidity, ignominiously losing their states, without any show of being virtuoso.[20]

As Machiavelli stressed in the famous opening passage of Chapter XIV of *Il Principe*, a ruler

> should have no other objective, nor thought, nor take anything else for his profession except war and its methods and rules.[21]

Instead, Italy's princes had given themselves up to an existence of effeminate culture, thinking it sufficient,

> to write handsome letters, or to compose clever responses at their writing desks, to show wit and wisdom in conversation and repartee, to know how to weave a web of deceit, to decorate themselves with jewels and gold, to eat and sleep in greater magnificence and luxury than their peers, to surround themselves with lasciviousness, to govern their subjects in a haughty and avaricious manner, to fester in inactivity, to

---

before the end of the sixteenth century. In a translated and plagiarised form it appeared as Diego de Salazar's *Tratado de re militari* in Valencia in 1536, and by the 1560s it was widely known in English and French translations. By the early seventeenth century it was available in German and Latin translations, and in the eighteenth it was admired by both Voltaire and Frederick II of Prussia, despite their co-authorship of the so-called *Antimachiavel*, a reworking of the Prussian crown prince's earlier *Réfutation du Prince de Machiavel*. In the early nineteenth century the great military theorist Clausewitz was making frequent reference to it in his writings on war. On the long-term influence of the work see the Introduction by N. Wood to the E. Farneworth trans. of Machiavelli, *The art of war* (New York, revised edn, 1990), xxix-xlvii. On Clausewitz see P. Paret, *Clausewitz and the state. The man, his theories and his times* (Princeton, 1985), 169-79.

[18] N. Machiavelli, *Opere*, vol. 2, 511.
[19] N. Machiavelli, *Opere*, vol. 2, 643.
[20] N. Machiavelli, *Opere*, vol. 2, 662.
[21] N. Machiavelli, *Opere*, vol. 2, 54-5.

> dispense their military preferments as favours, to despise anyone who showed the slightest merit, and to wish that their words be considered the sayings of oracles...[22]

According to Machiavelli it was this mentality that had led directly to the disastrous defeats of 1494 -'i grandi spaventi, le súbite fughe e le miracolose perdite' - that had resulted in the sack and destruction of three of Italy's greatest states. But what was infinitely more reprehensible was that those of Italy's princes who had not been overthrown as a result of Charles's invasion had continued to conduct themselves in the same fashion: they persisted in the same errors, refusing to learn either from recent history or from the wisdom of the ancients.[23]

Machiavelli's sense of Italian decadence is equally clear in the *Discorsi sopra la prima Deca di Tito Livio*. However, rather than singling out Italian princes for particular attack, he saves his bitterest criticism for the Papacy. Admittedly Machiavelli was critical of Christianity generally because, unlike the pagan beliefs of the ancients, it was of little worth in instilling military and civic *virtù*.[24] He also denounced the Church for having betrayed its original principles, upbraiding the court of Rome for having set such a poor example

---

[22] N. Machiavelli, *Opere*, vol. 2, 662.

[23] In both the *Discorsi* and the *Arte della Guerra*, Machiavelli specifically inveighs against his contemporaries' habit of valuing the artistic legacy of the ancients rather than their military and civic *virtù*. Hence in the Preface to Book One of the *Discorsi*, he attacks the way in which 'a bit of old statue' will fetch an exaggerated price as a decoration for a house or as a model for artists to copy, but that no one is prepared to learn from the 'le virtuosissime operazioni che la storia ci mostrono', and to act as the ancients did in order to emulate their success 'nello ordinare la milizia ed amministrare la guerra, nel iudicare e' sudditi, nello accrescere l'imperio'. N. Machiavelli, *Opere*, vol. 2, 101-2. Similarly he has Fabrizio Colonna, criticise Cosimo Rucellai's grandfather for choosing to lay out a garden in the fashion of the ancients, as symptomatic of the modern Italian readiness to copy their luxuries, but not to emulate their virtues: see 478-9.

[24] N. Machiavelli, *Opere*, vol. 2, 137-41.
Later in Book Two of the *Discorsi* Machiavelli returns to the subject of Christianity, arguing that it does not prepare men well for public or military life, because it inspires neither a love of liberty nor a thirst for glory. 'La religione antica, oltre a di questo, non beatificava, se non uomini pieni di mondana gloria; come erano capitani di eserciti e principi di republiche. La nostra religione ha glorificato piú gli uomini contemplativi, che gli attivi. Ha dipoi posto il sommo bene nella umilitá, abiezione, e nel dispregio delle cose umane: quell'altra lo poneva nella grandezza dell'animo, nella fortezza del corpo, ed in tutte le altre cose atte a fare gli uomini fortissimi. E se la religione nostra richiede che tu abbi in te fortezza, vuole che tu sia atto a patire piú che a fare una cosa forte. Questo modo di vivere, adunque, pare che abbi renduto il mondo debole, e datolo in preda agli uomini scelerati; i quali sicuramente lo possono maneggiare, veggendo come l'universitá degli uomini, per andarne in Paradiso, pensa piú a sopportare la sue battiture che a vendicarle. E benché paia che si sia effeminato il mondo, e disarmato il Cielo, nasce piú sanza dubbio dalla viltá degli uomini, che hanno interpretato la nostra religione secondo l'ozio, e non secondo la virtú. Perché, se considerassono come la ci permette la esaltazione e la difesa della patria, vedrebbono come la vuole che noi l'amiamo ed onoriamo, e prepariamoci a essere tali che noi la possiamo difendere.' See 254-5.

that Italians had lost their faith and lapsed into immorality.[25] But his fiercest objection to the Papacy was little concerned with Christian teaching on love and humility. For, by keeping Italy weak and divided, the Papacy was the cause of 'la rovina nostra'.[26]

> And truly, no land was ever united or happy, if not under the rule of a single republic or prince as has occurred in France and Spain. And the reason that Italy is not in the same position... is solely the fault of the Church, because although the Church is based in Italy and has its temporal domains there, it has not been of sufficient strength or of sufficient virtù to be able to occupy a position of absolute power and to dominate Italy; yet, on the other hand, nor has it been so weak that, when fearful of losing its temporal domain, it could not call on a power that could defend it against an Italian state that was becoming too powerful... Therefore, the Church, being neither strong enough to occupy the whole of Italy, nor being allowed by others to do so, has been the reason for its not coming under a single head; but, instead, it has been under many princes and masters, from which has been born such weakness and disunion, that it has become prey not only to powerful barbarians, but to whoever attacks it. Which situation we Italians owe the Church and no one else.[27]

Only a strong and 'united' state, such as France or Spain, could hope to achieve domestic stability and success on the battlefield.[28]

The views expressed by Machiavelli in both the *Arte della Guerra* and the *Discorsi* on Italian decadence and the need for military reform, and the anxiety displayed in the latter over the division of Italy into separate states unable to compete with the growing power of France and Spain, appear to receive their bluntest expression in *Il Principe*. In Chapter Twelve he once again treats us to his arguments on the superiority of armies drawn from the citizenry to mercenaries,[29] specifically identifies 1494 and the subsequent years of defeat as punishment for the Italian princes' refusal to attend seriously to matters military,[30] and names the Papacy as fundamental to the peninsula's weaknesses and divisions.[31] But Machiavelli puts his case at its plainest in the

---

[25] N. Machiavelli, *Opere*, vol. 2, 142-3.

[26] N. Machiavelli, *Opere*, vol. 2, 143.

[27] N. Machiavelli, *Opere*, vol. 2, 143-4.

[28] It should be noted that Machiavelli did not always identify France with a position of military strength. In one passage in the *Discorsi* he chose to rank it alongside contemporary Italy and ancient Carthage, in contrast to the military strength of the ancient Romans and the Swiss. However, at least France had the merit of unity. See N. Machiavelli, *Opere*, vol. 2, 280.

[29] 'Le mercenarie e ausiliarie sono inutile e periculose... la ruina di Italia non è causata da altro che per essere in spazio di molti anni riposatasi in sulle arme mercenarie.' N. Machiavelli, *Opere*, vol. 2, 47.

[30] 'E chi diceva come e' n'erano cagione e' peccati nostri, diceva il vero; ma non erano giá quelli che credeva, ma questi che io ho narrati: e perché elli erano peccati de' principi, ne hanno patito la pena ancora loro.' *Opere*, vol. 2, 47.

[31] Machiavelli's censure of the Papacy for keeping Italy divided is expressed more briefly but in much the same terms as in *I Discorsi*. In the same passage his condemnation of the

final chapter: the 'Exhortation to liberate Italy from barbarian domination'. In the 'Exhortation' Machiavelli reveals that, in a way, 1494 and the resulting barbarian yoke are to be welcomed: Italy had become so corrupt that the old system needed to be proved totally rotten so that it might be swept away, and *virtù* restored.[32] Yet at the same time he makes an impassioned plea to the Medici to provide the necessary reforming leader to heal *Italy*'s festering wounds. He is quite explicit that not only Tuscany, but also Lombardy and Naples should be liberated from foreign oppression.[33] Italian fighting men, he argues, equal if not surpass those of other European nations in single combat and duels - they have no lack of native bravery. However, this needs to be channelled by a prince redeemer, prepared to combine the techniques of both Spanish and Swiss infantry, in organising a citizen army which will achieve Italian liberty.[34]

The powerful sense of *italianità* evident in the 'Exhortation' is also obvious in the only one of Machiavelli's works to deal explicitly - albeit briefly - with the invasion of 1494 and its aftermath. This is his *Decennale primo*, which, written in 1504, deals with the events in Italy over the ten year period that began with Charles VIII's invasion. Rarely looked at by scholars in the English-speaking world, the *Decennale primo* is of dubious literary merit.[35] On the other hand, it is revealing of Machiavelli's political stance. Two points are quite certain from the opening lines. First, that the events of 1494 initiated a

---

popes' readiness to use foreign troops is well nigh identical to the criticisms he was to voice later in the *Istorie*. *Opere*, vol. 2, 50.

[32] '...cosí al presente, volendo conoscere la virtú di uno spirito italiano, era necessario che la Italia si riducessi nel termine che ella è di presente, e che la fussi piú stiava che gli Ebrei, piú serva ch'e' Persi, piú dispersa che gli Atenesi; sanza capo, sanza ordine; battuta, spogliata, lacera, corsa; ed avessi sopportato d'ogni sorte ruina.' N. Machiavelli, *Opere*, vol. 2, 92-3.

[33] 'In modo che, rimasa come sanza vita, espetta qual possa essere quello che sani le sue ferite, e ponga fine a' sacchi di Lombardia, alle taglie del Reame e di Toscana, e la guarisca di quelle sue piaghe giá per lungo tempo infistolite. Vedesi come la prega Dio, che le mandi qualcuno che la redima da queste crudeltá ed insolenzie barbare...' N. Machiavelli, *Opere*, vol. 2, 93.

[34] N. Machiavelli, *Opere*, vol. 2, 93-5.
Sasso suggests that the emphasis on the Swiss and Spanish (with only a brief aside to the merits of French cavalry) had much to do with the fact that when the *Principe* was written in 1513 or, at the very latest in the early months of 1514, the French had been driven from Milan and no longer posed a significant threat in the peninsula. 'Il «Principe» ebbe due redazioni?', in *Machiavelli e gli antichi e altri saggi*, 2 vols (Milan-Naples, 1988), vol. 2, 197-273. See especially, 207-13. However, Machiavelli's emphasis on Swiss and Spanish infantry can be traced more simply to his belief that when their two styles of fighting were combined they closely approximated to ancient Roman legionaries.

[35] Writing of both the *Decennale primo* and the *Decennale secondo*, Chabod remarked, 'Dal punto di vista artistico i due lavori valgono assai poco; sono invece notevoli per i giudizi politici del Machiavelli sugli eventi del suo tempo'. *Dizionario letterario Bompiani delle opere e dei personaggi* (Milano, 1947), vol. 2, 586.

period of disaster for the whole of Italy,[36] and second that the cause of this disaster was as much internal division as foreign invasion.[37]

Given the sentiments he expressed regarding Italian disunity and foreign domination, it is easy to see why champions of nationalism from the early nineteenth century onwards were to seize upon Machiavelli as an early prophet of the nation-state. As Villari wrote:

> the practical side and the real aim of his work are clearly seen. It is a question of achieving the unity of his Italian motherland and delivering it from foreign rule. This was certainly the holiest of objects.[38]

Writing in the immediate aftermath of the wars of Italian unification, it is obvious why Villari should have wished to emphasise Machiavelli's patriotic credentials. Few historians today would be prepared to adopt so simplistic an interpretation of his goals. However, many modern scholars, particularly in the anglophone world, are evidently ill at ease with addressing Machiavelli's outspoken *italianità* and shy away from treating his calls for wars of national liberation. Quentin Skinner, for example, in his masterful brief study of Machiavelli, side-steps the whole issue of the obviously central theme of Italian patriotism, and in particular ignores the message of the 'Exhortation'.[39] Likewise in the introduction to his recent translation of *Il Principe*, Skinner makes no attempt to explain (or even explain away) Machiavelli's clear calls for a war of patriotic liberation: while he acknowledges the 'Exhortation' as magnificent rhetoric, he overlooks its content entirely.[40] In contrast, Mary Dietz has adopted a position which at least seeks to locate Machiavelli's plans for Italy as central to his work. Dietz suggests that Machiavelli's appeal to the Medici to liberate Italy from foreign domination was part of a deliberate republican strategy. The aim of *Il Principe* was on the one hand to encourage the Medici to adopt policies which would make them vulnerable to popular rebellion, and on

---

[36] 'Io canterò l'italiche fatiche/ Seguíte giá ne'duo passati lustri/ Sotto le stelle al suo bene inimiche...' N. Machiavelli, *Opere*, vol. 1, 790.

[37] '...in sé discordante, Italia aperse/ La via a' Galli, e... esser calpesta/ Da le genti barbariche sofferse.' N. Machiavelli, *Opere*, vol. 1, 790.

[38] P. Villari, *Life and times of Machiavelli*, 515.

Mazzini, who found Machiavelli's political pragmatism essentially distasteful, had no doubt about his importance in the development of Italian patriotism. Indeed, such views were widespread during the *Risorgimento*, and it is no surprise that, when in the early 1820s political radicals in Naples began to print a periodical entitled *Annali del patriotismo*, its 'manifesto' should have carried a quotation from *Il Principe* at its head. For a description of this publication see the reports of the Austrian censors for Venetia: Venice, Archivio di Stato, Presidio di Governo (1820-23) VI 2/1.

[39] Skinner, *Machiavelli*.

[40] N. Machiavelli, *The Prince*, ed. Q. Skinner and R. Price (Cambridge, 1988), x, xiv and xxiii.

the other to persuade them to embark on a patriotic war of expansion which would lead them to overstretch themselves and quicken their collapse.[41]

Neither of these approaches to Machiavelli's *italianità* and his response to foreign rule is really adequate: Skinner's, simply because it fails to address fundamental themes in Machiavelli's work; Dietz's, because it does not acknowledge the obvious centrality of the liberation of Italy elsewhere in his writings. It is evident from reading any of Machiavelli's work from the *Decennali* to the *Discorsi* that his concern for Italy is much more than simple 'bait' to lure a vainglorious Medici into an ill-conceived war aimed at bringing about their destruction.[42] A more convincing treatment of Machiavelli's calls for a war against the foreigner is to be found in the work of Sidney Anglo. Anglo points out that:

> despite its naïveties, inconsistencies, and stylistic lapses, [Il Principe] is a deliberately structured work; and the apex of that structure is the call to the Medici to unite Italy - or rather North Italy - and lead it from the dominion of the barbarians.[43]

To Anglo it is quite clear that, however passionately Machiavelli longed for such a war, it was wishful thinking. Whatever the Florentine's 'personal

---

[41] M. Dietz, 'Trapping the Prince: Machiavelli and the politics of deception', *American Political Science Review*, 80 (1986), 777-99.

[42] 'We might read Machiavelli's final call to action as the "bait" ... he offers Lorenzo. If the chapter does its work, Lorenzo... will "forget every other good" and so become not only Machiavelli's puppet, but the dupe of his own grandiose expectations of earthly power and political immortality.' Dietz, 'Trapping the Prince', 796.

[43] Anglo, *Machiavelli*, 77. Judging from the text of Machiavelli's 'Exhortation' it is not clear that Anglo is right to point simply to 'North Italy'. If the final chapter really was a call for Italian unification, then Machiavelli's programme seems to extend to Kingdom of Naples as well.

Some scholars, however, have questioned whether the final chapter of *Il Principe* was written as a later appendage, suggesting that it is of a rather different style from rest of the book, which has more the character of technical treatise. Indeed, there is a long tradition of debate between those students who have backed Meinecke's assertion of the work's essential dualism, and those who follow Federico Chabod's defence of its intrinsic unity. Recent research by Gennaro Sasso should have laid to rest once and for all the thesis of the later composition of the 'Exhortation'. The most articulate of recent studies within the dualistic tradition is M. Martelli, 'Da Poliziano a Machiavelli. Sull'epigramma «dell'Occasione» e sull'occasione', *Interpres*, 2 (1979), 230-54. For a refutation see G. Sasso, 'Il «Principe» ebbe due redazioni?'. See also F. Chabod, 'Sulla composizione de «Il Principe» di Niccolò Machiavelli, *Scritti su Machiavelli* (Torino, 1964), 139-93. For the view that the 'Exhortation' is central to our understanding of Machiavelli's thought, regardless of whether it was written at the same time as or independently of the rest of the treatise, see F. Gilbert, 'The concept of nationalism in Machiavelli's *Prince*', *Studies in the Renaissance*, 1 (1954), 38-48, reprinted in De Lamar Jensen (ed.), *Machiavelli, cynic, patriot, or political scientist?* (Lexington, Mass., 1960), 35-41.

anguish' at the decadence of Italy, he was aware that nothing would come of his 'heartfelt plea'.[44]

But what really lay behind Machiavelli's constant emphasis on the need to cleanse Italy of *oltramontani*, to purge the legacy of 1494? To understand his position properly it is essential to realise that his strong sense of Italy as a political unit was by no means unusual. As Felix Gilbert observed, by the time Machiavelli was writing there was nothing new either in 'the idea that Italy was distinguished from the surrounding world' or 'in the demand for the expulsion of foreigners'.[45] On the contrary, that Machiavelli was able to end his 'Exhortation' with a quotation from Petrarch's *Italia mia* is a straightforward indication that he was operating within a long-standing political and artistic tradition. Admittedly the relative freedom from non-Italian interference experienced during much of the fifteenth century meant that it witnessed rather fewer expressions of such sentiments. Yet freedom from outside meddling also reinforced a sense of Italy's right to political autonomy. Moreover, there is little doubt that the sense of intellectual primacy and of close ties with ancient Rome, which was fostered by the fifteenth-century flowering of Italian humanism, led to an intensification of the sense 'of the separateness of Italy from the rest of Europe'. Similarly, the increasing tendency for Italians to identify with the ancient Romans, was matched by an equal readiness to equate *oltramontani* with the barbarians who had brought ruin to the Roman Empire. It is no coincidence that Guicciardini's opening paragraphs of his *Storia d'Italia* compare the prosperity of pre-1494 Italy with that enjoyed by ancient Rome, or that Italy's subsequent invaders are dismissed laconically as 'barbari'.[46]

Machiavelli was not alone in feeling so passionately about Italy's humiliation. His views were common to many of the best minds in Italy: not only Guicciardini but the likes of Pontano, Vettori, Bernardo Rucellai, and even

---

[44] S. Anglo, *Machiavelli*, 78-80. Anglo demonstrates Machiavelli's greater realism by pointing to his August 1513 correspondence with his friend Vettori in which he remarked that the latter's suggestion of co-operation between the different Italian states had simply made him laugh. For this letter see N. Machiavelli, *Opere*, vol. 2, 798.

[45] F. Gilbert, 'The concept of nationalism'. Elsewhere Gilbert writes: 'Before 1494 the Italian view about the position of Italy in Europe was clear and simple: there was Italy; and there was the indistinct mass of all other nations of Europe which the Italians regarded as culturally inferior. The Italians of the Renaissance liked to repeat the classical adage that God - or Nature - had placed the Alps as a protecting wall around Italy. People living beyond the Alps were foreigners and it was unnatural for *oltramontani* to interfere in Italian affairs.' F. Gilbert, *Machiavelli and Guicciardini*, 255.

[46] Elsewhere Guicciardini wrote in his *Ricordi*, 'Tre cose desidero vedere innanzi alla mia morte, ma dubito, ancora che io vivessi molto, non ne vedere alcuna: uno vivere di repubblica bene ordinato nella città nostra, Italia liberata da tutti e barbari e liberato el mondo dall tirannide di questi scelerati preti.' Francesco Guicciardini, *Ricordi*, ed. Sergio Marconi (Milan, 1983), 115-16.

the urbane Castiglione shared his dismay.[47]   By the time Machiavelli was penning his major works of politics and history, it was quite clear that 1494 had initiated a period of foreign domination which could not easily be dislodged. No longer could Italians entertain the earlier optimism of Francesco Gonzaga who, on learning of Charles VIII's withdrawal from the peninsula, had ordered that medals be struck bearing the legend *ob restitutam Italiae libertatem*.[48] But were Machiavelli's calls for a war of liberation merely premised on a desire to see Italy free from Swiss, Spanish and French power? Surely not. However fervent, Machiavelli's espousal of Italian patriotism served another end: to legitimate the rest of his political programme. Take, for example, his constant harping on the inadequacies of mercenaries and need for a militia. In some senses, there was nothing especially unusual about his views. After all, as Michael Mallett has recently shown, Florence's experiences with *condottieri* had rarely been happy.[49]   Moreover, in the sort of humanist milieu in which Machiavelli was educated, there was a strong tradition of extolling the virtue of a citizen army.[50] Add to this Machiavelli's eagerness to adopt ancient Roman models wherever possible, and it is simple to understand why he argued so energetically in favour of a prince relying on his own arms rather than mercenaries.   On the other hand, it is easy to see a hidden agenda in Machiavelli's writings. In *Il Principe* especially, he can be seen as justifying his own past errors. His experiments with both infantry and cavalry under the Soderini régime had proved pretty disastrous. If his treatise was designed to get him back into favour with the Medici, then it was essential for him to explain his rationale for raising an essentially ineffective militia force. Alternatively, as Chabod hinted and Dietz states specifically,[51] arming the people, rather than to relying on hired professionals, was extremely bad advice: citizen-soldiers could not be easily dictated to, and liberty would be guaranteed. It is hard to be certain whether Machiavelli was trying deliberately to undermine the position of the restored Medici, blindly pursuing his own military obsession, or genuinely

---

[47] The treatment of Italy's humiliation in *Il Cortegiano* is particularly revealing. Castiglione tended to shy away from a direct discussion of Italian politics, but frequently hinted at the need to raise Italians from their decadence. One particularly revealing passage is in Book Two in which he bemoans the reluctance among Italians to adopt a distinctive national style of dress and their preference for wearing French or Spanish fashions. This he suggests is symbolic of Italy's subjugation by foreigners, but also reflected the decadence that had led to that subjugation. B. Castiglione, *Il libro del cortegiano*, ed. G. Carnazzi (Milan, 1987), 140-41.

[48] P. Laven, *Renaissance Italy, 1464-1534* (London, 1966), 112.

[49] M. Mallett, 'The theory and practice of warfare in Machiavelli's republic', in G. Bock, Q. Skinner and M. Viroli (eds), *Machiavelli and republicanism* (Cambridge, 1991), 173-80.

[50] On the Florentine humanist tradition of defending the militia see C.C. Bayley, *War and society in Renaissance Florence. The* De Militia *of Leonardo Bruni* (Toronto, 1961).

[51] M. Dietz, 'Trapping the Prince', 785-6.

seeking to offer wise counsel in the hope of easing his return to government office. However, what is clear is that, whatever his motives, by associating his arguments with the pursuit of Italian liberty, Machiavelli was able to make them appear less controversial. The author of *Il Principe* might have loathed the 'barbaro dominio'; he might also have sought means to hasten its end. But there is no question that he also found it extremely useful.

In retrospect Machiavelli must have viewed 1494 with considerable ambivalence. In common with members of the educated élites throughout the peninsula, the realisation of Italy's intrinsic weakness must have come as a brutal and depressing shock. Yet by revealing the fundamental bankruptcy of the political and military institutions of Florence and her sister states, 1494 initiated a period which would once and for all destroy the complacent assumptions both of *quattrocento* civic humanism and of Italy's style of princely government. If Machiavelli loathed the legacy of 1494, it was his experience of that same legacy which shaped his thought, which moulded his poltical career and which was to result in his radical redefinition of political *virtù*.

'Traitres Lombardi': the expedition of Charles VIII in the Lombard sources up to the mid-sixteenth century

Paolo Margaroli

I

In August 1494, before the king of France had crossed the Alps, the *bon mot* was circulating in Milan: 'el non è ni savio ni matto che intendi la guerra dil novantaquattro'.[1] The following month Charles VIII's expedition departed, but in the Sforza duchy it generated neither apocalytic expectations nor hopes of renewal. Indeed, in the years that followed the Lombards were never quite sure where to place these events in the context of other significant changes that came to a head around this time. In fact, of all the expedition's aspects, that concerned with the attitude it generated in the different regions of Italy, whether analysed from a political, diplomatic or cultural angle, remains one of the most open issues, best known through the negative myth of the 'ruin of Italy' recorded by Guicciardini. Not just the local context but the cultural level of the observer are crucial factors in determining that observer's outlook. Interacting with such approaches and attitudes is a whole 'popular' level of responses, of fears and expectations, fed by the Messianic predictions of local preachers or the tales purveyed by rhyming narrators, to which historians have access through the widespread popular prints of the time, through songs in *ottava rima* and through the text of prophecies.[2] A notary of Piacenza, Marco Antonio Gatti, inserted among some blank pages of his acts dating between 1473 and 1501 some brief notes on the passage of Charles VIII through his city, but alongside them he also

---

[1] So indicates Marin Sanudo, *La spedizione di Carlo VIII in Italia*, ed. R. Fulin (Venice, 1873).

[2] O. Niccoli, *Profeti e popolo nell'Italia del Rinscimento* (Bari, 1987), 35-6; A. Denis, *Charles VIII et les Italiens: Histoire et Mythe* (Geneva, 1979), 19-25. *Guerre in ottava rima*, vol. 2, *Guerre d'Italia (1483-1527)*, ed. M. Beer, D. Diamanti, C. Ivaldi (Modena, 1989).

copied a section of the so-called 'Prophecy of San Cataldo' and a verse dialogue attributed to Antonio Cammelli.[3]

Materials like these possessed an extraordinary capacity for circulation and for adaptation to particular circumstances. Thus the prophecy called the 'Second Charlemagne' was composed for Charles VI of France, but was adapted to the case of Charles VIII's Italian invasion, and yet again later on to the needs of Emperor Charles V.[4] The 'Pater noster dei Lombardi' was probably composed in 1494-95, but was utilised again a century later against the Spaniards.[5] It is thus very difficult (and no such attempt will be made here) to trace in these popular themes sure evidence for precise knowledge of current events in the duchy of Milan, while even exact links with the expectations and fears of the time are hard to hazard. Thus no attention will be paid here to either learned or popular poetry, which needs a closely focussed study of its diffusion, its audience and the literary, perhaps even courtly, environment in which it emerged. The aim, rather, will be to follow the ways that Charles VIII's expedition was understood in other materials, above all by looking at the political and military impact of the expedition; this can be examined by way of the *Carteggi* in the Archivio di Stato at Milan devoted to internal and to external affairs, in other words the diplomatic correspondence and letters exchanged with officials operating in the lands of the duchy. A second approach adopted here will be to look at the reflection of these events in the historical writing of the decades after the invasion.

The Bolognese writer Giovanni Sabadino degli Arienti wrote these verses to the new Charlemagne:

> D'arme et de cavalli bolle il mondo,
> per che tu porai toi inimici in fondo[6]

Such an approach took little account in Lombardy of the earlier intrusions of French princes in the politics of the Italian peninsula: to cite some of the most recent examples, the useless involvement of René of Anjou in the war between Francesco Sforza and the Venetians, the ephemeral conquest of Genoa in 1458, the unsuccessful Angevin campaigns against Ferrante of Naples defeated at

---

[3] A.G. Tononi, 'Note storiche e rime politiche e morali tra gli atti di un notaio piacentino del secolo XV', *Strenna Piacentina*, 18 (1892), 28-44.

[4] Niccoli, *Profeti e popolo*, 35-6.

[5] F. Novati, 'Una poesia politica del Cinquecento: il Pater Noster dei Lombardi', in *Giornale di filologia romanza*, 2 (1879), 121; G. Gorni-S-Longhi, 'La parodia', in *Letteratura italiana Einaudi*, vol. 5, *Le questioni*, (Turin, 1986), 459-87 (480). An early sixteenth-century version can be found in Marin Sanudo, *I Diarii (1496-1533)*, ed. R. Fulin, F. Stefani, G. Berchet, N. Barozzi, M. Allegri, 58 vols. (Venice, 1877-1902), vol. 4, 292.

[6] Giovanni Sabadino degli Arienti to Ludovico il Moro, Bologna, 28 August 1494 (Milan, Archivio di Stato, Sforzesco Potenze Estere [henceforth ASMi, SPE] Romagna 1044). For the myth of the new Charlemagne see Denis, *Charles VIII*, 19-30.

Troia and at Ischia in 1462 and 1465. The Italian powers were completely unaware of the possible consequences of the descent of a foreign ruler into Italy, and continued to make use of the Italian League or of more particular leagues in order to arrange the territorial shape of Italy. It has often been shown that the collapse after 1494 must be understood in the context of the longer term development of the European monarchies, in the face of which the Italian League had and was understood to have no defensive power. Nor indeed is it helpful to speak of the summoning of the French to Italy, or to discuss who was responsible for what occurred.[7] Awareness of this was particularly clear in Milanese government circles; the words of Ludovico il Moro to his brother Ascanio Sforza, the Cardinal Vice-Chancellor based in Rome, reveal as much:

> Comprehendo che la Beatitudine sua non intende forse quello che è in questa cosa de Francia et sta in errore del animo et opera mia, però che stimando che in mia facultà debia essere fare o intermettere l'impresa o vero differirla, pare presupporre che'l movimento debia anche procedere da me: el che è alieno dal vero perché el Christianissimo Re è quello che sponte sua si è mosso sono zà mesi multi et anni.[8]

Even clearer are the words of Ascanio Sforza to his brother in cypher, when writing about the preparation of the troops to be sent in support of the French king; he tells Ludovico that 'li desiderii de questi conducteri sariano che le conducte loro fusseno facte sotto el nome de la Excellentia Vostra facendo però la spesa Francesi', since this way Pope Alexander VI will be prevented by the terms of the Italian League from moving against the troops of Milan's ally.[9] But even if the political game was played with such subtlety, what was lacking was a real ability to assess the possible consequences of the events that were unfolding.

Some aspects of the impact of the French expedition stand out prominently. The events of the king's journey into Italy are well known, but less known are the frequent acts of violence committed in Lombardy against the civil population, resulting from the impossibility of handling immense numbers of soldiers. The officials assigned the task of following the troop movements threw up their hands in horror at the daily episodes of disorder: at Vigevano,[10]

---

[7] G. Pillinini, *Il sistema degli stati italiani 1454-1494* (Venice, 1970), 139-49.

[8] Vigevano, 10 March 1494; see also the letter of 18 March, ASMi, SPE, Rome, 108).

[9] Roma, 26 May 1494, *post scriptum* (ASMi, SPE, Roma, 109).

[10] Il Moro to Lorenzo Mozzanica, segretario ducale e commissario generale delle genti d'arme, Vigevano, 3 October 1494 (Milan, Archivio di Stato, Sforzesco, Carteggio Interno [henceforth SCI] Parma 1174).

Palestro,[11] Rosasco,[12] Annone,[13] Binasco,[14] Voghera (where a girl was raped),[15] Tromello,[16] Castel San Giovanni,[17] Lomello,[18] Pavia.[19] And the same happened in the countryside around Piacenza[20] and around Parma, in the latter case at Castellana:

> in el dito alozamento li era una gravida per parturire et uno de questi [soldati francesi] volea dormire in quello lecto, che era cossa dishonesta, volendolivi dare uno altro, et sbatete la vechia per tera che la gridava et ferì sopra la testa il patre vechio...[21]

Borgo San Donnino (the modern Fidenza), was also affected; here some Gascon soldiers wounded an innkeeper;[22] so too was Parma,[23] as was Varano de' Melogare and Serravalle,[24] and also Pontremoli.[25] Only in Genoa much more dangerous political tensions opened up, in addition to the ever-present problems

---

[11] Cottino Cotta to il Moro, Palestro, 5 October 1494 (SPE, Francia, 554).

[12] Leonino Biglia to il Moro, Mortara, 10 October 1494 (SCI, Pavia, 1179).

[13] Conte Borella to Giovanni Giacomo Cotta, *commissario ducale*, Novi, 9 October 1494 (SPE, Genova, 1212); cf. also the Comune and the men of Annone to il Moro, Novi, 11 October 1494 (SPE, Genova 1212) and Giovanni Giacomo Cotta to il Moro, Alessandria, 11 October 1494 (SCI, Alessandria 1146).

[14] Pietro Reina, castellan of Binasco, to Giacometto de Latella (SPE, Francia 554).

[15] Giovanni Beccaria, *commissario ducale*, to Lorenzo Mozzanica, Voghera, 6 October 1494 (SCI, Pavia of 1179): è acaduto a vegnire a la terra una puta da marido et como è stato zonta a presso a dicta compagnia [del duca d'Orléans] gli sonno molti andati ad essa puta et l'hano et manizada et facto grande deshonestà...'.

[16] Cottino Cotta to il Moro, Tromello, 11 October 1494 (SCI, Pavia, 1179).

[17] Giovanni Antonio Guiscardo to an unknown addressee, Castel San Giovanni, s.d. (SCI, Cremona, 1162, wrongly classified under 1495): questi del duca de Orliens che sono stati qui due nocte et hanno facto mille insolentie, non hanno voluto pagare pane né vino a molti dove erano allogiati. Non è homo de questa terra che non sia stato robato et molti batuti et tra li altri heri sera a una hora de nocte, andando Paulino da Cilegno da una casa a una altra, el fu asaltato da sey Franciosi che li deteno una frota de ferite et li tolseno la capa et portata via et uno povero massaro per pagamento de pane e vino et altre sue robe senza parole gli tagliorno una sguanza e sta male.

[18] Angelo *de Lavello* to il Moro, Lomello, 14 October 1494 (SCI, Pavia, 1179).

[19] Giacomo Pusterla, castellan of Pavia, and Dionisio to il Moro, Pavia, 13 October 1494 (SPE, Francia, 554).

[20] Lorenzo Mozzanica to il Moro, Piacenza, 17 October 1494; and Borrino Colli, *commissario* of Piacenza, to il Moro, Piacenza, 27 October 1494 (SCI, Piacenza, 876).

[21] Angelo *de Lavello* to Lorenzo Mozzanica, Castellana, 23 September 1494 (SCI, Parma 1174).

[22] Lorenzo Mozzanica to il Moro, Fidenza, 3 and 4 October 1494, and two letters of Giovanni Nicolì *de Regio*, Fidenza, 4 October 1494 (SCI, Parma, 1174).

[23] Antonio Trotti, governor of Parma, to il Moro, Parma, 13 October 1494 (two letters), and the Anziani and Presidenti of Parma to il Moro, Parma, 13 October 1494 (SCI Parma, 1174): le grandissimo deshonestade et maltractamenti è facto per li Francesi e a li citadini nostri e contadini, cioè di volere vituperare le done nostre, havere le robe senza pagamento, de sachezare le case, de assassinare li homini a la Strata et de ferirli, ne li quali deshordini et manchamenti prosequeno di continuo imo multiplicano.

[24] Bernardino da Corte and Giovanni Andrea Landriani to Lorenzo Mozzanica, Parma, 13 and 14 October 1494 (SCI, Parma 1174).

[25] Cornelio *de Nibia* to il Moro, Pontremoli, 7 December 1494 (SCI, Piacenza, 876).

of providing lodgings for the troops; this was exactly what il Moro had feared since the beginning of the French invasion,[26] and events a few months later confirmed his worst fears:

> Perché la magior parte de questa città, maxime la parte Fregosa e guelfa incomenza havere grande inclinatione a Franzosi, in modo che dove prima erano tuti aragonesi in un subito hano prheso quest'altra volta.[27]

Leafing through the *carteggi*, there emerges a sense of disorientation among the Sforza officials observing these events, who tended to see the *cavalcata* of the French king as little more than a source of disorder at a local level, while they had no more expectations than they had had in the past of any real change in the political map of Italy. This is thus a situation far removed from those expectations of renewal which animated the Florentines, and which for better or worse, enabled them to see in the king the catalyst for a whole series of epoch-making earthquakes: the fall of the Medicean régime, the renewal of the Church, the crusade against the Infidel. Such attitudes helped feed a myth of the French conquest which then underwent a process of demystification or demythologisation, as events themselves unfolded, with a resultant transformation into the negative image of the 'ruin of Italy'.[28]

The entry of the French king into Italy made a great impression on contemporaries because of the grand scale of the welcome that was accorded him, but also because of the power of his army and of his weaponry; the Sforza ambassadors at the courts of other Italian rulers seemed better aware of the crisis than their compatriots back home, even though their approach to events was conditioned by their preoccupation with legitimising the conduct of Ludovico il Moro. The emissary in Bologna Guidantonio Arcimboldi forwarded to Milan the fears expressed by Giovanni Bentivoglio, who from the end of July witnessed the passage of the French troops sent to Romagna against the duke of Calabria:

> per la lista de Franza quale se era lecta questo gli pareva lo exercito del re Xerxes qual havea passare per qui et tanto numeroso che gli era da fare non mediocre consideratione et che quando queste guerre fosseno solamente tra gente italice se poteriano pur meglio tollerare, perché Italiani son soliti governarse cum magior discretione, ma le gente barbare erano de altra perversa natura et li exempli passati ne sono testimonio, perché et per le ruine che anchora se vedano et per quello se lege in le historie sono assai note le grandissime strage et destructione facte in Italia et al presente destruariano le ville sue cum li zardini et altre cose de fora.[29]

---

[26] Il Moro to Antonio Maria Sanseverino e Corrado Stanga, Annone, 12 September 1494 (SPE, Genova 1212).

[27] Corrado Stanga to il Moro, Genoa, 8 February 1495 (SPE, Genova, 1202).

[28] On this issue, see Denis, *Charles VIII*.

[29] Guidantonio Arcimboldi to il Moro, Bologna, 2 July 1494 (SPE, Romagna, 1044).

As events occurred in Romagna there began to crystallise in Italy a sense of aversion to the whole enterprise, resulting in the first place from the violence committed by the troops:

> Qui se commenza ad dire che nuy Lombardi siamo adormentati et deventati Franzosi, che cum parole milantono gran cose, ma che saremo desvegliati. Sonno perhò parole del vulgo, del quale pur il parlare favorevele assay cresce et dimminuisce la fama et reputatione de ognuno ma molto più de le grande imprese.[30]

Indeed, it was in the Romagna that French ferocity was first witnessed in full flood, with the massacre at Mordano on 20 October 1494, the cruelty of which, Bernardo Dovizi says, 'hanno pieno lo stomacho ad ognuno'.[31] On this occasion Ludovico il Moro was content simply to congratulate Charles VIII on the power and efficiency of his artillery,[32] but Dovizi records that 'li lombardi si fuggirono come p......'.[33]

II

The very image of French royalty seems rather blurred in the Milanese sources. It is true that il Moro sought to match the eminence of his illustrious guest, bringing to Asti the gold brocade coverings of the altar in the Duomo at Milan and the most beautiful of the sacred hangings;[34] in addition, he took care to find out about the king's favourite diet ('se expectarà prima intendere s'el doverà fare de grasso o de magro'[35]). This brought him the praise of the French court poet André de la Vigne: 'la fut receu joyeusement et bien'.[36] A few months later, however, he was asking his faithful follower Giovanfrancesco Sanseverino to request of the king payment of the dues for 'alcuni pavilioni et stalle' which Charles had ordered to be prepared for him at Milan, arousing as a result the protests of the French ambassador in the city.[37] Embarrassing, too, were perhaps the words of the Sforza ambassadors who were following the king's army, for instance when Carlo Barbiano di Belgioioso wrote to al Moro that 'de li dinari el re non sa niente de le intrate sue, né sa se le intrate sue siano riscosse o non'.[38] Alienation of crown property seemed not to have any effect: 'dicono glie ne viene come un niente in borsa perché tutti vano in provisione de li

---

[30] Francesco Tranchedini to il Moro, Bologna, 6 August 1494 (SPE, Romagna, 1044).

[31] Bernardo Dovizi da Bibbiena, *Epistolario*, vol. 1 *(1490-1513)*, ed. G.L. Moncallero (Florence, 1955), 218.

[32] Il Moro to Charles VIII, Milan, 24 October 1494 (SPE, Francia, 554).

[33] Dovizi, *Epistolario*, 194.

[34] Il Moro to Bartolomeo Calco, San Nazzaro, 4 September 1494 (SPE, Francia, 554).

[35] Pietro Landriani to il Moro, Alessandria, 9 September 1494 (SCI, Alessandria, 1146).

[36] André de la Vigne, *Le Voyage de Naples*, ed. A.Slerca (Milan, 1981), 173.

[37] Il Moro to Sanseverino, Milan, 11 February 1495 (SPE, Napoli 252) and Bartolomeo Calco to il Moro (SPE, Francia, 555).

[38] Lyons, 15 July 1494 (SPE, Francia, 554).

officiali che li scodeno'.[39] The impression was still more reserved when the king began to demand subventions from Milanese merchants,[40] or when he delayed his journey because of the favours of a lady, or indeed when he was engaged in attempts to cure scrofula: 'debe signare un gran numero de infirmi de quello male che soleno guarire li re de Franza'.[41]

So too after the triumphal entry of the king into Florence, the Milanese emissaries remained for the most part thunderstruck by the disorder within a city in the grip of famine and civic strife[42]; either that, or they tried to square with current events the ambiguous set of alliances patched together by il Moro. In Rome they were full of wonder when 'la intrata del Re de Franza non fo honorata perché intrò a tre hore de nocte repentinamente'.[43] The result of this action was that more acts of violence broke out, particularly at the hands of the Swiss soldiers.[44]   This perspective continued to adjust as Charles VIII overwhelmed in a matter of days the kingdom of Naples 'senza lanze né spade et senza morte de alcuni homini'.[45] He was greeted in triumph by the southern towns, which surrendered to him of their own accord.[46] The change in direction came, of course, with the League of 31 March 1495 sealed in Venice to the background of the magnificent Palm Sunday processions. Now a powerful contrast between 'Italians' and 'barbarians' came very much to the fore, having

---

[39] Lyons, 15 July 1494 (SPE, Francia 554).

[40] Carlo Barbiano to Ludovico il Moro, Lyons, 17 and 18 July 1494 (SPE, Francia, 554) and Gaspare del Paradiso to il Moro, Lyons, 18 July 1494 (SPE, Francia, 554).

[41] Carlo Barbiano and Maffeo Treviglio to Ludovico il Moro, la Côte-Saint-André, 22 August 1494 (SPE, Francia, 554). On this rite cf. M. Bloch, *Les rois Thaumaturges* (Strasbourg, 1924).

[42] Giovanni Stefano Castiglioni to Bartolomeo Calco, Florence, 21 e 24 November 1494 (SPE, Firenze 940) and Galeazzo Sanseverino to Bartolomeo Calco, Firenze, 21 November 1494 and to il Moro, 27 November 1494 (SPE, Florence, 940).

[43] Carlo Barbiano di Belgioioso and Stefano Taverna, Rome, 28 December 1494 (SPE, Roma, 111).

[44] Francesco de Curte to il Moro, Roma, 11 January 1495 (SPE, Roma, 112): Ultra questo Svixari medesimamente mixti cum l'altre gente francese da li doi giorni amazorono multi iudei che sogliono stantiare in Roma et li sacomanorono la case...

[45] Maneto detto Sconfioto, knight of the king of France to il Moro, s.l., 27 February 1495 (SPE, Napoli, 252).

[46] The attitude of Ludovico il Moro here is interesting, in view of his attempt to hold on to the duchy of Bari even under the new régime (il Moro to Giovanfrancesco Sanseverino, Milan, 27 February 1495, SPE, Napoli, 252 and 6 March 1495, SPE, Napoli 253, in which he requests the recovery of the lands of Felice Orsini, prince of Salerno; cf. the *comunità* of Bari to il Moro, Bari, 13 March 1495 (SPE, Napoli, 253), and the information provided on the raising of horses in Apulia (Antonio *de Bresello* and Giovanni Antonio *dal Castelazo* to il Moro, Palo del Colle, 7 March 1495, SPE, Napoli, 253: per Dio graci [*sic*] abiamo trovato tuta la raza de V.S. salva che non n'è stato robato nessuna et avemo trovato ch'el n'era figliati circha aquaranta et era nassuti dissidoto politri [*puledri*] masscoli et vintidoe femine; questo ano abiamo circha acento quaranta ziumente pregne... Also symbolic of such adaptation to the course of events are the digressions of the count of Caiazzo at Poggioreale, when he writes about the horse-riding of the beautiful daughter of the duchess of Amalfi (Giovanfrancesco Sanseverino to il Moro, Naples, 23 March 1495, SPE, Napoli, 253).

already been present in Italy for a couple of centuries as a literary *topos*, in particular in the mid-fifteenth century as a way of marking the difference between Italians and northerners.[47] At first this was put on one side to allow for the use to which the French invaders were being put, but the new consciousness of their difference from Italians began to affect the French themselves, as when on 31 March several of them in Venice had 'vestito un matto chiamato il Conte con una vesta coperta di gigli et menatolo in Rialto con uno bastone in mano, si dizea essere capitaneo della legha'.[48] Charles VIII aimed to pass 'sopra el ventre a tuti',[49] feeding further among his men their disdain for Italians and Lombards.[50] Meanwhile in France, according to the Italian merchants at Lyons and Avignon a great army was being preparerd to cross the Alps and come 'a riscodere il suo Rey che è assediato da Italiani, che tutti li hano coniurato e facto traison adosso'.[51]

Ludovico il Moro, with his sudden volte-face, became the keenest supporter of the new campaign against the French, to chase out of 'Liguria et Lombardia Gallorum impetus'.[52] Now that the ambition of the French king to the 'monarchia' of Italy became obvious, all the tools of propaganda that had previously been used against Florence and Venice could be turned against him.[53] No longer the hero of myth, Charles became Antichrist, or more simply a common nobody, while the French as a whole were accused of the traditional capital crimes elaborated upon in medieval literature, not least by Dante: luxury, pride, avarice.[54]

---

[47] G. Galasso, *L'Italia come problema storiografico*, introductory volume in the *Storia d'Italia*, ed. G. Galasso (Turin, 1979); A. Tenenti, 'Profilo e limiti delle realtà nazionali in Italia fra Quattrocento e Seicento', in A. Tenenti, *Stato: un'idea, una logica. Dal Comune italiano all'assolutismo francese* (Bologna, 1987), 139-55; P. Margaroli, 'L'Italia come percezione di uno spazio politico unitario negli anni Cinquanta del XV secolo', *Nuova rivista storica*, 74 (1990), 517-36.

[48] Agostino [?] to il Moro, Venice, 31 March 1495 (SPE, Venezia, 383).

[49] Summary of letters from Naples and from Rome, April 1495 (SPE, Napoli, 253).

[50] Giovanni *de Monte* to the duke of Bourbon, Acquapendente, 11 June 1495 (SPE, Francia, 555): Alchuni hano voluto dire dopo che siamo partiti da Roma che li Italiani et Lombardi obviarano ch'el Re non passarà. Questotome pare impossibile considerato la possanza ch'el Re ha et la voluntà grande de le gente d'arme et non domandano altro che havere a fare cum li inimici.

[51] Bartolomeo Zambeccari to Nestore Pallioto, Rome, 23 May 1495 (SPE, Roma, 113).

[52] Il Moro to the Governor and Anziani of Genoa, Milan, 26 June 1495 (SPE, Genoa, 1214).

[53] Taddeo Vimercati to il Moro, Venice, 20 June 1495 (SPE, Venezia, 383).

[54] That is, luxury, pride and avarice; as a result of this prudence, the most traditional virtue of the prince was undermined, making Charles the archetypal anti-Prince: cf. Denis, *Charles VIII*, 119-26.

non possono fare cossa notabile per suo vigore se non quanto gli è stato concesso per li Italiani et adesso non gli è speranza che Italiano alchuno li adherischa et se alchuni fussero con loro novello Antichristo et falsi propheti, se troverano mal contenti per essere loro odiati et exossi dal nome italiano. Et credo anchora Francesi farano contra loro le vendete, como quilli per loro superbia et insolentia non credeno havere victoria per opera humana, ma a pena da Dio et attribuisseno il tuto alla loro possanza bestiale.[55]

In Piacenza, a Benedictine monk was given a warning after striking fear into the faithful with his menaces of 'Galli e Galleti'.[56] Andrea Ghilini was arrested at Pavia for painting French insignia which were to be displayed in the event that the French were victorious.[57]

A massive attack against the very image of the king of France was now launched, with the intention of entirely demolishing the artificial epic of his divine mission. This is apparent from the words of Marquis Giovan Francesco Pallavicino to Ludovico il Moro on the subject of the French army which was working its way out of Italy after being attacked by the League's troops at Fornovo:

se intende per zente che vengono da Berceto che questi Franzosi non sono como quelli che andoreno a Napole, che erano grassi et rubicondi et havovano li soi cavalli che tuti parevano corseri, et pare che al presente sia tuto el contrario, prima sono pocha zente et la mitade mancho che non se diceva et li corpi loro pareno astinuati et li soi panni strazati et sono male armati, che non anno lance alcuna et li soi cavalli smagrati, siché si pò dire sieno malissimo a cavallo e più forte che intendo veneno como fa la bissa al percanto [la serpe all'incantesimo], che sono tuti impauriti et dice che sono quasi afamati che non hanno vitualia et di là a Berceto se tene opinione debiano piliare altro camino.[58]

After Fornovo the symbols of royalty became merely a booty to be divided between the Venetians and the Milanese, including the ornate sword covered with pearls and precious stones.[59] But in the same booty there were also more shameful objects such as the book remarked upon also by Bernardo Corio 'nel quale sotto diversi habiti et etate al naturale erano depicte molte femine per loro violate in molte citate'.[60] While the flight of Charles VIII in the course of the

---

[55] Fabrizio Marliani to il Moro, Piacenza, 14 July 1495 (SCI, Piacenza, 876).

[56] Anon. letter, Piacenza, 19 May 1495 (SCI, Piacenza, 876).

[57] Giovanni Galeazzo Visconti to il Moro, Pavia, 21 June 1495 (SCI, Pavia, 1180).

[58] Zibello, 1 July 1495 (SCI, Parma, 1175).

[59] Taddeo Vimercati to il Moro, Venice, 25 July 1495 (SPE, Venezia, 384); cf. also Brizio Giustiniano to il Moro, Genoa, [26] July 1495 (SPE, Genova, 1214), who claims he has captured the banner of the royal galley.

[60] Bernardino Corio, *Storia di Milano*, ed. A. Morisi Guerra, 2 vols. (Torino, 1978), vol. 2, 1584; this book was also mentioned by Alessandro Benedetti, a humanist and physician in the Venetian army who had fought at Fornovo, *Diaria de bello carolino*, ed. D.M. Schullian (New York, 1967).

battle was seen as an example of baseness, the time he spent between Turin and Chieri in the arms of the daughter of an artisan simply gave rise to caricature.[61]

The disdain of il Moro reached its peak when the target was the traitor Gian Giacomo Trivulzio, as can be seen from the instructions handed to one of Trivulzio's trumpeters containing the message that was to be passed on to the French on his return:[62]

> M. Zo. Jacomo, havendo lo Illustrissimo Signore mio, el Signore duca de Milano, inteso che ve doleti ch'el vi habia scripto di farvi impicare se li capitati in le mane, la sua Signoria ha commisso che io venesse a fare intendere alla presentia de questi Signori Francesi che non haveti causa de dolervene et che ciascuno chi con rasone considera alli grandi demeriti et rebellione vostra, iudicarà che questo scrivere sii stato molto conveniente et non se debii anche mancare del effecto, como la sua Signoria è per farlo capitandoli in le mane. Et perché voi, Signori Francesi, cognoscati meglio quanto capitale haveti fare de questo vostro homo, ho commissione de farvi intendere questa cosa certissima et notissima a gente assai, che essendo m. Jo. Jacomo in lo campo de lo prefato Illustrissimo Signore mio et havendosi a fare facto d'arme col Signore Roberto,[63] el valenthomo se misa una giornea d'uno trombeta et montò su uno roncino per non essere cognosciuto et potere fugire, dubitando che s'el fosse capitato in le mane de lo prefato S.Roberto non li havesse facto impicare; et se da epso S., dal quale non haveva dependentia alcuna, temeva questo et fece una cossa tanto vile et vituperosa, se ha essere certissimi che essendo al prefato Illustrissimo Signore, in lo stato del quale è nato subdito, rebelle con tanta ingratitudine et oblivione de infiniti beni et honori fac[ti] da la sua Illustrissima Signoria, haverà molto più pagura adess[o] non li intervenga questo de essere impicato se sarà preso [ ] et farà medesimamente quello fece quella volta de fugirs[e] s'el porrà et se allora s'è miso una giornea d'uno trombeta, se mettarà adesso uno sacco per non essere cognosciuto et potere fugire et chi li cerca in le casse trovarà qualche giornee de qualcuni conducteri del prefato Illustrissimo Signore a fine de usarle a questo effecto de scapare et non essere cognosciuto et chi per sue vane persuasione sarà in damno et periculo, suo damno.

However, beyond personal attack, and beyond the increasingly bitter debate concerning Italians and barbarians, it is hard to see in these statements anything substantially different from what can be seen in the tone of the ideological polemics which, for over a century, had formed an integral part of the political propaganda generated by the competing states of Italy.

III

In 1496 the situation seemed to have returned to normal, and it appeared that nothing much had changed, even if the problem of Pisa's freedom left a serious problem festering. However, these years saw a turning inwards to the internal

---

[61] Cf. the letters written to il Moro by Galeotto della Mirandola, Parma, 8 August 1495 (SPE, Francia, 555), by an anonymous author, s.l., s.d. (SPE, Francia, 555) and by Francesco Rudiano, podestà of Vigevano, Vigevano, 14 August 1495 (SCI, Pavia 1182).

[62] Milan, 11 September 1495 (SCI, Pavia, 1182).

[63] The battle of Montorio against the papal troops under the command of Roberto di Sanseverino (7 May 1486).

problems of each state: Florence was in the grip of Savonarola, Milan was the theatre of an increasingly dangerous confrontation between the duke and the leading citizens, for which the fate of Trivulzio offered a worrying precedent.[64] Another source of concern was the oppressive fiscal policy put into effect by il Moro to meet the vast expenses occasioned by Charles VIII's expedition.[65] The Milanese ambassador in Venice, Taddeo Vimercati, was anxious about this, and discussed with some Venetian patricians 'la mala dispositione de li populi de Vostra Excellentia et universalmente per li carichi insoliti, cum dire che quando uno populo o uno maligno che poria facilmente tirare dreto el vulgo et multitudine facesse uno scandalo poria essere causa de gran ruina de Vostra Excellentia et de tutta Italia, non tanto perché havesse voluntà né inclinatione a Francesi, quanto per vindicta et desperatione'.[66]

That the events of these years signalled a fundamental divide in the history of the Italian states, or that they were leading to a more serious, definitive crisis in the rule of the Sforzas, was not understood at once; in Milan an awareness of the significance of the events was particularly slow in coming, even on the part of the historians who wrote in subsequent decades. Long term events have to be taken into account, partularly following the definitive invasion of Milan in 1499. In the first place it is necessary to underline the failure of the Milanese aristocracy, little involved up to now in the life of the state,[67] to make sense of the developing crisis in the Sforza duchy, and indeed in the whole of Italy. The major concern was with the preservation of their own privileges, even after the arrival of Louis XII's troops, and they sought to re-organise themselves as an autonomous body in 1499, in the same way as had happened in 1447 with the Ambrosian Republic. They submitted their *capitoli* to the French and sought to strengthen their privileges through the newly reformed channel of the Milanese Senate.[68] A second point was the awareness of the lack of a true historiographical tradition, in a position to explain the links between what was happening locally and what was happening in Italy or indeed Europe, the result of the domination of literary life by the Sforza court and above all by the figure

---

[64] G. Chittolini, 'Dagli Sforza alle dominazioni straniere', in *Giovanni Antonio Amadeo. Scultura e architettura del suo tempo*, 19-35

[65] F. Leverotti, 'La crisi finanziaria del ducato di Milano alla fine del Quattrocento', in *Milano nell'età di Ludovico il Moro*, 2 vols. (Milan, 1983), vol. 2, 585-632 (especially 593-95).

[66] Vimercati to il Moro, Venezia, 22 June 1495 (SPE, Venezia, 383).

[67] G. Chittolini, 'Di alcuni aspetti della crisi dello stato sforzesco', in *Milano e Borgogna due stati principeschi tra Medioevo e Rinascimento*, ed. J-M. Cauchies and G. Chittolini (Rome, 1990), 21-34.

[68] G. Chittolini, 'Dagli Sforza alle dominazioni straniere'; on the Milanese Senate, cf. U. Petronio, *Il Senato di Milano. Istituzioni giuridiche ed esercizio del potere nel ducato di Milano da Carlo V a Giuseppe II* (Milan, 1972).

of the ruler himself; the result was a rhetorical, apologetic tradition ill-suited to these new circumstances.[69]

The first to occupy himself with the tragic events of 1494-95 was the Milanese Giovan Pietro Cagnola, a lawyer and diplomat from an old patrician family, involved in a number of different ducal offices. In his *Storia di Milano* from 1023 to 1497 he could not do other than celebrate the achievements of il Moro and defend his policies vis-à-vis Charles VIII;[70] his exposition and discussion do not go much deeper than a modern account fairly similar to what can be found in the diplomatic *carteggi*, nor is there any awareness of the significance of the wider changes taking place: 'E così come in poco tempo Carlo aveva aquistato Napoli, in poco tempo lo perse... Carlo re, facta questa pace, retornò in Francia sencia altra gloria'.[71] The most striking element is the accentuation of the strong contrast between Italians and barbarians, and it is quite significant that here it is presented as a contrast between Lombards and barbarians. When describing the defeat of the French at Bosco in 1447 he says (for instance) that 'molti de loro Francesi ancora fonno morti ne la zuffa; ma non tanti come de Lombardi, perché non sono i Lombardi così crudeli'.[72] Again, he says of the insult levelled by Charles VIII, *traitres lombardi*, 'veramente più si convene a loro Francesi che a Lombardi'.[73] Such characterisations are rooted in fixed stereotypes: 'Carlo re, non degienerando a la galica natura, che nel signoregiare a niuno termine sono contenti'.[74] He says too: 'non degienerando esso Duca [di Milano] a li antichi suoi, che sempre fonno amatori del bene e quiete de questa Italia'.[75] The insistent recourse to the cruelty and ferocity of the French is rooted in the standard *topoi*, and was probably of classical derivation, but also it circulated widely in these years.[76] There are thus echoes of Tacitus in

---

[69] L. Pesavento, 'La *pulcherrima urbs Mediolani* di Pietro Lazzaroni e la storiografia milanese di età sforzesca', in *La Memoria e la Città*, atti del convegno internazionale, Bologna/San Marino, 24-7 March 1993 (in press). On Milanese historiography at this time see also G.L. Barni, 'La vita culturale a Milano dal 1500 alla scomparsa dell'ultimo duca Sforza', in *Storia di Milano* Treccani, vol. 8 (Milan, 1957), 423-53 (in particular 427-34); E. Cochrane, *Historians and Historiography in the Italian Renaissance* (Chicago-London, 1981), 177-81, and G. Soldi Rondinini, 'Ludovico il Moro nella storiografia coeva', in *Milano nell'età di Ludovico il Moro*, vol. 1, 29-56.

[70] Giovan Pietro Cagnola, 'Storia di Milano dall'anno 1023 sino al 1497', ed. C. Cantù, *Archivio storico italiano*, 3 (1842), 1-215; cf. E. Cochrane, *Historians*, 177-9; G. Soldi Rondinini, 'Ludovico il Moro', 46-7.

[71] Cagnola, 'Storia di Milano', 202-4.

[72] Cagnola, 'Storia di Milano', 80.

[73] Cagnola, 'Storia di Milano', 202.

[74] Cagnola, 'Storia di Milano', 195.

[75] Cagnola, 'Storia di Milano', 195.

[76] Denis, *Charles VIII*, 91.

Cagnola's comment about Frederick Barbarossa: 'non perdonando nè a sexo alcuno nè ad etate'.[77]

The important point is that Cagnola is not a lone case; one can find a similar outlook in Jacopo d'Atri, the humanist and secretary to Francesco II Gonzaga, marquis of Mantua, who decided to commence his historical account in the *Croniche del marchese di Mantova* with the entry on the scene of his master, at the head of the League's troops at the battle of Fornovo, and as Captain-General of the Venetian Signoria.[78]

To see how events were understood more widely it is necessary to look at the period following the flight of il Moro, the period, that is, of Bernardo Corio's *Historia patria*, in which the events of the late fifteenth century are placed in a much wider European context.[79] The author had access to the ducal archives and was also an eye-witness of the events he described, even though he was never officially charged by il Moro with the task of writing such a history. The work was composed on the basis of many, and contradictory, influences, including without any doubt, the humanistic historiography of Florence and Merula's *Antiquitates*, but it can also be traced back to medieval chronicle traditions and to popular traditions, including some rejected by Merula himself, notably the foundation of Milan by Noah's descendant Subres.[80] The result is an eclectic and uneven work, the main element of which was arguably the firm desire of the author to reach a wide public. It is significant that it was already sent to press on 25 March 1503 at the workshop of Alessandro Minuziano, obtaining such a vast circulation in Italy that Eric Cochrane justly saw it as the Milanese equivalent of Sabellico's famous Venetian history. As Felix Gilbert remarked, what made its historical perspective important was the author's capacity to rise above the specific events of his time and to recognise in them a

---

[77] Cagnola, 'Storia di Milano', 193 and 7. Cf. also Sigismondo de' Conti di Foligno, *Le storie dei suoi tempi dal 1475 al 1510* (Rome, 1883), 79: 'non perdonarono nè a fanciulli, nè a donne, nè a vecchi cadenti'; and the summary of letters of Francesco da Casate and Stefano Taverna, Naples-Rome, November-[6] December 1495 (SPE, Napoli, 253), concerning the violence committed by the Swiss soldiers at Guglionesi: 'fecero tanto sforzo che introrno dentro et senza rispecto né de età né de sexo menorno ogniuno per il ferro cum tanta crudeltà quanto mai se oldesse'. The expression derives from Tacitus, *Annales*, I, 51, 1: 'non sexus, non aetas miserationem attulit'.

[78] Edited by C.E. Visconti, *Archivio storico lombardo*, 6 (1879), 38-68, 333-56, 500-13. Cf. Cochrane, *Historians*, 167.

[79] Corio, *Storia di Milano*, on which Cochrane, *Historians*, 117-18; F. Petrucci, 'Corio B.', in *Dizionario Biografico degli Italiani*, 29 (Rome, 1983) s.v.; E. Fueter, *Geschichte der neueren Historiographie* (Munich/Berlin, 1911, revised and extended, 1936), Italian edition, italiana *Storia della storiografia moderna* (Milan/Naples, 1970), 58-60; G. Soldi Rondinini, 'Spunti per una interpretazione della *Storia di Milano* di Bernardino Corio', in G. Soldi Rondinini, *Saggi di storia e storiografia visconteo-sforzesche* (Bologna, 1984), 205-20.

[80] Corio, *Storia di Milano*, vol. 1, 58-9.

significant watershed in Italian history.[81] However, the fundamental problem for Corio remained that of il Moro's responsibility, not simply as a major actor within the rational terms laid down by Guicciardini, but also in a more negative sense, as someone who made a political miscalculation: 'imperò li disegni suoi non erano che Carlo passasse'.[82] All this was also subject to the 'volunta divina';[83] moreover, the rapid fall of the kingdom of Naples was not attributable so much to the *virtù* of the French king as to inscrutable destiny, whose instrument Charles really was. This approach has been examined at greater length by Anne Denis in her study of Italian reactions to Charles VIII.[84] As for the image of the French, we find once again all the expected stereotypes about 'gallica superbia';[85] these, however, were mitigated by the recognition that the soldiers of the League were also guilty of atrocities at Fornovo,[86] and by the open verdict on who actually won that battle.[87] Rather than emphasising the objectivity of Corio it is important to recall that he wrote and published under the newly imposed rule of the French, to whom perhaps he was also paying some sort of homage when he included in the first edition an etching showing an open book with the words 'Mediolanum Gallis conditum'.

Another important work of the very early sixteenth century which has been wrongly ignored is the *De bello italico* of the Milanese lawyer Giorgio Floro or Florio.[88] This was composed without a doubt under French rule; nearly two centuries later Louis XIV's courtier and Historiographer Royal Godefroy understood it to be one of the official accounts of the expedition of Charles VIII, and saw in it 'multa in ea bona iudicia, multa libera'.[89] The work contains a large gap after the arrival of the French king in the kingdom of Naples, but it is rich in data apparently acquired at first hand, such as the description of the French fleet at Rapallo, and it attempts to make overall sense of the political and diplomatic setting of events in 1494. Cochrane recognised the author's ability to draw together the principal causes of the expedition, such as the fact that France was now free of other international complications.[90] However, it is important

---

[81] F. Gilbert, *Machiavelli e Guicciardini. Politics and History in Sixteenth-Century Florence* (Princeton, 1965), *Machiavelli e Guicciardini. Pensiero politico e storiografia a Firenze nel Cinquecento* (Torino, 1970), 220-27. 1, 58-9.

[82] Corio, Storia di Milano, vol. 2, 1565.

[83] Corio, Storia di Milano, vol. 2, 1565.

[84] Denis, *Charles VIII*, 143-54.

[85] Corio, *Storia di Milano*, vol. 2, 1579; cf. also 1568-9 and 1573-4.

[86] Corio, *Storia di Milano*, vol. 2, 1577.

[87] Corio, *Storia di Milano*, vol. 2, 1584.

[88] Partially published as 'De expeditione Caroli VIII in Neapolitanum Regnum libri duo', in *Histoire de Charles VIII roy de France*, ed. Godefroy (Paris 1684), 216-37; another edition exists, entitled 'De bello italico et rebus Gallorum preclarae gestis libri VI', ed. J.G. Graeve in *Thesaurus Antiquitatum et historiarum Italiae*, vol. 9/6 (Lugduni, 1724).

[89] Floro, 'De expeditione', 216.

[90] Cochrane, *Historians*, 180.

also to bear in mind the entirely French perspective adopted by Floro, who underplays significantly the acts of violence and cruelty committed by the French,[91] and overplays the glory and honour that the king acquired from his expedition.[92]

From this point onwards Lombard historiography seems to undergo a decline, visible above all in a strong process of provincialisation. There was a tendency to ignore the years 1494-95 and to begin accounts of Milan's recent history with the flight of il Moro and the beginning of French domination of the duchy, while the Italian and international setting of these events was more or less ignored. This can be seen in the works of the Milanese Giovanni Andrea Prato and Giovanni Marco Burigozzo.[93] The former was motivated more by his outlook as a 'cittadino curioso' than by a sense of himself as a historian, even though he was also perfectly capable of working in ambitious descriptions of France or Spain based on models going back to Herodotus, Caesar and Tacitus.[94] The latter was a modest 'merzaro' or mercer enclosed within the walls of his deep piety, full too of animosity against the 'gentiluomini' of Milan.[95] More interesting is in fact the *Cronaca milanese* of Ambrogio da Paullo which, within the limited horizons of Lombardy, makes sense of the central issue in the political life of the duchy at this time: the breach between the duke and the aristocracy, as well as the internal discord among the aristocrats themselves.[96] A good example of this is his use of a chronological scale beginning with the assassination of Galeazzo Maria Sforza in 1476. However, the arrival of King Charles is given rather little weight compared to the blindness attributed to

---

[91] Montefortino and Monte San Giovanni, where the French committed some of their worst atrocities, but which are here only noted briefly: 'in predamque militibus datis, ac omnibus fere oppidanis ferro trucidatis, tantus repente rei fama pavor finitimos invasit, ut de salute potius quam de pugna consultarent' (Floro, 'De expeditione', 234).

[92] Floro, 'De expeditione', 220: 'Constantem iam esse in omni terra Italiae fama de eius in Neapolitanum regnum expeditione. Quae si omitteretur, non sine ignominia id fieri posse'.Ambrogio da Paullo, 'Cronaca milanese dall'anno 1476 al 1515', ed. A. Ceruti in: *Miscellanea di storia italiana*, ser. 1, 13 (Torino, 1871), 91-378; cfr. G. Martini, 'Note biografiche e critiche su Ambrogio da Paullo cronista del primo Cinquecento', *ACME*, 10 (1957), 95-125 e Soldi Rondinini, 'Ludovico il Moro', 47-9.

[93] Giovanni Andrea Prato, 'Storia di Milano' and Giovanni Marco Burigozzo, 'Cronaca di Milano', both in *Archivio storico italiano*, 3 (1842), 220-418 and 419-552; on them, cf. G.L. Barni, 'La vita culturale', 431-4. It is not however worth paying attention to the *Commentarii* of Giovanni Maruzzi da Tolentino, ed. C. Marcora, *Archivio storico lombardo*, 90 (1963), 330-39, nothing more than a brief private memoir (up to 1517 but full of holes) without historical significance for the events of the time.

[94] Soldi Rondinini, 'Ludovico il Moro', 49; Cochrane, *Historians*, 178.

[95] G. De Caro, 'Burigozzo G.M.', in *Dizionario Biografico degli Italiani*, vol. 15 (Rome, 1972) s.v.

[96] Ambrogio da Paullo, 'Cronaca milanese dall'anno 1476 al 1515', ed. A. Ceruti in *Miscellanea di storia italiana*, ser. 1, 13 (Torino, 1871), 91-378; cf. G. Martini. '/Note biografiche e critiche su Ambrogio da Paullo cronista del primo Cinquecento', *ACME*, 10 (1957), 95-125 and Soldi Rondinini, '*Ludovico il Moro*', 47-9.

Ludovico il Moro and his favourites and compared to the civil discord which this author mourned with the sad tones of Virgil's *Eclogues*; the following verses concerning Louis XII were put by Ambrogio in the mouth of il Moro:

> Ma il suo sforzo non era potente
> A torme il Stato, se la giente mia
> M'avesse aiutato più fidatamente.[97]

It was also important to recognise that in 1494 there had occurred what would elsewhere have been termed the crossing of the Rubicon: 'Como diceva un certo proverbio bergamasco, che dice così: che Dio ha fatto li monti per tramontani stia de là, et taliani de zà'.[98]

Provincial too is the perspective of Antonio Grumello of Pavia.[99] He was a less polished writer, interested almost exclusively in military events, and inclined to a deluded pessimism. He provides no ordered exposition of the events of 1494-95, but only a moralistic condemnation of all parties in the struggle: the French 'canaglia' and the awful atrocities committed at Mordano;[100] il Moro's role in the ruin of 'casa Sforcescha, et ruina de tuta la Italicha nacione';[101] the Italian troops at Fornovo, easily led astray by Trivulzio's scheming ('cognosco lo Italiano ingordo de la roba') and ready to hurl themselves on the loaded carts in order to gain booty;[102] the Venetian stradiots who, promised a reward by il Moro for every enemy head, started to massacre their Italian colleagues, offering their heads to the duke in hope of gain.[103] Only King Ferrandino of Naples emerges better, carried off by 'Morte ingorda' from his role as 'Novo Camillo al Gallico furore'.[104]

Another approach to the process of provincialisation is to observe the local chronicles which began to die out later in the sixteenth century. A good example is the *Cronaca di Cremona*,[105] which mentions the arrival of Charles in

---

[97] Ambrogio da Paullo, 'Cronaca milanese', 111.

[98] Ambrogio da Paullo, 'Cronaca milanese', 103. The expression was already long in common use, as is shown by the words of the Venetian Doge Agostino Barbarigo reported in the letter of Taddeo Vimercati to il Moro, Venice, 7 February 1494 (SPE, Venezia 383): Poi intrò a dire che questa Italia è pur una bella provincia et la più bella parte del mondo et che è pur da golderla in pace et che pare che Iddio sempre ne habi bona et speciale cura per haverli posto da dui lati li monti, aciò che et Franzosi et Todeschi stesino ne le lhoro patrie et quando pur voleseno invaderla Italiani haveseno maiore comodità et facilità de defenderla et perservarla, da l'altro el mare per conservarla da Turchi et quelle altre gente barbare...

[99] *Cronaca di Antonio Grumello pavese dal MCCCCLXVII al MDXXIX*, ed. G. Muller (Milan, 1856); cf. Soldi Rondinini, 'Ludovico il Moro', 49, 11-12.

[100] *Cronaca*, 4-5.

[101] *Cronaca*, 2.

[102] *Cronaca*, 10.

[103] *Cronaca*, 11-12.

[104] *Cronaca*, 16.

[105] 'Cronaca di Cremona dal MCDXCIV al MDXXV', ed. F. Robolotti in *Bibliotheca Historica Italica*, vol. 1 (Milan, 1876), 189-276.

Italy without emotion, amid notes on rain, snow and wheat prices.[106] Even the fall of Milan to Louis XII did not appear especially traumatic to its author, at least compared to the heavy tax demands of il Moro: 'et li mugiti andaseveno al celo'.[107] In such a situation the most interesting sources appear to be the elegant narratives supplied by some Milanese humanists such as Scipione Vega, Gaudenzio Merula, Giovan Battista Speziano and Galeazzo Capra or Capella.[108] Here attempts were made to build an annalistic method on the model of the classical authors such as Livy, Sallust and Ammianus Marcellinus; there is perhaps an analogy with Venetian attempts around this time to create a 'memoria defensionale' of contemporary events.[109] The Milanese humanists offer a very full picture of events between 1515 and 1530, but there is absolutely no attention to the problem of how and when the ruin began. Another work in this vein is the unpublished *Historia* of the Milanese lawyer Bernardino Arluno, running from the city's origins to 1525;[110] here the very brief references to the expedition of Charles VIII in the first part of the work seem to be suffocated underneath the massive weight of a rather artificial synthesis of Milanese history up to 1500 in a classicising style, of little historical interest *per se*.[111]

IV

The changes in the duchy of Milan were certainly not favourable to the development of a mature historiographical tradition. While in 1520 the prospect of becoming a 'canton de' sguizari', a Swiss Canton, seemed in the air,[112] after

---

106 'Cronaca di Cremona', 189-90.

107 'Cronaca di Cremona', 191.

108 Scipione Vegio, 'Historia rerum in Insubribus gestarum sub Gallorum dominio' and 'Ephemeridum libri duo' , in *Bibliotheca Historica Italica*, vol. 1, 1-80; Gaudenzio Merula 'Suae aetatis rerum gestarum libri IV', *Bibl. Hist. Italica*, 81-106; Giovan Battista Speziano, 'De Bello Gallico Commentarii', 107-51, all ed. A. Ceruti; Galeazzo Capella *De bello Mediolanensi seu de rebus in Italia gestis pro restitutione Francisci Sfortiae II mediolanensium ducis ab anno MDXXI usque ad MDXXX libri VIII* (Mediolani, 1531), then translated into Italian (Venice, 1539) and finally edited by J.G. Graeve in *Thesaurus Antiquitatum et historiarum Italiae*, vol. 2/2 (Lugduni, 1704), coll. 1249-1335.

109 G. Arnaldi, 'Il notaio cronista e le cronache cittadine in Italia', in *La storia del diritto nel quadro delle scienze storiche* (Florence, 1966), 293-309 (293-7); cf. F. Gaeta, 'Storiografia, coscienza nazionale e politica culturale nella Venezia del Rinascimento', in *Storia della cultura veneta*, vol. 3/1 (Venice, 1980), 1-91 (80-81).

110 Milan, Biblioteca Trivulziana, codice 706; only the second part of the work (from 1500 to the battle of Marignano) was published under the title 'De bello veneto', ed. J.G. Graeve in *Thesaurus Antiquitatum et historiarum Italiae*, vol. 5/4 (Lugduni, 1704). Cf. N. Raponi, 'Arluno B.', in *Dizionario biografico degli Italiani*, vol. 4 (Rome, 1962) s.v.

111 Arluno, *Historia*, in which the conquest is reduced to: 'Parthenopeos reges... Italiae totius crepitatione, et omnium admiratione delevit' (f.74v); or the battle of Fornovo: 'quanquam Parmensi bello circumventum armisque paenis nostris interceptum...' (f.75r).

112 'Relazione del ducato di Milano del secretario Gianiacopo Caroldo 1520', in *Relazioni degli ambasciatori veneti al Senato*, ed. A. Segarizzi (Bari, 1912), reprinted in the anthology

the battle of Pavia in 1525 the ephemeral régime of Francesco II Sforza was on the brink of being permanently incorporated in Charles V's empire. Historical reflections were frequently redirected towards a type of antiquarian erudition evinced in the works of Bonaventura Castiglioni and Andrea Alcato.[113] However in Lombardy there was also room for more fully informed thought about recent events. This can be seen in Como, where from the 1520's the lawyer Francesco Muralto was putting together a history beginning in 1492.[114] Here he paid due attention to the European context of the events of 1492, writing in concise and effective Latin. His own experience laid the way for the much more important endeavours of the ecclesiastic Paolo Giovio.[115] Giovio worked for thirty years on a full history of his times, and succeeded in fusing his solid humanist training with an ability to handle a great mass of rich data; his research in the sources took him as far as the study of Commynes' work.[116] His narrative of events is precise and well based, even when dealing with the fall of Naples, for Neapolitan sources too were certainly known to him. But he goes further still, placing Charles VIII's policies within a framework of European links, as the result of the long-term project attributed to the fifteenth-century kings of France aiming at the conquest of Naples. On the other hand, he does not omit a weighty condemnation of the Italian mercenary bands, expressed in tones reminiscent of Machiavelli.[117] In fact his work does not stand so very far apart from Guicciardini's *Storia d'Italia*, to which it bears similarity in, for instance, offering a speech attributed to Carlo Barbiano di Belgioioso and addressed to the king of France; this text bears the clearest humanistic imprint.[118]

---

of the same title ed. A. Ventura (Bari, 1980), 3-29 (29); on this theme, cf. Chittolini, 'Dagli Sforza alle dominazioni straniere', 30-31.

[113] Bonaventura Castiglioni, *De Gallorum Insubrium antiquis sedibus* (Mediolani, 1541); Andrea Alciato, *Rerum Patriae libri IV* (Mediolani, 1625).

[114] *Annalia Francisci Muralti I.U.D. patricii comensis*, ed. P.L. Donini (Milano, 1861).

[115] The *Historiarum sui temporis libri* were published for the first time in Florence between 1550 and 1557 and were at once translated under the title *Istorie del suo tempo*, by L. Domenichini (Venice, 1555); the modern edition used here is in the *Opera*, vol. 2-5, ed. D. Visconti (Rome, 1957-85); on Giovio see F. Chabod, 'Paolo Giovio' in *Scritti sul Rinascimento* (Turin, 1957), 241-67, and C. Dionisotti, 'Machiavellerie IV', *Rivista storica italiana*, 87 (1975). Basti leggere l'*attacco* della parte relativa alla spedizione di Carlo VIII, con il suo piglio deciso e il tono critico, per misurare la distanza rispetto alla precedente storiografia lombarda: 'In Gallia autem longe lateque imperabat Carolus eius nominis octavus; qui, tametsi neque manu neque consilio multum valebat, tamen, ut mox dicemus, amplissimis maximi atque opulenti regni viribus innixus, viginti trium annorum adolescens, et pacem in Italiam evertit et rem Gallicam, quae nobis erat obscurior, armis atque ausu plurimum illustravit' (Giovio, *Historiarum*, 9).

[116] It is sufficient to read the *attacco* of the section dealing with Charles VIII's expedition, with its critical and contemptuous tone, to see the difference from earlier historical writing.

[117] Chabod, 'Paolo Giovio', 257.

[118] Giovio, *Historiarum*, 19-21; Francesco Guicciardini, *Storia d'Italia*, ed. E. Scarano (Torino, 1981), book 1, cap. 4, 110-13.

This survey of the Lombard sources must end here. Henceforward, especially outside Milan, the basis was laid for an interpretation of Italian history able to relate the present predicament to a series of causal connections and to a longer term historical trend. There is no escaping the retarded character of the situation in Lombardy, a deep, institutional retardation, as against the more profound awareness of the European significance of the Italian political drama after 1494; some hints are present in Corio's work, but the basis for such a view was securely laid in Bernardo Rucellai's *De bello italico*, and indeed in the still unedited *Historia de bellis italicis* of Girolamo Borgia.[119] A fuller expression of such an outlook may then be found in Guicciardini's corpus of works. The Milanese themselves were incapable of understanding and accounting for this retardation, with the result that the best source for the political history of the duchy of Milan in the first two decades of the sixteenth century is not even a Lombard source; it is, arguably, the diaries of the Venetian writer Marin Sanudo. This retardation had its roots in the incapacity of the Milanese to build solid state structures; the leading groups in Milan had missed their chance by failing to understand when the ruin of Milan, and of Italy, had actually commenced.

---

[119] Gilbert, *Machiavelli e Guicciardini*, 220-27. On the relationship between the two works, see M. De Nichilo, 'Un plagio dichiarato: Girolamo Borgia e Bernardo Rucellai', in: *La Memoria e la Città* (in corso di stampa).

Milan in the face of the Italian wars (1494-1535): between the crisis of the state and the affirmation of urban autonomy

Giorgio Chittolini

I

The second half of the fifteenth century saw the coming of Sforza dominion in Lombardy. This dominion did not, however, achieve its highest objective, that is, the creation of a strong and stable régime. In the 1470s Galeazzo Maria Sforza tried to set out a full programme of action, based on new energetic, centralising methods of government; but within a few years this programme had disintegrated as the result of a conspiracy, seen in the latest research not as the irrational gesture of a few people left on the margins, but as the product of a grander design supported by significant members of the Milanese aristocracy. Indeed, the plot must be placed in the wider context of the balance of power within Italy as a whole. Certainly it was a crucial moment, because it reveals in a dramatic way how difficult it really was for the Sforza dynasty to achieve recognition for its authority within a powerful principality and over the heads of the leading elements in Lombard society.[1]

These difficulties did not go away even when the crisis was at an end. 'Mirum fuit quod in toto dominio ducali nulla civitas, nulla terra, nullum castrum fecerit novitatem', as a chronicler commented in the weeks that followed.[2] In reality, though in secret, a long succession crisis began to unfold, which was only resolved some years later with the success of Ludovico il Moro, who even then felt obliged to affirm his power by appealing to higher authority

---

[1] Cf. especially R. Fubini, 'Osservazioni e documenti sulla crisi del ducato di Milano nel 1477 e sulla riforma del Consiglio segreto ducale', in *Essays presented to Myron P. Gilmore*, ed. S. Bertelli and G. Ramakus, Florence, 1978, vol. 1, 47-103.

[2] *Cronica gestorum in partibus Lombardiae et reliquis Italiae [Diarium parmense]*, ed. G. Bonazzi (Città di Castello, 1904-10) [R.I.S.², 22/3], 4.

and also to the consent of his subjects. On the other hand, the late Quattrocento sources, including chronicles and diplomatic reports of the 1480s and 1490s, reveal a considerable amount of information about the disaffection of the ruler's subjects, sometimes expressed as a real hatred by 'li populi de Milano' for their regent or for the entire dynasty.[3] Such ill-feeling often merged with other similar sentiments of hostility towards the 'gente nuova' who surrounded the Sforzas. Corio talked of them as 'gente nova e di minimo essere'; Ambrogio da Paullo said that they were people who 'de una sorte vile e abiecta ... per favore del Moro erano fatti grandi. Et aveva depresso li omini da bene de nobil sangue di Milano per esaltare tale sorte'. The nobly-born lawyer of Como Francesco Muratto lamented 'quot susceptiones hominum ex humili loco natorum, quot nobilium depositiones!'[4] The Sforza too could be dismissed as men of humble origins, a point Gian Giacomo Trivulzio was fond of making, by calling il Moro simply 'Ludovico da Colignola'; il Moro answered back by calling Trivulzio disparagingly 'Giacomo mugnaio', the Miller, since the family possessed quite a few mills in the countryside to the south of Milan.[5]

This disaffection 'di populi' should not be understood simply as a hostile critique of the lack of consent for Sforza power, nor of the limited popularity of the ruler or his house. It involved above all a wide detachment of the ruler's subjects from him, expressed above all in the lack of involvement by the local élites in the management of public affairs, and in the impossibility of mobilising essential mechanisms for the government of the Milanese state, notably in the fiscal arena and in the area of public order. First in the areas where co-operation between the ruler and his subjects seemed most vital, it was lacking. This created a vicious circle of ever more suffocating fiscal policies, and disaccord with the Milanese and Lombard nobility became ever more acute.[6] Generally, then, one can appreciate Machiavelli's judgment as the government of the Sforzas, amid a series of observations that certainly go still deeper.[7] At the same time, such a situation opened the way to the possibility of an alternative

---

[3] G. Soldi Rondinini, 'Ludovico il Moro nella storiografia coeva, in Milano nell'età di Ludovico il Moro', in G. Soldi Rondinini, *Saggi di storia e storiografia visconteo-sforzesca* (Bologna, 1984), 163, 167, etc.

[4] B. Corio, *Storia di Milano*, ed. A. Morisi Guerra (Turin, 1978), vol. 2, 1476; Ambrogio da Paullo, *Cronica milanese dall'anno 1476 al 1515*, ed. D. Ceruti, in *Miscellanea di Storia italiana*, 13 (1874), 93-378, 105; *Annalia descripta per Franciscum Muraltum iuris utriusque doctorem, patricium Comi* (Milan, 1861), 11: cited in F. Leverotti, 'La crisi finanziaria del ducato di Milano alla fine del Quattrocento, in Milano nell'età di Ludovico il Moro', 585-632, 591.

[5] G.P. Bognetti, *La città sotto i Francesi*, in *Storia di Milano*, Treccani, vol. 8 (Milan, 1957), 3-80, 17.

[6] Leverotti, 'Crisi finanziaria', 602 and *passim* (also for the discontent of 'artesani' and 'contadini').

[7] N. Machiavelli, *Il principe*, ed. S. Bertelli, (Milan, 1960), 15, 97.

régime, stimulating a positive attitude towards the French which is documented by Machiavelli and some of his contemporaries.

These difficulties in governing the state, and in affirming the authority of the Sforzas, make the causes of the crisis that occurred with the fall of il Moro in 1499 easier to understand. It was, to be sure, the crisis of a dynasty, which managed later on to reassert itself but never very credibly or strongly, becoming the plaything of others rather than a powerful force in its own right. A few days after Maximilian Sforza arrived in Milan following the French retreat and the battle of Ravenna, the Venetian ambassador was writing that the young duke was 'tamquam signum', and that one could say Milan was really governed by 'Germans, Swiss and Spaniards'.[8] In the chanceries and courts of Europe, in the branches of the banks on the great piazzas, discussion of the fate of Milan revolved more and more around the capacity of the Sforza dynasty to survive.[9]

This was the crisis of a political organism, an independent and indigenous principality, which had been in existence since the fourteenth century, and which was until now seen as the only viable type of government for Lombardy.[10] Now, however, times had changed decisively, and stability had come to depend on the presence of a foreign lord. As Guicciardini commented, with Charles VIII there had come to Italy 'una fiamma ed una peste che non solo mutò gli stati, ma è modi ancora del governargli ed è modi delle guerre'.[11] The result would be submission to the great European powers, despite ephemeral periods of Sforza restoration. Hence the deprecation of the 'barbarians' familiar from the work of Priuli, whose lament for the fall of Milan ('O poor Milan! O glorious city! O famous Milan!) is intermingled with his complaint against 'le genti barbare da le quale sei stata violata, vergognata e rubata'.[12] This marks the beginning of that long tradition of reflection on the decadence of Italy, which was understood as part and parcel of the assertion of foreign overlordship.

Yet the experience of these decades bears witness to a crisis that is not simply one of the Sforza dynasty, and of the independence of Milan and of Italy. Beyond the weakened figures of those who aspired to the ducal title, there also lay the structural weakness of a political institution, the duchy of Milan, which continued as evidence also under French overlordship. French rule never

---

[8] G. Franceschini, 'Le dominazioni straniere e le dominazioni sforzesche, in Storia di Milano', vol. 8, 83-332, 134 (cf. 125).

[9] See for instance the texts gathered together in *Guerre in ottava rima*, published by the Istituto di Studi rinascimentali di Ferrara: vol. 2, *Guerre d'Italia (1482-1527)*, ed. M. Beer, D. Diamanti, C. Ivaldi, Modena 1989; vol. 3, *Guerre d'Italia (1528-1559)*, ed. M. Bardini, M.C. Cabani, D. Diamanti. Cf. *infra* the 'relazioni' of the Venetian ambassadors in n.17.

[10] G. Tabacco, *Egemonie sociali e strutture del potere nel Medioevo italiano* (Turin, 1979), 352.

[11] F. Guicciardini, *Storie fiorentine*, ed. R. Palmarocchi (Bari, 1931), 38.

[12] *I Diari di Gerolamo Priuli (aa. 1494-1512)*, vol. 1 (*a. 1494-1500*), ed. A. Segre (Città di Castello, 1912) [R.I.S.², 24/3], 312.

succeeded in striking solid roots; the French were not perhaps expected and welcomed with quite the enthusiasm that has sometimes been suggested, but they were certainly not greeted with hostility when they arrived. Priuli was confounded by the scenes he witnessed, referring to the Lombards who not merely 'erano sì mal contenti de questo tirano, del signor Ludovico, che non vedevano l'hora di poter cazarlo del stato', but also 'aspectavano questo campo francese cum la bocha aperta, et quando si acostava ale terre e ale citade, li andavano incontro a quelli cum la palma in manno'.[13] Such scenes are recorded by the Lombard chroniclers in other towns too, revealing generally favourable expectations, all the more so with the involvement in this power structure of Gian Giacomo Trivulzio, who for his part posed as heir to the Milanese aristocratic tradition.[14]

II

It has been indicated that the French did not manage to strike deep roots, neither during the first nor the second period of their involvement in Milan. This depended certainly on the outside situation, which left their power fragile in Milan, and from the general weakness of the French within Italian politics; both Machiavelli and Guicciardini expounded the errors of King Louis XII, and other observers too were well aware of this. But it was a fragility which was never counter-balanced by the existence of strong internal state structures, as both Florentine commentators clearly saw. Their fascination with French weakness gave both writers considerable pause for thought, while they sought to explain the many changes in political fortune they themselves had witnessed. They saw Milan as a crucial example, worth examining for its special features, especially since to both of them it had seemed possible that the French presence would turn into a stable occupation, due to become the 'sedia firma e perpetua dei popoli francesi', as il Moro, according to Guicciardini, imagined. Or Milan might turn into a new province or colony of France, to all intents incorporated into it, as Machiavelli supposed.[15] Thus they could not ignore the different outcome.

The reason things turned out differently was identified, especially by Machiavelli, in the timidity of King Louis XII, who, perhaps fearful of annoying 'li populi', did not put into action the energetic style of government that he could have initiated. The effect was to maintain a degree of consensus, above all among the patricians, but without succeeding in rooting his authority effectively

---

[13] *I Diari di Gerolamo Priuli*, vol. 1, 173.
[14] G.P. Bognetti, 'La città sotto i Francesi', 13.
[15] F. Guicciardini, *Storia d'Italia*, ed. Silvana S. Menchi (Turin, 1971), vol. 1, 400; N. Machiavelli, *Il principe*, 16-25.

'in una provincia disforme di lingua, di costumi, di ordini'. At the same time he was unwilling or unable to 'rendere più secura e più durabile la sua possessione' by means of a new and more efficacious system of government.[16] Indeed, the scattered notices that survive of the French dominion in Milan testify to the same difficulties and weaknesses as were visible in the last years of Sforza rule, with the same inconsistency in applying rigid forms of control and in making substantial concessions to local interest groups, to greater and lesser families. The inadequacy of fiscal revenues and the difficulties balancing the government's books were confronted by extraordinary provisions; then, later, there followed the alienation of rights and of fiscal revenues, but all this simply hardened further an increasingly rigid fiscal structure. Feudal concessions multiplied. A Venetian ambassador, Gian Jacopo Caroldo, would remember in 1520 the great number of fiefs for 'gentilomeni': 'adeo che el re, da la cità in fuori, non ha pur un torre: tute le castella del ducato sono state antiqua e modernamente alienate per li duchi de Milano e re de Franza'.[17] Some major centres such as Monza, Vigevano and Lecco, close to the capital, became separate feudal jurisdictions; the result was the further weakening of the authority of the ruler, and of his capacity to control the state. It is worth adding that Maximilian Sforza had recourse to the same methods when he returned to the city in 1512, so that they survived during the new Sforza dominion, as did traditional methods of governing the state.[18]

III

Against this image of a rather fragile state power can be set another that highlights Milanese society, with its towns, institutions, great houses, social organisms and different social strata. These too were all affected by the crisis, while still showing signs of vitality and durability. These are aspects to which historians have paid much less attention, but which may suggest important new directions of research.

To begin with Milan itself, 'il povero Milano' as many contemporary chroniclers termed the city. And yet despite the damage caused by military occupation, warfare and economic difficulties, the city's old grandeur was not completely overshadowed. Gian Jacopo Caroldo, around 1520, provides an image of the city in chiaroscuro, in which there are many bright patches too:

---

[16] N. Machiavelli, *Il principe*, 18.

[17] 'Relazione del Ducato di Milano del secretario Gianjacopo Caroldo', in *Relazioni degli ambasciatori veneti al Senato*, ed. A. Segarizzi, vol. 2 (Bari, 1913), 3-29, 22.

[18] G. Franceschini, 'Le dominazioni straniere e le dominazioni sforzesche'; F. Chabod, *Lo Stato di Milano nell'impero di Carlo V* (1934), in F. Chabod, *Lo stato e la vita religiosa a Milano nell'epoca di Carlo V* (Turin, 1971), 1-226.

> La città de Milano è grande, e la più populosa de Italia. Sono molti poveri, e si consuma pan de mestura. Sono *etiam* gran quantità de gentilomini, che hano grossa intrata fino a ducati 8 in 10,000. Fano gran spese in fameglia: cavali, vestiti e viver ed *etiam* in elimosine; *adeo* che in capo de l'anno vengono ad intacar la intrata de l'altro. Sono grandissimo numero de artefici più che in città de cristiani, li quali fano ogni sorta lavori e merce, che vano per tuto el mondo, come armature, briglie, sele, ecc.; e però ditta città sempre voria guerra, per dar spazamento a le robe sue. Sono *etiam* molti mercadanti, qual fano per Venezia, Puglia, Lion, Spagna ed Alemagna lavorano asai pani de seda, se fano boni veluti, metteno in opera poca seda spagnola, el forzo traesi in vicentina, nè hano queli ordeni son qui al mestier de la seda. Sono *etiam* molte botege de lana; se fa gran numero de panni e de barete, se manda per ogni fiera de lion in Bona summa, lavorano lane, el forzo da Perpignan ancora, e qualche poca de Ingelterra, vano a Verceli a comprar lane, dove capitano in gran quantità, e mandano *etiam* in Linguadoca, fano etiam fostagni e bombasine in gran quantità....[19]

Milan was not just a prosperous city; there was also a continuity in the great families, in the institutions of urban life. Caroldo dedicates much of his *relazione* to a rich and detailed portrait of the great Milanese and Lombard houses: in Milan, the Visconti, the Trivulzio, the Landriani, the Borromeo, the Castiglioni, those who had the staying-power and the resources to take part in the political jockeying which was getting under way. As well as the great fiefs, he mentions the large ecclesiastical benefices they had acquired with their revenues; alongside a total revenue for the state of 350 to 400,000 ducats he indicates that a 'gran quantità di gentilhomini' received an income 'fino a ducati 8 in 10,000', and the various branches of the Visconti alone could expect 80,000 ducats. He mentions their position of power, their wider relationships.[20] For just at this time many families were heavily involved in the building of alliances among themselves and with outside forces: Guelfs, Ghibellines, French, imperialists, Sforza supporters, and so on. Giampiero Bognetti presciently observed in the Treccani *Storia di Milano* that these decades represent a period of renewed political activity by the great Milanese houses. It is true that the main expression of this was in a renewal of factional strife, rather than in the creation of unitary authority in the city and the state;[21] and there was very little sense of a common Milanese *patria* or of a *res publica*; one thinks of the illustrious Lombard gentlemen of Machiavelli, uninterested in republics or political acts.[22] Moments of concord were rare, and they occurred when a limited objective had to be attained, such as joint negotiation with greater outside powers.

A significant characteristic of this period is the emergence in greater relief than is visible under the Sforzas of group structures built around parishes, neighbourhoods, city gates, taking the form of assemblies and licensed

---

[19] 'Relazione del Ducato di Milano del secretario Gianjacopo Caroldo', 18.
[20] 'Relazione del Ducato di Milano del secretario Gianjacopo Caroldo', 18 and following.
[21] G.P. Bognetti, 'La città sotto i Francesi', 3 and following.
[22] *Discorsi sopra la prima deca di Tito Livio*, 1, lv.

deputations; these organisms appear plainly enough in the chronicles of the time.[23]   Other groups retained their collective power: merchants, lawyers,, notaries, artisans, groups which in fact reinforced their old group structures in the form of colleges, trade associations and confraternities.   Charitable enterprises and hospitals remained active and possessed a greater degree of flexibility, without the heavy-handed control of the signoria.[24]

This continuity and autonomy of corporate institutions in Milan can be used to explain the resistance of such institutions and groups to assimilation into a Sforza 'system' of government, giving them rather the character of an internal opposition to the régime; this phenomenon further helps explain the difficulties the Sforzas faced in attempts to impose their own system of government.   On the other hand, it is reasonable to ask why the vitality of Milan in these respects did not give rise to a strong citizen-based state, in the way that the republics of Venice and Florence were developing at this period.   This question was familiar, at least by implication, to contemporary observers, including even some Milanese writers: the idea existed of a free republican state, or at least of a republic whose existence was guaranteed by the patronage, preferably remote, of an outside ruler who was prepared to recognise the autonomy of the Milanese state.

In fact there had already been one such experience, several decades earlier: that of the Ambrosian Republic.   And indeed in 1499 a provisional government came into being for just a few days, taking as its badge the old seal of St Ambrose and aspiring to achieve, in its *capitoli* intended for French approval, a completely autonomous republic, incorporating all the territory under Sforza rule 'salvo el stato de Zenoa'.   This republic would accept the suzerainty of the king of France, paying him a yearly tribute, but it would be completely independent in arranging its internal affairs and would retain control of the entire Sforza lordship.   These *capitoli* are rather unusual in their insistence that the king 'non si impacciasse di nulla: né di gravezze e imposizione ordinarie e straordinarie, né delle nomine negli offici e magistrature, né degli appelli', except in cases touching the defence 'a proprie spese' of the Milanese state and the collection of the tribute due to him.   Taxes

---

[23] Cf. e.g. Giovanni Andrea Prato, 'Storia di Milano in continuazione ed emendazione del Corio dall'anno 1499 al 1519', in *Cronache Milanesi*, *Archivio Storico Italiano*, 2 (1842), 217-417, 237, 237, 240; G.M. Burigozzo, 'Cronica milanese dal 1500 al 1544', ibid., 426, 501.

[24] On the relations between charitable institutions and the Sforza dynasty see e.g. Giuliana Albini, 'Continuità e innovazione: la carità a Milano nel Quattrocento fra tensioni private e strategie pubbliche', in *La carità a Milano nei secoli XII-XV. Atti del Convegno di Studi, Milano 6-7 novembre 1987*, ed. M.P. Alberzoni, O. Grassi (Milan, 1989), 137-52; on the 'chiesa cittadina' in the duchy, a brief notice in *Gli Sforza, la chiesa lombarda e la corte di Roma.   Strutture e pratiche beneficiarie nel ducato di Milano (1450-1535)*, ed. G. Chittolini (Naples, 1989), introduction, xv-xvi.

and appointments to office were reserved to the Milanese 'parlamento', as were reforms of the statutes. Moreover, there was the unusual request that should Louis XII die without male heirs, an eventuality 'quod Deus avertat', but which could not be excluded, then Milan and its lands would not pass to anyone else, but would remain 'in libertà'.[25]

This project replicated quite closely that which had been voiced fifty years before in the days of the Ambrosian Republic, when the city had sought to enter into a relationship with the Holy Roman Emperor, proposing a relationship similar to that of the German imperial cities with the crown. The emperor, represented by such an authoritative figure as Aeneas Sylvius Piccolomini, was disposed to accept; but the case was compromised by the argument which no German imperial or free city would have dared present that the whole territory of the former Visconti duchy of Milan should remain under the authority of the civic government, without the right of interference by imperial officials but with the obligation imposed on the empire to come to Milan's military aid when necessary.[26] This project thus had no success, any more than the project of 1499; and there was any number of reasons: the bad faith of the parties to negotiation, the secessionist movements in many cities in Milan's orbit,[27] the traditional lack of support for such moves elsewhere in Italy and Europe,[28] but most of all the inability of the city's political institutions to assure such a solution, in view of the lack of a Milanese élite capable of becoming the élite of a great city republic within the framework of Milan's regional authority in Lombardy. Such a group was the necessary condition for the exercise of genuine independence.

---

[25] G. P. Bognetti, 'La città sotto i francesi', 14-16. The document in L. Pélissier, *Documents pour l'histoire de la domination française dans le Milanais* (Tolouse 1891), doc. no. 2, 5 September 1499, 5. Cf. also L. Pélissier, *Louis XII et Ludovic Sforza (8 avril 1498 - 29 julliet 1500)*, 2 vols. (Paris 1896), vol. 2, 217.

[26] *Der Briefwechsel des Aeneas Silvius Piccolomini*, ed. R. Wolkan, *2: Briefe als Priester und Bischof von Triest (1447-1450)* (Vienna, 1912), 263-78, in particular 268-70; cf. also M. Spinelli, 'Ricerche per una nuova storia della Repubblica Ambrosiana', *Nuova Rivista storica*, 70 (1986), 231-52, and 71 (1987), 27-48.

[27] On the lack of cohesion between the lands of the duchy, see G. P. Bognetti, 'La città sotto i francesi', 14, 16; for Pavia also P. Vaccari, *Profilo della storia di Pavia*, 94.

[28] Already in August 1447, in the first days of the Ambrosian republic, the Venetians were opposed to a Lombard regional state under Milanese direction, because the union of Milan 'col ducato suo saria sempre sufficiente ad mettere Italia sotto sopra': G. Soldi Rondinini, 'Ludovico il Moro nella storiografia coeva', 171 (and also 98).

IV

The fact that Milan had been ruled by dynasts for two centuries had several crucial consequences. The lords of Milan of necessity restricted the participation of the Milanese aristocracy in government; and Milan itself was transformed from being the dominant city in the region (as it had been in twelfth and thirteenth-century Lombardy) into the capital of a regional state. Meanwhile it proved impossible to create that sort of symbiosis between the ruling élite and the structure of government, involving a close identification between patrician public and private interests, which came into being most notably at Venice and in Florence, and which resulted in the forceful, organic identification of the leading groups with the government of the state. This could be an especially powerful force at times of crisis. But after two centuries of *signoria* the municipal aristocracy of the capital and of the major subject cities no longer had any self-consciousness as a 'dominant' group, possessing sovereign rights within Milan's territory and possessing too the means to govern these lands; so too these groups had no sense of the need for a broadly-based common programme, and had no real idea how to put one together.[29]

In the decades between the end of the fifteenth century and the assertion of Spanish rule (1535) the city of Milan witnessed events without really participating in them, full of regret at the ruinous struggles that beset the region, but without the will or the force to take any initiative. There were few who identified the 'salvezza' of Milan and its future fortune with the preservation of an independent principality; the Milanese élite, though taken aback at the course of events and brought in willy-nilly as intermediaries between the powers that were competing for control of the duchy, seemed incapable of working out a strategy for governing Milan. For they were well aware that the fate of the city and of the state lay in the hands of others, and there was little room for their own intervention. The great families were thus still on the stage, but they pursued their own political objectives, by means of factional strife. Every now and again, with other social groups, they put together 'governi provvisori' or 'comitati d'affari', negotiating groups whose task it was to make a deal with the overlords competing for control of the region. None of this energy was directed towards the creation of a major republic or a substantial regional power. The chroniclers, politicians and men of letters of the great centres of urban culture, such as Florence and Venice, viewed this aspect of Milan as a failure worthy of condemnation, arguing that the Milanese had no idea how to rule themselves, and had no tradition of self-rule, no sense of civic spirit. The élite did not

---

[29] G. Chittolini, 'Di alcuni aspetti della crisi dello stato sforzesco', in *Milan et les États bourguignons: deux ensembles politiques princiers entre Moyen Age et Renaissance (XIV-XVI e s.)*, Publication du centre d'Études bourguignonnes, 28 (Basle, 1988), 21-34.

understand how to function within the framework of a citizen-based republic with substantial regional commitments. Machiavelli expresses this view particularly scornfully, seeing Milan as a corrupt republic, or rather it is one of those provinces in which no true republic has ever emerged, nor 'alcuno vivere politico', in this respect similar to Naples. Pursuing the parallel further, he insisted that no event, however serious or violent, could bring freedom to Milan or Naples, 'per essere le loro membre tutte corrotte'. Such a judgment, coloured by the incurable republicanism of Machiavelli, nonetheless also reveals a clarity of analysis which matches well the situation in Milan, a situation where the longstanding exclusion of the urban aristocracy from government rendered vain any prospect of creating a regional state within a republican framework. In this respect, Florence and Venice remained exceptional, even if they too had to face fearsome new challenges in the changed context of early sixteenth-century European politics.

This persistent feature of the social and institutional structure of Milan was not, however, conducive to an entirely passive behaviour. There was an attempt to create the space, if not for a large territorial state, at least for an autonomous existence which the leading groups within the cities (Milan above all) felt able to claim as their right, as subordinate, minor entities, 'terre franche', within the much larger framework of Italian politics. That larger framework was seen as beyond the power of the Lombards to determine; but something more restricted could be achieved by following models that were familiar within and outside Italy.[30] Thus there were political programmes which the Milanese, with their action committees and at the prompting of the great families, began to put into effect at the start of the sixteenth century, even if there was little concord among the leading families in implementing them. What they sought was not full sovereignty so much as the space and conditions for autonomy within the dominion of an outside power. In fact this was achieved with some degree of success, given the rapid changes and frequent weakness of outside overlords, and the general disorder in Italy at the time.

The problem was to work out who was the best patron for Milan, allowing for the contrasting ambitions of the contending parties. Not all patrons were equally acceptable. The prospect of French government, witnessed early on in these developments, and supported notably by the Milanese 'gentiluomini', was soon discredited by its poor record and the progressive enfeeblement of France in the face of the Habsburg challenge. The Venetian Republic was another possibility. But 'Milanesi senza dubio non amano Veneziani', as Caroldo warned around 1520. 'Dubitano non devenio sotto el dominio nostro; il

---

[30] T. A. Brady, *Turning Swiss. Cities and Empire, 1450-1550* (Cambridge, 1985); E. Fasano Guarini, 'La crisi del modello repubblicano: patriziati e oligarchie', in *La storia*, ed. N. Tranfaglia, M. Firpo, vol. 3 (Turin, 1987), 553-84.

che per la superbia sua aboriscono, maxime li gentilomeni, li quali un gran numero hano feudi'. However:

> li mercadanti et artefici *etiam* dubitano che, essendo Milano subiecto a Venezia, se veniriano a minuir le facende con devedàrli el comprar, come se fa a le cità nostre. Ma quello che più importa è, e non se li po' risponder, *videlicet* che nel Stato de Milano non vi è alcun francese abia un solo beneficio: tuti li benefici sono de subiecti al dominio o de qualche forestier per favor de corte de Roma; e dicono che, quando milano fusse de' Veneziani, quasi tutti li benefici seriano de' veneziani, come ne le altre nostre terre, *adeo* che milanesi non averiano cosa alcuna.[31]

Other powers excited greater sympathy. The idea of 'turning Swiss', to cite a phenomenon identified by Thomas Brady, was discussed in several German cities at this period, and similar aspirations can be seen at work in Italy. Indeed, the idea of Milan as a Swiss canton continued to circulate persistently, even though it was not articulated in formal proposals despite the credibility it possessed as a result of the strong and continuous expansionist pressure of the Swiss confederates. The Swiss, armed and hence free, pressed on the edges of the Milanese state, were occasionally called in to decide the power balance, and became the real protectors of Maximilian Sforza when he was installed in the duchy.[32] There was also sympathy for an imperial solution to Milan's troubles, with the old Ghibelline faction showing itself ever ready in response to the growing prestige of the empire; and this readiness to serve the empire was eventually expressed, after the death of the last Sforza, in a request to remain 'perpetuamente nel poter et regimine imperiale de Sua Maestà [Carlo V] et Sacro Romano Imperio':[33] Such an attitude was based on memories of the Ambrosian Republic, or at least it followed the model of those Venetian Terraferma cities which after the battle of Agnadello sought imperial patronage. Indeed, the outcome, after the final fall of the Sforzas, was not so very different, even though the exact course of events proved slightly at variance.

---

[31] 'Relazione del Ducato di Milano del secretario Gianjacopo Caroldo', 22. On anti-Venetian hostility see also Franceschini, 'Le dominazioni straniere', 124 and *passim*.

[32] 'Relazione', 29: 'E opinion de molti che a la fine Milano si farà canton de' sguizari, tolendo la protezion sua, li quali hano l'ochio a Como; ed a la prima mutazione sguizari salterano in Como e, come mettino el piede, serà difficil cosa cazarli, e serano sempre su le porte de Milano. Sguizari sugano ben el danaro, ma se contentano de poco; e, quando era el duca Maximilian in Stato, sguizari davano poca graveza;... Sguizari etiam lo meritorono, perchè feceno due giornate a Novara ed a Marignan e persino molta gente; poi sguizari fano iustizia e ne lo allogiar si portano benissimo a comparazion degli altri. Concludo e replico che, expulsi francesi e barbari de Italia, facilmente Milano potria farsi canton de' sguizari'.

[33] F. Chabod, *Lo Stato di Milano nell'impero di Carlo V*, 12.

V

The decades of French and Sforza domination in the early sixteenth century were not simply a period of programme making and project building. They were also a time for the serious testing of new institutional models. It was towards this that the energies of Milanese society were directed, with fruitful results, especially in the definition of a new type of autonomy for the city and its component elements. It was the very changes in régime, frequent and rapid, that during this thirty-year period resulted paradoxically in the reinforcement of the institutions and high offices which were the primary expression of local municipal forces, despite the disruptive effects of factional strife. It was the uncertainty and changeability of the times that stimulated greater coherence and tighter structure in these institutions. Some aspects of this development can be seen as especially significant, not least in Milan, though much the same can be said of the other cities of the Sforza duchy and their changing position in the state.

The first example is the constitution of the Senate, and in particular its considerable strengthening after the Visconti and Sforza periods. In fact this institution, on which were based the two ancient *Consigli*, the *Consiglio Secreto* and the *Consiglio di giustizia*, acquired a new, different character in the French period. Having under the dukes been very much in the shadow of the court, the *Consigli* acquired a new significance when the ruler was far off, for the representative of the French crown in Milan could not match the authority of an on-the-spot ruler. The prerogatives of the Senate expanded considerably; composed of leading elements of Milanese and of Lombard society, the Senate became the most authoritative representative institution, the weightiest organ of government in the city and in the state, in the face of weak or absentee rulers.[34] Alongside the Senators, 'sotto la ragione de' quali tutto il ducato di Milano era regulato',[35] and closely linked to them, the College of Lawyers of the city of Milan, and parallel bodies in the lesser cities, played an important role. The Visconti and the Sforza had sought to make out of the Doctors of Laws a group of jurists wedded to the service of the duke and his régime.[36] The fall of the Sforzas signalled the end of this scheme, and indeed the disappearance of the *Consiglio di giustizia*. What emerged in its place was the link between the

---

[34] U. Petronio, *Il senato di Milano. Istituzioni giuridiche ed esercizio del potere nel Ducato di Milano da Carlo V a Giuseppe II* (Milan, 1972), 9-32 (the author underlines the elements of continuity with the Sforza councils).

[35] G.A. Prato, *Storia di Milano*, 254.

[36] E. Brambilla, *Genealogie del sapere. Per una storia delle professioni giuridiche nell'Italia padana, secoli XIV-XVI*, relazione presentata alla 'Tredicesima Settimana di Studio' dell'Istituto internazionale di Storia Economica Francesco Datini di Prato, 1981, now in *Schifanoia*, 8 (1989), 123-50.

lawyers and their setting in the urban patriciates, and this link became clearer still when the Spaniards reorganized the local Colleges of Doctors at the beginning of their rule.[37] Meanwhile, the *Consiglio di governo* of the city of Milan acquired a lasting place in government, leading ultimately to its transformation into the College of Decurions (as it was known for short), which became the place where the urban patriciate expressed its political existence. Milan had sought for a long time its own organs of municipal government, first cautiously under the Visconti, then more energetically after the fall of the Sforzas. The right to a government elected by the citizens was, as Louis XII was reminded in 1502, one that was possessed by 'fere omnes Italiae civitates', which had the power to create 'ex civibus suis presidentes qui publice utilitati preessent et providerent'. Such aspirations were negated by the lack of support of the Council of Nine Hundred and by the practice of ducal nomination for members of the *Ufficio di Provvisione*, in the same way that the officials of the city governments were nominated by the lord of Milan.[38]

However, at the start of the sixteenth century, as French and Sforza domination alternated, the importance of citizen-based representation was brought to the fore, with new characteristics. The root of the system lay in the decurional structure of Milan, which was to be so significant under the Spaniards, as a group focus and as a framework for patrician activity. Such developments paralleled the general trend in Italian society at this time, but in Milan the effect was to define the shape of the controlling group in Milanese society and how it would operate, including the existence in its midst of pro-French, pro-Sforza and pro-imperial tendencies.[39]

---

[37] G. Vismara, 'Le istituzioni del patriziato lombardo', in *Storia di Milano*, vol. 9 (Milan, 1958), repr. in G. Vismara, *Scritti di storia giuridica*, vol. 3, *Istituzioni lombarde* (Milan, 1987), 217-85, 224 and following; C. Mozzarelli, 'Strutture sociali e formazioni statuali a Milano e Napoli tra '500 e '600', in *Società e storia*, 1 (1978), 431-63; per Pavia, M.C. Zorzoli, 'Il Collegio dei giudici di Pavia e l'amministrazione della giustizia', *Bollettino della società pavese di storia patria*, 85 (1981), 56-90.

[38] E. Verga, 'Delle concessioni fatte da Massimiliano Sforza alla città di Milano', in *Archivio Storico Lombardo*, 21 (1894), 331-49; the quotation is from the requests of the Milanese to Louis XII in 1502, printed in G. Pelissier, *Documents pour servir à l'histoire de la domination française das le Milannais*, 77. For municipal institutions in the Quattrocento see also C. Santoro, *Gli offici del comune di Milano e del dominio visconteo-sforzesco (1216-1515)* (Milan, 1968), 61-5, 75-84; F. Cognasso, 'Istituzioni comunali e signorili a Milano sotto i Visconti, in Storia di Milano', vol. 6 (Milan, 1955), 61-5, 75-84; A. Colombo, 'L'ingresso di Francesco Sforza in Milano e l'inizio di un nuovo principato', in *Archivio storico lombardo*, ser. 4, vol. 3 (1905), 295-344; vol. 4 (1905), 33-101.

[39] G. Vismara, *Le istituzioni del patriziato lombardo*, 239-40; see also M. Formentini, *Il ducato di Milano* (Milan, 1877).

VI

A possible conclusion wouild be that the period either side of 1500 reveals the failure of state development; but on the other hand it is possible to see the emergence of strong and substantial components of the Milanese society of the sixteenth century, which were to prove fundamental to the political organisation of Spanish-ruled Milan. The advent of Charles V as ruler of Milan confirmed the city's state of subjection, and Milan and its dependencies were thus again deprived of the chance to express their aspiration for full liberty, aspirations not lacking in Charles V's other dominions, in both Spain and Flanders, where they stimulated a violent imperial reaction. And yet Milan had by now developed a robust and mature tradition of administration and jurisdiction, accompanied by a powerful self-consciousness, with the result that the Milanese could indeed lay claim to defined areas of self-rule.[40]

---

[40] On self-awareness and on the growth of the authority of the Milanese magistrates, see F. Chabod, *Lo Stato di Milano nell'impero di Carlo V*, 161, 181.

YALE UNIVERSITY

STERLING MEMORIAL LIBRARY

MICROFORM ROOM

The Ilardi Microfilm Collection of Renaissance Diplomatic Documents ca. 1450-ca. 1500

INDEX

Compiled by Vincent Ilardi

YALE UNIVERSITY LIBRARY
INTERLIBRARY LOAN POLICIES

Address

Interlibrary Loan - Lending
Yale University Library
P.O. Box 208240
New Haven, CT 06520-8240
(203-432-1789)

Form of requests

Requests for loan cannot be taken over the telephone. The Library requires a written request, submitted either through RLIN (our LI is CTYG), OCLC (our symbol is YUS, enter it twice), or typed on an ALA or IFLA form. Requests can also be submitted via Ariel (130.132.80.19) and by fax (203-432-7231).

Citation in requests

Requests must cite the Ilardi Collection, the Archive and series' names, and the document and reel numbers. (e.g. Ilardi Collection: Genoa, Archivio di Stato, Antico Comune, Politicorum, B.1648 (1451-81), Reel 257.)

Fees

A $20.00 fee is charged for each completed transaction. Postage for sending the material by Air is added to this fee if the loan is shipped abroad. A transaction is defined as a filled request for four reels of microfilm being supplied. Invoices for payment will usually be received before the material itself and act as notification of the fulfillment of the request. Not more than four reels of microfilm may be sent for one reader in any library at one time.

Loan period

Films are usually loaned for two weeks' use with no renewals. Exceptions will be considered if an unusual situation exists in the borrowing library, but a specific request must be made, and no automatic extension of the loan period should be assumed.

Conditions of use

Material may be loaned for use in the library only and/or with restriction on photocopying.

Copying

Permission to duplicate a few frames with microfilm-reader-printers is hereby granted. To facilitate research, the Italian government has generously authorized Sterling Memorial Library in exceptional circumstances to duplicate at its discretion one or two reels of the Italian holdings. Non-Italian films cannot be duplicated without written permission from the repositories. In all cases it is preferable for researchers to deal directly with the repositories for any duplication beyond the capabilities of microfilm-reader-printers.

List of entries

Note

Combined list of photocopies

1: Repositories in Italy

Bologna: Biblioteca Comunale dell'Archiginnasio

Ferrara: Archivio di Stato; Biblioteca Comunale Ariostea

Florence: Archivio di Stato; Archivio della Famiglia Guicciardini; Biblioteca Nazionale Centrale

Forli: Biblioteca Comunale

Genoa: Archivio di Stato

Isola Bella: Archivio Borromeo

Mantua: Archivio di Stato

Milan: Archivio di Stato; Biblioteca Ambrosiana; Biblioteca Nazionale Braidense; Biblioteca della Societa' Storica Lombarda; Biblioteca Trivulziana

Modena: Archivio di Stato

Pavia: Biblioteca Civica "Bonetta"

Rome: Archivio di Stato (see also *Vatican City*)

Siena: Archivio di Stato

Turin: Archivio di Stato

Vatican City: Archivio Segreto Vaticano

Venice: Archivio di Stato; Archivio di Stato; Biblioteca Nazionale
Marciana; Biblioteca Querini Stampalia

Veroli: Biblioteca Giovardiana

2. Repositories outside Italy

Austria
Vienna: Haus-, Hof- und Staatsarchivs; Österreichische Nationalbibliothek

: see end

Croatia

England
London: British Library

France
Dijon: Archives Départementales de la Cote-D'or

Lille: Archives Départementales du Nord

Marseilles: Archives Départementales des Bouches-Du-Rhone

Paris: Archives Nationales; Bibliothèque Nationale

Great Britain: see **England**

Spain
Barcelona: Arxiu de la Corona d' Aragó

Seville: Archivo General de las Indias

Simancas: Archivo General

Turkey
Istanbul: Top Kapi Sarayi Arsivi

United States of America
Chicago: University of Chicago, Joseph Regenstein Library

Croatia
Dubrovnik (Ragusa): Historijski Arhiv

Note

Vincent Ilardi

The following microfilm reel **Index** represents the second revision since its first compilation in 1985. Some fifty reels have been added and each reel has been assigned a sequential number. The entire collection now consists of 1856 reels and 179 photocopies, reproducing approximately two million documents. The microfilms, which were at first deposited temporarily in the Library of the University of Massachusetts, Amherst, were donated in March 1990 to the Sterling Memorial Library of Yale University and transferred in July. The collection has been catalogued with the title, **The Ilardi Microfilm Collection of Renaissance Diplomatic Documents ca. 1450 - ca. 1500.** The entire **Index** is now (April 1994) being inserted in the Internet database to facilitate access and borrowing through national and international interlibrary loans.

Begun in 1959, the collection now includes most if not all significant unpublished collections of diplomatic documents and related papers for the second half of the fifteenth century held in western European archives and libraries. Series of documents containing instructions, dispatches, credentials, ambassadorial powers and passports, treaties, letters of rulers, ciphers, and other pertinent records such as foreign policy memoranda and debates, ambassadorial expense accounts and travel diaries have been filmed in their entirety. An ample selection of other records, such as state internal correspondence and unpublished chronicles with relevance to diplomatic affairs, has also been included. In the relatively few cases where a selection had to be made, readers are so notified by means of an asterisk or by other appropriate means. Manuscript inventories have also been filmed whenever possible with the special permission of the archivists.

Scholars in the United States and abroad have used the collection for various studies not only in diplomacy, statecraft, and military affairs, but also in such diverse fields as literature, biography, musicology, economic and social history, religion, art history, optics, and even animal husbandry. Such is the richness of information included in diplomatic and state correspondence of the age. This comprehensive and diversified feature makes the collection unique in the world for the period. Assembled in one place, these records from numerous European repositories facilitate research, and provide a wide variety of samples from a great number of chanceries.

In using the collection researchers are urged to keep in mind the normal limitations inherent in the process of assembling vast quantities of microfilms from different countries. The filming was done over three decades by a great number of state and private photographers operating with varying skills under different conditions without a uniform standard. Although care was taken to be as complete and accurate as possible, there is no guarantee that in filming tens of thousands of records some may not have been omitted from a particular file or series through error. Generally the dates have been given in the modern style, but the accuracy of all the dates could not be checked. Often a file contains undated documents or documents wrongly dated by archivists. The extreme dates of the collection, 1450-1500, have sometime been transgressed in cases where files contained a few documents beyond these limits or for other compelling reasons. Normally the addresses of dispatches/letters have not been photographed unless they refer to persons other than the rulers or if the verso of the folio contains other writing or notations. Since dispatches were nearly always directed to rulers, and often consisted of only one page, the omission of these addresses has allowed additional filming with the saved funds.

The preceding paragraph should serve as a reminder that microfilms are an aid to research and are not intended to substitute for direct study of archival records *in situ*. Experienced reseachers know the value of personal visits in archives and treat microfilm collections as convenient tools to become familiar with the sources and use their time abroad more efficiently. This is, indeed, an enormous advantage for researchers worldwide for which all of us are grateful to the great number of archivists, librarians, and photographers who have collaborated in creating the collection: a long list, which will appear in a later publication. Equally crucial for the initiation and success of the project was the financial support generously extended by the following foundations and agencies: Fulbright Program for Italy (1959-60); American Philosophical Society (1960-63); Rockefeller Foundation Research and International Research Programs (two grants, 1961-63, 1963-64); John Simon Guggenheim Memorial Foundation (1970-71), National Endowment for the Humanities, Research Resources Division (three grants, 1976-85), and the National Italian American Foundation (1985).

The present **Index** is being included in this volume to serve as a convenient, condensed guide to a giant "database" from which researchers can draw most of the needed documentation for a fuller assessment of that fateful half century ending with the debacle of 1494-95, which changed the history of Europe for ever. I am grateful to the editor, David Abulafia, who suggested it as a fitting piece for the appendix. I also wish to thank Dr Susanne F. Roberts, Humanities Bibliographer at Sterling Memorial Library, and her assistant, Ms. Shalane Hansen for their dedicated assistance in the preparation of the present edition of the **Index.** It will be republished substantially in its present form, but with the appropriate scholarly apparatus and with extensive descriptions of archival collections, as part of my forthcoming book on the development of the permanent resident embassy, tentatively titled, *Renaissance Origins of Modern Diplomacy: Institutions, Archives, Microfilms.*

1) REPOSITORIES IN ITALY

BOLOGNA

I: BIBLIOTECA COMUNALE DELL'ARCHIGINNASIO

1. Cod. 16-CII-6 (A.325). Lettere e istruzioni di Jacopo Barbarigo sulla guerra della Morea (1465 June 5-1466 Mar.19).

FERRARA

I: ARCHIVIO DI STATO

ARCHIVIO BENTIVOGLIO

2. Guerini, Giacopo Filippo. Indice generale cronologico delle scritture e documenti dell'Archivio dell'Ecc.ma Casa Bentivoglio d'Aragona. Vol. I, fols. 5-92 (1449-1496).

Contratti di condotta, trattati e altri documenti riguardanti le relazioni politiche tra i Bentivoglio e Stati italiani.

3. Mazzo 1, F. 1 (1471-1499); F. 2 (1459-1499)
4. Mazzo 2, F. 1 (1446-1460); F. 2 (1500-1509); F.3 (1565-1566)

II: BIBLIOTECA COMUNALE ARIOSTEA

ANTONELLI COLLEZIONE

5. No.495(178). Original letters of Dukes Borso and Ercole d'Este to F. Ariosto, N. Bendedei (amb. in Florence, 1476), and others, 1462-1496).
No.396. Original letter of Duke Borso to L. Caselle, Venice, 15 Apr. 1467.

FLORENCE

I: ARCHIVIO DI STATO

ARCHIVIO DIPLOMATICO DELLA REPUBBLICA

RIFORMAGIONI, ATTI PUBBLICI

6. Selections. Roma (1451-1483); Francia (1451-1494); Spagna e Aragona (1453-1475);Napoli e Sicilia (1450-1486); Ristretto cronologico degli Atti Pubblici del Comune di Firenze. Vol.I, Roma, fols. 8lv-191; Vol.II, Francia, fols. 5v-9; Inghilterra, 65-66; Spagna e Aragona, 89-91; Napoli e Sicilia, 164v-88; Duca di Savoia, 203v-05.
7. Selections. Duca di Milano (1451-1494); Duca di Ferrara e di Modena (1454-1483); Venezia (1454-1486); Genova (1451-1486); Siena (1462-1487); Sarzana (1467); Città di Castello (1482); Ristretto cronologico... Vol.III, Soldano di Egitto e Re di Tunisi, fols. 1v-3; Duca di Milano, 50v-66; Duca di Ferrara e di Modena, 77v-81; Venezia, 100v-09; Duca di Urbino, 116-18; Genova, 146v-48; Lucca, 159v-62; Bologna, 177v-80; Perugia, 185v-89; Rimini, 195; Pesaro, 199; Siena, 214-20. Vol. V, Sarzana, fols.

85v-86; Città di Castello. 91v-92, 125v-26; Capitani, comandanti di compagnie e masnade estere, 215v-22.

SIGNORI, CARTEGGI DELLA PRIMA CANCELLERIA

19. Brunetti, Filippo. Spoglio del carteggio universale della Repubblica fiorentina. Vol.IV (1451-1475); Vol.V (1476-1495); Vol.VI (1496-1500).

MISSIVE

20. Reg.38 (1452 Dec.12-1453 June 9).
21. Reg.39 (1453 June 5-Dec.5).
22. Reg.40 (1453 June 12-1456 Nov.30).
23. Reg.41 (1456 Dec.4-1458 Apr.16).
24. Reg.42 (1458 Apr.24-1460 Feb.13).
25. Reg.43 (1460 Feb.13-1462 Feb.8).
26. Reg.44 (1462 Mar.13-1464 Sept.15).
27. Reg.45 (1465 Apr.20-1468 Dec.15).
28. Reg.46 (1469 Jan.4-1475 Nov.16)
29. Reg.47 (1474 July 29-1484 Jan.15).
30. Reg.48 (1480 Mar.27-1481 Sept.18).
31. Reg.49 (1475 Nov.21-1490 Dec.31).
32. Reg.50 (1494 Nov.9-Dec.31).

MISSIVE ORIGINALI

33. Selections. F.1 (1452-1494); B.3 (1479-1487; F.4 (1452-1494).

MINUTARI DELLE LETTERE MISSIVE

34. Reg.7 (1466 Apr.5-1471 Apr.11).
35. Reg.8 (1467 July 2-1479 May 24; Reg.9 (1468 Mar.5-1471 Sept.21).
36. Reg.10 (1473 Jan.27-1478 Mar.10).
37. Reg.11 (1478 Mar.18-1484 July 16).
38. Reg.12 (1481 Sept.18-1482 Sept.2).
39. F.13 (1484 Oct.19-1494 Dec.25); Reg.14 (1491 Mar.30-1495 Aug.13).
40. F.16 (1491 Feb.19-1502).
41. F.18 (1494 Sept.13-Nov.8).

MISSIVE. LEGAZIONI E COMMISSARIE, ELEZIONI E ISTRUZIONI A ORATORI

42. Reg.12 (1447 Apr.14-1451 Jan.18).
43. Reg.13 (1451 Jan.12-1456 Feb.7).
44. Reg.14 (1456 Feb.7-1458 Apr.11).
45. Reg.15 (1458 Aug.30-1465 Aug.17).
46. Reg.16 (1465 Apr.19-1470 Apr.14).
47. Reg.17 (1469 Sept.13-1474 May 19).
48. Reg.18 (1474 Mar.26-1476 July 30).
49. Reg.19 (1476 Jan.10-1478 July 13).

50. Reg.20 (1478 Apr.2-1482 Apr.2).

51. Reg.21 (1480 Apr.27-1495 Dec.24).

52. Reg.22 (1491 Oct.7-1495 June 6; Reg.28 (1452 Dec.7-1487 Aug.13).

LEGAZIONI E COMMISSARIE, RISPOSTE VERBALI DI ORATORI FORESTIERI

53. Reg.1 (1458 Apr.-1462 Feb.); Reg.2 (1465 May 23-1496 July).

RESPONSIVE ORIGINALI

54. F.7, fols. 190-91 (1474 July 18); F.8, fols. 210-329 (1450 July 27-1530?); Responsive Originali, Inventario: vol.I, pp. 126-43; F.9, fols. 1-4, 6-9, 13 (1483 Dec.8-1494); F.31 (1491 July 11).

COPIARI DI RESPONSIVE

55. Inventario.

56. Reg.1 (1453 Jan.6-1468 Oct.3).

57. Reg.2 (1468 Oct.5-1483 Apr.18).

DIECI DI BALIA

CARTEGGI

58. Gabbrielli, Pietro Domenico. Alfabeti che servono a spiegare le lettere in cifra del carteggio dei Dieci di Balia dal 1424 al 1530 (1864). Vol. I.

MISSIVE, LEGAZIONI E COMMISSARIE, ISTRUZIONI E LETTERE A ORATORI

59. Reg.4 (1451 June 26 - 1454 May 14).

60. Reg.5 (1482 Sept. 21 - 1484 Jan. 3).

61. Reg.6 (1485 Dec. 9 - 1487 Aug. 9).

62. Reg.7 (1486 Apr. 24 - Oct. 27).

63. Reg.8 (1488 Jan. 29 - 1490 Mar. 22).

64. Reg.9 (1488 June 27 - 1490 Mar. 24).

65. Reg.10 (1490 Mar. 29 -1492 Aug. 14).

66. Reg.11 (1491 Sept. 7 - 1493 Aug. 2).

67. Reg.12 (1492 Aug. 17 - 1494 Oct. 22).

68. Reg.13 (1493 Aug. 2 - 1494 Jan. 17); Reg.14 (1494 Dec. 3 - 1495 June 1).

RESPONSIVE ORIGINALI

69. Reg.9 (1430 - 1431, 1453 - 1519).

70. Reg.15 (1440 May 8 - 31).

71. Reg.21 (1451 July 12 -1454 Dec. 18).

72. Reg.22 (1451 Jan. 27 - 1453 Sept. 21).

73. Reg.23 (1467 Apr. 24 - 1468 Mar. 23); (1455 Mar. 26);(1465 Sept. 26).

74. Reg.24 (1468 Jan. 3 - 1469 Mar. 12); 1476 Dec. 22 - 1478 Dec. 24).

75. Reg.25 (1479 Apr. 2 - Dec. 31).

76. Reg.26 (1482 Mar. 24 - 1483 July 2); (1480 Feb. 6 - June 26).

77. Reg.27 (1483 Mar. 25 - 1484 Mar. 24).

78. Reg.28 (1483 June 1 - Aug. 15).

79. Reg.29 (1483 Aug. 16 - Dec. 31).

80. Reg.30 (1484 Jan. 1 - Mar. 31).

81. Reg.31 (1484 Apr. 2 - July 31).

82. Reg.32 (1484 Aug. 2 - Nov. 30).

83. Reg.33 (1484 Dec. 1 - Dec. 31); (1485 Jan.1-Mar. 31).

84. Reg.34 (1485 Apr. 1 - Sept. 30).

85. Reg.35 (1485 Oct. 1 - 1486 Mar. 31).

86. Reg.36 (1486 Apr. 1 - June 29).

87. Reg.37 (1486 July 12 - 1494 Feb. 13).

88. Reg.38 (1494 Mar. 27 - 1495 Mar. 19).

89. Reg.39 (1495 Mar. 2 - 1497 May 21); (1454 - 1494)

SOMMARI DI MISSIVE E RESPONSIVE E RICORDI

91. Reg.1 (1478 July 16 - 1479 Mar. 23).

92. Reg.2 (1479 Mar. 26 - 1496 Feb. 3).

OTTO DI PRATICA

CARTEGGI

93. Gabbrielli, Pietro Domenico. Alfabeti che servono a spiegare le lettere in cifra del carteggio degl'Otto di Pratica dal 1482 al 1530 e della Signoria, Missive, dal 1481 al 1530 e Responsive dal 1414 al 1530 (1864). Vol. II.

MISSIVE ESTERNE, LEGAZIONI E COMMISSARIE, LETTERE E ISTRUZIONI A ORATORI

94. Reg.1 (1480 May 2 - June 17); Reg.2 (1484 Jan. 3 - July 21).

95. Reg.3 (1484 Jan. 1 - 1485 Dec. 9).

96. Reg.4 (1484 Jan. 1 - 1486 Apr. 23).

97. Reg.5 (1485 Aug. 23 - 1487 Sept. 11).

98. Reg.6 (1488 Jan. 29 - 1489 Mar. 8).

99. Reg.7 (1488 Jan. 29 - 1489 Sept. 20).

100. Reg.8 (1489 Sept. 19 - 1491 July 9).

101. Reg.9 (1491 Sept. 19 - 1493 Feb. 28).

RESPONSIVE

102. Reg.1 (1471 May 16 -1481 Sept. 30).

103. Reg.2 (1481 Oct. 1 - 1482 Sept. 23).

104. Reg.3 (1483 Apr. 11 - 1487 Aug. 30).

105. Reg.4 (1487 Sept. 1 - 1488 May 31).

106. Reg.5 (1488 June 1 - Aug. 31).

107. Reg.6 (1488 Sept. 1 - 1489 July 31).

108. Reg.7 (1489 Aug. 1 - 1491 Jan. 9).

109. Reg.8 (1491 Apr. 1 - 1492 Aug. 31).

110. Reg.9 (1492 Sept. 1 - 1494 Apr. 30).

111. Reg.10 (1494 May 1 - 1497 July 19).

SIGNORI, DIECI DI BALIA, OTTO DI PRATICA

LEGAZIONI E COMMISSARIE, MISSIVE E RESPONSIVE

112. Inventario sommario No.318, pp.7-10, 12-31, 40-42, 46-51, 59, 69-82, 91-92.

113. B.4, fols.11-97 (1479 Oct. 20 - 1496 May).

114. F.6 (1446 Nov. 17 - 1455 Feb. 25).

115. B.9 (1448 Aug. 13 - 1479 Oct. 28).

116. B.10 (1479 Feb. 22 - 1480 July 26).

117. Reg.11 (1482 Sept. 4 - 1492 June 16).

118. Reg.12 (1483 Dec.29 - 1484 Mar. 10).

119. B.13 (1484 Aug. 5 - 1487 Apr. 19).

120. B.14 (1479 Mar. 12 - 1517 Oct. 25).

121. F.15 (1488 Jan. 16 - 1499 Apr. 4).

122. Reg.16 (1488 Jan. 23 - Sept. 19).

123. Reg.17 (1488 Nov. 15 - 1490 Jan. 2).

124. B.18 (1450 Mar. 24 - Nov. 30).

125. Reg.19 (1490 Dec. 16 - 1492 Mar. 14).

126. Reg.20 (1488 Mar. 1 - 1489 July 30).

127. Reg.21 (1488 June 2 - 1489 June 24).

128. Reg.22 (1489 July 19 - 1490 Oct. 23).

129. Reg.23 (1490 Mar. 4 - 1491 Jan. 28).

130. Reg.24 (1492 Mar. 8 - July 3; Reg.25 (1491 Apr. 10 - Nov. 23).

131. Reg.26 (1491 Apr. 23 - Nov. 19).

132. B.27, fols.1-162 (1446 Aug. 14 - 1500 Feb. 10).

133. Reg.28 (1493 Feb. 28 - 1494 Feb. 15).

134. Reg.29 (1494 July 21 - Oct. 18).

135. B.48 (1484 Mar. 20 - 1530 Feb. 2).

136. B.60, fols.1-59, 126-97 (1452 Sept. - 1478 Nov. 29).

137. B.62 (1444 Dec. 28 - 1458 Oct. 17).

138. B.63 (1461 Sept. 26 - 1482 Dec. 30).

139. F.65 (1487 Apr. 16 - 1527 May 2).

140. B.67 (1487 June 25 - 1497 Jan. 14).

141. F.74, fols. 206-08, 216-18 (1480, 1486, 1497); B.75, fols. 23-236 (1470 Oct. 29 - 1491).

142. B.77 (1451 Jan. 5 - 1509 Feb. 22).

143. B.78, fols. 14-106 (1471 Sept. 17 - 1494 June 9).

CARTE DI CORREDO

LEGAZIONI E COMMISSARIE

144. Reg.17(51), fols.95-100, 108-69 (1450 - 1460); Reg.8(61), fols.1-19, 23-30v (1451 - 1492).

ARCHIVIO MEDICEO AVANTI IL PRINCIPATO

145. F.I (1458-95); F.II (1453-72); F.IV (1464, 1470, 1478); F.V (1455-80); F.VI (1451-68); F.VII (1452-94); F.VIII (1450-63); F.IX (1454-63).
146. F.X (1452-92); F.XI (1450-78); F.XII (1455-66).
147. F.XIV (1455-95); F.XV (1492, 1494); F.XVI (1460-94).
148. F.XVII (1451-79); F.XVIII (1489-94).
149. F.XIX (1492-94).
150. F.XX (1455-81); F.XXI (1464-79); F.XXII (1464-77).
151. F.XXIII (1422-76); F.XXIV (1466-92); F.XXV (1470-77).
152. F.XXVI (1467-91); F.XXVII (1470-72); F.XXVIII (1472).
153. F.XXIX (1471-74); F.XXX (1473-75); F.XXXI (1472-88).
154. F.XXXII (1474-89); F.XXXIII (1475-77).
155. F.XXXIV (1466-82); F.XXXV (1477-78).
156. F.XXXVI (1478-79).
157. F.XXXVII (1479); F.XXXVIII (1480-87).
158. F.XXXIX (1483-89).
159. F.XL (1483-88).
160. F.XLI (1487-90).
161. F.XLII (1490-91).
162. F.XLIII (1474-91).
163. F.XLV (1411-94).
164. F.XLVI (1435-94).
165. F.XLVII (1425-1524).
166. F.XLVIII (1470-87).
167. F.XLIX (1475-94).
168. F.L (1478-1515). 2 reels.
169. F.LI (1431-93). 2 reels.
170. F.LII (1472-92).
171. F.LIII (1483-92).
172. F.LIV (1466-94).
173. F.LV (1481-94).
174. F.LVI (1477-94).
175. F.LVII (1487, 1489).
176. F.LVIII (1487-94).

177. F.LIX (1485-1520).

178. F.LX (1490-93).

179. F.LXI (1466-90).

180. F.LXVI (1462-94); F.LXVII (1481-93).

181. F.LXVIII (1454-94); F.LXXII (1459-94).

182. F.LXXIII (1469-94).

183. F.LXXIV (1492-94).

184. F.LXXV (1481, 1492-94).

185. F.LXXVI (1489-91).

186. F.LXXX (1466, 1479, 1480); F.LXXXIII (1459, 1460, 1487); F.LXXXIV (1482); F.LXXXVI (1458).

187. F.LXXXVII (1454-87); F.LXXXVIII (1457-89); F.LXXXIX (1458-88); F.XC (1478-79).

188. F.XCIII (1479-91); F.XCIV (1459-82); F.XCVI (1476-94).

189. F.XCVII (1455-73, 1514); F.XCVIII (1455-93); F.C (1491-94).

190. F.CI (1454-89, 1537, 1542); F.CII (1480-94).

191. F.CIII (1455, 1491-94); F.CIV (1464, 1492); F.CV (1486, 1492-98); F.CVI (1462-75); F.CXIX (undated: cifre della segreteria di Lorenzo il Magnifico).

192. F.CXXIV (1478-94).

193. F.CXXXVII (1402-1555). 2 Reels.

194. F.CXXXVIII (1425-1538).

195. F.CXXXIX (1473-94); F.CXLVI (1472-92); F.CXLVII (1415-1534: entire); F.CXLIX (1478); F.CL (1464,1474,1482).

196. F.CLXIII (1464-65).

CARTE STROZZIANE

SERIE PRIMA

197. F.3 (1458-1494.

198. F.4 (1494-1495).

199. F.10 (1488); F.12 (1461, 1454-94, 1494); F.15 (1488); F.23 (1492 + undated); F.111 (1455, 1475 + undated); F.113 (1472).

200. F.136 (1454-71); F.137 (1466-93); F.229 (1474-82); F.230 (1459-84); F.238 (1475); F.241 (1459-93); F.151 (1457-94).

201. F.253 (1467-71); F.256 (1463, 1477-78); F.293 (1493-95); F.294 (1469, 1487 + undated); F.295 (1461, 1465); F.302 (1475 + undated); F.324 (1459-85); F.325 (1456-79); F.351 (1482).

202. F.352 (1463-70); F.357 (1488); F.358 (1459); F.369 (1476-91); F.371 (1492); SERIE SECONDA: F.96 (1479, 1470-80); F.97 (1471-84 + undated).

SERIE TERZA

203. F.103 (1481-82, 1492); F.106 (1475); F.114 (1482-83); F.131 (1460. 1465); F.138 (1465 + undated); F.149 (1465 + undated).

204. F.133. Lettere scritte da diversi di Casa Strozzi dal 1470 al 1500.

205. F.178. Lettere di Filippo Strozzi e d'altri (1450-1536).

206. F.247. Volume (segnato delle lettere ZQ) contenente una raccolta di lettere di molto conto storico... scritte dal 1424 al 1518.

207. F.249. Volume (segnato delle lettere ZS) contenente diverse lettere di grande importanza storica scritte a individui della famiglia Strozzi da varie persone. In principio del MS stanno spiegazioni di diverse cifre impiegate nei carteggi della nostra Repubblica coi suoi ambasciatori, Girolamo, Francesco e Luigi Guicciardini ed altre tavole decifrate... 1460-78 [ca.1361-ca.1529].

ACQUISTI E DONI

208. DONO DEL SEMINARIO DI PISTOIA.

F.1, No.1e. Commissione degli Otto di Pratica a Piero Vettori, 1490 Jan.28. PROVENIENZA MAGLIABECHIANA.

F.3. Francesco Gaddi. Spese per la sua ambasciata di Roma, 1487.

F.4. F. Gaddi. Spese per la sua ambasciata di Milano, 1488.

F.5. F. Gaddi. Spese per la sua ambasciata a Venezia, 1492. ACQUISTO CALAMANDREI-BIGAZZI.

F.140, Inserto 6(1). I Conservatori delle Leggi e gli Ufficiali dell'Abbondanza a F.de' Medici, Arcivescovo di Pisa, e ad altri oratori fiorentini presso il Pontefice, 1464 Oct.27; Inserto 9 (4). Minuta di discorso tenuto da un oratore fiorentino al Santo Padre, 15th cent.

F.142, Inserto 7(3). Sei lettere dei X di Balia a Giovanni Lanfredini e a Francesco Gualterotti, 1485 Feb.11-1509 June 3.

F.234, II(1). Tre lettere concernenti il duca di Ferrara e il marchese Sadoleto, suo ambasciatore, 1470-94.

F.286, XXX. Credenziale della Rep. Veneta per Bernardo Bembo, inviato a Lorenzo il Magnifico, 1478 July 2.

ARCHIVIO DELLA FAMIGLIA GUICCIARDINI

LEGAZIONI E COMMISSARIE. CARTEGGI

209. B.I, Nos.86-147. Lettere a Piero di Iacopo Guicciardini, Console di Mare a Pisa, 1491 Sept.5-1492 Aug.16.
210. B.II, Nos.1-15. Istruzioni a Piero di Luigi di P. Guicciardini, 1423-1440.
Nos.16-41. Lettere a Giovanni Girolami, Averardo de' Medici e Piero Guicciardini, Commissari a Faenza, 1425 Apr.18-Oct.30.
Nos.43-52. Lettere a Nerone Neroni, Bernardo Guadagni e Piero Guicciardini, ambasciatori a Venezia, 1430.
Nos.41bis-42, 53-54. Lettere a Piero Guicciardini, scritte da varie persone, 1416, 1424, 1431, 1435, 1498.
No.58. Copialettere della legazione di Piero Guicciardini a Venezia, 1430 July 1-1431 Jan.26.
211. B.III, Nos.1-14. Istruzioni, copialettere e vari documenti relativi a più legazioni e commissarie di Luigi Guicciardini, 1435-82.
Nos.17-48. Lettere a Luigi Guicciardini, ambasciatore al Duca di Milano, 1469 June 3-Dec.9.
Nos.15-16, 49-69. Lettere varie, scritte a Luigi Guicciardini da più persone, 1436, 1459, 1470-1480.

211.1. B.IV, Nos.32-43. Lettere a Jacopo Guicciardini, 1459 Aug. 6-Dec. 22.

Nos.93-134. Lettere a Jacopo Guicciardini, 1466 Jan. 28-July 26.

Nos.44-70, 135. Lettere a Jacopo Guicciardini, 1467 Jan. 25-Sept. 17.

Nos.137-57. Lettere a Jacopo Guicciardini, 1470 Sept. 13-1471 Feb. 15.

Nos.158-63. Lettere a Jacopo Guicciardini, 1471 Aug. 7-22.

Nos.164-84. Lettere a Jacopo Guicciardini, 1476 Mar. 16-Sept. 14.

Nos.185-305. Lettere a Jacopo Guicciardini, 1478 Sept. 2-1479 Oct. 29.

Nos.1-31. Lettere varie a Jacopo Guicciardini, 1450-1487.
Nos.80-85, 88-91, 306-08. Istruzioni e patenti, relative a più legazioni e commissarie di Jacopo Guicciardini, 1465, 1468, 1483-4, 1488.
Nos.309-15. Libri di conti appartenti alle commissarie di Jacopo Guicciardini, 1478-87.

212-13. B.V. a). Lettere a Iacopo Guicciardini, ambasciatore a Ferrara, 1483 Mar.28-July 27.

b). Lettere a detto Iacopo, Commissario Generale nella guerra coi genovesi, 1484 Aug.22-1485 Jan.28.

c). Lettere allo stesso, ambasciatore a Milano, 1485 Dec.21-1486 Sept.29.

d). Lettere di vari a vari, ca.1483-ca.1486.

e). 1. Registro di lettere scritte per Iacopo quando era ambasciatore a Ferrara per la guerra, 1483 Mar.22-June 25.
2. Copie di lettere scritte ai X da Iacopo Guicciardini, Commissario in Lombardia nella guerra contro i veneziani, 1483 Sept.5-Nov.23.
3. Copialettere dello stesso, Commissario Generale nella guerra contro i genovesi, 1485 Jan.18-Feb.8.
4. Registro di lettere scritte dallo stesso, ambasciatore a Milano, 1485 Dec. 1486-Apr.18.

f). Documenti vari: 1482, 1486 + undated.

214. B.VI. No.1. Salvocondotto del Duca Galeazzo Maria Sforza a Piero di Iacopo Guicciardini, 1476 Apr.14.

No.2. Lettera di Orfeo da Ricavo a P. Guicciardini, 1476 Sept.22.

Nos. 3-8. Lettere degli Otto di Balia a P. Guicciardini, ambasciatore a Milano, 1493 May, July, Oct.

CARTE PATRIMONIALI

215. B.XLIX. Minutario di Iacopo Guicciardini, ambasciatore a Roma e a Napoli, 1470 Sept.8-1471 Feb.22.

CARTE DI FRANCESCO GUICCIARDINI

216. B.XXVI. a). Lettera di Giovan Battista Ridolfi, ambasciatore al Duca di Milano, agli Otto di Pratica, 1494 Sept.15.

B.XIII. b). 4. Lettere scritte per Luigi Guicciardini, ambasciatore a Milano, 1466 Dec.1-1467 May 26.

5. Minutario di Luigi Guicciardini, ambasciatore a Milano, 1469 June 9-July 9.

6. Copie di lettere scritte alla Signoria per Iacopo Guicciardini e Otto Niccolini, ambasciatori a Roma, 1469 July 8-Dec.21.

7. Copialettere di Luigi Guicciardini, amb. a Venezia, 1475 Jan.23-May 13.

d). 2. Lettere di Piero Nasi, ambasciatore a Napoli, 1483 Jan.1-31.

II. BIBLIOTECA NAZIONALE CENTRALE

217. Cod.II.III.256. Minutario di brevi di Sisto IV (1481 Aug.25-1482 Aug. 24).
218. Cod.II.IV.169. Historia fiorentina di Piero di Marco Parenti. Vol.I, 1476-96.
219. Cod.II.IV.170. Storia fiorentina di Piero di Marco Parenti, scritta di sua propria mano, dal 1497 al 1501.
220. Cod.II.IV.171. Diario fiorentino di Piero di Marco Parenti, dal settembre 1507 all'agosto 1518. .
221. Cod.II.II.130. Parenti, Pietro. Istorie fiorentine. Vol.II, 1496 Apr.-1497 Mar.
222. Cod.II.II.133. Parenti, Pietro. Istorie fiorentine. Vol.V, 1502 Mar.-1504 Feb.
223. Cod.II.II.134. Parenti, Pietro. Istorie fiorentine. Vol.VI, 1504 Mar.-1507 Aug.
224. Cod.Magl.XXV,272. Parenti, Marco. Diverse notizie istoriche d'Italia, delle potenze che la dominavano nel 1464 e delle cose seguite in Firenze contro la fazione de' Medici fino al 1467.
225. Cod.II.V.12. Lettere a Giovanni Lanfredini, ambasciatore fiorentino a Venezia e a Napoli, di vari dal 1468 al 1485.
226. Cod.II.V.15. Minutario di lettere dell'oratore Giovanni Lanfredini, Napoli 1484-85, a vari. Precedono quattro minute di lettere della Signoria al Lanfredini, del 1477.
227. Cod.II.V.16. Minutario di lettere dell'oratore Giovanni Lanfredini, dal 1 settembre 1477 al maggio 1483.
228. Cod.II.V.18. Minutario di lettere di G. Lanfredini, oratore della Signoria a Napoli, dal 10 maggio 1485 al 26 settembre 1486 e senza data.
229. Cod.II.V.19. Lettere autografe di vari, per lo più da Firenze, a Giovanni Lanfredini, oratore della Signoria a Napoli ed a Roma, dal 1485 al 1487.
230. Cod.II.V.20. Lettere originali dei Dieci di Balìa di Firenze a G. Lanfredini, oratore a Napoli e a Roma, dal 1485 al 1487.
231. Cod.II.IV.311. Miscellanea, 15th cent.
232. Cod.Palatino 1091. Lettere latine e volgari a diversi Principi del 1400 [1479 Dec.15-1480 Apr. 21).
232.1. Indici e Cataloghi, IV: Manoscritti Palatini, Tomo 3, pp. 136-56 (Pal. 1103). Cod. Palatino 1103. Copialettere della Prima Cancelleria della Rep. Fiorentina comprendente le Missive dal 20 maggio 1465 al 23 luglio 1474.

MANOSCRITTI GINORI CONTI

233. Catalogo 77. Inventario dei Manoscritti Ginori Conti.
234. No.1. Registro di lettere dal 1493 al 1494 di Dionigi di Puccio de' Pucci ed altri.
235. No.7. Libro Giornale di Bernardo di Giovanni Cambi dal 1455 al 1460.
236. No.12. Ambascerie di Dionigi Pucci ed altri in Romagna, Ferrara e Bologna, 1490-92.
237. No.13. Ambascerie di Puccio di Antonio Pucci in Faenza e Romagna, 1493-95.
238. No.18. Ricordanze originali di Pietro Capponi, dal 1466 al 1475.

MANOSCRITTI GINORI CONTI, CARTE MICHELOZZI

239. No.29/8. Lettere (40) di vari commissari della Repubblica a Pietro Vettori, 1478-79, 1487.
No.29/10. Lettere (10) di Virginio Orsini d'Aragona, governatore della Lega italiana, 1485-93.
No.29/10h. Ambasceria fiorentina a Bologna, 1494.
240. No.29/15. Lettera di Battista Campofregoso a Nicolò da Uzzano, 1420.
No.29/16. Lettera di Paolo da Siena a Paolo da Diacceto, 1448.
No.29/17. Lettere (44) di Alessandro Bracci, da Siena, 1470-1502.

No.29/18. Lettere (47) di Baccio Ugolini, da Roma, a Niccolo Michelozzi e a Lorenzo il Magnifico, 1476-93.
241. No.29/21. Lettera di Battista Campofregoso a Luigi XI, 1479.
No.29/22. Lettere (45) di Andrea Cambini, da Ferrara, 1482-1483.
No.29/23. Lettera di Onofrio Tornabuoni, da Roma, 1493.
No.29/29. Fascicoli (18) contenenti documenti per la storia della Repubblica fiorentina, sec.XIV-XVI.
Fasc.7. Alleanza fra Firenze e Ferrara dopo la congiura dei Pazzi, 1478.
Fasc.10. Cronichetta fiorentina, 1491-96.
Fasc.11. Riforma al tempo di Savonarola, dopo l'espulsione dei Medici, 1494.
No.29/30. Lettera che annunzia alla Repubblica di Firenze la morte di Innocenzo VIII, 1492 July 26.
242. No.29/33. Lettera di Piero di Cosimo de' Medici, 1450.
No.29/34. Lettere (11) di Giuliano de' Medici, 1472-77.
No.29/35. Lettere (25) di Pietro di Lorenzo de' Medici, 1480-92.
No.29/36. Lettere (9) di Lucrezia Tornabuoni, 1473-80.
No.29/37. Lettere (3) di Giovanni di Pier Francesco de' Medici, 1489-98.
No.29/38. Lettera di Giovanni de' Medici, 1497.
No.29/38bis. Lettere (36) di Clarice Orsini, 1472-89.
No.29/39. Lettere (5) di Giovanni de' Medici, 1490-92.
243. No.29/91. Lettere da Roma ai Michelozzi, 1471-96.
No.29/95. Corrispondenza di commissari e capitani della Repubblica fiorentina, 1478-1513.
244. No.29/97. Ambascerie fiorentine in Francia presso Luigi XI, Carlo VIII, Luigi XII e Francesco I, 1478-1529.
No.29/98. Dispacci (6) degli ambasciatori fiorentini presso Carlo V, 1529.
No.29/99. Lettere (16) di Bonsignore Bonsignori, commissario nel Levante, 1497-98.
No.29/100. Lettere (2) di Pier Francesco Portinari, ambasciatore fiorentino a Londra, a Nicolo Capponi, 1527-28.
No.29/101. Lettere (45) di ambasciatori fiorentini a Napoli, 1480-89: Ser Francesco di Ser Barone, 1480-90; Bernardo Rucellai, 1486-87; Francesco Nacci, 1487-89.
245. No.29/102. Ambasciatori fiorentini a Milano, 1474-1519: Donato Acciaioli (12), 1474-75; Pier Filippo Pandolfini (9), 1478-88; Antonio de' Medici (38), 1477-80; Andrea Bartolini (14 fols.), 1480-84; Agnolo Niccolini (11 fols.), 1476-92; Bernardo Rucellai (2 fols.), 1484-85.
No.29/103. Ambasceria fiorentina a Roma, 1477-1528: Leonardo Bartolini, 1490-1500; Donato Acciaioli, 1477; Filippo Pandolfini, 1479-92; Giovanni Lanfredini, 1484-88; Nofri Tornabuoni, 1490-92; Filippo Valori, 1490-92.
No.29/104. Ambasceria di Pietro Alamanni a Milano, Roma e Napoli (13 fols.), 1486-92.
No.29/105. Ambasciatori fiorentini a Venezia, 1479-1514: Paolo Antonio Soderini (23 fols.), 1479-91; Piero da Bibbiena (15 fols.), 1513-14.
No.29/106. Istruzioni di Ferdinando d'Aragona a Francesco Accolti d'Arezzo, mandato ambasciatore all'Imperatore Federico, undated.
246. No.29/115. Istruzioni ad ambasciatori fiorentini, 1479-1505. No.29/116. Istruzioni della Repubblica, 1482-1528.
247. No.29/117. Lettere (2) di Lorenzo de' Medici a Niccolò Michelozzi: 1489, 1490.
No.29/118. Lettere (4) di Lorenzo de' Medici a Niccolò Michelozzi a Pitigliano, 1489.
No.29/119. Lettera di Loreno de' Medici a Niccolò Michelozzi, undated.
No.29/120. Lettere (2) di Lorenzo de' Medici a Niccolò Michelozzi, 1479.
No.29/121. Lettere (22) di Lorenzo de' Medici a vari. 1478-1490.
No.29/122. Lettere (5) di Lorenzo de' Medici a N. Michelozzi in Perugia, 1488.
No.29/123. Lettere (8) di L. de' Medici a N. Michelozzi a Napoli: 1479, 1492.
No.29/124. Lettere (7) di L. de' Medici a N. Michelozzi a Milano, 1479-83.
No.29/125. Lettere (10) di L. de' Medici agli ambasciatori, 1479-84.
No.29/125bis. Lettere (6) di L. de' Medici a N. Michelozzi nel campo della Lega, 1484.
No.29/126. Lettere (2) di L. de' Medici a N. Michelozzi: 1472, 1491.

No.29/127. Lettere (5) di L. de' Medici a N. Michelozzi in Firenze, 1472 and undated.

No.29/127bis. Lettere (3) di L. de' Medici a N. Michelozzi, 1478-82.

No.29/128. Lettere (19) di L. de' Medici a N. Michelozzi in Firenze, 1472-84.

No.29/129. Lettere (56) di L. de' Medici a N. Michelozzi in Firenze, 1485-90.

No.29/130. Lettere (8) di L. de' Medici e appunti (11) o copie di lettere riguardanti la sua cancelleria, 1478-87 and undated.

No.29/131. Lettera di L. de' Medici a Giovanni Antonio d'Arezzo in Roma, 1489.

248. No.29/132. Lettere (35) di Lorenzo de' Medici a Niccolò Michelozzi e Giovanni Antonio d'Arezzo in Roma, 1489-91.

No.29/133. Lettera e appunti (4) in originale o copia di Lorenzo de' Medici: 1485, 1492 and undated.

No.29/134. Minute (4) di lettere di N. Michelozzi a L. de' Medici (da Milano), 1482-84.

No.29/135. Minute (2) di lettere di N. Michelozzi a Giuliano de' Medici, 1513.

No.29/136. Lettere (4) di L. de' Medici a N. Michelozzi e a Giovanni Antonio d'Arezzo in Roma, 1490.

No.29/137. Minute (65) d'istruzioni e lettere della cancelleria di L. de' Medici, dettate da lui o da N. Michelozzi, 1477-1515.

No.29/138. Lettere (6) di L. de' Medici in copia decifrata, 1479-82.

No.29/139. Lettere (4) di Agnolo della Stufa a L. de' Medici in Napoli, 1480.

FORLI

I. BIBLIOTECA COMUNALE

COLLEZIONE PIANCASTELLI, SEZIONE AUTOGRAFI

249. Carbonari, Giuliana. Indice del materiale umanistico che si conserva fra gli autografi della collezione Piancastelli (Tesi di laurea, 1955-56), pp.52-53, 59, 65-66, 90, 117, 203-04, 206.

250. Autografi. Selections, 15th-early 16th cent.

GENOA

I. ARCHIVIO DI STATO

ANTICO COMUNE

TRATTATI E NEGOZIAZIONI POLITICHE

251. Selections, 1458-1493.

INSTRUCTIONES ET RELATIONES

252. B.2707A (1396-1464; selections, 1450-64).

253. F.2707B (1433-99); selections, 1464-93).

254. F.2707G (1439-1621; selections, 1481-1503).

255. F.22(3042). (1456-57; selections, Mazzo 1: 1456 Jan. 26, Nov.10, Dec.1; Mazzo 2: 1457 Apr.30, Oct.19.
F.23(3043). (1458-59; selections: 1458 June 15, Nov.21; 1459 Jan. 24.
256. F.24(3044). (1460).

POLITICORUM

257. B.1648 (1451-81).

REGISTRI LITTERARUM

258. Reg.18/1794. (1451-58; selections, 1455-57).
259. Reg.18A/1794A. (1454-55; selections, 1455).
Reg.18B/1794B. (1454-55; selections, 1455).
260. Reg.21/1797. (1455-64; selections, 1458-64).

LETTERE DI PRINCIPI ALLA REPUBBLICA

261. Selections: B.4/2780. Ferrara, 1593-94; Francia, 1466-88. B.10/2786.Milano, 1468-78.
B.16/2792. Sicilia (Napoli), 1480, 1496.
B.17/2793. Spagna, 1473-74.
B.21/2797. Venezia, 1465.
B.22B/2798B. Savoia, 1476; Spagna, 1492.

ARCHIVIO DEL BANCO DI S. GIORGIO. PRIMI CANCELLIERI

262-3. B.82. Savoia, Monferrato, Saluzzo, Asti (1458-1537?).

264. B.83. Milano (1458-1508).

265. B.87. Francia, Spagna, Inghilterra, Fiandre, Germania (1456-1519; Francia, selections, 1456-94).

REGISTRI LITTERARUM

266-266.1. Reg.1778 (1426-1503).

RACCOLTE E MISCELLANEE, MANOSCRITTI

267. MS.652. Franzone, Agostino. Informazioni date dalla Repubblica genovese a suoi ambasciatori mandati a diversi Potentati del mondo dall'anno 1423 all'anno 1596, pp.277-527 (1450-76).

ISOLA BELLA

I. ARCHIVIO BORROMEO

FONDO GOVERNI E STATI, ATTI DIVERSI

Cart. I. Milano [Selections].

Appendix. 1. Authenticated notarial copy of feudal investiture of Genoa and Savona, granted by King Louis XI of France to the Duke and Duchess of Milan, Francesco and Bianca Maria Sforza (22 Dec., 1463), and related instruments of alliance between the above rulers, executed in Milan on 21 Jan., 1469 by order of Duke Galeazzo Maria Sforza [15 photocopies].

Appendix. 2. Contemporary copies of instructions and letters by Duke Galeazzo Maria Sforza to his ambassadors at the Papal court, Giovanni Borromeo and Giovanni Jacobo Riccio or Ricci, for the renewal of the Italian League, Oct. - Dec., 1470 [21 photocopies].

MANTUA

I. ARCHIVIO DI STATO

ARCHIVIO GONZAGA

SERIE E. DIPARTIMENTO AFFARI ESTERI (CORRISPONDENZA ESTERA)

268. Davari, Stefano. Indici Serie "E". Nos.I-XXVI. Pareri Politici, Cifrari-Pesaro e Urbino.
269. Davari, Indici... Nos.XXVII-XLI. Rimini-Parma e Piacenza.
270. Davari, Indici... Nos.XLII-XLIX. Guastalla-Milano.
271. Davari, Indici... Nos.L-LXI.2. Pavia-Corrispondenza col Cardinale Ercole Gonzaga.

PARERI POLITICI, CIFRARI

272. E.I.2. B.423. Cifre sciolte: filmed for 15th century.

AFFARI IN CORTE CESAREA

273. E.II.1. B.426. Istruzioni agli Inviati e Residenti: filmed 1474-75.
E.II.2. B.428. Lettere Imperiali: filmed 1452-94.
E.II.3. B.439. Carteggio degli Inviati e Residenti: filmed 1458-93.

CORTI ELETTORALI

274. E.IV.1. B.510. Istruzioni agli Inviati e Residenti: filmed 1460.
E.IV.2a. B.514. Lettere degli Elettori e Principi dell'Impero ai Gonzaga: filmed 1376-1507.
E.IV.3. B.522. Carteggio di Inviati e Diversi: filmed 1460-94.

INNSBRUCK E GRATZ

275. E.VI.2. B.536. Lettere degli Arciduchi d'Austria ai Gonzaga: filmed 1460-90.
E.VI.3. B.544. Carteggio di Inviati e Diversi: filmed 1364-1493.

426

DANIMARCA

276. E.IX.1. B.563. Lettere Reali ai Principi di Mantova (1458-96, 1512).

FIANDRE

277. E.XI.3. B.567*. Carteggio di Inviati e Diversi: filmed 1466-94.

SPAGNA

278. E.XIV.2. B.583. Lettere Reali ai Principi di Mantova: filmed 1486-92.
E.XIV.3. B.585. Carteggio di Inviati e Diversi: filmed 1460, 1485-93.

FRANCIA

279. E.XV.2. B.626*. Lettere dei Re di Francia ai Gonzaga: filmed 1459-94.
E.XV.3. B.629*. Carteggio di Inviati e Diversi: filmed 1461-94.
E.XV.5. B.705*. Scritture e stampe diverse d'interesse della corte di Francia: filmed 1475.
E.XV.6. B.708*. Scritture e stampe sulle guerre di Francia: filmed 1475.

SAVOIA

280. E.XIX.2. B.729. Lettere dei Sabaudi ai Gonzaga: filmed 1450, 1487.
E.XIX.3. B.731. Carteggio di Inviati e Diversi: filmed 1478-94.

MONFERRATO

281. E.XX.1. B.740. Lettere dei Marchesi di Monferrato ai Gonzaga: filmed 1461-94.
E.XX.2. B.745. Carteggio di Inviati e Diversi: filmed 1458-94.

GENOVA

282. E.XXI.2. B.756. Lettere della Repubblica di Genova ai Gonzaga: filmed 1480-88.
E.XXI.3. B.757. Carteggio di Inviati e Diversi: filmed 1452-94.

NAPOLI E SICILIA

283. E.XXIV.1. B.801*. Istruzioni agli Inviati e Residenti: filmed 1465, one document.
E.XXIV.2. B.802*. Lettere Reali ai Principi di Mantova: filmed 1450-94.

284. E.XXIV.2a. B.804*. Lettere dei Duchi di Calabria ai Gonzaga: filmed 1447-94.

285. E.XXIV.3. B.805*. Carteggio di Inviati e Diversi:filmed 1449-81.

286. "   B.806. Carteggio... (1482-90).

287. "   B.807. Carteggio... (1491-98).

ROMA

288. E.XXV.1. B.831*.. Istruzioni agli Inviati e Residenti: filmed 1502-12.

289. E.XXV.2. B.834*. Brevi Papali ai Signori di Mantova: filmed 1454-96.

290. E.XXV.3. B.840*. Carteggio di Inviati e Diversi: filmed 1444-60.

291-2. "   B.841*. Carteggio... (1461-62).

293-4. "   B.842*. Carteggio... (1463-65).
295. "   B.843*. Carteggio... (1466-69).
296. "   B.844*. Carteggio... (1470-72).
297. "   B.845*. Carteggio... (1473-76).
298. "   B.846*. Carteggio... (1477-83).
299-300." B.847. Carteggio... (1484-88).
301. "   B.848. Carteggio... (1489-91).
302. "   B.849. Carteggio... (1492-93).
303. "   B.850. Carteggio... (1494-95).
304. E.XXV.5. B.1062*. Scritture e stampe diverse riflettenti la curia romana: filmed 1425, 1471, 1512.

FIRENZE

305. E.XXVIII.2. B.1085*. Lettere della Signoria e dei Medici ai Gonzaga: filmed 1445-1523.
306. E.XXVIII.3. B.1099*. Carteggio di Inviati e Diversi: filmed 1458-60 + undated.
307. "   B.1100*. Carteggio... (1461-71).
308-9. "   B.1101. Carteggio... (1472-80).
310. "   B.1102. Carteggio... (1481-99).

FERRARA

311. E.XXXI.1. B.1179*. Istruzioni agli Inviati e Residenti di Mantova: filmed 1440, 1472, 1484, 1494?
    E.XXXI.2. B.1181*. Lettere degli Estensi ai Signori di Mantova: filmed 1451-62.
312. E.XXXI.2. B.1182*. Lettere degli Estensi... (1463-76).
313. "   B.1183. Lettere degli Estensi... (1477-85).
314. "   B.1184. Lettere degli Estensi... (1486-90).
315. "   B.1185. Lettere degli Estensi... (1491-93).
316. "   B.1186. Lettere degli Estensi...: filmed 1494.
317. E.XXXI.3. B.1228. Carteggio di Inviati e Diversi: filmed 1454-76.
318. "   B.1229. Carteggio... (1477-81).
319-20. "   B.1230. Carteggio... (1482).
321-2. "   B.1231. Carteggio... (1483-90).
323. "   B.1232. Carteggio... (1491-93).
324. "   B.1233. Carteggio... (1494).
325. E.XXXI.5. B.1278*. Scritture e stampe diverse su Ferrara e gli Estensi: filmed 1471-80.

MODENA-REGGIO

326. E.XXXII.3. B.1288*. Carteggio di Inviati e Diversi: filmed 1449-76.
327. "   B.1289. Carteggio... (1477-99).

VENEZIA

328. E.XLV.1. B.1417*. Istruzioni agli Inviati e Diversi: filmed 1448-83.

329. E.XLV.2. B.1419. Lettere dei Dogi ai Gonzaga: filmed 1444-53.

330. 	" 	B.1420*. Lettere dei Dogi... (1454-69).

331. 	" 	B.1421*. Lettere dei Dogi... (1470-84).

332. 	" 	B.1422. Lettere dei Dogi... (1485-91).

333. 	" 	B.1423. Lettere dei Dogi... (1492-99).

334-5. E.XLV.3. B.1431*. Carteggio di Inviati e Diversi: filmed 1445-76.

336. 	" 	B.1432. Carteggio... (1477-89).

337. 	" 	B.1433. Carteggio... (1490-92).

338. 	" 	B.1434. Carteggio... (1493-94).

MILANO

339. E.XLIX.1. B.1602. Istruzioni agli Inviati e Diversi: filmed 1446, 1459, 1461-84.

340. E.XLIX.2. B.1607. Lettere dei Signori di Milano ai Gonzaga (1402-76).

341. 	" 	B.1608*. Lettere dei Signori di Milano... (1477-83).

342. 	" 	B.1609. Lettere dei Signori di Milano... (1484-86).

343. 	" 	B.1610. Lettere dei Signori di Milano... (1487-91).

344. 	" 	B.1611. Lettere dei Signori di Milano... (1492).

345. 	" 	B.1612. Lettere dei Signori di Milano... (1493-94).

346-7. E.XLIX.3. B.1620. Carteggio di Inviati e Diversi (1401-59).

348-9. 	" 	B.1621. Carteggio... (1460-61).

350-2. 	" 	B.1622. Carteggio... (1462-64).

353-4. 	" 	B.1623. Carteggio... (1465-70).

355-6. 	" 	B.1624. Carteggio... (1471-74).

357-8. 	" 	B.1625. Carteggio... (1475-76).

359-60. 	" 	B.1626. Carteggio... (1477-79).

361. 	" 	B.1627. Carteggio... (1480-82).

362-3. 	" 	B.1628. Carteggio... (1483-84).

364. 	" 	B.1629. Carteggio... (1485-90).

365. 	" 	B.1630. Carteggio... (1491-95).

366. E.XLIX.5. B.1783*. Scritture e stampe diverse riflettenti Milano: filmed 1465-94.

SERIE F. LEGISLAZIONE E SISTEMAZIONE DEL GOVERNO

(CORRISPONDEZA INTERNA)

F.II.6. LETTERE ORIGINALI DEI GONZAGA

367. B.2094 (1412-50).

368. B.2095 (1451-59).

369. B.2096 (1460-61).

370. B.2097 (1462-63).

371. B.2098 (1464-65).

372. B.2099 (1466-67).

373. B.2100 (1468-71).
374. B.2101 (1472-73).
375. B.2102 (1474-75).
376. B.2103 (1476-78).
377. B.2104 (1479-81).
378. B.2105 (1482-83).
379. B.2106 (1484-90).
380. B.2107 (1491).
381. B.2108 (1492-93).
382. B.2109 (1494).

F.II.7. MINUTE DELLA CANCELLERIA

383. B.2186 (filmed 1457-63).
384-5. B.2187 (1464-75).
386-7. B.2188 (1476-81).
388-9. B.2189 (1482-83).
390-1. B.2190 (1484-94).

F.II.8. LETTERE AI GONZAGA DA MANTOVA E PAESI DELLO STATO

392. Davari, Stefano. Indici Serie F.II.8. Lettere ai Gonzaga da Mantova e Paesi dello Stato (14th cent.-1601).
393. B.2390. Lettere da Mantova (1400-59).
394. B.2391. Lettere dai Paesi (1400-57).
395. B.2392. Lettere dai Paesi, A-O (1458).

F.II.9. COPIALETTERE DEI GONZAGA

A). COPIALETTERE ORDINARI E MISTI

396-7. B.2883 (1449-52).
398-9. B.2884 (1452-55).
400-1. B.2885 (1455-60).
402-3. B.2886 (1455-61).
404-5. B.2887 (1462-64).
406-7. B.2888 (1460-66).
408-9. B.2889 (1464-67).
410-11. B.2890 (1465-69).
412-13. B.2891 (1468-74).
414-15. B.2892 (1471-73).

MILAN

I. ARCHIVIO DI STATO

ARCHIVIO DIPLOMATICO (SEZIONE STORICO-DIPLOMATICA)

AUTOGRAFI

416. Inventario Sommario No.84. Inventario No.84bis. Cartelle 107-59. Uomini celebri.
417. Inventario No.85. Ecclesiastici: Pontefici, santi e beati, predicatori e gerarchie ecclesiastiche.
418. Inventario No.86. Case regnanti, principi, grandi dignitari.
419. Inventario No.87. Pittori, architetti, ingegneri, scultori, artisti diversi.
420. Inventario No.88. Autorità civili e militari, avvocati, medici, notai, uomini di stato, armaiuoli.

FAMIGLIE

421. Inventario No.90.
422. **Famiglie**, selections: Cart.20. Bianchi Giovanni (1467-76); Cart.176. Simonetta Angelo, Cicco, Giovanni ed altri (1438, 1466-68, 1470-72, 1474-80, 1483, 1491, 1497, 1499, 1513-14, 1521, 1530, 1532, 1549, 1552, 1560, 1580, 1583, 1593 + undated); Cart.188. Tranchedini Francesco e Nicodemo (1470-72, 1476, 1479, 1481, 1489 + undated).

MISCELLANEA STORICA

423. Selections: Cart.5 (1451, 1461-63, 1468-69, 1472, 1474, 1478, 1492, 1532). Cart.6 (1478?). Cart.7 (1469). Cart.11 (undated). Cart.26 (1480 + undated).
423.1. Cart. 9A. **Cicco Simonetta**, documenti biografici (various dates).
423.2. Cart. 9B. **Cicco Simonetta**, Quaderni di conti (1452-1479).

ARCHIVIO SFORZESCO DUCALE, CARTEGGIO

POTENZE SOVRANE

424. Bassino Viola. "La serie Potenze Sovrane dell'Archivio Ducale, anni 1450-1460. Proposta di riordinamento." Tesi di laurea. Milano, Università degli Studi, 1968-69.
425. Frati Giuliana. "La serie Potenze Sovrane dell'Archivio Ducale, anni 1461-1468. Proposta di riordinamento." Tesi di laurea. Milano, Università degli Studi, 1968-69.
426-7. Cart.1455 (12th - 16th cent.).
428. Cart.1457 (1452-64).
429. Cart.1458 (1465-66, 1473).
430. Cart.1459 (1450-67: Bianca Maria Visconti Sforza).
431. Cart.1460 (1468-79).
432. Cart.1461 (1450-76 + undated: Galeazzo Maria Sforza).
433. Cart.1462 (1451-78: Galeazzo Maria Sforza).
434. Cart.1463 (1468-1526 + undated: Bona di Savoia).
435. Cart.1465 (1462-1514: Ascanio Maria Sforza).

436. Cart.1466 (1482-99: Isabella d'Aragona).

437. Cart.1467 (1472-98: Bianca Maria Sforza).

438. Cart.1468 (1464-1500: Ludovico Maria Sforza).

439. Cart.1469 (1466-1500: Ludovico Maria Sforza).

440. Cart.1480 (1451-96 + undated: Sforza Secondo, figlio naturale di Francesco Primo).

441. Cart.1483 (1444-1535 + undated: Feste, giuochi, spettacoli, giostre, cacce, animali,argenterie, gioie, abiti, spese di corte, tesoreria, bilanci, inventari, etc.).

442. Cart.1486 (1451-65 + undated: corrispondenza interna fra la Duchessa Bianca Maria Visconti Sforza ed altri).

CANCELLERIA SEGRETA, SOMMARI

443. Cartelle 1560 - 1561 (1461-99): Bologna, Firenze, Francia, Genova, Germania, Lucca, Lunigiana, Napoli, Oltre Po, Pisa.

CANCELLERIA SEGRETA, CIFRARI

444. Cart.1591: selections, 15th cent.

445. Cart.1597: selections, 15th cent.

CARTEGGIO INTERNO

446. Inventario No.1 (old and revision, 1972): Carteggio Interno e Carteggio Estero (Potenze Estere).

MILANO CITTA' E DUCATO

446.1. Cart.664 (1454 Jan. - Dec. + undated).

446.2. Cart.665 (1455 Jan. - Dec.).

446.3. Cart.666 (1456 Jan. - Dec.).

446.4. Cart.667 (1457 Jan. - Dec.).

446.5. Cart.668 (1458 Jan. - Dec.).

446.6. Cart.669 (1459 Jan. - Dec.).

446.7. Cart.670 (1460 Jan. - Dec. + undated).

446.8. Cart.671 (1461 Jan. - Dec. + undated).

447. Cart.880 (1467 May - June).

MILANO CITTA'

447.1. Cart.1083 (1453-54), 1456-57, 1461-65, 1468, 1474-76, 1478, 1479 Jan. - Dec. + undated; carte di Cicco Simonetta).

CARTEGGIO ESTERO (POTENZE ESTERE)

448. Cart.1201 [Miscellanea]: Napoli, 1468-1513; Marca, 1460-98; Mirandola, 1495; Monferrato, 1474-77; Francia, 1475-99; Lunigiana, 1470-1534; Mantova, 1455-1535;

Ferrara, 1466; Lucca, 1471-99; Inghilterra, 1471-98; Carpi, 1452-83; Firenze, 1477, 1497-98; Correggio, 1466-83; Guastalla, 1470-97; Francia, 1452-98; Borgogna e Fiandra, 1468-78; Alemagna, 1452-1531; Napoli, 1531; Asti, 1452-95; Polonia, 1533; Tunisi, 1535.

P. E. ALEMAGNA

449. Cartt.569-571 (1450-73).

450. Cart. 572 (1474-75).

451. Cart. 573 (1476-82).

452. Cart. 575 (1480, 1482-85).

453. Cartt.576-577 (1486-90).

454. Cart. 578 (1490-93).

455. Cart. 579 (1494 + undated).

456. Cart. 580 (1495 Jan.-June).

457. Cart. 581 (1495 July-Dec.+ undated).

458. Cart. 590 (undated).

459. Cart. 591 (Istruzioni ca.1468-ca.1535).

460. Cart. 933 (1469-83).

461. Cart. 1331 (Istruzioni ca.1468-ca.1535).

P. E. ARAGONA E SPAGNA

462. Cart.652 (1452, 1455-66).

463. Cart.653 (1467-95 + undated).

464. Cart.656 (1465-99, 1513, 1535 + undated).

465. Cart.1061 (1469-76,1478-79)

465.1. Cart.l203 (1494-1497 Mar.).

P. E. ASTI

466. Cart.476 (1452-65 + undated).

467. Cart.477 (1466-1531+ undated)

468. Cart.933 (1469-83).

P. E. BORGOGNA E FIANDRE

469. Cart.514 (1452-65).

470. Cart.515 (1466-74).

471. Cart.516 (1475 Feb.-June).

472. Cart.517 (1475 July-Dec.).

473. Cart.518 (1476 Jan.-Mar.).

474. Cart.519 (1476 Apr.-May).

475. Cart.520 (1476 June-Nov.+ undated).

476. Cart.521 (filmed 1477-80, 1494).

477. Cart.523 (undated).

P. E. FERRARA

478. Cart.318 (1450-53 + undated).
479. Cart.319 (1454-57).
480. Cart.320 (1458-60).
481. Cart.321 (1461-67).
482. Cart.322 (1468-70).
483. Cart.323 (1471-75).
484. Cart.324 (1476-79).
485. Cart.325 (1480 Jan.-Dec.).
486. Cart.326 (1481 Jan.-Dec.).
487. Cart.327 (1482 Jan.-May).
488. Cart.328 (1482 June-Dec.).
489. Cart.329 (1483 Jan.-Aug.).
490. Cart.330 (1483 Sept.-1484 Dec.).
491. Cart.331 (1485-89).
492. Cart.333 (1490-92).
493. Cart.334 (1493-94).
494. Cart.335 (1495 Jan.-June).
495. Cart.336 (1495 July-1496 Apr.).

P. E. FIRENZE

496. Cart.265 (1450 May-1451 Dec.).
497. Cart.266 (1452 Jan.-1453 Dec. + undated).
498. Cart.267 (1454 Jan.-Dec.).
499. Cart.268 (1455 Jan.-1456 Dec. + undated).
500. Cart.269 (1457 Jan.-1458 Dec. + undated).
501. Cart.270 (1459 Jan.-1462 Dec.).
502. Cart.271 (1463 Jan.-1464 Dec.).
503. Cart.272 (1465 Jan.-1466 Dec.).
504. Cart.273 (1467 Jan.-Dec.).
505. Cart.274 (1468 Jan.-June).
506. Cart.275 (1468 July-Dec.).
507. Cart.276 (1469 Jan.-July).
508. Cart.277 (1469 Aug.-Dec.).
509. Cart.278 (1470 Jan.-Apr.).
510. Cart.279 (1470 May-Aug.).
511. Cart.280 (1470 Sept.-Dec.).
512. Cart.281 (1471 Jan.-July).
513. Cart.282 (1471 Aug.-Dec.).
514. Cart.283 (1472 Jan.-Dec. + minute di lettere, 1469-73).
515. Cart.284 (1473 Jan.-Apr. + undated).

516. Cart.285 (1473 May-Dec.).

517. Cart.286 (1474 Jan.-June).

518. Cart.287 (1474 July-Sept.).

519. Cart.288 (1474 Oct.-Dec. + minutario, Aug.11-Dec.27).

520. Cart.289 (1475 Jan.-June + minutario, 1474 Dec.27-1475 Apr.9).

521. Cart.290 (1475 July-Dec. + minutario, 1475 July 23-1476 Jan.2).

522. Cart.291 (1476 Jan.-Dec.).

523. Cart.292 (1477 Jan.-Oct.).

524. Cart.293 (1477 Nov.-Dec. + minutario, 1477 Jan.1-Dec.30).

525. Cart.294 (1478 Jan.-May).

526. Cart.295 (1478 June-Aug.+ minutario, May 6-June 7).

527. Cart.296 (1478 Sept.-Dec.).

528. Cart.297 (1479 Jan.-May).

529. Cart.298 (1479 June-Dec.).

530. Cart.299 (1480 Jan.-June + minutario, May 30-June 10).

531. Cart.300 (1480 July-Sept.).

532. Cart.301 (1480 Oct.-Dec.).

533. Cart.302 (1481 Jan.-June + copiario, 1480 Oct. 12-1481 Jan. 1).

534. Cart.303 (1481 July-Dec.).

535. Cart.304 (1482 Jan.-Apr.).

536. Cart.305 (1482 May-Dec.).

537. Cart.306 (1483 Jan.-Dec.+ undated).

538. Cart.307 (1484 Jan.-Dec.).

539. Cart.308 (1485 Jan.-Dec.).

540. Cart.309 (1486 Jan.-Dec.).

541. Cart.310 (1487 Apr.-1489 Dec. + undated).

542. Cart.311 (1490 Jan.-Aug.).

543. Cart.312 (1490 Sept.-1491 Aug.).

544. Cart.937 (1491 Sept.-1492 June + undated).

545. Cart.938 (1492 July-Dec.+ undated).

546. Cart.939 (1493 Jan.-Dec.).

547. Cart.940 (1494 Jan.-Dec.).

548. Cart.941 (1495 Jan.-Dec.+ undated).

549. Cart.953 (undated: fascicles 2-3, 11-12).

P. E. FRANCIA

550. Cart.524 (1451 Mar.-1459 Dec. + undated).

551. Cart.525 (1460 Jan.-1461 July + undated).

552. Cart.526 (1461 Aug.-Dec. sel.).

553. Cart.527 (1462 Jan.-Dec. sel.).

554. Cart.528 (1463-64 sel.).

555. Cart.529 (1465 Jan.-Sept. sel.).

556. Cart.530 (1465 Oct.-Dec. sel.).

557. Cart.531 (1466 Jan.-Mar.8 + undated sel.).
558. Cart.532 (1466 Mar.3-Dec. + undated).
559. Cart.533 (1467 Jan.-Dec. + undated).
560. Cart.534 (1468 Jan.-Sept.).
561. Cart.535 (1468 Oct.-Dec. + undated).
562. Cart.536 (1469 Jan.-Dec.).
563. Cart.537 (1470 Jan.-Dec.).
564. Cart.538 (1471 Jan.-Dec.).
565. Cart.539 (1472 Jan.-Dec. + undated).
566. Cart.540 (1473 Jan.-Dec.).
567. Cart.541 (1474 Jan.-Dec.).
568. Cart.542 (1475 Jan.-1476 Dec.).
569. Cart.543 (1477 Jan.-1478 Dec. + undated).
570. Cart.544 (1479 Jan.-Dec.).
571. Cart.545 (1480-83 + undated).
572. Cart.546 (1484-89 + undated).
573. Cart.547 (1490 Jan.-Dec. + undated).
574. Cart.548 (1491 Jan.-Dec.).
575. Cart.549 (1492 Jan.-Apr.).
576. Cart.550 (1492 May-1493 June + undated).
577. Cart.551 (1493 July-Dec.+ undated).
578. Cart.552 (1494 Jan.-Apr.+ undated).
579. Cart.553 (1494 May-June).
580. Cart.554 (1494 July-Dec.+ undated).
581. Cart.555 (1495 Jan.-Dec.+ undated).
582. Cart.559 (1452, 1464-69, 1479, 1493-94, 1496 + undated).
583. Cart.560 (1473, 1475 + undated).
584. Cart.561 (1450-98, 1461-94?, 1496-98, 1534 + undated).
585. Cart.562 (1462-1512 + undated).
586. Cart.563 (1483-96 + undated).
587. Cart.564 (1483-1551 + undated).
588. Cart.565 (1447-1535? + undated).
589. Cart.1312 (1469-83).

P. E. GENOVA

590-1. Cart.407 (1450-52).
592-3. Cart.408 (1453 Jan.-Dec.).
594. Cart.409 (1454 Jan.-Dec.).
595. Cart.410 (1455 Jan.-Dec.).
596. Cart.411 (1456 Jan.-Sept.).
597. Cart.412 (1456 Oct.-Dec.; 1457-58).
598. Cart.413 (1459-60).
599. Cart.414 (1461 Jan.-Dec.).

600. Cart.415 (1462 Jan.-Aug.).
601. Cart.416 (1462 Sept.-Dec.; 1463 Jan.-June).
602. Cart.417 (1463 July-Dec.; 1464 Jan.-Feb.).
603. Cart.418 (1464 Mar.-May).
604. Cart.419 (1464 June-Aug.).
605. Cart.420 (1464 Sept.-Dec.).
606. Cart.421 (1465 Jan.-Mar.).
607. Cart.422 (1465 Apr.-June).
608. Cart.423 (1465 July-Sept.).
609. Cart.424 (1465 Oct.-Dec.).
610. Cart.425 (1466 Jan.-Mar.).
611. Cart.426 (1466 Apr.-June).
612. Cart.427 (1466 July-Sept.).
613. Cart.428 (1466 Oct.-Dec.).
614. Cart.429 (1467 Jan.-Mar.).
615. Cart.430 (1467 Apr.-June).
616. Cart.431 (1467 July-Sept.).
617. Cart.432 (1467 Oct.-Dec.).
618. Cart.433 (1468 Jan.-Apr.).
619. Cart.434 (1468 May-July).
620. Cart.435 (1468 Aug.-Oct.).
621. Cart.436 (1468 Nov.-Dec.; 1469 Jan.-Feb.).
622. Cart.437 (1469 Mar.-June).
623. Cart.438 (1469 July-Oct.).
624. Cart.439 (1469 Nov.-Dec.; 1470 Jan.-Mar.).
625. Cart.440 (1470 Apr.-July).
626. Cart.441 (1470 Aug.-Dec.).
627. Cart.442 (1471 Jan.-Apr.).
628. Cart.443 (1471 May-Aug.).
629. Cart.444 (1471 Sept.-Dec.).
630. Cart.445 (1472 Jan.-Apr.).
631. Cart.446 (1472 May-Aug.).
632. Cart.447 (1472 Sept.-Dec.).
633. Cart.448 (1473 Jan.-Mar.).
634. Cart.449 (1473 Apr.-June).
635. Cart.450 (1473 July-Sept.).
636. Cart.451 (1473 Oct.-Dec.).
637. Cart.452 (1474 Jan.-Mar.).
638. Cart.453 (1474 Apr.-May).
639. Cart.454 (1474 June-July).
640. Cart.455 (1474 Aug.-Sept.).
641. Cart.456 (1474 Oct.-Dec.).
642. Cart.457 (1475 Jan.-Mar.).

643. Cart.458 (1475 Apr.-May).
644. Cart.459 (1475 June-July).
645. Cart.961 (1475 Aug.-Sept.).
646. Cart.962 (1475 Oct.-Dec.).
647. Cart.963 (1476 Jan.-Apr.).
648. Cart.964 (1476 May-July).
649. Cart.965 (1476 Aug.-Dec.).
650. Cart.966 (1477 January).
651. Cart.967 (1477 February).
652. Cart.968 (1477 March).
653. Cart.969 (1477 April).
654. Cart.970 (1477 May).
655. Cart.971 (1477 June).
656. Cart.972 (1477 July).
657. Cart.973 (1477 August).
658. Cart.974 (1477 September).
659. Cart.975 (1477 Oct.-Dec.).
660. Cart.976 (1478 January).
661. Cart.977 (1478 February).
662. Cart.978 (1478 March).
663. Cart.980 (1478 April).
664. Cart.981 (1478 May).
665. Cart.982 (1478 June).
666. Cart.983 (1478 July).
667. Cart.984 (1478 August).
668. Cart.985 (1478 September).
669. Cart.986 (1478 October).
670. Cart.987 (1478 November).
671. Cart.988 (1478 December).
672. Cart.989 (1479 Jan.-May).
673. Cart.990 (1479 June-Dec.).
674. Cart.991 (1480 Jan.-June).
675. Cart.992 (1480 July-Dec.; 1481)
676. Cart.993 (1482).
677. Cart.994 (1483-85).
678. Cart.995 (1486-90 Mar.).
679. Cart.996 (1490 Apr.-July).
680. Cart.997 (1490 Aug.-Dec.).
681. Cart.998 (1491 Jan.-July).
682. Cart.999 (1491 Aug.-Dec.).
683. Cart.1209 (1492 Jan.-July).
684. Cart.1210 (1492 Aug.-Dec.).
685. Cart.1211 (1493).

686. Cart.1212 (1494, 1495 Jan.-Feb.).

687. Cart.1319 (undated).

688. Cart.1514 (1408-71 + undated).

P. E. ILLIRIA, POLONIA, RUSSIA, SLAVONIA

688.1. Cart.640 (Illiria: Cilli, 1453; Spalato, 1464; Veglia, 1454-1466; Ragusa, 1454-1499). (Polonia, 1461-1531). (Russia, 1450-1493). (Slavonia: Bosnia, 1458-1474 +undated; Serbia, 1461-1498).

P. E. INGHILTERRA E SCOZIA

689. Cart.566 (1458, 1460-62, 1465?, + undated).

690. Cart.567 (1467, 1469-71, 1475-76, 1484, 1486-92, 1494, 1496-97).

P. E. LUCCA

691. Cart.314 (1451-79).

691.1. Cart.1594 (1480-1485, 1489-1497).

P. E. LUNIGIANA

692. Cart.315 (1452-66).

693. Cart.316 (1467-70).

694. Cart.317 (1471-76).

695. Cart.1000 (1477-78).

696. Cart.1001 (1479 Jan.-Apr.).

697. Cart.1002 (1479 May-Dec.).

698. Cart.1003 (1480).

699. Cart.1004 (1481-82).

700. Cart.1006 (1483-84).

701. Cart.1232 (1485-87, 1489-95).

P. E. MANTOVA

702. Cart.390 (1450-55).

703. Cart.391 (1456-1459 May).

704. Cart.392 (1459 June-Sept.).

705. Cart.393 (1459 Oct.-Dec.).

706. Cart.394 (1460-65).

707. Cart.395 (1466-74).

708. Cart.396 (1475-1480).

709. Cart.397 (1478-82).

710. Cart.398 (1483-84).

711. Cart.399 (1485-95).

712. Cart.1013 (1469-80).

P. E. Marca (Marche)

713. Cart.143 (1450-58 + undated).
714. Cart.144 (1459 Jan.-1460 Mar.).
715. Cart.145 (1460 Apr.-1461 Dec. + undated).
716. Cart.146 (1462 Jan.-1464 Dec. + undated).
717. Cart.147 (1465 Jan.-1469 Oct.).
718. Cart.148 (1470 Jan.-1475 Nov. + undated).
719. Cart.149 (1476 Feb.-1479 Dec.).
720. Cart.150 (1480 Jan.-1482 Dec. + undated).
721. Cart.151 (1483 Jan.-1489 Nov.).
722. Cart.152 (1490 Jan.-1492 Dec.).
723. Cart.153 (1493 Feb.-1497 Dec. + undated).

P. E. Monaco

723.1. Cart.460 (1451-1469).
724.   Cart.461 (1470-1477).
724.1. Cart.462 (1478-1576 + undated).

P. E. Monferrato

725. Cart.464 (1450-56).
726. Cart.465 (1457-66 + undated).
727. Cart.466 (1466-70).
728. Cart.467 (1471-77).
729. Cart.468 (1478).
730. Cart.469 (1479).
731. Cart.470 (1480-82; one doc. 1479).
732. Cart.471-472 (1483-94).
733. Cart.475 (undated).
734. Cart.1017 (1469-77).
735. Cart.1019 (1478-83).
736. Cart.1238 (1484-1497 June).

P. E. Napoli

737. Cart.195 (1450-54; 1455 Jan.-Dec.).
738. Cart.196 (1456 Jan.-Dec. + undated).
739. Cart.197 (1457 Jan.-Dec. + undated).
740. Cart.198 (1458 Jan.-Aug.).
741. Cart.199 (1458 Sept.-Dec. + undated).
742. Cart.200 (1459 Jan.-June).
743. Cart.201 (1459 July-Dec.).
744. Cart.202 (1460 Jan.-Apr.).

745. Cart.203 (1460 May-July).
746. Cart.204 (1460 Aug.-Oct.).
747. Cart.205 (1460 Nov.-1461 Feb. + undated).
748. Cart.206 (1461 Mar.-July).
749. Cart.207 (1461 Aug.-Dec.).
750. Cart.208 (1462 Jan.-June).
751. Cart.209 (1462 July-Dec.).
752. Cart.210 (1463 Jan.-June).
753. Cart.211 (1463 July-Dec.).
754. Cart.212 (1464 Jan.-July).
755. Cart.213 (1464 Aug.-Dec.).
756. Cart.214 (1465 Jan.-July).
757. Cart.215 (1465 Aug.-1466 Dec.+ undated).
758. Cart.216 (1467 Jan.-Dec.).
759. Cart.217 (1468 Jan.-Dec.).
760. Cart.218 (1469 Jan.-1470 June).
761. Cart.219 (1470 July-Dec.).
762. Cart.220 (1471 Jan.-Dec.).
763. Cart.221 (1472 Jan.-Apr.).
764. Cart.222 (1472 May-Sept.).
765. Cart.223 (1472 Oct.-1473 Apr.).
766. Cart.224 (1473 May-Oct.).
767. Cart.225 (1473 Nov.-1474 June).
768. Cart.226 (1474 July-Dec.).
769. Cart.227 (1475 Jan.-Dec.).
770. Cart.228 (1476 Jan.-1478 Dec.).
771. Cart.229 (1479 Jan.-1480 Mar.).
772. Cart.230 (1480 Apr.-July).
773. Cart.231 (1480 Aug.-Oct. + undated).
774. Cart.232 (1480 Nov.-1481 Apr.).
775. Cart.233 (1481 May-June).
776. Cart.234 (1481 July-Aug.).
777. Cart.235 (1481 Sept.-Oct.).
778. Cart.236 (1481 Nov.-Dec. + undated).
779. Cart.237 (1482 Jan.-Feb.).
780. Cart.238 (1482 Mar.-Apr.).
781. Cart.239 (1482 May-June).
782. Cart.240 (1482 July-Oct.).
783. Cart.241 (1482 Nov.-1483 Apr.).
784. Cart.242 (1483 May-Dec.).
785. Cart.243 (1484 Jan.-May).
786. Cart.244 (1484 June-Dec. + undated).
787. Cart.245 (1485 Jan.-July).

788. Cart.246 (1485 Aug.-Dec.).
789. Cart.247 (1486 Jan.-1489 Dec.).
790. Cart.248 (1490 Jan.-Dec.).
791. Cart.249 (1491 Jan.-Dec. + undated).
792. Cart.250 (1492 Jan.-Dec.).
793. Cart.251 (1493 Jan.-Dec.).
794. Cart.252 (1494 Jan.-1495 Feb.).
795. Cart.253 (1495 Mar.-Dec. + undated).
796. Cart.1248 (ca.1454-ca.1499).
797. Cart.1249 (undated).
798. Cart.1250 (undated).

P. E. PIOMBINO

799. Cart.313 (1453-56, 1458-60, 1462-66, 1468-71, 1476-78, 1483-90, 1492-98 + undated).

P. E. ROMA

800. Cart.40 (1450 Mar.-1453 Dec.).
801. Cart.41 (1454 Jan.1-1455 Jun. 30).
802. Cart.42 (1455 July 2-Nov. 30).
803. Cart.43 (1455 Dec.1-1456 Apr.30).
804. Cart.44 (1456 May 1-Dec. + undated).
805. Cart.45 (1457 Jan.2-Aug.31).
806. Cart.46 (1457 Sept.3-1458 Apr.30).
807. Cart.47 (1458 May 1-Dec.31).
808. Cart.48 (1459 Jan.3-1460 Oct.31).
809. Cart.49 (1460 Nov.1-1461 Jan.31 + undated 1460).
810. Cart.50 (1461 Feb.1-May 31).
811. Cart.51 (1461 June 1-Oct.31 + undated).
812. Cart.52 (1461 Nov.2-1462 Feb.28 + undated 1461).
813. Cart.53 (1462 Mar.1-Dec.31 + undated).
814. Cart.54 (1463 Jan.1-May 31).
815. Cart.55 (1463 June 1-Dec.31 + undated).
816. Cart.56 (1464 Jan.1-Oct.31).
817. Cart.57 (1464 Nov.2-1465 Jun.29).
818. Cart.58 (1465 July 1-1466 Mar.8 + undated 1465).
819. Cart.59 (1466 Mar.9-June 30).
820. Cart.60 (1466 July 1-Oct.31).
821. Cart.61 (1466 Nov.1-1467 Mar.31).
822. Cart.62 (1467 Apr.1-July 31).
823. Cart.63 (1467 Aug.1-Dec.31).
824. Cart.64 (1468 Jan.1-Apr.30 + undated).
825. Cart.65 (1468 May 1-Dec.31).

826. Cart.66 (1469 Jan.-Dec.; 1470 Jan.-Dec.).
827. Cart.67 (1471 Jan.2-July 31).
828. Cart.68 (1471 Aug.1-Dec.31).
829. Cart.69 (1472 Jan.1-Apr.30).
830. Cart.70 (1472 May 1-Aug.30).
831. Cart.71 (1472 Sept.1-Dec.31 + undated).
832. Cart.72 (1473 Jan.1-June 30).
833. Cart.73 (1473 July 2-Nov.30).
834. Cart.74 (1473 Dec.1-1474 Feb.28).
835. Cart.75 (1474 Mar.1-Apr.30).
836. Cart.76 (1474 May 1-July 31).
837. Cart.77 (1474 Aug.1-Nov.30).
838. Cart.78 (1474 Dec.1-1475 Apr.30).
839. Cart.79 (1475 May 1-Dec.31 + undated).
840. Cart.80 (1476 Jan.2-Mar.31).
841. Cart.81 (1476 Apr.1-June 26).
842. Cart.82 (1476 July 1-Dec.30 + undated).
843. Cart.83 (1477 Jan.1-July 31).
844. Cart.84 (1477 Aug.2-Dec.31).
845. Cart.85 (1478 Jan.1-May 31).
846. Cart.86 (1478 June 1-Dec.31 + undated; 1479 Jan.16-Dec.21 + undated).
847. Cart.87 (1480 Jan.1-Aug.31).
848. Cart.88 (1480 Sept.1-1481 Mar.30).
849. Cart.89 (1481 Apr.1-Aug.31).
850. Cart.90 (1481 Sept.1-Dec.31).
851. Cart.91 (1482 Jan.2-Nov.27).
852. Cart.92 (1482 Dec.1-31 + undated; 1483 Jan.1-Mar.31).
853. Cart.93 (1483 Apr.1-Aug.31).
854. Cart.94 (1483 Sept.1-Dec.29 + undated).
855. Cart.95 (1484 Jan.1-May 30).
856. Cart.96 (1484 June 1-Dec.31).
857. Cart.97 (1485 Jan.3-June 30).
858. Cart.98 (1485 July 2-Oct.30).
859. Cart.99 (1485 Nov.1-Dec.31; 1486 Jan.14-Dec.30).
860. Cart.100 (1487 Jan.6-Dec.27; 1488 Jan.1-Dec.20; 1489 Jan.25-Dec.31).
861. Cart.101 (1490 Jan.1-Apr.30).
862. Cart.102 (1490 May 1-Dec.30).
863. Cart.103 (1491 Jan.1-June 28 + undated).
864. Cart.104 (1491 July 1-Dec.29 + undated).
865. Cart.105 (1492 Jan.4-June 28).
866. Cart.106 (1492 July 1-Dec.29).
867. Cart.107 (1493 Jan.9-Dec.30; 1491-93 undated).
868. Cart.108 (1494 Jan.2-Mar.31).

869. Cart.109 (1494 Apr.1-May 31 + undated).

870. Cart.110 (1494 June 2-July 31 + undated).

871. Cart.111 (1494 Aug.1-Dec.31 + undated).

872. Cart.112 (1495 Jan.1-Apr.30).

873. Cart.113 (1495 May 2-Aug.31).

874. Cart.114 (1495 Sept.2-Dec.31 + undated).

875. Cart.1202 (1456 - 1513).

876. Cart.1303 (15th cent., undated, selections).

877. Cart.1304 (15th cent., undated, selections).

P. E. ROMAGNA

878. Cart.155 (1450 May-1453 Dec.).

879. Cart.156 (1454 Jan.-1455 May).

880. Cart.157 (1455 June-1457 Dec.).

881. Cart.158 (1458 Jan.-1459 Sept.).

882. Cart.159 (1459 Oct.-1460 Mar.).

883. Cart.160 (1460 Apr.-Dec.).

884. Cart.161 (1461 Jan.-Dec.).

885. Cart.162 (1462 Jan.-Dec.).

886. Cart.163 (1463 Jan.-Dec.).

887. Cart.164 (1464 Jan.-1465 May).

888. Cart.165 (1465 June-1466 Mar.).

889. Cart.166 (1466 Apr.-1467 Apr.).

890. Cart.167 (1467 May-July).

891. Cart.168 (1467 Aug.-Dec.).

892. Cart.169 (1468 Jan.-1469 May).

893. Cart.170 (1469 June-Dec.).

894. Cart.171 (1470 Jan.-July).

895. Cart.172 (1470 Aug.-1471 Jan.).

896. Cart.173 (1471 Feb.-June).

897. Cart.174 (1471 July-Oct.).

898. Cart.175 (1471 Nov.-1472 Jan.).

899. Cart.176 (1472 Feb.-May).

900. Cart.177 (1472 June-Nov.).

901. Cart.178 (1472 Dec.-1473 Apr.).

902. Cart.179 (1473 May-Aug.; copiario May-Dec.).

903. Cart.180 (1473 Sept.-Dec. + undated)

904. Cart.181 (1474 Jan.-Mar.; copiario Mar.-Oct.).

905. Cart.182 (1474 Apr.-June).

906. Cart.183 (1474 July-Dec.).

907. Cart.184 (1475 Jan.-Dec. + undated).

908. Cart.185 (1476 Jan.-Dec.).

909. Cart.186 (1477 Jan.-Oct.).

910. Cart.187 (1477 Nov.-1478 Sept.).
911. Cart.188 (1478 Oct.-1479 Aug.).
912. Cart.189 (1479 Sept.-1480 May).
913. Cart.190 (1480 June-Oct.).
914. Cart.191 (1480 Nov.-1481 June).
915. Cart.192 (1481 July-1482 May).
916. Cart.193 (1482 June-Dec.).
917. Cart.194 (1483 Jan.-Dec.).
918. Cart.1039 (1484 Jan.-1488 Dec.).
919. Cart.1040 (1489 Mar.-1491 Aug.)
920. Cart.1041 (1491 Sept.-1492 Mar.).
921. Cart.1042 (1492 Apr.-Dec.).
922. Cart.1043 (1493 Jan.-1494 June).
923. Cart.1044 (1494 July-Dec.).
924. Cart.1045 (1495 Jan.-Dec.).

P. E. ROMAGNA-VENEZIA

925. Cart.1199 [Miscellanea]. (1452-1535).

P. E. SAVOIA

926. Cart.478 (1450-57).
927. Cart.479 (1458-59).
928. Cart.480 (1460-63).
929. Cart.481 (1464-66 Mar.4).
930. Cart.482 (1466 Mar.10-1467).
931. Cart.483 (1468-69).
932. Cart.484 (1470).
933. Cart.485 (1471 Jan.-Aug.).
934. Cart.486 (1471 Sept.-Dec. + undated).
935. Cart.487 (1472 Jan.-Apr.).
936. Cart.488 (1472 May-Aug.).
937. Cart.489 (1472 Sept.-Dec. + undated)
938. Cart.490 (1473 Jan.-Dec.).
939. Cart.491 (1474 Jan.-Dec.).
940. Cart.492 (1475 Jan.-June).
941. Cart.493 (1475 July-Dec.).
942. Cart.494 (1476 Jan.-Mar.).
943. Cart.495 (1476 Apr.-June).
944. Cart.496 (1476 July-Sept.).
945. Cart.497 (1476 Oct.-Dec. + undated).
946. Cart.498 (1477 Jan.-Dec.).
947. Cart.499 (1478-79).

948. Cart.500 (1480-84).
949. Cart.501 (1485-89).
950. Cart.502 (1490 Jan.-Aug.).
951. Cart.503 (1490 Sept.-1491 Dec.)
952. Cart.504 (1492-95).
953. Cart.512 (undated).
954. Cart.513 (undated).
955. Cart.1060 (1469-83).
956. Cart.1258 (1484-96).
957. Cart.1259 (undated).
958. Cart.1261 (undated).
959. Cart.1322 (15th cent.: undated fragments).

P. E. SIENA

960. Cart.255 (1450-1455 July).
961. Cart.256 (1455 Aug.-1456 Dec.).
962. Cart.257 (1457 Jan.-1458 Dec.).
963. Cart.258 (1459 Jan.-1460 Feb.).
964. Cart.259 (1460 Mar.-May).
965. Cart.260 (1460 June-July).
966. Cart.261 (1460 Aug.-Dec.).
967. Cart.262 (1461 Jan.-1462 Aug.).
968. Cart.263 (1462 Sept.-1463 June).
969. Cart.264 (1464 Jan.-1467 Dec.).
970. Cart.1262 (1468 Jan.-1482 Nov.).
971. Cart.1263 (1483 Mar.-1496 Dec.)

P. E. SVIZZERA

972. Cart.592 (1450-66).
973. Cart.593 (1467-70).
974. Cart.594 (1471-77).
975. Cart.595 (1478 Jan.-Nov.).
976. Cart.596 (1478 Dec.).
977. Cart.597 (1479 Jan.-July).
978. Cart.598 (1479 Aug.-Dec. + undated).
979. Cart.599 (1480 Jan.-Dec. + undated).
980. Cart.600 (1481-82).
981. Cart.601 (1483 Jan.-Dec.).
982. Cart.602 (1484 Jan.-Dec.).
983. Cart.603 (1485 Jan.-Dec. + undated).
984. Cart.604 (1486 Jan.-Dec.).
985. Cart.605 (1487 Jan.-Dec.).

986. Cart.606 (1488 Jan.-Dec.).
987. Cart.607 (1489-1490 May).
988. Cart.608 (1490 June-Dec.).
989. Cart.609 (1491 Jan.-Dec. + undated).
990. Cart.610 (1492 Jan.-Dec.).
991. Cart.611 (1493 Jan.-Dec. + undated).
992. Cart.612 (1494 Jan.-May).
993. Cart.613 (1494 June-Dec. + undated).
994. Cart.1318 (undated, 15th-16th cent.).
995. Cart.1335 (undated, 15th-16th, 18th? cent.).

P. E. UMBRIA E SABINIA

996. Cart.139 (1452-61).
997. Cart.140 (1462-66 + undated).
998. Cart.141 (1467-68, 1470-83, 1485, 1491, 1493-94, 1496-99 + undated).

P. E. UNGHERIA

998.1. Cart.642 (1490 Jan.-Nov. + undated).
998.2. Cart.645 (1491-1497, 1513, 1514, 1524, 1530, 1533-1535, 1537, + undated).
998.3. Cart.650 (1452-1489 + undated).

P. E. VENEZIA

999. Cart.340 (1450 Mar.-1453 Dec.).
1000. Cart.341 (1454 Jan.-Dec. + undated).
1001. Cart.342 (1455 Jan.-Dec. + undated).
1002. Cart.343 (1456 Jan.-Dec.).
1003. Cart.344 (1457 Jan.-Dec.).
1004. Cart.345 (1458 Jan.-Dec.).
1005. Cart.346 (1459 Jan.-Dec.).
1006. Cart.347 (1460 Jan.-Dec.).
1007. Cart.348 (1461 Jan.-Dec. + undated).
1008. Cart.349 (1462 Jan.-Dec. + undated).
1009. Cart.350 (1463 Jan.-Dec.).
1010. Cart.351 (1464 Jan.-Dec.).
1011. Cart.352 (1465 Jan.-1466 Mar.5 + undated).
1012. Cart.353 (1466 Mar.9-1467 Dec.).
1013. Cart.354 (1468 Jan.-1469 Dec.).
1014. Cart.355 (1470 Jan.-Dec.).
1015. Cart.356 (1471 Jan.-Dec.).
1016. Cart.357 (1472 Jan.-1473 Dec.).
1017. Cart.358 (1474 Jan.-June).
1018. Cart.359 (1474 July-Dec.).
1019. Cart.360 (1475 Jan.-June).

1020. Cart.361 (1475 July-Dec. + undated).

1021. Cart.362 (1476 Jan.-Dec.).

1022. Cart.363 (1477 Jan.-July).

1023. Cart.364 (1477 Aug.-Dec.).

1024. Cart.1062 (1477 Jan.-Dec.).

1025. Cart.365 (1478 Jan.-Dec.).

1026. Cart.1063 (1478 Jan.-1480 Dec.)

1027. Cart.366 (1479 Jan.-Dec.).

1028. Cart.368 (1480 Jan.-Dec. + undated).

1029-30. Cart.369 (1481 Jan.-1485 Dec. + undated).

1031. Cart.370 (1480 Jan.-Dec. + undated).

1032. Cart.1064 (1483 Aug.-Dec.).

1033. Cart.375 (1486-1490 June).

1034. Cart.376 (1490 June-Dec.).

1035. Cart.377 (1491 Jan.-Aug.).

1036. Cart.378 (1491 Sept.-Dec. + undated).

1037. Cart.379 (1492 Jan.-Dec. + undated).

1038. Cart.380 (1493 Jan.-May).

1039. Cart.381 (1493 June-Dec.).

1040. Cart.382 (1494 Jan.-Dec.).

1041. Cart.383 (1495 Jan.-June).

1042. Cart.384 (1495 July-Dec. + undated 1492-95).

1043. Cart.1268 (1498 Jan.-July).

1044. Cart.1270 (1498 Aug.-Dec.).

1045. Cart.1314 (15th-16th cent. + undated: istruzioni).
1046. Cart.1315 (Miscellanea con dati riguardanti la Cancelleria, 1460 e successivamente. Istanza di Francesco Sforza per l'investitura del Ducato, 1457).

TRATTATI

1047. Perletti Stefania, "La serie Trattati dell'Archivio Ducale (Sforzeco) relativamente ai rapporti con i Cantoni svizzeri, i Grigioni e il Vallese." Tesi di laurea. Milano, Università degli Studi, Facoltà di Lettere e Filosofia, 1968-69.

1048. Cart.1526 (1455-56 selections).

1049. Cart.1527 (1457-58 selections).

1050. Cart.1528 (1459-61 selections).

1051. Cart.1529 (1462-64 selections).

1052. Cart.1530 (1464-66 selections).

1053. Cart.1531 (1467 Jan.-Apr. selections).

1054. Cart.1532 (1467 May-1468 May).

1055. Cart.1533 (1468 June-Nov.).

1056. Cart.1534 (1468 Dec.-1469 Dec.).

1057. Cart.1535 (1470 Jan.-Oct.).

1058. Cart.1536 (1470 Mar.20).

1059. Cart.1537 (1470 Mar.20).

1060. Cart.1538 (1470 Nov.-1471 July).

1061. Cart.1539 (1471 Aug.-1472 Dec.)

1062. Cart.1540 (1473 Jan.-Dec.).

1063. Cart.1541 (1474 Jan.-Dec.).

1064. Cart.1542 (1475-76).

1065. Cart.1543 (1477 Jan.-Oct.).

1066. Cart.1544 (1477 Nov.-1478 Nov.).

1067. Cart.1545 (1479 Jan.-1480 Apr.)

1068. Cart.1546 (1480 May-Dec.).

1069. Cart.1547 (1481 Jan.-Dec.).

1070. Cart.1548 (1482 Jan.-1483 Dec.).

1071. Cart.1549 (1484 Jan.-Dec.).

1072. Cart.1550 (1485-87).

1073. Cart.1551 (1488-90).

1074. Cart.1552 (1491-94).

ARCHIVIO SFORZESCO DUCALE, REGISTRI

REGISTRI DUCALI

1075. Inventario No.3. Registri Ducali (Per ordine cronologico).

1076. Reg.2 (1183-1480). Privilegi del Ducato di Milano. Matrimoni e legittimazioni dei principi delle famiglie ducali.

1077. Reg.3 (1183-1469). Privilegi del Ducato di Milano. Matrimoni e legittimazioni dei principi delle famiglie ducali.

1078. Reg.4 (1460-70). Investiture, delegazioni, ambascerie, Duchessa Bianca.

1079. Reg.5 (1461-65). Lettere a principi ed oratori, Duca Francesco I.

1080. Reg.7 (1463-78). Donazioni, concessioni e feudi: Duchi Francesco I, Galeazzo Maria e Gian Galeazzo.

1081. Reg.13 (1467-70). Paci, ratificazioni ed aderenze: Bianca e Galeazzo.

1082. Reg.17 (1470-71). Aderenze, ratificazioni e leghe, Duca Galeazzo Maria.

1083. Reg.18 (1414-67). Leghe, paci ed altre cose d'importanza: Duchi Filippo Maria e Francesco I.

1084. Reg.22 (1474-78). Aderenze, trattati e ratificazioni, Duca Galeazzo Maria.

1085. Reg.24 (1454-73). Matrimoni, delegazioni, concessioni etc.: Duchi Francesco I e Galeazzo Maria.

1086. Reg.25 (1452-61). Trattazioni, carteggio con Roma, Duca Francesco I.

1087. Reg.32 (1477-87). Leghe, condotte, ratificazioni, donazioni ed altro: Duchessa Bona e Duca Gian Galeazzo.

1088. Reg.34 (1477-87). Vicende della famiglia ducale. Trattative e convenzioni diplomatiche, condotte etc.

1089. Reg.35 (1414-67). Paci, leghe e capitoli.

1090. Reg.37 (1426-74). Convenzioni colle Potenze italiane.

1091. Reg.39 (1433-81). Leghe, capitoli e convenzioni: Duchi Filippo Maria, Francesco I, Galeazzo Maria, Bianca Maria e Gian Galeazzo.

1092. Reg.42 (1454-58). Paci, leghe ed aderenze, Duca Francesco I.

1093. Reg.50 (1487-97). Trattazione coi genovesi.

1094. Reg.55 (1489-93). Trattazioni, Genova: Duca Gian Galeazzo.

1095. Reg.56 (1490-99). Trattazioni coi Grigioni, Svizzeri e Vallesani: Duchi Gian Galeazzo e Lodovico.

1096. Reg.105 (1468-70). Miscellanea di varii registri. Littere passus, lettere di giustizia etc.
1097. Reg.170 (1466-79). Castellani nel Genovesato. Istruzioni.
1098. Reg.171 (1466-81). Castellani, conestabili. Istruzioni.
1099. Reg.183 (1486-98). Oratori ducali: procure.
1100. Reg.195 (1440-53). Lettere e concessioni ducali.
1101. Reg.196 (1458-69). Lettere e concessioni ducali.
1102. Reg.197 (1470-74). Lettere e concessioni ducali.
1103. Reg.199 (1475-79). Lettere e concessioni ducali.
1104. Reg.200 (1487-99). Lettere e concessioni ducali.

REGISTRI DELLE MISSIVE

1105. Inventario No.5. Registri delle Missive.
1106. Reg.1 (1447 Sept.21-1458 Aug.7). Ordini di Francesco I ai Castellani.
1107. Reg.2 (1450 Feb.3-1451 June 15). Lettere diverse.
1108. Reg.3 (1450 Oct.5-1451 June 28). Lettere diverse.
1109. Reg.4 (1450 Dec.19-1451 Oct.23). Lettere diverse.
1110. Reg.5 (1451 June 11-Dec.17). Lettere diverse.
1111. Reg.6 (1451 June 10-Nov.4). Lettere diverse.
1112. Reg.7 (1451 July 22-1452 Dec.23). Cremona, Piacenza, Brescia, Mantova, Ferrara.
1113. Reg.8 (1451 Nov.20-1452 Apr.7). Lettere di giustizia.
1114. Reg.9 (1452 May 1-1464 July 18). Licenze ai Castellani.
1115. Reg.10 (1452 Apr.17-Dec.16). Lettere di giustizia.
1116. Reg.11 (1452 Mar.13-1453 May 21). Lettere di giustizia.
1117. Reg.12 (1451 Dec.26-1453 July 31). Pavia, Lodi, Bergamo, Geradadda etc.
1118. Reg.13 (1451 Oct.26-1453 Mar.31). Novara, Tortona, Alessandria, Genova, Asti, Monferrato ed estero.
1119. Reg.14 (1451 Dec.26-1453 June 18). Parma, Piacenza, Firenze, etc.
1120. Reg.15 (1452 Jan.7-1458 Dec.21). Lettere di pagamento.
1121. Reg.16 (1453 Aug.1-1454 Aug.26). Pavia, Lodi, Piacenza, Geradadda, Bergamo, etc.
1122. Reg.17 (1453 May 20-1454 Apr.18). Lettere di giustizia.
1123. Reg.18 (1453 Oct.24-1455 May 24). Lettere relative alla guerra con Venezia e Monferrato.
1124. Reg.19 (1453 June 18-1455 Nov.28). Piacenza, Parma, Pontremoli, Firenze.
1125. Reg.19bis (1453 Nov.4-1461 Sept.24). Missive a Firenze, etc.
1126. Reg.20 (1453 Mar.30-1456 Jan.19). Alessandria, Tortona, Genova ed estero.
1127. Reg.21 (1453 Oct.22-1457 Mar.18). Cremona, Brescia.
1128. Reg.22 (1454 Mar.12-Sept.7). Lettere di giustizia.
1129. Reg.23 (1454 Mar.14-1455 Jan.13). Lettere di giustizia.
1130. Reg.24 (1454 Sept.7-1456 Mar.6). Lettere di giustizia.
1131. Reg.25 (1454 Aug.17-1458 Dec.18). Milano, Novara, Como, Valtellina ed estero.
1132. Reg.26 (1454 Aug.22-1455 Dec.7). Pavia, Piacenza, Lodi, Bergamo, Crema, Geradadda.
1133. Reg.27 (1455 Mar.6-Dec.23). Lettere di giustizia.
1134. Reg.28 (1455 Jan.13-Nov.29). Lettere di giustizia.
1135. Reg.29 (1455 Aug.1-1458 Mar.9). Mantova, Parma, Verona, Padova, estero.
1136. Reg.30 (1455 Dec.29-1456 Aug.13). Lettere di giustizia.
1137. Reg.31 (1456 Aug.14-Dec.30). Lettere diverse.
1138. Reg.32 (1456 Apr.12-1457 Mar.12). Pavia, Piacenza, Lodi, Bergamo, Cremona, Crema, Ferrara, Venezia, Geradadda, Vigevano.
1139. Reg.33 (1455 Aug.26-1458 Dec.20). Licenze relative alle granaglie.
1139.1. Reg.34 (1456 Jan.18-1458 Mar.11). Alessandria, Genova, Tortona ed estero occidentale.
1140. Reg.35 (1456 Dec.31-1457 July 26). Lettere di giustizia.
1141. Reg.36 (1457 July 26-Dec.27). Lettere di giustizia.
1142. Reg.37 (1457 June 16-1459 July 2). Pavia, Piacenza, Lodi, Bergamo, Vigevano, Crema etc.

1142.1. Reg.38 (1457 Jan.1-1459 July 18). Milano, Novara, Como, Valtellina ed estero - Ungheria.
1143. Reg.39 (1457 Mar.19-1461 Feb.1). Cremona, Brescia, Mantova, etc.
1144. Reg.40 (1458 Sept.6-Dec.28). Lettere diverse: Milano, Parma, Piacenza, Brescia, Pavia, Tortona, Alessandria, Pontremoli etc.
1145. Reg.41 (1457 Dec.29-1458 Sept.27). Lettere di giustizia.
1146. Reg.42 (1458 Mar.2-1460 May 3). Parma, Venezia e Stati italiani centrali e meridionali.
1147. Reg.43 (1457 Aug.?-1461 Mar.22). Lettere dirette al Commissario di Parma e viceversa.
1147.1. Reg.44 (1458 Mar.15-1461 Jan.31). Lombardia, Genova, Spagna, Savoia, Francia, Borgogna, Monferrato, Inghilterra.
1148. Reg.45 (1459 Jan.1-Sept.30). Lettere diverse.
1149. Reg.45bis (1459 June 18-1476 Mar.17). Registrum statutorium privilegiorum et iurium terre Cotignole.
1150. Reg.46 (1459 Oct.5-Dec.31). Milano, Parma, Cremona, Lodi, Como, Piacenza, Alessandria, Pavia.
1151. Reg.47 (1459 July 2-1461 Jan.31). Pavia, Lodi, Piacenza, Bergamo, Lomellina, Geradadda.
1152. Reg.47bis (1460 Jan.3-Dec.22). Salvacondotti.
1153. Reg.48 (1459 June 1-1461 July 10). Milano, Como, Novara, Bellinzona, Venezia, Ungheria, Austria, Monferrato.
1154. Reg.49 (1460 Jan.2-Dec.28). Lettere di giustizia.
1154.1. Reg.50 (1460 May 3-1462 June 30). Parma, Bologna, Ferrara, Venezia, Firenze, Siena, Regno di Napoli, Roma, Albania.
1155. Reg.51 (1461 Feb.2-1462 Aug.18). Piacenza, Lomellina, Geradadda, Lodi, Pavia, Bergamo, Crema.
1155.1. Reg.52 (1461 Jan.28-1463 May 21). Alessandria, Genova, Monferrato, Asti, Piemonte, estero: Borgogna, Francia, Inghilterra.
1155.2. Reg.53 (1461 July 10-1464 Oct.12). Milano, Como, Novara, estero: Francia, Borgogna.
1156. Reg.54 (1461 Jan.3-1464 Oct.23). Lettere diverse: Vigevano, Pavia, Lodi, Cremona, Alessandria, Parma, Piacenza, etc.
1157. Reg.55 (1461 Feb.2-1464 May 1). Cremona, Brescia, Casalmaggiore, Mantova etc.
1157.1. Reg.56 (1462 Jan.5-Dec.30). Lettere di giustizia.
1157.2. Reg.57 (1460 - 1466). Azienda di Sartirana.
1157.3. Reg.58 (1462 July 10-1463 Oct.10). Pavia, Padova, Piacenza, Lodi, Bergamo, Crema, Geradadda.
1157.4. Reg.59 (1462 May 1-1463 Oct.4). Parma, Modena, Reggio, Bologna, Romandiola, Ancona, Venezia, Ferrara, Firenze, Illiria, Albania, Grecia, Rodi, etc.
1157.5. Reg.60 (1461 Mar.26-1465 Mar.12). Lettere dirette da Parma al Duca di Milano dal Commissario ducale, Lorenzo da Pesaro.
1158. Reg.61 (1462 Oct.25-1466 May 29). Napoli, Toscana, Perugia, Parma etc.
1158.1. Reg.62 (1463 Sept.30-1464 Sept.30). Milano, Pavia, Lodi, Piacenza.
1158.2. Reg.63 (1463 May 15-1465 Oct.31). Ovada, Tortona, Alessandria, Monferrato, Savoia ed estero.
1158.3. Reg.64 (1463 Oct.2-1465 July 19). Parma e Stati italiani.
1158.4. Reg.65 (1463 May 31-1465 Jan.23). Ducato di Milano, Novara e suo territorio, Como e suo territorio, Valtellina, Alemagna, etc.
1158.5. Reg.66 (1464 Jan.2-Oct.29). Lettere di giustizia.
1158.6. Reg.67 (1464 Jan.17-1465 Apr.17). Genova e Genovesato.
1158.7. Reg.68 (1464 Sept.31-1465 Oct.20). Parma, Lodi, Piacenza, Crema, Bergamo, Geradadda.
1159. Reg.69 (1464 May 2-1469 Mar.17). Cremona, Brescia.
1160. Reg.70 (1465 Apr.17-1466 May 25). Genova e Stati italiani.
1161. Reg.71 (1465 Mar.12-1467 June 7). Milano, Valtellina e regioni diverse: Como, Novara, Austria, Pavia.
1162. Reg.72 (1465 Oct.29-1467 Mar.6). Milano, Pavia, Lodi, Piacenza.

1163. Reg.73 (1465 Jan.?-1467 Dec.?). Estratti di lettere interne ed estere.
1164. Reg.74 (1465 Oct.30-1469 Mar.27). Alessandria, Tortona, Piemonte, Monferrato, Francia, Aragona, Borgogna, Inghilterra.
1165. Reg.75 (1465 Oct.9-1469 Mar.5). Parma, Modena, Venezia, Bologna, Mantova etc.
1166. Reg.76 (1466 May 27-1469 Feb.26). Genova, Savona etc.
1167. Reg.77 (1466 Jan.2-1468 June 3). Napoli, Firenze etc.
1168. Reg.78 (1466 Jan.1-1469 Jan.1). Roma.
1169. Reg.79 (1467 May 16-1468 Jan.2). Novara, Pavia, Como, Lodi, Piacenza, Roma, Firenze, Parma, Modena etc.
1170. Reg.80 (1467 Feb.3-1469 May 4). Milano, Novara, Como, Alemagna.
1171. Reg.81 (1468 Jan.5-Feb.29). Lettere diverse.
1172. Reg.82 (1468 Sept.21-Dec.26). Lettere diverse.
1173. Reg.83 (1468 Apr.1-1469 May 2). Lombardia, Novara, Piacenza, Alessandria.
1174. Reg.84 (1468 July 3-Aug.26). Milano, Parma, Asti, Piacenza, Pavia.
1175. Reg.85 (1468 Dec.9-1469 Aug.28). Copialettere di Sagramoro da Rimini in Firenze.
1176. Reg.86 (1469 Jan.8-Dec.27). Lettere diverse.
1177. Reg.87 (1469 Aug.28-Dec.31). Lettere diverse.
1178. Reg.88 (1469 May 27-Aug.28). Lettere diverse.
1179. Reg.89 (1468 Dec.28-1469 Apr.22). Milano, Lodi, Como, Novara, Genova etc.
1180. Reg.90 (1469 Jan.18-Aug.4). Pavia, Cremona, Parma, Piacenza, Alessandria, Tortona.
1181. Reg.91 (1469 July 19-1470 Feb.14). Milano, Como, Novara, Lodi, Genova, Pontremoli.
1182. Reg.92 (1469 Oct.23-1470 May 23). Pavia, Cremona, Parma.
1183. Reg.93 (1469 Apr.29-1471 Apr.29). Lettere diverse.
1184. Reg.94 (1469 Jan.25-1471 June 12; one doc. 1472 Apr.14). Estero.
1185. Reg.95 (1470 Jan.1-1471 Jan.3). Lettere diverse.
1186. Reg.96 (1470 Jan.1-1472 Jan.2). Magistrati straordinari.
1187. Reg.97 (1470 Sept.1-1471 May 10). Pavia, Cremona, Parma, Alessandria, Tortona, Piacenza, Vigevano etc.
1188. Reg.98 (1470 Nov.30-1471 May 8). Milano, Como, Novara, Lodi, Genova, Pontremoli, etc.
1189. Reg.99 (1471 Jan.3-Dec.31). Lettere diverse.
1190. Reg.100 (1471 May 7-Oct.18). Milano, Como, Novara, Lodi, Genova, etc.
1191. Reg.101 (1471 May 10-Oct.31). Parma, Cremona, Pavia, Alessandria, Tortona, Piacenza etc.
1192. Reg.102 (1471 Sept.10-1472 Jan.28). Milano, Como, Novara, Genova, Pavia, Vigevano.
1193. Reg.103 (1471 Nov.1-1472 May 18). Pavia, Cremona, Parma, Alessandria, Tortona, Piacenza, Milano, Vigevano.
1194. Reg.104 (1472 Jan.2-July 31). Vicario di Provvisione ed altre diverse.
1195. Reg.105 (1472 June 19-Nov.14). Lettere diverse.
1196. Reg.106 (1472 Jan.28-June 12). Como, Novara, Lodi, Genova.
1197. Reg.107 (1472 May 12-Nov.14). Pavia, Cremona, Parma, Alessandria, Tortona, Piacenza.
1198. Reg.108 (1471 June 12-1472 July 5). Estero.
1199. Reg.109 (1472 Jan.2-1473 Aug.13). Ai magistrati straordinari e varie altre.
1200. Reg.110 (1472 July 16-1473 Aug.13). Milano, Piacenza, Lodi, Cremona, Novara, Pavia ed altre.
1201. Reg.111 (1472 July 5-1473 Dec.10). Estero.
1202. Reg.112 (1473 July 14-Dec.2). Milano, Como, Lodi, Novara, Genova etc.
1203. Reg.113 (1473 Mar.11-Apr.30). Milano, Genova, Como, Lodi, Novara etc.
1204. Reg.114 (1473 Apr.11-Aug.28). Pavia, Cremona, Piacenza, Parma, Alessandria, Tortona.
1205. Reg.115 (1473 Dec.3-1474 June 14). Milano, Lodi, Genova, Como, Novara.
1206. Reg.116 (1473 Sept.20-1474 May 16). Pavia, Cremona, Parma, Piacenza, Alessandria, Tortona etc.
1207. Reg.117 (1473 Dec.11-1475 Apr.8). Estero.

1208. Reg.118 (1474 Jan.14-1475 Feb.18). Milano, Como, Novara, Lodi, Genova etc.
1209. Reg.119 (1474 May 16-1475 Jan.30). Pavia, Parma, Cremona, Tortona, Alessandria, Piacenza etc.
1210. Reg.120 (1475 Jan.5-July 12). Milano, Como, Novara, Lodi, Genova.
1211. Reg.121 (1475 Feb.16-Dec.4). Parma, Pavia, Cremona, Piacenza, Alessandria, Tortona.
1212. Reg.122 (1475 July 18-1476 Jan.19). Milano, Como, Novara, Genova, Lodi.
1213. Reg.123 (1475 Dec.4-1476 Oct.1). Pavia, Cremona, Piacenza, Alessandria, Tortona.
1214. Reg.124 (1475 Sept.3-1477 Aug.9). Milano ed altre città del Dominio ed estero.
1215. Reg.125 (1476 Mar.14-June 18). Lodi, Como, Novara, Genova ed estero.
1216. Reg.125bis (1475 Apr.10-1477 Jan.18). Estero.
1217. Reg.126 (1476 Oct.13-1477 Mar.30). Milano, Lodi, Como, Genova, Novara.
1218. Reg.126bis (1475 Apr.5-1479 Jan.12). Registro di Corsica.
1219. Reg.127 (1476 Oct.2-1477 Jan.16). Pavia, Piacenza, Parma, Alessandria, Tortona, Cremona.
1220. Reg.128 (1477 Jan.23-Oct.16). Pavia, Cremona, Piacenza, Parma, Alessandria, Tortona etc.
1221. Reg.129 (1477 Jan.16-Apr.28). Milano, Como, Lodi, Novara ed altre varie.
1222. Reg.130 (1476 Dec.26-1477 July 11). Lettere diverse.
1223. Reg.132 (1477 July 28-Dec.31). Pavia, Cremona, Piacenza, Parma, Alessandria, Tortona.
1224. Reg.133 (1477 Jan.18-1478 Apr.1). Lettere diverse extra dominium.
1225. Reg.136 (1478 Jan.10-June 9). Pavia, Parma, Piacenza, Cremona, Alessandria, Tortona.
1226. Reg.137 (1478 June 7-Nov.21). Pavia, Parma, Piacenza, Cremona, Alessandria, Tortona.
1227. Reg.138 (1478 Jan.23-1479 Feb.24). Lettere diverse.
1228. Reg.139 (1478 Jan.23-1479 Nov.10). Registro camerale.
1229. Reg.140 (1478 Jan.23-1479 Apr.30). Pavia, Cremona, Piacenza.
1230. Reg.141 (1478 Jan.23-1479 Sept.14). Lodi, Parma, Novara.
1231. Reg.142 (1478 Apr.1-1479 Sept.10). Estero.
1232. Reg.143 (1479 Jan.1-July 20). Atti del Consiglio Segreto.
1233. Reg.144 (1479 Jan.15-Sept.9). Lettere diverse.
1234. Reg.144bis (1479 Jan.9-May 15). Cremona, Pavia, Piacenza, Alessandria, Parma, Tortona, Vigevano etc.
1235. Reg.145 (1479 May 15-Sept.11). Pavia, Parma, Piacenza, Alessandria, Tortona, Cremona.
1236. Reg.146 (1479 Nov.11-1480 May 22). Lettere diverse.
1237. Reg.147 (1479 Sept.16-1480 Nov.13). Cremona, Alessandria, Tortona.
1238. Reg.148 (1479 Sept.18-1481 Oct.27). Estero.
1239. Reg.149 (1479 Nov.10-1494 Dec.10). Ai maestri delle entrate.
1240. Reg.150 (1480 May 17-Sept.13). Lettere di giustizia ed altre.
1241. Reg.151 (1480 Sept.13-Nov.12). Lettere diverse.
1242. Reg.152 (1480 Sept.1-1481 Apr.14). Milano, Lodi, Como, Novara, Genova, Bellinzona, Gallarate, Varese, Savona etc.
1243. Reg.152bis (1480 June 22-1481 May 7). Pavia, Parma, Piacenza, Cotignola, Vigevano, Pontremoli etc.
1244. Reg.152ter (1482 Jan.31-Oct.24). Cremona, Alessandria, Tortona, Casalmaggiore, Soncino etc.
1245. Reg.153 (1481 Apr.16-Dec.26). Milano, Novara, Como, Lodi, Bellinzona, Caravaggio, Varese.
1246. Reg.154 (1481 May 8-Dec.31). Pavia, Parma, Piacenza, Cotignola, Pontremoli, Vigevano.
1247. Reg.155 (1481 Nov.4-1485 Jan.3). Estero, lettere diverse: Austria, Siena, Roma, Mantova, Firenze, Venezia, Ferrara, Vercelli, Lucca, Napoli, Genova, Spagna, Urbino, Savoia, Monferrato, Svizzera, Francia, Bologna, Ungheria, Bavaria, Forlí, Saluzzo, Perugia, Asti etc.

1248. Reg.156 (1482 Jan.1-1483 Jan.3). Cremona, Alessandria, Tortona, Soncino, Casalmaggiore, Parma, Piacenza, Pavia, Cotignola, Pontremoli.
1249. Reg.157 (1482 Sept.23-1483 Apr.29). Milano, Lodi, Como, Novara, Bellinzona, Lugano, Parma, Caravaggio.
1250. Reg.158 (1483 May 1-Nov.8). Lettere diverse.
1251. Reg.159 (1483 Jan.1-1484 Jan.2). Pavia, Piacenza, Parma, Cotignola, Pontremoli.
1252. Reg.160 (1483 Nov.9-1484 Apr.21). Milano, Lodi, Novara, Como, Caravaggio, Locarno.
1253. Reg.161 (1483 Jan.4-1484 Mar.16). Cremona, Alessandria, Tortona, Casalmaggiore, Soncino.
1254. Reg.162 (1484 Apr.23-Oct.16). Lettere diverse.
1255. Reg.163 (1484 Jan.1-Dec.27). Pavia, Parma, Piacenza, Pontremoli, Cotignola.
1256. Reg.164 (1485 June 1-1486 June 16). Cremona, Alessandria, Tortona, Soncino, Casalmaggiore.
1257. Reg.165 (1485 Jan.5-1487 July 5). Lettere extra dominium: Roma, Ungheria, Venezia, Bologna, Monferrato, Firenze, Mantova, Svizzera, Asti, Savoia, Forlí, Inghilterra, Austria, Lucca, Napoli, Germania, Ferrara, Genova, Siena, Spagna, Francia etc.
1258. Reg.165bis (1485 Jan.2-1486 Feb.23). Piacenza, Pavia, Parma, Pontremoli, Cremona, Cotignola.
1259. Reg.166 (1486 June 17-1487 Aug.16). Cremona, Alessandria, Tortona, Casalmaggiore, Soncino.
1260. Reg.167 (1486 Mar.11-1487 Jan.11). Pavia, Parma, Piacenza, Bobbio, Cotignola, Pontremoli, Bellinzona.
1261. Reg.167bis (1487 Jan.10-1488 Jan.25). Parma, Pavia, Pontremoli, Piacenza, Cotignola, Bobbio.
1262. Reg.168 (1487 July 2-1488 Feb.10). Milano, Como, Novara, Lodi, Bellinzona, Caravaggio, Varese.
1263. Reg.169 (1487 Aug.17-1488 June 5). Cremona, Alessandria, Tortona, Casalmaggiore, Soncino.
1264. Reg.170 (1487 July 5-1489 Apr.3). Estero: Austria, Firenze, Savoia, Svizzera, Roma, Monferrato, Lucca, Venezia, Bologna, Ferrara, Asti, Mantova, Forlí, Siena, Ungheria, Napoli, Urbino, Spagna, Germania, Pesaro, Portogallo etc.
1265. Reg.171 (1487 July 31-1499 Aug.20). Genova, Spezia, Savona.
1266. Reg.172 (1488 Feb.10-July 12). Milano, Como, Novara, Lodi, Caravaggio, Bellinzona, Vigevano.
1267. Reg.172bis (1488 July 13-Nov.29). Svizzera, Milano, Como, Lodi, Varese, Novara, Bellinzona, Caravaggio.
1268. Reg.173 (1488 Dec.3-1489 May 22). Milano, Como, Novara, Lodi, Caravaggio, Varese, Bellinzona.
1269. Reg.174 (1488 June 7-1489 Sept.30). Cremona, Alessandria, Tortona, Soncino ed altre.
1270. Reg.175 (1488 Dec.19-1490 May 14). Pavia, Parma, Piacenza, Bobbio, Cotignola.
1271. Reg.176 (1489 May 23-Aug.29). Como, Novara, Lodi.
1272. Reg.177 (1489 Aug.30-1490 Jan.29). Milano, Como, Novara, Varese, Lodi.
1273. Reg.178 (1489 Apr.7-1490 Nov.27). Estero, lettere diverse: Roma, Savoia, Forlí, Monferrato, Lucca, Napoli, Siena, Bologna, Ferrara, Ungheria, Vercelli, Venezia, Francia, Firenze, Austria, Asti, Faenza, Pesaro, Bavaria, Spagna etc.
1274. Reg.179 (1489 Oct.10-1491 Mar.24). Cremona, Alessandria, Tortona, Soncino.
1275. Reg.180 (1489 Jan.12-1520 May 24). Salvacondotti.
1276. Reg.181 (1490 July 9-1491 Jan.4). Milano, Como, Lodi, Novara, Caravaggio, Varese, Bellinzona ed altre.
1277. Reg.182 (1490 May 15-1491 Dec.31). Pavia, Parma, Piacenza, Bobbio, Cotignola.
1278. Reg.183 (1491 Jan.1-June 7). Milano, Como, Novara, Lodi, Caravaggio, Bellinzona, Domodossola etc.
1279. Reg.184 (1491 June 14-1492 July 11). Milano, Como, Novara, Lodi, Caravaggio, Domodossola, Bellinzona etc.
1280. Reg.184A (1491 May 26-Aug.30). Decreti del Senato. Reg.184B (1491 Aug.31-Dec.7). Decreti del Senato.

1281. Reg.185 (1491 Nov.1-1492 Mar.28). Milano, Novara, Lodi, Caravaggio, Varese, Bellinzona, Domodossola.
1282. Reg.186 (1491 Mar.24-1492 Nov.4). Cremona, Alessandria, Tortona etc.
1283. Reg.187 (1492 Mar.28-Oct.7). Milano, Como, Lodi, Novara, Caravaggio etc.
1284. Reg.188 (1492 Oct.8-1493 Apr.23). Milano, Como, Lodi, Valtellina, Novara, Caravaggio, Varese etc.
1285. Reg.189 (1492 Jan.3-1493 Oct.26). Pavia, Parma, Piacenza, Bobbio, Cotignola.
1286. Reg.190 (1492 Nov.5-1494 Aug.2). Cremona, Tortona, Alessandria, Soncino.
1287. Reg.191 (1493 Apr.25-Sept.30). Milano, Como, Novara, Lodi, Domodossola.
1288. Reg.192 (1493 Sept.30-1494 Mar.3). Milano, Como, Novara, Lodi, Bellinzona, Varese, Vigevano etc.
1289. Reg.193 (1493 Oct.26-1495 June 10). Parma, Piacenza, Pavia, Pontremoli, Bobbio, Cotignola etc.
1290. Reg.194 (1493 Mar.10-1495 May 2). Estero: Ferrara, Savoia, Pesaro, Germania, Monferrato, Firenze, Roma, Asti, Venezia, Francia, Austria, Rimini, Vercelli, Lucca, Pesaro, Mantova, Bologna, Siena, Spagna, etc.
1291. Reg.195 (1494 Mar.4-Oct.18). Milano, Como, Novara, Lodi, Domodossola, Bellinzona.
1292. Reg.196 (1494 Oct.18-1495 Mar.4). Milano, Como, Novara, Lodi, Caravaggio, Vigevano, Domodossola etc.
1293. Reg.197 (1494 Aug.5-1496 June 26). Cremona, Alessandria, Tortona etc.
1294. Reg.198 (1494 June 26-1495 Jan.11). Frammenti dei Registri delle Patenti.
1295. Reg.198bis (1495 May 8-1497 Feb.13). Extradominium: Firenze, Monferrato, Vercelli, Venezia, Lucca, Bologna, Forlí, Mantova, Ferrara, Roma, Saluzzo, Savoia, Francia, Faenza, Siena, Germania, Spagna, Genova, Pesaro etc.

FRAMMENTI I REGISTRI DUCALI DE DELLE MISSIVE

1296-8. Cart.1 (1426-63).

1299-1301. Cart.2 (1457-67).

1302-3. Cart.3 (1469-87).

1304.　Cart.5 (1413-68: filmed 1446-68).

1305.　Cart.6 (1468-72, selections);

　　　Cart.7 (1472-76, selections);

　　　Cart.8 (1476-79, selections);

　　　Cart.11 (ca.1227-ca.1498, selections: 1459, 1478, 1450-62).

ACQUISTI E DONI

1306. Cart.22. **Dono Vittani Giovanni**: Lettera di Luigi XI alla Duchessa Bianca Maria, [1467], June 13.
　　　Cart.48(ex 43). **Dono Mario Minniti** (1941): 58 lettere che riguardano il periodo dell'esilio pisano di Ludovico il Moro, 1477-79.

II. BIBLIOTECA AMBROSIANA

1307. Cod.Z.68.Sup. Entrate e spese del Ducato di Milano per l'anno 1463.
1308. Cod.Z.88.Sup. Trattati, convenzioni e capitolazioni riguardanti gli Svizzeri e li Grigioni dal 1315 al 1552.
1309. Cod.Z.198.Sup. Formularium Cancellarie Ducali Mediolani.
1310-11. Cod.Z.219.Sup. Selections. Roma. Corrispondenza epistolare col Duca Francesco Sforza. Documenti di vari Papi e Cardinali (ca.1450-ca.1479).
1312. Cod.Z.226.Sup. Arte militare dei secoli XIV-XVI.

1313. Cod.Z.227.Sup. Corrispondenza diplomatica tra Milano e Venezia (1450-66 + undated).
1314. Cod.Z.247.Sup. Selections. Corrispondenza diplomatica tra Milano e Firenze (ca.1440-ca.1491 + undated).
1315. Cod.I.290.Inf. Liber antiquus diversorum matrimoniorum.

III. BIBLIOTECA NAZIONALE BRAIDENSE

1316. Cod.AD.XI.59. Istrumentario di Nicodemo da Pontremoli, della famiglia dei Tranchedini, segretario di Francesco I Sforza, Duca di Milano, 1437-61.
Cod.AD.XIII.41. No.15. Lettera a Francesco I Sforza per esortarlo alla guerra. Anonima, 1431 Aug.26.
MS. Morbio 19. No.3. Lettera di Ferrante d'Aragona a Gian Galeazzo Sforza, 1491 July 3.
No.4. Lettera di Ferrante d'Aragona a Gian Galeazzo Sforza, 1490 Apr.4.
No.6. Lettera di Alfonso II di Napoli a Gian Galeazzo Sforza, 1494 Jan.25.

IV. BIBLIOTECA DELLA SOCIETA' STORICA LOMBARDA

1317. Codice Formentini. Entrate e spese del Ducato di Milano per l'anno 1463.
Appendix 3. Carte Morbio. Nos.53-54 (1491); 59 (1479); 62 (1478); 66-68 (1491); 78 (1491); 110 (1474); 206 (1474); 221 (1491); 231-50 (1491-92). [34 photocopies].

V. BIBLIOTECA TRIVULZIANA

1319. Cod. Nuovi Acquisti N.7, Coll.A35. Liber diversarum dotum, 1472-99.
1320. Cod. Nuovi Acquisti N.8, Coll.F48. Atti di Bona di Savoia, 1468-77.
1321. Cod.101. Itinerari diversi per l'Italia e per altre parti d'Europa.
1322. Cod.682. Miscellanea Latina.
1323. Cod.700. Franciscus Petrasancta, De laudibus Galeacii Sfortiae oratio.
1324. Cod.1130. Miscellanea Storica.
No. III. Arbitrato di re Renato tra Francesco Sforza e Giovanni Marchese del Monferrato e fratelli per il possesso della città di Alessandria e suo distretto, 1453 Sept.15.
No.XII. Capitoli della pace tra il Duca di Milano e il Duca di Savoia, 1469 Mar.22.
1325. Cod.1325. Varia a Iacobo Alifero collecta.
1326. Cod.1458. Relazione d'Ungheria dell'anno 1490, o poco dopo, senza nome del relatore.

MODENA

I. ARCHIVIO DI STATO

ARCHIVIO SEGRETO ESTENSE

a. CANCELLERIA, SEZIONE GENERALE

REGISTRI DI LETTERE

1327. Reg.1(937). (1443-52; filmed 1450-52).
Reg.2(938). (1445-49, 1469-71; filmed 1469-71).
Reg.3(939). (1471-75).

1328. Reg.4(940). (1476).
1329. Reg.5(941). (1478).
1330. Reg.6(942). (1479).
1331. Reg.7(943). (1481).
1332. Reg.8(944). (1482).
1333. Reg.9(945). (1482-83).
1334. Reg.10(946). (1486-88).

MINUTARIO CRONOLOGICO, LETTERE SCIOLTE

1335. B.1. (1454-82).
1336-7. B.2. (1483-86).
1338-9. B.3. (1487-93).
1340. B.4. (1494-1500 + 15th undated; filmed 1494 + undated).

CIFRARI

1341. B.2. Cifrari con Principi Estensi e con Principi esteri (15th-18th cents.; filmed 1450-94).
B.4. Cifrari con ambasciatori e agenti estensi all'estero (15th cent.; filmed 1450-94).

b. CANCELLERIA, SEZIONE ESTERO

CARTEGGI DI ORATORI, AGENTI E CORRISPONDENTI PRESSO LE CORTI

(CARTEGGIO AMBASCIATORI)

(1.) CARTEGGIO AMBASCIATORI, ITALIA:

BOLOGNA

1342. B.1. (Filmed 1463-94).

FIRENZE

1343. B.1. (Filmed 1462-78).
1344-5. B.2. (1479-81).
1346-7. B.3. (1482-84).
1348. B.4. (1479-94).
1349. B.5. (1486-89).
1350. B.6. (1485-89).
1351. B.7. (1485-91).
1352. B.8. (1492-94).

GENOVA, MANTOVA

1353. **GENOVA** B.1. (Filmed 1462). **MANTOVA** B.1. (Filmed 1454-94).

MILANO

1354. B.1. (1442-78; filmed 1454-78).
1355-6. B.2. (1478-83).
1357-8. B.3. (1479-83).
1359-60. B.4. (1484-86).
1361-2. B.5. (1487-88).
1363-4. B.6. (1489-91).
1365-6. B.7. (1492-93).
1367-8. B.8. (1494).
1369-70. B.9. (1482-95).

NAPOLI

1371. B.1. (1448-81; filmed 1458-81).
1372. B.2. (1479-82).
1373. B.3. (1480-83).
1374. B.4. (1483-85).
1375-6. B.5 (1482-89).

ROMA

1377. B.1. (1374-1491; filmed 1459-91).
1378-9. B.2. (1480-82).
1380. B.3. (1481-85).
1381-3. B.4. (1483-85).
1384-7. B.5. (1482-91).
1388-90. B.6. (1482-91).
1391. B.7. (1486-90).
1392. B.8. (1483-1502).
1393-4. B.9. (1491-95).
1395. B.10. (1491-99).
1396. B.11. (1498-1504).

ROMAGNA

1397. B.1. (Filmed 1463-93).

VENEZIA

1398. B.1. (1406-78).
1399-1400. B.2. (1476-82).
1401. B.3. (1481-84).
1402. B.4. (1484-85).
1403. B.5. (1484-87).
1404. B.6. (1486-89).

1405. B.7. (1489-92).
1406. B.8. (1493-96).

(2) CARTEGGIO AMBASCIATORI, FUORI D'ITALIA

FRANCIA

1407. B.1. (1470-95; filmed 1470-94).

GERMANIA, INGHILTERRA

1408. **GERMANIA**. B.1. (1482-1522; filmed 1482-94).
INGHILTERRA. B.1. (1470-1674; filmed 1470, 1479).

LEVANTE, SPAGNA

1409. **LEVANTE**. B.1. (1477-1732; filmed 1477-94).
SPAGNA. B.1. (1468-1526; filmed 1468, 1482, 1491).

UNGHERIA

1410. B.1. (1479-88).

CARTEGGI CON PRINCIPI E RETTORI DI STATI ESTERI

ITALIA

BOLOGNA

1411. B.1/1134. (1460-94). Lettere di Sante e Giovanni II Bentivoglio.

FAENZA

1412. B.1/1151. (1450-94). Lettere di Astorre II, Carlo II, Galeotto e Taddeo Manfredi.

FIRENZE

1413. B.1/1152. (1467-94). Lettere di Piero I, Lorenzo e Piero II dei Medici.
B.16/1166B. (1454-92). Lettere della Signoria, X di Balia e VIII di Pratica.

FORLI, IMOLA

1414. **FORLI** B.1/1167. (1474-80). Lettere di Pino II e Sinibaldo II Ordelaffi.
IMOLA. B.1/1177. (1476-94). Lettere di Girolamo Riario e Caterina Sforza.

MANTOVA

1415. B.1/1181. (1454-96). Lettere di Lodovico III, Federico I e Gian Francesco II Gonzaga.

MILANO

1416. B.1/1213. (1451-94). Lettere di Francesco I, Galeazzo Maria, Bona e Gian Galeazzo Sforza.

1417. B.2/1214. (1480-92). Lettere di Lodovico Maria Sforza.

1418. B.3/1215. (1493). Lettere di Lodovico Maria Sforza.

B.4/1215A. (1494). Lettere di Lodovico Maria Sforza.

1419. B.7/1217. (1484-1500; filmed 1484-94). Lettere di Lodovico Maria Sforza.

MONFERRATO

1420. B.1/1244. (1452-83). Lettere di Giovanni IV, Guglielmo VIII, Bonifacio III e Teodoro Paleologo.

NAPOLI E SICILIA

1421. B.1/1245. (1450-93). Lettere di Giovanni d'Angió, Alfonso I e Ferdinando I.

B.2/1246. (1468-94). Lettere di Alfonso II e Ferdinando II.

PESARO, RIMINI

1422. **PESARO**. B.1285/A. (1452-92). Lettere di Alessandro, Costanzo, Giovanni e Camilla Sforza.
RIMINI. B.1286. (1462-92). Lettere di Roberto, Pandolfo, Ursina, Novello, Sigismondo Pandolfo e Galeotto Malatesta.

ROMA

1423. B.7/1293. (1450-63). Lettere di Niccoló V, Calisto III e Pio II.

1424. B.8/1293A. (1466-84). Lettere di Paolo II e Sisto IV.

1425. B.9/1294. (1484-92). Lettere di Innocenzo VIII.

1426. B.10/1295. (1493-1502). Lettere di Alessandro VI.

CARTEGGI CON PRINCIPI E RETTORI DI STATI ESTERI FUORI D'ITALIA

FRANCIA

1427. B.1/1559. (1456?-1550?). Lettere di Carlo VII, Luigi XI, Carlo VIII, Luigi XII, Francesco I, Luigia di Savoia.

AVVISI E NOTIZIE DALL'ESTERO

1428. B.5157/101. (1446-96; filmed 1450-94).

CARTEGGIO DIPLOMATICO ESTERO

SOMMARI E COPIE DI LETTERE

1429-30. B.1/5301. (965-1487; filmed 1450-87).
1431. B.2/5302. (1488-1500; filmed 1488-95).

1432. B.1736. Faenza-Milano (1465-1522).

   B.1737. Napoli-Parma (1480-1500).

   B.1742. Saluzzo-Venezia (1479-80).

PAVIA

II. BIBLIOTECA CIVICA "BONETTA"

MANOSCRITTI, SECONDA SEZIONE

1433. A.II.11 [già A.122]. Registrum diversarum litterarum ducalium ac decretorum et ordinum diversorum annorum (1382-1496).

1434. A.II.22 [già B.64]. Registrum decretorum ac litterarum ducalium diversorum annorum (1380-1535).

1435. A.II.23 [già B.65]. Registro-regesto di lettere e documenti ducali per tutto il secolo XV.

1436. A.II.26 [già B.68]. Registrum litterarum ducalium anni MCCCCLV.

1437. A.II.30 [già B.72]. I. Registrum litterarum et privilegiorum canzellarie communitatis Papie per il 1464-66.

   II. Frammento del "Liber Provisionum" del Comune di Pavia per il 1466.

1438. A.II.33 [già B.75]. Registrum litterarum ducalium anni 1480 et anni 1481.

1439. A.II.34 [già B.76]. Registro di lettere ducali per gli anni 1486-89.

1440. A.II.38 [già B.80]. Registro di lettere ducali per gli anni 1496-1499.

1441. A.III.30 [già A.45]. Sacco Jacopo. Raccolta di decreti e lettere ducali su vari argomenti (Sec. XIV-XV).

ROME

I. ARCHIVIO DI STATO

ACQUISTI E DONI

1442. No.50. Brevia Communia (1476 Aug.27-1477 Jan.31).

SIENA

I. ARCHIVIO DI STATO

CAPITOLI

1443. No.174 (1454 Dec.17-1455 May 7); 177 (1455 Jan.26); 178 (1456 May 30); 179 (1456 Aug.17); 181 (1459 Oct.1); 195 (1468 Apr.25); 196 (1468 Sept.10); 203 (1477 Dec.24); 204 (1478 May 17-July 23); 205 (1480 Mar.13); 206 (1480 Mar.13); 207 (1480 Apr.14); 208 (1480 Apr.30); 213 (1487 June 5); 226 (1480 Oct.); 230 (1480?).

ARCHIVIO DEL CONCISTORO

COPIALETTERE

1444. Reg.1676 (1456 Jan.1-Dec.31).
1445. Reg.1677 (1459 Jan.1-Dec.31).
1446. Reg.1678 (1460 Jan.1-Dec.31).
   Reg.1679 (1461 Mar.1-June 5).
1447. Reg.1680 (1462 Jan.1-Dec.31).
1448. Reg.1681 (1463 Jan.1-Dec.31).
1449. Reg.1682 (1464 Jan.1-Dec.31).
1450. Reg.1683 (1465 Jan.1-Dec.31).
1451. Reg.1684 (1466 Jan.1-Dec.31).
1452. Reg.1685 (1467 Jan.2-Dec.31).
1453. Reg.1686 (1468 Jan.1-Dec.30).
1454. Reg.1687 (1469 Jan.1-Dec.31).
1455. Reg.1688 (1471 Jan.1-Dec.31).
1456. Reg.1689 (1472 Jan.1-Dec.31).
1457. Reg.1690 (1473 Jan.1-Dec.31).
1458. Reg.1691 (1476 Jan.1-Dec.31).
1459. Reg.1692 (1477 Jan.1-Dec.31).
1460. Reg.1693 (1478 Jan.1-Dec.31).
1461. Reg.1694 (1480 Jan.1-June 22).
1462. Reg.1695 (1482 Jan.1-Dec.31).
1463. Reg.1696 (1483 Jan.1-Dec.31).

COPIARII

1464. Reg.1771 (1436 Jan.1-1483 July 6; filmed 1450 Feb.3-1483 July 6). Copie di lettere di imperatori, re, pontefici, principi e repubbliche, e copie di trattati e convenzioni internazionali.

CARTEGGIO

1465. Indice, fols.109-218 (1449-94).
1466. F.1982 (1455 Jan.2-Mar.24).
   F.1983 (1455 Mar.26-May 15).
1467. F.1984 (1455 May 16-June 30).
   F.1985 (1455 July 1-Sept.30).
1468. F.1986 (1455 Oct.4-1456 Mar.23).
   F.1987 (1456 Mar.29-June20).
1469. F.1988 (1456 June 21-July 31).
   F.1989 (1456 Aug.1-Aug.30).
1470. F.1990 (1456 Sept.6-1457 Mar.14).
   F.1991 (1457 Mar.27-1458 Mar.18).
1471. F.1992 (1458 Mar.25-Oct.31).

F.1993 (1458 Nov.1-1459 Mar.24).

1472. F.1994 (1459 Mar.28-Aug.10).

F.1995 (1459 Aug.11-Oct.31).

1473. F.1996 (1459 Nov.2-1460 Mar.22).

F.1997 (1460 Mar.25-June 30).

1474. F.1998 (1460 July 1-Oct.29).

F.1999 (1460 Nov.1-1461 Mar.24).

1475. F.2000 (1461 Mar.25-July 31).

F.2001 (1461 Aug.1-Nov.30).

1476. F.2002 (1461 Dec.1-1462 Mar.26).

F.2003 (1462 Mar.25-June 30).

1477. F.2004 (1462 July 1-Oct.31).

F.2005 (1462 Nov.1-1463 Mar.22).

1478. F.2006 (1463 Mar.25-Sept.30).

F.2007 (1463 Oct.1-1464 Mar.24).

1479. F.2008 (1464 Mar.27-Sept.16).

F.2009 (1464 Sept.17-1465 Mar.23).

1480. F.2010 (1465 Mar.25-June 10).

F.2011 (1465 June 12-Oct.31).

1481. F.2012 (1465 Nov.1-1466 Mar.23).

F.2013 (1466 Mar.26-Sept.4).

1482. F.2014 (1466 Sept.8-1467 Mar.22).

F.2015 (1467 Mar.25-May 31).

1483. F.2016 (1467 June 1-Sept.12).

F.2017 (1467 Sept.18-Nov.30).

1484. F.2018 (1467 Dec.1-1468 Mar.23).

F.2019 (1468 Mar.26-Aug.31).

1485. F.2020 (1468 Sept.1-1469 Mar.23).

F.2021 (1469 Mar.26-Aug.28).

1486. F.2022 (1469 Sept.1-1470 Mar.22).

F.2023 (1470 Mar.26-Oct.31).

1487. F.2024 (1470 Nov.1-1471 Mar.24).

F.2025 (1471 Mar.25-May 31).

1488. F.2026 (1471 June 1-Sept.26).

F.2027 (1471 Oct.1-1472 Mar.24).

1489. F.2028 (1472 Mar.26-July 30).

F.2029 (1472 Aug.1-1473 Mar.21).

1490. F.2030 (1473 Mar.25-Sept.28).

F.2031 (1473 Oct.6-1474 Mar.24).

1491. F.2032 (1474 Mar.26-Sept.30).

F.2033 (1474 Oct.1-1475 Mar.21).

1492. F.2034 (1475 Mar.25-Sept.30).

F.2035 (1475 Oct.1-1476 Mar.19).

1493. F.2036 (1476 Mar.25-Aug.30).

F.2037 (1476 Sept.10-1477 Mar.23).

1494. F.2038 (1477 Mar.25-July 24).

F.2039 (1477 July 25-1478 Mar.14).

1495. F.2040 (1478 Mar.25-July 31).

F.2041 (1478 Aug.1-Sept.30).

1496. F.2042 (1478 Oct.1-1479 Mar.23).

F.2043 (1479 Mar.26-1481 Mar.22).

1497. F.2044 (1481 Mar.26-Oct.31).

F.2045 (1481 Nov.1-1482 Jan.30).

1498. F.2046 (1482 Feb.1-Mar.24).

F.2047 (1482 Mar.25-May 14).

1499. F.2048 (1482 May 15-June 30).

F.2049 (1482 July 1-Sept.30).

1500. F.2050 (1482 Oct.2-1483 Jan.24).

F.2051 (1483 Jan.25-Mar.24).

1501. F.2052 (1483 Mar.25-July 29).

F.2053 (1483 Aug.1-Nov.29).

1502. F.2054 (1483 Dec.1-1484 Mar.24).

CIFRARI E LETTERE CIFRATE

1503. F.2308 (14th-16th cents.; filmed Nos.6-16, 15th cent.).

LEGAZIONI E COMMISSARIE

1504. Reg.2408, fols.18-291 (1450-1483 Oct.3). Andate degli ambasciatori, commissari e castellani.
1505. Reg.2409, fols.1-36v (1482 Sept.1-1495). Andate degli ambasciatori, commissari e castellani.
1506. Reg.2416 (1453 Jan.31-1475 Nov.4). Libro VIII delle notule o istruzioni agli ambasciatori e commissari con relazioni di ambasciatori.
1507. Reg.2417, fols.1-96 (1476 Jan.13-1494 Nov.4). Libro IX delle notule o istruzioni agli ambasciatori e commissari con relazioni di ambasciatori.
1508. Reg.2418, fols.45-110 (1450 Dec.24-1470 Apr.12). Libro V delle notule. Lettere credenziali di ambasciatori stranieri, loro notule e risposte date dal Concistoro.
1509. Reg.2420 (1477 July 12-Aug.1). Entrata e uscita di Andrea Piccolomini, commissario presso il conte Antonio da Montefeltro.
1510. Reg.2421 (1478 June 28-Aug.5). Copialettere di Antonio Bichi, ambasciatore a Sisto IV.
    Reg.2422 (1478 Nov.8-1479 May 17). Copialettere di Antonio Bichi, ambasciatore a re Ferdinando di Napoli.
1511. Reg.2423 (1480 Nov.6-1481 Mar.7). Copialettere di Placido Placidi e Sinolfo Ottieri, ambasciatori a Sisto IV.
1512. Reg.2434 (1477 July 14-Aug.30). Copialettere di Andrea Piccolomini, commissario senese in Valdichiana al tempo dell'invasione del conte Carlo da Montone.
    Reg.2443 (1471 Mar.30-1472 June 14). Copialettere di Andrea Piccolomini, ambasciatore al papa e al re di Napoli.
    Reg.2448 (1385-1553; filmed 1455, 1472-73, 1478). Notule e istruzioni ad ambasciatori senesi presso potentati esteri.

Reg.2452 (1387-1555; filmed 1453-93). Lettere scritte da principi, signorie e particolari ad ambasciatori senesi, durante le loro missioni.
Reg.2459 (15th-16th cent.; filmed Nos.63, 67-68, 84, 95, 99, 112, 115, 143). Relazioni di ambasciatori, senza data.

ARCHIVIO DI BALIA

COPIALETTERE

1513. Reg.396 (1455 July 16-Dec.31).

1514. Reg.397 (1456 Jan.1-Dec.31).

1515. Reg.398 (1458 Jan.1-Oct.13).

1516. Reg.399 (1477 Aug.1-Oct.16).

 Reg.400 (1478 Nov.1-Dec.31).

1517. Reg.401 (1479 Jan.1-Dec.31).

1518. Reg.402 (1480 Jan.1-Apr.30).

 Reg.403 (1482 June 11-Dec.31).

1519. Reg.404 (1483 Jan.27-Dec.31).

CARTEGGIO

1520. Indice, fols.2-63 (1455-94).

1521. F.488 (1455 Mar.27-Oct.31).

1522. F.489 (1455 Nov.1-1456 Mar.24).

1523. F.490 (1456 Mar.3-Oct.26).

1524. F.491 (1456 Nov.1-1457 Jan.31); F.492 (1457 Feb.1-Mar.24).

1525. F.493 (1457 Mar.25-Sept.30); F.494 (1457 Oct.1-1458 Mar.24).

1526. F.495 (1458 Mar.25-1460 Mar.18); F.496 (1460 Apr.1-1478 Jan.19).

1527. F.497 (1478 Aug.5-1479 Mar.21); F.498 (1479 Mar.25-May 31).

1528. F.499 (1479 June 1-July 15); F.500 (1479 July 16-Dec.31).

1529. F.501 (1479 Oct.14-1480 Mar.24); F.502 (1480 Mar.27-1481 Mar.20).

1530. F.503 (1481 Mar.26-1482 Mar.24); F.504 (1482 Apr.10-July 31).

1531. F.505 (1482 Aug.1-Sept.30); F.506 (1482 Oct.1-Dec.31).

1532. F.507 (1483 Jan.1-Feb.10); F.508 (1483 Feb.6-Mar.23).

1533. F.509 (1483 Mar.25-Apr.30); F.510 (1483 May 1-May 31).

1534. F.511 (1483 June 1-June 20); F.512 (1483 June 21-July 31).

1535. F.513 (1483 Aug.1-Aug.19); F.514 (1483 Aug.20-Sept.30).

1536. F.515 (1483 Oct.1-Nov.30); F.516 (1483 Dec.1-1484 Feb.10);

 F.517 (1484 Feb.11-Mar.24).

TURIN

I. ARCHIVIO DI STATO

ARCHIVIO DI CORTE

TRATATI INTERNAZIONALI

1537. Traités anciens avec la France, les Dauphins, et autres Princes confinans au Duché de Savoie, depuis l'an 1257 jusqu'à 1489. Selections:

Mazzo 9, No.11:Trattato d'alleanza tra il Delfino e il Duca di Savoia (1451 Mar.13).
No. 12: Amedeo di Savoia, Principe di Piemonte, promette perpetua assistenza al Delfino (1451 Mar.13).
No.13: Anna di Cipro, Duchessa di Savoia, promette assistenza al Delfino (1451 Dec. 15).
No.15: Patenti di Carlo VII, Re di Francia, con cui si rinnovano col Duca Lodovico di Savoia le antiche alleanze fatte tra i loro predecessori (1452 Oct.27), colla ratifica del Duca (1455 Dec.16).
No.16: Trattato di pace, a mediazione del Duca di Borgogna, dei Signori di Berna col Duca di Savoia e col Delfino (1454 Sept.11).
No.17: Ratifica del suddetto Trattato pel Delfino (1454 Sept.11 e 20).
No.19: Dichiarazione del Re di Francia (1456 Dec.9).
No.20: Altra dichiarazione del Re di Francia (1456 Dec.9).
Mazzo 10, No.4: Ratifica del Duca Filippo di Borgogna e di Carlo di Charolais dell'alleanza conchiusa a Chalons col Duca di Savoia (1467 Mar.29).
No.5: Trattato di lega difensiva tra il Duca di Borgogna e il Duca Amedeo di Savoia (1467 Apr.4).
No.6: Ratifica del suddetto Trattato pel Conte di Charolais (1467 Apr.4).
No.7: Trattato di lega difensiva tra il Duca Carlo di Borgogna e Filippo di Savoia (1467 July 20).
No.12: Promessa di Luigi XI di assistere la Duchessa Iolanda di Savoia (1469 Mar.11).
No.13: Duca Amedeo e Duchessa Iolanda promettono assistenza al Conte Ianus di Ginevra (1470 Dec.23).
No.14: Trattato di alleanza tra Luigi XI e Filippo di Savoia (1471 Oct.6).
No.15: Lettere di Duca Carlo di Borgogna, per cui si confermano le alleanze difensive col Duca Amedeo (1473 June 8).
No.16: Trattato di alleanza difensiva tra Luigi XI e la Duchessa Iolanda (1476 Nov.2).
No.18: Donazione fatta da Carlo I a Carlo VIII, Re di Francia, di 1200 scudi d'oro (1489 Mar.17).
No.19: Patenti di Carlo VIII, con cui si obliga a difendere il Duca Carlo di Savoia (1489 Aug.26).
Addizioni. Mazzo 1, No.20. Propositions faites par Guillaume de Vaudrey de la part du Duc de Bourgogne pour entretenir les anciennes alliances avec le Duc de Savoye, avec le reponse faite à ce sujet (1457).
Trattati Diversi. Selections. Mazzo 5, No.4: Trattato di accessione del Duca di Savoia e del Marchese di Monferrato alla Lega conchiusa tra Re Alfonso d'Aragona e la Repubblica di Venezia (1451 Apr.16).

LETTERE MINISTRI, FRANCIA

Selections. Mazzo 1, No.2: Lettera scritta alla Duchessa Bianca da ambasciatore alla Corte di Francia (1492?).

1538. **FRANCIA**. Selections. Mazzo 1, No.16: Istruzione del Duca Galeazzo Maria Sforza ad Emanuele de Iacopo, suo ambasciatore al Re di Francia (1467 Mar.24).
No.17: Salvacondotto e passaporto del Re di Francia al Duca Carlo I di Savoia e al suo seguito (1488 Mar.2).
SVIZZERI. Selections. Mazzo 1: Trattato di lega perpetua tra Carlo VIII, Re di Francia, e i Cantoni Svizzeri (1453). Convenzione tra Luigi XI, Re di Francia, e i Cantoni Svizzeri contro il Duca di Borgogna (1470 Sept.23). Rinnovazione di lega tra il Re di Francia e i Cantoni Svizzeri (1474 Jan.26).
Mazzo 1bis, No.6: Trattato di confederazione ed alleanza perpetua tra la Duchessa Iolanda e i Cantoni Svizzeri (1477 Apr.23).
No.7: Altro di rinnovazione e conferma delle antiche alleanze tra la Duchessa Iolanda e le città di Berna e di Fribourg (1477 Aug.20).
No.10: Istruzioni della Duchessa Bianca di Savoia al suo segretario Giovanni Forno (1491 Aug.29).
Nos.11-13: Altre istruzioni della Duchessa Bianca a Giovanni Forno (1491 Sept.22, Oct.6, Nov.12; 1492 Dec.10).
VALLESANI. Selections. Mazzo 1, No.1: Istruzioni del Duca Galeazzo Maria Sforza a Giovanni Battista Cotignola, spedito al vescovo di Lyon e alla Repubblica di Valley (1476 July 4).

1539. **FRANCIA**. Selections. Mazzo 1, No.2: Tréve entre Louis, roi de France, et Charles, duc de Bourgogne (1475 Sept.13).
No.3: Traité de paix signé à Arras entre Louis XI et Charles Dauphin par une part, et Maximilien, Archiduc d'Autriche, Philippe et Marguerite, ses enfans, de l'autre (1482 Dec.23).
No.4: Traité de paix entre Charles VIII et Maximilien, Roi des Romains (1494).

LETTERE PRINCIPI DI SAVOIA

SERIE I, DUCHI E SOVRANI

1540. Mazzo 1, fasc.6: Ludovico (1437-62).
fasc.7: Amedeo IX (1459, 1468, 1471).
fasc.8: Iolanda (145?, 1469, 1472, 1475, 147?).

RACCOLTA MONGARDINO

ROMA, ISTRUZIONI DIPLOMATICHE (SISTO IV)

1541. Selections. Vol.63, fols.213-25v (undated).
Vol.114, fols.77-89, 105-12v (undated);
fols.116-18v (1481 Oct.14).

VATICAN CITY

I. ARCHIVIO SEGRETO VATICANO

ARM. XXXIX: REGISTRA BREVIUM

1542. Reg.7 (1456 May-1458 June).

1543. Reg.8 (1457 June 15-1459 Nov.4).
1544. Reg.9 (1458 Oct.1-1461 Nov.).
1545. Reg.10 (ca.1460-ca.1482).
1546. Reg.12 (1470 Sept.13-1471 July 23).
1547. Reg.13 (1480 Aug.26-Dec.16).
1548. Reg.14 (1471 Oct.10-1472 Sept.18).
1549. Reg.15 (1482 Aug.25-1483 Aug.24).
1550. Reg.16 (1483 Aug.25-Dec.30).
1551. Reg.16A (1484 Jan.1-Aug.30).
1552. Reg.17 (1482-1503).
1553. Reg.18 (1484 Aug.30-1485 Aug.30).
1554. Reg.19 (1485 Sept.12-1486 Aug.8).
1555-6. Reg.20 (1488 May 1-Oct.6).
1557-8. Reg.21 (1490 Jan.2-Mar.31).

DATARIA APOSTOLICA

BREVIA LATERANENSIA

1559. Reg.1 (1490 July 1-Aug.31).
1560-1. Reg.2 (1493 Mar.-May, July).

ARM. XL: MINUTAE BREVIUM

1562. Vol.1 (1478-1513?; filmed fols.1-179, 1478-90).

REGISTRA VATICANA

RUBRICELLAE

1563. Regs.436-438, 440-453, 465-467.
1564. Regs.468-487.
1565. Regs.488-497, 515-519.
1566. Regs.540, 542-43, 545, 655-59, 662, 664-80, 691-92, 694-97.

REGISTRA

1567. Reg.465 (1455 Apr.20-1457 Nov.30). Litterae officiorum.
1568. Reg.466 (1457 Dec.17-1458 Apr.6). Litterae officiorum.
1569. Reg.467 (1455 Apr.14-1458 Apr.26). Litterae officialium.
1570. Reg.515 (1458 Sept.4-1460 Dec.29). Litterae officiorum.
1571. Reg.516 (1461 Jan.23-1464 May 25). Litterae officiorum.
1572. Reg.517 (1461 Feb.16-1464 Aug.7). Litterae officiorum.
1573. Reg.518 (1461 Feb.8-1464 July 31). Litterae mere de Curia.
1574. Reg.519 (1463 Nov.24-1468 Apr.21). Litterae Sancte Cruciatae.
1575. Reg.540 (1467 Jan.20-1471 June 22). Litterae mere de Curia.

1576. Reg.542 (1464 Sept.16-1469 Sept.17). Litterae officiorum.

1577. Reg.543 (1468 Feb.25-1471 June 10). Litterae officiorum.

1578. Reg.544 (1464-71). Litterae officialium.

1579. Reg.545 (1464-71). Litterae officialium.

SEGRETERIA DI STATO

SS NUNZIATURE DIVERSE

1580. Vol.237, fols.1-8, 33-305. Istruzioni latine e volgari a Nunzii e ad altri di Eugenio IV, Sisto IV, Innocenzo VIII e Lodovico XI ai suoi ambasciatori, mandati a Roma con diverse doglianze e per protestare un Concilio al detto Sisto, e altri affari.

1581. Vol.244 (ca.1484-ca.1492). Istruzioni di Innocenzo VIII a nunzi ed a legati.

1582. Vol.245 (ca.1484-ca.1492).

ARCHIVUM ARCIS

1583. Indici: No.1001, fols.497v-98 (1418-1501).
No.1003, fols.191v-92v (1436-95).
No.1004, fols.40-49, 378v-81v (1449-1510).
No.1008, fols.358v-59 (1450-1513).
No.1011, pp.192-94 (1431-16th cent.).

1584. Arm.I-XVIII, 1443 (1460-1539, filmed fols.1-121, 209-17v (1460-92). Liber rubeus diversorum memorabilium inceptus ab anno 1460 in civitate Senarum tempore Pii papae secundi.

1585. Armaria: E.43 (1461 June 30); E.44 (1464 Feb.16); E.45 (1464 Apr.1); E.46 (1459 Nov.24); E.47 (1474 Aug.23); E.49 (1474 Sept.9); E.50 (1478 Feb.10); E.51 (1478 Apr.5); E.52 (1481 Sept.26); E.53 (1477 Dec.17); E.54 (1487); E.55 (1485); E.56 (1486 Nov.10); E.57 (1486 May 20); E.62 (1494 Mar.1); E.86 (1494 Dec.3); E.95 (1491 July 4); E.96 (1494); E.48 (1474 Oct.12); E.92 (1488 Jan.4-5, Dec.30-31).

1586. Arm. C.1135 (1460 Aug.2). Arm. C.1176: Cifre antiche e moderne ad uso delle Nunziature dal sec. XIV al XVIII.

1587. Arm.I-XVIII, 517 (1459 Jan.14); 518 (1472 Feb.29); 5018 (1464 Aug.31); 6217 (1493 Oct.10); 2088 (1493 Sept.19); 2089 (1493 Sept.19); 4973 (1466 June 6); 6216 (1470 Jan.9); 639 (1458 May 6); 4430 (1492 Feb.7); 4431 (1494 Mar.9).

1588. Arm.I-XVIII, 5020 (ca.1493-ca.1494). Lettere di Principi e altri Signori, scritte a Papa Alessandro Sesto. 5021 (ca.1494-ca.1495). Lettere di Cardinali scritte a Papa Alessandro Sesto. 1772 (1457 Apr.1); 1677 (1487 Mar.15); 1634 (1494 Sept.28); 1410 (1485 Oct.23); 1055 (1490 Apr.8); 1056 (1492 Apr.12); 1058 (1490 Mar.25); 1059 (1487 Mar.24); 1061 (1493 Jan.29); 1052 (1491 Apr.2); 1051 (1483 July 16); 838 (1492 May 2); 455 (1493 Oct.31); 816 (undated: Discorso del principio et origine della republica di Venetia).

1589. Arm.I-XVIII, 6251 (ca.1484); 6273 (1474 June 11); 6274 (1474 June 30); 6275 (1487 Oct.31); 6291 (1459 Aug.25, 1463 Oct.25, 1482 Jan.8); 515 (1494 Mar.28); 4171

(1490-92); 834 (1483, 1459, 1509, 1510); 841 (1471); 6518 (1463 Oct.22); 6006 (1472, 1478, 1445, 1523, 1539, 1551, 1570, 1594, 1600, 1611); 6554 (1462 June 5 + undated).

MISCELLANEA

ARM. II

1590. Vol.2 (14th cent.-1585?).

1591-2. Vol.7 (13th cent.-ca.1492).

1593. Vol.9 (Biblioteca Apostolica Vaticana, Cod. Vat. Lat. 11713), fols.86-91: Conventiones et capitula inter Sixtum Quartum, Ferdinandum Siciliae regem ex una, et Baptistam de Campofregoso, Ianuae Ducem altera (undated). Vol.13, fols.293-301v: Commissio data R.mo Mantuano legato Bononiam destinato per P. Sixtum Quartum (undated); fols.1012-1018: Capitula celebrata A.D. 1459 inter Pium II.m et Marchionem Mantuae.

Vol.15, fols.398-413v. Littera Sixti Quarti ad Venetorum Ducem I. Mocenigo (1482 Apr.19); fols.453-70v: Responsio Sixti Quarti ad obiecta sibi per Venetos in causa belli Ferrariae (undated).

1594. Vol.20, fols.1-155: Istruzioni diverse di Federico III, Sisto IV, Luigi XI, Massimiliano I e Innocenzo VIII (ca. 1471-ca.1494).
Vol.21, fols.9-20: Responsio Pii Papae Secundi data oratoribus Serenissimi Regis Franciae (1462 Mar.16).

1595. Vol.22, fols.145-45v: Littera Pii Papae Secundi ad Federicum Romanorum Imperatorem (1460 Feb.9); fols.153-64v: Acta et gesta nuntios Pii Papae Secundi pro pace inter Regem Boemie et clerum et civitates Vuritislammen (1460). Vol.23, fols.117-24v: Sixtus IV ad oratores Italici Foederis (undated); fols.145-50v: Consilium de gestis per legati in Anglia (undated). Vol.29, fols.43-82v: Innocentius VIII. Considerationes generales super introducenda materia expeditionis decernendae contra Turcos (undated); fols.83-106v: Sixtus IV ad Patres in pleno Consistorio pro expeditione in Turcas (undated); fols.147-64: Sixtus IV. Preparatio expeditionis contra Turcos (undated); fols.165-74: Responsio Reipublicae Florentinae ad Sixtum IV (undated); fols.191-93v: Conclave Calixti Papae Tertii (undated).

1596. Vol.30, fols.27-133v: Istruzioni diverse di Sisto IV e Innocenzo VIII (ca.1471-ca.1492).
Vol.35, fols.284-311: Viaggio di Pio II fino a Mantova per far il Concilio (undated). Vol.41, fols.171-75v: Conclave Pii Papae II; fols.176-76v: Conclave Pauli II.

1597. Vol.56, fols.3-296, 467-524: Istruzioni di Sisto IV e Innocenzo VIII (ca.1471-ca.1492).

1598. Vol.104, fols.169-71v: Capitula inter Papam et Regem Siciliae (1458 Nov.10); fols.232-37: Vicariatum Terracinae (1458 Nov.10); fols.137v-38: Super solutione census (1494 Aug.1); fols.238v-40v: Litterae Regis Ferdinandi ad Papam (1487 July 3, 1492 May 14);fol.241: Iuramentum Principis Capuae (1492 June 4); fols.241v-42: Littera Ioannis Galeaz Maria Sfortia super pace (1486 July 4); fols.242v-46v: Super discordiis Regni Neapolis (1486-87).

VENICE

1. ARCHIVIO DI STATO

ARCHIVIO DEL COLLEGIO

COMMISSIONI

1599. B.1 (1473-79).
1600. Reg.1 (1482-95).

LETTERE SOTTOSCRITTE DELLA SERENISSIMA SIGNORIA: TERRA

1601. F.1 (1488 Sept.1-Nov.30).
1602. F.2 (1492 Mar.1-Aug.31).

LETTERE SOTTOSCRITTE DELLA SERENISSIMA SIGNORIA: MAR

1603. F.164 (1492 Mar.12-Nov.7).

LETTERE SEGRETE

1604. F.1 (1486-89).
1605. Reg. (1484-85).
1606. Reg. (1490-94).

NOTATORIO

1607. Reg.8 (1444 Mar.17-1453 May 13).
1608. Reg.9 (1453 May 15-1460 June 19).
1609. Reg.10 (1460 June 14-1467 Apr.11).
1610. Reg.11 (1467 Apr.11-1474 Mar.28).
1611. Reg.12 (1474 Mar.27-1481 Nov.23).
1612. Reg.13 (1481 Dec.20-1489 July 7).
1613. Reg.14 (1489 July 15-1499 Feb.27).
1614. Reg.15 (1499 Mar.1-1507 Apr.5).

ARCHIVIO DEL SENATO

DELIBERAZIONI SEGRETE (SENATO SECRETA)

1615. Reg.18 (1448 June 1-1450 Aug.17).
1616. Reg.19 (1450 Aug.17-1453 Dec.31).
1617. Reg.20 (1454 Jan.3-1460 Feb.22).
1618. Reg.21 (1460 Mar.1-1464 Feb.28).
1619. Reg.22 (1464 Mar.2-1466 Sept.12).
1620. Reg.23 (1466 Sept.16-1469 Feb.28).
1621. Reg.24 (1469 Mar.2-1471 Feb.28).

1622. Reg.25 (1471 Mar.1-1473 Feb.27).

1623. Reg.26 (1473 Mar.1-1475 Feb.27).

1624. Reg.27 (1475 Mar.4-1477 Feb.27).

1625. Reg.28 (1477 Mar.4-1479 Feb.25).

1626. Reg.29 (1479 Mar.2-1481 Feb.28).

1627. Reg.30 (1481 Mar.3-1483 Feb.27).

1628. Reg.31 (1483 Mar.1-1484 Feb.21).

1629. Reg.32 (1484 Mar.5-1486 Feb.22).

1630. Reg.33 (1486 Mar.10-1489 Feb.24).

1631. Reg.34 (1489 Mar.5-1494 Feb.27).

1632. Reg.35 (1494 Mar.17-1496 Feb.28).

1633. Reg.36 (1496 Mar.7-1498 Feb.28).

1634. Reg.37 (1498 Mar.1-1500 Feb.28).

1635. Reg.38 (1500 Mar.5-1502 Feb.28).

DISPACCI DEGLI AMBASCIATORI AL SENATO, COSTANTINOPOLI

1636. F.1A (Pietro Bembo, 1484 Jan.16-1485 Feb.9). (Giovanni Dario, 1484 May 31-1485 Feb.28). (Antonio Ferro, 1487 Feb.19-Mar.31).

DISPACCI DEGLI AMBASCIATORI AL SENATO, ARCHIVI PROPRI, EGITTO

1637. F.1 (Pietro Diedo, 1489 Sept.17-1490 Feb.19). (G. Borghi, 1490 Feb.19-May 18).

DISPACCI AL SENATO, RETTORI ED ALTRE CARICHE

1638. B.2 (Francesco Marcello, Console in Damasco, 1483 Oct.28; 1484 Mar.31). (Dispacci originali di Luca Pisani e Niccolò da Pesaro, Provveditori presso Roberto di Sanseverino, Luogotenente Generale, 1484 July 7-Sept.1). (Dispacci diversi e qualche altro documento del periodo della Pace di Bagnolo, 1484 Aug.8-Sept.8).

ARCHIVIO DEL CONSIGLIO DEI DIECI

PARTI MISTE

1639. Reg.14 (1450 Aug.26-1454 May 22).

1640. Reg.15 (1454 June 5-1460 Feb.27).

1641. Reg.16 (1460 Mar.5-1466 Sept.24).

1642. Reg.17 (1466 Oct.1-1473 Feb.26).

1643. Reg.18 (1473 Mar.3-1477 Feb.26).

1644. Reg.19 (1477 Mar.5-1480 May 31).

1645. Reg.20 (1480 June 2-1482 Dec.28).

1646. Reg.21 (1482 Dec.28-1484 Feb.27).

1647. Reg.22 (1484 Mar.4-1486 Feb.28).

1648. Reg.23 (1486 Mar.6-1488 June 30).

1649. Reg.24 (1488 July 9-1491 Feb.26).

1650. Reg.25 (1491 Mar.4-1493 Feb.27).

1651. Reg.26 (1493 Mar.4-1495 Dec.29).

1652. F.3 (1489, selections). F.4 (1490, selections).

Collezione Benedetto Soranzo, Archivio di Cipro

1653. Indice No.98.

1654. B.I: a). Lettere di B. Soranzo a diversi per ordine cronologico, 1481-94.
   b). Lettere di diversi a B. Soranzo per ordine alfabetico d'autore e per ordine cronologico da A a E, 1481-94.

1655. B.II. Lettere di diversi a B. Soranzo per ordine alfabetico d'autore e per ordine cronologico da F a Q, 1477-95.

1656. B.III: a). Lettere di diversi a B. Soranzo per ordine alfabetico d'autore e per ordine cronologico da R a Z, 1480-95.
   b). Lettere di Pietro e Vettore, fratelli Soranzo, al fratello Benedetto, 1481-83.

1657. B.IV. Lettere di Pietro e Vettore, fratelli Soranzo, al fratello Benedetto, 1484-94 and undated.

1658. B.V: a). Lettere di diversi a diversi per ordine alfabetico d'autore e per ordine cronologico, 1404-1530.
   b). Scritture di vario argomento sopratutto beneficiario, 1457-95 and undated. Selections, 1482, 1484-87.

Archivio dei Capi del Consiglio dei Dieci

Lettere

1659. F.1 (1473 Mar.4-1476 Feb.27).

1660. F.2 (1476 Mar.1-1484 Feb.28).

ARCHIVI DEI REGGIMENTI

Archivio del Duca di Candia

1661. B.2. Ducali e lettere ricevute, 1441-90; filmed 1461-78.

1662. B.8. Missive e responsive, 1417-1550; filmed 1465-89.

COLLEZIONI E MISCELLANEE VARIE

Libri Pactorum

1663. Reg.5 (1336-1473).

1664. Reg.6 (1380-1486).

1665. Reg.7 (1094-1496).

Ducali ed Atti Diplomatici

1666. B.XX. Selections, 1485-94.

Miscellanea di Atti Diplomatici e Privati

1667. Indice Cronologico No.243, Sec.VIII-XVIII, pp.95-123 (1449-95).

1668. B.39 (1450 Feb.15-1454 June 27; selections, 1450 July 2-1454 June 19).

1669. B.40 (1454 July 12-1458 Apr.29; selections, 1454 Aug.3-1456 Aug.4).

1670. B.41 (1459 Nov.4-1467 Aug.31; selections, 1459 Nov.27-1467 Aug.31).

1671. B.42 (1468 Jan.21-1470 Feb.8; selections, 1468 Feb.24-1469 Oct.4).

1672. B.43 (1470 Apr.30-1472 June 23; selections, 1470 Dec.22-1472 June 23).

1673. B.44 (1473 Mar.3-1477 Nov.19; selections, 1474 Jan.6-1477 Jan.8).

1674. B.45 (1478 Jan.7-1484 Dec.2; selections, 1478 Jan.9-1484 Dec.2).

1675. B.46 (1485 Jan.2-1492 Nov.14; selections, 1485 Jan.2-1492 Nov.14).

1676. B.47 (1493 Feb.16-1495?; selections, 1493 Apr.22-1494 Nov.5).

MISCELLANEA DI ATTI DIPLOMATICI E PRIVATI, COLLEZIONE PODOCATARO

1677. Indice No.242 II. Atti della Curia Romana.

1678. Serie I, B.I. Lettere di Papi (1320, 1428 Dec.12-1484 July 30; selections, 1461 Feb.18-1484 July 30).

1679. Serie I, B.II. Lettere di Papi (1484 Sept.1-1491 Aug.28; selections, 1484 Sept.1-1491 Aug.28).

1680. Serie I, B.III. Lettere di Papi e del Collegio dei Cardinali (1492 Sept.3-1547 Mar.; selections, 1492 Nov.24-1494 Dec.22).

1681. Serie II, B.IV. Lettere di Principi al Papa. Selections. Italia: Firenze (1471-93); Mantova (1487-92); Milano (1471-94); Napoli e Sicilia (1473-94); Savoia (1475-93); Venezia (1471-93).

1682. Serie II, B.V. Lettere di Principi Esteri al Papa. Selections. Danimarca (1478), Francia (1478-88); Germania, Federico III (1474-93).

1683. Serie II, B.VI. Lettere di Principi Esteri al Papa. Selections. Germania, Massimiliano (1477-94); Austria (1472-91); Germania, Principi diversi (1471-1500).

1684. Serie II, B.VII. Lettere di Principi Esteri al Papa. Selections. Inghilterra (1476-93); Polonia (1479-94); Portogallo (1475-93); Spagna (1474-91); Svezia e Norvegia (1485-94).

1685. Serie II, B.VIII. Lettere di Principi Esteri al Papa. Selections. Ungheria e Boemia (1475-97).

1686. Serie II, B.IX. Lettere di Prelati al Papa. Selections. Prelati italiani (1484, 1487-90); Prelati stranieri (1489?). Atti diversi. No.5: Domande da sottoporsi ad alcuni testimoni sulla vita dell'ambasciatore veneto a Roma, 1484-88.

RACCOLTA DI BOLLE PONTIFICIE

1687. Inventario No.235 (1053-1796), pp.50-77 (1444-95).

1688. Bolle Pontificie. Selections, 1455-91.

MISCELLANEA

1689. Cod.823. Registro di lettere del Provveditore Generale in Terraferma, Lorenzo Loredan (1477 Sept.1-1478 Oct.15)

BIBLIOTECA, MISCELLANEA

1690. Cod.122. Gradenico Pietro. Memorie istorico-cronologiche spettanti ad ambasciatori della Serenissima Repubblica di Venezia spediti a varii Principi.

SALA DIPLOMATICA "REGINA MARGHERITA"

1691. Selections, 1453-91.

II. BIBLIOTECA NAZIONALE MARCIANA

1692. It.VII, Cod.398(8170). Dispacci di Zaccaria Barbaro, ambasciatore a Napoli, inviati alla Signoria veneta dal 1 novembre 1471 al 7 settembre 1473.
1693. It.VII, Cod.1196(8884). Dispacci di Francesco Contarini, ambasciatore a Siena (1454 Mar.1-1455 Sept.17).
1694. It.VII, Cod.547(8529). Dispacci di Sebastiano Badoer e Benedetto Trevisan, ambasciatori a Milano (1494 Nov.22-1495 June 4).
1695. It.VII, Cod.1044(9608). Miscellanea, fols.88-121v. [Zaccaria Contarini e Girolamo Lion, ambasciatori all'imperatore Massimiliano]. Registro delle lettere al Senato (1493 Nov.13-1494 Mar.18).
1696. It.VII, Cod.1795(7679). Miscellanea, fols.25-105. Andrea de Franceschi. "Itinerario de Germania" degli ambasciatori veneti Giorgio Contarini e Paolo Pisani, all'imperatore Federico III, 1492.
1697. It.VII, Cod.794(8503). Dolfin Giorgio. Cronaca Veneta dalle origini al 1458, fols.417v-60v (1450-58).
1698. It.VII, Cod.81(7304). Cronaca Veneta dal 1424 al 1521, fols. 77v-165 (1449-95).
1699. It.VII, Cod.51(8528). Cronaca Veneta dalle origini al 1476, fols.278v-327v (1446-76).
1700. It.VII, Cod.66(7766). Cronaca Veneta sino all'anno 1545, fols.215v-68 (1449-95).
1701. It.VII, Cod.321(8838). Cronaca detta Savina, sino al 1588, fols.175-97v (1464-95).
1702. It.VII, Cod.53(7419). Cronaca di Venezia dal principio al 1478, fols.326-56 (1450-78).
1703. It.VII, Cod.129(8323). Tiepolo Giorgio?. Cronaca Veneta sino al 1538, fols.201-28 (1449-98).
1704. It.VII, Cod.1(8356). Degli Agostini Agostino. Cronaca Veneta (1421-1570), fols.147v-75 (1449-1500).
1705. It.VII, Cod.54(8140). Cronaca di Venezia dal principio al 1490 circa. Origine delle famiglie nobili, ecc.; fols.311v-73v (1449-90).
1706. It.VII, Cod.791(7589). Famiglie nobili. Cronaca detta Veniera fino al 1580, fols.146-67v (1449-1500).
1707. It.VII, Cod.56(8636). Erizzo Marcantonio. Cronaca Veneta fino al 1495, fols.447v-611 (1449-95).
1708. It.VII, Cod.323(8646). Cronaca Veneta sino al 1528, fols. 160v-214 (1447-1503).
1709. It.VII, Cod.762(7668). Miscellanea. No.IV: Paolo Morosini. Lettera a Cicco Simonetta in difesa della Rep. Veneta, undated.
1710. Pélissier, Léon G., *Inventaire de la Collection Podocataro à la Bibliothèque de Saint-Marc Venise* (Leipzig, 1901). Separate publication from *Centralblatt für Bibliothekswesen* XVIII (1901), pp.473-93, 521-41, 576-98.
1711. Collezione Podocataro. Lat.X, Cod.174(3621). (1351, 1465-1502, 1548).
1712. Collezione Podocataro. Lat.X, Cod.175(3622). Epistolae latinae et italicae principum et illustrium virorum ad Sixtus IV., Innocentium VIII. et Alexandrum VI. summos pontifices magna ex parte autographae (1472-1500).
1713. Collezione Podocataro. Lat.X, Cod.176(3623). (1476-1500).
1714. Collezione Podocataro. Lat.X, Cod.177(3624). Epistolae et acta de rebus Italiae sub Sixto IV., Innocentio VIII. et Alexandro VI., summis pontificibus (1329, 1474-1500, 1552).

1715. Collezione Podocataro. Lat.X, Cod.178(3625). Epistolae et acta de rebus extra Italiam gestis sub Sixto IV., Innocentio VIII. et Alexandro VI., summis pontificibus (1456, 1471-1502, 1517).

1716. It.XI, Cod.187(7363). Commissio Ducalis Nicolai Marcelli ad Leonardum Sanutum oratorem ad Summum Pontificem, 1474 Sept.2.
It.VII, Cod.143(8951). Scritture sugli Interdetti di Sisto IV e di Paolo V. Fols.1-4: Informatione sopra l'Interdetto di Sisto IV contro Venetia, a 23 di giugno dell' anno 1483 nell'assedio di Ferrara.

1717. Lat.XI, Cod.88(3818). Francisci Philelphi, oratio parentalis de divi Franc. Sfortiae Mediolanensium ducis felicitate.

1718. Lat.XI, Cod.81(4155). Documenta varia, ca.1478-ca.1483.

1719. Lat.XIV, Cod.252(4718), fols.69-79: Oratio pro Francisco Sfortia Duca Mediolanensi ad Paulum II. P. M.; fols. 249-57v: Bernardi Iustiniani, oratio apud Sistum IIII. Pontificem Maximum, 1471 Dec.2.
Lat.XI, Cod.145(4371), fols.69-109: Orazione funebre per Pio II.
Lat.XI, Cod.80(3057), fols.123-24. Copie di lettere: Bianca Maria Sforza ai fiorentini con la risposta di questi, 1466 Mar.9 e senza data; Signoria di Firenze a Galeazzo Maria Sforza, 1468 Oct.31.

1720. Lat.XIV, Cod.289(4615). Commissione ducale di Cristoforo Moro a Giovanni Capello, capitano di tre galere per viaggio in Barbaria, 1462 May 13. Commissione ducale di Agostino Barbadico a Domenico Contarini, capitano di tre galee, 1491 Apr.21.

1721. Lat.X, Cod.304(3789). No.I: Litterae ducales decem authenticae Augustini Barbadici, principis Venetiarum ad Zachariam Contarenum et Hieronymum Leonem, reipubl. Venetae oratores apud Maximilianum Romanorum regem, 1493 Nov.5-1494 Feb.11.
Lat.XIV, Cod.228(4498), pp.159-67: Iacobus de Utino, oratio ad P. Maripetrum, 1457.
Lat.XI, Cod.82(3816), fols.1-10v. Copie di lettere alla Signoria di Venezia: Re Ferrante, 1481; Duca Giovanni Galeazzo Sforza, 1481 Dec.21; Signoria di Firenze, 1481. Gli ambasciatori di Napoli, Milano e Firenze ai loro principi, 1481 Mar.24.

1722. Lat.XI, Cod.83(4360). Miscellanea, ca.1403-ca.1553.

1723. Lat.XIV, Cod.251(4685). Zaccaria Contarini, oratio ad Maximilianum Regem Romanorum de obitu Imperatoris patris et de nuptiis cum Blanca Sfortia initis (undated).
Lat.XI, Cod.108(4365), fols.196-97: Breve di Pio II al Doge Cristoforo Moro, 1463 Oct.25; fols.255-58v: Donato Acciaiuoli, oratoris florentini, oratio habita coram Summo Pontifice Sixto Quarto, 1471 Oct.; fols.261v-68v: Oratio Bartolomee Scalae, florentini oratoris ad Summum Pontificem Innocentium Octavium, undated; fols.303-13: Vladislai Vetesii, oratio ad Summum Pontificem Sixtum IIII., 1475 Feb.9; fols.313-19: Lettera di Francesco Filelfo a Sisto IV, 1476 Mar.1.
Lat.XIV, Cod.244(4681), fols.127-38: Sixti IV. Pont. Max. et Collegii Cardinalium, epistolae ad Venetos et Venetorum responsiones de bello Ferrariensi, 1482.

1724. Lat.XI, Cod.9(4516), fols.8-17v: Bernardi Iustiniani, oratoris Venetorum, oratio ad Serenissimum Regem Franciae Ludovicum et responsio ad Universitatem Parisiensem [1462 Jan.6]; fols.18-48v: B. Iustiniani, oratio funebris habita in obitu Francisci Fuscari Ducis, undated.

1725. Lat.XI, Cod.106(4363), fols.1-10: Pauli Barbi, oratio ad Ludovicum Francorum Regem, 1461 Dec.8.
Lat.X, Cod.76(3842), fols.1-24: Pauli Mauroceni, defensio Venetorum ad Europae principes contra obtrectatores, undated.
Lat.XIV, Cod.126(4664). Ambroxii Michete, oratio congratulatoria ad Pasqualem Maripetrum, Illustrissimum Venetorum Ducem, 1458 Feb.1. Lelii Iusti, oratio ad Pasqualem Maripetrum, 1458 Dec.19.

1726. Lat.XIV, Cod.265(4501). Miscellanea, fols.85v-114v, 142v-159v, 193-95 (ca.1457-ca.1468).

Lat.XIV, Cod.266(4502). Miscellanea, fols.246-47, 270-71, 275-77, 279 (ca.1464-ca.1473).

Lat.XIV, Cod.267(4344). Miscellanea, fols.23v-25, 28v-29, 34v, 36v-39v (1492-93).

Lat.XIV, Cod.252(4718), fols.162-65v: Leonardi Sanuti Marini filii, legati veneti, oratio habita apud Sixtum Quartum Pontificem Maximum, 1474.

1727. Lat.XIV, Cod.252(4718), fols.27-30v: De felice successu belli Venetorum adversus Herculem Ferrarie Ducem, undated.

Lat.XI, Cod.72(4113), fols.18v-19v: Oratio in laudem clarissimi viri Cosme de Medicis habita in convivio apud priores Volaterranos, undated.

Lat.XI, Cod.77(4193), fols.136-48v: Oratio Iacobi Calcaterre habita Rome in pleno concistorio... Calisti Papae III, 1455 July 9?.

III. BIBLIOTECA QUERINI STAMPALIA

1728. Classe IV, Cod.CCLIIIbis. Ambasciarie ordinarie e estraordinarie espedite a diversi Potentati del Mondo dalla Republica di Venetia di tempo in tempo dalla sua Fondatione sino il presente Anno MDCXXXVI, con li tempi delle Espeditioni così delli uni come delli altri et Sostanza delle commissioni e delle Estraordinarie.

VEROLI

I. BIBLIOTECA GIOVARDIANA

1729. Cod.14 (42.2.24). Litterae ms. Sixti pp. IV, annus IX, communes (1479 Aug.26-Nov.26).

2) REPOSITORIES OUTSIDE ITALY

AUSTRIA

VIENNA

I. HAUS-, HOF- UND STAATSARCHIVS

HANDSCHRIFTEN

1730. B.12(27). Traités de paix de Maximilian I roi des Romains avec Louis XI et Charles VIII rois de France, 1482, 1489, 1493.

1731. W479(953). Privilegia Ducatus Mediolani et Lombardiae atque Comitatus Papiae, 1493-95.

ITALIEN, DIPLOMATISCHE KORRESPONDENZ

1732. **Toskana**, Fz.1. Florentinorum Lucensiumque foedus et liga, 1482 June 12.
Rom, Fz.1. Selections, 1480-81, 1488, 1490.

II. ÖSTERREICHISCHE NATIONALBIBLIOTHEK

1733. Cod.441, fols. 11-354v: Ludovicus Foscarini. Epistolae (ca.1455-ca.1466).
fols.371-95: L. Foscarini. De laudibus Isotae Nogarolae.

1734. Cod.2398. Franciscus Tranchedinus. Furtivae litterarum notae, quibus auctor usus fuisse videtur in cancellaria Vicecomitum Mediolanensium ab anno 1450 ad annum 1496. Praecedit series nominum eorum, cum quibus de arcanis notis et eorum usu auctor convenerat.

1735. Cod.5972. (? Daniele Barbaro). Cronica veneta, 1228-1501.

1736. Cod.6254. Miscellanea, fols.276-308v: Giosafatte Barbaro. Lettere scritte al Senato Veneto dalla Dalmazia e dalla Grecia, 1472-73.

1737. Cod.6461. Nomina legatorum Venetorum ad principes et civitates per universum orbem seculis XIV. XV, XVI et XVII currentibus missorum . Videtur opus esse Marci Fuscareni.

1738. Cod.6568. Ambasciarie ordinarie et straordinarie espedite a diversi Potentati del mondo della republica di Venetia di tempo in tempo dalla sua prima fondatione sino il presente anno MDCLXXVIII con li tempi dell'espeditioni cosí dell'uni come delli altri et sostanza delle commissioni delle estraordinarie.

1739. Cod.6620, fols.1-342v: Ferdinandus Aragonensis rex Siciliae. Instructiones diversis suis legatis alijsque officialibus datae Italicae d. d. Neapoli (1486 May 10-1488 Jan.4). fols.346-590: various papal instructions to legates and other documents (16th cent.).

1740. Cod.7094. Rélation et actes de la négociation faicte par les ambassadeurs de Louis XI pour traicter la paix entre le pape Sixte IV et le roy de Naples d'une part et la republique de Venize, les ducz de Milan et de Ferrare et la republique de Florence d'autre, ez années 1478 et 1479.

Appendix 4. Cod.10348, fols.9v-16: Instruttione a Hermolao Barbaro quando andò nuntio alla Corte Cesarea (undated). [7 photocopies].

1742. Cod. Ser. N.12281. Rechnungsbuch des Herzogtums Mailand für die Jahre 1481-1488.

ENGLAND

LONDON

I. BRITISH LIBRARY (formerly BRITISH MUSEUM)

1743. Add. MSS. 48067 (Yelverton LXXIII). Letter-book of Girolamo Zorzi, as Venetian ambassador to Milan and France (1485 Sept.13-1487 Sept.24).

FRANCE

DIJON

I. ARCHIVES DÉPARTEMENTALES DE LA COTE-D'OR
CHAMBRE DES COMPTES DE BOURGOGNE

Appendix 5. B.11.934. (1474-75). [5 photocopies].

LILLE

1. ARCHIVES DÉPARTEMENTALES DU NORD

CHAMBRE DES COMPTES

1745. Livre de detail des paiements effectués.
   Vol.6, selections (1449-1453 July).
   Vol.7, selections (1453 Aug.-1494).

TRÉSOR DES CHARTES. TRAITÉS, TREVES, NÉGOCIATIONS

1746. B.855: No.16.030 (1463 Oct.19); No.16.027 (1463 Oct.24).
   B.331: No.16.122 (1467 July 20); No.16.164 (1469 Sept.18).
   B.334: No.16.218 (1471?); No.16.191 (1471 Feb.15); No.16.190 (1471 Mar.5);
   No.16.206 (1471 Aug.15).
   B.335: No.16.204 (1471 Feb.20).
   B.575: No.16.110 (1466).
1747. B.846: No.23.627 (1466 Apr.18); No.23.628 (1466 Aug.4); No.23.630 (1466 Nov.27);
   No.23.631 (1466 Dec.19); No.23.632 (1466 Dec.24); No.23.633 (1466 Jan.16);
   No.23.634 (1467 Aug.7); No.23.636 (1467 Jan.5).
   B.18.842: Nos. 29.445 - 29.446 (1472 Feb.23).

Appendix 6. B.340: No.16.277 (1475 Jan.30). [28 photocopies].

MARSEILLES

I. ARCHIVES DÉPARTEMENTALES DES BOUCHES-DU-RHONE

CHAMBRE DES COMPTES DE PROVENCE

1748. B.673. (1453 Jan.26, Apr.11).
B.675. (1454 Mar.4).
B.678. (1458 Nov.27).
B.686. (1467 May 13).
Supplement B.4. (undated, 1494?).

PARIS

I. ARCHIVES NATIONALES

TRÉSOR DES CHARTES

1749. J.496. **Gênes,** Nos. 2-9 (1463-75).
J.498. **Gênes,** Nos. 28-31, 33-36 (1458-76).
J.499. **Gênes,** No. 37 (1488).
J.502. **Savoie,** Nos. 21-22, 25-29 (1452-76).
J.505. **Milan,** No. 8 (1476).
J.507. **Milan,** Nos. 34-35 (1476).

II. BIBLIOTHEQUE NATIONALE

FONDS ITALIEN

1750. Cod.1583 (1433-1447).

1751. Cod.1584 (1447).

1752. Cod.1585 (1448-51).

1753. Cod.1586 (1452-54).

1754. Cod.1587 (1455-57).

1755. Cod.1588 (1458-60).

1756. Cod.1589 (1461-63).

1757. Cod.1590 (1464).

1758. Cod.1591 (1465-66).

1759. Cod.1592 (1467-1500).

1760. Cod.1593 (1463-66).

1761. Cod.1594 (1183-1461+ undated).

1762. Cod.1595 (1454-76).

1763. Cod.1596 (1446-68).

1764. Cod.1610 (1466-1500).

1765. Cod.1611 (1463-66).

1766. Cod.1649 (1455-74; fols.100-330: 1466 May 20-1474 Dec.26).

1767. Cod.2245 (ca.1447-ca.1471).

FONDS FRANÇAIS

1768. Cod.2897. Recueil de lettres et de pièces originales, et de copies de pièces, 15th-16th cents.

1769. Cod.2907. Recueil de lettres et de pièces originales, et de copies de pièces, 15th cent.

1770. Cod.2909. Recueil de lettres et de pièces originales, et de copies de pièces, 15th-17th cents.

1771. Cod.2911. Recueil de lettres et de pièces originales, ed de copies de pièces, 15th cent.

1772. Cod.3880. [Mèlanges, 15th-16th cents.]. Copies, 17th cent.

1773. Cod.3884. Recueil de copies de pièces, 14th-15th cents. + undated. Copies, 17th cent.

1774. Cod.3887. Recueil de lettres originales et de copies de pièces, 15th cent.

1775. Cod.4054. Recueil de lettres et pièces originales, et de copies de pièces, relatives aux querelles de la France et de l'Angleterre, 1308-1531.

1776. Cod.5040. Recueil de pièces diplomatiques de la seconde moitié du XVe siècle, relatives la plupart aux rapports entre la France et la Bourgogne.

1777. Cod.5041. Recueil de pièces relatives principalement aux rapports de la France et de la Bourgogne sous les règnes de Charles VII et de Louis XI, 1447-78.

1778. Cod.5042. Recueil de pièces relatives aux rapports de la France et de la Bourgogne sous Charles VII et Louis XI, ca.1445-ca.1479 + undated.

1779. Cod.5044. Recueil de pièces relatives principalement à la Bourgogne, au Portugal et à l'Allemagne, 1343-1575.

1780. Cod.6963. Papiers de l'abbé Le Grand sur l'histoire de Louis XI. Pièces originales, 1444?-69.

1781. Cod.6964. Papiers de l'abbé Le Grand sur l'histoire de Louis XI. Pièces originales, 1469-1580?.

1782. Cod.10187. Registre de Pierre Doriolle, chancelier de France, contenant des instructions, mémoires, traités, lettres et ordonnances de Louis XI, 1474-80.

1783. Cod.15537. Recueil de pièces originales relatives principalement aux différends entre Louis XI, alors dauphin, et Charles VII, 1420-1500.

1784. Cod.15538. Lettres et pièces principalement du temps de Louis XI et de Charles VIII, la plupart originales, et servant à l'histoire de leur règnes, et pièces du règne de François Ier, 1459-1521.

1785. Cod.15539. Copie du Registre du chancelier Doriolle, depuis 1474 jusques en 1480.

1786. Cod.15540. Règnes de Louis XI et de Charles VIII; lettres originales adressèes à ces souverains, 1477-88.

1787. Cod.17293. Recueil de traités entre les rois de France et les ducs de Bourgogne au XVe siècle.

1788. Cod.18983. Recueil de pièces concernant principalement les relations diplomatiques entre la France et la Savoie, sous les règnes de Charles VII et de Louis XI, provenant en partie au moins des papiers du chancelier d'Oriole, 1447-77. Originaux et copies.

FONDS LATIN

1789. Cod.10133. Pièces relatives à l'histoire d'Italie, de 1460 à 1494, recueillies par Cicchus Simonetta, XVe siècle.

COLLECTION DUPUY

1790. Cod.760. Recueil de pièces relatives à l'histoire de l'Italie, de l'Allemagne, de l'Angleterre, de la Suisse et de la Lorraine, de 1365 à 1651 environ. Copies; quelques originaux.

SPAIN

BARCELONA

I. ARCHIVO GENERAL DE LA CORONA DE ARAGON

CANCILLERIA REAL

Registros Curiae

1791. Reg.2661 (1453-58).
1792. Reg.2662 (1455-58).
1793. Reg.3406 (1458-59).
1794. Reg.3407 (1458-64).
1795. Reg.3408 (1459-60).
1796. Reg.3409 (1459-64).
1797. Reg.3410 (1461-64).
1798. Reg.3411 (1461-67).
1799. Reg.3412 (1465-69).
1800. Reg.3413 (1468-74).
1801. Reg.3414 (1474-78).
1802. Reg.3415 (1474-78).
1803. Reg.3416 (1476-78).

Registros Curiae Sigilli Secreti

1804. Reg.3303 (1454-58).
1805. Reg.3304 (1455-58).
1806. Reg.3305 (1456-58).

Registros Diversorum Sigilli Secreti

1807. Reg.3393 (1474-78).
1808. Reg.3394 (1476-78).

Registros Secretorum

1809. Reg.2700 (1452-58).

SEVILLE

I. ARCHIVO GENERAL DE LAS INDIAS

PATRONATO REAL

1810. Leg.8, No.11. "Extracto breve y curioso de la vida de Don Cristobal Colon." Anonimo (1486-93).

SEVILLE

I. ARCHIVO GENERAL DE LAS INDIAS

PATRONATO REAL

1810. Leg.8, No.11. "Extracto breve y curioso de la vida de Don Cristobal Colon."
Anonimo (1486-93).

BULAS Y BREVES

Appendix 7. Leg.1, Nos.1-3 (1493 May 5, Sept.23). [4 photocopies].

SIMANCAS

I. ARCHIVO GENERAL

PATRONATO REAL

1812. **Negociaciones con Francia.** Tratados y Negociaciones. K.1638(D.1.2.). Nos.1-2
(ante 1474, ante 1488).
Secretaría de Estado. K.1680B(i.1). Nos.18-19 (1458, 1464).
Documentos Diplomaticos Diversos. K.1710(Q.1). Nos.9-11 (1494).
1813. **Capitolaciones con Aragón y Navarra.** No.12-54 (1244): 1471.
Capitolaciones con Pontifices. Nos.: 16-56 (1412):1476; 16-39 (1413): 1476?; 16-7
(1414): 1477-78?; 16-11 (1415): 1478?; 16-12 (1416): 1478?; 14-48 (1417): 1478?;
16-16 (1418): 1478?; 16-17 (1420): 1479?; 16-50 (1421): 1479; 16-1 (1422): 1481;
16-2 (1423): 1481-93?; 16-51 (1424): 1482-85?; 16-17 (1433): 1485-93?.
Papeles de Estado de la Correspondencia y Negociación de Roma. Serie 2,
Leg.847 (1381-1527). Selection: Registro del acta de la paz entre el papa Inocencio,
el Rey Católico Fernando V y el Rey de Francia, 1486.
1814. **Patronato Real, Nápoles y Sicilia.** Nos.: 41-13 (3592): 1464; 41-15 (3594): 1471;
41-16 (3595): 1487.
Papeles de Estado de la Correspondencia y Negociación de Nápoles. Leg.1003
(1339-1509). Selections: Nos.11-12 (1476, 1488).
Papeles de Estado, Negociación de Venecia. Serie I, Leg.1308 (1484-1528).
Selections: Nos.1-4 (1484, 1484, 1486, 1490).

SECRETARIA DE ESTADO, LIBROS DE BERZOSA

1815. Libro 3 (2004). Instrucciones y despachos de Eugenio IV, Sixto IV, Inocencio VIII,
Alejandro VI, Julio II, Léon X y Paulo III a sus nuncios en diversos reinos, sobre
negocios públicos así eclesiásticos como seculares... Hay también algunas
instrucciones de príncipes a sus ministros en cortes extranjeras.

TURKEY

ISTANBUL

I. TOP KAPI SARAYI ARSIVI

Appendix 8. Latin File. Nos.9-18, 21-23, 29-30 (1482-94 + undated). Mainly letters to the
Sultan by King Ferrante of Naples (3), Innocent VIII (1), and others. [21 photocopies].

UNITED STATES OF AMERICA

UNIVERSITY OF CHICAGO

I. JOSEPH REGENSTEIN LIBRARY

1816. Volpicella, Luigi, ed. Regis Ferdinandi Primi Instructionum Liber (10 maggio 1486-10 maggio 1488). Napoli, Soc. Napoletana di Sto. Pat., 1916.

CROATIA (EX-YUGOSLAVIA)

DUBROVNIK (RAGUSA)

I. HISTORIJSKI ARHIV

Appendix 9. Iosip Gelcich, 'Dubrovacki Arhiv' *Glasnik, Zemaljskog muzeja u Bosni i Hercegovini,* 22, No.4 (1910), pp.545-88. [44 photocopies].

1818. Luka Curlica. Protocollo Generale dell'Antico Archivio di Ragusa, fols.47-78 (15th cent.). (Serie LXXVI. Diplomata et Acta).

SERIE XXVII. LETTERE E COMMISSIONI

LETTERE DI LEVANTE

1819. Reg.5 (1403-11, 1413, 1473-92, 1501, 1568-70, 1595). Fols.112-30 (1473-92).
1820. Reg.14 (1448-62, 1464-66, 1468-70, 1472-79, 1481-83, 1485-90, 1492-94, 1496, 1546).
1821. Reg.15 (1449-53).
1822. Reg.16 (1454-60).
1823. Reg.17 (1493-1568, 1569, 1575, 1593-94, 1596, 1606-07, 1612, 1623, 1635, 1654, 1656, 1664).
1824. Johannes Radonic, ed., *Acta et diplomata Ragusina,* Tom.1, fasc.2 (*Fontes Rerum Slavorum Meridionalium, Series Prima*). Belgrade, 1934.

General index

compiled by Eleni Sakellariou